Praise for *Center Church*

In a fast-changing culture that seems alien to many Christians (just as Christians seem alien to many in the culture!), it is easy for Christians to throw up their hands in despair and adopt a purely defensive mode. In this important book, Tim Keller unpacks the gospel and gently but firmly reminds us that it is nonnegotiable. At the same time, he enables us to think through how we can responsibly interact with the culture, how we can—indeed, must—appreciate good things within it, and how we can firmly and faithfully apply the gospel to it. But this is not a mechanical how-to book; rather, it is a reflective meditation on some hugely important themes in Scripture written by someone who has exercised faithful pastoral ministry in a major city for two decades.

D. A. Carson, research professor of New Testament, Trinity Evangelical Divinity School

No one has listened more closely to the harmonies of city, culture, church, and Scripture than Tim Keller. In *Center Church*, he not only describes the different strains of music but also tells us how he has orchestrated the results for the sake of ministry outreach and renewal. Now it's our turn to listen, as Tim practically yet powerfully prepares us to participate in this great symphony of the gospel.

Bryan Chapell, president, Covenant Theological Seminary

Center Church is an immensely helpful resource for the next generation of church leaders. It is theologically profound, thought-provoking, and energizing, and it will make you uncomfortable in measure. Once again, Tim Keller has hit the bull's-eye!

Alistair Begg, senior pastor, Parkside Church, Cleveland, Ohio

We don't need another "do ministry like my church does ministry" book. Nor do we need another book that critiques other church models. We need a book that helps us think critically and biblically as we structure our churches. *Center Church* is packed with Tim Keller's experience, humility, and wisdom. This book will help you if you are serious about seeing your city transformed by the gospel of grace.

Darrin Patrick, lead pastor, The Journey, St. Louis, Missouri

As our culture continues to move toward a post-Christian secularism, it is more vital than ever that Christians know the gospel well and know how to communicate it effectively. In *Center Church*, Tim Keller masterfully explains what the gospel is and how to relate it successfully wherever we serve. This is more than an academic analysis; it is pastoral coaching of the best sort, based on three decades of successful practice. Thanks, Tim.

Sandy Willson, senior minister, Second Presbyterian Church, Memphis, Tennessee

Most of us observe and see the obvious. Tim observes and sees that which is unseen by others—especially when it comes to the truth of God's Word and the culture of the day. Once again, he has given us deeper insights—this time regarding the church and how she can experience her healthiest potential. How foolish to know of this book and not read it!

Randy Pope, pastor, Perimeter Church, Atlanta, Georgia

This outstanding book, like the Manhattan ministry out of which it has come, shows how Reformed theological acumen and wise pastoral intelligence may combine to achieve spiritual fruitfulness in urban contexts everywhere. Every page illuminates. Keller is a huge gift to today's church.

J. I. Packer, professor emeritus, Regent College

Center Church is not only a doctrinally rigorous and socially perceptive explanation of a sustained and remarkable work of God in Manhattan but also a hugely important, original, and timely call to mission that is appropriately contextualized for contemporary urban culture. We need to carefully learn from these principles if we are to reach our cities for Christ.

Richard Coekin, director, Co-Mission church planting network, London, England

Cities are challenging and complex but also important and strategic. And those who are called to minister in cities need encouragement and resources that fuel hope and effectiveness. That's why I'm so glad that Tim Keller has written this book. His passion for the gospel, heart for the city, and vision of a movement of the Holy Spirit that will transform lives and bring hope and peace to our cities has compelled him to share his insights and thinking with us. What's more, the church he serves speaks to the integrity of his heart and the possibility of the reality of this vision. Be prepared. Your thinking will be sharpened, and your heart will be moved.

Dr. Crawford W. Loritts Jr., senior pastor, Fellowship Bible Church, Roswell, Georgia

Tim Keller has given us the must-read book on gospel-shaped ministry. Robustly theological and profoundly practical, it is a top-to-bottom survey of gospel implications for the life and ministry of the church. The gap between biblical and practical theology is masterfully bridged. Having worked with Tim and Redeemer City to City, I have benefited from the content of this book and can also attest to its profound influence on ministers and churches throughout the world. This is not simply curriculum content; it is exactly the kind of life-giving, generative gospel theology our churches need. No thoughtful Christian's bookshelf should be without it.

Stephen T. Um, senior minister, Citylife Presbyterian Church, Boston, Massachusetts

Church leaders abandon their unique calling if they merely think theologically to the exclusion of seeing the world in light of the gospel and helping their churches live in the world with gospel wisdom. No one makes this case more clearly today than Tim Keller. He resists the all-too-easy pattern of selling a simple model of what it means to be the church that fits every setting. Instead he brings to life the myriad ways churches are called to be faithful and fruitful in their own unique cultural context. Read this book if you want to learn how to ask the really important (and difficult) questions by which the gospel confronts our ecclesial identity.

Richard Lints, Andrew Mutch distinguished professor of theology, Gordon-Conwell Theological Seminary

I'm not exaggerating when I say that *Center Church* is my favorite book Tim Keller has written thus far. Perhaps this book simply represents the distillation of Tim's wisdom—the synthesis of years of marinating in the gospel, exegeting the text of Scripture, and engaging the soul of our culture; his willingness to dialogue without diatribe; his ongoing commitment to think through the radical implications of God's grace; his great love for Jesus' bride, God's kingdom, and the history of redemption. It's all refreshingly here. What an awesome and practical read! I cannot wait to use this book with emerging leaders and churches willing to dream.

Scotty Smith, founding pastor, Christ Community Church, Franklin, Tennessee

Many know Tim Keller the pastor, apologist, and theologian. But he is also an urban evangelist—an evangelist for the city. In *Center Church*, we find all of the unique facets of his vision and calling in one place. More than essential reading, it is a gift because Tim Keller has given his heart and life to the work of the kingdom in the city.

Mark R. Gornik, director, City Seminary of New York

In *Center Church*, one of the great missionary statesmen of our times lays out a vision of the church vigorous enough to transform entire cities through its agency of the gospel. Tim is a gifted teacher, an outstanding leader, and an exemplary disciple of Jesus. A worthy read!

Alan Hirsch, founder of Forge Missional Training Network

We live in a day of remarkable church leaders and wonderful Christian thinkers, but I'm not sure there's a more thoughtful church leader in our day than Tim Keller. *Center Church* is his call for church ministry formed by deep theological reflection and sensitive cultural exegesis executed by courageous leaders so that the city may once more flourish under the gospel.

John Ortberg, senior pastor, Menlo Park Presbyterian Church, Menlo Park, California

Tim Keller's church in New York City serves as one of the world's best models for gospel-centered ministry that wisely, biblically, and fruitfully connects with its community. This is mainly due to Dr. Keller's deep understanding of the gospel and his exceptional gift for interpreting culture. His latest book will be immensely helpful to anyone doing ministry anywhere. *Center Church* is not a manual for replicating Keller's ministry, but something much more important: a theological vision for how the gospel of Jesus Christ relates to culture, ministry, and the Christian life.

Philip Ryken, president, Wheaton College

Doing Balanced, Gospel-Centered Ministry in Your City

CENTER CHURCH

TIMOTHY KELLER

 ZONDERVAN®

 REDEEMER
CITY to CITY

ZONDERVAN.com/
AUTHORTRACKER
follow your favorite authors

ZONDERVAN

Center Church
Copyright © 2012 by Redeemer City to City and Timothy J. Keller

This title is also available as a Zondervan ebook. Visit www.zondervan.com/ebooks.

This title is also available in a Zondervan audio edition. Visit www.zondervan.fm.

Requests for information should be addressed to:
Zondervan, *Grand Rapids, Michigan 49530*

Library of Congress Cataloging-in-Publication Data

Keller, Timothy J., 1950-
    Center church : doing balanced, Gospel-centered ministry in your city / Timothy J. Keller.
      p. cm.
    ISBN 978-0-310-49418-8 (hardcover)
    1. City missions. 2. City churches. 3. Church work. 4. Evangelistic work. I. Title.
  BV2653.K45. 2012
  253.09173'2 — dc23
                                                                           2012012176

Cover design: *Kristin Spix Design*
Cover photography: *Last Refuge/Robert Harding*
Interior design: *Kristin Spix Design/Ben Fetterley/Matthew Van Zomeren*

Printed in the United States of America

13 14 15 16 17 18 19 20 /DCI/ 22 21 20 19 18 17 16 15 14 13 12 11 10 9 8 7 6 5 4

To Terry Gyger,
founder of the Redeemer Church Planting Center,
missions pioneer, colleague, and friend.

And to the staff,
church planters,
and network leaders
of Redeemer City to City,
for living out this vision
in the global cities of the world.

CONTENTS

ABBREVIATIONS

BIBLE BOOKS

Gen	Genesis
Exod	Exodus
Lev	Leviticus
Num	Numbers
Deut	Deuteronomy
Josh	Joshua
Judg	Judges
Ruth	Ruth
1–2 Sam	1–2 Samuel
1–2 Kgs	1–2 Kings
1–2 Chr	1–2 Chronicles
Ezra	Ezra
Neh	Nehemiah
Esth	Esther
Job	Job
Ps/Pss	Psalm/Psalms
Prov	Proverbs
Eccl	Ecclesiastes
Song	Song of Songs
Isa	Isaiah
Jer	Jeremiah
Lam	Lamentations
Ezek	Ezekiel
Dan	Daniel
Hos	Hosea
Joel	Joel
Amos	Amos
Obad	Obadiah
Jonah	Jonah
Mic	Micah
Nah	Nahum
Hab	Habakkuk
Zeph	Zephaniah
Hag	Haggai
Zech	Zechariah
Mal	Malachi
Matt	Matthew
Mark	Mark
Luke	Luke
John	John
Acts	Acts
Rom	Romans
1–2 Cor	1–2 Corinthians
Gal	Galatians
Eph	Ephesians
Phil	Philippians
Col	Colossians
1–2 Thess	1–2 Thessalonians
1–2 Tim	1–2 Timothy
Titus	Titus
Phlm	Philemon
Heb	Hebrews
Jas	James
1–2 Pet	1–2 Peter
1–2–3 John	1–2–3 John
Jude	Jude
Rev	Revelation

BIBLE VERSIONS

ESV	English Standard Version
KJV	King James Version
NASB	New American Standard Bible
NIV	New International Version
NJB	New Jerusalem Bible

GENERAL

AD	*anno Domini* (in the year of [our] Lord)
cf.	*confer*, compare
ch(s).	chapter(s)
diss.	dissertation
ed(s).	editor(s), edited by, edition
e.g.	*exempli gratia*, for example
esp.	especially
et al.	*et alii*, and others
ff.	and the following ones
ibid.	*ibidem*, in the same place
idem	that which was mentioned before, same, as in same author
i.e.	*id est*, that is
n.	note
NT	New Testament
OT	Old Testament
p(p).	page(s)
repr.	reprinted
rev.	revised
trans.	translator, translated by
v(v).	verse(s)

CENTER CHURCH THEOLOGICAL VISION

SUCCESSFUL, FAITHFUL, OR FRUITFUL?

Once we embark on a life of ministry, it is only natural to ask, "How am I doing? And how will I know?" One answer for ministers today is *success*. Many say that if your church is growing in conversions, members, and giving, your ministry is effective. This view of the ministry is on the rise because the expressive individualism of modern culture has deeply eroded loyalty to institutions and communities. Individuals are now "spiritual consumers" who will go to a church only if (and as long as) its worship and public speaking are immediately riveting and attractive. Therefore, ministers who can create powerful religious experiences and draw large numbers of people on the power of their personal appeal are rewarded with large, growing churches. That is one way to evaluate a ministry.

In reaction to this emphasis on quantifiable success, many have countered that the only true criterion for ministers is *faithfulness*. All that matters in this view is that a minister be sound in doctrine, godly in character, and faithful in preaching and in pastoring people. But the "faithful — not successful" backlash is an oversimplification that has dangers as well. The demand that ministers be not just sincere and faithful but also *competent* is not a modern innovation. The famous nineteenth-century English Baptist preacher Charles Spurgeon pointed out that it takes more than faithfulness to make a minister:

> Certain good men appeal to me who are distinguished by enormous [passion] and zeal, and a conspicuous absence of brains; brethren who would talk forever and ever upon nothing — who would stamp and thump the Bible, and get nothing out of it at all; earnest, awfully earnest, mountains in labor of the most painful kind; but nothing comes of it all … therefore I have usually declined their applications.[1]

Notice that Spurgeon has obvious affection for these men. He is not ridiculing them. He says they are faithful and deeply committed to the work of the ministry, but "nothing comes of it all." When they teach, there is little or no learning; when they evangelize, there is little or no converting. And so he declines their application to his college for ministers. In short, it is an oversimplification to say that faithfulness is all that matters. No — something more than faithfulness is needed to assess whether we are being the ministers we should be.

As I read, reflected, and taught, I came to the conclusion that a more biblical theme for ministerial evaluation than either success or faithfulness is *fruitfulness*. Jesus, of course, told his disciples that they were to "bear much fruit" (John 15:8). Paul spoke even more specifically. He spoke of conversions as "fruit" when he desired to preach in Rome: "that I might have some fruit among you also, even as among other Gentiles" (Rom 1:13 KJV). Paul also spoke of the "fruit" of godly character that a minister can see growing in Christians under his care. This included the "fruit of the Spirit" (Gal 5:22). Good deeds, such as mercy to the poor, are called "fruit" as well (Rom 15:28).

Paul spoke of the pastoral nurture of congregations as a form of gardening. He told the Corinthian Christians they were "God's field" in which some ministers planted, some watered, and some reaped (1 Cor 3:9). The gardening metaphor shows that both success and faithfulness by themselves are insufficient criteria for evaluating ministry. Gardeners must be faithful in their work, but they must also be skillful, or the garden will fail. Yet in the end, the *degree* of the success of the garden (or the ministry) is determined by factors beyond the control of the gardener. The level of fruitfulness varies due to "soil conditions" (that is, some groups of people have a greater hardness of heart than others) and "weather conditions" (that is, the work of God's sovereign Spirit) as well.

The church growth movement has made many lasting contributions to our practice of ministry. But its overemphasis on technique and results can put too much pressure on ministers because it underemphasizes the importance of godly character and the sovereignty of God. Those who claim that "what is required is faithfulness" are largely right, but this mind-set can take too much pressure off church leaders. It does not lead them to ask hard questions when faithful ministries bear little fruit. When fruitfulness is our criterion for evaluation, we are held accountable but not crushed by the expectation that a certain number of lives will be changed dramatically under our ministry.

THE "SECRET" OF REDEEMER'S FRUITFULNESS

After nearly a decade of pastoral ministry in a small town in Virginia, I moved to Philadelphia, where I served on the faculty of Westminster Seminary in the mid-1980s. There I was called to teach preaching, pastoral leadership, evangelism, and the doctrine of the church. The academic position afforded me my first chance to reflect on what I had learned in my first busy years of church leadership. It also gave me the opportunity to study about ministry at a depth that had been impossible previously. In 1989, our family moved to New York City to begin Redeemer Presbyterian Church. A few years later, we began getting inquiries from pastors around the country (and eventually overseas) who asked if they could visit us because "we want to see what you are doing that is working so well in Manhattan." After a while, it became impossible to see everyone individually, and so we began to host regular weekends for visitors to observe the church.

Those conferences called for me to summarize what we were doing that was bearing fruit in the city. The talks I gave were based on the syllabi I had developed at Westminster to answer the question, "What makes gospel ministry faithful and fruitful?" But those lectures had been more theoretical.

Now I was being asked for principles of ministry grounded in our everyday experience of gospel work in Manhattan.

But the process of identifying "principles of ministry" was not easy for me because what I wanted to say to observers didn't fit very well into existing categories.

You see, two kinds of books are ordinarily written for pastors and church leaders. One kind lays out general biblical principles for all churches. These books start with scriptural exegesis and biblical theology and list the characteristics and functions of a true biblical church. The most important characteristic is that a ministry be faithful to the Word and sound in doctrine, but these books also rightly call for biblical standards of evangelism, church leadership, community and membership, worship, and service. All of this is critical, but I knew many ministers who conducted their ministry on these sound principles and who had seen a great deal of fruit elsewhere, but when they moved to New York City — still working on the same sound foundation — they had far less impact than they had elsewhere. I concluded that an understanding of the biblical marks of a healthy church was absolutely foundational and necessary, but that something more should be said if gospel ministry was going to be productive.

Another category of book operates at the opposite end of the spectrum. These books do not spend much time laying biblical theological foundations, though virtually all of them cite biblical passages. Instead, they are practical "how-to" books that describe specific mind-sets, programs, and ways to do church. This genre of book exploded onto the scene during the church growth movement of the 1970s and 1980s through the writing of authors such as C. Peter Wagner and Robert Schuller. A second generation of books in a similar vein appeared with personal accounts of successful churches, authored by senior pastors, distilling practical principles for others to use. A third generation of practical church books began more than ten years ago. These are volumes that directly criticize the church growth "how-to" books. Nevertheless, they also consist largely of case studies and pictures of what a good church looks like on the ground, with practical advice on how to organize and conduct ministry. Again, from these volumes I almost always profited, coming away from each book with at least one good idea I could use. But by and large, I found the books less helpful than I hoped they would be. Implicitly or explicitly, they made near-absolutes out of techniques and models that had worked in a certain place at a certain time. I was fairly certain that many of these methods would not work in New York and were not as universally applicable as the authors implied. In particular, church leaders outside of the United States found these books irritating because the authors assumed that what worked in a suburb of a U.S. city would work almost anywhere.

As people pressed me to speak and write about our experience at Redeemer, I realized that most were urging me to write my own version of the second type of book. Pastors did not want me to recapitulate biblical doctrine and principles of church life they had gotten in seminary. Instead, they were looking for a "secrets of success" book. They wanted instructions for specific programs and techniques that appealed to urban people. One pastor said, "I've tried the Willow Creek model. Now I'm ready to try the Redeemer model." People came to us because they knew we were thriving in one of the least churched, most secular cities in the U.S. But when visitors first started coming to Redeemer in the early and mid-1990s, they were disappointed because they did not discern a new "model" — at least not in the form of unique, new programs. At first glance, Redeemer seems so traditional. To reach unchurched, postmodern young adults, many ministers preach in warehouses, dress informally, sit on stools, show video clips, and use indie-rock music. At Redeemer we did none of these things, yet we had thousands of the very kind of secular, sophisticated young adults the church was not reaching.

So, for example, Redeemer has had classical music in its morning services and jazz music in its evening services. This is unusual, so some have asked, "Is this how you reach urban people? Is this a key?" My immediate response is, "No, it isn't. Not only is it likely you will come to different conclusions about music in different world cities, but there have been and are other effective ways to use music in worship that are effective in New York City." Others have concluded that the type of preaching at Redeemer has been the key. They noticed my style of quoting liberally from literary and secular media sources and conclude that this is the way to reach large numbers of urban people. But it is possible to adopt this style to little effect. Preaching is compelling to young secular adults not if preachers use video clips from their favorite movies and dress informally and sound sophisticated, but if the preachers understand their hearts and culture so well that listeners feel the force of the sermon's reasoning, even if in the end they don't agree with it. This is not a matter of style or program.

During these years of conferences, it became clear that the real "secret" of Redeemer's fruitfulness did not lie in its ministry programs but in something

BOOKS ON BIBLICAL CHURCHES

Mark Dever's book *Nine Marks of a Healthy Church* (2nd ed.; Wheaton, Ill.: Crossway, 2004) is one of the most practical and useful of all the "biblical principles for churches" books. Written at a similarly popular level but from a Presbyterian perspective are Edmund P. Clowney's *Living in Christ's Church* (Philadelphia: Great Commission Publications, 1986) and Philip Graham Ryken's *City on a Hill: Reclaiming the Biblical Pattern for the Church in the 21st Century* (Chicago: Moody, 2003). A similar kind of book, but less doctrinally oriented, is Christian A. Schwarz's *Natural Church Development: A Guide to Eight Essential Qualities of Healthy Churches* (St. Charles, Ill.: ChurchSmart, 1996). An introduction from an Anglican perspective is John Stott's *The Living Church* (Downers Grove, Ill.: InterVarsity, 2007). The best single academic (though still accessible) theology of the church is Edmund P. Clowney's *The Church* (Downers Grove, Ill.: InterVarsity, 1995).

The original generation of practical church growth books was exemplified by C. Peter Wagner's *Your Church Can Grow* (Ventura, Calif.: Regal, 1984) and *Your Church Can Be Healthy* (Nashville: Abingdon, 1979). More recently, influential church growth books have been written by highly successful large-church pastors. Examples include Bill and Lynne Hybels's *Rediscovering Church: The Story and Vision of Willow Creek* (Grand Rapids: Zondervan, 1997), Rick Warren's *The Purpose Driven Church* (Grand Rapids: Zondervan, 1995), and Andy Stanley's *Seven Practices of Effective Ministry* (Sisters, Ore.: Multnomah, 2004). Many of these second-generation church growth books share the effectiveness of one particular ministry program or practice. Take, for example, such books as Larry Osborne's *Sticky Church* (Grand Rapids: Zondervan, 2008), which lifts up the helpfulness of sermon-based small groups, and Nelson Searcey's *Fusion: Turning First-Time Guests into Fully Engaged Members of Your Church* (Ventura, Calif.: Regal, 2008), which stresses new visitor follow-up and assimilation.

The third generation of practical books directly reacts to the church growth, megachurch movement. Most offer a new way to do church through the perspective of a key concept. Thom Rainer's *Simple Church: Returning to God's Process for Making Disciples* (Nashville: Broadman & Holman, 2006) sees discipleship as the key. Tim Chester and Steve Timmis's *Total Church: A Radical Reshaping around Gospel and Community* (Wheaton, Ill.: Crossway, 2008) rethinks church in terms of community. Colin Marshall and Tony Payne's *The Trellis and the Vine: The Ministry Mind-Shift That Changes Everything* (Kingsford, Australia: Matthias Media, 2009) understands the heart of ministry

that functioned at a deeper level. What was important for observers to grasp was not so much the particular ministry expression but the way in which we arrived at the expressions we used at Redeemer. We had thought long and hard about the character and implications of the gospel and then long and hard about the culture of New York City, about the

---

The "secret" of Redeemer's fruitfulness was not so much the particular ministry expression but the way in which we arrived at the expressions we used at Redeemer.

---

sensibilities of both Christians and non-Christians in our midst, and about the emotional and intellectual landscape of the center city. It was the character of that analysis and decision-making process rather than its specific products that was critical to the fruitfulness of our ministry in a global city center. We wanted to be shaped by what Jonathan Edwards called "the rules of the gospel."[2] We did not simply choose music or sermon illustrations to please our own tastes and make us happy, any more than Christ lived to please himself.

HARDWARE, MIDDLEWARE, SOFTWARE

What was this deeper level, exactly? As time went on, I began to realize it was a middle space between two more obvious dimensions of ministry. All of us have a *doctrinal foundation* — a set of theological beliefs — and all of us conduct particular *forms of ministry*. But many ministers take up programs and practices of ministry that fit well with neither their doctrinal beliefs nor their cultural context. They adopt popular methods that are essentially "glued on" from the outside — alien to the church's theology or setting (sometimes both!). And when this happens, we find a lack of fruitfulness. These ministers don't change people's lives within the church and don't reach people in their city. Why not? Because the programs do not grow naturally out of reflection on both the gospel and the distinctness of their surrounding culture.

For example, imagine that a minister who had a flourishing ministry in an exurban area moves to an urban setting. He continues to preach and pastor in exactly the same way he did before, and soon he sees an alarming drop in attendance and in lives being changed. He may go in one of three directions. First, he may simply keep doing the same thing, attributing lack of fruit to the hard-heartedness of urban dwellers. Second, he may read books, looking for new programs that worked elsewhere — usually in suburban U.S. contexts — and finding that when he adopts them, they are also ineffective in his new setting. Third, he may actually come to believe he needs to reengineer and change his doctrinal foundation, reasoning that contemporary people can't accept traditional teachings on judgment and atonement. In each case, however, he is failing to notice the middle space between doctrine and practice — the space where we reflect deeply on our theology and our culture to understand how both of them can shape our ministry. This leads to better choices of existing ministry forms, or to the development of promising new ones.

Therefore, if you think of your doctrinal foundation as "hardware" and of ministry programs as "software," it is important to understand the existence of something called "middleware." I am no computer expert (to say the least), but my computer-savvy friends tell me that middleware is a software layer that lies between the hardware and operating system itself and the various software applications being deployed by the computer's user. In the same way, between one's doctrinal beliefs and ministry practices should be a well-conceived vision for how to bring the gospel to bear on the particular cultural setting and historical moment. This is something more practical than just doctrinal beliefs but much more theological than "how-to steps" for carrying out a particular ministry. Once this vision is in place, with its emphases and values, it leads church leaders to make good decisions on how to worship, disciple, evangelize, serve, and engage culture in their field of ministry — whether in a city, suburb, or small town.

to be the training of lay ministers of the Word. Robert Lewis's *The Church of Irresistible Influence: Bridge-Building Stories to Help Reach Your Community* (Grand Rapids: Zondervan, 2001) and Rick Rusaw and Eric Swanson's *The Externally Focused Church* (Loveland, Colo.: Group, 2006) lift up community involvement and service as the way forward.

A sharply different set of "church growth pushback" books have appeared under the heading of "missional church." Early examples include Eddie Gibbs's *ChurchNext: Quantum Changes in How We Do Ministry* (Downers Grove, Ill.: InterVarsity, 2000) Reggie McNeal's *The Present Future* (2003), and Ryan Bolger's *Emerging Churches: Creating Christian Community in Postmodern Cultures* (Grand Rapids: Baker, 2005). More recent examples include Reggie McNeal's *Missional Renaissance* (2009) and *Missional Communities* (2011), published by Jossey-Bass, and M. Scott Boren's *Missional Small Groups: Becoming a Community that Makes a Difference in the World* (Grand Rapids: Baker, 2010). See part 6 ("Missional Community") for much more on the missional church movement.

THEOLOGICAL VISION

This "middleware" is similar to what Richard Lints, professor of theology at Gordon-Conwell Theological Seminary, calls a "theological vision."[3] According to Lints, our doctrinal foundation, drawn from Scripture, is the starting point for everything:

> *Theology must first be about a conversation with God … God speaks and we listen… The Christian theological framework is primarily about listening — listening to God. One of the great dangers we face in doing theology is our desire to do all the talking… We most often capitulate to this temptation by placing alien conceptual boundaries on what God can and has said in the Word… We force the message of redemption into a*

cultural package that distorts its actual intentions. Or we attempt to view the gospel solely from the perspective of a tradition that has little living connection to the redemptive work of Christ on the cross. Or we place rational restrictions on the very notion of God instead of allowing God to define the notions of rationality.[4]

However, the doctrinal foundation is not enough. Before you choose specific ministry methods, you must first ask how your doctrinal beliefs "might relate to the modern world." The result of that question "thereby form[s] a theological vision."[5] In other words, a theological vision is a vision for what you are going to *do* with your doctrine in a particular time and place. And what does a theological vision develop from? Lints shows that it comes, of course, from deep reflection on the Bible itself, but it also depends a great deal on what you think of the culture around you.

Lints explains why we cannot stop with our doctrinal foundation but must also look at our setting — our historical moment and our cultural location:

Having recognized the source of the conversation [God], we must then take into account those with whom he speaks. God does not speak in a vacuum but to and through people and in and through history. The speech of God ... is addressed to people across different cultural histories, and for this reason (among others), it is often misunderstood and misinterpreted ...

Nicodemus and the Pharisees stood in a tradition, were conditioned by a culture, and applied certain principles of rationality to their own conversations with Jesus. We do the same today. It is ... [critical that] the people of God [come] to an awareness of their historical, cultural, and rational filters so that they will not be ruled by them.[6]

This reveals, I believe, one (among others) of the key reasons for failures in fruitfulness. We must discern where and how the culture can be challenged and affirmed. The answers to these questions have enormous impact on how we preach, evangelize, organize, lead, disciple, and shepherd people. Lints offers this important observation:

A theological vision allows [people] to see their culture in a way different than they had ever been able to see it before ...Those who are empowered by the theological vision do not simply stand against

the mainstream impulses of the culture but take the initiative both to understand and speak to that culture from the framework of the Scriptures ... The modern theological vision must seek to bring the entire counsel of God into the world of its time in order that its time might be transformed.[7]

"The modern theological vision must seek to bring the entire counsel of God into the world of its time in order that its time might be transformed." — Richard Lints

---

I propose a similar but slightly more specific set of questions for the development of a theological vision. As we answer these questions, a theological vision will emerge:

- What is the gospel, and how do we bring it to bear on the hearts of people today?
- What is this culture like, and how can we both connect to it and challenge it in our communication?
- Where are we located — city, suburb, town, rural area — and how does this affect our ministry?
- To what degree and how should Christians be involved in civic life and cultural production?
- How do the various ministries in a church — word and deed, community and instruction — relate to one another?
- How innovative will our church be and how traditional?
- How will our church relate to other churches in our city and region?
- How will we make our case to the culture about the truth of Christianity?

This concept of a theological vision explains how, for example, our conservative Presbyterian denomination, in which all churches share the same detailed doctrinal foundation (Westminster Confession of Faith) can be deeply divided over ministry expressions and methods, such as music, preaching style, approach to organization and leadership, forms of outreach, and so on. The reason is that churches with the same basic doctrine are shaped by different theological visions because they are answering these questions about culture, tradition, and rationality differently.

For example, some churches believe nearly all popular culture is corrupt, and therefore they will not use popular music in worship. Others have no problem doing so. Why? It is not merely a matter of personal preference. Implicit questions of theological vision are being posed and answered when we make such decisions. The fundamental differences are often between competing theological visions, yet because theological vision is largely invisible, people inevitably (and unfortunately) conclude that the differences are doctrinal.

It could be argued that an acquaintance with the category of theological vision will help us understand many of the conflicts in local churches and denominations. Our doctrinal statements of faith and confessions do not tell us what in our culture can be affirmed and what can be challenged, nor do they speak directly to our relationship to tradition and the Christian past or reflect much on how human reason operates. Yet our ministries are shaped profoundly by our assumptions about these issues. When we see other people who say they believe our doctrine but are doing ministry in a way we greatly dislike, we tend to suspect they have fallen away from their doctrinal commitments. They may have, of course; yet it's equally likely that they haven't strayed but are working from a different theological vision. Unless we can make these assumptions more visible and conscious, we will misunderstand one another and find it difficult to respect one another.

Perhaps we can diagram it like this (see next page). Our theological vision, growing out of our doctrinal foundation but including implicit or explicit readings of culture, is the most immediate cause of our decisions and choices regarding ministry expression.

So what is a theological vision? It is a faithful restatement of the gospel with rich implications for life, ministry, and mission in a type of culture at a moment in history.

THE FORMATION OF THEOLOGICAL VISION

According to Richard Lints in *The Fabric of Theology*, four factors influence the formation of a theological vision. The foundation is, of course, *listening to the Bible to arrive at our doctrinal beliefs* (pp. 57–80). The second is *reflection on culture* (pp. 101–16), as we ask what modern culture is and which of its impulses are to be criticized and which are to be affirmed. A third is our particular *understanding of reason* (pp. 117–35). Some see human reason as being able to lead a nonbeliever a long way toward the truth, while others deny this. Our view of the nature of human rationality will shape how we preach to, evangelize, argue with, and engage with non-Christians. The fourth factor is the role of *theological tradition* (pp. 83–101). Some believers are antitraditionalists who feel free to virtually reinvent Christianity each generation without giving any weight to the interpreters of the Christian community in the past. Others give great weight to tradition and are opposed to innovation with regard to communicating the gospel and practicing ministry.

Lints argues that what we believe about culture, reason, and tradition will influence how we understand what Scripture says. And even if three ministers arrive at the same set of doctrinal beliefs, if they hold different views of culture, reason, and tradition, then their theological visions and the shapes of their ministries will be very different.

WHY A WHOLE BOOK ON THEOLOGICAL VISION?

The need to explain and chart these insights became more acute as we began to plant churches — first in New York City and then in many other global cities. We wanted to help church planters learn as much as they could from our reflection and experience, but we had no interest in starting little copies of Redeemer because we knew that every city — indeed, every neighborhood — was different. We believed a city needed all kinds of churches to reach all kinds of people. And we knew that church planters need to *create* ministry, not replicate it. We wanted to help plant churches that would be unlike Redeemer in many particulars but still be like Redeemer in certain ineffable ways. For that to happen, we had to begin articulating a theological vision that lay somewhere between doctrinal beliefs on the one hand and specific ministry programs on the other.

A theological vision is a faithful restatement
of the gospel with rich implications for
life, ministry, and mission in a type of
culture at a moment in history.

Redeemer City to City is a nonprofit organization involved in global city church planting on every continent, across a wide array of theological traditions. It should not be surprising that nearly all of our training and coaching centers on the theological vision outlined in this book. Once we assess prospective church planters for their gifts and theological soundness, we spend relatively little time on doctrinal foundations (though our training is highly theological) or ministry expression (though church planters are wrestling with concrete issues of expression and form in their respective churches). Here is what we have found in two decades of experience.

1. Theological vision is hard, but it is what pastors need. Urban pastors struggle to connect doctrinal foundations to ministry expression in a meaningful way. There is a tendency either to overcontextualize to the city (which usually leads to weakening or relativizing a church's commitment to orthodoxy) or to undercontextualize (which leads to inward-facing churches that reach only certain kinds of people and fail to advance a movement of the gospel in the community). But we find that the quality of

WHAT TO DO

How the gospel is expressed
in a particular church in one
community at a point in time

- *Local cultural adaptation*
- *Worship style & programming*
- *Discipleship & outreach processes*
- *Church governance & management*

MINISTRY EXPRESSION

HOW TO SEE

A faithful restatement of
the gospel with rich
implications for life, ministry,
and mission in a type of
culture at a moment in
history

- *Vision and values*
- *Ministry "DNA"*
- *Emphases, stances*
- *Philosophy of ministry*

THEOLOGICAL VISION

WHAT TO BELIEVE

Timeless truths from the Bible
about God, our relationship
to Him, and His purposes
in the world

- *Theological tradition*
- *Denominational affiliation*
- *Systematic & biblical theology*

DOCTRINAL FOUNDATION

the theological vision often determines the vitality of the ministry, particularly in urban settings.

2. It is transferable and adaptable. We find that this theological vision is highly transferable to orthodox, confessing churches in many cultural contexts and styles. Focusing on the theological vision allows us truly to serve a movement rather than to just create or inspire churches in our own image. It also suits those entrepreneurial leaders who neither want to reengineer doctrine nor be given a template to implement but who want to create new and beautiful ministry expressions.

3. It goes beyond churches. We have found that this theological vision not only fuels the planting and leading of churches but also relates to all kinds of ministry and even to the mission and vocation of people who are not professional ministers.

CENTER CHURCH

In this book, we will call our theological vision — this particular set of emphases and stances for ministry — "Center Church." I know there has been a trend over the last few years to publish books with the title _____ *Church*, and I join this trend with two particular perils in mind. My first concern is that the term will be used as a label or a diagnostic tool, as in "*This* is a Center Church, but *that* one isn't." I will certainly try to avoid this kind of unhelpful shorthand, and I ask you to do the same. My second concern is that people will read political or doctrinal overtones into the term, as if Redeemer is advocating that to be a faithful Christian you must occupy some neutral center between liberal and conservative political views. This has nothing to do with what we mean by the term.

Those issues notwithstanding, we chose this term for several reasons.

1. The gospel is at its center. In the first section, I will seek to make the case that it is one thing to have a ministry that is gospel believing and even gospel proclaiming but quite another to have one that is gospel centered.

2. The center is the place of balance. In this book, you will hear a great deal about the need to strike balances as Scripture does: of word *and* deed

ministries; of challenging *and* affirming human culture; of cultural engagement *and* countercultural distinctiveness; of commitment to truth *and* generosity to others who don't share the same beliefs; of tradition *and* innovation in practice.

3. This theological vision is shaped by and for urban and cultural centers. Redeemer and the other churches we have helped to start minister in the center city. We believe ministry in the center of global cities is the highest priority for the church in the twenty-first century. While this theological vision is widely applicable, it is distinctly flavored by the urban experience.

4. The theological vision is at the center of ministry. As described above, a theological vision creates a bridge between doctrine and expression. It is central to how all ministry happens. Two churches can have different doctrinal frameworks and ministry expressions but the same theological vision — and they will feel like sister ministries. On the other hand, two churches can have similar doctrinal frameworks and ministry expressions but different theological visions — and they will feel distinct.

CENTER CHURCH COMMITMENTS

The Center Church theological vision can be expressed most simply in three basic commitments: Gospel, City, and Movement.[8]

Gospel. Both the Bible and church history show us that it is possible to hold all the correct individual biblical doctrines and yet functionally lose our grasp on the gospel. D. Martyn Lloyd-Jones argues that while we obviously lose the gospel if we fall into heterodoxy, we can also operationally stop preaching and using the gospel on ourselves through dead orthodoxy or through doctrinal imbalances of emphasis. Sinclair Ferguson argues that there are many forms of both legalism and antinomianism, some of which are based on overt heresy but more often on matters of emphasis and spirit.[9] It is critical, therefore, in every new generation and setting to find ways to *communicate the gospel clearly and strikingly*, distinguishing it from its opposites and counterfeits. This particular subject is not just hardware but also middleware. Parties who agree on all doctrinal basics can still differ sharply on

MIDDLEWARE, THEOLOGICAL VISION, AND DNA

As we found ourselves driven away from both the general (foundational discussions of what the church should be) and the particular (detailed programs and styles), we had to find a way to talk about what we meant. We have not typically employed the term "theological vision" or the "middleware" metaphor. More often at Redeemer, we use the language of city-gospel "DNA."

Why use this particular image? DNA is a set of instructions deep within the cells of an organism that directs how it develops, grows, and self-replicates. At the core of Redeemer's ministry is orthodox evangelical theology—the classic doctrines of the biblical gospel. We want our doctrine to act as a control and driver of our ministry, and this will only happen if we use doctrine to generate a theological vision. We do so by asking, "*How* should this unchanging gospel doctrine be communicated and embodied in a great, global city like New York in this day and age?" Our answers to this question—our theological vision—are the DNA that enables us to choose or develop ministry expressions that are not only consistent with our doctrinal commitments but that fit our time, place, and culture. As a result, our ministry can develop, grow, and self-replicate fruitfully.

In the end, different metaphors, such as middleware and DNA, are useful in drawing out certain aspects of how a theological vision works.

ing toward legalism. On the other hand, communicating the gospel rightly in your time and place is not just a matter of "how-to" programming.

City. A second major area of a Center Church theological vision has to do with our cultural context. All churches must understand, love, and identify with their local community and social setting, and yet at the same time be able and willing to critique and challenge it. Because Redeemer was a ministry operating in a major urban center, we had to spend time studying the Bible to see what it said about cities in particular — and to our surprise we found that it said a lot. Every church, whether located in a city, suburb, or rural area (and there are many permutations and combinations of these settings), must become wise about and conversant with the distinctives of human life in those places. But we must also think about how Christianity and the church engages and interacts with culture in general. This has become an acute issue as Western culture has become increasingly post-Christian. Churches with similar doctrinal foundations have come to strikingly divergent conclusions about how to relate to culture, and their "Christ and Culture" model always has a drastic impact on ministry expression. Again, the development of a theology of the city and of culture is neither a matter of systematic theology nor of concrete ministry practice. It is an aspect of *theological vision.*

Movement. The last area of theological vision has to do with your church's *relationships* — with its community, with its recent and deeper past, and with other churches and ministries. Richard Lints points out that one of the elements of a theological vision has to do with our understanding of tradition. Some churches are highly institutional, with a strong emphasis on their own past, while others are anti-institutional, fluid, and marked by constant innovation and change. Some churches see themselves as being loyal to a particular ecclesiastical tradition — and so they cherish historical and traditional liturgy and ministry practices. Those that identify very strongly with a particular denomination or newer tradition often resist change. At the other end of the spectrum are churches with

emphasis, tone, and spirit, as can be seen in the "Marrow Controversy" in the Church of Scotland during the early eighteenth century when all parties agreed wholeheartedly with the Westminster Confession of Faith, yet a significant portion of the church was slid-

little sense of a theological and ecclesiastical past that tend to relate easily to a wide variety of other churches and ministries. All of these different perspectives have an enormous impact on how we actually do ministry. Again, they are not included in systematic theology — these issues are not solved by historical confessions or statements of faith. On the other hand, they pose deeper concerns than the practical ministry books can address.[10]

THE BALANCE OF THREE AXES

One of the simplest ways to convey the approach to the rest of this volume — and the principles of theological vision under each of these headings — is to think of three axes.

1. The *Gospel* axis. At one end of the axis is legalism, the teaching that asserts or the spirit that implies we can save ourselves by how we live. At the other end is antinomianism or, in popular parlance, relativism — the view that it doesn't matter how we live; that God, if he exists, loves everyone the same. But the gospel, as we will argue in a later chapter, is neither legalism nor relativism. We are saved by faith and grace alone, but not by a faith that remains alone. True grace always results in changed lives of holiness and justice. It is, of course, possible to lose the gospel because of heterodoxy. That is, if we no longer believe in the deity of Christ or the doctrine of justification, we will necessarily slide toward relativism. But it is also possible to hold sound doctrine and yet be marked

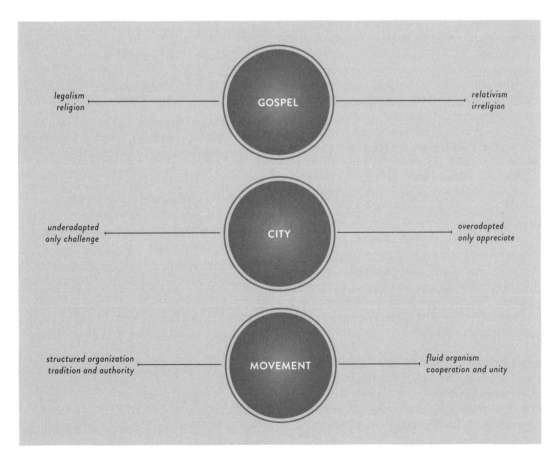

legalism
religion — GOSPEL — relativism
irreligion

underadapted
only challenge — CITY — overadapted
only appreciate

structured organization
tradition and authority — MOVEMENT — fluid organism
cooperation and unity

by dead orthodoxy (a spirit of self-righteousness), imbalanced orthodoxy (overemphasis on some doctrines that obscure the gospel call), or even "clueless orthodoxy," which results when doctrines are expounded as in a theology class but aren't brought together to penetrate people's hearts so they experience conviction of sin and the beauty of grace. Our communication and practices must not tend toward either law or license. To the degree that they do, they lose life-changing power.[11]

2. The *City* axis (which could also be called a *Culture* axis). We will show that to reach people we must appreciate and adapt to their culture, but we must also challenge and confront it. This is based on the biblical teaching that all cultures have God's grace and natural revelation in them, yet they are also in rebellious idolatry. If we overadapt to a culture, we have accepted the culture's idols. If, however, we underadapt to a culture, we may have turned our own culture into an idol, an absolute. If we overadapt to a culture, we aren't able to change people because we are not calling them to change. If we underadapt to a culture, no one will be changed because no one will listen to us; we will be confusing, offensive, or simply unpersuasive. To the degree a ministry is overadapted or underadapted to a culture, it loses life-changing power.

3. The *Movement* axis. Some churches identify so strongly with their own theological tradition that they cannot make common cause with other evangelical churches or other institutions to reach a city or work for the common good. They also tend to cling strongly to forms of ministry from the past and are highly structured and institutional. Other churches are strongly anti-institutional. They have almost no identification with a particular heritage or denomination, nor do they have much of a relationship to a Christian past. Sometimes they have virtually no institutional character, being completely fluid and informal. As we will show later, a church at either extreme will stifle the development of leadership and strangle the health of the church as a corporate body, as a community.[12] To the degree that it commits either of these errors, it loses its life-giving power.

The more that ministry comes "from the center" of all the axes, the more dynamism and fruitfulness it will have. Ministry that is out toward the end of any of the spectrums or axes will drain a ministry of life-changing power with the people in and around it.

I hope this book will be especially useful for those ministering in urban and cultural centers. But even if you are not literally in such a center, I believe you can still minister "from the center" by being aware of these three axes and adjusting your ministry expressions accordingly.

In the rest of the book, I explain as best I can what it means to center on the three commitments of Gospel, City, and Movement. The Center Church theological vision is further broken down into eight elements, which are treated in the eight parts of this volume:[13]

Section 1: GOSPEL

Part 1: Gospel Theology. We seek to be characterized by our gospel-theological depth rather than by our doctrinal shallowness, pragmatism, nonreflectiveness, and method-driven philosophy.

Part 2: Gospel Renewal. A constant note of grace is applied to everything, so that ministry is not marked by legalism or cold intellectualism.

Section 2: CITY

Part 3: Gospel Contextualization. We are sensitive to culture rather than choosing to ignore our cultural moment or being oblivious to cultural differences among groups.

Part 4: City Vision. We adopt city-loving ways of ministry rather than approaches that are hostile or indifferent to the city.

Part 5: Cultural Engagement. We are culturally engaged and avoid being either too triumphalistic or too withdrawn and subcultural in our attitude.

Section 3: MOVEMENT

Part 6: Missional Community. Every part of the church is outward facing, expecting the presence of nonbelievers and supporting laypeople in their ministry in the world.

Part 7: Integrative Ministry. We minister in word and deed, helping to meet the spiritual and physical needs of the poor as well as those who live and work in cultural centers.

Part 8: Movement Dynamics. We have a mindset of willing cooperation with other believers, not being turf conscious and suspicious but eagerly promoting a vision for the whole city.[14]

We are not, then, laying out a "Redeemer model" in this book. This is not a "church in a box." Instead, we are laying out a particular theological vision for ministry that we believe will enable many churches to reach people in our day and time, particularly where late-modern Western globalization is influencing the culture. This is especially true in the great cities of the world, but these cultural shifts are being felt everywhere, and so we trust that this book will be found useful to church leaders in a great variety of social settings. We will be recommending a vision for using the gospel in the lives of contemporary people, doing contextualization, understanding cities, doing cultural engagement, discipling for mission, integrating various ministries, and fostering movement dynamics in your congregation and in the world. This set of emphases and values — a Center Church theological vision — can empower all kinds of church models and methods in all kinds of settings. We believe that if you embrace the process of making your theological vision visible, you will make far better choices of model and method.

INTRODUCTION — CENTER CHURCH THEOLOGICAL VISION *(pages 13–25)*

1. Charles H. Spurgeon, *Lectures to My Students*. There are many editions of this book, and some are online. This quote is taken from Lecture 2 — "The Call to the Ministry."

2. Jonathan Edwards, "Christian Charity: The Duty of Charity to the Poor Explained and Enforced," in *The Works of Jonathan Edwards*, ed. E. Hickman (Carlisle, Pa.: Banner of Truth, 1974), 2:171. In this treatise, Edwards uses the phrase "rules of the gospel" to refer to the shape of Christ's work of salvation (sacrificial self-giving to those who are spiritually poor and bankrupt), which must in turn shape how we behave in the world. He infers from the gospel that we should (1) forgive those who wrong us, (2) give to the poor — even the "undeserving poor," and (3) help others, even when we cannot afford to. Edwards draws out the implications of Christ's substitutionary atonement and our free justification for every area of life. He gives us a good example in this essay of how reflection on the core elements of the gospel leads to a commitment to ministry to the poor.

3. Richard Lints, *The Fabric of Theology: A Prolegomenon to Evangelical Theology* (Grand Rapids: Eerdmans, 1993), 9.

4. Ibid., 82.

5. Ibid., 315.

6. Ibid., 83.

7. Ibid., 316–17.

8. These three areas correspond roughly to Richard Lints's four theological vision factors in this way: (1) *Gospel* flows from how you read the Bible, (2) *City* flows from your reflections on culture, and (3) *Movement* flows from your understanding of tradition. Meanwhile the fourth factor — your view of human rationality — influences your understanding of all three. It has an impact on how you evangelize non-Christians, how much common grace you see in a culture, and how institutional (or anti-institutional) you are in your thinking about ministry structure.

9. See D. Martyn Lloyd-Jones, *Revival* (Wheaton, Ill.: Crossway, 1982); see also Sinclair Ferguson's three lectures on the Marrow Controversy, www.sermonaudio.com/search.asp?seriesOnly=true&currSection=sermonstopic&SourceID=gpts&keyworddesc=The+Marrow+Controversy&keyword=The+Marrow+Controversy (accessed December 30, 2011).

10. For example, virtually all of the popular church growth books assume that churches have no distinctive ecclesiastical traditions. The volumes treat Reformed, Anglican, Methodist, Baptist, and Lutheran churches as if they are all alike. But there is no theological or exegetical argument offered for this. It is simply assumed that historical tradition means little or nothing.

11. It can be argued that the Gospel axis is not like the other two. In the other two axes, the desired position is a midpoint, a balance between extremes. However, Sinclair Ferguson (in his lectures on the Marrow Controversy) and others have argued that the gospel is not at all a balance between two opposites but an entirely different thing. In fact, it can also be argued that legalism and antinomianism are not opposites but essentially the same thing — self-salvation — opposed to the gospel. So please note that putting Gospel between these two extremes is simply a visual shorthand.

12. Astute readers will notice later in this book that I advise churches to *not* occupy an exact midpoint on the spectrum between a structured organization and a fluid organism. I suggest you occupy a position a couple of steps toward the organism end to maintain a spirit of innovation and creativity. So while this three-axis schematic does not precisely convey all we want to say about each topic, it is a good way to remember the basic themes and emphases.

13. Some have pointed out that these eight elements cover roughly the same territory covered by Francis Schaeffer in his seminal short book titled *2 Contents, 2 Realities* (Downers Grove, Ill.: InterVarsity, 1975), based on his address to the first Lausanne Congress on World Evangelization held in July 1974. Schaeffer's address covers four things he saw as "absolutely necessary if we as Christians are to meet the need of our age and the overwhelming pressure we are increasingly facing" (p. 7). These four things are sound doctrine; contextual, cultural engagement ("honest answers to honest questions"); a spiritual recovering of the gospel for our hearts ("true spirituality"); and remarkable, vital Christian community ("the beauty of human relationships"). I hope the balance of Schaeffer's elements will be reflected in my similar but somewhat more specific list.

14. Those who are familiar with Redeemer will certainly wonder why preaching doesn't have its own section in the book. The answer is that it embodies all of the elements of theological vision. You will find, for example, that suggestions on preaching appear in more than half of the eight elements: how to preach for renewal, how to contextualize in your preaching, how to preach in a way that engages culture, and so on.

GOSPEL

legalism
religion

relativism
irreligion

*The gospel is neither religion nor irreligion, but
something else entirely — a third way of relating
to God through grace. Because of this, we minister
in a uniquely balanced way that avoids the
errors of either extreme and faithfully
communicates the sharpness of the gospel.*

GOSPEL

It is quite easy to assume that if we understand the gospel accurately and preach it faithfully, our ministry will necessarily be shaped by it — but this is not true. Many churches subscribe to gospel doctrines but do not have a ministry that is shaped by, centered on, and empowered through the gospel. Its implications have not yet worked their way into the fabric of how the church actually does ministry. These churches' theological vision has likely arisen from something other than sustained reflection on the gospel.

Gospel-centered ministry is more theologically driven than program driven. To pursue it, we must spend time reflecting on the essence, the truths, and the very patterns of the gospel itself. It is an unfortunate development within the history of thought in general and the history of the church in particular that has insisted on driving a wedge between theory and practice. The two belong together in dialogical relationship. Theology here is understood to be *fides quaerens intellectum*, the ministry of Christian understanding — an understanding that aims for the church's fitting participation within the drama of God's redemption.[*]

The first section of this book addresses several current discussions and conflicts pertaining to the nature of the gospel itself. In part 1 (**Gospel Theology**), we look at what the gospel *is* and *is not*. In part 2 (**Gospel Renewal**), we reflect on the history and patterns of revival — how individual and corporate gospel renewal occurs — and what happens as a result.

---

[*] See Kevin J. Vanhoozer, *The Drama of Doctrine: A Canonical-Linguistic Approach to Christian Theology* (Louisville: Westminster John Knox, 2005).

THE GOSPEL IS NOT EVERYTHING

What do we mean by "the gospel"? Answering this question is a bit more complex than we often assume. Not everything the Bible teaches can be considered "the gospel" (although it can be argued that all biblical doctrine is necessary background for understanding the gospel). The gospel is a *message* about how we have been rescued from peril. The very word *gospel* has as its background a news report about some life-altering event that has already happened.[1]

1. The gospel is good news, not good advice. The gospel is not primarily a way of life. It is not something we do, but something that has been done for us and something that we must respond to. In the Greek translation of the Old Testament — the Septuagint — the word *euangelizō* (proclaim good news) occurs twenty-three times. As we see in Psalm 40:9 (ESV) — "I have told the glad news of [your] deliverance in the great congregation" — the term is generally used to declare the news of something that has happened to rescue and deliver people from peril. In the New Testament, the word group *euangelion* (good news), *euangelizō* (proclaim good news), and *euangelistēs* (one who proclaims good news) occurs at least 133 times. D. A. Carson draws this conclusion from a thorough study of gospel words:

> Because the gospel is news, good news ... it is to be announced; that is what one does with news. The essential heraldic element in preaching is bound up with the fact that the core message is not a code of ethics to be debated, still less a list of aphorisms to be admired and pondered, and certainly not a systematic theology to be outlined and schematized. Though it properly grounds ethics, aphorisms, and systematics, it is none of these three: it is news, good news, and therefore must be publicly announced.[2]

2. The gospel is good news announcing that we have been rescued or saved. And what are we rescued *from*? What peril are we saved from? A look at the gospel words in the New Testament shows that we are rescued from the "coming wrath" at the end of history (1 Thess 1:10). But this wrath is not an impersonal force — it is God's wrath. We are out of fellowship with God; our relationship with him is broken.

In perhaps the most thoroughgoing exposition of the gospel in the Bible, Paul identifies God's wrath as the great problem of the human condition (Rom 1:18 – 32). Here we see that the wrath of God has many ramifications. The background text is Genesis 3:17 – 19, in which God's curse lies on the entire created order because of human sin. Because we are alienated from God, we are *psychologically* alienated within ourselves — we experience shame and fear (Gen 3:10). Because we are alienated from God, we are also *socially* alienated from one another (v. 7 describes how Adam and Eve must put on clothing, and v. 16 speaks of alienation between the genders; also notice the blame shifting in their dialogue with God in vv. 11 – 13). Because we are alienated from God, we are also *physically* alienated from nature itself. We now experience sorrow, painful toil, physical degeneration, and death (vv. 16 – 19). In fact, the ground itself is "cursed" (v. 17; see Rom 8:18 – 25).

Since the garden, we live in a world filled with suffering, disease, poverty, racism, natural disasters, war, aging, and death — and it all stems from the wrath and curse of God on the world. The world is out of joint, and we need to be rescued. But the root of our problem is not these "horizontal" relationships, though they are often the most obvious; it is our "vertical" relationship with God. All human problems are ultimately symptoms, and our separation from God is the cause. The reason for all the misery — all the effects of the curse — is that we are not reconciled to God. We see this in such texts as Romans 5:8 and 2 Corinthians 5:20. Therefore, the first and primary focus of any real rescue of the human race — the main thing that will save us — is to have our relationship with God put right again.

3. The gospel is news about what has been done by Jesus Christ to put right our relationship with God. Becoming a Christian is about a change of status. First John 3:14 (emphasis added) states that "we *have passed* from death to life," not we *are passing* from death to life.[3] You are either in Christ or you are not; you are either pardoned and accepted or you are not; you either have eternal life or you don't. This is why Dr. Martyn Lloyd-Jones often used a diagnostic question to determine a person's spiritual understanding and condition. He would ask, "Are you now ready to say that you are a Christian?" He recounts that over the years, whenever he would ask the question, people would often hesitate and then say, "I do not feel that I am good enough." To that, he gives this response:

> At once I know that … they are still thinking in terms of themselves; their idea still is that they have to make themselves good enough to be a Christian … It sounds very modest but it is the lie of the devil, it is a denial of the faith … you will never be good enough; nobody has ever been good enough. The essence of the Christian salvation is to say that He is good enough and that I am in Him![4]

Lloyd-Jones's point is that becoming a Christian is a change in our relationship with God. Jesus' work, when it is believed and rested in, instantly changes our standing before God. We are "in him."

Ever since reading J. I. Packer's famous essay introducing John Owen's *Death of Death in the Death of Christ*, I have liked "God saves sinners" as a good summary of gospel:

> God saves sinners. God — *the Triune Jehovah, Father, Son and Spirit; three Persons working together in sovereign wisdom, power and love to achieve the salvation of a chosen people, the Father electing, the Son fulfilling the Father's will by redeeming, the Spirit executing the purpose of Father and Son by renewing. Saves — does everything, first to last, that is involved in bringing man from death in sin to life in glory: plans, achieves and communicates redemption, calls and keeps, justifies, sanctifies, glorifies. Sinners — men as God finds them, guilty, vile, helpless, powerless, unable to lift a finger to do God's will or better their spiritual lot.*[5]

THE GOSPEL IS NOT THE RESULTS OF THE GOSPEL

The gospel is not about something we do but about what has been done for us, and yet the gospel results in a whole new way of life. This grace and the good deeds that result must be both distinguished and connected. The gospel, its results, and its implications must be carefully related to each other — neither confused nor separated. One of Martin Luther's dicta was that we are saved by faith alone but not by a faith that remains alone. His point is that true gospel belief will always and necessarily lead to good works, but salvation in no way comes through or because of good works. Faith and works must never be confused for one another, nor may they be separated (Eph 2:8 – 10; Jas 2:14, 17 – 18, 20, 22, 24, 26).

I am convinced that belief in the gospel leads us to care for the poor and participate actively in our culture, as surely as Luther said true faith leads to good works. But just as faith and works must not be separated or confused, so the results of the gospel must never be separated from or confused with the gospel itself. I have often heard people preach this way: "The good news is that God *is* healing and *will* heal the world of all its hurts; therefore, the work of the gospel is to work for justice and peace in the world." The danger in this line of thought is not that the particulars are untrue (they are not) but that it mistakes effects for causes. It confuses what the gospel *is* with what the gospel *does*. When Paul speaks of the renewed material creation, he states that the new heavens and new earth are guaranteed to us because on the cross Jesus restored our relationship with God as his true sons and daughters. Romans 8:1 – 25 teaches, remarkably, that the redemption of our bodies and of the entire physical world occurs when we receive "our adoption." As his children, we are guaranteed our future inheritance (Eph 1:13 – 14, 18; Col 1:12; 3:24; Heb 9:15; 1 Pet 1:4), and *because* of that inheritance, the world is renewed. The *future* is ours because of Christ's work finished in the *past*.

We must not, then, give the impression that the gospel is simply a divine rehabilitation program for the world, but rather that it is an accomplished substitutionary work. We must not depict the gospel as primarily *joining* something (Christ's kingdom program) but rather as *receiving* something (Christ's finished work). If we make this error, the gospel becomes another kind of a salvation by works instead of a salvation by faith. As J. I. Packer writes:

> The gospel does bring us solutions to these problems [of suffering and injustice], but it does so by first solving … the deepest of all human problems, the problem of man's relation with his Maker; and unless we make it plain that the solution of these former problems depends on the settling of this latter one, we are misrepresenting the message and becoming false witnesses of God.[6]

A related question has to do with whether the gospel is spread by the doing of justice. Not only does the Bible say over and over that the gospel is spread by preaching, but common sense tells us that loving deeds, as important as they are as an accompaniment of preaching, cannot by themselves bring people to a saving knowledge of Jesus Christ. Francis Schaeffer argued rightly that Christians' relationships with

---

The gospel is news that creates a life of love, but the life of love is not itself the gospel.

---

each other constitute the criterion the world uses to judge whether their message is truthful — so Christian community is the "final apologetic."[7] Notice again, however, the relationship between faith and works. Jesus said that a loving community is necessary for the world to know that God sent him (John 17:23; cf. 13:35). Sharing our goods with each other and with the needy is a powerful sign to nonbelievers (see the relationship between witness and sharing in Acts 4:31 – 37 and Acts 6). But loving deeds — even though they embody the truths of the gospel and cannot be separated from preaching the gospel — should not be conflated with it.

The gospel, then, is preeminently a report about the work of Christ on our behalf — that is why and how the gospel is salvation by grace. The gospel is news because it is about a salvation accomplished for us. It is news that creates a life of love, but the life of love is not itself the gospel.[8]

THE GOSPEL HAS TWO EQUAL AND OPPOSITE ENEMIES

The ancient church father Tertullian is reputed to have said, "Just as Jesus was crucified between two thieves, so the gospel is ever crucified between these two errors."[9] What are these errors to which Tertullian was referring? I often call them *religion* and *irreligion*; the theological terms are *legalism* and *antinomianism*. Another way to describe them could be *moralism* and *relativism (or pragmatism)*.

These two errors constantly seek to corrupt the message and steal away from us the power of the gospel. Legalism says that we have to live a holy, good life in order to be saved. Antinomianism says that because we are saved, we don't have to live a holy, good life.

This is the location of the "tip of the spear" of the gospel. A very clear and sharp distinction between legalism, antinomianism, and the gospel is often crucial for the life-changing power of the Holy Spirit to work. If our gospel message even slightly resembles "you must believe and live right to be saved" *or* "God loves and accepts everyone just as they are," we will find our communication is not doing the identity-changing, heart-shaping transformative work described in the next part of this book. If we just preach general doctrine and ethics from Scripture, we are not preaching the gospel. The gospel is the good news that God has accomplished our salvation for us through Christ in order to bring us into a right relationship with him and eventually to destroy all the results of sin in the world.

Still, it can be rightly argued that in order to understand all this — who God is, why we need salvation, what he has done to save us — we must have knowledge of the basic teachings of the entire Bible. J. Gresham Machen, for example, speaks of the biblical doctrines of God and of man to be the "presuppositions of the gospel."[10] This means that an understanding of the Trinity, of Christ's incarnation, of original sin and sin in general — are all necessary. If we don't understand, for example, that Jesus was not just a good man but the second person of the Trinity, or if we don't understand what the "wrath of God" means, it is impossible to understand what Jesus accomplished on the cross. Not only that, but the New

Testament constantly explains the work of Christ in Old Testament terms — in the language of priesthood, sacrifice, and covenant.

In other words, we must *not* just preach the Bible in general; we must preach the gospel. Yet unless those listening to the message understand the Bible in general, they won't grasp the gospel. The more we understand the whole corpus of biblical doctrine, the more we will understand the gospel itself — and the more we understand the gospel, the more we will come to see that this is, in the end, what the Bible is really about. Biblical knowledge is necessary for the gospel *and* distinct from the gospel, yet it so often stands in when the gospel is not actually present that people have come to mistake its identity.

THE GOSPEL HAS CHAPTERS

So, the gospel is good news — it is not something we do but something that has been done for us. Simple enough. But when we ask questions like "Good news about what?" or "Why is it good news?" the richness and complexity of the gospel begin to emerge.

USE WORDS IF NECESSARY

The popular saying "Preach the gospel; use words if necessary" is helpful but also misleading. If the gospel were primarily about what we must do to be saved, it could be communicated as well by actions (to be imitated) as by words. But if the gospel is primarily about what God has done to save us, and how we can receive it through faith, it can *only* be expressed through words. Faith cannot come without hearing. This is why we read in Galatians 2:5 that heresy endangers the truth of the gospel, and why Philippians 1:16 declares that a person's mind must be persuaded of the truth of the gospel. Ephesians 1:13 also asserts that the gospel is the word of truth. Ephesians 6:19 and Colossians 1:23 teach that we advance the gospel through verbal communication, particularly preaching.

There are two basic ways to answer the question "What is the gospel?" One is to offer the biblical good news of how you can get right with God. This is to understand the question to mean, "What must *I* do to be saved?" The second is to offer the biblical good news of what God will fully accomplish in history through the salvation of Jesus. This is to understand the question as "What hope is there for the world?"

If we conceive the question in the first, more individualistic way, we explain how a sinful human being can be reconciled to a holy God and how his or her life can be changed as a result. It is a message about *individuals*. The answer can be outlined: Who God is, what sin is, who Christ is and what he did, and what faith is. These are basically propositions. If we conceive of the question in the second way, to ask all that God is going to accomplish in history, we explain where the world came from, what went wrong with it, and what must happen for it to be mended. This is a message about the *world*. The answer can be outlined: creation, fall, redemption, and restoration. These are chapters in a plotline, a story.

As we will see in the next chapter, there is no single way to present the biblical gospel. Yet I urge you to try to be as thoughtful as possible in your gospel presentations. The danger in answering only the first question ("What must I do to be saved?") without the second ("What hope is there for the world?") is that, standing alone, the first can play into the Western idea that religion exists to provide spiritual goods that meet individual spiritual needs for freedom from guilt and bondage. It does not speak much about the goodness of the original creation or of God's concern for the material world, and so this conception may set up the listener to see Christianity as sheer escape from the world. But the danger in conceiving the gospel too strictly as a story line of the renewal of the world is even greater. It tells listeners about God's program to save the world, but it does not tell them how to actually get right with God and become part of that program. In fact, I'll say that without the first message, the second message is not the gospel. J. I. Packer writes these words:

In recent years, great strides in biblical theology and contemporary canonical exegesis have brought new precision to our grasp of the Bible's overall story of how God's plan to bless Israel, and through Israel the world, came to its climax in and through Christ. But I do not see how it can be denied that each New Testament book, whatever other job it may be doing, has in view, one way or another, Luther's primary question: how may a weak, perverse, and guilty sinner find a gracious God? Nor can it be denied that real Christianity only really starts when that discovery is made. And to the extent that modern developments, by filling our horizon with the great metanarrative, distract us from pursuing Luther's question in personal terms, they hinder as well as help in our appreciation of the gospel.[11]

Still, the Bible's grand narrative of cosmic redemption is critical background to help an individual get right with God. One way to proceed is to interleave the two answers to the "What is the gospel?" question so that gospel truths are laid into a story with chapters rather than just presented as a set of propositions. The narrative approach poses the questions, and the propositional approach supplies the answers.

How would we relate the gospel to someone in this way? What follows is a "conversational pathway" for presenting the gospel to someone as the chapters in a story. In the Bible, the term *gospel* is the declaration of what Jesus Christ has done to save us. In light of the biblical usage, then, we should observe that chapters 1 (God and Creation), 2 (Fall and Sin), and 4 (Faith) are not, strictly speaking, "the gospel." They are prologue and epilogue. Simon Gathercole argues that both Paul and the Gospel writers considered the good news to have three basic elements: the identity

of Jesus as Son of God and Messiah, the death of Jesus for sin and justification, and the establishment of the reign of God and the new creation.[12] The gospel, then, is packed into chapter 3, with its three headings — incarnation, substitution, and restoration. Chapter 1 on God and chapter 2 on sin constitute absolutely critical background information for understanding the meaning of the person and work of Jesus, and chapter 4 helps us understand how we must respond to Jesus' salvation. Nevertheless, it is reasonable and natural to refer to the entire set of four chapters as "the gospel."

WHERE DID WE COME FROM?

Answer: God. There is one God. He is infinite in power, goodness, and holiness and yet also personal and loving, a God who speaks to us in the Bible. The world is not an accident, but the creation of the one God (Genesis 1). God created all things, but *why* did he do that? Why did he create the world and us? The answer is what makes the Christian understanding of God profound and unique. While there is only one God, within God's being there are three persons — Father, Son, and Holy Spirit — who are all equally God and who have loved, adored, served, and enjoyed one another from all eternity. If God were unipersonal, then he would have not known love until he created other beings. In that case, love and community would not have been essential to his character; it would have emerged later. But God is triune, and therefore love, friendship, and community are intrinsic to him and at the heart of all reality. So a triune God created us (John 1:1 – 4), but he would not have created us to get the joy of mutual love and

CHAPTERS	GOSPEL NARRATIVE	GOSPEL TRUTHS
Chapter 1	Where did we come from?	From God: the One and the relational
Chapter 2	Why did things go so wrong?	Because of sin: bondage and condemnation
Chapter 3	What will put things right?	Christ: incarnation, substitution, restoration
Chapter 4	How can I be put right?	Through faith: grace and trust

service, because he already had that. Rather, he created us to share in his love and service. As we know from John 17:20 – 24, the persons of the Trinity love and serve one another — they are "other-oriented."[13] And thus God created us to live in the same way. In order to share the joy and love that God knew within himself, he created a good world that he cares for, a world full of human beings who were called to worship, know, and serve him, not themselves.[14]

WHY DID THINGS GO SO WRONG?

Answer: Sin. God created us to adore and serve him and to love others. By living this way, we would have been completely happy and enjoyed a perfect world. But instead, the whole human race turned away from God, rebelling against his authority. Instead of living for God and our neighbors, we live lives of self-centeredness. Because our relationship with God has been broken, all other relationships — with other human beings, with our very selves, and with the created world — are also ruptured. The result is spiritual, psychological, social, and physical decay and breakdown. "Things fall apart; the center cannot hold. Mere anarchy is loosed upon the world"[15] — the world now lies under the power of sin.

Sin reaps two terrible consequences. One consequence is spiritual bondage (Rom 6:15 – 18). We may believe in God or we may not believe, but either way, we never make him our greatest hope, good, or love. We try to maintain control of our lives by living for other things — for money, career, family, fame, romance, sex, power, comfort, social and political causes, or something else. But the result is always a loss of control, a form of slavery. Everyone has to live for something, and if that something is not God, then we are driven by that thing we live for — by overwork to achieve it, by inordinate fear if it is threatened, deep anger if it is being blocked, and inconsolable despair if it is lost. So the novelist David Foster Wallace, not long before his suicide, spoke these words to the 2005 graduating class at Kenyon College:

Everybody worships. The only choice we get is what to worship. And the compelling reason for maybe choosing some sort of god or spiritual-type thing to worship … is that pretty much anything else you worship will eat you alive. If you worship money and things, if they are where you tap real meaning in life, then you will never have enough, never feel you have enough … Worship your body and beauty and sexual allure and you will always feel ugly. And when time and age start showing, you will die a million deaths before they finally grieve you … Worship power, you will end up feeling weak and afraid, and you will need ever more power over others to numb you to your own fear. Worship your intellect, being seen as smart, you will end up feeling stupid, a fraud, always on the verge of being found out. But the insidious thing about these forms of worship is … they're unconscious. They are default settings.[16]

The second basic consequence of sin is condemnation (Rom 6:23). We are not just suffering because of sin; we are *guilty* because of sin. Often we say, "Well, I'm not very religious, but I'm a good person — and that is what is most important." But is it? Imagine a woman — a poor widow — with an only son. She teaches him how she wants him to live — to always tell the truth, to work hard, and to help the poor. She makes very little money, but with her meager savings she is able to put him through college. Imagine that when he graduates, he hardly ever speaks to her again. He occasionally sends a Christmas card, but he doesn't visit her; he won't answer her phone calls or letters; he doesn't speak to her. But he lives just like she taught him — honestly, industriously, and charitably. Would we say this was acceptable? Of course not! Wouldn't we say that by living a "good life" but neglecting a relationship with the one to whom he owed everything he was doing something condemnable? In the same way, if God created us and we owe him everything and we do not live for him but we "live a good life," it is not enough. We all owe a debt that must be paid.

WHAT WILL PUT THINGS RIGHT?

Answer: Christ. First, Jesus Christ puts things right through his *incarnation*. C. S. Lewis wrote that if there is a God, we certainly don't relate to him as people on the first floor of a building relate to people on the second floor. We relate to him the way Hamlet relates to Shakespeare. We (characters) might be able to know quite a lot about the playwright, but only to the degree that the author chooses to put information about himself in the play.[17]

In the Christian view, however, we believe that God did even more than simply give us information. Many fans of Dorothy Sayers's detective stories and mystery novels point out that Sayers was one of the first women to attend Oxford University. The main character in her stories — Lord Peter Wimsey — is an aristocratic sleuth and a single man. At one point in the novels, though, a new character appears, Harriet Vane. She is described as one of the first women who graduated from Oxford — and as a writer of mystery novels. Eventually she and Peter fall in love and marry. Who was she? Many believe Sayers looked into the world she had created, fell in love with her lonely hero, and wrote herself into the story to save him. Very touching! But that is not nearly as moving or amazing as the reality of the incarnation (John 1:14). God, as it were, looked into the world he had made and saw our lostness and had pity on his people. And so he wrote *himself* into human history as its main character (John 3:16). The second person in the Trinity, the Son of God, came into the world as a man, Jesus Christ.

The second way Jesus puts things right is through *substitution*. Because of the guilt and condemnation on us, a just God can't simply shrug off our sins. Being sorry is not enough. We would never allow an earthly judge to let a wrongdoer off, just because he was contrite — how much less should we expect a perfect heavenly Judge to do so? And even when we forgive personal wrongs against us, we cannot simply forgive without cost. If someone harms us and takes money or happiness or reputation from us, we can either make them pay us back or forgive them — which means *we* absorb the cost ourselves without remuneration. Jesus Christ lived a perfect life — the only human being to ever do so (Heb 4:15). At the end of his life, he deserved blessing and acceptance; at the end of our lives, because every one of us lives in sin, we deserve rejection and condemnation (Rom 3:9 – 10). Yet when the time had fully come, Jesus received in our place, on the cross, the rejection and condemnation we deserve (1 Pet 3:18), so that, when we believe in him, we can receive the blessing and acceptance he deserves (2 Cor 5:21).

There is no more moving thought than that of someone giving his life to save another. In Charles Dickens's *A Tale of Two Cities*, two men — Charles Darnay and Sydney Carton — both love the same woman, Lucie Manette, but Lucie chooses to marry Charles. Later, during the French Revolution, Charles is thrown in prison and awaits execution on the guillotine. Sydney visits Charles in prison, drugs him, and has him carried out. When a young seamstress (also on death row) realizes that Sydney is taking Charles's place, she is amazed and asks him to hold her hand for strength. She is deeply moved by his substitutionary sacrifice — and it wasn't even for her! When we realize that Jesus did the very same thing for us, it changes everything — the way we regard God, ourselves, and the world.

The third way Jesus will put things right is through the eventual *restoration* of all that has gone wrong with the world. The first time Jesus came from heaven to earth, he came in weakness to suffer for our sins. But the second time he comes, he will judge the world, putting a final end to all evil, suffering, decay, and death (Rom 8:19 – 21; 2 Pet 3:13). This means that Christ's salvation does not merely save our souls so we can escape the pain of the curse on the physical world. Rather, the final goal is the renewal and restoration of the material world, and the redemption of both our souls *and* our bodies. Vinoth Ramachandra notes how unique this view is among the religions of the world:

> So our salvation lies not in an escape from this world but in the transformation of this world ... You will not find hope for the world in any religious systems or philosophies of humankind. The biblical vision is unique. That is why when some say that there is salvation in other faiths I ask them, "What salvation are you talking about?" No faith holds out a promise of eternal salvation for the world the way the cross and resurrection of Jesus do.[18]

HOW CAN I BE PUT RIGHT?

Answer: Faith. Jesus died for our sins and rose again from the grave. By faith in him, our sins can be forgiven and we can be assured of living forever with God and one day being raised from the dead like

Christ. So what does it mean to believe, to have faith? First, it means to grasp what salvation "by faith" means. Believing in Christ does not mean that we are forgiven for our past, get a new start on life, and must simply try harder to live better than we did in the past. If this is your mind-set, you are still putting your faith in yourself. You are your own Savior. You are looking to your moral efforts and abilities to make yourself right with God. But this will never work. No one lives a perfect life. Even your best deeds are tainted by selfish and impure motives.

The gospel is that when we believe in Christ, there is now "no condemnation for those who are in Christ Jesus" (Rom 8:1). Putting our faith in Christ is not about trying harder; it means *transferring our trust* away from ourselves and resting in him. It means asking, "Father, accept me not because of what I have done or ever will do but because of what Jesus has done in my place." When we do that, we are adopted into God's family and given the right to his eternal, fatherly love (John 1:12 – 13).

The second thing to keep in mind is that it is not the quality of the faith itself that saves us; it is what Jesus has done for us. It is easy to assume that being "saved by faith" means that God will now love us *because* of the depth of our repentance and faith. But that is to once again subtly make ourselves our own Savior rather than Jesus. It is not the amount of our faith but the object of our faith that saves us. Imagine two people boarding an airplane. One person has almost no faith in the plane or the crew and is filled with fears and doubts. The other has great confidence in the plane and the crew. They both enter the plane, fly to a destination, and get off the plane safely. One person had a hundred times more faith in the plane than the other did, but they were equally safe. It wasn't the amount of their faith but the object of their faith (the plane and crew) that kept them from suffering harm and arriving safely at their destination. Saving faith isn't a level of psychological certainty; it is an act of the will in which we rest in Jesus. We give ourselves wholly to him because he gave himself wholly for us (Mark 8:34; Rev 3:20).

THE RIGHT RELATIONSHIP OF THE GOSPEL TO ALL OF MINISTRY

There is always a danger that church leaders and ministers will conceive of the gospel as merely the minimum standard of doctrinal content for being a Christian believer. As a result, many preachers and leaders are energized by thoughts of teaching more advanced doctrine, or of deeper forms of spirituality, or of intentional community and the sacraments, or of "deeper discipleship," or of psychological healing, or of social justice and cultural engagement. One of the reasons is the natural emergence of specialization as a church grows and ages. People naturally want to go deeper into various topics and ministry disciplines. But this tendency can cause us to lose sight of the whole. Though we may have an area or a ministry that we tend to focus on, the gospel is what brings unity to all that we do. Every form of ministry is empowered by the gospel, based on the gospel, and is a result of the gospel.

Because the gospel is endlessly rich, it can handle the burden of being the one "main thing" of a church.

Perhaps an illustration here will help. Imagine you're in an orchestra and you begin to play, but the sound is horrific because the instruments are out of tune. The problem can't be fixed by simply tuning them to each other. It won't help for each person to get in tune to the person next to her because each person will be tuning to something different. No, they will all need to be tuned properly to one source of pitch. Often we go about trying to tune ourselves to the sound of everything else in our lives. We often hear this described as "getting balance." But the questions that need to be asked are these: "Balanced to what?" "Tuned to what?" The gospel does not begin by tuning us in relation to our particular problems and surroundings; it first re-tunes us to God.[19]

If an element of ministry is not recognized as a

result of the gospel, it may sometimes be mistaken *for* the gospel and eventually supplant the gospel in the church's preaching and teaching. Counseling, spiritual direction, doing justice, engaging culture, doctrinal instruction, and even evangelism itself may become the main thing instead of the gospel. In such cases, the gospel as outlined above is no longer understood as the fountainhead, the central dynamic, from which all other things proceed. It is no longer the center of the preaching, the thinking, or the life of the church; some other good thing has replaced it. As a consequence, conversions will begin to dwindle in number because the gospel is not preached with a kind of convicting sharpness that lays bare the secrets of the heart (1 Cor 14:24 – 25) and gives believers *and* nonbelievers a sense of God's reality, even against their wills.

Because the gospel is endlessly rich, it can handle the burden of being the one "main thing" of a church. First Peter 1:12 and its context indicate that the angels never tire of looking into and exploring the wonders of the gospel. It can be preached from innumerable stories, themes, and principles from all over the Bible. But when the preaching of the gospel is either confused with or separated from the other endeavors of the church, preaching becomes mere exhortation (to get with the church's program or a biblical standard of ethics) or informational instruction (to inculcate the church's values and beliefs). When the proper connection between the gospel and any aspect of ministry is severed, *both* are shortchanged.

———————

The gospel is "heraldic proclamation" before it is anything else.[20] It is news that creates a life of love, but the life of love is not itself the gospel. The gospel is *not* everything that we believe, do, or say. The gospel must primarily be understood as good news, and the news is not as much about what we must do as about what has been done. The gospel is preeminently a report about the work of Christ on our behalf — salvation accomplished for us. That's how it is a gospel of grace. Yet, as we will see in the next chapter, the fact that the gospel is news does not mean it is a *simple* message. There is no such thing as a "one size fits all" understanding of the gospel.

QUESTIONS FOR DISCUSSION AND REFLECTION

1. This chapter looks at several truths that are not the gospel. In what sense are each of these not the gospel?

   - everything the Bible teaches
   - a way of life; something we do
   - joining Christ's kingdom program; a divine rehabilitation plan for the world

   If the gospel is not everything, what is the gospel?

2. Keller writes, "The gospel is not about something we do but about what has been done for us, and yet the gospel results in a whole new way of life. This grace and the good deeds that result must be both distinguished and connected." How can an individual or ministry go about distinguishing between "the gospel" and "the results of the gospel"?

3. The section titled "The Gospel Has Chapters" shows how to present the gospel to someone as chapters in a larger story. What other "conversational pathways" have you found to be fruitful in relating the gospel to non-Christians? To Christians?

4. What happens when the gospel is proclaimed without its results, or when its results are pursued without proclamation?

CHAPTER 1 — THE GOSPEL IS NOT EVERYTHING {pages 29-37}

1. Mark 1:1; Luke 2:10; 1 Corinthians 1:16 – 17; 15:1 – 11.
2. D. A. Carson, "What Is the Gospel? — Revisited," in *For the Fame of God's Name: Essays in Honor of John Piper*, ed. Sam Storms and Justin Taylor (Wheaton, Ill.: Crossway, 2010), 158.
3. The verb translated "passed" in 1 John 3:14 is *metabainō*, which means to "cross over." In John 5:24, Jesus states, "Whoever hears my word and believes him who sent me has eternal life and will not be condemned; he has *crossed over* [*metabainō*] from death to life." A parallel passage is Colossians 1:13, where it is said that Christ-followers have been transferred from the dominion of darkness into the kingdom of the Son.
4. D. Martyn Lloyd-Jones, *Spiritual Depression: Its Causes and Cure* (Grand Rapids: Eerdmans, 1965), 34.
5. J. I. Packer, "Introductory Essay to John Owen's *Death of Death in the Death of Christ*," www.all-of-grace.org/pub/others/deathofdeath.html (accessed January 4, 2012).
6. J. I. Packer, *Knowing God* (Downers Grove, Ill.: InterVarsity, 1973), 171.
7. Francis Schaeffer, *The Mark of the Christian* (Downers Grove, Ill.: InterVarsity, 1977) 25. Cf. Timothy George and John Woodbridge, *The Mark of Jesus: Loving in a Way the World Can See* (Chicago: Moody, 2005).
8. See Carson, "What Is the Gospel? — Revisited," in *For the Fame of God's Name*, 158.
9. Having heard and read this in the words of other preachers, I have never been able to track down an actual place in Tertullian's writings where he says it. I think it may be apocryphal, but the principle is right.
10. J. Gresham Machen, *Christianity and Liberalism*, new ed. (Grand Rapids: Eerdmans, 2001), 99.
11. J. I. Packer, *In My Place Condemned He Stood: Celebrating the Glory of the Atonement* (Wheaton, Ill.: Crossway, 2007), 26 – 27.
12. Simon Gathercole, "The Gospel of Paul and the Gospel of the Kingdom," in *God's Power to Save*, ed. Chris Green (Leicester, UK: Inter-Varsity, 2006), 138 – 54.
13. D. A. Carson (*The Difficult Doctrine of the Love of God* [Wheaton, Ill.: Crossway, 2000], 39, 43) writes, "What we have, then, is a picture of God whose love, even in eternity past, even before the creation of anything, is other-oriented. This cannot be said (for instance) of Allah. Yet because the God of the Bible is one, this plurality-in-unity does not destroy his entirely appropriate self-focus as God ... There has *always* been an other-orientation to the love of God ... We are the friends of God by virtue of the intra-Trinitarian love of God that so worked out in the fullness of time that the plan of redemption, conceived in the mind of God in eternity past, has exploded into our space-time history at exactly the right moment."
14. See "The Dance of Creation," in Tim Keller, *The Reason for God: Belief in an Age of Skepticism* (New York: Dutton, 2008), 225 – 26; "The Dance," in Tim Keller, *King's Cross: The Story of the World in the Life of Jesus* (New York: Dutton, 2011), 3 – 13.
15. From the poem "The Second Coming" (1920) by William Butler Yeats.
16. Emily Bobrow, "David Foster Wallace, in His Own Words" (taken from his 2005 commencement address at Kenyon College), http://moreintelligentlife.com/story/david-foster-wallace-in-his-own-words (accessed January 4, 2012).
17. See C. S. Lewis, *Christian Reflections* (Grand Rapids: Eerdmans, 1967), 167 – 76.
18. Vinoth Ramachandra, *The Scandal of Jesus* (Downers Grove, Ill.: InterVarsity, 2001), 24.
19. Thanks to Michael Thate for this illustration.
20. Carson, "What Is the Gospel? — Revisited," in *For the Fame of God's Name*, 158.

chapter 2

THE GOSPEL IS NOT A SIMPLE THING

The gospel is not everything, yet in the final analysis it cannot be tamed into a single simple formula with a number of points that must be recited to everyone, in every time and place. There is an irreducible complexity to the gospel. I do not mean that the gospel can't be *presented* simply and even very briefly. Paul himself does so on numerous occasions (e.g., Rom 10:9). The gospel is a clear and present word, but it is not a simplistic word.[1] Though in the previous chapter I gave an example of a gospel outline that I believe is broadly useful today, I want to resist the impulse, mainly among conservative evangelicals, toward creating a single, one-size-fits-all gospel presentation that should be used everywhere, that serves as a test of orthodoxy.

THE BIBLE DOESN'T GIVE ONE STANDARD GOSPEL OUTLINE

In Galatians 1:8, Paul condemns anyone who preaches "a gospel other than the one we preached to you." In 1 Corinthians 15:11, he takes pains to show that the gospel he declares is the same as that preached by Peter, John, and the others: "Whether, then, it was I or they, this is what we preach, and this is what you believed." It would be impossible for Paul to condemn a "false gospel" and affirm the preaching of Peter as "the gospel" without assuming a consensus body of gospel content. And yet it is obvious that the various biblical writers express the gospel in significantly different ways.

For example, when the Synoptic writers speak about the gospel, they constantly use the concept of "the kingdom," but this phrase is virtually missing in John's gospel, which emphasizes, rather, receiving "eternal life." On the one hand, we can say that this difference does not at all constitute a contradiction, because when we compare Matthew 25:31 – 46 and

Mark 10:17 – 31 with John 3:3 – 6, 17, we see that entering God's kingdom and receiving eternal life are virtually the same thing. Reading Matthew 18:3; Mark 10:15; and John 3:3 – 6 together reveals that conversion, the new birth, and receiving the kingdom of God like children are basically the same move.[2]

Nonetheless, the terms "eternal life" and "the kingdom" are not mere synonyms. The Synoptics use "kingdom" so often because their orientation is more toward the future.[3] The terms convey somewhat different aspects of God's salvation. As many have pointed out, John seems to emphasize the individual and the inward aspects of being in the kingdom of God. He takes pains to show that the kingdom is *not* an earthly, sociopolitical order (John 18:36). On the other hand, when the Synoptic writers speak of the kingdom, there is a somewhat more external and corporate emphasis. They lay out the social and behavioral changes that the gospel brings.[4] The kingdom of God *does* take corporate shape, and it *does* have major implications for how we live. It is a new order of things in which money is not made an idol (Mark 10:17 – 31) and the hungry, naked, and homeless are cared for (Matt 25:31 – 46). John and the Synoptic writers reveal complementary aspects of the gospel, stressing both the individual and corporate dimensions of our salvation.

So John and the Synoptic writers present the gospel in somewhat different ways. And when we look at the apostle Paul, we find yet another, different set of emphases. While Paul uses both "kingdom" and "life," he more centrally focuses on the concept of justification. So is this a different gospel? No. Paul stresses the intercanonical theme of the law court. Jesus takes the curse of the law, the legal penalty for sin, so we can receive the blessing of Christ's obedience (Gal 3:13 – 14). Simon Gathercole has shown that there is no real contradiction between the Synoptic writers, John, and Paul.[5] In Jesus, God substitutes himself for us and, on our behalf, pays the debt (Mark 10:45; John 12:20 – 36; 1 Tim 2:6); defeats the evil powers (Col 2:15; 1 John 3:8); bears the curse and divine wrath (Matt 27:45; Gal 3:13; 1 John 2:2; 4:10), secures for us salvation by grace, not by our works (Eph 2:8 – 9; 2 Tim 1:9), and even becomes for us an exemplar (1 Tim 1:16; Heb 12:2; 1 Pet 2:21). At the heart of all of the biblical writers' theology is redemption through substitution.

At the heart of all of the biblical writers' theology is redemption through substitution.

THE GOSPEL MUST BE TIED TO THE BIBLE'S STORY LINE AND THEMES

Over the last several decades, as anthropologists and linguists studied "meaning making" through language in a given society, they began to divide their study into two approaches: a *synchronic* approach, which is concerned with the whole structure of a language at a given time, and a *diachronic* approach, which looks at how language and meaning change as a result of life experience.

Theologians also stress reading the Bible both synchronically and diachronically. The synchronic approach is sometimes called the systematic-theological method (STM), which tends to deal with Scripture topically. It organizes what the Bible says by categories of thought: *The Bible is about God, sin, the Holy Spirit, the church, marriage and family, prayer, and so on.* It looks at every text on a particular topic and synthesizes them into a coherent set of statements or principles. This method is especially sensitive to the Bible's unity in expressing a view of God, humanity, sin, grace, the world, and so on. As I pointed out in the previous chapter, it tends to be particularly useful in answering the gospel question "What must I do to be saved?" We believe we can read the Bible this way because it has a single author — God — and because as rational creatures we respond to the

beauty of truth. In this perspective, the gospel appears as *God, sin, Christ,* and *faith.* It brings out the *means* of salvation, namely, the substitutionary work of Christ and our responsibility to embrace it by faith.[6]

To read the Bible diachronically is to read along its narrative arc, and this is often called the redemptive-historical method (RHM), which tends to deal with Scripture historically. It organizes what the Bible says by stages in history or by the plotline of a story: *The Bible is about God's creating the world, the fall of man, God's reentry into history to create a new people for himself, and eventually about a new creation that emerges out of a marred and broken world through Christ.* The method discerns the basic plotline of the Bible as God's story of redemption, as well as the biblical themes (e.g., covenant, kingship, sanctuary) that run through every stage of history and each part of the canon, climaxing in Jesus Christ. This approach is especially sensitive to the differences in historical eras and among biblical authors. It is particularly helpful in answering the gospel question "What hope is there for the world?" We believe we can read the Bible this way because God used human beings to write his revelation — and because as hope-based creatures we respond to the beauty of narrative. In this perspective, the gospel appears as *creation, fall, promise and prefigurement, Israel, Christ's redemption,* and *restoration.* It brings out the *purpose* of salvation, namely, a renewed creation.

There is no ultimate reason these two approaches should contradict one another.[7] In fact, using both approaches does justice to the miraculous fact that the Bible is both unmistakably divine and providentially human. I would go even further and warn that failing to use both approaches invites danger. The STM, carried out in isolation from the RHM, can produce a Christianity that is rationalistic, legalistic, and individualistic. Similarly the RHM, carried out in isolation from the STM, tends to produce a Christianity that loves narrative and community but shies away from sharp distinctions between grace and law and between truth and heresy.

One approach that draws from both the story line and the themes of Scripture is to read the Bible through *intercanonical themes.* In his essay "The Biblical Gospel," D. A. Carson warns against reductionistic versions of the gospel that do not tie into the Bible's story line.[8] Carson has posited that there may be twenty or so intercanonical themes that hold the Bible together.[9] The gospel unifies and gives meaning to these many threads that run through the Old and New Testaments. A person can explain the gospel from beginning to end through any of these themes, but no single theme gives the full picture.

The table below highlights a few of these. In the next three sections, we will highlight how the gospel can be expressed through each theme.

THE EXILE AND OUR HOMECOMING

Home, according to Scripture, is a place where life flourishes fully — spiritually, physically, and socially. It is a place where physical life and health are sustained and where our most intimate love *relationships* are nurtured. It is place of rest, of shalom.

The story of the human race, however, is one of exile and longing for homecoming. Death and disease have distorted and defaced God's good physical creation. Society is a Babel filled with selfishness, self-exaltation, and pride. Exploitation and violence mar and ruin human community. The world as it now exists is not our true home. We were made for a place without death or parting from love, without decay, and without disease and aging. We are, therefore, exiles and aliens here. Why? Because the human race turned from God to live for itself; our first parents were turned out of the garden of God and banished from the face of God, in whose presence is our true home. We are alienated from God, our true selves, one another, and the creational environment.

Some of the questions that arise when we look at the story of the Scriptures through this theme are these: "How can we be brought home? How can the creation be healed and restored? How can death and decay be overcome?" The gospel answers these questions by telling us that Jesus leaves his own true home (Phil 2:6 – 7), is born away from his earthly parents' home, wanders without a place to lay his head and without a home (Matt 8:20), and is finally

HOME/EXILE	YAHWEH/COVENANT	KINGDOM
AT CREATION MADE FOR:		
a place of rest and shalom	a faithful covenant love relationship with God	God's kingdom and kingliness
SIN IS/RESULTS IN:		
self-centeredness, destroying shalom	unfaithfulness, causing God's curse and wrath	idolatry, causing enslavement
ISRAEL IS:		
exiled in Egypt, then Babylon	called to faithfulness but is unfaithful	looking for a true judge/king
JESUS IS:		
the rejected but resurrected Lord, who breaks the power of death	the suffering servant but new covenant Lord, who takes the curse of sin	the returning true king, who frees us from the world, flesh, Devil
RESTORATION:		
the garden-city of God	the marriage supper of the Lamb	true freedom under the reign of God

crucified outside the city gate, a sign of his exile and rejection (Heb 13:11 – 12). He takes our place and experiences the exile — the alienated state — that the human race deserves. He is cast out so we can be brought home. This is summed up in Luke 9:31 (the Greek *exodos* is translated "departure" here) — Jesus' death and resurrection are the ultimate exodus and the ultimate escape from exile. When Jesus rises from the grave, he breaks the power of death and becomes a living foretaste of the new heavens and the new earth that will be our true home. He will reconcile "all things" (Col 1:16 – 20) and remake the world into the garden-city of God (Rev 21:1 – 8; 22:1 – 2).[10]

This "home" and our sense of it are hinted at in all of our varying forms of homesickness. And it is this sense of home that steers us clear from any number of false home-goings and idolatries.

HOME /EXILE: RELATED THEMES

Rest and Sabbath. Sin has left us restless. How can we enter God's rest?

Justice and Shalom. The fabric of the world is broken. How can we restore shalom?

Trinity and Community. We were made for personal and interdependent community with God and his people because we reflect the triune God. How can we become part of this community?

THE COVENANT AND ITS FULFILLMENT

Yahweh reveals himself to be the faithful covenant God. In the covenant relationship, the covenant Lord becomes *our* God, and we become *his* people. A covenant is absolutely binding, and indeed the Lord always does what he says. He is absolutely faithful to his word and promises. In turn, he asks us to also be faithful, to do what *we* say we will do. This poses a problem, for we continually break our word.

Just as the exile/homecoming theme points to our need for the world healer, the Yahweh/covenant theme shows us our need to be saved from our transgressions of the law. This theme raises

questions like these: "How can God be *both* faithful and true to his law and word *and* faithful and committed to us? How can God be holy and still love his people? How do the holiness and love of God relate in the covenant?" Isaiah points to a resolution when he speaks of the need for both a covenant Lord and a suffering covenant servant. Jesus takes the curse of the covenant so that the blessing of the covenant could come to us (Gal 3:7 – 14). He fulfills the covenant promise of Genesis 3:15 — he is wounded and yet destroys the work of Satan. Jesus fulfils the Abrahamic covenant as well — he truly is the blessing that comes to all nations. His life as the perfect sacrifice fulfills the Mosaic law (Heb 8 – 10).

So, in response to the great question "Are the covenant blessings of God conditional or unconditional?" — the answer is *yes*. Jesus, as the obedient and faithful covenant servant, absolutely fulfilled the conditions of the covenant through his life and his suffering in our place, making it possible for him, as our faithful covenant Lord, to love us *un*conditionally. At the cross, both the law of God and the love of God were fulfilled and satisfied. In the city of God, there is no more curse (Rev 22:3) because the Passover Lamb of God bore the sins of his people. We will be his people — his bride — and he will be our God (Rev 21:2 – 3). History is consummated in the marriage supper of the Lamb (Rev 19:6 – 9). The ultimate love relationship we were built for will be fulfilled.

YAHWEH/COVENANT: RELATED THEMES

Righteousness and Nakedness. We experience shame and guilt. How can our sins be covered?

Marriage and Faithfulness. We long for true love and closure. How can we find it?

Presence and Sanctuary. We are made to flourish in the presence of God. How can we stand in it?

As the exile/homecoming theme points to our need for the world healer and the Yahweh/covenant theme shows our need to be saved from our transgressions of the law, the kingdom theme shows us the need for a liberator from slavery. As Romans 1:25 tells us, whatever we worship we serve, and since we all must worship something, we are enslaved to various forces and powers in this world. The search for a true leader, judge, and king absorbs much of the history of God's people (see Deut 17:14 – 20; 2 Sam 7). None of these leaders fully succeed in protecting the people from falling into idolatry, servitude, and exile. This raises one key question: "How can any king be powerful enough to liberate us from slavery this great?"

The answer announced in the gospel is that God himself must come. Mark 1:1 – 3 declares that Jesus is the divine King returning to take up his kingdom.[11] The power of Christ's kingly rule is now present among gathered Christians (Luke 17:20 – 21), liberating people from false masters and enslaving idols. Among the disciples, the kingdom is a new human order in which power, money, recognition, and success are properly reordered in light of the registry of the kingdom. It is not that these things no longer matter but that they become transposed by the unleashing of Christ's new creation — by service, generosity, and humility (Luke 6:17 – 49). Jesus' kingship is not like human kingships, for it wins influence through suffering service, not coercive power. We enter it not through strength but through the weakness of repentance and the new birth (John 3) and becoming like a child (Matt 18:3 – 4).

Christ's liberating rule is not fully here. All his disciples are to pray for it to come, according to Matthew 6:10, and at the end of time we will receive it in completion (Matt 25:34). But finally the day comes when the city of God will descend. It contains the throne of God — the seat of the kingdom (Rev 22:3) — from which the renewal of all things proceeds (Rev 21:3 – 6). This is the ecstatic enthronement depicted in Psalms 96 – 98. When God returns to rule, even the rivers will clap their hands and the mountains will sing for joy that their liberator has finally come (Ps 98:8; Rom 8:21 – 22). The freedom and joy of the kingdom of heaven will come to earth.

Although each of these themes emphasizes a unique aspect of the story of the Bible, there is no contradiction — only harmony — among these different ways of communicating the gospel. The Bible's story line tells us at least four things:

1. What God wants for us (Creation)
2. What happened to us and what went wrong with the world (Fall)
3. What God has done in Jesus Christ to put things right (Redemption)
4. How history will turn out in the end as a result (Restoration)

This story can be — and is — told in multiple ways, using multiple themes, since both sin and salvation are multidimensional. This does not mean the gospel cannot be presented simply, nor does it contradict the earlier statement that "the gospel is not everything." All of these ways of presenting the gospel must still emphasize that it is news — an announcement of what God has done and will do. However, whenever we flesh out the good news, even in a very brief way, we will put it into the context of one or some of these themes, and when we do this, we will shade things a bit toward some aspects of the biblical story and away from others.

KINGDOM: RELATED THEMES

Image and Likeness. Loving God supremely is the only way to truly love anything else and become your true self, to become truly free (2 Cor 4:4; Col 1:15).

Idolatry and Freedom. Serving God supremely is the only way to freedom.

Wisdom and the Word. Submission to the Word of God is the way to wisdom.

THE GOSPEL MUST BE CONTEXTUALIZED

The gospel is not a simple thing. We know this because its expression in the themes of the Bible is inexhaustibly deep and rich. But a second reason we know it is that humanity, in both its perfect design and fallen nature, is also complex and varied. The gospel

---

The gospel has supernatural versatility to address the particular hopes, fears, and idols of every culture and every person.

---

has supernatural versatility to address the particular hopes, fears, and idols of every culture and every person. This points us to the need for contextualization.

In 1 Corinthians 1:22 – 25, for example, Paul explains that when he spoke to Greeks, he first confronted their culture's idol of speculation and philosophy with the "foolishness" of the cross, and then he presented Christ's salvation as true wisdom. When he spoke to Jews, however, he first confronted their culture's idol of power and accomplishment with the "weakness" of the cross, and then he presented the gospel as true power. One of these gospel forms was tailored to Bible-believing people who thought they would be justified by works on judgment day, while the other

was tailored to pagans. These two approaches can also be discerned in Paul's speeches in Acts, some of which were given to Jews and some to pagans. Luke provides three summaries of Paul's gospel preaching.

1. In Acts 13, Paul communicates to Jews and Gentile God-fearers.
2. In Acts 14, Paul addresses noneducated pagans.
3. Acts 17 is a digest of Paul's sermon to philosophers and educated pagans.

It is instructive to see how his audience's capacities and beliefs shape the way Paul presents and argues for the gospel. Different cultural audiences respond to different approaches of nuancing and shaping the same message.

Gospel contextualization is an enormous subject requiring great care, and so the third part of this book is dedicated to it. It is only necessary at this point to observe that one of the reasons the gospel is never given in exactly the same form is not only the diverse richness of the biblical material itself, with all of its intercanonical themes, but the diverse richness of humanity. Paul himself presented the gospel content in different ways — using different orders, arguments, levels of emphasis, and so on — to different cultures. And we should too. The gospel is so rich that it can be communicated in a form that fits every situation. It is a *singular* message, but it is not a *simple* message.

QUESTIONS FOR DISCUSSION AND REFLECTION

1. Have you or others you know ever felt a pressure to create or adopt a "single, one-size-fits-all gospel presentation that should be used everywhere, that serves as a test of orthodoxy"? What is the appeal of this? What are the risks?

2. Which of the intercanonical themes described in this chapter most resonated with you? Which intercanonical theme would best resonate with non-Christians in your minis-

try context? With people in your own church? What new ways of communicating the gospel does this open up for you?

3. Read the three passages in Acts cited at the end of the chapter. Jot down a few notes about the differences among Paul's gospel presentations. What does this exercise tell you about your own audience's "capacities and beliefs" and how they should shape the way you present and argue for the gospel?

CHAPTER 2 — THE GOSPEL IS NOT A SIMPLE THING *(pages 39–44)*

1. See Mark D. Thompson, *A Clear and Present Word: The Clarity of Scripture* (New Studies in Biblical Theology 21; Downers Grove, Ill.: InterVarsity, 2006).
2. See Paul Woodbridge, " 'Kingdom of God' and 'Eternal Life' in the Synoptic Gospels and John," in *God's Power to Save: One Gospel for a Complex World?* ed. Chris Green (Nottingham, UK: Inter-Varsity, 2006).
3. Ibid., 72.
4. Ibid., 64.
5. Simon Gathercole, "The Gospel of Paul and the Gospel of the Kingdom," in *God's Power to Save*, ed. Chris Green (Leicester, UK: Inter-Varsity, 2008), 138–54.
6. Thanks to Dr. John Thomas for helping to bridge the worlds of anthropology, linguistics, and theology in this area.
7. In the previous chapter, I gave one example of how to mix the two approaches in a single blended gospel presentation.
8. See D. A. Carson, "The Biblical Gospel," in *For Such a Time as This: Perspectives on Evangelicalism, Past, Present and Future*, ed. Steve Brady and Harold Rowdon (London: Evangelical Alliance, 1996), 80–81.
9. See D. A. Carson, "Systematic Theology and Biblical Theology," in *New Dictionary of Biblical Theology*, ed. T. Desmond Alexander and Brian S. Rosner (Downers Grove, Ill.: InterVarsity, 2000), 89–104, especially 97–98. See also the "Series Prefaces" to the New Studies in Biblical Theology series, where Carson gives a third definition of biblical theology as "the delineation of a biblical theme across all or part of the biblical corpora."
10. There is an interesting way the Greek translators of the Hebrew Bible (the Septuagint) handle references to the garden, namely, Eden. In places like Genesis 2:9, 15–16; 3:1, 8, 10, and in Ezekiel 31:8, the Greek word *paradeisos* is used to translate as "Eden" or "garden." This word is used in Luke 23:43 when Jesus says to the penitent criminal on the cross, "Today you will be with me in paradise" (*en tō paradeisō*), as well as by Paul in 2 Corinthians 12:4, when Paul reports being caught up to paradise (*eis ton paradeison*), and by John in Revelation 2:7, when one "like a son of man" (1:13) says to those in the church of Ephesus, "To him who overcomes, I will give the right to eat from the tree of life, which is in the paradise of God" (*en tō paradeisō tou theou*).
11. See also Isaiah 40:9–11; Mark 1:14–15.

chapter 3

THE GOSPEL AFFECTS EVERYTHING

We have seen that *the gospel is not everything*, meaning it must be distinguished as an announcement of news, distinct from its results and implications, and that *the gospel is not a simple thing*, meaning it cannot be packaged in a single standard form. My third contention, that *the gospel affects virtually everything*, builds on these two statements.

In his article "The Gospel of Jesus Christ (1 Corinthians 15:1–19)," D. A. Carson surveys the ethical directives of 1 Corinthians and draws this conclusion:

> [This] book ... *repeatedly shows how the gospel rightly works out in the massive transformation of attitudes, morals, relationships, and cultural interactions ...*
>
> *Just as Paul found it necessary to hammer away at the outworking of the gospel in every domain of the lives of the Corinthians, so we must do the same today ...*
>
> *It does not take much to think through how the gospel must also transform the business practices and priorities of Christians in commerce, the priorities of young men steeped in indecisive but relentless narcissism, the lonely anguish and often the guilty pleasures of single folk who pursue pleasure but who cannot find happiness, the tired despair of those living on the margins, and much more. And this must be done, not by attempting to abstract social principles from the gospel, still less by endless focus on the periphery in a vain effort to sound prophetic, but precisely by preaching and teaching and living out in our churches the glorious gospel of our blessed Redeemer.*[1]

Even though the gospel is a set of truths to understand and believe, it cannot *remain* a set of beliefs if it is truly believed and understood. As Lesslie Newbigin states, "The Christian story provides us with such a set of lenses, not something for us to look *at*, but for us to look *through*."[2] Paul says as much in Romans 12:1, when he looks back

on his rich exposition of the doctrine of justification in chapters 1–11 and states, "Therefore, I urge you, brothers, in view of God's mercy, to offer your bodies as living sacrifices." Scripture teaches that the gospel creates an entire way of life and affects literally everything about us. It is a power (Rom 1:16–17) that creates new life in us (Col 1:5–6; 1 Pet 1:23–25).

THE RICHNESS OF THE GOSPEL

New Testament scholar Simon Gathercole offers the following outline of the gospel taught in common by Paul and the Gospel writers:

1. The Son of God emptied himself and came into the world in Jesus Christ, becoming a servant.
2. He died on the cross as a substitutionary sacrifice.
3. He rose from the grave as the firstfruits of a whole renewed world.[3]

Each of these three truths can be fleshed out to show that the implications of the gospel are endless.

THE INCARNATION AND THE "UPSIDE-DOWN" ASPECT OF THE GOSPEL

Because Jesus was the king who became a servant, we see a reversal of values in his kingdom administration (Luke 6:20–26). In Jesus' kingdom, the poor, sorrowful, and persecuted are above the rich, recognized, and satisfied. The first shall be last (Matt 19:30). Why would this be?

This reversal is a way of imitating the pattern of Christ's salvation (Phil 2:1–11). Though Jesus was rich, he became poor. Though he was a king, he served. Though he was the greatest, he made himself the servant of all. He triumphed over sin not by taking up power but by serving sacrificially. He "won" through losing everything. This is a complete reversal of the world's way of thinking, which values power, recognition, wealth, and status. The gospel, then, creates a new kind of servant community, with people who live out an entirely alternate way of being human. Racial and class superiority, accrual of money and power at the expense of others, yearning for popularity and recognition — all are marks of living in the world. They represent the opposite of the gospel mind-set.

THE ATONEMENT AND THE "INSIDE-OUT" ASPECT OF THE GOSPEL

The Pharisees tended to emphasize the externals of the covenant — the covenant boundary markers of Sabbath observance, circumcision, Torah, and so on — rather than a regenerated heart (Luke 11:39 – 41). God's kingdom, however, "is not a matter of eating or drinking, but of righteousness, peace and joy in the Holy Spirit" (Rom 14:17). Why would this be?

Jesus took our place on the cross and accomplished salvation for us, which we receive freely as a gift. Traditional religion teaches that if we do good deeds and follow the moral rules in our external behavior, God will come into our hearts, bless us, and give us salvation. In other words, if I obey, God will love and accept me. But the gospel is the reverse of this: If I know in my heart that God has accepted me and loves me freely by grace, then I can begin to obey, out of inner joy and gratitude. Religion is outside in, but the gospel is inside out. We are justified by grace alone, not by works; we are beautiful and righteous in God's sight by the work of Christ. Once we gain this understanding on the inside, it revolutionizes how we relate to God, to ourselves, and to others on the outside.

THE RESURRECTION AND THE "FORWARD-BACK" ASPECT OF THE GOSPEL

Jesus is resurrected, but we are not. He has inaugurated the kingdom of God, but it is not fully present. The coming of the messianic King occurs in two stages. At his first coming, he saved us from the

penalty of sin and gave us the presence of the Holy Spirit, the down payment of the age to come (2 Cor 1:21 – 22; Eph 1:13 – 14). At the end of time, he will come to complete what he began at the first coming, saving us from the dominion and very presence of sin and evil. He will bring a new creation, a material world cleansed of all brokenness.

Christians now live in light of that future reality. We evangelize, telling people about the gospel and preparing them for the judgment. We also help the poor and work for justice, because we know that this is God's will and that he will ultimately overcome all oppression. We teach Christians to integrate their faith and their work so they can be culture makers, working for human flourishing — the common good. The "already but not yet" of the kingdom keeps us from utopian, triumphalistic visions of cultural takeover on the one hand, and from pessimism or withdrawal from society on the other.

A church that truly understands the implications of the biblical gospel, letting the "word of Christ dwell in [it] richly" (Col 3:16), will look like an unusual hybrid of various church forms and stereotypes. Because of the inside-out, substitutionary atonement aspect, the church will place great emphasis on personal conversion, experiential grace renewal, evangelism, outreach, and church

---

A church that truly understands the implications of the biblical gospel will look like an unusual hybrid of various church forms and stereotypes.

---

planting. This makes it look like an evangelical-charismatic church. Because of the upside-down, kingdom/incarnation aspect, the church will place great emphasis on deep community, cell groups or house churches, radical giving and sharing of resources, spiritual disciplines, racial reconciliation, and living with the poor. This makes it look like an Anabaptist "peace" church. Because of the forward-back, kingdom/restoration aspect, the church will place great emphasis on seeking the welfare of the city, neighborhood and civic involvement, cultural engagement, and training people to work in "secular" vocations out of a Christian worldview. This makes it look like a mainline church or, perhaps, a Kuyperian Reformed church. Very few churches, denominations, or movements integrate all of these ministries and emphases. Yet I believe that a comprehensive view of the biblical gospel — one that grasps the gospel's inside-out, upside-down, and forward-back aspects — will champion and cultivate them all. This is what we mean by a Center Church.

THE GOSPEL CHANGES EVERYTHING

The gospel is not just the ABCs but the A to Z of the Christian life. It is inaccurate to think the gospel is what saves non-Christians, and then Christians mature by trying hard to live according to biblical principles. It is more accurate to say that we are saved by believing the gospel, and then we are transformed in every part of our minds, hearts, and lives by believing the gospel more and more deeply as life goes on (see Rom 12:1 – 2; Phil 1:6; 3:13 – 14).

In the first chapter, we introduced the idea that there are two errors that constantly seek to steal the gospel from us. On the one hand, "moralism/religion/legalism" stresses truth without grace, for it claims we must obey the truth to be saved. On the other hand, "relativism/irreligion/liberalism" stresses grace without truth, for it claims we are all accepted by God (if there is a God), and we each have to decide what is true for us. We must never forget that Jesus was full of grace *and* truth (John 1:14). "Truth" without grace is not really truth, and "grace" without truth is not really grace. Any religion or philosophy of life that de-emphasizes or loses one or the other of these truths falls into legalism or into license. Either way, the joy and power and "release" of the gospel are stolen — by one thief or the other.

Edward Fisher's *The Marrow of Modern Divinity* is a classic, comprehensive description of how important it is to remember the two enemies of the gospel. Fisher discusses how legalism can be of two types, either of the theological type (a theol-

ogy that mixes faith and works and is not clear on free justification) or simply of a moralistic spirit and attitude. He also warns of the opposite error of antinomianism, an attitude that is afraid to ever say, "You *ought*," and refrains from insisting that God's law must be obeyed.[4]

The power of the gospel comes in two movements. It first says, "I am more sinful and flawed than I ever dared believe," but then quickly follows with, "I am more accepted and loved than I ever dared hope." The former outflanks antinomianism, while the latter staves off legalism. One of the greatest challenges is to be vigilant in both directions *at once*. Whenever we find ourselves fighting against one of these errors, it is extraordinarily easy to combat it by slipping into the other. Here's a test: if you think one of these errors is much more dangerous than the other, you are probably partially participating in the one you fear less.

Unlike legalism or antinomianism, an authentic grasp of the gospel of Christ will bring increasing transformation and wholeness across all the dimensions of life that were marred by the fall. By removing the primary cause of all of our alienations — our separation from God — it also treats the alienations that flow from it. The gospel addresses our greatest need and brings change and transformation to every area of life. Let's look at just a few of the ways that the gospel changes us.

Discouragement and depression. When a person is depressed, the moralist says, "You are breaking the rules. Repent." On the other hand, the relativist says, "You just need to love and accept yourself." Absent the gospel, the moralist will work on behavior, and the relativist will work on the emotions — and only superficialities will be addressed instead of the heart. Assuming the depression has no physiological base, the gospel will lead us to examine ourselves and say, "Something in my life has become more important than God — a pseudo-savior, a form of works-righteousness." The gospel leads us to embrace repentance, not to merely set our will against superficialities.

Love and relationships. Moralism often turns relationships into a blame game. This occurs when a moralist is traumatized by severe criticism and in reaction maintains a self-image as a good person by blaming others. Moralism can also cause people to procure love as the way to earn salvation; gaining love convinces them they are worthy persons. This, in turn, often creates codependency — you must save yourself by saving others. On the other hand, much relativism reduces love to a negotiated partnership for mutual benefit. You relate only as long as it does not cost you anything. Without the gospel, the choice is to selfishly use others or to selfishly let yourself be used by others. The gospel leads us to do neither. We selflessly sacrifice and commit, but not out of a need to convince ourselves or others that we are acceptable. We can love a person enough to confront, yet stay with the person even when it does not benefit us.

Sexuality. The moralist tends to see sex as dirty, or at least as a dangerous impulse that leads constantly to sin. The relativist/pragmatist sees sex as merely a biological and physical appetite. The gospel shows us that sexuality is supposed to reflect the self-giving of Christ. He gave himself completely, without conditions. Consequently, we are not to seek intimacy while holding back the rest of our lives. If we give ourselves sexually, we are also to give ourselves legally, socially, and personally. Sex is to be shared only in a totally committed, permanent relationship of marriage.

Family. Moralism can make a person a slave to parental expectations, while relativism/pragmatism sees no need for family loyalty or keeping promises and covenants if they do not meet one's needs. The gospel frees us from making parental approval a form of psychological salvation by pointing to how God is the ultimate Father. Grasping this, we will be neither too dependent nor too hostile toward our parents.

Self-control. Moralists tell us to control our passions out of fear of punishment. This is a volition-based approach. Relativists tell us to express ourselves and find out what is right for us. This is an emotion-based approach. The gospel tells us that the free, unshakable grace of God "teaches us to say 'No'" to our passions (Titus 2:12) if we will only

listen to it. It gives us new appetites and affections.[5] The gospel leads us to a whole-person approach that begins with truth descending into the heart.

Race and culture. The moralist/conservative bias is to use truth to evaluate cultures. Feeling superior to others in the impulse of self-justifying pride, moralists idolize their culture as supreme. The relativist/liberal approach is to relativize all cultures ("We can all get along because there is no truth"). The gospel leads us, on the one hand, to

---

Christianity is universal in that it welcomes everybody, but it is also particular in its confession that Jesus is Lord, and culture and ethnicity (or whatever other identity) are not.

---

be somewhat critical of all cultures, including our own (since truth *is* objective and real). On the other hand, it leads us to recognize we are morally superior to no one, since we are saved by grace alone. In this instance, the gospel is the grand leveler. Both sin and grace strip everyone of every boast. "*All* have sinned" (Rom 3:23, emphasis added); "there is *no one* righteous, not even one" (Rom 3:10, emphasis added; cf. Ps 143:2); therefore, "*whoever* believes in [Jesus] shall not perish but have eternal life" (John 3:16, emphasis added; cf. Mark 16:16; John 3:36; 5:24; 7:38; 11:26). For *in Christ* "there is neither Jew nor Greek, slave nor free, male nor female" (Gal 3:28, emphasis added). Christianity is universal in that it welcomes *everybody*, but it is also particular in its confession that Jesus is Lord, and culture and ethnicity (or whatever other identity) are not. Gospel-relying Christians will exhibit both moral conviction and compassion with flexibility.

Witness. The moralist believes in proselytizing, because "we are right, and they are wrong." Such an approach is almost always offensive. The relativist/pragmatist approach denies the legitimacy of evangelism altogether. Yet the gospel produces a constellation of traits in us. We are compelled to share the gospel out of generosity and love, not guilt. We are freed from the fear of being ridiculed or hurt by others, since we have already received the favor of God by grace. Our dealings with others reflect humility because we know we are saved only by grace alone, not because of our superior insight or character. We are hopeful about everyone, even the "hard cases," because we were saved only because of grace, not because we were people likely to become Christians. We are courteous and careful with people. We don't have to push or coerce them, for it is only God's grace that opens hearts, not our eloquence or persistence or even their openness (Exod 4:10 – 12). Together, these traits create not only an excellent neighbor in a multicultural society but also a winsome evangelist.

Human authority. Moralists tend to obey human authorities (family, tribe, government, and cultural customs) too anxiously, since they rely heavily on their self-image as upright persons. Relativists/pragmatists will either obey human authority too much (since they have no higher authority by which they can judge their culture) or else too little (since they may obey only when they know they can't get away with it). The result is either authoritarianism or a disregard for the proper place of authority. The gospel gives a standard by which to oppose human authority (if it contradicts the gospel), as well as an incentive to obey the civil authorities from the heart, even when we could get away with disobedience. To confess Jesus as Lord was simultaneously to confess that Caesar was not. Though there have been several studies of late that discuss the "counter-imperial" tenor of various texts, it is important to stress that the Bible is not so much against governing authorities or "empire" as such but that it prescribes a proper reordering of power. It is not that Jesus usurped the throne of Caesar but that when we allow Caesar to overstep his bounds, he is usurping the throne of Christ and leading people into idolatry.

Guilt and self-image. When someone says, "I can't forgive myself," it indicates that some standard or condition or person is more central to this person's identity than the grace of God. God is the only God who forgives — no other "god" will. If you cannot forgive yourself, it is because you have failed your true god — that is, whatever serves as your real righteousness — and it is holding you captive. The moralists' false god is usually a god of their imagination, a god that is holy and demanding but not gracious. The relativist/pragmatist's false god is usually some achievement or relationship.

This is illustrated by the scene in the movie *The Mission* in which Rodrigo Mendoza, the former slave-trading mercenary played by Robert de Niro, converts to the church and as a way of showing penance drags his armor and weapons up steep cliffs. In the end, however, he picks up his armor and weapons to fight against the colonialists and dies at their hand. His picking up his weapons demonstrates he never truly converted from his mercenary ways, just as his penance demonstrated he didn't get the message of forgiveness in the first place. The gospel brings rest and assurance to our consciences because Jesus shed his blood as a "ransom" for our sin (Mark 10:45). Our reconciliation with God is not a matter of keeping the law to earn our salvation, nor of berating ourselves when we fail to keep it. It is the "gift of God" (Rom 6:23).

Without the gospel, our self-image is based on living up to some standards — either our own or someone else's imposed on us. If we live up to those standards, we will be confident but not humble; if we don't live up to them, we will be humble but not confident. Only in the gospel can we be both enormously bold and utterly sensitive and humble, for we are *simul justus et peccator*, both perfect and sinner!

Joy and humor. Moralism eats away at real joy and humor because the system of legalism forces us to take our self (our image, our appearance, our reputation) *very* seriously. Relativism/pragmatism, on the other hand, tends toward pessimism as life goes on because of the inevitable cynicism that grows from a lack of hope for the world ("In the end, evil will triumph because there is no judgment or divine justice"). If we are saved by grace alone, this salvation is a constant source of amazed delight. Nothing is mundane or matter-of-fact about our lives. It is a miracle we are Christians, and the gospel, which creates bold humility, should give us a far deeper sense of humor and joy. We don't have to take ourselves seriously, and we are full of hope for the world.

Attitudes toward class. Moralists, when they look at the poor, tend to see their entire plight stemming from a lack of personal responsibility. As a result, they scorn the poor as failures. Relativists tend to underemphasize the role of personal responsibility and see the poor as helpless victims needing the experts to save them. The poor themselves either feel like failures or angrily blame their problems on others.

When the gospel is expounded and applied in its fullness in any church, that church will look unique.

The gospel, however, leads us to be humble, free from moral superiority, because we know we were spiritually bankrupt yet saved by Christ's free generosity. It leads us to be gracious, not worried too much about people getting what they deserve because we are aware that *none* of us deserve the grace of Christ. It also inclines us to be respectful of poor Christian believers as our brothers and sisters in Christ, people from whom we can learn. The gospel alone can produce a humble respect for and solidarity with the poor (see Pss 140:12; 146:9; Prov 14:31; 21:13; 22:22 – 23; 29:7).

In James 1:9 – 10, the poor Christian "ought to take pride in his high position" but the rich Christian "should take pride in his low position, because he will pass away like a wild flower." Here James is using the gospel on his listeners' class-consciousness. Everyone in Christ is at the same time a sinner who deserves death and also an adopted child of God, fully accepted and loved. But James proposes that the well-off believer would spiritually benefit by thinking about his or her sinfulness before God, since out in the world he or she gets a lot of acclaim. The poor believer, however, would spiritually benefit by thinking about his or her new high spiritual status, since out in the world he or she gets nothing but disdain.

In a remarkable, similar move, Paul tells the Christian slave owner Philemon that his slave, Onesimus, must be treated as a fellow "man and as a brother in the Lord" (Philemon 16). Therefore, Paul says, he should welcome and treat his slave "as you would welcome me" (v. 17). By teaching that Christians who understand the gospel should have a radically different way of understanding and wielding power, Paul deeply undermines the very institution of slavery. When both master and slave recognize each other as sinners saved by grace and beloved siblings, "slavery has been abolished even if its outer institutional shell remains." The gospel "emptied [slavery] of its inner content."[6]

Most of our problems in life come from a lack of proper orientation to the gospel. Pathologies in the church and sinful patterns in our individual lives ultimately stem from a failure to think through the deep implications of the gospel and to grasp and believe the gospel through and through. Put positively, the gospel transforms our hearts and our thinking and changes our approaches to absolutely everything. When the gospel is expounded and applied in its fullness in any church, that church will look unique. People will find in it an attractive, electrifying balance of moral conviction and compassion.

D. A. Carson writes the following:

The gospel is regularly presented not only as truth to be received and believed, but the very power of God to transform (see 1 Cor 2; 1 Thess 2:4; [Rom 1:16 – 17]) . . .

One of the most urgently needed things today is a careful treatment of how the gospel, biblically and richly understood, ought to shape everything we do in the local church, all of our ethics, all of our priorities.[7]

But how does this happen? What does a church that believes in the centrality of the gospel actually look like? How does a church, or even a group of churches, change to become a gospel-centered community of faith? There must first be a life-changing recovery of the gospel — a revival in the life of the church and in the hearts of individuals. We call this *gospel renewal.*

QUESTIONS FOR DISCUSSION AND REFLECTION

1. Keller writes, "Here's a test: if you think one of these errors [legalism or license] is much more dangerous than the other, you are probably partially participating in the one you fear less." Which error have you tended to fear less, and why?

2. Keller writes, "The primary cause of all of our alienations [is] our separation from God." How has the gospel mended this primary ailment in you and how has it helped curb the many other symptoms that flow from it? How does this experience prepare you to minister to alienated people?

3. Keller writes, "The gospel addresses our greatest need and brings change and transformation to every area of life." The gospel also treats the alienations that flow from our alienation from God. Rehearse, in your own words, how the gospel treats at least three of the following areas:

- discouragement and depression
- love and relationships
- sexuality
- family and parental expectations
- self-control
- racial and cultural differences
- our motive for witness
- obedience to human authority
- guilt and self-image
- joy and humor
- our attitudes toward class

4. Look at the three aspects of the gospel dealt with in this chapter: incarnation/upside-down, atonement/inside-out, and resurrection/forward-back. Compare these to the similar outline in the section titled "The Gospel Has Chapters" in chapter 1. How can you sharpen and clarify the way you set the gospel within the story line of the Bible?

CHAPTER 3 — THE GOSPEL AFFECTS EVERYTHING {pages 46-52}

1. D. A. Carson, "The Gospel of Jesus Christ (1 Corinthians 15:1 – 19)," *The Spurgeon Fellowship Journal* (Spring 2008): 10 – 11, www.thespurgeonfellowship.org/Downloads/feature_Sp08.pdf (accessed January 5, 2012); see also Carson's chapter "What Is the Gospel? — Revisited," in *For the Fame of God's Name: Essays in Honor of John Piper*, ed. Sam Storms and Justin Taylor (Wheaton, Ill.: Crossway, 2010), 164 – 66, where he writes that "the gospel is not just for unbelievers but also for believers" and makes the biblical case.
2. Lesslie Newbigin, *The Gospel in a Pluralist Society* (Grand Rapids: Eerdmans, 1989), 38, italics in original.
3. Simon Gathercole, "The Gospel of Paul and the Gospel of the Kingdom," in *God's Power to Save*, ed. Chris Green (Nottingtham, UK: InterVarsity, 2006), 138 – 54.
4. Edward Fisher, *The Marrow of Modern Divinity* (1645; repr., Fearn, Scotland: Christian Focus Publications, 2009).
5. See Thomas Chalmers, "The Expulsive Power of a New Affection" (sermon, date unknown), www.theologynetwork.org/historical-theology/getting-stuck-in/the-expulsive-power-of-a-new-affection.htm (accessed January 6, 2012).
6. Miroslav Volf, *A Public Faith: How Followers of Christ Should Serve the Common Good* (Grand Rapids: Baker, 2011), 92.
7. Carson, "What Is the Gospel? — Revisited," in *For the Fame of God's Name*, 165.

chapter 4

THE NEED FOR GOSPEL RENEWAL

Gospel renewal is a life-changing recovery of the gospel. *Personal* gospel renewal means the gospel doctrines of sin and grace are actually experienced, not just known intellectually. This personal renewal includes an awareness and conviction of one's own sin and alienation from God and comes from seeing in ourselves deeper layers of self-justification, unbelief, and self-righteousness than we have ever seen before. There is a new, commensurate grasp of the wonder of forgiveness and grace as we shed these attitudes and practices and rest in Christ alone for salvation. Perhaps we have previously said that we were "resting in Christ's work, not our own work" for salvation, but when we experience gospel renewal, we have a new clarity about what this means in our mind and a new experience of actually doing it with our heart.

Corporate gospel renewal — what has sometimes been called "revival" — is a season in which a whole body of believers experience personal gospel renewal together.[1] Over time, all churches, no matter how sound their theology, tend to lose sight of the uniqueness of the gospel and fall into practices that conform more to other religions or to irreligion. Their doctrinal instruction loses sight of how each doctrine plays a role in the gospel message, and their moral instruction is not grounded in and motivated by the finished work and grace of Christ. The leaders of the church must always be bringing the gospel to bear on people's minds and hearts so that they see it as not just a set of beliefs but as a power that changes us profoundly and continually. Without this kind of application of the gospel, mere teaching, preaching, baptizing, and catechizing are not sufficient.

Richard Lovelace was a student of the history of revivals. He sought to discover what, for all their apparent differences, they had in common. He concluded that while Christians know intellectually that their justification (acceptance by God) is the basis for their sanctification (their actual moral behavior), in their actual "day-to-day existence ... they rely on their sanctification for their justification ... drawing their assurance of acceptance with God from their sincerity, their past experience of conversion, their recent religious performance or the relative infrequency of their conscious, willful disobedience."[2]

In other words, revivals and renewals are necessary because the default mode of the human heart is works-righteousness — we do not ordinarily live as if the gospel is true. Christians often believe in their heads that "Jesus accepts me; therefore I will live a good life," but their hearts and actions are functioning practically on the principle "I live a good life; therefore Jesus accepts me." The results of this inversion are smug self-satisfaction (if we feel we are living up to standards) or insecurity, anxiety, and self-

DEFINITIONS OF REVIVAL

This understanding of gospel renewal differs from two widespread views of what revival is. The first view sees revival primarily as the adding of the extraordinary operations of the Holy Spirit (such as miracles, healings, and revelations). A second view sees revival as an especially vigorous season of preaching, gatherings, and evangelistic activity. In contrast to both, I am arguing that gospel renewal or revival is an intensification of the normal operations of the Spirit (conviction of sin, regeneration and sanctification, assurance of grace) through the ordinary means of grace (preaching the Word, prayer, and the sacraments).

hatred (if we feel we are failing to live up). In either case, the results are defensiveness, a critical spirit, racial or cultural ethnocentricity to bolster a sense of righteousness, an allergy to change, and other forms of spiritual deadness, both individual and corporate. In sharp contrast, the gospel of sheer grace offered to hopeless sinners will humble and comfort all at once. The results are joy, a willingness to admit faults, graciousness with all, and a lack of self-absorption.[3]

Because we don't really believe the gospel deep down — because we are living as if we save ourselves — our hearts find ways of either rejecting or reengineering the doctrine (as in liberal theology) or of mentally subscribing to the doctrine while functionally trusting and resting in our own moral and doctrinal goodness (as in "dead orthodoxy"). As a result, individuals and churches experience a slow spiritual deadening over the years, unless some sort of renewal/revival dynamic arrests it.

Revival can be widespread, affecting a whole region or country, or more narrow in scope, influencing just one congregation or even just a part of one. It can be fairly gentle and quiet or rather sensational. But all revivals are seasons in which the ordinary operations of the Holy Spirit are intensified manyfold. In revival, the ordinary means of grace produce a great wave of newly awakened inquirers, soundly converted sinners, and spiritually renewed believers. The church growth that inevitably results cannot be accounted for by demographical-sociological shifts or efficient outreach programs.

So revival is not a historical curiosity; it is a consistent pattern of how the Holy Spirit works in a community to arrest and counteract the default mode of the human heart. It is surely relevant to ministry in twenty-first-century global cultures, as it is relevant in every culture.

CRITIQUING REVIVALS

We cannot sufficiently cover a full history of revivals here. We know that revivals have often had powerful, society-changing effects.[4] The most famous revival in American history, the Great Awakening of the early and mid-eighteenth century, had a major impact on the culture and history of both Britain

and the United States. And of course there have been other well-known revivals in many other parts of the world.[5] Throughout history, revivals have also drawn sharp criticism and suspicion. When William B. Sprague, a Presbyterian minister in Albany, New York, published his lectures on revival in 1832, he devoted his longest lecture to a "Defence of Revivals," fielding several objections and addressing many of the most common criticisms of revival. He addressed concerns that revivals were unbiblical and "modern," that they led to emotional excesses and fanaticism, that they split families, and that they undermined established churches.[6]

Revival is not a historical curiosity; it is a consistent pattern of how the Holy Spirit works in a community to counteract the default mode of the human heart.

This last charge — that revivals undermine the role and importance of the church — is the most persistent today. I want to examine this charge by looking back at the conditions that led to revivalism in the first place. Before the eighteenth century, a person became a Christian through a process that was corporate, gradual, formal, and completely church-centric. First came the presentation of an infant for baptism by the whole family. After that came a long period of catechetical instruction in the church's historic creeds and traditions. Finally, it was expected that the child would be admitted to the Lord's Supper as a full communicant. Weddings and funerals in the church were also significant milestones, all observed with one's family in the presence of the congregation and through forms and traditions that tied all participants in the present to the lives of believers in the past. One's faith was first inherited and then personally confirmed by the individual through a highly communal process that entailed the support and approval of his or her family, church, and religious authorities.

However, the Industrial Revolution brought profound social changes. Many people were displaced to the big cities to work in factories, which took them away from their parish churches and small towns where everyone knew everyone else and where norms of behavior and participation in institutions could be enforced through social pressure. Second, market capitalism gave individuals (who could now act more autonomously) more goods and services to choose from.

The revivalist ministries of the Wesleys in England and of George Whitefield in America were responses to these cultural realities. They took preaching directly to the masses in outdoor meetings that called people to conversion, not waiting for them to be processed by their local parish churches in the traditional way, because (revivalists felt) this was less and less likely to happen. Revivalists emphasized the decisions of individuals rather than the incorporation of families into a community

and called on a dramatic turning experience, rather than a process of liturgy and catechism, for spiritual formation.[8]

Now we see why Sprague in the 1830s had to respond to the charges that revivalists were undermining the authority of the ordained ministry and the local church. Detractors of revivals said that, in the long run, stressing conversion and revival undermines churches' ability to instruct and discipline their members. Participation in church comes to be viewed as optional, since salvation comes directly through personal faith and experience — it is not mediated through the church. Emotional experience is placed above doctrinal soundness and holiness of life. Christianity becomes a way to meet felt needs instead of a means of re-forming a person into the image of Christ. The individual is privileged at the expense of the community, so every Christian becomes his or her own spiritual authority, and there is no true accountability.[9]

They were partly right, of course. These criticisms of revivalism hit home in the eighteenth century (and are equally valid today). In fact, Sprague's second-longest lecture was on "Evils to Be Avoided in Connection to Revivals," and here he leveled his own criticisms of the excesses of revivalism, excesses that eventually came to full flower in Charles Finney's ministry.[10] Sprague was part of an influential stream of nineteenth-century Reformed theology that was able to find a middle ground in the debate. Archibald Alexander, the founding faculty member of Princeton Seminary, remained a strong promoter of revivals, despite his recognition of all their possible negative effects. He believed those effects were not inherent to revival and could be avoided or minimized.

Alexander and his successors at Princeton continued to support the basic insights of revival while insisting on the critical importance of both evangelism and spiritual formation. As believers in infant baptism, they understood that baptized children were part of the church and recipients of God's grace in the life of the family through the sacrament. But they continued to exhort children to put their faith in Christ and counseled them about

CATECHISM IN TODAY'S CHURCH

The Princeton thinkers stressed the importance of catechetical instruction. In an important book titled *Grounded in the Gospel: Building Believers the Old-Fashioned Way*, Gary Parrett and J. I. Packer urge contemporary Christians to restore catechetical instruction to the life of the church.[7] This approach to spiritual formation has declined so drastically in modern churches that most Protestants, particularly evangelicals, think of it as a "Catholic thing."

Parrett and Packer make a great case for reinventing catechesis. Catechesis is much more than a document to memorize — it is a communal, lifelong commitment to learning and study. Memorization and recitation help deepen, elongate, and reinforce the theology and practice of the church. This depth of understanding forms a basis for ongoing life change and encourages assimilation into the church, more so than most contemporary seminars and programs.

what conversion looked like.[11] When it came time to admit children to the Lord's Supper, they looked for a "credible profession of faith" rather than simply admitting any child who completed church instruction. While continuing to affirm the importance of the church in the process of spiritual formation, they emphasized the ongoing need to preach and teach the gospel message — even to their own children and congregations.

REVIVALISM TODAY

The same debate continues today, as the perils of unbalanced revivalism are still apparent in the church. Extreme revivalism is certainly too individualistic. Our truth-allergic, experience-addicted populace wants transformation but doesn't want the loss of freedom and control associated with submitting to authority within a committed community. Many "converts" seem to make decisions for Christ but soon lose their enthusiasm because they are offered quick programs for follow-up and small group fellowship rather than a lifelong, embodied experience of community. Many churches do not even have a process for becoming a member. As a result, converts' lives are often not visibly different from those in the culture around them. The older,

---

The basic insights and practices of gospel renewal ministry are right for two reasons: they fit our times, and they center on the heart in a biblical way.

---

more communal processes of traditional churches are better at bringing about a more thorough transformation of life.

However, many of today's critics do more than lament these effects; they deny the basic premises of revival. They reject the idea that we should call people to conversion if they are in the church. Many aim to recapture something similar to the traditional church life of pre-eighteenth-century Europe, where

THE UNIQUE ROLE OF THE HEART

J. I. Marais, a theology professor at Stellenbosch in South Africa, wrote, "In the 'heart' God's Spirit dwells with might (Eph 3:16, *eis ton esō anthrōpon*); in the 'heart' God's love is poured forth (Rom 5:5). The Spirit of his Son has been 'sent forth into the heart' (Gal 4:6); the 'earnest of the Spirit' has been given 'in the heart' (2 Cor 1:22). In the work of grace, therefore, the heart occupies a position almost unique."[12]

no one could "become a Christian" except through incorporation into a local congregation. And once baptized and incorporated, this person was a Christian by definition, regardless of personal experience.

I believe this is a mistake for two fundamental reasons. To use biblical terms, this position does not know the times and seasons, and it does not sufficiently account for the heart. Or, to put it more positively, the basic insights and practices of gospel renewal ministry are right for two reasons: they fit our times, and they center on the heart in a biblical way.

Gospel renewal fits our times. What do I mean when I say that revival "fits our times"? The traditional, highly church-centered approach worked well when there was one dominant church and religious tradition in a culture and when the private and public sectors put far fuller weight behind the church. The institutions of society and the shared symbols and practices of common life expressed, confirmed, and reinforced religious beliefs. In such an environment, the culture's God seemed inevitable and the worldview of our society's religion seemed plausible to everyone. The traditional model also depended on not having many kinds of churches to choose from. Alternative denominations or religions were absent or were heavily stigmatized. Citizens could choose to be active in their society's inherited faith (and the local parish) or to just be fairly inactive, but those were the only two realistic options. The social realities were such

Revival and spiritual forgetting. Israel constantly "forgets" the great salvation they had received from God (Deut 4:9; 8:11, 14, 19; cf. Josh 4:20–24). Peter warns that it is possible for Christians to lose their awareness of the spiritual reality that they have been cleansed from their past sins (2 Pet 1:9). We need to continually renew the spiritual remembrance of our salvation.

Revival and cycles of decline. The books of Judges, Kings, and Chronicles depict constant cycles of decline and revival. The cycle starts when the Israelites assimilate to the pagan culture around them. The result is suffering that leads them to return to God in repentance. God responds by sending leaders who spark a revival (Judges 2:11–20; 10:6–16). New Testament churches can go through the cycle too; Christ calls the Ephesian church to "return to your first love" (Rev 2:1–7).

Revival and the Spirit. At Pentecost, the disciples were "filled with the Holy Spirit" and preached the word of God so boldly that there were many conversions (Acts 2:4, 14–41). Though this event is unique, the Christians were again filled with the Spirit so that their community life and outreach were empowered (Acts 4:7–31; 13:9, 49–52). David Peterson states that in this context the phrase "suggests … a fresh filling of the Spirit so that with great power they were able to continue their work of testifying to the resurrection."[13] As in the Old Testament, God's response to prayer and persecution is the sending of the Spirit to revive individuals and churches.

that virtually no one *chose* their own faith, let alone their own congregation.

This church-centric model broke down as people became increasingly mobile and society slowly but surely became more pluralistic. North America was the first place where churches had to *appeal* for members and converts. Americans only came to church if they chose to do so.[14] Now wind the clock forward a couple of centuries to today's pluralistic societies, where the important institutions of our public life do not all point to a unified set of beliefs about life and reality. No one really inherits their belief systems as they once did. People actively choose among competing sets of beliefs and worldviews and must be persuaded through personal appeals to do so.[15] I believe this state of affairs demands the revivalist emphasis on persuasion, conversion, and individual self-examination.

Gospel renewal focuses on the heart. I believe this second reason for retaining the basic insights and practices of revival is the more important one. Revivalism's core insight — that salvation is a matter of the heart — has ample grounding in the Bible. In Romans 10:9, Paul writes, "If you confess with your mouth, 'Jesus is Lord,' and believe in your heart that God raised him from the dead, you will be saved." Virtually all commentaries observe that this means it is not enough to agree with Christian truth intellectually ("confess with your mouth"). There must also be personal trust, a heart conviction.

When the Bible speaks of the heart, it means more than just our emotions. It is true that we feel our emotions in our hearts (Lev 19:17; Pss 4:7; 13:2), but we also think and reason in our hearts (Prov 23:7; Mark 2:8) and even act from our hearts (Eccl 10:2). Our heart is the center of our personality, the seat of our fundamental commitments, the control center of the whole person. What is in the heart determines what we think, do, and feel — since mind, will, and emotions are all rooted there. Paul states in Romans 10:9–10 that it is not enough to grasp and assent rationally to Christian truth, though that is absolutely necessary. Saving faith is never less than intellectual assent, but it is always more than that. It combines rational knowledge with the conviction and trust of the heart.

For an example of revival preaching in the Old Testament, consider Jeremiah's call to the Israelites and his demand to "circumcise your hearts" (Jer 4:4; cf. 9:26; Acts 7:51). Jeremiah's listeners had the outward sign of the covenant, yet Jeremiah informed them they did not have the inward reality of a new heart (Jer 31:33). The rite of circumcision was the sign of belonging to the covenant community. It functioned much like baptism in the Christian church (Col 2:11 – 12). Anyone who was circumcised had been visibly incorporated into the community of God's people. And yet, according to Jeremiah, there was more required of them than just the outward signs. Salvation required the removal of a stony heart (Ezek 11:19). The heart had to be cleansed (Ps 51:10) and made steadfast (Ps 112:7).

The New Testament continues to make this distinction between the outward and the inward. In Romans, Paul makes the case that many who were members of God's covenant people "outwardly" were not so "inwardly," because "circumcision is … of the heart, by the Spirit" (Rom 2:28 – 29). In his letter to the Philippians, Paul declares that in Christ, Christians become the "[true] circumcision, we who worship by the Spirit of God" (Phil 3:3). Here he ties Christian conversion to the "heart circumcision" of the Old Testament.[16] In this chapter, Paul describes his reliance on law keeping and moral attainments ("put no confidence in the flesh" — v. 3) and how he once lacked this inward spiritual reality. The renewal and heart change in Paul's life came only when he transferred his trust from law keeping to Christ's imputed righteousness for his confidence before God (vv. 4b, 7 – 9). When Jesus called a religious leader to be "born again" by the Holy Spirit (John 3:7), he was making essentially the same exhortation that Jeremiah had made in calling the people to circumcise their hearts.

Another warrant for emphasizing the heart is the biblical teaching on the relationship between repentance and faith. The summary of Jesus' gospel given in Mark 1:15 highlights this relationship: "The kingdom of God is near. Repent and believe the good news!" In Luke 24:46 – 47, Jesus states that "repentance and forgiveness of sins will be preached in

Revival and inner reality. In Ephesians 3:14 – 21, Paul prays that the Spirit will strengthen his readers with power in their inner being. For what? "So that Christ may dwell in your hearts through faith" and so we may know the love of Christ "that surpasses knowledge — that you may be filled to the measure of all the fullness of God." But elsewhere Paul states that Christians already have Christ dwelling in them (Eph 2:22) and already have come to fullness in him (Col 2:9 – 10). Taken together, these passages must mean that while these things are objectively true of Christians, the Spirit can make the love of God so spiritually real and affecting that it changes how we live. He wants us not just to know the fact of Christ's love but to have power to grasp the infinity and wonder of it (Eph 3:18 – 19). This is what happens when the fullness of the Spirit is mentioned. The truth begins to shine out to us. We hear in our hearts, "You are my child" (see Rom 8:16; cf. Luke 3:22), and it makes us effective ambassadors of his kingdom.

Revival and conversion. Revival consists not only of the renewal of true believers but also of the conversion of those within the covenant community who are only nominal believers. The prophets preach to the circumcised — full members of the covenant outwardly — yet call them to inner conversion: "Circumcise yourselves to the LORD, circumcise your hearts" (Jer 4:4; cf. Deut 10:16; 30:6; Joel 2:13). In the New Testament too, it is possible to be a baptized member of the Christian community and still have a heart "not right before God" and in need of conversion (Acts 8:9 – 23). Through revival stagnant Christians come alive and nominal Christians become converted.

[my] name to all nations, beginning at Jerusalem." And when people ask Peter how to be saved in Acts 2 he tells them to repent (v. 38; see Acts 3:19; 5:31). Repeatedly throughout the New Testament, we see that saving faith and repentance are inseparable and that true repentance includes grief and sorrow over our sin (2 Cor 7:10). Second Corinthians 7:11 tells us that repentance includes zeal, indignation, and longing, using a variety of terms to show that repentance is a deep experience that profoundly affects the mind, will, and emotions. Repentance changes the heart. It will never be enough to ask if a person has learned the faith, has been baptized, or has joined the church. If he or she has not repented, it is all to no avail.

Gospel renewal does not simply seek to convert nominal church members; it also insists that *all* Christians — even committed ones — need the Spirit to bring the gospel home to their hearts for deepened experiences of Christ's love and power.

Unbalanced revivalism indeed undermines the work of the established church. But balanced revivalism is the work of the church.

In Paul's great prayer for the Ephesians in chapter 3, he prays for his readers that Christ will dwell in their hearts and they may be filled with all the fullness of God. This is noteworthy, since *he is writing to Christians*, not nonbelievers. By definition, all Christians already have Christ dwelling in them (1 Cor 6:19; Col 1:27) and have the fullness of God (Col 2:9 – 10) by virtue of their union with Christ through faith (see sidebar on "A Biblical Theology of Revival" on pp. 58 – 59). What does Paul mean, then, by his prayer? He must be saying that he hopes the Ephesians will *experience* what they already believe in and possess — the presence and love of Christ (Eph 3:16 – 19). But how does this experience happen? It comes through the work of the Spirit, strengthening our "inner being" and our "hearts" so that as believers we can know Christ's

love (see v. 16). It happens, in other words, through gospel renewal.

This fits perfectly with what Jesus declares about the work of the Holy Spirit in John's gospel: "[The Holy Spirit] will bring glory to me by taking from what is mine and making it known to you" (John 16:14). The phrase "making it known" indicates a momentous announcement, a declaration that grabs attention. The Holy Spirit's job is to unfold the meaning of Jesus' person and work in such a way that its infinite importance and beauty are brought home to the mind and heart. This is why in the letter to the Ephesians Paul hopes that Christians, who already know rationally that Christ loves them, will have "the eyes of [their] heart … enlightened" (1:18) so they will "have power … to grasp how wide and long and high and deep is the love of Christ" (3:17 – 18). Paul's prayers in Ephesians show that Christians can expect the Holy Spirit to continually renew their boldness, love, joy, and power as they go beyond merely believing in the things that Jesus has done to experiencing them by the work of the Spirit.

Unbalanced revivalism indeed undermines the work of the established church. But balanced revivalism — a commitment to corporate and individual gospel renewal through the ordinary means of grace — *is* the work of the church. This is because it is possible (even common) for a person to be baptized, to be an active member of the church, to subscribe to all biblical doctrines, and to live according to biblical ethics, but nonetheless to be wholly unconverted. Revivalist ministry emphasizes conversion and spiritual renewal, not only for those outside the church, but also for those *inside* the church. Some need to be converted from clear unbelief; others need to see, to their surprise, that they've never been converted; still others need to sense their spiritual stagnation.

In commenting on "the truth of the gospel" (Gal 2:5), Martin Luther says the gospel is for us "the principal article of all Christian doctrine … Most necessary it is, therefore, that we should know this article well, teach it unto others, and beat it into their heads continually."[17] If it were natural or even possible for our hearts to operate consistently from the truth and in the life-giving power of the gospel, we wouldn't need to have it beat into our heads continually. We wouldn't need a persistent, balanced, revivalist ministry of gospel renewal. But of course it isn't possible; and so we do.

QUESTIONS FOR DISCUSSION AND REFLECTION

1. Have you ever experienced spiritual renewal in a corporate setting as described in this chapter? If so, how would you describe it? How did it differ from a more personal experience of renewal?

2. The sidebar on "Catechism in Today's Church" argues for the need to recover and reinvent catechism for the church today. What training currently takes place in your church for teaching children and new believers, and what three things could you do differently after reading this chapter?

3. What does it mean to say that "the basic insights and practices of gospel renewal ministry are right for two reasons: they fit our times, and they center on the heart in a biblical way." How does gospel renewal ministry fit our times, and how is it uniquely focused on the heart?

4. How can you bring more of a gospel renewal focus to your existing ministry?

CHAPTER 4 — THE NEED FOR GOSPEL RENEWAL *(pages 54–61)*

1. I am going to use the terms *renewal* and *revival* interchangeably.
2. Richard F. Lovelace, *Dynamics of Spiritual Life: An Evangelical Theology of Renewal* (Downers Grove, Ill.: InterVarsity, 1979), 101.
3. See ibid., 212.
4. For a varied reading list on revival, see Thomas S. Kidd, *The Great Awakening: The Roots of Evangelical Christianity in America* (New Haven, Conn.: Yale University Press, 2007); Mark Noll, "The New Piety: The Conversion of the Wesleys," in *Turning Points: Decisive Moments in the History of Christianity* (Grand Rapids: Baker, 2001), 221 – 44; D. Martyn Lloyd-Jones, *Revival* (Wheaton, Ill.: Crossway, 1987); Iain H. Murray, *Revival and Revivalism: The Making and Marring of American Evangelicalism 1750 – 1858* (Carlisle, Pa.: Banner of Truth, 1994); C. Goen, ed., *The Works of Jonathan Edwards: The Great Awakening* (New Haven, Conn.: Yale University Press, 1972); Richard F. Lovelace, *Dynamics of Spiritual Life* (Downers Grove, Ill.: InterVarsity, 1979).
5. For a recent survey, see Collin Hansen and John Woodbridge, *A God-Sized Vision: Revival Stories That Stretch and Stir* (Grand Rapids: Zondervan, 2010).
6. William B. Sprague, *Lectures on Revivals of Religion* (1832; Edinburgh: Banner of Truth, 1958), 25 – 60.
7. Gary A. Parrett and J. I. Packer, *Grounded in the Gospel: Building Believers the Old-Fashioned Way* (Grand Rapids: Baker, 2010); see discussion in "Churchly Piety and 'Ecclesial Revivalism'" in chapter 25.
8. See Noll, "The New Piety," in *Turning Points*, 221 – 44.
9. In the last several years, many young evangelical leaders have adopted this same critique. They have read neo-Anabaptist thinkers such as Stanley Hauerwas and William Willimon; older Anabaptist thinkers such as John Howard Yoder; "new monastics" such as Shane Claiborne; "high church Calvinists" such as Michael Horton and Darryl Hart; Federal Vision leaders such as Douglas Wilson; and those who follow Lesslie Newbigin and N. T. Wright. As different as these thinkers and groups are, they all put much emphasis on liturgy, catechism, thick and deep community, and weekly observance of the Lord's Supper. Revivalist religion is critiqued as being "Gnostic" (not involving the body, not caring for the physical), as being individualistic, and as seeking to ground assurance in shifting subjective experience rather than in more solid community participation and tradition. The call is to look to the sacraments and church involvement for assurance rather than to personal experience.
10. Sprague warns against these "evils" of revivalism: "undervaluing divine institutions and divine truth" (p. 242), "certain things … that are fitted to impair the dignity and lessen the influence of the ministerial office" (p. 247), "setting up false standards of Christian character" (p. 249), and "admitting persons to the communion with little or no probation" (p. 254). It is remarkable that many of these criticisms are similar to those of modern social historians, theologians, and young evangelical leaders.
11. See Archibald Alexander, *Thoughts on Religious Experience* (Edinburgh: Banner of Truth, 1978), 13 – 35.
12. J. I. Marais, "Heart," in *The International Standard Bible Encyclopedia*, gen. ed. James Orr (Grand Rapids: Eerdmans, 1960), 2:1351.
13. David G. Peterson, *The Acts of the Apostles* (Pillar New Testament Commentary; Grand Rapids: Eerdmans, 2009), 203.
14. See Mark Noll, *The Old Religion in a New World: The History of North American Christianity* (Grand Rapids: Eerdmans, 2001), 51.
15. For two classic explanations of how pluralistic culture forces everyone to choose their faith, see Peter L. Berger, *The Homeless Mind: Modernization and Consciousness* (New York: Vintage, 1974); Peter L. Berger, *The Heretical Imperative: Contemporary Possibilities of Religious Affirmation* (New York: Doubleday, 1980).
16. Philippians 3:3 reads, "we who are *the* circumcision …" "Circumcision" here is particular, communicating distinguishment. There is debate over whether "faith in Christ" in verse 9 is to be understood as an objective genitive ("faith in Christ") or subjective genitive ("faith/faithfulness of Christ"), but this doesn't affect our point. The passage is about what marks our identity — what we do (works of the flesh) or what has been done for us in Christ.
17. Martin Luther, *Commentary on Galatians* (Lafayette, Ind.: Sovereign Grace, 2002), 103.

THE ESSENCE OF GOSPEL RENEWAL

Revival is necessary because religion ("I obey; therefore I am accepted") is so different from the gospel ("I am accepted by God through Christ; therefore I obey") but is such an effective counterfeit. Though these systems of motivation and purpose have utterly different lineages, on the surface they may look like twins. Two people basing their lives on these two systems may sit right beside each other in church. Both strive to obey the law of God, to pray, to give generously, and to be good family members. Yet they do so out of radically different motives, in radically different spirits, and resulting in radically different kinds of inner personal character. One of them (the "religious" one) may even be lost altogether. Even the one operating out of the gospel will naturally drift into religion unless constantly challenged and renewed.

If these insights from the last chapter addressed the *why* of gospel renewal, the question for this chapter is the *what* of gospel renewal. What does the gospel do that actually changes people in a congregation? How can the distinct and unique theological truths of the gospel be formulated in ways that produce new, Spirit-led, Christ-centered motivation in people, whether their starting point is religion or irreligion? First we will look further at the distinction between religion, irreligion, and the gospel. Then we will see how these insights are applied to the heart.

THREE WAYS OF RESPONDING TO GOD

Christians typically identify two ways to respond to God: follow him and do his will, or reject him and do your own thing. Ultimately this is true, but there are actually *two ways to reject God* that must be distinguished from one another. You can reject God by rejecting his law and living any way you see fit. And you can also reject God by embracing and obeying

God's law so as to earn your salvation. The problem is that people in this last group — who reject the gospel in favor of moralism — *look* as if they are trying to do God's will. Consequently, there are not just two ways to respond to God but three: irreligion, religion, and the gospel.

Irreligion is avoiding God as Lord and Savior by ignoring him altogether. "Religion," or moralism, is avoiding God as Lord and Savior by developing a moral righteousness and then presenting it to God in an effort to show that he "owes" you.[1] The gospel, however, has nothing to do with our developing a righteousness we give God so he owes us; it is God's developing and giving us righteousness through Jesus Christ (1 Cor 1:30; 2 Cor 5:21). The gospel differs from both religion and irreligion, from both moralism and relativism.

There are not just two ways to respond to God but three: irreligion, religion, and the gospel.

This theme runs the length of the Bible. When God saves the Israelites from slavery in Egypt, he first leads them out and *then* gives them the law to obey. Law obedience is the result of their deliverance and election, not the cause of it (Exod 19:4 – 5; Deut 7:6 – 9). As God makes a covenant with the Israelites, he warns them that it is still possible for them to be uncircumcised in heart (Lev 26:41; Deut 10:16; 30:6; Jer 4:4) — even as they are completely compliant and obedient to all the laws, observances, and rituals of worship. As we saw in the previous chapter, it took the New Testament to lay out what it meant to be the true circumcision (Phil 3:3). Paul tells us that the circumcised in heart do not rely on their law keeping for confidence before God. Paul explains the three ways to live according to the Old Testament: (1) literally uncircumcised (pagans and nonbelievers who do not submit to God's laws); (2) circumcised only in the flesh (submitted to God's law but resting and relying on it); and (3) circumcised in heart (submitted to God's law in response to the saving grace of God).

In the New Testament, these three ways appear most prominently in Romans 1 – 4. Beginning in Romans 1:18 – 32, Paul shows how the pagan, immoral Gentiles are lost and alienated from God. In Romans 2:1 – 3:20, Paul counterintuitively states that the moral, Bible-believing Jews are lost and alienated from God as well. "What shall we conclude then? Are we any better? Not at all! We have already made the charge that Jews and Gentiles alike are all under sin. As it is written: 'There is no one righteous, not even one; there is no one … who seeks God'" (Rom 3:9 – 11). The last part of this statement is particularly shocking, since Paul concludes that thousands of men and women who were diligently obeying and believing the Bible were *not seeking* God, even in all their religion. The reason is that if you seek to be right with God through your morality and religion, you are not seeking God for your salvation; you are using God as a means to achieve your own salvation. Paul proceeds in the rest of Romans to explain the gospel as seeking God in Christ for salvation through grace alone and through faith alone.

Throughout the Gospels, these three ways — religion, irreligion, and the gospel — are repeatedly depicted in Jesus' encounters. Whether a Pharisee or a tax collector (Luke 18), a Pharisee or a fallen woman (Luke 7), or a respectable crowd and a man possessed by a demon (Mark 5), in every instance the less moral, less religious person connects more readily to Jesus. Even in John 3 and 4, where a similar contrast occurs between a Pharisee and an immoral Samaritan woman, the woman receives the gospel with joy, while Nicodemus the Pharisee evidently has to go home and think about it. Here we have the New Testament version of what we saw in earlier pages of the Bible — that God chooses the

foolish things to shame the wise, the weak things to shame the strong, to show that his salvation is by grace (see 1 Cor 1:26 – 31).

It is so much easier to move from the gospel to religion than the other way round. One of Martin Luther's fundamental insights is that religion is the default mode of the human heart. Even irreligious people earn their acceptability and sense of worth by living up to their set of values.[2] And the effects of "works-religion" persist so stubbornly in the heart that Christians who believe the gospel at one level will continually revert to religion, operating at deeper levels as if they are saved by their works. Richard F. Lovelace develops this train of thought:

Only a fraction of the present body of professing Christians are solidly appropriating the justifying work of Christ in their lives. Many … have a theoretical commitment to this doctrine, but in their day-to-day existence they rely on their sanctification for justification … drawing their assurance of acceptance with God from their sincerity, their past experience of conversion, their recent religious performance or the relative infrequency of their conscious, willful disobedience. Few know enough to start each day with a thoroughgoing stand upon Luther's platform: you are accepted, looking outward in faith and claiming the wholly alien righteousness of Christ as the only ground for acceptance, relaxing in that quality of trust which will produce increasing sanctification as faith is active in love and gratitude …

Much that we have interpreted as a defect of sanctification in church people is really an outgrowth of their loss of bearing with respect to justification. Christians who are no longer sure that God loves and accepts them in Jesus, apart from their present spiritual achievements, are subconsciously radically insecure persons … Their insecurity shows itself in pride, a fierce defensive assertion of their own righteousness and defensive criticism of others. They come naturally to hate other cultural styles and other races in order to bolster their own security and discharge their suppressed anger.[3]

PREACHING THE THIRD WAY FOR EVERYONE

If you are communicating the gospel message, you must not only help listeners distinguish between obeying God and disobeying him; you must also

A QUICK COMPARISON OF RELIGION AND THE GOSPEL[4]

RELIGION	GOSPEL
"I obey; therefore I'm accepted."	"I'm accepted; therefore I obey."
Motivation is based on fear and insecurity.	Motivation is based on grateful joy.
I obey God in order to get *things* from God.	I obey God to get *God*—to delight and resemble him.
When circumstances in my life go wrong, I am angry at God or myself, since I believe, like Job's friends, that anyone who is good deserves a comfortable life.	When circumstances in my life go wrong, I struggle, but I know that while God may allow this for my training, he will exercise his fatherly love within my trial.
When I am criticized, I am furious or devastated because it is essential for me to think of myself as a "good person." Threats to that self-image must be destroyed at all costs.	When I am criticized, I struggle, but it is not essential for me to think of myself as a "good person." My identity is not built on my performance but on God's love for me in Christ.
My prayer life consists largely of petition and only heats up when I am in need. My main purpose in prayer is to control circumstances.	My prayer life consists of generous stretches of praise and adoration. My main purpose is fellowship with him.
My self-view swings between two poles. If and when I am living up to my standards, I feel confident, but then I am prone to be proud and unsympathetic to people who fail. If and when I am not living up to standards, I feel humble but not confident—I feel like a failure.	My self-view is not based on a view of myself as a moral achiever. In Christ I am at once sinful and lost, yet accepted. I am so bad he *had* to die for me, and so loved he was *glad* to die for me. This leads me to deeper humility as well as deeper confidence, without either sniveling or swaggering.
My identity and self-worth are based mainly on how hard I work or how moral I am, so I *must* look down on those I perceive as lazy or immoral. I disdain and feel superior to others.	My identity and self-worth are centered on the One who died for his enemies, including me. Only by sheer grace am I what I am, so I *can't* look down on those who believe or practice something different from me. I have no inner need to win arguments.
Since I look to my pedigree or performance for my spiritual acceptability, my heart manufactures idols—talents, moral record, personal discipline, social status, etc. I absolutely *have* to have them, so they are my main hope, meaning, happiness, security, and significance, whatever I say I believe about God.	I have many good things in my life—family, work, etc., but none of these good things are *ultimate* things to me. I don't absolutely *have* to have them, so there is a limit to how much anxiety, bitterness, and despair they can inflict on me when they are threatened and lost.

make clear the distinction between obeying God as a means of self-salvation and obeying God out of gratitude for an accomplished salvation. You will have to distinguish between general, moralistic religion and gospel Christianity. You will always be placing three ways to live before your listeners.

The most important way to gain a hearing from postmodern people, confront nominal Christians, wake up "sleepy" Christians, and even delight committed Christians — *all at the same time* — is to preach the gospel as a third way to approach God, distinct from both irreligion and religion. Why?

The only way into a ministry that sees people's lives change is through preaching the gospel to deconstruct both legalism and relativism.

First, many professed Christians are only nominal believers; they are pure "elder brothers" (see Luke 15:11 – 32), and often making this distinction can help to convert them. Second, many genuine Christians are elder-brother*ish* — angry, mechanical, superior, insecure — and making this distinction may be the only way to reach them. Third, most postmodern people have been raised in or near churches that are heavily "religious." They have observed how religious people tend to bolster their own sense of worth by convincing themselves they are better than other people, which leads them to exclude and condemn others. Most contemporary nonbelievers have rejected these poisonous fruits of religion, but when they did so, they thought they had rejected Christianity. If they hear you calling them to follow Christ, even if you use biblical language such as "receive Christ and you will be adopted into his family" (see John 1:12 – 13), they will automatically believe you are calling them into the "elder brother," moralistic, religious approach to God. Unless you are constantly and clearly showing them that they have misunderstood the gospel and that you are talking about something else besides religion, they won't be listening for the true gospel.

Some claim that to always strike a note of "grace, grace, grace" in our sermons is not helpful. The objection goes like this: "Surely Pharisaism and moralism are not the current problem in our culture. Rather, our problem is license and antinomianism. People lack a sense of right or wrong. It is redundant to talk about grace all the time to postmodern people." I don't believe this is true. First, unless you point to the "good news" of grace, people won't even be able to bear the "bad news" of God's judgment. Second, unless you critique moralism, many irreligious people will not grasp the difference between moralism and what you are offering in the gospel. A deep grasp of the gospel is the antidote to license and antinomianism.

In the end, legalism and relativism in churches are not just equally wrong; they are basically the same thing. They are just different strategies of self-salvation built on human effort. No matter whether a local church is loose about doctrine and winks at sin or is marked by scolding and rigidity, it will lack the power it promises. The only way into a ministry that sees people's lives change, that brings joy and power and electricity without authoritarianism, is through preaching the gospel to deconstruct both legalism and relativism.

MORALISTIC BEHAVIOR CHANGE

People typically try to instill honesty in others this way: "If you lie, you'll get in trouble with God and other people," or, "If you lie, you'll be like those terrible people, those habitual liars, and you are better than that!" What motivations are being encouraged? They are being called to change their behavior out of fear of *punishment* ("you'll get in trouble") and out of *pride* ("you'll be like a dirty liar; you wouldn't want to be like one of them"). Both fear of punishment and pride are essentially self-centered. The root motivation is, then, "Be honest because it will pay off for you." This approach puts pressure on the will and stirs up the ego to more selfishness in order to force a person to curb his or her inclinations to do wrong. We can call this "moralistic behavior change" because its basic argument is this: "Will yourself to change your behavior, and you can save yourself."

Christians who are taught to act morally primarily to escape punishment or to win self-respect and salvation are learning to be moral to serve themselves. At the behavioral level, of course, they may be performing actions of great self-sacrifice. They may be sacrificing time, money, and much more to help the poor, to love their family, or to be faithful to God's law. Yet at a deeper level they are behaving this way so God will bless them, so they can think of themselves as virtuous, charitable persons. They are not loving God for himself. They are not obeying him simply because of his greatness and because he has done so much for them in Christ. Rather, they are using God to get the things they want. They want answered prayers, good health, and prosperity, and they want salvation in the afterlife. So they "do good," not for God's sake or for goodness' sake, but for their own sake. Their behavior is being changed by the power of their own self-interest.

Stirring up self-centeredness in order to get someone to do the right thing does not get at the fundamental self-regard and self-absorption that is the main problem of the human heart. Consequently, it does nothing to address the main cause of the behavior you are trying to change (such as lying). Moralistic behavior change simply manipulates and leverages radical selfishness without challenging it. It tries to use that selfishness against itself by appealing to fear and pride. But while this may have some success in *restraining* the heart's self-centeredness, it does absolutely nothing to *change* it. Indeed, it only confirms its power.

Moralistic behavior change *bends* a person into a different pattern through fear of consequences rather than *melting* a person into a new shape. But this does not work. If you try to bend a piece of metal without the softening effect of heat, it is likely to snap back to its former position. This is why we see people who try to change through moralistic behaviorism find themselves repeatedly lapsing into sins they thought themselves incapable of committing. They can't believe they embezzled or lied or committed adultery or felt so much blind hatred that they lashed out. Appalled at themselves, they say, "I wasn't raised that way!" But they were. For moralistic behaviorism — even deep within a religious environment — continues to nurture the "ruthless, sleepless, unsmiling concentration on self

that is the mark of Hell."[5] This is the reason people embezzle, lie, and break promises in the first place. It also explains why churches are plagued with gossip and fighting. Underneath what appears to be unselfishness is great self-centeredness, which has been enhanced by moralistic modes of ministry and is marked by liberal doses of sanctimony, judgmentalism, and spite.

To complete our illustration, if you try to bend metal without the softening effect of heat, it may simply break. Many people, after years of being crushed under moralistic behaviorism, abandon their faith altogether, complaining that they are exhausted and "can't keep it up." But the gospel of God's grace doesn't try to bend a heart into a new pattern; it *melts* it and *re-forms* it into a new shape. The gospel can produce a new joy, love, and gratitude — new inclinations of the heart that eat away at deadly self-regard and self-concentration. Without this "gospel heat" — the joy, love, and gratitude that result from an experience of grace — people will simply snap. Putting pressure on their will may temporarily alter their behavior, but their heart's basic self-centeredness and insecurity remain.

GOSPEL BEHAVIOR CHANGE

In light of all this, let's look at how the Bible calls us to change. In 2 Corinthians 8 and 9, Paul writes to believers to encourage them to give an offering to the poor, but he wants them to do so without a direct command from him. He does not begin by pressuring them into it or asserting his authority as an apostle. He doesn't force their wills by saying, "I'm an apostle and this is your duty to me," or, "God will punish you if you don't do this." Nor does he put pressure directly on their emotions by telling them stories about how deeply the poor are suffering and how much more money the Corinthians have than the sufferers. Instead, Paul vividly and unforgettably writes, "You know the grace of our Lord Jesus Christ, that though he was rich, yet for your sakes he became poor, so that you through his poverty might become rich" (2 Cor 8:9). When Paul states, "You know the grace," he is reminding his readers of the grace of God by means of a powerful image, one that shifts Jesus' salvation into the realm of

COMMON MORALITY AND TRUE VIRTUE

Jonathan Edwards explored the difference between genuine gospel-triggered heart change and moralistic compliance with God's law. In *The Nature of True Virtue*, he contrasted these two kinds of moral behavior as "common morality" and "true virtue." Edwards argued that if our highest love is our family, we will ultimately choose our family's good over the good of other families; if our highest love is our nation, we will choose our nation's interests and ignore those of other countries; if our highest love is our own individual interests, we will choose to serve ourselves over seeking to meet the needs of others.

Only if our highest love is God himself can we love and serve all people, families, classes, races; and only God's saving grace can bring us to the place where we are loving and serving God for himself alone and not for what he can give us. Unless we understand the gospel, we are *always* obeying God for our sake and not for his.[6]

wealth and poverty. He moves their hearts through a spiritual recollection of the gospel. Paul, in essence, urges, "Think about his costly grace, until the gospel changes you from the heart into generous people."

We find another example in Ephesians, where Paul is addressing spouses — but particularly, it seems, husbands (Eph 5:25 – 33). Many of these men had no doubt retained attitudes and understandings of marriage from their pagan backgrounds, attitudes in which marriage was primarily a business relationship that entailed marrying as profitably as they could. In his letter, Paul wants not only to encourage husbands to be sexually faithful but also to cherish and honor their wives. Here again (as in 2 Cor 8 and 9), Paul exhorts his readers

to change their lives by showing unloving husbands the salvation of Jesus, our ultimate Spouse in the gospel, who showed sacrificial love toward us, his "bride." He did not love us because we were lovely (5:25 – 27), but to make us lovely.

In his letter to Titus, Paul calls his readers to "say 'No' to ungodliness and worldly passions, and to live self-controlled, upright and godly lives" (Titus 2:12).[7] Think for a moment of all the ways you can say no to ungodly behavior. You can say:

No — because I'll look bad.
No — because I'll be excluded from the social circles I want to belong to.
No — because then God will not give me health, wealth, and happiness.
No — because God will send me to hell.
No — because I'll hate myself in the morning and lose my self-respect.

Virtually all of these incentives use self-centered impulses of the heart to force compliance to external rules, but they do very little to *change* the heart itself. The motive behind them is not love for God. It is a way of using God to get beneficial things: self-esteem, prosperity, or social approval.

Paul does not urge his readers to use any of these arguments to attempt to change themselves. In the Titus passage, how does he call Christians to gain self-control? Paul states that it is the "grace of God that brings salvation … [that] teaches us to say 'No' to ungodliness" (Titus 2:11 – 12). In Titus 3:5, Paul explains what he means by this grace: "[God] saved us, not because of righteous things we had done, but because of his mercy." Paul is saying that if you want true change, you must let the gospel *teach* you. This word we translate *teach* is a Greek word that means to train, discipline, and coach someone over a period of time. In other words, you must let the gospel argue with you. You must let the gospel sink down deeply until it changes your views and the structures of your motivation. You must be trained and discipled by the gospel.

The gospel, if it is truly believed, helps us out of the extreme neediness that is natural to the human heart. We have the *need* to be constantly respected, to be appreciated, and to be highly regarded. We *need* to control our lives — not trusting God or anyone else with them. We *need* to have power over others in order to boost our self-esteem. The image of our glorious God delighting over us with all his being (Isa 62:4; Zeph 3:14; cf. Deut 23:5; 30:9) — if this is a mere concept to us, then our needs will overwhelm us and drive our behavior. Without the power of the Spirit, our hearts don't really believe in God's delight or grace, so they operate in their default mode. But the truths of the gospel, brought home by the Spirit, slowly but surely help us grasp in a new way how safe and secure, how loved and accepted, we are in Christ. Through the gospel, we come to base our identity not on what *we* have achieved but on what has been achieved for us in Christ.

And when the gospel, brought home to our hearts (see Eph 3:16 – 19), eats away at this sin-born neediness, it destroys the inner engines that drive sinful behavior. We don't have to lie, because our reputation isn't so important to us. We don't have to respond in violent anger against opponents, because no one can touch our true treasure. The gospel destroys both the pride and the fearfulness that fuel moralistic behavior change. The gospel destroys *pride,* because it tells us we are so lost that Jesus had to die for us. And it also destroys *fearfulness,* because it tells us that nothing we can do will exhaust his love for us. When we deeply embrace these truths, our hearts are not merely restrained but changed. Their fundamental orientation is transformed.

We no longer act morally simply because it profits us or makes us feel better about ourselves. Instead, we tell the truth and keep our promises simply out of love for the One who died for us, who kept a promise despite the unfathomable suffering it brought him. The gospel leads us to do the right thing not for our sake but for God's sake, for Christ's sake, out of a desire to know, resemble, please, and love the One who saved us. This kind of motivation can only grow in a heart deeply touched by grace.

The Bible's solution to stinginess, then, is a reorientation to the gospel and the generosity of Christ, who poured out his wealth for us (2 Cor 8:9). We don't have to worry about money, because the cross proves

IS SANCTIFICATION BY "FAITH ALONE"?

People who agree that (1) salvation is strictly by grace through faith and (2) this free salvation results in a gratitude-motivated obedience to the law of God nevertheless disagree over the precise role and nature of effort in Christian growth. If, as Martin Luther states, all sin is rooted in idolatry, which is a failure to believe in Christ for our salvation and justification, then it appears that the only effort any Christian should put forth is an effort to believe the gospel. This seems to mean that Christian sanctification is by "faith alone," just as justification is — that it is only a matter of believing the gospel fervently enough. This kind of language has led some to charge that Luther (and those following him) are reducing Christians' efforts to live a holy life to nothing but believing in justification. They counter that sanctification takes strenuous effort beyond that.

I won't get into that debate at length here, but I think both sides are making a point that is right, yet easily misconstrued. In the moment, Christians should use every possible means to do God's will. If you feel an impulse to pick up a rock and hurl it at someone — do anything necessary to keep yourself from doing it! Remind yourself, "I'll go to jail. I'll disgrace my family!" It would be wrong to give in to the sinful impulse simply because, on the spot, you do not believe the gospel enough to refrain. There is no reason in the short run that a Christian can't simply use pure willpower if necessary. God deserves our obedience, and we should give it, even if we know our motives are mixed and impure.

Those who say, "We need to put in strenuous effort to obey, even if our belief in the gospel is wanting" are right, at least in the short term. But obedience is not the same thing as change. In the end, all effort is fueled by *some* motivation, and if our motivation is not the gospel, then we are not obeying God for his own sake (see sidebar on "Common Morality and True Virtue," p. 68); neither will we be able to permanently change our character.

Imagine that a baby bird falls from its nest in the sight lines of a fox. The bird cannot yet fly (hence the fall), but there is a small protective hole at the base of tree that is within a scurry's reach. The fox pounces and sets out after the bird. What should the little bird do? Of course, it should scamper into the hole to get out of immediate danger. But if as time goes on all the bird ever does is scamper, it will never learn what it has been designed for: to fly. And eventually it will surely be eaten by the predators it is designed to escape.[8]

In the short run, we should simply obey God because it is his right and due. But in the long run, the ultimate way to shape our lives and escape the deadly influence of our besetting sins is by moving the heart with the gospel.

God's care for us and gives us security. Likewise, the Bible's solution to a bad marriage is a reorientation to the radical, spousal love of Christ communicated in the gospel. "You shall not commit adultery" (Exod 20:14) makes sense in the context of his spousal love, especially on the cross, where he was completely faithful to us. Only when we know this sacrificial, spousal love of Christ will we have real fortitude to combat lust. His love is fulfilling, so it keeps us from looking to sexual fulfillment to give us what only Jesus can.

What will truly make us sexually faithful spouses or generous persons or good parents or faithful children is *not* a redoubled effort to follow the example of Christ. Rather, it is deepening our understanding of the salvation of Christ and living out of the changes this understanding makes in our hearts — the seat of our minds, wills, and emotions. Faith in the gospel restructures our motivations,

our self-understanding, our identity, and our view of the world. It changes our hearts.[9]

Behavioral compliance to rules without heart change will be superficial and fleeting. The purpose of preaching, pastoring, counseling, instructing, and discipling is, therefore, to show people these practical implications of faith in the gospel.

THE IMPORTANCE OF IDOLATRY

One of the most important biblical and practical ways to help people come to see how they fail to believe the gospel is by instructing them on the nature of idolatry.[10] In his *Treatise on Good Works*, an exposition of the Ten Commandments, Martin Luther states that the call to "have no other gods before me" (Exod 20:3) and the call to believe in Jesus alone for our justification (Rom 3 – 4) are, in essence, the same thing. To say we must have no other gods but God and to say we must not try to achieve our salvation without Christ are one and the same:

> Now this is the work of the First Commandment, which commands: "Thou shalt have no other gods," which means: "Since I alone am God, thou shalt place all thy confidence, trust and faith on Me alone, and on no one else."[11]

Luther's teaching is this: Anything we look to *more* than we look to Christ for our sense of acceptability, joy, significance, hope, and security is by definition our god — something we adore, serve, and rely on with our whole life and heart. In general, idols can be *good* things (family, achievement, work and career, romance, talent, etc. — even gospel ministry) that we turn into *ultimate* things to give us the significance and joy we need. Then they drive us into the ground because we must have them. A sure sign of the presence of idolatry is inordinate anxiety, anger, or discouragement when our idols are thwarted. So if we lose a good thing, it makes us sad, but if we lose an idol, it devastates us.

Luther also concludes from his study of the commandments that we never break one of the other commandments unless we are also breaking the first.[12] We do not lie, commit adultery, or steal unless we first make something else more fundamental to our hope and joy and identity than God. When we lie, for example, our reputation (or money or whatever) is at that moment more foundational to our sense of self and happiness than the love of Christ. If we cheat on our income tax form, then money and possessions — and the status or comfort from having more of them — have become more important to our heart's sense of significance and security than our identity in Christ. Idolatry, then, is also the root of our other sins and problems.[13]

Those who preach and counsel for gospel renewal should constantly speak about underlying idols, which show us our hearts' particular, characteristic ways of failing to believe the gospel.

So if the root of every sin is idolatry, and idolatry is a failure to look to Jesus for our salvation and justification, then the root of every sin is a failure to believe the gospel message that Jesus, and *Jesus alone*, is our justification, righteousness, and redemption.

What, then, is the essence of behavior change? What will help us lead godly lives? The solution is not simply to force or scare ourselves into doing the right thing, but to apply the gospel to our hearts' idols, which are always an alternate form of self-salvation apart from Jesus. Our failures in *actual* righteousness, then, generally come from a failure to rejoice in our *legal* righteousness in Christ. Our failures in sanctification (living Christlike, godly lives) come mainly from a lack of orientation to our justification. We will never change unless we come to grips with the particular, characteristic ways our hearts resist the gospel and continue their self-salvation projects through idolatry.

Those who preach and counsel for gospel renewal should constantly speak about underlying idols, which show us our hearts' particular, characteristic ways of failing to believe the gospel. To do so will prevent people from trying to solve all problems and make all changes through moralistic behaviorism, which leads to insecurity, suppressed anger and guilt, and spiritual deadness.[14] Instead it keeps the focus on the gospel and the work of Christ. In the next chapter, we'll look at how churches can cooperate with the Holy Spirit to bring about gospel renewal.

QUESTIONS FOR DISCUSSION AND REFLECTION

1. How would you articulate the three ways of responding to God? What are the differences and similarities between the two ways of rejecting God? How do both of these contrast with a response to the gospel?

2. Where do you find yourself in the chart titled "A Quick Comparison of Religion and the Gospel"? Go back and honestly take stock: Do the majority of your descriptors fall to the left column or to the right? In what situations do you find yourself turning to religion instead of the gospel? How have your patterns changed over the last five years, and why?

3. Keller writes, "The only way into a ministry that sees people's lives change, that brings joy and power and electricity without authoritarianism, is through preaching the gospel to deconstruct both legalism and relativism." Why is it necessary to confront and deconstruct both of these errors? Which is more prevalent in your context? Which are you more likely to confront, and what can you do to restore balance to your ministry?

4. The apostle Paul uses pictures of the gospel rather than pressure to lead people to change. This chapter gives three examples (generosity, husbands honoring wives, and self-control). Choose another area of life change and take notes on how you would bring the gospel to bear on the motivation of someone in your congregation. If you are in a group setting, practice this with someone else.

CHAPTER 5 — THE ESSENCE OF GOSPEL RENEWAL *(pages 63–71)*

1. Throughout this chapter and much of the book, I use "religion" as a synonym for moralism and legalism. Certainly we can refer to the "Christian religion," but I will use "religion" more negatively, as a heuristic device, and I have a couple of good reasons for doing so: (1) The New Testament uses two words for "religion" or "religious" — *thrēskeia* and *deisidaimonia* — which Luke and Paul only use negatively (Acts 25:19; 26:5; Col 2:18 [NIV, "worship"]). James uses *thrēskeia* positively once (Jas 1:27), but negatively in 1:26. Hebrews has a number of similar terms for works-religion as well. (2) Sometime people contrast "religion" with "relationship," as in "Christianity isn't a religion; it is a relationship." This isn't what I mean, and some make such a statement to mean Christianity requires only an inner love relationship with God, not obedience, holiness of life, life in community, and discipline. Dietrich Bonhoeffer (*The Cost of Discipleship* [New York: Touchstone, 1995]. 44 – 45) calls this "cheap grace" — the love of a non-holy God who didn't require costly atonement in order to reconcile us and whose love, therefore, does not require or provoke life change. The gospel is distinct from both cheap grace and religion.
2. The truth is that even seemingly irreligious people are actually religious. See the quote from David Foster Wallace referenced in chapter 1 (p. 34; Emily Bobrow, "David Foster Wallace, in His Own Words" [taken from his 2005 commencement address at Kenyon College], http://moreintelligentlife.com/story/david-foster-wallace-in-his-own-words [accessed January 4, 2012]).
3. Richard F. Lovelace, *Dynamics of Spiritual Life: An Evangelical Theology of Renewal* (Downers Grove, Ill.: InterVarsity, 1979), 101, 211 – 12.
4. A version of this table is found in Timothy Keller, *Gospel in Life Study Guide: Grace Changes Everything* (Grand Rapids: Zondervan, 2010), 16.
5. C. S. Lewis, *The Screwtape Letters* (New York: Macmillan, 1961), vii.
6. We should add here that Edwards did not disdain common morality. He believed that it was the main way in which God restrained evil in the world and led the great majority of people to tell the truth, to re-frain from stealing, to keep their promises, and so on. Nevertheless, Edwards did not want Christians to settle for anything less than the development of true virtue (see esp. Paul Ramsey, ed., *Ethical Writings: The Works of Jonathan Edwards*, vol. 8 (New Haven, Conn.: Yale University Press, 1989).
7. Paul is engaging the Stoic virtues. Fulfilling these virtues through Stoicism — a functional moralism of suppressing your emotions and denying your passions — is not sufficient. It takes being "taught" by the gospel to truly attain these virtues. Thanks to Dr. Mark Reynolds for this insight.
8. Thanks to Michael Thate for this illustration.
9. This "indicative-imperative" order and balance is everywhere in the letters of Paul. For example, Paul in the first three chapters of 1 Corinthians repeatedly reminds the Corinthian Christians that they *are* "holy" — set apart and accepted. Then in 1 Corinthians 4, 5, and 6, he tells them to "*be* what you *are*; practice your identity."
10. For considerably more on this subject, see Timothy Keller, *Counterfeit Gods* (New York: Penguin, 2009).
11. Martin Luther, *A Treatise on Good Works* (Rockville, Md.: Serenity, 2009), 28.
12. Luther (*Treatise on Good Works*, 29) writes, "All those who do not at all times trust God ... but seek His favor in other things or in themselves, do not keep this Commandment, and practice real idolatry, even if they were to do the works of all the other Commandments."
13. Theologian Paul Tillich also provides helpful categories for understanding idolatry. Tillich (*Dynamics of Faith* [New York: HarperCollins, 2001]) defined faith as "ultimate concern" (p. 1). Whatever you are *living for* — whether you are religious or not — is your god. Idolatry is "the elevation of something preliminary to ultimacy" (p. 133).
14. See Timothy Keller, *Gospel in Life Study Guide* (Grand Rapids: Zondervan, 2010), for more detail on much of what is included in this chapter.

chapter 6

THE WORK OF GOSPEL RENEWAL

We have talked about the *need* for gospel renewal and the *essence* of the gospel in revival and renewal, and now we will look at the *work* of gospel renewal — the practical ways and means by which the Holy Spirit brings lasting change to the lives of individuals and to congregations.

We will also focus in more detail on one of these means — the work of preaching — and examine several signs that give evidence of gospel renewal.

THE MEANS OF GOSPEL RENEWAL

While the ultimate source of a revival is the Holy Spirit, the Spirit ordinarily uses several "instrumental," or penultimate, means to produce revival.

EXTRAORDINARY PRAYER

To kindle every revival, the Holy Spirit initially uses what Jonathan Edwards called "extraordinary prayer" — united, persistent, and kingdom centered. Sometimes it begins with a single person or a small group of people praying for God's glory in the community. What is important is not the number of people praying but the nature of the praying. C. John Miller makes a helpful and perceptive distinction between "maintenance" and "frontline" prayer meetings.[1] Maintenance prayer meetings are short, mechanical, and focused on physical needs inside the church. In contrast, the three basic traits of frontline prayer are these:

1. A request for grace to confess sins and to humble ourselves
2. A compassion and zeal for the flourishing of the church and the reaching of the lost
3. A yearning to know God, to see his face, to glimpse his glory

These distinctions are unavoidably powerful. If you pay attention at a prayer meeting, you can tell quite clearly whether these traits are present. In the biblical prayers for revival in Exodus 33; Nehemiah 1; and Acts 4, the three elements of frontline prayer are easy to see. Notice in Acts 4, for example, that after the disciples were threatened by the religious authorities, they asked not for protection for themselves and their families but only for boldness to keep preaching! Some kind of extraordinary prayer beyond the normal services and patterns of prayer is always involved.

GOSPEL REDISCOVERY

Along with extraordinary, persistent prayer, the most necessary element of gospel renewal is *a recovery of the gospel itself,* with a particular emphasis on the new birth and on salvation through grace alone. D. Martyn Lloyd-Jones taught that the gospel emphasis on grace could be lost in several ways. A church might simply become heterodox — losing its grip on the orthodox tenets of theology that undergird the gospel, such as the triune nature of God, the deity of Christ, the wrath of God, and so on. It may turn its back on the very belief in justification by faith alone and the need for conversion and so move toward a view that being a Christian is simply a matter of church membership or of living a life based on Christ's example. This cuts the nerve of gospel renewal and revival.[2]

But it is possible to subscribe to every orthodox doctrine and nevertheless fail to communicate the gospel to people's hearts in a way that brings about repentance, joy, and spiritual growth. One way this happens is through dead orthodoxy, in which such pride grows in our doctrinal correctness that sound teaching and right church practice become a kind of works-righteousness. Carefulness in doctrine and life is, of course, critical, but when it is accompanied in a church by self-righteousness, mockery, disdain of everyone else, and a contentious, combative attitude, it shows that, while the doctrine of justification may be believed, a strong spirit of legalism reigns nonetheless. The doctrine has failed to touch hearts.[3]

Lloyd-Jones also speaks of "defective orthodoxy" and "spiritual inertia."[4] Some churches hold to orthodox doctrines but with imbalances and a lack of proper emphasis. Many ministries spend more time defending the faith than propagating it. Or they may give an inordinate amount of energy and attention to matters such as prophecy or spiritual gifts or creation and evolution. A church may become enamored with the mechanics of ministry and church organization. There are innumerable reasons that critical doctrines of grace and justification and conversion, though strongly held, are kept "on the shelf." They are not preached and communicated in such a way that connects to people's lives. People see the doctrines — yet they do not see them. It is possible to get an "A" grade on a doctrinal test and describe accurately the doctrines of our salvation, yet be blind to their true implications and power. In this sense, there are plenty of orthodox churches in which the gospel must be rediscovered and then brought home and applied to people's hearts. When this happens, nominal Christians get converted, lethargic and weak Christians become empowered, and nonbelievers are attracted to the newly beautified Christian congregation.

One of the main vehicles that sparked the first awakening in Northampton, Massachusetts, was Jonathan Edwards's two sermons on Romans 4:5 ("Justification by Faith Alone") in November 1734. And for both John Wesley and George Whitefield, the primary leaders of the British Great Awakening, it was an understanding of salvation by grace *rather* than moral effort that touched off personal renewal and made them agents of revival.

GOSPEL APPLICATION

How do we bring the gospel home to people so they see its power and implications? This can take place in a church in several ways. First, a church recovers the gospel through preaching. Preaching is the single venue of information and teaching to which the greatest number of church people are exposed. Are some parts of the Bible "better" for gospel preaching than others? No, not at all. Any time you preach Christ and his salvation as the meaning of the text rather than simply expounding biblical principles for life, you are preaching toward renewal. Preaching this way is not at all easy, however. Even those who commit to Christ-centered preaching tend toward inspirational sermons about Jesus, with little application. Realizing that this is an enormous topic to digest, I point you to Bryan Chapell's *Christ-Centered Preaching: Redeeming the Expository Sermon* (2nd ed.; Grand Rapids: Baker, 2005) for a place to begin your study.[5]

The second way for a pastor or leader to recover the gospel in the church is through the training of lay leaders who minister the gospel to others. It is critical to arrange a regular and fairly intense time of processing these gospel renewal dynamics with the lay leaders of a church. The components of this training include both content and life contact. By "content," I propose studying elementary material such as D. Martyn Lloyd-Jones's chapter "The True Foundation" in *Spiritual Depression* or working through my book *The Prodigal God* along with the discussion guide.[6] More advanced materials would include books by Richard Lovelace and Jonathan Edwards (several of which are listed in the sidebar on p. 78).

By "life contact," I mean finding ways in personal meetings and counseling to help your leaders repent of idols and self-righteousness. Once the gospel "penny drops" and begins its ripple effects, you will have plenty of this type of pastoral work to do. Your leaders can then begin leading groups in which they guide people to the truths in the Bible that have helped them and have changed their lives.[7]

A third way for a church to foster gospel renewal dynamics is to inject an experiential element into its small group ministry or even to form several groups dedicated to it. Many small group meetings resemble classes in which the Bible is studied or fellowship meetings in which people talk about their burdens and needs, help each other, and pray for each other. While these functions are extremely important, we can learn from leaders of the revivals of the past, such as George Whitefield and John Wesley, who encouraged people to form groups of four to eight people to share weekly the degree to which God was real in their hearts, their besetting sins, ways God was dealing with them through the Word, and how their prayer lives were faring. *The Experience Meeting* by William Williams is a classic guide to how a Welsh *seiat* or "experience meeting" ran (see sidebar).[8]

A fourth way the gospel becomes applied to people's hearts in a church is through the most basic and informal means possible — what the older writers simply called "conversation." Gospel renewal in the church spreads through renewed individuals talking informally to others. It is in personal conversations that the gospel can be applied most specifically and pointedly. When one Christian shares how the gospel has "come home" to him or her and is bringing about major life changes, listeners can ask concrete questions and receive great encouragement to move forward spiritually themselves. William Sprague writes, "Many a Christian has had occasion … to reflect that much of his usefulness and much of his happiness was to be referred under God … to a single conversation with some judicious Christian friend."[9] Sprague states that it is often not so much the actual content of what a Christian says but their gospel-renewed spirit and character that has an impact. Christians must have the infectious marks of spiritual revival — a joyful, affectionate seriousness and "unction," a sense of God's presence.[10] Visible, dramatic life turnarounds and unexpected conversions may cause others to do deep self-examination and create a sense of spiritual longing and expectation in the community. The personal revivals going on in these individuals spread informally to others through conversation and relationship. More and more people begin to examine themselves and seek God.

A fifth way to do gospel application is to make sure that pastors, elders, and other church leaders

---

QUESTIONS TO GUIDE AN "EXPERIENCE MEETING"

To be admitted to an experience meeting, a prospective member had to answer the following questions in the affirmative:

1. Are you seeking God with all your heart?
2. Are you willing to take rebukes, chastening, and instruction from others?
3. Will you refrain from repeating the confidential things we discuss?
4. Are you willing to use your spiritual gifts to edify others in the group?
5. Are you resolved to forsake your idols and inordinate loves?

To spark discussion in the group, these questions were typically asked:

1. Do you have spiritual assurance of your standing in Christ? How clear and vivid is it?
2. How does the Holy Spirit bear witness with your spirit that you are his child? Are you conscious of a growing spiritual light within, revealing more of the purity of the law, the holiness of God, the evil of sin, and the preciousness of the imputed righteousness of Christ?
3. Is your love for Christians growing? Do you find yourself having a less censorious, judgmental spirit toward weak Christians, those who fall, or those who are self-deceived? Have you been cold to anyone?
4. Is your conscience growing tenderer to convict you of the very first motions of sin in the mind, such as the onset of resentment; worry, pride, or jealousy; an inordinate desire for power, approval, and material comfort; and an overconcern for your reputation? Are you becoming more aware of and convicted about sins of the tongue, such as cutting

remarks, rambling without listening, deception and semi-lying, gossip and slander, inappropriate humor, or thoughtless statements?

5. Do you see signs of growth in the fruit of the Spirit? Can you give examples in which you responded in a new way — with love, joy, patience, honesty, humility, or self-control — in a situation that a year or two ago you would not have?

6. Are you coming to discern false, idolatrous motives for some of the good service you do? Are you seeing that many things you thought you did for God you are actually doing for other reasons? Are you coming to see areas of your life in which you have resisted the Lord's will?

7. Are you seeing new ways to be better stewards of the talents, gifts, relationships, wealth, and other assets that God has given you?

8. Are you having any seasons of the sweet delight that the Spirit brings? Are you finding certain promises extremely precious? Are you getting answers to prayers? Are you getting times of refreshing from reading or listening to the Word?

know how to use the gospel on people's hearts in pastoral counseling — especially people who are coming under a deep conviction of sin and are seeking counsel about how to move forward. Sprague shows how the gospel must be used on seekers, new believers, and stagnant Christians alike.[11] For example, Sprague tells pastoral counselors to "determine ... what is his amount of knowledge and his amount of feeling."[12] He tells counselors to help those who have little doctrinal knowledge but much feeling — or little feeling but a good grasp on doctrine — to bring those two things into balance.

Sprague advises to look for forms of self-righteousness and works-righteousness and tells how to help people escape them. He also makes a surprisingly up-to-date list of common doubts and problems that spiritual seekers have and gives advice on how to respond to each one. The gospel must be used to cut away *both* the moralism and the licentiousness that destroy real spiritual life and power.[13]

GOSPEL INNOVATION

We can identify another important factor in movements of gospel renewal — creativity and innovation. Sprague rightly points out that revivals occur mainly through the "instituted means of grace" — preaching, pastoring, worship, and prayer. It is extremely important to reaffirm this. The Spirit of God can and does use these ordinary means of grace to bring about dramatic, extraordinary conversions and significant church growth. Nevertheless, when we study the history of revivals, we usually see in the mix some innovative method of communicating the gospel. The Great Awakening of the eighteenth century adopted two ministry forms that had seldom been used: public, outdoor preaching and extensive small group "society" meetings. In the 1857 – 1859 New York City revival, massive numbers of people were converted and joined the churches of Manhattan. Yet the most vital ministry form turned out to be lay-led, weekday prayer meetings all around the business district of Wall Street. Many historians have pointed out that the Protestant Reformation in Europe was greatly powered by new uses of a major technological innovation — the printing press.

No revival will completely repeat the experiences of the past, and it would be a mistake to identify any specific method too closely with revivals. D. Martyn Lloyd-Jones points to a few sad cases where people who came through the Welsh revival of 1904 – 1905 became wedded to particular ways of holding meetings and hymn singing as the *only* way that God brings revival. (This kind of nostalgia for beloved methods abounds yet today.) Instead, while the core means of revival are theological (rediscovery of the gospel) and ordinary (preaching, prayer, fellowship, worship), we should always be looking for new modes of gospel proclamation that the Holy Spirit can use in our cultural moment. As C. S. Lewis noted in The Chronicles of Narnia, things never happen the same way twice, so it is best to keep your eyes open.

PREACHING FOR GOSPEL RENEWAL

Let's return to our discussion of preaching's role in gospel renewal, for it can hardly be overemphasized. We'll begin by looking at five characteristics that define preaching for gospel renewal.

1. Preach to distinguish between religion and the gospel. We have already laid out much of this imperative in the previous chapter. Effective preaching for gospel renewal will critique both religion and irreligion. It will also address the core problem of idolatry by helping listeners look beneath the level of behavior to their hearts' motivation to see the way the gospel functions (or does not function) in the human heart.

2. Preach both the holiness and the love of God to convey the richness of grace. Preaching should not emphasize only God's judgment, holiness, and righteousness (like moralistic preachers) or emphasize only God's love and mercy (like liberal preachers). Only when people see God as absolutely holy *and* absolutely loving will the cross of Jesus truly electrify and change them. Jesus was so holy that he *had* to die for us; nothing less would satisfy his holy and righteous nature. But he was so loving that he was *glad* to die for us; nothing less would satisfy his desire to have us as his people. This humbles us out of our pride and self-centeredness yet at the same time affirms us out of our discouragement. It leads us to hate sin yet at the same time forbids us to morbidly hate ourselves.

3. Preach not only to make the truth clear but also to make it *real*. We have seen how Paul seeks greater generosity from people by appealing to them to *know* the grace and generosity of Christ (2 Cor 8). In other words, if Christians are materialistic, it is not merely a failure of will. Their lack of generosity comes because they have not *truly* understood how Jesus became poor for them, how in him we have all true riches and treasures. They may have a super-

ficial intellectual grasp of Jesus' spiritual wealth, but they do not truly, deeply grasp it. Preaching, then, must not simply tell people what to do. It must re-present Christ in such a way that he captures the heart and imagination more than material things. This takes not just intellectual argumentation but the presentation of the *beauty* of Christ.

For Jonathan Edwards, the main spiritual problem for most Christians is that while they have an intellectual grasp of many doctrines, these are not real to their hearts and thus do not influence their behavior.[14] In the case of materialism, the power of money to bring security is more "spiritually real" to people than the security of God's loving and wise providence. Clear preaching, then, is a means to the end of making the truth more real to the hearts of the listeners than it has been before. D. Martyn Lloyd-Jones summarizes it this way:

> *The first and primary object of preaching ... is to produce an impression. It is the impression at the time that matters, even more than what you can remember subsequently ... Edwards, in my opinion, has the true notion of preaching. It is not primarily to impart information; and while [the listeners are taking] notes you may be missing something of the impact of the Spirit. As preachers we must not forget this. We are not merely imparters of information. We should tell our people to read certain books themselves and get the information there. The business of preaching is to make such knowledge live.[15]*

4. Preach Christ from every text. The main way to avoid moralistic preaching is to be sure that you always preach Jesus as the ultimate point and message of every text. If you don't point listeners to Jesus before the end of the sermon, you will give them the impression that the sermon is basically about *them* — about what they must do. However, we know from texts such as Luke 24:13 – 49 that Jesus understood every part of the Bible as pointing to him and his saving work. This is not to suggest that the author of every biblical passage intentionally made references to Jesus but that if you put any text into its full, canonical context, it is quite possible to discern the lines that point forward to Christ.

For example, in Judges 19, we have the jarring account of a Levite who is surrounded by violent

BASIC

Keller, Timothy. *The Prodigal God: Recovering the Heart of the Christian Faith*. New York: Dutton, 2008.

Lloyd-Jones, D. Martyn. "The True Foundation." Pages 23 – 36 in *Spiritual Depression: Its Causes and Cures*. Grand Rapids: Eerdmans, 1965.

INTERMEDIATE

Lloyd-Jones, D. Martyn. *Revival*. Wheaton, Ill.: Crossway, 1987.

Lovelace, Richard F. *Dynamics of Spiritual Life: An Evangelical Theology of Renewal*. Downers Grove, Ill.: InterVarsity, 1979.

ADVANCED

Edwards, Jonathan. *The Nature of True Virtue*. Eugene, Ore.: Wipf and Stock, 2003.

_____. *Thoughts on the New England Revival: Vindicating the Great Awakening*. Carlisle, Pa.: Banner of Truth, 2004.

_____. *Religious Affections*. Carlisle, Pa.: Banner of Truth, 1961.

Edwards has numerous other works on revival that are worth examining. See also his sermons "A Divine and Supernatural Light" and "Justification by Faith."

Sprague, William B. *Lectures on Revivals of Religion*. Edinburgh: Banner of Truth, 1958.

men in an alien city and who, in order to save his own life, offers his concubine (a second-class wife) to them to gang-rape. There is no way to preach this without talking about the fact that this is a horrible, direct contradiction of all that the Bible demonstrates a husband should be. A husband must protect his wife — and beyond that, he is to sacrifice

himself for his wife (Eph 5). And how do we know what a true husband should be? Well, the author of Judges doesn't know it as clearly as we do, but we know what a true husband is when we look at Jesus; Paul writes about this in Ephesians 5. And therefore we must bring the sermon forward to Christ. Only he shows us what husbands should be like, and only when we recognize his saving work can we be free from the fear and pride that makes us bad spouses. This message convicts, but it also gives deep encouragement. We are not trying to desperately earn our salvation by being good spouses; we are applying an accomplished and full salvation to our marriage. We must always turn to Jesus in our sermon because we want to put what the Bible declares in *any one particular place* into context with what the Bible says about it *as a whole*. And this journey always leads us through the gospel to Jesus.

There are, in the end, only two questions to ask as we read the Bible: Is it about me? Or is it about Jesus? In other words, is the Bible basically about what *I* must do or about what *he* has done? Consider the story of David and Goliath. If I read David and Goliath as a story that gives me an example to follow, then the story is really about me. It is an exhortation that *I* must summon up the faith and courage to fight the giants in my life. But if I accept that the Bible is ultimately about the Lord and his salvation, and if I read the David and Goliath text in that light, it throws a multitude of things into sharp relief! The very point of the Old Testament passage is that the Israelites could *not* face the giant themselves. Instead, they needed a champion who would fight in their place — a substitute who would face the deadly peril in their stead. And the substitute that God provided is not a strong person but a weak one — a young boy, too small to wear a suit of armor. Yet God used the deliverer's weakness as the very means to bring about the destruction of the laughing, overconfident Goliath. David triumphs through his weakness and his victory is imputed to his people. And so does Jesus. It is through his suffering, weakness, and death that the sin is defeated. This vivid and engaging story shows us what it means to declare that we have died with Christ (Rom 6:1 – 4) and are raised up and seated with him (Eph 2:5 – 6). Jesus is the ultimate champion, our *true* champion, who did not merely risk his life for us, but who gave it. And now his victory is our victory, and all he has accomplished is imputed to us.

There are, in the end, only two questions to ask as we read the Bible: Is it about me? Or is it about Jesus?

5. Preach to both Christians and non-Christians at once. When I first came to New York City in the late 1980s, I realized I had not come to a normal part of the United States. Thirty percent of Manhattan residents said they had "no religious preference" compared with (at the time) 6 percent of U.S. residents. Only 5 percent of Manhattanites attended any Protestant church, compared with 25 percent of Americans.[16] I realized that New York City was, religiously and culturally, more like secular, post-Christian Europe. So I looked at the work of Dr. Lloyd-Jones, one of the great preachers who had labored in London in the mid-twentieth century, and I reread his book *Preaching and Preachers*. In addition, I listened to scores (eventually hundreds, I think) of his sermon recordings.

I found particularly fascinating the structure he designed for his preaching. Lloyd-Jones planned his evening sermons to be evangelistic, while the morning sermons were intended to instruct and build up Christians. The evening sermons contained direct appeals to people to come to Christ and believe the gospel but were still richly theological and expository. On the other hand, while the morning sermons assumed a bit more knowledge of Christianity, they always returned to the clear themes of sin, grace, and Christ — the gospel. Lloyd-Jones urged his church members to attend both services. While he saw the evening service as an ideal setting to which to bring a nonbelieving friend, he wanted the professing Christians to attend regularly for their own good. Nor was he concerned when nonbeliev-

ers showed up regularly at the morning services. In fact, he wrote, "We must be careful not to be guilty of too rigid a classification of people saying, 'These are Christians, therefore...' [or] 'Yes, we became Christians as the result of a decision we took at an evangelistic meeting and now, seeing that we are Christians, all we need is teaching and edification.' I contest that very strongly."[17] I learned these lessons from him: Don't just preach to your congregation for spiritual growth, assuming that everyone in attendance is a Christian; and don't just preach the gospel evangelistically, thinking that Christians cannot grow from it. Evangelize as you edify, and edify as you evangelize.

THE SIGNS OF RENEWAL

Revival occurs as a group of people who, on the whole, *think* they already know the gospel discover they do *not* really or fully know it, and by embracing the gospel they cross over into living faith. When this happens in any extensive way, an enormous release of energy occurs. The church stops basing its justification on its sanctification. The nonchurched see this and are attracted by the transformed life of the Christian community as it grows into its calling to be a sign of the kingdom, a beautiful alternative to a human society without Christ.

Often, the first visible sign of renewal is when nominal church members become converted. Nominal Christians begin to realize they had never understood the gospel, experienced the new birth, or entered a living relationship with Christ by grace. Congregations are electrified as longtime church

Evangelize as you edify, and edify as you evangelize.

members speak of their conversions, talk about Christ in radiant terms, or express repentance in new ways. These early adopters of renewal stir up other church members into renewal. Soon, "sleepy" Christians also begin to receive a new assurance

HOW D. MARTYN LLOYD-JONES USED THE GOSPEL

Why use the gospel to edify Christians? D. Martyn Lloyd-Jones gave two reasons. First, we should not "assume that all ... who are members of the church are ... Christians. This, to me, is the most fatal blunder of all."[18] Second, many people have accepted Christianity intellectually but have never come under the power of the Word and the gospel and therefore have not truly repented. In other words, it is important to always remember that *some of your members are not really converted.* "One of the most exhilarating experiences in the life of a preacher is what happens when people whom everybody had assumed to be Christians are suddenly converted and truly become Christians. Nothing has a more powerful effect upon the life of a church than when that happens to a number of people."[19]

Not only have many professing Christians never truly repented and rested in grace; regenerate Christians, in order to grow, need to constantly feel the power of the gospel and rehearse the experience of conversion again and again. Lloyd-Jones adds, "If our preaching is always expository and for edification and teaching it will produce church members who are hard and cold, and often harsh and self-satisfied. I do not know of anything that is more likely to produce a congregation of Pharisees than that."[20] He also warns against "preaching morality and ethics without the Gospel as a basis."[21]

Why, however, give nonbelievers fairly theologically "meaty" expositions, as Lloyd-Jones did in his evening services? He makes this observation:

> I have often had the experience of people who have been converted, and have then gone on and grown in the church, coming to me some

of and appreciation for grace. They wake up to the reasons they have been living in anxiety, envy, anger, and boredom. They gain a sense of God's reality in the heart as well as higher, immediate assurances of his love. Along with a new and deeper conviction of sin and repentance — concerning not only major behavioral sins but inner attitudes — they have a far more powerful assurance of the nearness and love of God. The deeper their sense of sin debt, the more intense their sense of wonder at Christ's payment of it. As a result, they become simultaneously humbler and bolder.

Of course, the church also begins to see non-Christian outsiders converted as people are attracted to the newly beautified church and its authentic worship, its service in the community, and the surprising absence of condemning, tribal attitudes. Christians become radiant and attractive witnesses — more willing and confident to talk to others about their faith, more winsome and less judgmental when they do so, and more confident in their own church and thus more willing to invite people to visit it. The resulting conversions — sound, lasting, and sometimes dramatic — generate significant, sometimes even astounding, church growth.

Richard Lovelace describes a phenomenon common to churches before and after awakenings and revivals. Ordinarily, various Christian traditions and denominations tend to strongly emphasize one or two ministry functions while being weaker in others. For example, Presbyterians are historically strong in teaching and doctrine, Pentecostals and Anglicans (in their own ways!) in worship, Baptists in evangelism, Anabaptists in community and care for the poor, and so on. During times of gospel renewal, however, these strengths are often combined in churches that are otherwise one-sided. Churches experiencing gospel renewal find that some of the "secondary elements" — areas that typically fell outside of their primary focus — emerge during gospel renewal.[22]

This change is often first felt in the vibrancy of a church's *worship*. When the gospel "comes home" — when both God's holiness and his love become far more magnificent, real, and affecting to the heart — it leads naturally to a new "God reality" in worship. Irrespective of the mode or tradition, renewed churches worship in a way that is no longer one-dimensional — neither merely emotional nor merely formal. A clear, widely felt sense of God's transcendence permeates worship services, which edifies believers while also attracting and helping nonbelievers.

In addition, renewed interest in the gospel always piques interest in an expression of *biblical theology* that is deeply connected to real life. During revival, liberal-leaning churches may grow more biblical, while fundamentalist-leaning churches may grow less sectarian and more focused on the gospel itself rather than on denominational distinctives.

When the gospel comes home — when believers no longer have to maintain their image as competent and righteous — it naturally breaks down barriers that impede relationships and leads to more authentic experiences of *community* with others. Pretense and evasion become unnecessary. The gospel also creates a humility that makes believers empathetic and patient with others. All of this enables relationships within the church to thicken and deepen. During times of renewal, the distinct countercultural nature of the church becomes attractive to outsiders.

Finally, gospel renewal will produce people who are humbled (and thus not disdainful or contemptuous toward those who disagree with them) yet loved (and thus less concerned about others' opinions of them). Therefore every believer becomes a natural evangelist. Times of renewal are always times of remarkable church growth, not through membership transfer and "church shopping," but through conversion. There is also a renewed emphasis on poverty and justice ministries. When Christians realize they did not save themselves but were rescued from spiritual poverty, it naturally changes their attitudes toward people who are in economic and physical poverty. This kind of humble concern is the message of James 1 – 2 and many other biblical texts. Christians renewed by the gospel render sacrificial service to neighbors, the poor, and the community and city around them.

time later and telling me about what happened to them. What they have so often said is, "When we first came to the Church we really did not understand much of what you were talking about." I have then asked what made them continue coming, and have been told again and again that, "There was something about the whole atmosphere that attracted us … We gradually began to find that we were absorbing truth … It began to have meaning for us more and more …" They had continued to grow in their understanding until now they were able to enjoy the full service, the full message.[23]

Why were his evangelistic sermons not simpler; and why was it possible for people to slowly but surely find Christ through his edification-based sermons? It was because he addressed believers' questions and problems by always pointing in some way to the truths of the gospel. That way, as believers were edified, nonbelievers could also hear a gospel presentation. What made this such a good practice is that as nonbelievers came to faith they didn't have to graduate to a whole different service. And they weren't led to believe they had graduated from the gospel. They might begin coming to the Friday night lectures on theology or Romans, but on Sunday they were able to come to faith *and* grow in grace through rich expositions of the Bible.

All of these changes, both within the church and the surrounding community, will eventually have a broad effect on the culture. Gospel-shaped believers who belong to churches that are experiencing gospel renewal often have a deep, vital, and healthy impact on the arts, business, government, media, and academy of any society. The past two decades have produced a far greater acknowledgment that major social justice and social change movements in Britain and the United States — such as the abolition of slavery and the strengthening of child labor laws — had strong roots in the revivals. Because true religion is not merely a private practice that provides internal peace and fulfillment, holiness affects both the private and civic lives of Christians. It transforms behavior and relationships. The active presence of a substantial number of genuine Christians thus changes a community in all its dimensions — economic, social, political, intellectual, and more.

Notice the interdependence of these "secondary

Churches experiencing gospel renewal find that some of the "secondary elements" emerge during gospel renewal.

---

elements" flowing naturally from hearts renewed by the gospel. First, many individuals are renewed by the gospel because they are drawn into a church marked by these qualities. Second, the vitality of each factor depends not only on the gospel-renewed heart but also on each of the other factors. They stimulate each other. For example, as Christians give their lives sacrificially for the poor, their neighbors become more open to evangelism. Deep, rich community could be said to *result* from gospel evangelism, but just as frequently it is a *means* to evangelism, because it makes the gospel credible. Often it is not through listening to preaching but listening to friends that brings us home spiritually. Although these factors are mutually strengthening, the specialists and proponents of each element will almost always pit them against the others. Thus, evangelists may fear that a social justice emphasis will drain energy, attention, and resources from evangelism. Social justice advocates, on the other hand, often resist an emphasis on cultural renewal because they maintain that Christians should be out in the streets identifying with the poor rather than trying to influence the elite worlds of art, media, and business. Community-focused leaders often view rapid church growth and evangelistic programs negatively because they do not like programs — they want everything to happen naturally and "organically." Leaders who grasp how the gospel inspires all of these dimensions must

overcome these tensions, and we will discuss these dynamics in greater depth in later chapters.

When the dynamics of gospel renewal are not in place, a church may increase in numbers but not in vitality. It may grow but fail to produce real fruit that has lasting results. It will exhibit symptoms of lifelessness. Most or all of the growth will happen through transfer, not conversion. Because no deep conviction of sin or repentance occurs, few people will attest to dramatically changed lives. Church growth, if it does occur, will make no impact on the local social order because its participants do not carry their Christian faith into their work, their use of monetary resources, or their public lives. However, with these gospel renewal dynamics strong in our hearts and in our churches, our lives and our congregations will be empowered and made beautiful by the Spirit of God.

Of all the elements of a Center Church theological vision, gospel renewal may be the single most difficult one to put into practice because, ultimately, we can only prepare for revival; we can't really bring it about. God must send it. That may discourage those of us who live in a technological society in which we seek to control everything through our competence and will. When we do not see renewal happening, we can get deeply discouraged. But we should not be. Derek Kidner's commentary on Psalm 126 can help us here. The first three verses of Psalm 126 look back to times of great spiritual flourishing, when the Israelites' "mouths were filled with laughter" (verse 2) and when all the nations around them said, "The LORD has done great things for them." But verse 4 tells us that times have changed. The people cry, "Restore our fortunes, O LORD!" Kidner looks closely at the final parts of the psalm:

> [4]*Restore our fortunes, O LORD,*
> *like streams in the Negev.*
> [5]*Those who sow in tears*
> *will reap with songs of joy.*
> [6]*He who goes out weeping,*
> *carrying seed to sow,*
> *will return with songs of joy,*
> *carrying sheaves with him.*

Kidner sees two very different pictures of how revival and renewal can come. The first is in verse 4b; it is "all suddenness, a sheer gift from heaven." Few places are more arid than the Negev, where the dry gulleys become rushing torrents after a rare downpour and can literally turn a desert into a place of grass and flowers overnight.[24] This points to times of revival that are sudden and massive, the kind that historians write about. The second picture is in verses 5 – 6, "farming at its most heartbreaking," a long and arduous process when the weather is bad and the soil is hard. The image is one of those who, in the absence of rain, still get a harvest through steady, faithful work, watering the ground with their tears if they have no other source of water. It depicts gospel workers who spend years of hard work, often weeping over the hardness of hearts that they see, and who bear little initial fruit.

And yet the psalmist is absolutely certain of eventual harvest — "God's blessing of seed sown and His visiting of His people." This is the final note. Kidner says that the modern translations tend to omit the extra words of emphasis in the final verb and therefore miss the psalmist's pointedness. No matter how long we may wait, nevertheless "he that surely goes forth weeping … will surely come home with shouts of joy."[25] Kidner concludes, "So the psalm, speaking first to its own times, speaks still. Miracles of the past it bids us treat as measures of the future; dry places as potential rivers; hard soil and good seed as the certain prelude to harvest."[26]

QUESTIONS FOR DISCUSSION AND REFLECTION

1. Keller writes, "Maintenance prayer meetings are short, mechanical, and focused on physical needs inside the church. In contrast, the three basic traits of frontline prayer are these: a request for grace to confess sins and to humble ourselves; a compassion and zeal for the flourishing of the church and the reaching of the lost; and a yearning to know God, to see his face, to glimpse his glory." How have you experienced God working through "frontline" prayer? If you do not currently have these prayer times in your church, how can you go about beginning them?

2. One way to engage in gospel application is by training lay leaders to minister the gospel to others. This involves personal meetings and counseling to help people learn how to repent of their idols and self-righteousness. Does this type of gospel application currently happen in your church? If not, how can you begin training people to apply the gospel? How is ministering the gospel different from other forms of counseling?

3. Look at the questions in the sidebar on "Questions to Guide an 'Experience Meeting.'" Which of these questions make you uncomfortable? Which ones do you find easiest to engage? Which are personally convicting?

4. Gospel innovation involves creatively communicating the gospel in new ways. How have you seen an overreliance on a particular communication style or methodology hinder a ministry? Why is it necessary to be innovative? What are some dangers associated with this?

5. The section titled "Preaching for Gospel Renewal" gives five characteristics that define preaching that leads to renewal. Which of these five do you need to strengthen? How can you incorporate these missing emphases into your preaching?

CHAPTER 6 — THE WORK OF GOSPEL RENEWAL *(pages 73 – 83)*

1. C. John Miller, *Outgrowing the Ingrown Church* (Grand Rapids: Zondervan, 1986, 1999), 98 – 101.
2. See D. Martyn Lloyd-Jones, *Revival* (Wheaton, Ill.: Crossway, 1987), 33 – 54 (chs. titled "Unbelief" and "Doctrinal Impurity").
3. See Lloyd-Jones, *Revival*, 68 – 79.
4. Ibid., 55 – 67, 80 – 91.
5. See the section on "Preaching for Gospel Renewal" below for more on this subject. However, I'm not going into depth on this topic here because I'm preparing a book-length treatment to be published in the near future.
6. D. Martyn Lloyd-Jones, *Spiritual Depression: Its Causes and Cure* (Grand Rapids: Eerdmans, 1965), 23 – 36; Timothy Keller, *The Prodigal God: Recovering the Heart of the Christian Faith* (New York: Dutton, 2008); Timothy Keller, *The Prodigal God Discussion Guide* (Grand Rapids: Zondervan, 2009).
7. Helpful resources for this process include Redeemer's *Paul's Letter to the Galatians: Living in Line with the Truth of the Gospel* (facilitator guide and participant guide, http://redeemercitytocity.com/resources/library.jsp?Library_item_param=376) and Timothy Keller, *Gospel in Life Study Guide: Grace Changes Everything* (Grand Rapids: Zondervan, 2010).
8. William Williams, *The Experience Meeting: An Introduction to the Welsh Societies of the Great Awakening*, trans. D. Martyn Lloyd-Jones (Vancouver, B.C.: Regent College Publishing, 2003).
9. William B. Sprague, *Lectures on Revivals of Religion* (1832; Carlisle, Pa.: Banner of Truth, 2007), 139.
10. Ibid., 118 – 29.
11. Ibid., 153 – 214 ("Lecture VI: Treatment Due to Awakened Sinners"; "Lecture VII: Treatment Due to Young Converts").
12. Ibid., 155.
13. The letters of John Newton, the famous hymn writer, provide another great resource for gospel counseling. A good place to start is the small paperback *The Letters of John Newton* (Carlisle, Pa.: Banner of Truth, 1960).
14. See Wilson H. Kimnach, "Jonathan Edwards's Pursuit of Reality," in *Jonathan Edwards and the American Experience*, ed. Nathan O. Hatch and Harry S. Stout (New York: Oxford University Press, 1988), 105.
15. D. Martyn Lloyd-Jones, "Jonathan Edwards and the Crucial Importance of Revival," in *The Puritans: Their Origins and Successors* (Edinburgh: Banner of Truth, 1976), 360.
16. This figure came from a *New York* magazine article in the early 1990s and included attendees at *all* Protestant congregations. Another study showed that the population attending *evangelical* Protestant congregations was less than 1 percent of Manhattanites at the end of the 1980s.
17. D. Martyn Lloyd-Jones, *Preaching and Preachers* (Grand Rapids: Zondervan, 1972), 151.
18. Ibid., 96.
19. Ibid., 152.
20. Ibid., 152 – 53.
21. Ibid., 35.
22. Richard F. Lovelace, *Dynamics of Spiritual Life: An Evangelical Theology of Renewal* (Downers Grove, Ill.: InterVarsity, 1979), 145 – 200.
23. Lloyd-Jones, *Preaching and Preachers*, 127 – 28.
24. Derek Kidner, *Psalms 73 – 150: A Commentary* (Downers Grove, Ill.: InterVarsity, 1973), 440.
25. Ibid.
26. Ibid.

GOSPEL BALANCE

 legalism
religion

relativism
irreligion

The gospel is neither religion nor irreligion, but something else entirely — a third way of relating to God through grace. Because of this, we minister in a uniquely balanced way that avoids the errors of either extreme and faithfully communicates the sharpness of the gospel.

- Remember that the gospel is not *everything*, neither is it a *simple* thing.
- Draw on both synchronic (STM) and diachronic (RHM) views of Scripture.
- Employ several intercanonical themes in our preaching and pastoring, not just one or two.

- Incorporate the upside-down, inside-out, and forward-back aspects of the kingdom.
- Acknowledge that there are individual and corporate aspects to salvation.
- Know that the kingdom is already *and* not yet.
- Demonstrate the harmony of grace and truth.
- Promote revivalism that recognizes the formative role of the church, yet also addresses the individual heart.
- Counsel believers to have both doctrine/knowledge and experience/feeling.

CITY

underadapted
only challenge

overadapted
only appreciate

Center Church ministry is neither undercontextual-
ized nor overcontextualized to the city and the
culture. Because the city has potential for both
human flourishing and human idolatry, we minister
with balance, using the gospel to both appreciate and
challenge the culture to be in accord with God's truth.

CITY

Fruitful ministry in this century must embrace the unavoidable reality of the city. A Center Church theological vision affirms that center cities are wonderful, strategic, and underserved places for gospel ministry and recognizes that virtually all ministry contexts are increasingly shaped by urban and global forces. Regardless of your particular cultural or geographical context, you will need to consider the city when forming a theological vision that engages the people you are trying to reach. In other words, because the world is on its way to becoming 70 percent urban, we all need a theological vision that is distinctly urban. Even if you don't go to the city to minister, make no mistake: the city is coming to you.

In part 3 (**Gospel Contextualization**), we look at the biblical foundations for balanced contextualization and examine how we can contextualize the gospel in our communication to the culture in a way that is both respectful and challenging.

Churches and ministries that flourish in urban and cultural centers are marked by what we call **City Vision**. In part 4, we examine the key characteristics of city vision. It is based in an understanding of how the city develops as a theme throughout Scripture, from its anti-God origins, to its strategic importance for mission, to its culmination and redemption in glory. Most important, a city vision will give us a genuine love for the place we are called to reach with the gospel, rather than hostility or indifference toward it.

We will also examine the need for thoughtful **Cultural Engagement**. In part 5, we will discuss four models for engaging culture, acknowledging that each model has strengths and weaknesses — ways in which it accurately reflects a particular biblical emphasis and other ways in which it reflects an unbiblical imbalance or idol. The Center Church model for cultural engagement blends the key insights of each model in a way that we believe is more biblically faithful and also fruitful for reaching urban culture.

INTENTIONAL CONTEXTUALIZATION

Redeemer City to City is an agency that promotes church planting and gospel movements in the great city centers of the world.[1] As part of our global ministry, we have had opportunities to talk with Chinese house church leaders. God is blessing the church in China with extraordinary growth. However, when Chinese churches and ministers who had experienced God's blessing in their rural ministries entered the mushrooming cities of China and tried to minister and communicate the gospel in the same ways that had been blessed in the countryside, they saw less fruitfulness.

Over a decade ago, several Dutch denominations approached us. While they were thriving outside of urban areas, they had not been able to start new, vital churches in Amsterdam in years — and most of the existing ones had died out. These leaders knew the gospel; they had financial resources; they had the desire for Christian mission. But they couldn't get anything off the ground in the biggest city of their country.[2]

In both cases, ministry that was thriving in the heartland of the country was unable to make much of a dent in the city. It would have been easy to say, "The people of the city are too spiritually proud and hardened." But the church leaders we met chose to respond humbly and took responsibility for the problem. They concluded that the gospel ministry that had fit nonurban areas well would need to be adapted to the culture of urban life. And they were right. This necessary adaptation to the culture is an example of what we call "contextualization."[3]

SOUND CONTEXTUALIZATION

Contextualization is not — as is often argued — "giving people what they want to hear."[4] Rather, it is giving people *the Bible's answers*, which they may not at all want to hear, *to questions about life* that people in their particular time and place are asking, *in language and forms* they can comprehend, and *through appeals and arguments* with force they can feel, even if they reject them.

Sound contextualization means translating and adapting the communication and ministry of the gospel to a particular culture without compromising the essence and particulars of the gospel itself. The great missionary task is to express the gospel message to a new culture in a way that avoids making the message unnecessarily alien to that culture, yet without removing or obscuring the scandal and offense of biblical truth. A contextualized gospel is marked by clarity and attractiveness, and yet it still challenges sinners' self-sufficiency and calls them to repentance. It adapts and connects to the culture, yet at the same time challenges and confronts it. If we fail to adapt to the culture or if we fail to challenge the culture — if we under- or overcontextualize — our ministry will be unfruitful because we have failed to contextualize well.

Perhaps the easiest way to quickly grasp the concept is to think about a common phenomenon. Have you ever sat through a sermon that was biblically sound and doctrinally accurate — yet so boring that it made you want to cry? What made it tedious? Sometimes it's the mechanics (e.g., a monotone delivery), but more often a boring sermon is doctrinally accurate but utterly irrelevant. The listener says to himself or herself, "You've shown me something that may be true, but in any case I don't care. I don't see how it would actually change how I think, feel, and act." A boring sermon is boring because it fails to bring the truth into the listeners' daily life and world. It does not connect biblical truth to the hopes, narratives, fears, and errors of people in that particular time and place. It does not help the listener to even *want* Christianity to be true. In other words, the sermon fails at contextualizing the biblical truth for the hearers.

When we contextualize faithfully and skillfully, we show people how the baseline "cultural narratives" of their society and the hopes of their hearts can only find resolution and fulfillment in Jesus. What do I mean by this? Some cultures are pragmatic and prod their members to acquire possessions and power. Some are individualistic and urge their members to seek personal freedom above all. Others are "honor and shame" cultures, with emphasis on respect, reputation, duty, and bringing honor to your family. Some cultures are discursive and put the highest value on art, philosophy, and learning.[5] These are called "cultural narratives" because they are stories that a people tell about themselves to make sense out of their shared existence. But whatever these personal and cultural narratives may be, sound contextualization shows people how the plotlines of the stories of their lives can only find a happy ending in Christ.[6]

So contextualization has to do with culture, but what exactly is culture? Effective contextualization addresses culture in the broadest sense of the word, along the maximum surface area. Culture is popularly conceived narrowly — as language, music and art, food and folk customs — but properly understood, it touches every aspect of how we live in the world. Culture takes the raw materials of nature

---

Sound contextualization shows people how the plotlines of the stories of their lives can only find a happy ending in Christ.

---

and creates an environment. When we take the raw material of the earth to build a building or use sounds and rhythms to compose a song or fashion our personal experiences into a story, we are creating an environment we call a culture. We do all this, however, with a goal: to bring the natural order into the service of particular "commanding truths," core beliefs, and assumptions about reality and the world we live in.

Missionary G. Linwood Barney speaks of culture as resembling an onion. The inmost core is a worldview — a set of normative beliefs about the world, cosmology, and human nature. Growing immediately out of that layer is a set of values — what is considered good, true, and beautiful. The third layer is a set of human institutions that carry on jurisprudence, education, family life, and governance on the basis of the values and worldview. Finally comes the most observable part of culture — human customs and behavior, material products, the built environment, and so on.[7] Some have rightly criticized this model — of an onion or a ladder — as not sufficient to show how much all these "layers" interact with and shape one another.[8] For example, institutions can produce something new like the United States interstate highway system, which created "car culture" behavior, which has in turn undermined older forms of communities and therefore many institutions. So the interactions are neither linear nor one-way.

But the main point here is that contextualizing the gospel in a culture must account for all these aspects. It does not mean merely changing someone's behavior, but someone's worldview. It does not mean adapting superficially — for example, in music and clothing. Culture affects every part of human life. It determines how decisions are made, how emotions are expressed, what is considered private and public, how the individual relates to the group, how social power is used, and how relationships, particularly between genders, generations, classes, and races, are conducted. Our culture gives distinct understandings of time, conflict resolution, problem solving, and even the way in which we reason. All these factors must be addressed when we seek to do gospel ministry. David Wells writes, "Contextualization is not merely a practical application of biblical doctrine but a translation of that doctrine into a conceptuality that meshes with the reality of the social structures and patterns of life dominant in our contemporary life."[9]

Skill in contextualization is one of the keys to effective ministry today. In particular, churches in urban and cultural centers must be exceptionally sensitive to issues of contextualization, because it is largely there that a society's culture is being forged and is taking new directions. It is also a place where multiple human cultures live together in uneasy tension, so cultural compounds are more complex and blended there.

A BRIEF HISTORY OF THE TERM

The term *contextualization* may have first been used in 1972 by Shoki Coe, a Taiwanese-born man who was one of the key figures in the formation of the World Council of Churches.[10] Coe questioned the adequacy of the older "indigenous church movement" model identified with Henry Venn and Rufus Anderson. Venn and Anderson directed Western missionaries to plant churches in new cultures that were "self-supporting, self-governing, and self-propagating." Older missionaries had planted churches in foreign cultures and maintained control of them indefinitely, using native Christians only in assisting roles. They also explicitly directed national Christians to adopt Western ways wholesale. The indigenous church movement, however, called missionaries to see themselves as temporary workers whose job was to do initial evangelism and then, as quickly as possible, to turn the churches over to indigenous, national leadership so the Christian churches could worship and minister in native languages, music, and culture.

This was a good and important step forward in our understanding of how Christian mission is conducted. But Coe, who served as principal of Tainan Theological College, argued that something more than just empowering national leaders was needed. He observed that the missionaries still gave national leaders *forms* of church ministry — ways of expressing and formulating the gospel and structuring churches — that were unalterably Western. National Christians were not being encouraged to think creatively about how to communicate the gospel message to their own culture.[11]

The Theological Education Fund of the World Council of Churches was the first agency to use this new term and pursue it within its mission. The earliest work under this name, however, caused grave concerns. Following the existential theological thinking of Rudolf Bultmann, who was still highly influential in the 1970s, and Ernst Käsemann, theologians connected to the WCC insisted that the New Testament was itself largely adapted to a Hellenistic worldview that did not have abiding validity. Therefore, it was argued, Christians were free to determine in whatever way that fit their particular culture the "inner thrust of Christian [biblical] revelation" and discard or adapt the rest.[12]

This approach to contextualization assumes that both the text (Bible) and context (culture) are relative and equally authoritative. Through a dialectical process in which the two are brought into relationship to one another, we search for the particular form of Christian truth (with a small *t*) that fits a culture for the time being. Virtually any part of the Christian faith, then — the deity of Christ, the triunity of God, the gracious basis of the gospel — can be jettisoned or filled with radically new content, depending on the particular cultural setting. In the name of contextualizing to its culture, a church has the potential to make radical changes to historic Christian doctrine.

The irony is deep. The original call for contextualization intended to allow national churches to do theological reflection without having extrabiblical, Western thought forms imposed on them. However, much of what the ecumenical WCC Theological Education Fund propagated was nonetheless deeply shaped by Western thinking. Contextualization based on the idea of a nonauthoritative Bible stems from the views of modern Western theologians who themselves accepted the European Enlightenment's skepticism about the miraculous and supernatural. The result was that, yet again, the Christian faith was overadapted to culture. This time it was not the older, more conservative Western culture of nineteenth-century missionaries, but the liberal culture of twentieth-century Western academia.

THE DANGER OF CONTEXTUALIZING

Because of this history, the word *contextualization* makes many people in conservative theological circles nervous, as indeed it should. As Craig Blomberg points out in an essay on contextualization,

"Many who have embraced universalism began life as evangelicals ... In the Spanish-speaking world, the same is true of many liberation theologians."[14] In all these cases, the values of a culture were given preference over the authority of Scripture.

Although the word *contextualization* was not around at the time, this was the same issue J. Gresham Machen faced in the Presbyterian Church in the early twentieth century. In his book *Christianity and Liberalism*, Machen states that liberal Christianity was trying to solve a problem:

> What is the relation between Christianity and modern culture; may Christianity be maintained in a scientific age?
>
> It is this problem which modern liberalism attempts to solve. Admitting that scientific objections may arise against the particularities of the Christian religion — against the Christian doctrines of the person of Christ, and of redemption through His death and resurrection — the liberal theologian seeks to rescue certain of the general principles of religion, of which these particularities are thought to be mere temporary symbols, and these general principles he regards as constituting "the essence of Christianity."
>
> As a matter of fact ... what the liberal theologian has retained after abandoning to the enemy one Christian doctrine after another is not Christianity at all, but a religion which is so entirely different from Christianity as to belong in a distinct category.[15]

Machen, speaking from the early twentieth century, declared that his culture had become "natu-

ralistic" — it had completely rejected any account of supernatural intervention by God. Everything, in this view, must have a natural, scientific explanation. The problem with the liberal Christianity of Machen's day is that it granted this cultural belief, even though it clearly contradicted Scripture. Liberal Christianity adapted to the culture when it should have been confronting it.[16] In order (they thought) to make Christianity palatable to modern people, liberal Christian leaders redefined all doctrine in naturalistic terms. The reformulated version of Christianity looked (and still looks) like this:

- The Bible is filled with divine wisdom, but this doesn't mean it is inerrant — it is a human document that has errors and contradictions.
- Jesus is the Son of God, but this doesn't mean he was the preexisting, divine Son of God. He was a great man infused with God's Spirit.
- Jesus' death is not a cosmic event that propitiates the wrath of God — it is an example of sacrificial love that changes us by moving us through his example.
- Becoming a Christian, then, doesn't entail the supernatural act of the new birth. It means to follow the example of Jesus, follow the teaching of the Sermon on the Mount, and live a life of love and justice in the world.

Machen goes on to argue forcefully and persuasively that the effort to reconcile Christianity to a naturalistic philosophy results not in an adapted version of biblical faith but an entirely new religion, one that directly contradicts classic Christianity at nearly every important point. Perhaps the most telling and devastating example is given in Machen's chapter titled "Salvation." There he points out that if Jesus' atonement is now just an example of how to live, and if being a Christian is not to be born again but to live like Jesus, we have replaced the Christian gospel of salvation by grace with a religion of salvation by good works. "Such teaching is just a sublimated form of legalism," he concludes.[17]

The call to contextualize the gospel has been — and still often is — used as a cover for religious syncretism. This means not *adapting* the gospel to a particular culture, but rather *surrendering* the gospel entirely and morphing Christianity into a different religion by overadapting it to an alien worldview. But how do we judge when we have moved from legitimate contextualization into fatal syncretism? In a helpful essay, Natee Tanchanpongs states that evangelicals usually try to defend contextualization by arguing that it is simply adapting the *less essential* parts of Christianity and that syncretism occurs when "the critical and basic elements" of the gospel are lost.[18] In this view, contextualization involves keeping the essentials while flexing on the nonessentials.

Tanchanpongs argues, however, that it is wrong to look at Scripture and imagine that some core, essential teachings are more important than other, more tangential ones. In fact, Harvie Conn argued that syncretism is most likely to occur when (in the name of culture) we forbid the *whole* of Scripture to speak. Every culture will find some parts of Scripture more attractive and other parts more offensive. It will be natural, then, for those in that culture to consider the inoffensive parts more "important" and "essential" than the offensive parts. This is exactly what the liberal Christianity of Machen's day did in rejecting the "offensive" supernatural elements of the Bible. Syncretism is, in fact, a rejection of the full authority of the Bible, a picking and choosing among its various teachings to create a Christianity that does not confront or offend.[19] Faithful contextualization, then, should adapt the communication and practice of *all* scriptural teaching to a culture (see below on the dangers of having a "canon within a canon" when contextualizing).

THE INEVITABILITY OF CONTEXTUALIZING

Here is a beautiful paradox that is easy to miss: the fact that we must express universal truth in a particular cultural context does not mean that the truth itself is somehow lost or less universal. D. A. Carson writes, "[While] no truth which human beings may articulate can ever be articulated in a culture-transcending way ... that does not mean that the truth thus articulated does not transcend culture."[20]

It is important to seek to maintain the balance of this careful and important statement. First, this means there is no one, single way to express the Christian faith that is universal for everyone in all cultures. As soon as you express the gospel, you are unavoidably doing it in a way that is more understandable and accessible for people in some cultures and less so for others. On the other hand, while there is no culture-transcending way to express the truths of the gospel, there is nonetheless only one true gospel. The truths of the gospel are not the products of any culture, and they stand in judgment over all human cultures. If you forget the first truth — that there is no culture-less presentation of the gospel — you will think there is only one true way to communicate it, and you are on your way to a rigid, culturally bound conservatism. If you forget the second truth — that there is only one true gospel — you may fall into relativism, which will lead to

LIBERALISM AND NATURALISM

When liberal Christianity adopted naturalism, it assumed this was a permanent change in human thinking that had to be accepted. Those who clung to supernatural Christianity were, it was said, "on the wrong side of history." But this was a category mistake. Early modernity was both naturalistic ("everything must have a natural, scientific explanation") and individualistic ("there can be no higher authority than the reasoning, choosing self"). Late modernity or postmodernity, however, while maintaining belief in the autonomous self, has rejected naturalism's confidence that science can eventually answer all-important questions and that technology can solve all significant problems. Liberal Christianity wedded itself to what is now seen as a fading, obsolete cultural view. Pentecostalism (the most supernaturalistic form of the faith) and other forms of orthodox Christianity have grown exponentially in the past hundred years, leaving liberal Christianity far behind.

a rudderless liberalism. Either way, you will be less faithful and less fruitful in ministry.

What should we conclude from this? If there is no single, context-free way to express the gospel, then contextualization is inevitable. As soon as you choose a language to speak in and particular words to use within that language, the culture-laden nature of words comes into play. We often think that translating words from one language to another is simple — it's just a matter of locating the synonym in the other language. But there are few true synonyms. The word *God* is translated into German as *Gott* — simple enough. But the cultural history of German speakers is such that the word *Gott* strikes German ears differently than the English word *God* strikes the ears of English speakers. *It means something different to them.* You may need to do more explanation if you are to give German speakers the same biblical concept of God that the word conveys to English speakers. Or maybe a different word will have to be used to have the same effect. As soon as you choose words, you are contextualizing, and you become more accessible to some people and less so to others. There is no universal presentation of the gospel for all people.[21]

However, even within the field of one language, numerous other factors unavoidably involve us in the work of contextualization. Let's think back for a moment to the boring sermon. Sometimes the sermon we hear is boring because it went on for too long (or it was not long enough) to engage the listeners. One of the most culturally sensitive areas of human life is this area of time. What various people and cultures consider "late" and "too long" varies widely. In the United States, African-American and Hispanic Christians have services in which singing, prayer, and preaching go on at least 50 percent longer than the attention spans and comfort zones of most Anglo people. Anyone who leads worship services will, then, unavoidably be contextualizing toward some people and away from others.

A sermon can also lose listeners because of the types of metaphors and illustrations that are chosen. When Jesus tells those who preach the gospel to hostile people to avoid throwing pearls to pigs

(Matt 7:6), he is uniting two fields of discourse. He is connecting preaching the gospel to the concrete world of raising pigs. By doing so, he is conveying meaning in a far more riveting and illuminating way than if he had simply said, "Don't preach the gospel indefinitely to people who are hostile to it." Jesus used an illustration, but every illustration by definition must use some concrete life experience. And so, as soon as we choose an illustration, we move toward some people (who share those life experiences) and become more remote and less accessible to others (who do not).

I once spoke to a mature British Christian believer from a working-class background. For a time, he attended a solidly evangelical church, but all the leaders and ministers were from the upper classes and the elite schools. The preaching referred to life situations and concepts that the speakers knew, which meant frequent illustrations drawn from the sports of cricket and rugby. This man shared, "People in my world know very little of these sports, and the constant references to them reminded me that I did not go to their schools or have their privileges. That was distracting, but not insurmountable, because we are all one in Christ now. But I realized that I could not bring to that church the working-class folks to whom I was ministering. The continual reminders that the leaders were from the upper

---

As soon as you express the gospel, you are unavoidably doing it in a way that is more understandable and accessible for people in some cultures and less so for others.

---

crust would make it very hard for my friends to listen to the Word. You might say to them, 'Why so touchy?' — but you can't expect people to be sanctified before they are justified. You can't expect people who are not yet believers to shed all their cultural sensitivities." Eventually he went to another church.

Does this example mean that the church in this situation failed in some way? It is possible that the church could have consulted with this man and others to discuss ways that it could have been less culturally strange and remote to working-class people. But there is always a limit to this flexibility. The preachers must choose *some* particular illustrations and concepts that will inevitably be more meaningful to some cultural groups than others. We need to stretch as much as we can to be as inclusive as possible. But we must also be aware of our limits. We should not live in the illusion that we can share the gospel so as to make it all things to all people at once.

Another reason a sermon can be accurate but still have little impact is that the level of emotional expressiveness is not calibrated to the culture of the person listening. I once had a Hispanic member of my church tell me, a bit sheepishly, that when he brought other Hispanic people to hear me preach at Redeemer, he had to tell them, "He really *does* believe what he is saying with all his heart, in spite of what it looks like." He had to do that because so many people from his culture felt that my level of emotional expression signaled indifference to my subject matter. "In our culture, if you *really* believe something and are committed to it, you express more *feeling*." I was struck by the fact that if I adapted to a certain type of culture and expressed my emotions more fervently, it would look to people from another culture like a rant and be completely unpersuasive to them. There is no universal presentation. We *cannot* avoid contextualization.

We have talked about the manner and mode of preaching, but contextualization also has much to do with the content. A sermon could be unengaging to a person because, though expressing accurate biblical truth, it does not connect biblical teaching to the main objections and questions people in that culture have about faith. A few years ago, I participated in a consultation on evangelism for several churches in London. One of the dilemmas we discussed was the two very different groups of non-Christians in a particular area of the city. On one side were millions of Hindus and Muslims who believed that Christianity was not moralistic enough; on the other side were secular British

---

GARDENS OR FIELDS?

Craig Blomberg points out that in Matthew's parable of the mustard seed, the sower sows his seed in a "field" (*agros*, Matt 13:31), while in Luke the sowing is in a "garden" (*kēpos*, Luke 13:19). Jews never grew mustard plants in gardens, but always out on farms, while Greeks in the Mediterranean basin did the opposite. It appears that each gospel writer was changing the word that Jesus used in Mark — the word for "earth" or "ground" (*gē*, Mark 4:31) — for the sake of his hearers. There is a technical contradiction between the Matthean and Lukan terms, states Blomberg, "but not a material one. Luke changes the wording precisely so that his audience is not distracted from … the lesson by puzzling over an … improbable practice." The result is that Luke's audience "receives his teaching with the same impact as the original audience."[22]

---

people who thought that Christianity was far too rigidly moralistic. Of course, the gospel is neither legalism nor antinomianism, and so it is possible to preach a single sermon on the gospel that engages listeners from both groups, but if we are ministering in a neighborhood or area dominated by one of these groups, we must preach each passage with the particular objections of that people group firmly in mind. No one single gospel presentation will be equally engaging and compelling to both sides.

Finally, as we will see below, contextualization doesn't simply include language and vocabulary, emotional expressiveness and illustrations. It goes even deeper. Contextualization affects the way we reason because people in one culture find one way of appealing persuasive, while those of another may not. Some people are more logical; some are more intuitive. When we choose a particular way to persuade and argue, we will unavoidably be adapting more to some kinds of people than to others.

I used a boring sermon as my case study for contextualization (or a lack of it), and so all my examples have been about verbal communication of the gospel. But culture has a pervasive impact on every aspect of how a Christian community is ordered — how people relate to each other, how leadership is exercised, how pastoral oversight and instruction is done. For example, some years ago, a Korean member of my staff watched our pastoral staff make a decision. He noticed that I as senior pastor would not betray my view at first but would try to get everyone, even the youngest and newest, to offer their opinion; then I would affirm them and try to incorporate their input into our final decision. He pointed out that in a first-generation Korean church, the senior pastor would give his full view first and then others would comment in order of age and seniority. Junior members of the pastoral staff only spoke after the decision was already a *fait accompli.* As I listened to him, I realized there was no culture-free way for the pastors of my church to make a decision. We were unavoidably going to be very contextualized to one culture.

As soon as we seek to communicate, we will automatically be making all sorts of cultural moves.

THE DANGER OF NOT CONTEXTUALIZING (OR OF THINKING YOU AREN'T)

All gospel ministry and communication are already heavily adapted to a particular culture. So it is important to do contextualization *consciously*. If we never deliberately think through ways to rightly contextualize gospel ministry to a new culture, we will unconsciously be deeply contextualized to some other culture. Our gospel ministry will be both overadapted to our own culture and underadapted to new cultures at once, which ultimately leads to a distortion of the Christian message.[23]

The subject of contextualization is particularly hard to grasp for members of socially dominant groups. Because ethnic minorities must live in two cultures — the dominant culture and their own subculture — they frequently become aware of how deeply culture affects the way we perceive things. In the movie *Gran Torino*, an older blue-collar American named Walt Kowalski (Clint Eastwood) lives alongside an Asian family in a deteriorating Detroit neighborhood. He finds it impossible to understand the cultural forms of the Hmongs, just as the elderly Hmongs (who cannot speak English and live completely within their ethnic enclave) find Walt strange and inexplicable. But the teenage Hmong girl, Sue, is bicultural — she lives in both worlds at once. So she understands and appreciates both Walt and her own parents and grandparents. As a result, she is able to communicate persuasively to both about the other. Isn't this the very thing we are doing whenever we present the truth of the gospel to a culture that has alienated itself from it?

In the United States, Anglo-Americans' public and private lives are lived in the same culture. As a result, they are often culturally clueless. They relate to their own culture in the same way a fish that, when asked about water, said, "What's water?" If you have never been out of water, you don't know you are *in* it. Anglo Christians sometimes find talk of contextualization troubling. They don't see any part of how they express or live the gospel to be "Anglo" — it is just the way things are. They feel that any change in how they preach, worship, or minister is somehow a compromise of the gospel. In this they may be doing what Jesus warns against — elevating the "traditions of men" to the same level as biblical truth (Mark 7:8). This happens when one's cultural approach to time or emotional expressiveness or way to communicate becomes enshrined as *the* Christian way to act and live. Bruce Nicholls writes the following:

A contemporary example of cultural syncretism is the unconscious identification of biblical Christianity with "the American way of life." This form of syncretism is often found in both Western and Third World, middle-class, suburban, conservative, evangelical congregations who seem unaware that their lifestyle has more affinity to the consumer principles of capitalistic society than to the realities of the New Testament, and whose enthusiasm for evangelism and overseas missions is used to justify [lives of materialism and complacency].[24]

Lack of cultural awareness leads to distorted Christian living and ministry. Believers who live in individualistic cultures such as the United States are blind to the importance of being in deep community and placing themselves under spiritual accountability and discipline. This is why many church hoppers attend a variety of churches and don't join or fully enter any of them. American Christians see church membership as optional. They take a nonbiblical feature of American culture and bring it into their Christian life. On the other hand, Christians in more authoritarian and patriarchal cultures often are blind to what the Bible says about freedom of conscience and the grace-related aspects of Christianity. Instead, their leaders stress duty and are heavyhanded rather than eager to follow Jesus' words that "if anyone wants to be first, he must be the very last, and the servant of all" (Mark 9:35).

An inability to see one's own enculturation has other results. One of the most basic mistakes ministers make is to regurgitate the methods and programs that have personally influenced them. After experiencing the impact of a ministry in one part of the world, they take up the programs and methods of that ministry and reproduce them elsewhere virtually unchanged. If they have been moved by a ministry that has forty-five-minute verse-by-verse expository sermons, a particular kind of singing, or a specific order and length to the services, they reproduce it down to the smallest detail. Without realizing it, they become method driven and program driven rather than theologically driven. They are contextualizing their ministry expression to themselves, not to the people they want to reach.

> If we never deliberately think through ways to rightly contextualize gospel ministry to a new culture, we will unconsciously be deeply contextualized to some other culture.

I have been moved to see how churches and ministries around the world have looked at what we do at Redeemer Presbyterian Church and how they have expressed their appreciation and have sought to learn from this ministry. But I have been disappointed to visit some congregations that have imitated our programs — even our bulletins — and haven't grasped the underlying theological principles that animate us. In other words, they haven't done the hard work of contextualization, reflecting on their own cultural situation and perspective to seek to better communicate the gospel to their own context. They have also failed to spend time reflecting on what they see in Redeemer and how *we* have adapted our ministry to an urban U.S. culture.

Everyone contextualizes — but few think much about how they are doing it. We should not only contextualize but also think about *how* we do it. We must make our contextualization processes visible, and then intentional, to ourselves and to others.

1. This chapter defines contextualization as "giving people *the Bible's answers*, which they may not at all want to hear, *to questions about life* that people in their particular time and place are asking, *in language and forms* they can comprehend, and *through appeals and arguments* with force they can feel, even if they reject them." Unpack the four parts of this definition. Which of these elements of contextualization do you tend to do best? Which do you tend to skip or overlook?

2. Evangelicals often try to defend contextualization by arguing that it is about adapting the less essential parts of Christianity and that syncretism and compromise occur when "the critical and basic elements" of the gospel are lost. In this view, contextualization involves keeping the essentials while flexing on the nonessentials. What is the danger of this approach, according to this chapter?

3. Keller writes, "There is no universal presentation of the gospel for all people." What do you think is meant by this statement? Do you agree or disagree?

4. D. A. Carson is quoted as stating that "no truth which human beings may articulate can ever be articulated in a culture-transcending way." What distinctive values or biases have you learned through your own cultural formation (family, hometown, nation, race, church, etc.) that affect your communication of truth? Which biblical themes are you most tempted to edit out? How did you become aware of these biases?

5. Keller writes, "One of the most basic mistakes ministers make is to regurgitate the methods and programs that have personally influenced them. After experiencing the impact of a ministry in one part of the world, they take up the programs and methods of that ministry and reproduce them elsewhere virtually unchanged ... They are contextualizing their ministry expression to themselves, not to the people they want to reach." How have you seen this mistake made in ministry? What do you need to do to begin intentionally contextualizing?

CHAPTER 7 — INTENTIONAL CONTEXTUALIZATION *(pages 89–98)*

1. See www.redeemercitytocity.com.
2. Today, by God's grace, this story is changing, and we see a vibrant movement of new churches in the city.
3. This part of the book that focuses on contextualization is really a bridge between the domains of Gospel and City. It contains significant material on the character of the gospel as well as on the nature of the culture we are trying to reach with the gospel. Why not place it in the section on Gospel? We chose to include it in City because in the end this material is more about what we *do* with the gospel than about what the gospel *is* in itself.
4. In scholarly discussions of contextualization, many words have been infused with technical meaning by various writers. So the words *adaptation, indigenization, translation, contextualization,* and *praxis* are all given specific and distinct meanings (see A. Scott Moreau, "Evangelical Models of Contextualization," in *Local Theology for the Global Church: Principles for an Evangelical Approach to Contextualization,* ed. Matthew Cook et al. [Pasadena, Calif.: William Carey Library, 2010], 165 – 93). Often "adaptation" is used for a method of missiological engagement that is not as deep or thorough as "contextualization." This chapter, however, is written for pastors and practitioners. I write with some awareness of the scholarly debates, but I will not seek to observe the very fine distinctions some missiologists make between methods. Besides, as Moreau states on p. 172, there is no consensus among scholars about how each term is defined. Therefore, I will use the terms *adapt, translate,* and *contextualize* as synonyms here. I will refer to the widely accepted distinction between indigenization, syncretism, and contextualization below.
5. These cultural narratives can change in a society over time. Andrew Delbanco (*The Real American Dream: A Meditation on Hope* [New Haven, Conn.: Harvard University Press, 1999]) explains the three baseline cultural narratives of American society: "God" (seventeenth to the mid-eighteenth century), "Nation" (mid-eighteenth century to the twentieth), and now "Self." The first narrative is a religious one — religious freedom and faithfulness to God. It yielded to the idea of being "the greatest nation on earth." Today the main narrative of our culture is self-fulfillment. For another interesting way to analyze cultural narratives, see Leslie Stevenson, *Seven Theories of Human Nature* (New York: Oxford University Press, 1974).
6. The idea of cultural narrative is well expressed by Andrew Delbanco (*The Real American Dream,* 1 – 3): "Human beings need to organize the inchoate sensations amid which we pass our days — pain, desire, pleasure, fear — into a story. When that story leads somewhere and thereby helps us navigate through life, it gives us hope. And if such a sustaining narrative establishes itself over time in the minds of a substantial amount of people, we call it a culture." Cultural narratives are necessary to create meaning in life. "We must imagine some end to life that transcends our own tiny allotment of days and hours if we are to keep at bay the 'dim, back-of-the-mind suspicion that one may be adrift in an absurd world' ... [We must overcome] the lurking suspicion that all our getting and spending amounts to nothing more than fidgeting while we wait for death."
7. Barney's ideas are discussed in David J. Hesselgrave, *Planting Churches Cross-Culturally: North America and Beyond,* 2nd ed. (Grand Rapids: Baker, 2000), 145; see Bruce J. Nicholls, *Contextualization: A Theology of Gospel and Culture* (Downers Grove, Ill.: InterVarsity, 1979), 11 – 12.
8. Nicholls (*Contextualization,* 11 – 12) writes, "Perhaps a better model would be a sphere of which each segment is in proximity to the others, or again of a pyramid with the worldview as the unseen base, and values, institutions, and observable behavior as the three sides each interacting with the other." But the pyramid model may still not be dynamic enough. It implies that changes in behavior, values, and institutions can interact with one another but cannot shape the underlying worldview.
9. David Wells, "The Painful Transition from Theoria to Praxis," in *Evangelicalism and Modern America,* ed. George Marsden (Grand Rapids: Eerdmans, 1984), 90. Compare this with Richard Lints's definition: "By 'contextualization of the gospel' I mean the manner in which the expression of the biblical message is shaped in and by the native conceptuality of a given culture" (*The Fabric of Theology: A Prolegomena to Evangelical Theology* [Grand Rapids: Eerdmans, 1991], 101 n.19).
10. Ray Wheeler, "The Legacy of Shoki Coe," *International Bulletin of Missionary Research* 26.2 (April 2002): 78.
11. Ibid.
12. Nicholls (*Contextualization,* 26 – 28) gives two examples of contextualization done by theologians in the ecumenical movement of the 1970s.
13. James D. Hunter, *Before the Shooting Begins* (New York: Free Press, 2007), 202.
14. Craig Blomberg, "We Contextualize More Than We Realize," in *Local Theology for the Global Church,* ed. Matthew Cook et al. (Pasadena, Calif.: William Carey Library, 2010), 37, n.2.
15. J. Gresham Machen, *Christianity and Liberalism,* new ed. (1923; Grand Rapids: Eerdmans, 2009) 5 – 6.
16. Ibid., 2.
17. Ibid., 121.

18. Natee Tanchanpongs, "Developing a Palate for Authentic Theology," in *Local Theology for the Global Church*, ed. Matthew Cook et al. (Pasadena, Calif.: William Carey Library, 2010]), 110. Tanchanpongs makes an excellent case that personal sanctification should be one of the tests of whether we have moved from contextualization into syncretism. Syncretism nullifies some part of biblical teaching in order to reshape Christianity into the image of a particular culture. The result of religious syncretism can be seen in the lives of the people who believe it. Syncretism does not produce people whose lives match the descriptions of Christian character — "the fruit of the Spirit" — or Christian behavior in the Bible.

19. Harvie Conn (*Eternal Word and Changing Worlds: Theology, Anthropology, and Mission in Trialogue* [Grand Rapids: Zondervan, 1984], 176 – 78, 184 – 90, 194 – 95) makes this point.

20. D. A. Carson, "Maintaining Scientific and Christian Truths in a Postmodern World," *Science & Christian Belief* 14.2 (October 2002): 107 – 22, www.scienceandchristianbelief.org/articles/carson.pdf (accessed January 13, 2012).

21. For a full essay making this argument from a conservative, evangelical point of view, see Craig Blomberg, "We Contextualize More Than We Realize," in *Local Theology for the Global Church*.

22. Ibid., 42.

23. For example, J. Gresham Machen, who founded Westminster Seminary, followed B. B. Warfield and others at Princeton Seminary in their approach to defending the faith through the use of rational proofs and historical evidences. Cornelius Van Til and other younger faculty at Westminster later made a sharp critique of this use of reason in apologetics, arguing that the Warfield/Machen approach gave too much authority to unaided human reason and therefore was unwittingly being too influenced by the Enlightenment. More recent scholarship by Mark Noll and others has brought to light how much old Princeton was shaped by the Scottish Enlightenment and "common sense realism." In summary, Machen was criticized by some of his own successors as being too adapted to the rationalism of the Enlightenment, and there is some warrant for that charge. Some blindness to one's own culture is inevitable, but it may also be that if you spend a great deal of energy, as Machen did, combating illegitimate contextualization, you may be unconscious of the fact that you are doing it.

24. Nicholls, *Contextualization*, 31.

chapter 8

BALANCED CONTEXTUALIZATION

John Stott's book on preaching, *Between Two Worlds*, likens Christian communication to building a bridge from the Scriptures to the contemporary world.[1] Some sermons are like "a bridge to nowhere." They are grounded in solid study of the biblical text but never come down to earth on the other side. That is, they fail to connect the biblical truth to people's hearts and the issues of their lives. Other sermons are like bridges *from* nowhere. They reflect on contemporary issues, but the insights they bring to bear on modern problems and felt needs don't actually arise out of the biblical text. Proper contextualization is the act of bringing sound biblical doctrine all the way over the bridge by reexpressing it in terms coherent to a particular culture.

How do we do this? Scholars point out that any reader of the Bible who wants to understand it must go back and forth between two different horizons, between the two banks of the river in Stott's analogy — the biblical text and the reader's cultural context. Scripture has supreme authority, and so it cannot be wrong and does not need to be corrected. But a Christian communicator's understanding of the Bible may definitely be wrong — indeed, is always partly so — and therefore must always be open to being corrected. The same goes for the gospel communicator's understanding of the hearer's context, which can also benefit from more insight and correction.

Many Christians seeking to preach the gospel to a new culture are simply unwilling or unable to deal with this issue; they believe their task is simply to carry biblical doctrine over the bridge into the new culture. In other words, they see gospel communication as a one-way bridge. They do not like the idea that information must come over the bridge in the other direction. They don't see its importance, or they see this as a threat to the authority of Scrip-

ture. The problem with this idea of mission is that it assumes we who are on one side of the bridge already have an undistorted grasp of the gospel, and that our knowledge of the culture on the other side is not important. This view is blind to the truth that we are not only sinful but also finite, and therefore we cannot have clear and exhaustive knowledge of anything. We are largely oblivious to the power of culture to shape our understanding of things.[2]

So how can we guard the authority and integrity of Scripture and remain open to being corrected in our understanding of it? How can our message to the new culture be both faithful and fruitful? The answer is to allow some two-way traffic on the bridge.

When we approach the biblical text, we come with a "pre-understanding," a set of already established beliefs about the subjects addressed in the Bible. These beliefs are strong and deep, and many are tacit — that is, they are difficult to verbalize, formulate, or even recognize in oneself.[3] They come from a variety of voices we have listened to within our own culture. This does not mean we cannot or have not arrived at a sufficient and true understanding of biblical teaching. But it does mean the process is not a simple one, for our existing beliefs — many of them virtually unconscious — make it difficult for us to read Scripture rightly, to let it correct our thinking, and to carry it faithfully over the bridge to someone who needs it.

Because of our cultural blinders, we must not only *speak* to the people over the bridge; we must *listen* to them as well. We need to listen to what they are saying and take seriously their questions, their objections to what we are saying, and their hopes and aspirations. More often than not, this interaction with a new culture shows us many things taught in the Bible — things we either missed altogether or thought unimportant, possibly even ways in which we misread the Bible through the lens of our own cultural assumptions.

When I was a professor at Westminster Seminary in Philadelphia, many of my students had traveled from Korea to study in our school. I often led case study seminars that discussed real-life ministry situations with both Korean and Anglo-American students. Despite the fact that all the students shared the same conservative Reformed theology, they approached ministry in very different ways. One of the key differences had to do with how my Asian students wielded and regarded human authority. Koreans cede far more power to pastors and fathers, while American culture is much more egalitarian and democratic. The Korean students were able to point out to American students that there is quite a lot in the Bible about the authority of civil magistrates, parents, elders, and ministers, which Americans tend to ignore or screen out because our culture is deeply suspicious of institutions and authority. But while Korean students could point to texts such as Romans 13 and Hebrews 13:17, American students could point Asian colleagues to passages such as Matthew 20:24 – 28 and 1 Peter 5:1 – 4 (warning against leaders "lording it over" others) or Acts 4:19 and 5:29 (telling us we must not let human authority usurp God's) or the book of Revelation (in which human authority overreaches and becomes demonic).[4]

What was happening? Information was going back and forth over the bridge. Our interaction with a different culture leads us to ask the text questions we may never have asked it before and to see many things we didn't see clearly before. Entering into the text from a different perspective provides a point of triangulation that can help us to identify our own culturally bound presuppositions about the gospel. As a result we begin to see truths and insights in the Bible that were there all along, yet we had simply been blind to them. The questions of the new culture reveal to us as communicators that we have our own unique cultural blind spots.

To provide another example, secular people in Western culture are highly individualistic, which makes them sensitive to violations of human dignity on the basis of race. Their commitment to individual freedom leads to sensitivity to racial prejudice wherever it exists. Many Christians who have interacted with secularists have gone back to the Scriptures and found that the Bible speaks far

---

Interactions with different cultures help us lose our blinders and slowly but surely move to a more rounded biblical Christianity.

---

more about the evil of racism than they had thought. Christians are not correcting the Bible, but they are correcting their understanding of the Bible through humble interaction with nonbiblical philosophies. We know that God in his mercy sometimes gives pagans morally informed consciences (Romans 2), which sense real evil and truth even if their overall worldview has no basis for their insights.

One of the main ways our understanding of the Bible remains distorted is through what has been called "the canon within the canon." That is, we treat some parts of Scripture as more important and ignore or discard other parts of it. All Christians fall victim to some form of this, depending on our temperament, experience, and culture. D. A. Carson notes many instances of this. For example, the Bible tells us that God loves everyone in the world with his providential love, and yet it also teaches us that he loves the saved with his gracious love and is angry at the wicked.[5] Different cultures will respond to these biblical aspects of God's love differently. Members of Western cultures love the concept of God's love for all and recoil from the doctrine of God's wrath on evil. More traditional tribal cultures will have no problem with a God of judgment but will bristle at the idea that he loves all people groups equally. Each culture, then, will tend to highlight certain biblical teachings and downplay others, creating a mini-canon within the canon of Scripture. But if we stress the first biblical teaching (about God's universal, providential love) and play down the second (about God's judgment) — or vice versa — we have distorted the faith. Interactions with different cultures help us lose our blinders and slowly but surely move to a more rounded biblical Christianity.

Other examples abound. The Bible has much to say about wealth and poverty, and what it says is enormously varied and nuanced. In some places it is very positive about private property and riches — such as when God blesses Abraham, Job, and others with great wealth. Other Bible passages contain severe warnings about the dangers of money and make strong statements about the responsibility of God's people to promote justice and care for the poor. People typically ignore much of the teaching on one side and latch on to other parts, largely dependent on whether they live in prosperous conditions or in poor ones. Carson summarizes, "The name of the game is reductionism," that is, taming Scripture by not letting all of it speak to us.[6] Our sociocultural location makes us prone to flatten the teachings of Scripture, ignoring some parts and exaggerating others. When we interact with people from other cultures and social settings, we find our particular distortions being challenged. So while gospel communicators should seek to correct their *hearers'* cultural beliefs with the gospel, it is inevitable that contact with a new culture will also end up correcting the *communicators'* understanding of the gospel.

The bridge, then, must run in both directions. While the Bible itself cannot be corrected by non-Christian cultures, individual Christians — and their culturally conditioned understanding of the Bible — can and should be. There should be heavy traffic back and forth across the bridge. We speak and listen, and speak and listen, and speak again, each time doing so more biblically *and* more compellingly to the culture.

THE BRIDGE AND THE SPIRAL

The two-way bridge image is important. In hindsight, we now recognize that the original call for "contextualization" in the 1970s was essentially a call for a two-way bridge rather than the older,

CONTEXTUAL THEOLOGY AND HARVIE CONN

Much of my thinking in this section is derived from Harvie Conn's "Contextual Theology" course, available as a course syllabus and recordings of twenty lectures from the Westminster bookstore.[7] Conn relates how cultural anthropologists in the late nineteenth and early twentieth century began to see each culture as a complex set of practices, beliefs, and customs that helped a people group adapt to its environment.

This view was called "functionalism," and it was a Darwinian approach. Culture enabled people to survive in a particular environment. A culture was studied to determine how it functionally met people's psychological and social needs. The functionalist approach saw culture as a fairly mechanical entity, like a set of keys on a ring. You could remove a couple of pieces and put others in their place without changing the whole.

The functionalist approach to culture fit in well with the pietistic impulse of much of European Christianity. Pietism focuses on the inner individual experience and does not expect or ask how the experience of salvation will change the way we use our money, do our work, create our art, pursue our education, etc. In the indigenous church movement, personal salvation is offered without much thought as to how Christianity substantially changes a people's attitude toward power and powerlessness, art and commerce, cultural ritual and symbolism. Conn states, "The Christian faith is consigned to the realm of mind and spirit rather than to the broad stream of the history of society and civilization."

RECOMMENDED READINGS

See Richard Lints's excellent survey of the issues in *The Fabric of Theology* (pp. 101–16). Other important works that occupy various points of view across the middle of the contextualization spectrum include the following:

Bevans, Stephen B. *Models of Contextual Theology*, rev. ed. Maryknoll, N.Y.: Orbis, 1992.

Carson, D. A. *Biblical Interpretation and the Church: The Problem of Contextualization*. Carlisle, UK: Paternoster, 1984.

Conn, Harvie. *Eternal Word and Changing World*. Grand Rapids: Zondervan, 1984.

_____. "Contextualization: Where Do We Begin?" Pages 90–119 in *Evangelicals and Liberation*, ed. Carl Amerding. Phillipsburg, N.J.: Presbyterian & Reformed, 1977.

_____. "The Missionary Task of Theology: A Love/Hate Relationship." *Westminster Theological Journal* 45 (1983): 1–21.

_____. "Normativity, Relevance, and Relativity." Pages 185–210 in *Inerrancy and Hermeneutic*, ed. Harvie Conn. Grand Rapids: Baker, 1988.

Cook, Matthew et al., eds. *Local Theology for the Global Church: Principles for an Evangelical Approach to Contextualization*. Pasadena, Calif.: William Carey Library, 2010.

Cortez, Marc. "Context and Concept: Contextual Theology and the Nature of Theological Discourse." *Westminster Theological Journal* 67 (2005): 85–102.

_____. "Creation and Context: A Theological Framework for Contextual Theology." *Westminster Theological Journal* 67 (2005): 347–62.

Hesselgrave, David J., and Edward Rommen. *Contextualization: Meanings, Methods, and Models*. Pasadena, Calif.: William Carey Library, 1989.

one-way bridge of the "indigenous church" model. The older model did not encourage national Christian leaders to engage in deep theological reflection on how profoundly the gospel challenges culture. It assumed that Western Christianity was the true, undistorted, universal expression of the faith. Transporting it across the bridge required only a few minor adaptations, such as language translation and appropriating native music and dress. Harvie Conn argued that the indigenous model was based on a "functionalist" view of culture, which saw culture as a set of unrelated practices that helped a people group adapt to its environment. In this view of culture, you can slip out one piece of a culture (say, by replacing Hinduism with Christianity) and not expect the rest of the culture to change (such as the music, art, family structures, relationships between classes, and so on). This encouraged national Christians to engage in wholesale adoption of much of their indigenous culture, uncritically embracing it without examining it in light of the Scriptures. The indigenous church movement also failed by not challenging Western missionaries to recognize the culturally adapted nature of their own theology and practices.

But for all its benefits, the two-way bridge has limitations as a metaphor for explaining contextualization. In the end, evangelicals believe that the two sides of the bridge do not have equal authority — the Bible is supreme. Yes, our interaction with culture helps us adjust and change our understanding of the Bible for the better, but in the final analysis, the Bible must be seen as the ultimate authority over both the culture and our consciousness.[8]

If the Bible is instead seen as a fallible product of human culture, then we are locked in an endless interpretive circle that goes back and forth between our culture and the Bible. In this view, the Bible and culture are equally authoritative, which is to say equally relative. Thus we may use the Bible to correct a culture, but we can also use the culture to argue that parts of the Bible are now obsolete. This is why, for example, some mainline denominations use the Bible to denounce various forms of economic injustice in the United States, but at the same time they insist that what the Bible teaches about sex and gender is oppressive and dated. Following this pattern, in every generation and culture Christianity will be changing radically, often contradicting the teaching of the church in other centuries and lands. There is no way for us to increasingly come to grasp the truth.

But the deeper flaw in this "hermeneutical circle" approach is that it cannot exist in real life. Though we may say we make the Bible and culture equally authoritative, in the end we really are not doing so. If we state that what the Bible says here is true but what the Bible says over here is regressive and outdated, we have absolutized our culture and given it final authority over the Bible. Either the Bible has final authority and determines what in the culture is acceptable or unacceptable, or the culture has final authority over the Bible and determines what in the text is acceptable or unacceptable. So the image of the circle (or of a completely symmetrical two-way bridge) falls short. In the end the circle must be broken, and, fallen creatures that we are, we will always break it by privileging our own cultural biases.

For these reasons evangelicals have insisted that while contextualization must be a two-way process,

---

If we state that what the Bible says here is true but what the Bible says over here is regressive and outdated, we have absolutized our culture and given it final authority over the Bible.

---

the final authority of the Bible must be maintained.[9] This is why many have come now to speak of contextualization as a hermeneutical *spiral* rather than a circle.[10] If Scripture and culture are equally authoritative, the movement back and forth between text and context is an endless circle of change. But if Scripture is the supreme authority and the interaction with culture is for the purpose of understanding the text more accurately (not to bring it into line with the culture), then the text-context movement is a spiral, moving us toward better and better

Kraft, Charles. *Communication Theory for Christian Witness.* Nashville: Abingdon, 1983.

_____. *Anthropology for Christian Witness.* Maryknoll, N.Y.: Orbis, 1996.

Nicholls, Bruce J. *Contextualization: A Theology of Gospel and Culture.* Downers Grove, Ill.: InterVarsity, 1979.

Ott, Craig, and Harold Netland, eds. *Globalizing Theology: Belief and Practice in an Era of World Christianity.* Grand Rapids: Baker, 2006.

Sanneh, Lamin. *Translating the Message: The Missionary Impact on Culture.* Maryknoll, N.Y.: Orbis, 1989.

understanding of the Word of God and how it can be brought to bear on and communicated to a particular culture.[11]

Using the hermeneutical spiral, evangelicals have been seeking to avoid either extreme on a spectrum described by Richard Lints in his book *The Fabric of Theology.*[12] At one end of his spectrum is a cultural fundamentalism that believes we can read the Bible and express its theology in culture-free, universal terms; at the other end is a cultural relativism that holds "that the Scripture can have no other meaning than that which is permitted by the conceptuality of the present-day situation."[13] Evangelicals seek to work in the middle of this spectrum, insisting that while there are no universal, culture-free *expressions* of biblical teachings, the Bible nonetheless expresses absolute and universal truths. I would call this approach "balanced contextualization" because it avoids these two extremes as it rests, ultimately and firmly, on the fulcrum of scriptural authority.

Lints writes that despite the effort to find this middle ground of balanced contextualization, there is still a lack of consensus about many particulars, and of course many evangelicals tend to lean toward one side of the spectrum or the other. Some are moving more toward giving the culture more say in how the gospel is communicated, and this is driving others toward the other end of the spectrum, refusing to acknowledge how culturally influenced our theological formulations are. Since this is a book for practitioners, I will not delve further into a discussion of the more theoretical issues related to contextualization other than to say how important

it is to maintain the balance that Lints and many others speak of.

But it's important not only to maintain this balance, but to do so in a way that is shaped by the patterns and examples of Scripture. I want to look at three biblical foundations for doing contextualization and then use Paul's ministry to provide some examples and practical "ways and means" to go about it.

QUESTIONS FOR DISCUSSION AND REFLECTION

1. When you err in the way you contextualize the gospel, do you tend to create a "bridge to nowhere," or a "bridge from nowhere?" What makes you suspect this is true? What factors or beliefs contribute to this tendency?

2. Keller writes, "Our interaction with a different culture leads us to ask the text questions we may never have asked it before and to see many things we didn't see clearly before ... As a result we begin to see truths and insights in the Bible that were there all along, yet we had simply been blind to them." Have you ever experienced the benefit of interacting with another culture in this way? What blind spots has this experience revealed to you in your own understanding of the Bible and the gospel?

3. What is your "canon within the canon"? Take a few moments to jot down the themes of

Scripture to which you typically give special prominence. Which parts do you notice other Christians emphasizing that you do not? Do you see a pattern? What does this tell you about your spiritual or cultural blind spots?

4. Keller writes, "Evangelicals have been seeking to avoid either extreme on a spectrum ... At one end ... is a cultural fundamentalism that believes we can read the Bible and express its theology in culture-free, universal terms; at the other end is a cultural relativism that holds 'that the Scripture can have no other meaning than that which is permitted by the conceptuality of the present-day situation.'" What dangers are associated with each of these two extremes? What examples have you seen of either extreme? On which side of the spectrum do you tend to err?

CHAPTER 8 — BALANCED CONTEXTUALIZATION {pages 101-6}

1. John R. W. Stott, *Between Two Worlds: The Challenge of Preaching Today* (Grand Rapids: Eerdmans, 1982).
2. Bruce J. Nicholls (*Contextualization*, 8) writes, "Evangelical communicators have often underestimated the importance of cultural factors in communication ... Some have been unaware that terms such as *God, sin, incarnation, salvation,* and *heaven* convey [very] different images in the minds of the hearer from those of the messenger."
3. See Natee Tanchanpongs, "Developing a Palate for Authentic Theology," in *Local Theology for the Global Church*, ed. Matthew Cook et al. (Pasadena, Calif.: William Carey Library, 116ff) for a discussion of tacit knowledge, Michael Polanyi's proposals about the nature of it, and the relationship of tacit knowledge and belief to contextualization.
4. D. A. Carson (*Biblical Interpretation and the Church* [Carlisle, UK: Paternoster, 1984], 22 – 23) writes, "Suppose, for instance, that a pastor wishes to encourage people to accept his authority and to follow his leadership almost without question. This might arise because he is a demagogue; or it might arise because in his cultural setting people naturally reverence leaders and eschew iconoclasm. He can foster what he regards as healthy spirituality in this respect by citing passages such as Heb. 13:17 ... but he will probably be less inclined to cite 1 Pet. 5:11ff or Matt. 20:24 – 28 ... [He may be] very concerned to get across to his congregation the responsibility for the church to pay good teachers with 'double honor' ... while the church leaders themselves may be very exercised about those passages which insist that spiritual leaders must be free from greed and covetousness and love of material goods."
5. See Carson's detailed case for various biblical teachings on God's love in his *The Difficult Doctrine of the Love of God* (Downers Grove, Ill.: InterVarsity, 2000).
6. Carson, *Biblical Interpretation and the Church,* 23.
7. See www.wtsbooks.com.
8. It is true, of course, that the biblical authors themselves wrote out of a particular culture. In order to understand a biblical writer's intended meaning — and therefore what a particular biblical text is actually teaching — it is critical to understand the historical, linguistic, and cultural setting of both the writer and the original readers. However, this does not mean we can somehow discover some inner kernel of timeless truth in the Bible to hold on to while discarding many less "essential" teachings as culturally conditioned. An evangelical theology of Scripture acknowledges that the Bible is a thoroughly human book, each author being embedded in human culture, but it believes that God specifically chose each author's culture and even the very life circumstances so that God's overruling providence sovereignly determined every word to be written just as it was. See J. I. Packer, *"Fundamentalism" and the Word of God* (Leicester, UK: InterVarsity, 1958), ch. 4, "Scripture"; Nicholls, *Contextualization,* 45 – 52.
9. See John Stott and R. Coote, eds., *Down to Earth: Studies in Christianity and Culture* (Grand Rapids: Eerdmans, 1980), esp. the appendix "The Willowbank Report."
10. See Anthony Thiselton, *The Two Horizons: New Testament Hermeneutics and Philosophical Description* (Grand Rapids: Eerdmans, 1980), 104, 439; J. I. Packer, "Infallible Scripture and the Role of Hermeneutics," in *Scripture and Truth*, ed. D. A. Carson and John D. Woodbridge (Downers Grove, Ill.: InterVarsity, 1983), 348 – 49; Grant R. Osborne, *The Hermeneutical Spiral: A Comprehensive Introduction to Biblical Interpretation* (Downers Grove, Ill.: InterVarsity, 1997).
11. For the sake of clarity, we won't enter into the complex details of contextualization through a hermeneutical spiral. In reality, there are at least *two* spirals and *three* horizons. First, you must go back and forth between the biblical text and your own cultural setting in order to let the text correct your understanding (i.e., you must seek to fuse your own horizon of understanding with the horizon of understanding of the text). After that, you must bridge the gap between your own understanding of the truth (now instructed by the biblical text) and that of the people you are trying to reach (see D. A. Carson, "A Sketch of the Factors Determining Current Hermeneutical Debate in Cross-Cultural Contexts," in *Biblical Interpretation and the Church* (Carlisle, UK: Paternoster, 1984), 17.
12. Richard Lints, *The Fabric of Theology: A Prolegomenon to Evangelical Theology* (Grand Rapids: Eerdmans, 1993), 101 – 3.
13. Lints (*Fabric of Theology,* 102) quotes David Wells: "In the one understanding of contextualization, the revelatory trajectory moves only [one way] from authoritative [text] into contemporary culture [context]; in the other, the trajectory moves ... from text to context and from context to the text." In the first view, the communicator assumes he has no cultural involvement himself. He can simply read the text, understand it, and then bring it home to the new culture without adapting to the new culture at all. In the latter view, the context and text relate in an endless circle, which ultimately means we can never conclude what the text "really" says.

chapter 9

BIBLICAL CONTEXTUALIZATION

The Bible has much to say about human culture and how the gospel frames our relationship to it. I'll begin by looking at three key passages that have proved helpful to me in developing a biblical view of contextualization. The first, Romans 1 and 2, provides the *basis* for contextualization, namely, that the Bible takes a mixed view of culture, and while many elements of a culture can be affirmed, we must avoid uncritically accepting aspects of culture without first examining them in light of the gospel. The second passage, 1 Corinthians 9, speaks to our *motive* for contextualization, reminding us that we need to be flexible toward culture, ready to adapt what we can to communicate the gospel message. Third, in 1 Corinthians 1, the Bible gives us a basic *formula* for contextualization and shows us how to keep a balance between affirming and confronting culture.

RESTRAINING THE POWER OF SIN

An interesting example of common grace can be seen in Isaiah 45:1, where we read about Cyrus, a pagan king whom God anoints with his Spirit and chooses for world leadership. God's use of Cyrus is an example of why common grace is often seen in a culture as a nonsaving, restraining force in the world. By giving people, regardless of what they believe about God, a measure of wisdom, courage, insight, and goodness, the Spirit works to check the power and influence of sin in the world and keeps it from being as bad a place to live as it could be.

ROMANS 1 – 2 AND THE MIXED NATURE OF CULTURE

Every culture is a mixed bag of good and bad elements, and we should avoid rejecting certain aspects of a culture simply because they differ from our own. While this idea seems true at a commonsense level, does the Bible actually give a warrant for it? A study of Romans 1 and 2 suggests it does.

Every culture assumes a set of answers to the big questions: Why are we here? What are therefore the most important things in life? What is wrong with the world? What will put things right? And every society considers something of supreme worth; accordingly, they seek to bring their environment into service to it. No culture is neutral on these matters, and in this sense all cultural work can be said to be "covenantal" — we are all committed to something, even when those presuppositions and assumptions aren't consciously identified. Romans 1 and 2 get this point across by telling us that all have sinned and fall short of God's glory — that both Jews and Gentiles alike are lost. The pagan Gentiles may make sensuality an idol, but the Jews make moral righteousness an idol — like every culture, they look to something else to justify and save them rather than God.

Yet at the same time we see in Romans 1 and 2 that all human beings possess a primordial knowledge of God. In Romans 2:14 – 15, Paul states that God's law is written on the heart of every human being. All people have an innate sense of the rightness of honesty, justice, love, and the Golden Rule.[1] Because we are made in the image of God (Gen 1:26 – 28), all people know at some deep level that there is a God, that we are his creatures, and that we should serve him and are accountable to him. There is "general revelation" or "common grace" — a nonsaving knowledge and likeness of God that he grants to all those who bear his image — present in some way in every culture. This is not saving knowledge. It does not tell us about Jesus or what he has done for us, for that can only be known through the "special revelation" of the Bible. But a general understanding of God exists, for God reveals a measure of his truth and wisdom to all.

This is why Isaiah 28:23 – 29 can state that anyone who is skillful in agriculture, who brings forth an advancement in farming science, has been "instructed by God." One commentator writes about this text: "What appears as a discovery (the proper season and conditions for sowing, farm management, rotation of crops, etc.) is actually the Creator opening his book of creation and revealing his truth."[2] And farming is just one aspect of human culture. The development of new music, new technologies that advance our ability to travel by air or communicate with others, wise political leadership — all of these things are the result of God's opening his book of creation and teaching us (cf. Exod 31:2 – 11; Jas 1:17).

> Our stance toward every human culture should be one of critical enjoyment and an appropriate wariness.

Romans 1:18 – 25 gives a dynamic and balanced picture of how general revelation (or common grace) actually works in people's lives. We read that the truth is being suppressed (v. 18), but it continues to bear down on us. The NIV translates verse 20 as "Since the creation of the world God's invisible qualities ... have been clearly seen, being understood from what has been made, so men are without excuse." But the verbs *nooumena* ("are being understood") and *kathoratai* ("are being seen") are in the form of present passive participles. In other words, the reality of God's nature and our obligations to him are *continuously* present to us. General revelation is not just a set of innate ideas or static principles. It is the continuous and insistent pressure of God's truth on the consciousness of every human being.

Every human culture is an extremely complex mixture of brilliant truth, marred half-truths, and overt resistance to the truth. Every culture will have some idolatrous discourse within it. And yet every culture will have some witness to God's truth in it. God gives out good gifts of wisdom, talent, beauty, and skill completely without regard for merit. He casts them across a culture like seed, in order to enrich, brighten, and preserve the world. Without this understanding of culture, Christians will tend to think that they can live self-sufficiently, isolated from and unblessed by the contributions of those in the world. Without an appreciation for God's gracious display of his wisdom in the broader culture, Christians may struggle to understand why non-Christians often exceed Christians in moral practice, wisdom, and skill. The doctrine of sin means that as believers we are never as good as our right worldview should make us. At the same time, the doctrine of our creation in the image of God, and an understanding of common grace, remind us that nonbelievers are never as flawed as their false worldview should make them.

This suggests that our stance toward every human culture should be one of critical enjoyment and an appropriate wariness. Yes, we should enjoy the insights and the creativity of other peoples and cultures. We should recognize and celebrate expressions of justice, wisdom, truth, and beauty in every culture. But we approach every culture with awareness that it has been distorted by sin and in particular, the sin of idolatry. All cultures contain elements of darkness and light. We can't simplistically conclude that traditional, conservative cultures are biblical and that liberal, secular cultures are immoral and evil. Traditional cultures have their own idols, often elevating the family or ethnicity to an absolute value — leading to the evils of racism, tribalism, patriarchy and other forms of moralism and oppression. Liberal cultures elevate the individual and the principle of human freedom to an absolute value — leading to the erosion of family, community, of integrity in both business and sexual practices. Yet both the importance of the family *and* the worth and freedom of the individual are to be found at

A river is nature, a canal culture; a raw quartz is nature, an arrowhead culture; a moan is natural, a word cultural.

H. Richard Niebuhr, *Christ and Culture*

Culture is ... a normative order by which we comprehend ourselves, others, and the larger world and through which we order our experience. At the heart of culture is a system of norms and values ... but these norms and values are better understood as commanding truths so deeply embedded in our consciousness and in the habits of our lives that to question them is to question reality itself.

James D. Hunter, *Before the Shooting Begins*

Culture ... is any and all human effort and labor expended on the cosmos, to unearth its treasures and riches and bring them into ... service ... to something.

Henry Van Til, *The Calvinistic Concept of Culture*

the center of a biblical worldview. A coherent and biblical understanding of the gospel (Christians are saved but sinners); of the image of God (people are lost but indelibly reflect the nature of God); and of common grace (all people suppress the truth about God but they nonetheless "hear" and "know" it) — provides us with a nuanced understanding of culture. This gives us the basis for contextualization.

FIRST CORINTHIANS 9 AND FLEXIBILITY TOWARD CULTURE

First Corinthians 9 is very likely the first Bible passage many people think of when the topic of contextualization is considered, and it is an important one to consider:

Though I am free and belong to no man, I make myself a slave to everyone, to win as many as possible.

To the Jews I became like a Jew, to win the Jews. To those under the law I became like one under the law (though I myself am not under the law), so as to win those under the law. To those not having the law I became like one not having the law (though I am not free from God's law but am under Christ's law), so as to win those not having the law. To the weak I became weak, to win the weak. I have become all things to all men so that by all possible means I might save some. I do all this for the sake of the gospel, that I may share in its blessings.

1 Corinthians 9:19 – 23

Prior to this part of his letter, Paul speaks about the *skandalon* — stumbling block — and provides as a case study a conflict in the Corinthian church. Jewish Christians occasionally purchased meat after it had been used in idol ceremonies. Jews knew that idols were nonentities and therefore believed there was nothing wrong with eating the meat. Gentile Christians, however, "stumbled" at this. As former pagans, they could not eat such meat without feeling spiritually defiled (1 Cor 8:7), and to see Jewish brothers doing this distressed them and tempted some of them to do what they weren't able to do with a clear conscience.

Paul responds by saying that the Jews were right theologically — indeed the meat was harmless, and thus the Gentile believers with "weak" consciences were being controlled by a strictly cultural taboo (1 Cor 8:4 – 5). Nevertheless, Paul says that the Jewish believers (whom he called the "strong") should not exercise their cultural freedom in this situation. They should refrain from eating the meat to remove the merely cultural offense, the stumbling block (1 Cor 8:9 – 12), from their Gentile brothers and sisters. Cultural adaptation here is seen as an expression of love. Later, in 1 Corinthians 10:32 – 11:1, Paul lays this out in the form of a principle: "Do not cause anyone to stumble, whether Jews, Greeks or the church of God — even as I try to please everybody in every way. For I am not seeking my own good but the good of many, so that they may be saved. Follow my example, as I follow the example of Christ."

In areas where the Bible has left us free, when we carry out Christian ministry, we should be constantly engaged in cultural adaptation — refraining from certain attitudes or behaviors to remove unnecessary stumbling blocks from the paths of people with culturally framed perceptions. For example, we may need to refrain from particular music, clothing, foods, and other nonessential practices and concepts that could distract or repulse people from clearly perceiving the gospel. Similarly, where the Bible has not spoken, we must not elevate relative human cultural norms to make them absolutes. For example, we should not absolutize styles of dress or insist that rhythmic music is less pleasing to God than melodic music and must be excluded from worship.

D. A. Carson makes this observation about this section of 1 Corinthians:

> When in the last century Hudson Taylor, the founder of the China Inland Mission (now the Overseas Missionary Fellowship), started to wear his hair long and braided like Chinese men of the time and to put on their clothes and to eat their food, many of his fellow missionaries derided him. But Hudson Taylor had thought through what was essential to the gospel (and was therefore nonnegotiable) and what was a cultural form that was neither here nor there, and might in fact be an unnecessary barrier to the effective proclamation of the gospel...
>
> This is not to say that all cultural elements are morally neutral. Far from it. Every culture has good and bad elements in it... Yet in every culture it is important for the evangelist, church planter, and witnessing Christian to flex as far as possible, so that the gospel will not be made to appear unnecessarily alien at the merely cultural level.[3]

"Every culture has good and bad elements in it," writes Carson. If some aspect of a new culture does not compromise the gospel itself and makes you more accessible to others, there is no reason not to adapt to that element out of courtesy and love — even if it is not your preference. Otherwise, the gospel may, because of you, appear "unnecessarily alien." We must avoid turning off listeners because *we* are culturally offensive rather than the gospel. Seen in this way, sound contextualization is an expression of unselfishness. It is choosing in love not to privilege yourself or to exercise your full freedom as a Christian so people can hear and follow Christ's call.

On the other hand, our message and teaching must not eliminate the offense, the *skandalon*, of the cross (1 Cor 1:23). What the Bible has clearly and absolutely taught we cannot soft-pedal or discard. If we do, we have not adapted to the culture; we have capitulated to it. If we never speak to our relatively wealthy congregation about social justice — an implication of the gospel (Jas 1 – 2) — we eliminate a biblical *skandalon*. Proper contextualization means causing the *right* scandal — the one the gospel poses to all sinners — and removing all unnecessary ones. This is the motive for contextualization.

FIRST CORINTHIANS 1 AND THE BIBLICAL BALANCE

Though Romans 1 – 2 and 1 Corinthians 9 establish the basis and motive for contextualization, no single biblical text is more helpful on the subject of contextualization than 1 Corinthians 1:22 – 25, which provides the basic formula for doing contextualization:

> Jews demand miraculous signs and Greeks look for wisdom, but we preach Christ crucified: a stumbling block to Jews and foolishness to Gentiles, but to those whom God has called, both Jews and Greeks, Christ the power of God and the wisdom of God. For the foolishness of God is wiser than man's wisdom, and the weakness of God is stronger than man's strength.

Here Paul assumes the mixed nature of culture. He tells us that when he spoke to Greeks, he confronted their culture's idol of wisdom. The Greek culture put a high value on philosophy, intellectual attainment, and the arts. To the Greeks, a salvation that came not through teaching or reflection but through a crucified savior was pure foolishness. Jewish culture, on the other hand, put its highest value on something entirely different, which Paul describes with three synonyms — miraculous signs, power, and strength. Unlike the Greek culture, Jewish culture was highly practical, valuing actions and results. Rather than discursive thought, the Jewish culture valued getting things done through power and skill. To the Jews, a salvation that came through a crucifixion was weak and ineffective. A messiah should overthrow the Romans; he should *do* something. A suffering, weak savior made no sense at all to the Jews.

Notice, however, that while the gospel offended each culture in somewhat different ways, it also drew people to see Christ and his work in different ways. Greeks who were saved came to see that the cross was the ultimate *wisdom* — making it possible for God to be both just and the justifier of those who believe. And Jews who had been saved came to see that the cross was true *power*. It meant that our most powerful enemies — sin, guilt, and death itself — have been defeated.

It is striking, then, to see how Paul applies the gospel to confront and complete each society's baseline cultural narrative. He does this both negatively and positively. He confronts each culture for its idols, yet he positively highlights their aspirations and ultimate values. He uses the cross to challenge the intellectual hubris of the Greeks and the works-righteousness of the Jews. But he also affirms their most basic collective longings, showing that Christ alone is the true wisdom the Greeks have looked for and is the true righteousness that the Jews have sought. Paul's approach to culture, then, is neither completely confrontational *nor* totally affirming. He does not simply rail against Greek pride in intellect and Jewish pride in power; instead he shows them that the *ways* they are pursuing these good things are ultimately self-defeating. He reveals the fatal contradictions and underlying idolatry within their cultures and then points them to the resolution that can only be found in Christ. This is the basic formula for contextualization. We will now examine how this formula is fleshed out in Paul's actual ministry practice.

PAUL'S SPEECHES IN ACTS

We have looked at the need to approach contextualization with an awareness of our own cultural presuppositions, those assumptions we make about the Bible and its message that we are unable to see until we are exposed to the questions another culture is asking of the Scriptures. We have also sought to establish some necessary biblical foundations, recognizing the mixed nature of every culture — that there are good and bad elements in every

culture — while still affirming the need to adapt the message of the Bible to a specific cultural context. Paul gives a basis for contextualization in Romans 1 – 2, a motive for contextualizing in 1 Corinthians 9, and a basic formula for contextualization in 1 Corinthians 1. Yet it is in his speeches in the book of Acts that we actually see him engaged in the *work* of contextualization, communicating the gospel to different people groups.

We immediately notice that Paul is able to adapt his message to communicate with a variety of people from very different backgrounds. In Acts 13:13 – 43, while in Antioch, Paul speaks to an audience of **Bible believers** — Jews, Gentile proselytes, and "God-fearers" (Gentiles who believed the Bible and met in synagogues but who had not been circumcised). Then, at Lystra, in Acts 14:6 – 16, Paul addresses a crowd of **peasant polytheists**, uneducated folk who still believed in the old gods. Next, while visiting Athens, in Acts 17:16 – 34, Paul speaks to **sophisticated pagans** who had largely abandoned belief in literal gods, instead holding to a variety of philosophical views (such as Stoicism and Epicureanism). In Acts 20:16 – 38, at Miletus, we

---

Paul applies the gospel to confront and complete each society's baseline cultural narrative.

---

see Paul delivering a farewell sermon to **Christian elders**, while in Acts 21:27 – 22:22, in Jerusalem, he speaks to a **hostile Jewish mob**. Finally in Acts 24 – 26, in Caesarea, Paul addresses Felix, Festus, and Herod Agrippa — **governing elites** with mixed cultural backgrounds and knowledge of both Judaism and paganism.

When reading these addresses, we are immediately struck by how Paul's gospel presentations differ markedly, depending on the culture of the listeners. What can we learn from them? Our conclusions must be drawn with great care. In every case, we must keep in mind that the biblical accounts of the speeches are fragmentary. In Acts 17, for example,

Paul is interrupted before he finishes his message. Nevertheless, with these cautions in mind, we can still detect some patterns in his public communication in Acts.[4]

First, let's take a look at the *differences* among the speeches. Paul's citation of authority varies with changing audiences. With Bible believers, he quotes Scripture and John the Baptist; with pagans he argues from general revelation and the greatness of creation. The biblical content in his presentation varies as well, depending on the audience. He changes the order in which various truths are introduced, as well as the emphasis he gives to different points of theology. With Jews and God-fearers, Paul spends little time on the doctrine of God and gets right to Christ. But with pagans, he concentrates most of his time on developing the concept of God. With Greeks and Romans, Paul goes to Christ's resurrection first — not the cross.

When it comes to speaking about sin, Paul is clear in his message to the Jews that the law cannot justify them, that moral effort cannot save them (Acts 13:39). In effect, Paul is saying to Bible believers, "You think you are good, but you *aren't* good enough!" However, his approach with a pagan audience is to urge them to turn from "worthless things" — idols — "to the living God," who is the true source of "joy" (Acts 14:15 – 17). In effect, Paul says, "You think you are free, but you are enslaved to dead idols." Paul varies his use of emotion and reason, his vocabulary, his introductions and conclusions, his figures of speech and illustrations, his identification of the audience's concerns, hopes, and needs. In every case, he adapts his gospel presentation to his hearers.[5]

Despite all these profound differences, the speeches show several important commonalities as well. David Peterson observes that while there is no standard "gospel presentation," it is assumed through the book of Acts that there is only one gospel for all peoples.[6] It is called "the good news about the Lord Jesus" (11:20), "the good news" (14:7, 21), "the message of salvation" (13:26), "the message of his grace" (14:3), "the message of the gospel" (15:7), "the gospel" (16:10), "the gospel of God's grace" (20:24), and "the word of his grace" (20:32). What do all the presentations have in common? What is the common core that Paul shares in his preaching?

In every gospel presentation, there is an *epistemological challenge*. People are being told that their understanding of God and ultimate reality is wrong. Jews are told that though they think they understand the God of the Bible, they have seriously misunderstood the Scriptures. Gentiles are told that though they think they understand the world, they have seriously misread creation and their instincts. There is only one true God who has created all things. Both audiences are told about a God who is powerful, yet good (Acts 13:16 – 22; 14:17).

There is also a *personal challenge* regarding sin and a depiction of the listeners' fallen condition. Jews are trying to obey the law (Acts 13:39) and pagans are giving themselves to idols and gods that cannot satisfy (14:15). One group is trapped by works-righteousness, the other by a more conventional idolatry. Both audiences are trying to save themselves, and both are failing.

Then there is a *proclamation of Christ* as the answer and solution to their sin. As David Peterson states, "The messianic kingship of Jesus and its implications remains the core of the message to pagan audiences, though the terminology and approach are very different from the preaching to Jews or Gentiles who were familiar with the Jewish Scriptures."[7] With pagans, Paul emphasizes the resurrection to prove that Jesus is the divine Savior come into the world, the only true King. With Jews, Paul demonstrates that the covenant promises are actually fulfilled in a suffering Messiah (cf. Luke 24:25 – 26). So both Jew and Gentile are told to turn from their schemes of performance because God has broken into history to accomplish our salvation.

In summary, there is truth about God ("you think you know who God is, but you do not"), truth about sin and our need for salvation ("you are trying to save yourself, but you cannot"), truth about Jesus ("he is the messianic King who comes to accomplish your salvation for you"), and a call to respond to these truths by repenting and believing in him.[8] These speeches of Paul give us a strong biblical case for engaging in careful contextualization. They remind us that there is no universal, culture-free formulation of the gospel for everyone. The Scriptures show numerous instances when gospel truths are brought out in different orders, argued for using different premises, and applied to hearts in distinctive ways. It is clear that Paul does not feel an obligation to give the whole gospel picture to his audience in one sitting. He puts the pagan Gentiles on a very gradual ramp and works to establish foundational principles without necessarily getting to the work of Christ right away. And yet, while these gospel truths are never expressed in the same way to all, it is clear they have the same content — the nature of God as just and loving, the state of our sin and lostness, the reality of Christ's accomplishment of salvation on our behalf, and the necessity of receiving that salvation by faith and through grace.

THE APPEALS OF THE BIBLE

Some years ago, I read a book based on Jesus' encounter with the rich young ruler. The book concluded that when we evangelize, we must always spend time "preaching the law for conviction," because Jesus in this passage takes pains to bring about a sense of guilt and need in this self-righteous, self-satisfied young man. The problem with the book's thesis is, of course, that this is not the only example of how Jesus evangelized someone. In John 4, with the woman at the well, Jesus spends very little time trying to bring her to a place of guilt and conviction of sin. He is considerably gentler and focuses not on the law but on his ability to satisfy spiritual thirst. (Jesus' behavior in John 4 can also be contrasted with his much more confrontational approach to Nicodemus in John 3.) To make any of these forms of persuasion *the* paradigm for gospel communication will lead to fruitlessness in ministry. We all tend to be blind to how much our own culture and temperament shape how we do gospel ministry, but careful attention to the remarkable diversity of gospel ministry in the Bible can broaden us.

People of a conservative temperament may want to stress judgment even more than the Bible itself does, while people of a liberal temperament may want to stress unconditional love more than the Bible does. Those of a rational bent need to see the importance of narrative, while those who love stories need to appreciate the extremely closely reasoned arguments of, say, Paul's letters. D. A. Carson has written an article that is a valuable resource for understanding the work of contextualization.[9] He argues that the biblical authors use a range of motivations when appealing to their readers to believe and obey the truth. They do not seek to persuade in just one way. As missiologists have pointed out, people of different temperaments and from different cultures reason differently. Some people are highly logical, others more intuitive, and others simply practical. In order to persuade people, you must adapt to these differences. Carson lists eight motivations to use when appealing to non-Christians to believe the gospel. I have combined and simplified his categories down to six:

1. **Sometimes the appeal is to come to God out of fear of judgment and death.** Hebrews 2:14 – 18 speaks about Christ delivering us from the bondage of the fear of death. In Hebrews 10:31, we are told it is a terrible thing to fall under the judgment of the living God.

2. **Sometimes the appeal is to come to God out of a desire for release from the burdens of guilt and shame.** Galatians 3:10 – 12 tells us we are under the curse of the law. Guilt is not only objective; it can also be a subjective inner burden on our consciences (Ps 51). If we feel we have failed others or even our own standards, we can feel a general sense of shame and low self-worth. The Bible offers relief from these weights.

3. **Sometimes the appeal is to come to God out of appreciation for the "attractiveness of truth."** Carson writes: "The truth can appear wonderful ... [they can] see its beauty and its compelling nature." In 1 Corinthians 1:18, Paul states that the gospel is foolishness to those who are perishing, but to those who are being

saved it is the power of God. Yet, immediately after this statement, Paul argues that the wisdom of the cross is the consummate wisdom. Paul is reasoning here, appealing to the mind. He is showing people the inconsistencies in their thinking (e.g., "your culture's wisdom is not wisdom by its own definition"). He holds up the truth for people to see its beauty and value, like a person holding up a diamond and calling for people to admire it.

4. **Sometimes the appeal is to come to God to satisfy unfulfilled existential longings.** To the woman at the well Jesus promised "living water" (John 4). This was obviously more than just eternal life — he was referring to an inner joy and satisfaction to be experienced now, something the woman had been seeking in men.

5. **Sometimes the appeal is to come to God for help with a problem.** There are many forms of what Carson calls "a despairing sense of need." He points to the woman with the hemorrhage (Matt 9:20 – 21), the two men with blindness (Matt 9:27), and many others who go to Jesus first for help with practical, immediate needs. Their heart language is, "I'm stuck; I'm out of solutions for my problems. I need help for this!" The Bible shows that Jesus does not hesitate to give that help, but he also helps them see their sin and their need for rescue from eternal judgment as well (see Mark 2:1 – 12; Luke 17:11 – 19).

6. **Lastly, the appeal is to come to God simply out of a desire to be loved.** The person of Christ as depicted in the Gospels is a compellingly attractive person. His humility, tenderness, wisdom, and especially his love and grace draw people like a magnet. Dick Lucas, longtime pastor at St Helen's Bishopsgate in London, has said that in the Bible God does not give us a watertight argument so much as a watertight *person* against whom, in the end, there can be no argument. There is an instinctive desire in all human beings to be loved. A clear depiction of Christ's love can attract people to want a relationship with him.

These are six ways that the biblical authors use to persuade people, and notice what a motley assortment they are. Some are what we might call "sticks," while others are "carrots." One is essentially logical ("attractiveness of the truth"), relying on thinking things out. Some are intuitive (the "attractiveness of Jesus" and "fulfillment of longings"), relying on narratives and stories that compel. Sometimes the need is short term ("a despairing sense of need"), while others want to escape judgment and hell in the long term — an equally practical concern!

In conclusion, Carson argues, "We do not have the right to choose only one of these motivations in people and to appeal to it restrictively." This addresses one of the greatest dangers for us as preachers and evangelists. Most of us come to Christ through one of these motivations, or we are part of a community of people who find one of these motivations to be persuasive. It is natural for us to exclusively use this motivation in our appeals to others. When expounding a particular text, we tend to use our "pet" motivation, even though the biblical author may not. This is a failure to be fully biblical in our preaching. And yet, Carson states, "On the other hand, we may have the right to emphasize one motivation more than others." Why? "In the same way that the structure and emphases of Paul's evangelistic addresses could change, depending on whether he was addressing biblically literate Jews and proselytes (Acts 13) or completely biblically illiterate pagans (Acts 17), so the particular motivations to which we appeal may vary according to our knowledge of our audience."[10] Here we see a strong biblical pattern of contextualization. In the long run, we must expose people to all that the Bible says. But, as Carson argues, it is right to lead with the passages and approaches that will be most effective in opening our audience to the message of the gospel.

THE GOSPEL AND CONTEXTUALIZATION

I believe that faithful contextualization is a direct implication of the gospel of salvation by grace alone through faith alone. Paul used the gospel of justification on Peter in Galatians 2:14 when he criticized Peter's failure to be culturally open to

Gentile believers. As we have seen, the gospel gives two impulses that lead us toward balanced, biblical contextualization. Religion ("I obey — therefore I am accepted") leads to pride if we are living up to standards, or to inferiority if we are failing to live up to standards. But the gospel ("I am accepted through Christ — therefore I obey") makes us both humble and confident at once. And these two attitudes are critical for doing faithful and sound contextualization. If we need the approval of the receiving culture too much (not enough gospel confidence), we will compromise in order to be liked. If we are too proudly rooted in any one culture (not enough gospel humility), we will be rigid and unable to adapt. Only the gospel gives us the balance we need.

The gospel makes us both humble and confident at once; these two attitudes are critical for doing faithful and sound contextualization.

A major reason the gospel is necessary for us to do contextualization is that in our default mode of self-justification we tend to turn neutral cultural traits into moral virtues. Some years ago, I performed a wedding in which the groom was from an Anglo culture and the bride from a Hispanic culture. At the hour the wedding was to begin, not only had the bride not arrived at the church; almost none of her family or friends of the family had arrived either. Not until forty-five minutes after the stated hour of the service did the bride and her family arrive at the church. The Anglo guests were filled with indignation about how rude, undisciplined, and insensitive this late arrival was. I heard some mutter, "No wonder those people can't ..." The Hispanic folks thought the Anglos were, as usual, rigid, uptight, and more oriented to goals and schedules than to relationships. What was happening? Each side was moralizing the time orientation of their particular culture.[11]

The gospel brings about great humility. A heart reoriented by a grasp of the gospel of grace does

not have the same need to get a leg up on everyone. Richard Lovelace writes the following:

> [Those] who are not secure in Christ cast about for spiritual life preservers with which to support their confidence, and in their frantic search they not only cling to the shreds of ability and righteousness they find in themselves, but they fix upon their race, their membership in a party, their familiar social and ecclesiastical patterns, and their culture as means of self-recommendation. The culture is put on as though it were armor against self-doubt, but it becomes a mental straitjacket which cleaves to the flesh and can never be removed except through comprehensive faith in the saving work of Christ. Once faith is exercised, a Christian is free to be enculturated, to wear his culture like a comfortable suit of clothes. He can shift to other cultural clothing temporarily if he wishes to do so, as Paul suggests in 1 Corinthians 9:19 – 23, and he is released to admire and appreciate the differing expressions of Christ shining out through other cultures.[12]

But it is not *only* the gospel that calls us to contextualization; a high view of the Bible does so as well. Why? If we believe in *sola scriptura*, that only the Bible has unquestioned authority over our lives, then at any place where the Bible leaves our consciences free we should be culturally flexible. Since the Bible never prescribes details on how to dress or on what kind of music to listen to, there is freedom to shape dress and music in such a way that both honors the biblical boundaries and themes and yet fits a culture.[13] To deny that much of our Christianity is culturally relative is to elevate human culture and tradition to a divine level and to dishonor Scripture.

Francis Schaeffer often spoke about the difference between biblically prescribed "form" and cultural "freedom": "Anything the New Testament does not command in regard to church form is a freedom to be under the leadership of the Holy Spirit for that particular time and place."[14] In the next chapter, we'll look at practical steps for engaging in active contextualization of the gospel message in a way that uses this freedom wisely. This involves a three-part process: *entering* the culture, *challenging* the culture, and *appealing* to the culture.

1. According to Romans 1 and 2, what is the basis for contextualization?

2. Keller writes, "Christians may struggle to understand why non-Christians often exceed Christians in moral practice, wisdom, and skill. The doctrine of sin means that as believers we are never as good as our right worldview should make us. At the same time the doctrine of our creation in the image of God, and an understanding of common grace, remind us that nonbelievers are never as flawed as their false worldview should make them." What does this understanding of common grace suggest about our stance toward the culture? How does this awareness provide balance to your engagement with the culture? What types of relationships, spiritual disciplines, readings, and exercises help you employ a balance of "critical enjoyment and an appropriate wariness"?

3. The formula for contextualization, as derived from 1 Corinthians 1, is defined as applying the gospel "to confront and complete each society's baseline cultural narrative." This must be done both negatively and positively, confronting each culture for its idols, while positively highlighting its aspirations and ultimate values. Name an idol in your own culture. How might Paul have exposed the futility of that idol while also affirming the God-given desires that led people to pursue it in the first place? How might he have persuaded his listeners that the true answer to their deepest desires can be found in Jesus?

4. This chapter summarizes six ways of making a biblical appeal to people to come to God:

   - out of fear of judgment and death
   - out of a desire for a release from the burdens of guilt and shame
   - out of appreciation for the "attractiveness" of truth
   - to satisfy unfulfilled existential longings
   - for help with a problem
   - simply out of a desire to be loved

   Which of the six ways of making appeals are most comfortable and natural for you? Which are most difficult? Why? What resources can help you become more adept at using all these appeals?

CHAPTER 9 — BIBLICAL CONTEXTUALIZATION {pages 108-17}

1. Francis Hutcheson, an eighteenth-century moral philosopher, uses a famous illustration to demonstrate this. He asks us to imagine that we hear of a man who discovers buried treasure in his backyard worth millions of dollars. But then we hear that he gives it all away to the poor. Even if we would never do so ourselves, and even if we swagger publicly that such an act is stupid, we cannot help but admire what was done. There is an indelible sense of the moral beauty of the act itself.

2. J. Alec Motyer, *The Prophecy of Isaiah* (Downers Grove, Ill.: InterVarsity, 1993), 235.

3. D. A. Carson, *The Cross and Christian Ministry: Leadership Lessons from 1 Corinthians* (Grand Rapids: Baker, 2004), 122. We have said we cannot choose between essentials and nonessentials in Scripture. However, in a culture there are things that do not directly contradict Scripture and therefore are neither forbidden nor commanded by the Bible. Carson is saying that, in general, the Christian in mission should adopt such cultural features to avoid making gospel communication unnecessarily strange.

4. See David G. Peterson, *The Acts of the Apostles* (Pillar Commentary on the New Testament; Grand Rapids: Eerdmans, 2009), 40; see also Jay E. Adams, *Audience Adaptations in the Sermons and Speeches of Paul* (Nutley, N.J.: Presbyterian & Reformed, 1976), esp. 61–64.

5. See Adams, *Audience Adaptations*, esp. 61–64.

6. Peterson, *Acts of the Apostles*, 44.

7. Ibid.

8. Another helpful survey of the gospel presentations in Acts is found in John Stott, *The Message of Acts* (Bible Speaks Today; Downers Grove, Ill.: InterVarsity, 1994), 79–81. Stott seems to be looking more at the speeches of Peter early in the book. Peter does not address pagan audiences; nevertheless, Stott (p. 81) comes up with a gospel outline similar to the one we discern in Paul: "Here, then, is a fourfold message. Two events (Christ's death and resurrection), as attested by two witnesses (the Bible and historical witnesses to resurrection), on the basis of which God makes two promises (forgiveness and the Spirit), on two conditions (repentance and faith) … We have no liberty to amputate this apostolic gospel."

9. D. A. Carson, "Pastoral Penseés: Motivations to Appeal to in Our Hearers When We Preach for Conversion," *Themelios* 35.2 (July 2010): 258–64, www.thegospelcoalition.org/publications/35–2/ (accessed January 19, 2012).

10. Carson's final point is important: "All of the biblically sanctioned motivations for pursuing God, for pursuing Christ, say complementary things about God himself, such that failure to cover the sweep of motivations ultimately results in diminishing God." As we have seen in this chapter, contextualization must roll out biblical truths in an order that is adapted to culture, but faithful gospel ministry must not hide from people any part of the whole counsel of God, lest the picture of God we give people be less than true and full.

11. See Sherwood G. Lingenfelter and Marvin K. Mayers, *Ministering Cross-Culturally* (Grand Rapids: Baker, 2003), 37–50.

12. Richard F. Lovelace, *Dynamics of Spiritual Life* (Downers Grove, Ill.: InterVarsity, 1979), 198–99.

13. Biblical principles about thrift and modesty must be applied here, but we must also recognize that terms such as *modesty* and *respectful*, while not infinitely elastic, will look different in different cultures.

14. Francis Schaeffer, *The Church at the End of the Twentieth Century* (Downers Grove, Ill.: InterVarsity, 1970), 67.

ACTIVE CONTEXTUALIZATION

To illustrate what is needed for effective contextualization, let's turn to the world of demolition. Say you are building a highway and want to remove a giant boulder. First, you drill a small shaft down into the center of the rock. Then you put explosives down the shaft into the core of the stone and detonate them. If you drill the shaft but never ignite the blast, you obviously will never move the boulder. But the same is true if you only blast and fail to drill — putting the explosives directly against the surface of the rock. You will simply shear off the face of it, and the boulder will remain. All drilling with no blasting, or all blasting with no drilling, leads to failure. But if you do both of these, you will remove the rock.

To contextualize with balance and successfully reach people in a culture, we must *both* enter the culture sympathetically and respectfully (similar to drilling) *and* confront the culture where it contradicts biblical truth (similar to blasting). If we simply "blast" away — railing against the evils of culture — we are unlikely to gain a hearing among those we seek to reach. Nothing we say to them will gain traction; we will be written off and dismissed. We may feel virtuous for being bold, but we will have failed to honor the gospel by putting it in its most compelling form. On the other hand, if we simply "drill" — affirming and reflecting the culture and saying things that people find acceptable — we will rarely see anyone converted. In both cases, we will fail to "move the boulder." We may feel virtuous for being sensitive and open-minded, but we will have failed to honor the gospel by letting it speak pointedly and prophetically. It is only when we do our blasting on the basis of our drilling — when we challenge the culture's errors on the basis of something it (rightly) believes — that we will see the gospel having an impact on people.

For example, consider the biblical doctrine of "the priesthood of all believers." This doctrine fits well with our Western concept of the freedom and rights of the individual, and Western churches can easily "drill" into this cultural narrative by stressing the importance of lay ministry. However, it is also possible for our Western individualism to have an unhealthy influence on the church. We see this problem when church members refuse to respond to church discipline and claim that no one — not even church leaders — has the right to tell anyone else how to live *their* Christian life. This is an area where some "blasting" work must be done, confronting the individualism of contemporary Christianity with the truth of God's Word.

The need for both drilling and blasting — for both respectful affirmation of culture and confrontation of culture — makes it challenging to engage in the work of contextualization.[1] We want to avoid both *cultural captivity* (the refusal to adapt to new times and new cultures) — and *syncretism* (bringing unbiblical views and practices into our Christianity). While the danger of the former is becoming incomprehensible and irrelevant, the danger of the latter is losing our Christian identity and distinctiveness.

So how do we proceed? Most books and chapters on gospel contextualization are (to me) frustratingly impractical. Christian leaders are therefore (1) ignorant of the very idea of contextualization, (2) naively against it, or (3) for it but don't know how to do it. As a result, most contextualization happens passively, and in this way we enculturate the gospel in all sorts of unconscious and unfruitful ways. Instead we need to engage in a process I call practical, active contextualization because it requires us to be proactive, imaginative, and courageous at every step.

What are these steps? Active contextualization involves a three-part process: *entering* the culture, *challenging* the culture, and then *appealing* to the listeners. These three parts generally relate to one another as steps, but they overlap.[2] And as we proceed through these stages, we will bring to bear all that we have learned about contextualization so far. We must

---

Active contextualization involves a three-part process: entering the culture, challenging the culture, and then appealing to the listeners.

---

make our assumptions and processes intentional (as discussed in chapter 7); we must stay aware of the need for balance (as discussed in chapter 8); and we must be faithful to the biblical patterns of contextualization (as discussed in chapter 9).

ENTERING AND ADAPTING TO THE CULTURE

The first step in active contextualization is to understand and, as much as possible, identify with your listeners, the people you are seeking to reach. This begins with a diligent (and never-ending) effort to become as fluent in their social, linguistic, and cultural reality as possible. It involves learning to express people's hopes, objections, fears, and beliefs so well that they feel as though they could not express them better themselves. In Francis Schaeffer's address to the 1976 Lausanne Congress (published as *2 Contents, 2 Realities*), he began by stressing the importance of sound doctrine. But he immediately added that this doctrine must be communicated in the form of "honest answers to honest questions." Truth should not be simply declared into a vacuum — it must be delivered as a response to the questions of particular people, and this means understanding their culture. He writes the following: "The lordship of Christ covers the whole man. That includes his so-called spiritual things and his intellectual, his creative and cultural things … Christianity demands that we have enough compassion to learn the questions of our generation …

Answering questions is hard work … Begin to listen with compassion."[3]

This emphasis on listening to questions is a crucial aspect of contextualization. When a church writes a "confession of faith," it is not simply writing down what the Bible says. A confession is a series of answers from the Bible to a particular set of questions the church is asking of it. There are some questions that almost everyone will ask of the Scriptures, but no one person or group will ask *all* the questions that can honestly and profitably be asked. Every church's questions depend on its experience, social location, historical period, and cultural situation.

Missions professor Harvie Conn used to point out that missionaries from the United States and Europe directed the new Presbyterian churches of Korea to adopt the Westminster Confession as their statement of faith. The Westminster standards were formulated in seventeenth-century Britain, and it should not surprise us that this confession contains very little about how to regard our ancestors, parents, and grandparents. Yet issues relating to respect for one's family and to ancestor worship are paramount in Korean culture. Koreans who want to live Christian lives need to know what the Bible says about the family, but the framers of the Westminster Confession simply did not ask the Bible much about that subject. This confession does not go into the level of detail necessary for most Asian believers.[4]

If twentieth-century Koreans had written their own confession, they would have likely asked several questions that the seventeenth-century British did not. And in doing so, they would have learned much truth from the Bible that would have been practically invisible to the British. Instead, opined Conn, Koreans never went through that exercise in contextualization and have in many cases uncritically adopted their culture's views of authority and family without examining them in light of the Bible. This does not mean that Korean and Hispanic confessions, by being different, would contradict British and older confessions. There would certainly be significant areas of overlap because many of the questions human beings ask of the Bible are common questions we all ask. Nevertheless, different times and cultures will lead to a different range of questions. You can have different contextual confessions that are not contradictory — all of them being quite biblically sound.

HOW TO ENTER A CULTURE

So the first task of contextualization is to immerse yourself in the questions, hopes, and beliefs of the culture so you can give a biblical, gospel-centered response to its questions. When Paul began to speak to the philosophers in Athens, he began by saying he had carefully studied their objects of worship (Acts 17:23). We should do the same. There are several ways to become familiar with the questions and beliefs of a particular culture. One way is to get the point of view of outside experts, often academicians. Because I was "from the North" when I went to Hopewell, Virginia, to serve as a minister, it was important for me to read up on their cultural history, particularly the history of the Civil War and of the civil rights movement. Again, when I moved to New York City, I spent time reading several studies of the city's demographics, as well as novels such as *The Bonfire of the Vanities*, which captured the spirit of the age of Manhattan in the 1980s.

Ultimately, the most important source for learning will be the hours and hours spent in close relationships with people, listening to them carefully. In the earliest days of my ministry in New York City, I preached at both morning and evening services. New Yorkers are gregarious, and after each sermon many people came up to give frank opinions about what they had heard. I made appointments to see them to discuss things at greater length, and I would often talk to fifteen or twenty people a week who bombarded me with feedback about my preaching. Christians were bringing a lot of non-Christian friends, and I was able to hear reactions to my preaching from people across the spectrum, from mature Christians to skeptics.

As I listened, I heard four categories of responses. Some told me about things I had said that *confused* them; some shared something that had

LEARNING A CULTURE FROM THE INSIDE

Most people know what IQ is, and many speak of EQ (emotional intelligence quotient), but ministry leaders should also be characterized by CQ (cultural quotient). Cultural resourcefulness is not easily developed.

First, cultural intelligence requires that we have a deep understanding of our own culture and how it shapes us. One of the biggest barriers to effective contextualization is the invisibility of our own cultural assumptions. Sometimes this blindness makes us disdainful of other cultures, particularly when we come to new cultures that are not wholly alien. For example, if a person from rural Indiana moves to Mumbai, he expects the culture to be different; accordingly, he sees the differences and tries to adapt to them. However, if this same person moves to downtown Chicago and discovers he isn't fitting in, he is more likely to see Chicagoans as snobs. Instead of seeing the problem as cultural difference, he is likely to disdain urban people as arrogant. If we cannot see or too uncritically accept our own cultural biases, we will be less likely to contextualize well. The Bible states we are "aliens and strangers" in this world (Hebrews 11:13) and so must never be completely at home in any culture, including our home culture. The gospel and its critique of every culture can give us a detachment from our home culture that will enable us to better see its features in a way that others in it cannot.

So know your cultural influences. Here are some questions to explore: What institutions, schools, theologies, worldviews, regional cultures, artistic expressions, ministries, churches, and leaders have shaped me? What forms of ministry have shaped me? What can

I adapt, and what must I discard? Where do I need to "detox and rehabilitate" from these influences?

Second, cultural intelligence requires a heart shaped by the gospel — a heart secure enough that we are liberated from our culture's idolatries and from the need for the approval of the new culture. We must also have the humility to respect and learn from others who hold very different views.

Third, cultural intelligence requires us to immerse ourselves in a culture, coming to love and seeking to understand its members as much as possible. Keep these points in mind:

- We can embrace the disorientation we feel when entering into a culture and allow this discomfort to yield fruitful inquiry and a relentless quest to understand more about the culture.
- We need lots of feedback from peers and mentors to help us get the most from our experiences. Most of us do not naturally seek the necessary debriefing with others to enable the implications of our learning to lodge deeper in our being.
- We can increase the number of cultural moments and artifacts that we are taking in on a weekly basis. Take time to evaluate the implications of what we are learning and experiencing for our ministry.[5]

moved and helped them; some related things that had *offended* them. This last category I divided into two. I came to see that some of the things that bothered people were simple, irreducible, biblical, gospel truths. But I also realized that some of my statements upset people because I had assumed beliefs listeners did not have and failed to clarify or qualify statements at crucial points. In other words, I had not known enough about the beliefs, fears, and prejudices of the listeners to speak

carefully enough to them. I had offended them unnecessarily. As time went on, these meetings had a profound impact on my sermon preparation. As I studied the biblical text with the objections and questions of my new friends still ringing in my ears, I saw implications and applications of the text I hadn't seen before. I would think of a skeptic I had met with that week and say, "That is *exactly* what she was complaining about!" or "This answers his question very well."

Immersion in the pastoral needs of people in our community and continued involvement in evangelistic venues could not be more important. If we are deeply involved in the lives, questions, and concerns of the people, then when we study the Bible in order to preach it to them, we will see God's answers to their questions. If we are living in the culture and developing friendships with people, contextualization should be natural and organic. It will simply bubble up from the relationships in our lives and in our pastoral ministry.

WHAT TO LOOK FOR AS YOU ENTER A CULTURE

Contextualized communication adapts to the "conceptuality" of the hearers. That is, the illustrations we use in communication are taken from the people's social world; the emotion expressed is within their comfort range; the questions and issues addressed are highly relevant to them; the authorities cited are respected by them.[6] Contextualized gospel communication will adapt to a culture in the way it persuades, appeals, and reasons with people. Missiologist David Hesselgrave speaks of three basic ways to reason. He calls them conceptual (or "Western"), concrete relational (or "Chinese"), and intuitional (or "Indian").[7] I summarize his categories this way:

- **Conceptual.** People make decisions and arrive at convictions through analysis and logic. This involves syllogistic reasoning in which premises are established and then necessary conclusions are drawn.
- **Concrete relational.** People make decisions and arrive at convictions through relationships

and practice. These are people likely to believe what their community believes. They also are concerned with practical living. They will believe a principle only if they see "how it works."

- **Intuitional.** People make decisions and arrive at convictions through insight and experience. Intuitional people find stories and narratives more convincing and mind-changing than proving propositions through reasoning.

No one way of persuasion is inherently better than the others. All of them can lead to (or away from) the knowledge of God. The conceptual person may demand that we prove the existence of God; the intuitional person may refuse to make commitments that go against feelings; the practical person may not care much about truth and focus only on results. Yet the biblical authors use all of these appeals. If we have "entered" a culture, we will begin to discern which of these approaches and their many variants will have the most impact with the people we seek to reach. For example, on the whole, less educated people are more concrete and intuitional than educated people. Western people are more rational and conceptual than non-Western people.

If we are deeply involved in the lives, questions, and concerns of the people, then when we study the Bible in order to preach it to them, we will see God's answers to their questions.

But keep in mind that culture is far more complex than these simple distinctions imply. Even within these broad categories there are generational and regional differences.

The eighteenth-century pastor and scholar Jonathan Edwards spent most of his career preaching at the Congregational Church of Northampton, the most important town in western Massachusetts, and a church filled with many prominent people. But when he was turned out of the congregation, he went to Stockbridge, Massachusetts, on the American frontier, where he preached often to a congregation that included many Native Americans. Edwards's sermons changed dramatically. Of course, they changed in content — they became simpler. He made fewer points and labored at establishing basic theological concepts. But in addition, he changed his very way of reasoning. He used more stories, parables, and metaphors. He made more use of narrative and insight and less use of syllogistic reasoning. He preached more often on the accounts of Jesus' life instead of on the propositions of the Pauline epistles.[8]

To enter a culture, another main task is to discern its dominant worldviews or belief systems, because contextualized gospel ministry should affirm the beliefs of the culture wherever it can be done with integrity. When we enter a culture, we should be looking for two kinds of beliefs. The first are what I call "A" beliefs, which are beliefs people already hold that, because of God's common grace, roughly correspond to some parts of biblical teaching. Because of their "A" beliefs, people are predisposed to find plausible some of the Bible's teaching (which we may call "A" doctrines). However, we will also find "B" beliefs — what may be called "defeater" beliefs — beliefs of the culture that lead listeners to find some Christian doctrines implausible or overtly offensive. "B" beliefs contradict Christian truth directly at points we may call "B" doctrines.

In this first stage, it is important to identify the "A" beliefs — the wisdom and witness to the truth that God, by his common grace, has granted to the culture. Remember that "A" beliefs differ from culture to culture, so we will need to listen carefully. To use an obvious example, in Manhattan, what the Bible says about turning the other cheek is welcome (an "A" belief), but what it says about sexuality is resisted (a "B" belief). In the Middle East, we see the opposite — turning the other cheek seems unjust and impractical, but biblical prohibitions on sexuality make sense.

In our gospel communication, we enter the culture by pointing people to the overlapping beliefs they can easily affirm: *Do you see this in your culture? Do you see this well-known belief? The Bible says the same thing — even more strongly, even more clearly*. Paul does this in his speech in Athens when he quotes pagan poets in order to establish the creation and providence of God (Acts 17:28). Spend time building in your listeners' minds a respect for biblical wisdom in this way. A culture that puts a high value on family relationships and community should be shown that there is a strong biblical basis for the family. A culture that puts a high value on individual human rights and justice should be shown how the biblical doctrine of the image of God is the historical and logical foundation for human rights. One of the reasons we should take great care to affirm the "A" beliefs and doctrines is that they will become the premises, the jumping-off points, for challenging the culture.

Keep in mind that you never stop entering or identifying with a culture. It is not just a "stage" that you leave behind. Always show respect and empathy, even when you are challenging and critiquing, saying things such as, "I know many of you will find this disturbing." Show that you understand. Be the kind of person about whom people conclude that, even if they disagree with you, you are someone they can approach about such matters.

CHALLENGING AND CONFRONTING THE CULTURE

As we saw in the previous chapter, Paul's strategy was not simply to rail against the Greeks' love of intellect and the Jews' love of power, but to show them that they were pursuing those things in a self-defeating way. Valuing strength (as the Jews did) was a good thing, but without Christ, the pursuit of power leads to weakness, as David Foster Wallace so poignantly argued, while Christ's apparent weakness brings true power.[9] Paul does not simply dismiss a culture's aspirations; rather, he both affirms and confronts, revealing the inner contradictions in people's understanding. This is why it is so important to enter a culture before challenging it. Our criticism of the culture will have no power to persuade unless it is based on something that we can affirm in the beliefs and values of that culture. We can challenge some of the wrong things they believe from the foundation of those right things they believe. As we have said,

each culture includes some rough areas of overlap between its own beliefs and Christian beliefs. These Christian beliefs (the "A" doctrines) will make a lot of sense to members of the culture. Others will be quite offensive (the "B" doctrines).[10] It is important to learn how to distinguish a culture's "A" doctrines from its "B" doctrines because *knowing which are which provides the key to compelling confrontation*. This happens when we base our argument for "B" doctrines *directly on* the "A" doctrines.

Here is an illustration of what I mean. We all know that logs float and stones sink. But if you lash several logs together and then put the stones on top of the logs, you can get both the logs and stones across the river. If you try lashing the stones together and putting the logs on top, the stones will sink and the logs will scatter, and nothing will get across the river. You always float stones on logs, not the other way around.

Our criticism of the culture will have no power to persuade unless it is based on something that we can affirm in the beliefs and values of that culture.

In the same way, we need to "float" "B" doctrines on top of "A" doctrines. Every culture (including our own) can readily grasp part of the truth but not all of it. And we know that biblical truth, because it is from God, is coherent and *consistent* with itself. What we refer to as "A" and "B" doctrines are equally true and interdependent, and they follow from each other. The confrontation occurs because every culture is profoundly *inconsistent*, conforming to some biblical truths but not to others. If those in a particular culture hold certain "A" beliefs, they are inconsistent not to hold "B" beliefs because the Scriptures, as the revealed truth of God, are always consistent. These inconsistencies reveal the points where a culture is vulnerable to confrontation.

Paul reasons this way in Acts 17 when he speaks on Mars Hill. In verse 28, Paul quotes pagan sources that teach the idea that God is the source of all existence and life. Then in verse 29, he states this: "Therefore, since we are God's offspring, we should not think that the divine being is like gold or silver or stone — an image made by man's design and skill." Notice that Paul does not call him "the Lord" or talk of creation *ex nihilo* — for these would have highlighted the differences between the Bible and pagan beliefs. Instead, for the sake of argument, Paul stresses the similarity between his hearers' beliefs and the Bible's. But then he turns on them, arguing something like this: "If we have been fashioned by God, how can he be fashioned by us — and worshiped as we wish, through images and temples we devise?" Paul is showing them that their beliefs fail *on the basis of their own premises.* He challenges idolatry by showing that it is *inconsistent* with the pagans' own (and better) impulses about God. He tells them, essentially, "If you believe 'A' about God — and you are right — how can you believe in 'B'?" David Peterson in his Acts commentary concludes, "Paul's critique seems to go out of its way to find common ground with philosophers and poets, but his presuppositions are not drawn from Platonism or Stoicism but unambiguously from the Old Testament."[11]

This, then, is how we confront a culture and persuade faithfully. Our premises must be drawn wholly from the Bible, yet we will always find some things in a culture's beliefs that are roughly true, things on which we can build our critique. We will communicate something like this: "You see this 'A' belief you have? The Bible says the same thing — so we agree. However if 'A' is true, then why do you not believe 'B'? The Bible teaches 'B,' and if 'A' is true, then it is not right, fair, or consistent for you to reject 'B.' If you believe *this* — how can you not believe *that*?" We reveal inconsistencies in the cultural beliefs and assumptions about reality. *With the authority of the Bible we allow one part of the culture — along with the Bible — to critique another part.*[12] The persuasive force comes from basing our critique on something we can affirm within the culture.

GOD'S LOVE AND JUDGMENT

I once spoke to a missionary who worked among prostitutes in Korea some years ago. He found that

In general, Western societies make an idol out of individual freedom and embrace love and acceptance as attributes of God. Grace and forgiveness sound attractive, but sin and retributive judgment are difficult to accept.

In other cultures that make an idol of honor, the Christian idea of deep human depravity is self-evident, while the biblical concepts of free grace and forgiveness are seen as weakness or injustice. Retribution is critical, not only to maintain dignity, but also to keep order in society. People in these cultures are naturally more comfortable with the sovereignty, justice, and holiness of God.

A real-life example of this dynamic comes from a discussion with a Korean-American pastor, Dr. Stephen Um, in which we talked about a book that contended that people could not accept the idea of a God who judged and sent people to hell. Stephen responded that the statement was culturally narrow. He related how his grandfather struggled with Christianity. His grandfather had no objection to the idea of hell. He had seen firsthand how evil human beings could be, and he had no problem with a God who judged people for their actions. His real concern was with the concept of free grace — that forgiveness could be extended to someone regardless of what they had done in the past. His culture did not value this idea, and so the "A" doctrine to him (the acceptable belief) was not God's love but God's justice. Free grace was the doctrine he found objectionable.

No culture has the full set of prerequisite mental furniture necessary to receive the gospel, which tells us that while God is holy and must punish sin, at the same time he is loving and doesn't want to punish us for our sin, and so Christ died in our place, making him both just and the justifier of those who believe.

women in that culture simply could not accept the idea of God extending grace to them. Their self-loathing was too great. No matter how much the missionary showed them narratives of Jesus' forgiveness or passages about God's love and grace, he got nowhere. Finally, the missionary, who was a Presbyterian, came up with a radical idea. He decided to talk to these non-Christian Asian prostitutes about the doctrine of predestination.

No one denies there are biblical texts that talk about God predestining and electing people to believe in him, though there is plenty of controversy about what these passages exactly mean. In our Western, democratic, egalitarian culture, the idea of God's sovereignty and his control of all things is definitely a "B" doctrine. We don't like those parts of the Bible that talk about God being completely in charge of history, or those parts where he opens the hearts of those chosen for eternal life (Acts 13:48; 16:14). So when sharing the gospel, we avoid this doctrine at all costs. For most of us in the West, predestination is not just a "B" doctrine; it's a "C" doctrine!

This missionary, however, realized that this was not necessarily true in mid-twentieth-century Korea. So he told the prostitutes about a God who is a King. Kings, he said, have a sovereign right to act as they saw fit. They rule — that's just what kings do. And this great divine King chooses to select people out of the human race to serve him, simply because it is his sovereign will to do so. Therefore, his people are saved because of his royal will, not because of the quality of their lives or anything they have done.

This made sense to the women. They had no problem with idea of authority figures acting in this way — it seemed natural and right to them. But this also meant that when people were saved, it was not because of pedigree or virtue or effort, but because of the will of God (cf. John 1:13). Their acceptance of this belief opened up the possibility of understanding and accepting the belief in salvation by grace. They asked my missionary friend a question that a non-Christian in the West would never ask: "How can I know if I am chosen?" He answered that if as they heard the gospel they wanted to accept and believe it, this was a sign that the Holy Spirit was

working on their hearts and that God was seeking them. And some of them responded. The missionary had discerned the difference between "A" and "B" beliefs and had built one on top of the other: "If you believe in a sovereign God, why won't you believe that you can be saved by grace despite all that you've done?"

A classic example of this type of argument is found in C. S. Lewis's appeal to his British readers to accept the idea of a jealous, holy God:

If God is Love, he is, by definition, something more than mere kindness ... He has paid us the intolerable compliment of loving us, in the deepest, most tragic, most inexorable sense ...

When we fall in love with a woman, do we cease to care whether she is clean or dirty, fair or foul? Do we not rather, then, first begin to care? ...

In awful and surprising ways, we are the objects of His love. You asked for a loving God: you have one ... not a senile benevolence that drowsily wishes you to be happy in your own way, not the cold philanthropy of a conscientious magistrate ... but the consuming fire Himself, the Love that made the worlds, persistent as the artist's love for his work ... provident and venerable as a father's love for a child, jealous, inexorable, exacting as love between the sexes. How this should be, I do not know: it passes reason to explain why any creatures, not to say creatures such as we, should have a value so prodigious in their Creator's eyes. It is certainly a burden of glory not only beyond our deserts but also, except in rare moments of grace, beyond our desiring.[13]

Note how Lewis confronts his own culture. He builds on an "A" doctrine held by Western people, namely, that if there is a God, he is a God of love. Lewis reasons that if this God is truly loving, he will also get angry. He must oppose sin and anything that hurts his beloved. A person may say, "I believe in a God of love, not a God of wrath against sin." But Lewis reasons that if we have a truly loving God, we will *have to* believe in a God of wrath against sin.

SIN AS IDOLATRY

When I first began ministry in Manhattan, I encountered a cultural allergy to the Christian concept of sin. I found that I got the most traction with people, however, when I turned to the Bible's extensive teaching on idolatry. Sin, I explained, is building your life's meaning on any thing — even a very good thing — more than on God. Whatever else we build our life on will drive our passions and choices and end up enslaving us. I often referred to Augustine's description of sin in his *Confessions* as a disorder of love. So, for example, if we love our own reputation more than the truth, it's likely that we'll lie. Or if we love making money more than our family, we'll neglect our children for our career. Disordered love always leads to misery and breakdown. The only way to "reorder" our loves is to love God supremely.

This approach was very effective with young, secular professionals for two reasons. First, it neutralized (for the moment) the postmodern person's sensitivity to cultural diversity. The moment you say to them, "Sin is breaking God's law," they will retort, "Well, but different cultures and different times had different moral standards. Everyone has different ones!" Of course, postmodern people must eventually be challenged about their naive view of truth, but the concept of idolatry is a way to move forward and give them a convicting sense of their need for Christ before getting into these philosophical issues. The concept of idolatry helps them understand their own drivenness, fears, addictions, lack of integrity, envy of others, and resentment in properly theological terms. It tells them they have been looking to their careers and romances to save them, to give them something they should have been looking for only in God. Most important, this approach makes a great case that supports a "B" doctrine ("you are a sinner before God") on the basis of an acceptable "A" doctrine ("you were created to be free"). Former generations in Western society believed it was most important for someone to be a *good* person. Today in the West, our values have shifted, and our cultural narrative tells us it is most important to be a *free* person. The biblical theme of idolatry challenges contemporary people precisely at that point. It shows them that, paradoxically, if they don't serve God, they are not, and can never be, as free as they aspire to be.

From the Old Testament prophets to Paul (who did so in his speeches in Acts 17 – 20) and beyond, Christian theologians and commentators have often used the category of idolatry for cultural critique. For example, Alexis de Tocqueville's famous book on the United States noted how Americans believed that prosperity could bring deep happiness. But such a hope was an illusion, Tocqueville argued, because "the incomplete joys of this world will never satisfy [the human] heart."[14] As a result, he spoke of a "strange melancholy often haunting inhabitants of democracies in the midst of abundance."[15] This melancholy is, of course, the bitter fruit of idolatry that always leads to disappointment. False gods never give us what they promise.

We have already looked at David Foster Wallace's powerful insight: "In the day-to-day trenches of adult life, there is actually no such thing as atheism. There is no such thing as not worshiping. Everybody worships. The only choice we get is what to worship."[16] Wallace was not a Christian, and his testimony is more powerful for it. First he argues that the biblical teaching — that we are *homo religioso*, "man the worshiper" — is true. It is a powerful exposé. Most people think, "I am just working hard to be a good writer. I am just seeking to find someone to love me. I am working out so I can be a good steward of my body. I am working hard to accomplish something in politics or have a good career or just make a little money for security." But Wallace won't let us off the hook. He calls all that activity "worship," even though we won't admit it. Then he shows that worshiping some created thing rather than God leads to spiritual devastation: "The compelling reason for maybe choosing some sort of god or spiritual-type thing to worship ... is that pretty much anything else you worship will eat you alive."[17] Until we recognize that what we are doing is worship, we will be eaten alive by it. We will feel enslaved and unhappy, and we won't know why.

I have found that when we describe the things that drive our lives in terms of idolatry, postmodern people do not put up much resistance. They quickly and even sheepishly admit that this is exactly what they are doing. The biblical message of heart idolatry adapts the message of sin to their cultural sensibilities, but it's far from telling them what they want to hear. It convicts them and makes sin more personal. Making an idol out of something means giving it the *love* you should be giving to your Creator and Sustainer. Depicting sin as an act of misplaced love, not just a violation of law, is more compelling to many people in our culture today.

Of course, a complete biblical description of sin and grace must recognize our rebellion against the authority of God's law. But I've found that if people become convicted about their sin as idolatry and misdirected love, it is easier to show them that one of the effects of sin is living in denial about our hostility to God. Why is this? In some ways, idolatry is much like addiction (and the vernacular of addiction is very familiar to the present generation). We become ensnared by our spiritual idols in much the same way that people are snared by drink and drugs. Once we understand this, it is possible to hear the message of Romans 1 and accept that we live in a state of denial — that we repress or "hold down" the truth that we live in rebellion and bear hostility toward God. Communicating the concept of sin through the biblical teaching on idolatry is an effective way to convey the idea of spiritual blindness and rebellion to postmodern people.

Does the understanding of sin as idolatry remain true to the Pauline gospel of justification by faith alone? It does; in fact it provides a natural stepping-stone to get there. Luther, in his Large Catechism, shows that idolatry (violating the first commandment) is the very same thing as trusting something besides Jesus for our justification.[18] Idolatry, then, is always a failure to accept salvation by grace alone through faith in Christ alone. Any sermon that calls for repentance from idols and offers freedom through Christ can also call people to move from justification by works to justification by faith alone.

OTHER PRESSURE POINTS

What are other ways we can challenge our contemporary secular, pluralistic, Western culture? There are several other "pressure points" at which our culture in the West is vulnerable to challenge. Western culture longs for community and for justice — these are "A" beliefs — but the culture's own commitments and beliefs end up destroying these very precious things. Here are a few examples:

1. The commodification of sex. Thinkers have long discerned the difference between a consumer relationship, which is characteristic of the marketplace, and a covenantal relationship, which has historically been characteristic of personal relationships, particularly within the family. A consumer relationship is maintained only as long as the consumer gets goods and services at an acceptable price. There is no obligation for the consumer to stay in the relationship if it is not profitable. However, a covenantal relationship is based not on favorable conditions of value but on a loving commitment to the good of the other person and to the relationship itself. Social historians tell us that increasingly the values of the market are being applied to areas of human life traditionally seen as covenantal. People now feel free to sever family and relational ties if they are not emotionally fulfilling for them. *Commodification* is a technical term for a process by which social relationships are reduced to the terms of economic exchange.

And this brings us to the subject of sex. Traditionally, you did not have sex with someone who was not your spouse. Put another way, you didn't give your body to someone unless you committed your whole life to them (and they to you) and you both gave up your individual freedom to bind yourself in the covenant of marriage. Contemporary adults, however, want freedom, including sexual freedom. So they have sex with each other without committing their lives to one another, which typically leads to chronic loneliness and a sense of being used — and well it should. Sex in our culture is no longer something that unites people together in binding community; it is a commodity for exchange. But the Bible tells us that sex is designed by God, not as a means of self-gratification, but as a means of self-donation that creates stable human community. If the Christian sex ethic is propounded in this way, using the culture's "A" belief in the goodness of community, it can be very persuasive.[19]

2. The problem of human rights. Western society also has a powerful concern for justice and human rights. At the same time, a secular worldview is being promoted that tells us there is no God. We are here by accident and evolution, and there is no supernatural world or afterlife. Increasingly, thoughtful non-Christians admit these two ideas run on tracks that can never meet: There is a contradiction between a belief in human rights and a disbelief in God. The philosopher Jacques Derrida states, "Today the cornerstone of international law is the sacred ... the sacredness of man as your neighbor ... made by God ... In that sense, the concept of crime against humanity is a Christian concept and I think there would be no such thing in the law today without the Christian heritage."[20] Jean-Paul Sartre makes the same point in a negative form: "God does not exist, and ... it is necessary to draw the consequences of his absence right to the end ... There can no longer be any good *a priori*, since there is no infinite and perfect consciousness to think it ... Dostoevsky once wrote 'If God did not exist, everything would be permitted' ... Everything is indeed permitted if God does not exist."[21]

You see, if we are merely the product of evolution — the strong eating the weak — on what basis can we object to strong nations oppressing weak ones, or powerful people oppressing marginalized ones? This is completely *natural* to the world if this material world is all there is. And if people are not made in the image of God but are simply the accidental product of blind forces, why would human beings be more valuable than, say, rocks and trees? This is a significant pressure point today. Because young adults are particularly sensitive to injustice, it is possible and necessary to show them that human rights and justice make far more sense in a world made by God than in a world that is not made by God.[22]

3. The loss of cultural hope. In his book *The Real American Dream: A Meditation on Hope*, Columbia University scholar Andrew Delbanco

gives a history of what American culture has put its hope in over the years, under the headings "God," "Nation," and "Self." He observes that the original Americans believed that life had meaning and our nation had a purpose because we lived for the glory of God. This later changed to a narrative of scientific and moral progress — and particularly of democratic values — promoted in the world through the growth of the United States. However, today "hope has narrowed to the vanishing point of the self alone," so that America's history of hope is "one of diminution."[23] In the last part of his short book, Delbanco argues that we are now in a cultural crisis. To say that the meaning of life is mere self-fulfillment cannot give a society the resources necessary to create a cohesive, healthy culture. A narrative must give people a reason for sacrifice — for living and dying — and the self-fulfillment narrative cannot do it.

Delbanco quotes the philosopher Theodor Adorno, who "recognized that in modern culture the 'pretense of individualism ... increases in proportion to the liquidation of the individual' — by which he meant that the modern self tries to compensate with posturing and competitive self-display as it feels itself more and more cut off from anything substantial or enduring."[24]

A few pages later, Delbanco writes the following:

[Alexis de] Tocqueville's detection of a "strange melancholy in the midst of abundance" has a special salience today — because while we have gotten very good at deconstructing old stories (the religion that was the subject of my first chapter was one such story; the nationalism that was the subject of my second chapter was another), when it comes to telling new ones, we are blocked ... We live in an age of unprecedented wealth, but ... the ache for meaning goes unrelieved.[25]

In short, if we are allowed the absolute freedom to define and create ourselves, we become untethered from anything bigger or more enduring than ourselves. The result is meaninglessness, loss of moorings, and increasing hopelessness about the future. This is an enormous opening and opportunity for persuasive gospel communication to contemporary secular people.

APPEALING TO AND CONSOLING THE LISTENERS

As we have seen in 1 Corinthians 1:18 – 2:16, Paul's approach to his listeners was not simply to denounce their culture. He does not merely critique the Greek passion for intellect and the Jewish desire for practical power. Instead, he shows them that the ways they are pursuing these good things are ultimately self-defeating and then urges them to find ultimate fulfillment of their cultural aspirations in Jesus Christ. And so he ends on a positive note, a note of invitation and consolation, though it always comes with a call to repent and believe.[26]

Having entered a culture and challenged its idols, we should follow the apostle Paul in presenting Christ to our listeners as the ultimate source of what they have been seeking. When we enter a culture with care, we earn the ability to speak to it. Then, after we challenge a culture's belief framework, our listeners will feel destabilized. Now, in this final stage of contextualization, we can reestablish equilibrium. Having confronted, we now console, showing them that what they are looking for can only be found in Christ. Put another way, we show our listeners that the plotlines of their lives can only find a resolution, a "happy ending," in Jesus. *We must retell the culture's story in Jesus.*

This aspect of appeal and invitation should not be seen as a third stage cut off from the other stages of contextualization. All throughout our gospel communication, we are seeking to connect to our listeners' deepest desires. We are trying to heed the advice of Blaise Pascal, who, in one of his Pensées, wrote, "Men despise religion; they hate it and fear it is true. To remedy this, we must begin by showing that religion is not contrary to reason; that it is venerable, to inspire respect for it; then we must make it lovable, to make good men hope it is true; finally, we must prove it is true."[27]

How can we make our appeal? As we saw in chapter 2, the intercanonical themes uniting the Bible are richly diverse. They speak of sin and salvation, using the language of exile and homecoming; of temple, presence, and sacrifice; of covenant and faithfulness; of kingdom and victory. When we seek to communicate the gospel to a particular culture,

we will find that some of these themes resonate more deeply than others. Paul was able to speak to a wisdom-obsessed culture by using one of the great themes of the Bible, the wisdom of God as it comes to its climax in Jesus Christ (see 1 Cor 1:18 – 2:16). The Bible has enough diversity to enable us to connect its message to any baseline cultural narrative on the face of the earth.

ATONEMENT "GRAMMARS"

It is commonly said that the Bible contains several different "models" of atonement. I prefer to call these different "languages" or "grammars" by which the saving work of Christ on the cross is presented.

1. **The language of the battlefield.** Christ fought against the powers of sin and death for us. He defeated the powers of evil for us.
2. **The language of the marketplace.** Christ paid the ransom price, the purchase price, to buy us out of our indebtedness. He frees us from enslavement.
3. **The language of exile.** Christ was exiled and cast out of the community so we who deserve to be banished could be brought in. He brings us home.
4. **The language of the temple.** Christ is the sacrifice that purifies us and makes us acceptable to draw near to the holy God. He makes us clean and beautiful.
5. **The language of the law court.** Christ stands before the judge and takes the punishment we deserve. He removes our guilt and makes us righteous.

It is sometimes implied we can choose which of these models we prefer and ignore the others, but this is misleading. Each way of communicating the atonement reflects a piece of inspired Scripture, and each tells us great things about our salvation that the others do not bring out as clearly. Each will have special resonance with certain temperaments and cultures. People who are fighting oppression or even enslavement and long for freedom will be helped by the first two grammars (the battlefield and the marketplace). People seeking relief for guilt and a sense of shame will be especially moved by the last two — the temple and the law court. People who feel alienated, rootless, and rejected will find the exile grammar intensely engaging.

But perhaps the single most consoling and appealing theme is what theologian Roger Nicole has called the one, irreducible theme that runs through every single one of these models — the idea of *substitution*.[28] Dr. Nicole taught that, regardless of the

---

The single most consoling and appealing atonement theme is substitution.

---

grammar being used, the essence of the atonement is always Jesus acting as our substitute. Jesus fights the powers, pays the price, bears the exile, makes the sacrifice, and bears the punishment *for* us, in our place, on our behalf. In every grammar, Jesus does for us what we cannot do for ourselves. *He* accomplishes salvation; we do nothing at all. And therefore the substitutionary sacrifice of Jesus is at the heart of everything.

This act — giving one's life to save another — is the most compelling, attractive, and electrifying story line there is. J. K. Rowling, for example, could hardly end her Harry Potter series in any other way because it is the ultimate drama, the most moving ending possible. Lifting up the substitutionary sacrifice of Christ is the ultimate way to appeal to any culture, to attract them to him. The various ways of speaking about the atonement furnish us with wonderfully fitting ways of showing each culture how this atoning work of Jesus specifically solves its greatest problems and fulfills its greatest aspirations.

We live in the first era of history that considers happy endings to be works of inferior art. Modern critics insist that life is *not* like that — rather, it is full of brokenness, paradox, irony, and frustration. Steven Spielberg was denied Oscars until he stopped making movies with happy endings and directed *Schindler's List*. Yet people continue to flock to movies and read books that have fairy-tale endings. There are deep human longings that modern realistic fiction can never satisfy: to escape death and live forever; to hold communion with other personal beings like elves or aliens or angels; to find love that perfectly heals and from which we never part. Most of all, we want to see and, if possible, participate in the final triumph over evil in the world. People turn to fairy tales because they depict these desires coming true.

The gospel is by no means a sentimental view of life. In fact, the Bible has a far darker vision of reality than any secular critic. It tells us that Satan and his legions of demons are at work in the world. It tells us we are so deeply flawed and cruel we can't save ourselves without God's intervention. And yet the gospel has an astonishing message about these longings for love and death and triumph. First, the gospel *explains* them. Human beings have been made in the image of God, which means we were originally designed to know and experience all these things. We were created to live forever. Second, the gospel tells us that the resurrection of Jesus Christ is hard *proof* that all these things will come true again. If you believe in Jesus Christ, you will see and know escape from death, love without parting, and triumph over evil. You will talk to angels and supernatural

IT'S IN OUR BLOOD

Ajith Fernando, a Sri Lankan evangelist, communicates the idea of substitutionary atonement to his listeners by using an illustration:

Have you ever had an infected wound or sore? When you open it, what comes rolling out? Pus. And what is that? It is basically the collective corpses of white blood cells fighting the infection that have died so that you may live. Do you see? Substitutionary salvation is in your very blood.

beings. You will live forever. And why will we get eternal life? Because he was killed. We get eternal love because he was forsaken. We triumph over evil because he was tortured, murdered, and defeated. In the salvation of Jesus Christ, we learn that the happy ending we long for is not a fairy tale.

The gospel is the deepest consolation you can offer to the human heart. Once you have taken care to enter and have found the courage to challenge the world of your hearers, be sure to offer this consolation with the passion of one who has experienced it firsthand.

QUESTIONS FOR DISCUSSION AND REFLECTION

1. Keller writes, "The first task of contextualization is to immerse yourself in the questions, hopes, and beliefs of the culture so you can give a biblical, gospel-centered response to its questions." What are some ways you have found to read and study the culture around you? What questions is the culture asking? How has involvement in the pastoral needs of your community helped you to better understand the culture and people you seek to reach?

2. This chapter highlights three ways of reasoning: conceptual, concrete relational, and intuitional.

   - *Conceptual.* People make decisions and arrive at convictions through analysis and logic.
   - *Concrete relational.* People make decisions and arrive at convictions through relationships and practice.
   - *Intuitional.* People make decisions and arrive at convictions through insight and experience.

   Which of these three approaches resonates most with you? With the people you are trying to reach? If they are different, what can you do to bridge the gap?

3. Another task of contextualization is discerning the dominant worldviews and belief systems of a culture. Keller writes, "Contextualized gospel ministry should affirm the beliefs of the culture wherever it can be done with integrity." He identifies "A" beliefs, which "roughly correspond to some parts of biblical teaching," and "B" beliefs, which contradict Christian truth ("B" doctrines) and "lead listeners to find some Christian doctrines implausible or overtly offensive."

   Take a moment to identify a key "A" doctrine — a teaching from the Bible that would be generally accepted and affirmed by your target culture — and how it expresses itself in the culture through "A" beliefs. What is an example of a "B" belief in your culture, and what "B" doctrines does it conflict with directly?

4. Keller writes, "It is important to learn how to distinguish a culture's 'A' doctrines from its 'B' doctrines because *knowing which are which provides the key to compelling confrontation.* This happens when we base our argument for 'B' doctrines *directly on* the 'A' doctrines." Using the examples you discussed in the last question, how might you do this?

5. This chapter gives a summary of several cultural pressure points and atonement grammars as it concludes. Which of these pressure points and grammars are less familiar or natural to you, but worth investigating? How might adding them to your repertoire strengthen your effectiveness in mission?

CHAPTER 10 — ACTIVE CONTEXTUALIZATION *(pages 119–32)*

1. See David F. Wells, "An American Evangelical Theology: The Painful Transition from Theoria to Praxis," in *Evangelicalism and Modern America*, ed. George Marsden (Grand Rapids: Eerdmans, 1984), 90, 93. Wells writes, "Where is the line between involvement and disengagement, acceptance and denial, continuity and discontinuity, being 'in' the world and not 'of' the world? Contextualization is the process through which we find answers to these questions. The Word of God must be related to our own context … The preservation of its identity is necessary for Christian belief; its contemporary relevance is required if Christians are to be believable."

2. Richard Cunningham, director of University Colleges and Christian Fellowship (UCCF) in Great Britain, gives practical training on how to give an evangelistic talk. He advises that every speaker *identify, persuade, and invite* (Alex Banfield Hicks and Richard Cunningham, "Identification, Persuasion and Invitation," Christian Persuaders Podcast #1, www.bethinking.org/what-is-apologetics/introductory/identification-persuasion-and-invitation.htm [accessed January 20, 2012]). These three stages (though they overlap too much to be called true "stages") correspond closely to my three steps of *enter, challenge, and appeal*.

3. Francis Schaeffer, *2 Contents, 2 Realities* (Downers Grove, Ill.: InterVarsity, 1975), 17 – 18.

4. Of course the Westminster Confession and catechisms treat the commandment "Honor your father and mother," but the answers it draws from Scripture show it was not searching the text with ancestor worship in mind. The Confession tends to generalize the command to mean respect for all in authority, such as civil magistrates.

5. Thanks to Mark Reynolds for the ideas in this section.

6. In Acts 17:26 – 28, Paul quotes pagan poets. If you are speaking biblical truth to those who are skeptical of the Bible's authority, it is good to reinforce your points with supplemental, respected authorities. So, for example, if you are teaching what the Bible says about something, and (in our Western society) you have some empirical, scientific study that confirms the Bible's statement — use the study. It gradually strengthens the skeptical listener's trust in the Word. Contextualization includes learning which supplemental authorities are credible to the listeners.

7. See David J. Hesselgrave, *Communicating Christ Cross-Culturally* (Grand Rapids: Zondervan, 1978), 198 – 236.

8. See the sermons from this period, with illuminating commentary by the editor, in *The Works of Jonathan Edwards: Sermons and Discourses, 1743 – 1758*, vol. 25, ed. Wilson H. Kimnach (New Haven, Conn.: Yale University Press, 2010).

9. See ch. 1, p. 34.

10. I believe this principle is implied in 1 Peter 2:12, a striking verse that assumes the world will in some respects praise and admire Christian faith and practice and yet in other respects will hate and persecute it; see Miroslav Volf's article on 1 Peter, "Soft Difference," www.yale.edu/faith/resources/x_volf_difference.html (accessed January 20, 2012). I am not arguing that this verse proves the principle — a principle more readily seen in Paul's actual reasoning with listeners, as in Acts 17.

11. David G. Peterson, *The Acts of the Apostles* (Pillar New Testament Commentary; Grand Rapids: Eerdmans, 2009), 496.

12. Thanks to Rochelle L. Cathcart for this insight.

13. C. S. Lewis, *The Problem of Pain* (New York: Macmillan, 1973), 29, 34 – 35.

14. Alexis de Tocqueville, *Democracy in America* (New York: HarperCollins, 1988), 296.

15. Ibid., 538.

16. Emily Bobrow, "David Foster Wallace, in His Own Words" (taken from his 2005 commencement address at Kenyon College), http://moreintelligentlife.com/story/david-foster-wallace-in-his-own-words (accessed January 20, 2012).

17. Ibid. When Wallace says we should worship "some sort of god or spiritual-type thing," he then lists "JC or Allah, be it YHWH or the Wiccan Mother-Goddess, or the Four Noble Truths, or some inviolable set of ethical principles." So he is counseling religious pluralism with a vengeance! But just as Paul in Acts 17:28 was careful — in the early stage of his argument — to express commonality between pagan poets and God, it is possible to accept Wallace's description of the *problem* as sound (i.e., that we need to build our lives around something that transcends this world).

18. See Martin Luther's comments on the first commandment in his Large Catechism (Birmingham, Ala.: CreateSpace, 2011), 1 – 3.

19. For an in-depth treatment of this subject, see chs. 1 and 3 of my book *The Meaning of Marriage* (New York: Dutton, 2011), esp. 80 – 82.

20. Richard Kearny, moderator, "On Forgiveness: A Roundtable Discussion with Jacques Derrida," in *Questioning God*, ed. John Caputo, Mark Dooley, and Michael Scanlon (Bloomington, Ind.: Indiana University Press, 2001), 70.

21. Jean-Paul Sartre, "Existentialism Is a Humanism," in *Existentialism from Dostoyevsky to Sartre*, ed. Walter Kaufmann (New York: Meridian, 1989), 352 – 53, www.marxists.org/reference/archive/sartre/works/exist/sartre.htm (accessed January 20, 2012).
22. It can be argued that belief in human rights makes far more sense if there is a God than if there is not. Nicholas Wolterstorff makes this case in "Is a Secular Grounding of Human Rights Possible?" and "A Theistic Grounding of Human Rights," in *Justice: Rights and Wrongs* (Princeton, N.J.: Princeton University Press, 2008), chs. 15 – 16. See also Christian Smith, "Does Naturalism Warrant a Moral Belief in Universal Benevolence and Human Rights?" in *The Believing Primate: Scientific, Philosophical, and Theological Reflections on the Origin of Religion*, ed. Jeffrey Schloss and Michael Murray (New York: Oxford University Press, 2009), 292 – 317; Timothy Keller, *Generous Justice: How God's Grace Makes Us Just* (New York: Dutton, 2010), ch. 7; Timothy Keller, *The Reason for God: Belief in an Age of Skepticism* (New York: Dutton, 2008), ch. 9.
23. Andrew Delbanco, *The Real American Dream: A Meditation on Hope* (Cambridge, Mass.: Harvard University Press, 1999), 103.
24. Ibid., 103 – 4.
25. Ibid., 106 – 7.
26. Theologian Dan Strange writes that non-Christian systems of thought are both antithetical to, yet practically "parasitic" on, Christian truth. That is, they must affirm some aspects of reality, of God's truth, even when they resist other parts of his truth. Strange concludes that ultimately the gospel is the "subversive fulfillment" for non-Christian systems. That is, the gospel challenges their aspirations and yet in another sense fulfills them (see "Perilous Exchange, Precious Good News: A Reformed 'Subversive Fulfillment' Interpretation of Other Religions," in *Only One Way? Three Christian Responses on the Uniqueness of Christ in a Religiously Plural World*, Gavin D'Costa, Paul Knitter, and Daniel Strange [London: SCM Press, 2011], 93).
27. Blaise Pascal, *Pensées* (New York: Collier, 1910), 68, #187.
28. See Roger Nicole, "Postscript on Penal Substitution," in *The Glory of the Atonement*, ed. Charles E. Hill and Frank A. James III (Downers Grove, Ill.: InterVarsity, 2004), 445 – 52.

THE TENSION OF THE CITY

Many Christians today, especially in the United States, are indifferent or even hostile toward cities. Some think of them as a negative force that undermines belief and morality, while others see them as inconsequential to Christian mission and living. It may also be true that some young Christians are adopting a romanticized view of the city.[1] But the attitude of the biblical authors is quite different. The biblical view of cities is neither hostile nor romantic. Because the city is humanity intensified — a magnifying glass that brings out the very best and worst of human nature — it has a dual nature.[2]

This is why the Bible depicts cities as places of perversion and violence and also as places of refuge and peace. Genesis 4 and 11 depict city builders as those in the line of Cain (the first murderer). Genesis also depicts the evil of the cities of Sodom and Gomorrah. Yet Psalm 107 speaks of a group of wandering people "finding no way to a city where they could settle . . . and their lives ebbed away. Then they cried out to the LORD . . . He led them by a straight way to a city where they could settle. Let them give thanks to the LORD" (vv. 4 – 8). The psalmist depicts life for people without a city as a bad thing. The assumption behind this psalm is that the city is a place where human life thrives — it is a positive social form. The depiction of the city in the Bible is therefore finely nuanced. It highlights how the capacities of this positive social form can be realized for God's glory yet also demonstrates how it can be a vehicle for enhancing human rebellion against God. And as we will see in chapter 12, the city plays a pivotal role in the arc of redemptive history.

In this chapter I want to look at this tension between the city's God-exalting promise and its man-exalting shadow. We will find this dual nature played out in the pages of Scripture and mirrored in our contemporary world, for in most ways our cities are still today as they have always been.

THE CITY DEFINED

But first we must ask: What do we mean by a city? Today, a city is usually defined in terms of population size. Large population centers are called "cities," smaller ones "towns," and the smallest "villages." We must be careful, however, not to impose our current cultural understanding of city onto the biblical term. The most common Hebrew word for city, *ʿir*, meant any human settlement surrounded by some fortification or wall.[3] Most ancient cities numbered only about one thousand to three thousand in population but the residents were tightly packed within the city wall.[4] Therefore, according to the Bible, the essence of a city was not the population's size but its density. A city is a social form in which people physically live in *close proximity* to one another.

Psalm 122:3 refers to this density: "Jerusalem, built as a city should be, closely compact."[5] In a fortified city, the people lived close to one another in small residences on narrow streets. City life was street life — physical human presence at all times and in all places. In fact, most ancient cities were estimated to be five to ten acres in size, containing an average of 240 residents per acre.[6] By comparison, the island of Manhattan in present-day New York City houses only 105 residents per acre — with high-rises! After Nehemiah rebuilt Jerusalem's city wall, there were far too many vacant homes for Jerusalem to flourish as a city (Neh 7:4). In other words, the city wasn't densely populated enough to function as a city should. So 10 percent of the nation was commanded to move into the city to fill it (Neh 11:1). When cities first arose, they created a distinct kind of human life within their walled, protected space. Out of this dense proximity flowed three signal features that mark urban human life.

SAFETY AND STABILITY

First, because early cities had walls, a city meant greater *safety* and therefore *stability*. Cities' primary importance lay in their resistance to hostile forces, whether opposing armies, marauders, blood feud avengers, or wild animals. The walled safety of a city allowed for a far more stable life than was possible outside the city, and this led to the growth of human civilization. *Civilized* literally means "citified." When the Israelites were conquering Canaan, they were amazed at the strength of its fortified cities (Deut 1:28; 9:1; Josh 14:12), and as they settled the land, they built cities for themselves (Num 32:16 – 42). It should not surprise us that in the Bible the city is used as a metaphor for confidence (Prov 21:22; cf. Deut 28:52). Proverbs 25:28 tells us that a man without self-control is like a city without

a wall. Cities were places where life was not dangerously out of control.

Because of this stability, systems of law and order were able to develop first in urban settings. Early cities had gates where the elders sat and decided cases according to the rule of law. Outside the gates, disputes were settled by the sword, which led to blood feuds, destruction, and social disorder. The wall and the gate made it both necessary and possible to develop systems of jurisprudence so matters could be settled fairly, without violence. God commanded the Israelites to build "cities of refuge" to which individuals who killed someone accidentally could flee and plead their case (Num 35:6).

The idea of the city as a place of safety and stability does not immediately strike modern readers as intuitive. We may accept that cities were safe places in earlier times, but today we think of cities as places of high crime. The latest studies indicate that this concept — that higher crime is inevitable in cities — is a mistake.[7] And we must broaden our definition of "the city as safe space." This concept continues to drive the growth and success of many cities in chaotic parts of the world. Even modern-day cities such as Hong Kong, Singapore, and Gaborone (in Botswana) have thrived because they have established themselves as bastions of the rule of law in disorderly parts of the world, thereby attracting a disproportionate amount of economic investment and human talent.

But another way in which most cities thrive is that they have become places of refuge to which minority groups and individuals can flee from powerful interests. In Bible times, accused criminals could flee blood avengers, seek refuge in the city, and have their case heard by the city elders (Num 35; Deut 19; Josh 20). Even today, economically pressed or politically oppressed people who need to move out of their homeland to achieve a better life usually emigrate to cities. It is in these places of density and proximity that immigrant groups can create "mini-cities" with their own institutions that enable newcomers to enter and learn the ways of the new country. And it's not just immigrants who feel cities are safe places to live. All demographic minorities (e.g., older single people, racial minorities) feel less conspicuous and odd in cities where more of the people in their group live. Cities, then, continue to thrive today because significant numbers of people perceive them to be safe places to live — in the broadest sense of the term.

DIVERSITY

Second, the biblical understanding of a city also implies greater *diversity*, which is a natural result of density and safety. In the church in Antioch, we see leaders from different ethnic groups (Acts 13:1) — a natural occurrence when the gospel goes forth in cities, in which many different people groups reside. Because minorities find them to be safe places to live, cities tend to become racially and culturally diverse. And this is not the full extent of their diversity. Cities are marked by diversity not just of population but of land use as well.

Human society requires several elements:

- an economic order, where people work and business transactions take place
- a cultural order, where people pursue scholarship, art, and theater
- a political-legal order, where cases are decided and governing officials meet

If you think of these elements as components of a pizza (tomato sauce, cheese, pepperoni, dough), the city is a place where every neighborhood is a slice of pizza. Along with residences, it has places to work, shop, read, learn, enjoy art and music, worship, and play, as well as public government buildings such as town halls and courts. All are mixed and compacted together within walking distance. In ancient times, rural areas and even villages could not provide all these elements; only cities could sustain them all. This is why some define a city as a "walkable, mixed-use settlement."[8] And in modern times, the dominant arrangement — the suburb — deliberately avoids this urban pattern. Suburbs are normally dedicated to large, single-use zones — so places to live, work, play, and learn are separated from one another and are reachable only by car, usually through pedestrian-

hostile zones. Suburbs and rural areas have the pizza ingredients, but not in pizza form. It is tomatoes here, dough there, and pepperoni over there.[10]

PRODUCTIVITY AND CREATIVITY

Third, in the Bible, cities were places of greater *productivity* and *creativity*. As we will see below, human culture — technology, architecture, the arts — began to develop as cities were built (see Gen 4; 11). The city features street life and marketplaces, bringing about more person-to-person interactions and exchanges in a day than are possible anywhere else. The more often people of the same profession come together, the more they stimulate new ideas and the faster these new ideas spread. The greater the supply of talent, the greater the productivity of that talent, and the demand for it follows. As a testimony to this fact, the purpose of modern conventions is *connection* — a place where people connect with expertise, peers, money, and other resources — and the best way to facilitate these connections is to create a temporary city! All the connections lead in the end to creativity — new alliances, ideas, art, and movements.

"Cities are the absence of physical space between people." — Edward Glaeser

---

So ever since the beginning of recorded history, cities have been the centers of cultural intensity — for better or for worse. And what makes a city a city is not so much population size but proximity. Edward Glaeser writes, "Cities are the absence of physical space between people."[11] This is what gives the city its distinctiveness and potency among all other human living arrangements.

THE CITY THROUGHOUT THE OLD TESTAMENT

We have said the Bible has a balanced understanding of how both good and evil operate in a city. We will call this the "tension" of the biblical view of the city. The tension takes time to come into focus, as the city plays a definite role at every stage in the history of salvation. As redemptive history progresses, the Bible moves from a largely negative view of the city (emphasizing the city's rebellion) to a more positive one (emphasizing the city's strengths, power, and strategic importance). To illustrate, we turn to a detailed study of the city in early biblical history.

THE PRIMEVAL CITY

The first occurrence of the word *city* (*'îr*) in the Bible is in Genesis 4:17, where Cain, after committing fratricide and being sent away from the presence of the Lord, settles east of Eden in the land of Nod (Gen 4:16). Cain, the rebel, then *builds a city*.[12] This has led some to see "a possible reflection of the anti-urban bias in Genesis."[13] But this association misses the subtleties of the narrative. First, the founding of the city comes as the result of Cain's search for security in the world and of God's granting his request (Gen 4:14 – 15). In other words, the city is seen as a refuge, even from the very beginning. In addition, Genesis 4:17 – 22 links the founding of the city with the beginnings of the creation of culture. Immediately after Cain establishes city life, we see the first development of the arts in the musicianship of Jubal (v. 21) and of technology in the tool making of Tubal-Cain (v. 22). Architecture, agriculture, the arts, and technology all begin when cities begin. Cities are places of human productivity.

This list of cultural expressions would have been shocking to Israel's ancient Near Eastern neighbors who believed that cultural advances like the sciences, writing, and the arts were the product of divine or mythological characters. The historical, human nature of their origins runs counter to the prevailing cultural view of the ancient Near East. In the Genesis narrative, we see man becoming a contributor under God in the ongoing work of creation, through the development of culture. We learn that city life is not to be seen as simply a punishment for humanity after the banishment from the garden. Rather the city has inherent capacities for bringing human beings together in such a way that enhances both security and culture making.

However, as can be seen in the line of Cain, these capacities, under the influence of sin and rebellion against God, can be generators of great evil. The song of Lamech, Cain's descendant, shows the Cainite city dwellers using all their advances to form a culture of death (Gen 4:23 – 24). Here is the first clear indicator of the dual nature of the city. Its capability for enormous good — for the culture-making creation of art, science, and technology — can be used to produce tremendous evil. Henri Blocher does not consider it a coincidence that the first mention of anti-God culture making is tied to the first instance of city building, but he warns against drawing the wrong conclusion:

> It is no doubt significant that [in Genesis 4] progress in arts and in engineering comes from the "city" of the Cainites. Nevertheless, we are not to conclude from this that civilization as such is … the fruit of sin. Such a conclusion would lead us to Manichaeism or to the views of Jean-Jacques Rousseau … The Bible condemns neither the city (for it concludes with the vision of the City of God) nor art and engineering.[14]

Blocher may be responding to writers such as Geerhardus Vos, who in his *Biblical Theology* points to "the problem of the city" and asserts that "the city, while an accumulator of the energies of culture, is also an accumulator of potencies of evil (Amos 3:9; Micah 1:5)."[15] Sometimes these seats of culture making can be established to bring glory to God's name (1 Cor 10:31) and therefore be a means of serving God and neighbor (e.g., Bezalel in Exod 31:3–5), or they can be erected to "make a name for ourselves" (Gen 11:4), resulting in a culture of human pride, self-salvation, violence, and oppression (Gen 4:17–24). Vos adds that what makes the human city fallen is not its density of population (indeed, this is what makes it an "accumulator of the energies of culture"), but its "spirit of rebellious self-dependence over against God."[16] A horse is a more valuable animal than a mouse, yet a crazed horse is capable of far more damage than a crazed mouse; so too a city's strengths under sin can unleash more destructive evil. As the Genesis narrative unfolds, we see that warring with the city's great potential is a profound bent toward corruption and idolatry.

For most of the rest of Genesis, the city is seen in a negative light. The city is mentioned in connection with the accursed Ham (Gen 10:12). The next substantive appearance is in Genesis 11:4 when the people dwelling in the plain of Shinar (11:2) gather together *to build a city*. The naming of Shinar is significant because of its associations with Babylon (see Gen 10:10; Isa 11:11; Dan 1:2). It is in this city that the people gather as one and say to each other, "Come, let's make bricks and bake them thoroughly." The writer of Genesis states:

HISTORY OR MYTH?

Jewish scholar Nahum Sarna states:

The list [in Gen 4:17–22] constitutes a silent polemic against the mythological concepts of the ancient world, which attributed the advance of culture to divine or semidivine figures. Mesopotamian tradition knew of the seven *Apkallu*, or mythical sages, half-fish and half-man, who rose out of the sea to reveal to man the sciences, the social system, writing, and art … For Egyptians, it was the god Thot who invented the scales and the balances; Osiris who taught humans agriculture and the arts of life; and Ptah who was the special patron of artists, artificers, and men of letters. In the Ugaritic-Phoenician area, the god Koshar, the divine artisan and smith, was credited with the discovery of the use of iron and the fishing tackle. In the Greek sphere, it was Athena who invented the plough and the rake and who taught both the useful and the elegant arts, while Apollo founded towns and invented the flute and the lyre.

This phenomenon, known as euhemerism or the divinization of the benefactors of humanity, was common to the ancient world. In [Gen 4:17–22] it is tacitly rejected. The development of human culture is demythologized and historicized … Man became a copartner with God in the world of creation. At the same time, the ascription of the origins of technology and urban life to Cain and his line constitute an unfavorable, or at least a qualified, judgment of man's material progress on the part of the Narrator, a recognition that it frequently outruns moral progress and that human ingenuity, so potentially beneficial, is often directed toward evil ends.[17]

They used brick instead of stone, and tar for mortar [again, the city is depicted as the place of technological achievement]. Then they said, "Come, let us build ourselves a city, with a tower that reaches to the heavens, so that we may make a name for ourselves and not be scattered over the face of the whole earth."

But the LORD came down to see the city and the tower that the men were building.

Genesis 11:3 – 5, emphasis mine

The spirit of the line of Cain reaches its climax in this effort to build the city of Babel. The new city and its tower are designed to help residents gain an identity apart from service to God. Here we see the essence of how cities can magnify our sinful drive for self-glorification and self-salvation. The efforts of the people working together for their own glory attract the notice of God, who reacts by confusing their language and scattering them "from there over all the earth," lest they succeed in their plans. The result of God's judgment was that they "stopped building the city" (v. 8).

THE PATRIARCHS AND THE CITY

The rest of Genesis continues to highlight the dark side of the city — particularly the infamous Sodom and Gomorrah. Again, God "goes down" to judge Sodom (Gen 18:21), just as he did with Babel. Babel, later called Babylon in the Bible, comes to serve as the archetype for urban culture arrayed against God (see Isa 13:19). The Sodom narrative stands in the midst of a long period in which we see city dwellers opposed to God, while God's people remain rural nomads. God called Abram to leave Ur, one of the great cities of the day, and remain a shepherd all his life. Genesis shows us that Abram's nephew Lot made a grave mistake in choosing urban life. While he remained a righteous man within Sodom and was distressed by the sinful lifestyle there, the behavior of his wife and daughters showed that Lot's decision to live in a city without a believing community led to spiritual disaster for his family.[18]

Nevertheless, we later learn that Abraham's refusal to enter the cities of his time and place lay in his longing for God's city: "By faith Abraham … lived in tents … For he was looking forward to the city with foundations, whose architect and builder is God" (Heb 11:8 – 10). If the city as a social form is intrinsically bad for human beings or for our faith, it wouldn't make sense for it to be idealized as the source of Abraham's sustaining hope. Cities in the service of human self-aggrandizement may work

to unravel and destroy the world God made and to contest his lordship over it. But as we will see, the city form, in service to God, actually fulfills the will of God for human life.

ISRAEL AND THE CITY

With the establishment of Israel in the Promised Land, the biblical depiction of cities becomes more positive. When God settled the Israelites in Canaan, he commanded them to build cities of refuge: "Select … your cities of refuge, to which a person who has killed someone accidentally may flee. They will be places of refuge from the avenger, so that a person accused of murder may not die before he stands trial before the assembly" (Num 35:11 – 12). Why did God command the building of cities? Cities with walls and a gathered population could protect an accused person and conduct a trial in a way that villages and rural areas could not. Without cities, a crime or accident could lead to an endless cycle of violence and reprisals. The safety and density of cities enabled a system of jurisprudence to develop around the rule of law. There the elders could hear and settle cases in peace (Deut 19:11 – 12). God commands the establishment of cities in Israel to establish justice.

But the biggest change in the city's role within redemptive history comes with the establishment of Jerusalem. Unlike Babel, established "to make a name for ourselves" (Gen 11:4), Jerusalem becomes the city that is the dwelling place for God's Name (1 Kgs 14:21). This begins when Jerusalem is captured by David (2 Sam 5), the ark of the covenant is brought to the city (2 Sam 6), and finally the temple is built by Solomon. Jerusalem is appointed to be an urban culture that is a witness to the nations and a symbol of the future City of God (2 Sam 7:8 – 16). God directs that the temple be built on Zion, an elevated location within the city, so it rises above the city as its "skyscraper." God's city is different from human cities (like Babel) where skyscrapers are designed for their builders' own prosperity and prominence. By contrast, God's city is "the joy of the whole earth" (Ps 48:2). The city's cultural riches are produced, not for the glory of the producers, but for the joy of the entire earth and the honor of God. The urban society in God's plan is based on service, not on selfishness.

THE PROPHETS AND THE CITY

From the time of David onward, the prophets speak of God's future world as an urban society. Bible scholar J. Alec Motyer writes, "The Isaianic literature could be accurately described as 'the book of the city.'"[19] He notes that in Isaiah, *Jerusalem, Zion, mount/mountain,* and *city* are interchangeable terms showing the city's centrality in the divine thought and plan.[20] At this point the spiritual battle lines of history become clear. The great spiritual conflict of history is not between city dwellers and country dwellers but is truly "a tale of two cities." It is a struggle between Babylon, representing the city of man, and Jerusalem, representing the city of God.[21] The earthly city is a metaphor for human life structured without God, created for self-salvation, self-service, and self-glorification. It portrays a scene of exploitation and injustice. But God's city is a society based on his glory and on sacrificial service to God and neighbor. This city offers a scene of peace and righteousness. As Saint Augustine put it, "The humble City is the society of holy men and good angels; the proud city is the society of wicked men and evil angels. The one City began with the love of God; the other had its beginnings in the love of self."[22]

John concludes his Apocalypse (Rev 22:19) by warning those who take words away (*aphelē*) from "this book of prophecy" that God will take away (*aphelei*) from them their "share in the tree of life and *in the holy city*" (*kai ek tēs poleōs tēs hagias*, emphasis mine). Throughout Revelation, John draws a consistent contrast between "the great city," Babylon,[23] and the city of God, or Jerusalem.[24] The former receives the eschatological judgment of God, while the latter receives (and mediates) eschatological blessing and salvation.[25]

THE CITY OF EXILE

When we get to the book of Jonah, we come to a new phase in the unfolding biblical theology of the city. Throughout Israel's history, prophets are raised up and sent to preach to God's people, to call them to repentance and renewal. But Jonah is given a unique mission. For the first time, a prophet is sent to preach to a pagan, foreign city — Nineveh. Jonah's response is first (in Jonah 1 – 2) to run away from the city. In chapter 3, after his famous encounter with the great fish, Jonah does preach to Nineveh — and the people respond in repentance. God does not destroy the city as he had warned he would. This

---

Cities have more of the image of God per square inch than any other place on earth.

---

response displeases Jonah greatly, and in Jonah 4:10 – 11, God scolds Jonah for his lack of compassion for the lost people of Nineveh. Listen to God's argument:

> Then the LORD said, "You had compassion on the plant for which you did not work and which you did not cause to grow, which came up overnight and perished overnight. Should I not have compassion on Nineveh, the great city in which there are more than 120,000 persons who do not know the difference between their right and left hand, as well as many animals?"
>
> Jonah 4:10 – 11 NASB

Here God makes a case for the importance of the city from the sheer number of the human beings in residence. He is saying, "How can you look at *so many* lost people and not find compassion in your heart?" This is a critical reason that the city is so important today. We might call it the *visceral* argument for the city. God "has compassion on all he has made" (Ps 145:9). But of all the things he has made, human beings have pride of place in his heart, because they were made in his image (Gen 9:6; James 3:9). Cities, quite literally, have more of the image of God per square inch than any other place on earth. How can we not be drawn to such masses of humanity if we care about the same things that God cares about?

Why did God send an Israelite prophet to a pagan city? Some have argued that this is intended to

THE CITY IN THE OLD TESTAMENT

Some basic sources that cover this topic
include the following:

Boice, James Montgomery. *Two Cities, Two
Loves.* Downers Grove, Ill.: InterVarsity, 1996.

Conn, Harvie, "Christ and the City: Biblical
Themes for Building Urban Theology
Models." Pages 222–86 in *Discipling the
City: Theological Reflections on Urban
Mission.* Roger Greenway, ed. Grand
Rapids: Baker, 1979.

Conn, Harvie M., and Manuel Ortiz. *Urban
Ministry: The Kingdom, the City, and
the People of God.* Downers Grove, Ill.:
InterVarsity, 2001.

Kline, Meredith G. "Eschatological Sanctions"
and "Prophetic Cult in the City of Man."
Pages 100–17 and 165–70 in *Kingdom
Prologue.* South Hamilton, Mass.: Gordon-
Conwell Theological Seminary, 1993.

Linthicum, Robert. *City of God, City of Satan:
A Biblical Theology of the Urban Church.*
Grand Rapids: Zondervan, 1990.

Ryken, Leland, James Wilhoit, and Tremper
Longman III, eds. "City." Pages 150–54 in
Dictionary of Biblical Imagery. Downers
Grove, Ill.: InterVarsity, 1998.

Timmer, J. "The Bible and the City."
Pages 21–25 in *The Reformed Journal* 23
(October 1973).

28–29? How will the people of God relate to the great human cities of the earth now?

A major part of the Babylonian Empire's strategy was to eradicate the spiritual identity of its conquered peoples. A defeated nation's professional and elite classes were often taken to Babylon to live before being allowed to return home.[26] Judah had been deported, partially in the hope that the children and grandchildren of the Israelites would assimilate and lose their identity as a distinct people. The false prophet Hananiah, who could not imagine Israel's life in Babylon long-term, dishonestly prophesied that God would bring Israel back to Jerusalem within two years (Jer 28:3–4). Had the exiles followed Hananiah's advice, they would have remained disengaged in Babylon, waiting indefinitely for God's imminent deliverance.

Instead God, through the prophet Jeremiah, contradicts both the Babylonians' strategy and the false prophet's counsel. On the one hand, God tells his people to "increase in number there; do not decrease" (Jer 29:6) to retain their distinct community identity and to grow, but he also tells them to settle down and engage in the life of the great city.[27] They are to build homes and plant gardens (v. 5). Most striking of all, God calls them to serve the city — to "seek the peace and prosperity of the

---

Loving and serving the city strengthens the hands of the people of God, who bear the message of the gospel to the world.

---

prepare the Jews for the next stage of their own history — the period of exile — in which they will be residing not in Jerusalem but literally in Babel — in Babylon. The importance of Jerusalem had been obvious; it was to be "the joy of the whole earth" (Ps 48:2), a model urban society demonstrating to the world what human life under God's lordship could be. But what happens when Israel goes to live in a wicked, pagan, bloodthirsty city in Jeremiah

city" and to "pray to the LORD for it" (v. 7). While living in Babylon, they are not simply to increase their tribe in a ghetto within the city; they are to use their resources to benefit the common good.

This is quite a balance! From Genesis 11 all the way through Revelation, Babylon is represented as the epitome of a civilization built on selfishness, pride, and violence — the ultimate city of man. The values of this city contrast absolutely with those of the city of God; yet here the citizens of the city of God are called to be the *very best* residents of this particular city of man. God commands the Jewish exiles not to attack, despise, or flee the city — but to seek its peace, to love the city as they grow in numbers.

God is still primarily concerned with his plan of salvation. He must establish his people; the gospel must be proclaimed; human beings must be reconciled to him. Yet he assures his people that serving the good of this pagan city is part of this very plan: "If it prospers, you too will prosper" (Jer 29:7). Loving and serving the city not only shows love and compassion; doing so also strengthens the hands of the people of God, who bear the message of the gospel to the world. Because the Jews in exile obeyed this command, they accrued the influence and leverage needed to eventually return to and restore their homeland. God ties, as it were, the fortunes of the people of God to the effectiveness of their urban ministry.

———————

Sadly, there has never been a city on earth that is not saturated with human sin and corruption. Indeed, to paraphrase a Woody Allen joke, cities are just like everywhere else, only much more so. They are both better and worse, both easier and harder to live in, both more inspiring and oppressive, than other places.

As redemptive history unfolds, we begin to see how the tension of the city will be resolved. The turn in the relationship between the people of God and the pagan city becomes a key aspect of God's plan to bless the nations and redeem the world. In the New Testament, we find cities playing an important role in the rapid growth of the early church and in spreading the gospel message of God's salvation.

QUESTIONS FOR DISCUSSION AND REFLECTION

1. How would you describe your own attitude toward cities? Indifferent? Hostile? Romanticized? Positive? In what way has this chapter challenged your attitude toward cities?

2. Cities are places of safety, diversity, and productivity. How do each one of these characteristics uniquely define urban culture?

3. Keller writes, "Cities, quite literally, have more of the image of God per square inch than any other place on earth. How can we not be drawn to such masses of humanity if we care about the same things that God cares about?" What are some of the reasons that people avoid ministry in the city? What are some of the reasons that they are attracted to urban ministry?

4. How can you and the community of believers to which you belong work to "seek the peace and prosperity of the city"? What does this look like in your context?

CHAPTER 11 — THE TENSION OF THE CITY *{pages 135 – 43}*

1. Cities have a glamorous attraction to young adults today, and some Christians may imbibe the depiction of cities as consumer heavens. See "Is London a Luxury Resort?" and "The Consumer City: Vancouver," in Edward Glaeser, *The Triumph of the City: How Our Greatest Invention Makes Us Richer, Smarter, Greener, Healthier, and Happier* (New York: Penguin, 2011).

2. The *Dictionary of Biblical Imagery* (ed. Leland Ryken, James C. Wilhoit, and Tremper Longman III [Downers Grove, Ill.: InterVarsity, 1998], 150) speaks of the city as "humanity *en masse*" and therefore "humanity 'writ large.'"

3. The *Dictionary of Biblical Imagery* (p. 150) defines *city* as a "fortified habitation."

4. See Frank Frick, *The City in Ancient Israel* (Missoula, Mont.: Scholars Press, 1977), 79.

5. Translation by Leslie C. Allen, *Psalms 101 – 150*, rev. ed. (Word Biblical Commentary 21; Nashville: Nelson, 2002), 210.

6. See Frick, *City in Ancient Israel*, 79.

7. See Franklin E. Zimring, *The City That Became Safe: New York's Lessons for Urban Crime and Its Control* (New York: Oxford University Press), 2011. Across all categories, New York City's crime rate is down 80 percent from twenty years ago. The drop came without an increase in prisoners incarcerated (the traditional conservative solution for crime) or a decrease in poverty (the traditional liberal solution for crime). Smarter law enforcement only accounts for about half of the drop. Zimring concludes that many of the factors that changed attitudes and behavior are simply being missed because social theorists — both conservative and liberal — simply don't know what to look for. He writes (p. 204), "The specific mechanisms at work in New York City [that have led to decreased crime] . . . are unknown." Nevertheless, he states (p. 202) that this twenty-year decline essentially proves the "inessentiality of crime to urban life," thus putting to rest one of the deepest fears generated in the last century about cities. At the end of his book, he writes (p. 217), "We now know that life-threatening crime is not an incurable urban disease in the United States." It is interesting to note that Zimring does not consider as one possible factor the growth of evangelical churches, adding somewhere between a half million to one million Christians to the NYC population over the past generation (see Michael Luo, "In New York, Billy Graham Will Find an Evangelical Force," *New York Times* [June 21, 2005], www.nytimes.com/2005/06/21/nyregion/21evangelical.html?ref=billygraham; see also the website www.nycreligion.info/).

8. See, e.g., Philip Bess, "A Realist Philosophical Case for Urbanism and against Sprawl: Part One," www.thepublicdiscourse.com/2011/07/3379 (accessed January 23, 2012).

9. Glaeser, *Triumph of the City*, 7 – 8.

10. The classic text describing and celebrating the density of population, mixed-land use, and street life is Jane Jacobs, *The Death and Life of Great American Cities* (New York: Vintage, 1961), esp. part 1 "The Peculiar Nature of Cities," and part 2, "The Conditions for City Diversity."

11. Glaeser, *Triumph of the City*, 6.

12. It should be noted that there is some scholarly debate about who actually builds the city: Is it Cain, or is it his son Enoch? The issue has to do with the name of the city. The name of Enoch's son, Irad, sounds like Eridu, generally regarded in Mesopotamian tradition to be the first city to be founded (see Gordon J. Wenham, *Genesis 1 – 15* [Word Biblical Commentary 1a; Nashville: Nelson, 1987], 110 – 12).

13. Robert Alter, *Genesis: Translation and Commentary* (New York: Norton, 1997), 19.

14. Henri Blocher, *In the Beginning: The Opening Chapters of Genesis*, trans. David G. Preston (Downers Grove, Ill.: InterVarsity, 1984), 199.

15. Geerhardus Vos, *Biblical Theology: Old and New Testaments* (Grand Rapids: Eerdmans, 1948), 294.

16. Gen 18:16 – 33; 19:16 – 36; see 2 Pet 2:7 – 8.

17. Nahum M. Sarna, *Genesis Commentary* (JPS Torah Commentary; Philadelphia: Jewish Publication Society, 1989), 35 – 36.

18. Ibid., 295. It should be noted that Vos generally saw the power of the city to create and influence culture as being a negative influence in human history. Meredith Kline in his *Kingdom Prologue* is more balanced, saying the city is a "divine ordinance" (p. 101). However, Kline sees the city as an instrument of God's common grace. Its effect on culture when used well is only "remedial," a way to resist the tendencies of human evil and is not a way to bring in the kingdom of God, contrary to those in the Kuyperian school (pp. 105 – 6). For more on the related debate about Christ and culture, see part 5 of this volume.

19. J. Alec Motyer, *The Prophecy of Isaiah: An Introduction and Commentary* (Downers Grove, Ill.: InterVarsity, 1993), 16.

20. Ibid., 17.

21. Note the idea of the two cities worked out in Isaiah 13 – 27. The theology is worked out most thoroughly in Augustine's *The City of God* (*De Civitate Dei*).

22. Augustine, *City of God*, 14:13.

23. Revelation 11:8, 13; 16:19; 17:18; 18:10, 16, 18 – 19, 21; see also 2:13 — Pergamum, "your city — where Satan lives."

24. Revelation 3:12; 11:2; 20:9; 21:2, 10, 14 – 27; 22:2 – 3, 14.

25. Jerusalem, as history has shown, was not the city of God per se. The prophets showed how far short the earthly Jerusalem fell from its future antitype (Jer 13:9 – 14; Mic 3:11 – 12). It was only a mixture of the city of man and the city of God, at its best pointing beyond itself to that ultimate city (see Jer 3:16 – 17).

26. See 2 Kings 24:14, where "all the officers and fighting men, and all the craftsmen and artisans" were exiled. The professional classes were taken and the poor left behind. Daniel 1:3 – 5 describes how the nobility and cream of Israel's ruling classes were to receive instruction in Babylonian ways and culture. Tremper Longman III (*Daniel* [NIV Application Commentary; Grand Rapids: Zondervan, 1999], 47) observes that Nebuchadnezzar wanted to assimilate conquered people groups into Babylonian culture so they would lose their distinct cultural identities and thus become compliant.

27. While Jeremiah 28 calls the Jews to invest in the life of the city, Daniel 1 warns them against defiling themselves through overassimilation to the pagan culture. Both of these texts were given to the exilic community for guidance. Thanks to Richard Coekin for this insight.

chapter 12

REDEMPTION AND THE CITY

As we saw in the last chapter, God unexpectedly calls Israel to serve the pagan city of Babylon — to seek its prosperity — while living in exile there. And in a sense, the people of God have yet to return from that state of exile. In this chapter, we will see how this exilic model helps us understand the relationship of the church to the city in New Testament times, and even today — and how God plans to resolve the great tension of the city at the end of time.[1]

During the exile, Israel no longer existed in the form of a nation-state with a government and laws. Instead, it existed as a countercultural fellowship contained within other nation-states. In many ways,

RESIDENT ALIENS AND CULTURE

In an article on 1 Peter titled "Soft Difference," Miroslav Volf shows how the tension Peter envisioned between persecution and attraction and between evangelism and service does not fit neatly into any of the historic models of relating Christ to culture. Unlike models that call for a transformation of culture or a Christendom-like alliance of church and state, Peter expects the gospel to always be highly offensive and never completely embraced or accepted by the world. This is a caution to those Christians who hope to bring about an essentially Christian culture. And unlike models that call solely for evangelism and are highly pessimistic about influencing culture, Peter nonetheless expects *some* aspects of Christian faith and practice to be highly attractive in any pagan culture, thus influencing people to praise God.[2]

this is also the form of the New Testament church, as Peter and James suggest when they address believers as "the Dispersion" (Jas 1:1 ESV) and "exiles" (1 Pet 1:1 ESV). Twice Peter uses *parepidēmoi* as a word for "exiles" — a word we sometimes translate as "resident aliens." *Parepidēmoi* were citizens of one country and yet full-time residents of another. Their primary allegiance was to another country, and that country's culture was formative for their beliefs and practices. Yet they lived in their country of residence as full participants in its life. In other words, "resident aliens" lived neither as natives nor as tourists. Though they were not permanently rooted, neither were they merely travelers who were just passing through.

Christians are now considered citizens of "the Jerusalem that is above" (Gal 4:26; see Phil 3:20). Indeed, in a significant statement, Jesus tells his followers that they are a "city on a hill" (Matt 5:14). Communities of Christ-followers are God's "city" within every earthly city. They are the renewed people of God (see Isa 32:14; Dan 9:16). Their ultimate allegiance belongs to God and his kingdom, yet, in keeping with the term used by Peter and James, believers are not just "passing through" their earthly cities. This reflects the same balanced attitude that Jewish exiles were called to have toward Babylon. The Jewish exiles were not to hate the pagan city as they bided their time, waiting for the day of their departure. They were to be fully involved in its life, working in it and praying for it. At the same time, they were not to adopt its culture or lose their distinctive identity as God's holy people. God called the Jewish exiles to accept and embrace the tension of the city for the sake of God's glory — and this is exactly what today's Christians are called to do as well.

Resident aliens will always live with both praise and misunderstanding. Jesus taught that Christians' "good deeds" are to be visible to the pagans (Matt 5:16), but he also warns his followers to expect misunderstanding and persecution (v. 10). In a similar way, Peter calls Christians to live in the midst of pagan society in such a way that others will

---

God called the Jewish exiles to embrace the tension of the city for the sake of God's glory — and this is exactly what today's Christians are called to do as well.

---

see their "good deeds and glorify God" (1 Pet 2:12), but he warns them to expect persecution nonetheless. Both Peter and Jesus indicate that these "good deeds" (which in the Greek meant not merely personal morality but also acts of service to others) will lead at least some pagans to glorify God.

Despite these similarities, the Christian church differs from the Jewish exiles in two significant ways. First, the Jews "increase in number" in Babylon almost exclusively by having children and growing families (Jer 29:6). The church must also multiply and increase in the pagan city as God's new humanity, but this happens especially through evangelism and discipling (Acts 6:1, 7; 9:31; 12:24). We also see a significant shift in God's call to mission between the Old and New Testaments. In the Old Testament, mission was *centripetal*; the flow was in toward the center. Israel was called to be an obedient people, becoming a society that displayed God's glory for the nations to see (Deut 4:6 – 8). The nations were called to look and to "come in" and worship God. But in the New Testament, mission becomes *centrifugal* — moving outward from the center. The people of God are sent out to the world to proclaim the gospel (Matt 28:16 – 20; Acts 1 – 2). The Babylonian exile and Jonah's mission are foreshadowings of this future change.

Second, despite their engagement with Babylonian society, the Jews still kept the Mosaic code, so that their dress, food, and other practices continued to set them culturally apart from the Babylonians (see, e.g., Dan 1:8). Their dietary laws alone virtually dictated that Jews eat separately from pagans. In the book of Acts, God has to send Peter a vivid and forceful vision to get him to even consider accepting an invitation to enter a Gentile soldier's home (10:28 – 29). In Christ, these ceremonial and cultural regulations and distinctions become obsolete (Mark 7; Acts 15:1 – 35). Jesus eats with tax collectors and sinners as a strategy for ministry. Adopting these New Testament teachings frees Christians to participate in a city's culture more fully than the Jews in Babylon could. However, this freedom also makes the danger of assimilation and compromise more acute for Christians. As future citizens of heaven, Christians must see and avoid the idolatries and injustices of their culture, even as they continue to enjoy its common-grace blessings.

So why should we apply the exhortations of Jeremiah 29 to the church today? In the Bible, we see the people of God living in three configurations. From Abraham's day onward, God's people existed as an *extended biological family*. From the days of Moses, they existed as a *nation-state*, with laws and a king and an army to enforce those laws by civil sanctions. During the exile, however, God's people existed as a *dispersed fellowship of congregations* (synagogues) living in many different nation-states. God's laws did not take a civil form during that period — the disobedient were expelled from the congregation, but they were not executed.

JONAH'S MISSION

The book of Jonah foreshadows the centrifugal New Testament mission (sending believers *out*) rather than the centripetal Old Testament mission (calling nonbelievers *in*). Jonah is the only Old Testament prophet sent to a pagan city to call it to repentance. God's final statement is striking. The Lord calls Jonah to love the great pagan city of Nineveh because of the vast number of its spiritually blind inhabitants (Jonah 4:10 – 11).[3]

THE "CRUCIALITY" OF CITY MINISTRY IN THE BIBLE

Many of the reasons that city ministry was so effective in the early church have been outlined by Wayne Meeks in *The First Urban Christians* and by Harvie Conn in his many books. They identify three "crucial" factors:

1. **Cultural cruciality.** In the village, someone might win its one or two lawyers to Christ. However, if you want to win the legal profession, which will influence all lawyers, you must go to the city, where you will find the law schools and the law journal publishers — the key institutions of influence in that profession.

2. **Global cruciality.** In the village, someone can win over the single people group living there, since rural areas are often sociologically homogeneous. But if you share the gospel in a city, you can reach dozens of different national and ethnic groups. Indeed, you can reach them through one language — the *lingua franca* of that place. The gospel then travels back into many different cultures through immigrants who return to visit or remain in their homelands.

3. **Personal cruciality.** In the village, people live in a culture that tends to resist change and is more conservative and traditional. However, because of the diversity and mobility of the cities, urbanites are more open to new ideas — such as the gospel! The pressure and diversity of the city environment make even the most gospel-hostile people open to new ways of thinking and living.

After the exile, the Jews went back to being a nation-state. Yet the New Testament does not envision the Christian church in this way. Instead, it shows that *the church continues to exist as a dispersion of people from every nation under heaven* (Acts 2), just as Israel did in the exile (see Jas 1:1; 1 Pet 1:1). Therefore, it seems reasonable to conclude that the church should continue to relate to the human cities of our time, not as the people of God did under Abraham, Moses, or David, but as they did during the time of the exile.

CITY MINISTRY IN THE EARLY CHURCH

In the early church, God's redemptive mission no longer centered on a particular city such as Jerusalem or Babylon. All of the cities of the world become primary targets of God's mission. The *Dictionary of Biblical Imagery* in its article on "City" states the following:

> The world that we enter in the book of Acts is the most modern in all the Bible by virtue of its urban identity. Most of the action occurs in the famous cities of the Greco-Roman world, not in the local villages or the countryside. This prevailingly metropolitan world is, moreover, international and cosmopolitan. There is a sense in which the city is vindicated in the history of the early church — not in the sense that the city is mainly good or cordial to the gospel but in the sense that the city is where most people now live and where the influential power structures exist … It is easy to see that the mission strategy of the early church was to evangelize the city. *It is no exaggeration to say that in Acts the church is almost exclusively associated with the city.*[4]

In Acts 17, Paul travels to Athens, the *intellectual* center of the Greco-Roman world. In Acts 18, he goes to Corinth, one of the *commercial* centers of the empire. In Acts 19, he arrives in Ephesus, perhaps the Roman world's *religious* center, the hub of many pagan cults and particularly of the imperial cult, with three temples for emperor worship. By the end of Acts, Paul has made it to Rome itself, the empire's capital of *military and political power*. John Stott concludes, "It seems to have been Paul's deliberate policy to move purposefully from one strategic city-centre to the next."[5]

Paul's ministry in Ephesus reveals several of the strengths of urban ministry. In Acts 19:1 we read,

"While Apollos was at Corinth, Paul took the road through the interior and arrived at Ephesus." Stott remarks that virtually all the roads in that part of the world went through Ephesus.[6] Similarly, all major cities are the unavoidable crossroads for their regions and societies. Paul entered Ephesus and rented the "lecture hall of Tyrannus" (v. 9). Stott notes that the lecture hall would have been a school that stood vacant for two to three hours at midday when people took a break from work for a meal and rest.[7] There Paul did gospel *dialegomenos*, arguing and persuading his hearers dialogically — not simply by preaching but by making his case that the Messiah was Jesus and engaging with people's questions and objections. "This went on for two years, so that all the Jews and Greeks who lived in the province of Asia heard the word of the Lord" (v. 10). Because Paul's ministry took place in the region's major city, virtually everyone in the Lycus River valley would have been exposed to the preaching of the gospel.

Stott observes that "all the inhabitants of Asia visited Ephesus from time to time, to buy or sell, visit a relative, frequent the baths, attend the games in the stadium, watch a drama in the theatre, or worship the goddess [Artemis]."[8] By reaching the city, Paul reached all segments of society, as evidenced in the letter to the Colossians. In this epistle, Paul follows up with disciples in cities along the Lycus Valley — Laodicea, Hierapolis, and Colossae (Col 4:13 – 16) — who were likely converted through his Ephesian ministry, even though he had never visited those places personally. This suggests that if the gospel is unfolded at the urban center, you can effectively reach the region and the surrounding society. Stott cites J. A. Alexander's insight that Acts shows the spread of the gospel "by the gradual establishment of radiating centres or sources of influence at certain salient points throughout a large part of the Empire."[10] Stott concludes:

> This process of urbanization … constitutes a great challenge to the Christian church. On the one hand, there is an urgent need for Christian planners and architects, local government politicians, urban specialists, developers and community social workers, who will work for justice, peace, freedom and beauty in the city. On the other, Christians need to move

AS THE CITY GOES, SO GOES THE CULTURE

In his book *The Rise of Christianity*, sociologist Rodney Stark discusses the strategic importance of the early Christians' reaching city dwellers to influence the broader culture:

> To cities filled with the homeless and impoverished, Christianity offered charity as well as hope. To cities filled with newcomers and strangers, Christianity offered an immediate basis for attachments. To cities filled with orphans and widows, Christianity provided a new and expanded sense of family. To cities torn by violent ethnic strife, Christianity offered a new basis for social solidarity …

> People had been enduring catastrophes for centuries without the aid of Christian theology or social structures. Hence I am by no means suggesting that the misery of the ancient world caused the advent of Christianity. What I am going to argue is that once Christianity did appear, its superior capacity for meeting these chronic problems soon became evident and played a major role in its ultimate triumph … [for what Christians] brought was not simply an urban movement, but a *new culture*.[9]

into the cities, and experience the pains and pressures of living there, in order to win city-dwellers for Christ. Commuter Christianity (living in salubrious suburbia and commuting to an urban church) is no substitute for incarnational involvement.[11]

The early church was largely an *urban* movement that won the people of the Roman cities to Christ, while most of the rural countryside remained pagan. Because the Christian faith captured the cities, however, it eventually captured the ancient Greco-Roman world. As the city went, so went the culture.[13] Why? The urban elites were, of course, important, but the Christian church did not focus

Bible scholar Meredith Kline notes how the development of culture in Genesis arises from the development of cities:

> The city is not to be regarded as an evil invention of ... fallen man ... The ultimate goal set before humanity at the very beginning was that human culture should take city-form ... There should be an urban structuring of human historical existence ... The cultural mandate given at creation was a mandate to build the city. Now, after the fall, the city is still a benefit, serving humankind as refuge from the howling wilderness condition into which the fallen human race, exiled from paradise, has been driven ... The common grace city has remedial benefits even in a fallen world. It becomes the drawing together of resources, strength, and talent no longer just for mutual complementation in the task of developing the resources of the created world, but now a pooling of power for defense against attack, and as an administrative community of welfare for the relief of those destitute by reason of the cursing of the ground.[12]

on them alone. Then, as now, the cities were filled with the poor, and urban Christians' commitment to the poor was visible and striking. Through the cities,

---

Through the cities, Christians changed history and culture by winning the elites as well as by identifying deeply with the poor.

Christians changed history and culture by winning the elites as well as by identifying deeply with the poor. Richard Fletcher, in *The Barbarian Conver-*

sion, shows that this same thing occurred during the Christian mission to Europe from AD 500 to 1500.[14]

CONSUMMATION: CULTIVATING THE CITY

Beginning with the Old Testament prophets, God's future redeemed world is depicted as a city. And in Revelation 21 – 22, when God's creational and redemptive intentions are fully realized, we see that the result is indeed a city, with walls and gates and streets. In some ways, this city is unlike our current cities, more of a "garden-city" that perfectly balances the glorious benefits of human density and diversity with the beauty and peace of nature. The city of God's old enemy, Babylon, is finally overthrown, and God's people thrive in peace and productivity (Rev 18).

What is most striking about this holy city is that it has not been built from scratch. In its midst flows a crystal river, and on each side of the river is "the tree of life" that bears fruit and leaves to heal the nations of all the effects of the divine covenant curse (Rev 22:1 – 3). This city is, in fact, the same garden we see in the Genesis account, which was also marked by a central river and the presence of the tree of life (Gen 2:8 – 10), but it has been expanded and remade into the garden-city of God. *It is the garden of Eden*, yet faithfully cultivated — the fulfillment of the purposes of the Eden of God.[15] Indeed, the very word used for "garden" in Genesis 2 denotes not a wilderness but a "park,"[16] a well-tended plot of land one would find in a city or near a royal palace.

Why is this important? God's directive that Adam and Eve "rule over" the earth (Gen 1:28) is often called "the cultural mandate." This is a call for them to "image God's work for the world by taking up our work in the world."[17] It is a call to develop a culture and build a civilization that honors God. Gardening (the original human vocation) is a paradigm for cultural development. A gardener neither leaves the ground as is, nor does he destroy it. Instead, he rearranges it to produce food and plants for human life. He *cultivates* it. (The words *culture* and *cultivate* come from the same root.) Every vocation is in some way a response to, and an extension of, the primal, Edenic act of cultivation. Artists, for example, take the raw material of the five senses and human experience to produce music and visual media; literature and painting; dance and architecture and theater. In a similar way, technologists and builders take the raw material of the physical world and creatively rearrange it to enhance human productivity and flourishing. Because we are called to create culture in this way, and because cities are the places of greatest cultural production, I believe that city building is a crucial part of fulfilling the mandate.

The city is an intrinsically positive social form with a checkered past and a beautiful future.

As we have already pointed out, the first evidence for this connection between the city, the culture, and the flourishing of human beings is found in Genesis 4, where Cain is "building a city" (v. 17). Immediately after the city is built, we see the first development of the arts, agriculture, and technology — the beginnings of the human cultural creativity that God had called for. Even though Cain's purpose in building the city was rebellious, its power was good. The tension of the city was present from its very start.

The cultural mandate, our failure to fulfill it in accord with God's design, its connection to city building, and the progressive importance of the city of man to the city of God — all these plotlines resolve at the end of the book of Revelation. Though the first Adam failed to faithfully heed God's call, the second Adam — Jesus Christ — *will* fulfill the mandate of the first Adam. He will save a people, subdue the earth, and bring in a civilization that honors the Father (1 Cor 15:22 – 25). Since the Bible reveals to us that a city is the final result of the work of the

second Adam on our behalf, it seems fair to assume this was what God had intended when he gave the cultural mandate to the first Adam. In other words, God called Adam and Eve to expand the borders of the garden, and when God's will is finally done and Jesus fulfills the cultural mandate on our behalf, the garden of Eden becomes a garden *city*.

Many Christians assume that the final goal of Christ's redemption is to return us to a rural, Edenic world. Based on this assumption, the work of Christians is exclusively to evangelize and disciple. But Revelation shows us this is not the case. God's intention for human endeavor is that it raise up civilizations — cities — that glorify him and steward the endless wonders and riches that God put into the created world. This insight has led Harvie Conn to write that the cultural mandate "could just as easily be called an urban mandate."[18]

The city is an intrinsically positive social form with a checkered past and a beautiful future. As redemptive history progresses, we see that God's people begin as wanderers and nomads outside of cities, and as city rebels (Babel). Then God directs them to be city builders and rebuilders (Jerusalem) and city-loving exiles (Babylon). In New Testament times, the people of God become city missionaries (indeed, New Testament writings contain few glimpses of nonurban Christianity). Finally, when God's future arrives in the form of a city, his people can finally be fully at home. The fallen nature of the city — the warping of its potential due to the power of sin — is finally overcome and resolved; the cultural mandate is complete; the capacities of city life are freed in the end to serve God. All of God's people serve him in his holy city.

1. Keller writes, "The church should continue to relate to the human cities of our time, not as the people of God did under Abraham, Moses, or David, but as they did during the time of the exile." In what ways is the situation of the Christian church different from that of the exiles in Babylon? In what ways is it similar? How does this affect the mission of the church today?

2. From Acts 17 through the end of the book of Acts, Paul has strategically traveled to the intellectual (Athens), commercial (Corinth), religious (Ephesus), and political (Rome) centers of the Roman world. What are the centers of power and influence in your own local context? How is your church seeking to strategically reach these different centers of cultural influence?

3. Keller writes, "Then, as now, the cities were filled with the poor, and urban Christians' commitment to the poor was visible and striking." Do you believe this is still true of the Christian church? If so, give an example. If not, how can this legacy be recaptured?

4. Keller writes, "Gardening (the original human vocation) is a paradigm for cultural development. A gardener neither leaves the ground as is, nor does he destroy it. Instead, he rearranges it to produce food and plants for human life. He *cultivates* it. (The words *culture* and *cultivate* come from the same root.) Every vocation is in some way a response to, and an extension of, the primal, Edenic act of cultivation." Discuss how different vocations are a response to our call to cultivate culture. How does the creation mandate transform our understanding of work and vocation?

CHAPTER 12 — REDEMPTION AND THE CITY {pages 146–52}

1. Note the references to "Pauline Christianity" in Wayne A. Meeks, *The First Urban Christians: The Social World of the Apostle Paul*, 2nd ed. (New Haven, Conn.: Yale University Press, 2003); see also Todd D. Still and David G. Horrell, eds., *After the First Urban Christians: The Social-Scientific Study of Pauline Christianity Twenty-Five Years Later* (Edinburgh: T&T Clark, 2009).

2. See Miroslav Volf, "Soft Difference," www.yale.edu/faith/resources/x_volf_difference.html (accessed January 20, 2012).

3. For more on mission in the Old Testament, see Christopher J. H. Wright, *The Mission of God: Unlocking the Bible's Grand Narrative* (Downers Grove, Ill.: InterVarsity, 2005); Walter C. Kaiser Jr., *Mission in the Old Testament: Israel as a Light to the Nations* (Grand Rapids: Baker, 2000).

4. Leland Ryken, James C. Wilhoit, and Tremper Longman III, eds., *Dictionary of Biblical Imagery* (Downers Grove, Ill.: InterVarsity, 1998), 153, emphasis mine.

5. John R. W. Stott, *The Message of Acts: The Spirit, the Church, and the World* (Bible Speaks Today; Downers Grove, Ill.: InterVarsity, 1990), 293.

6. Ibid., 314.

7. Ibid., 305.

8. Ibid., 314.

9. Rodney Stark, *The Rise of Christianity: How the Obscure, Marginal Jesus Movement Became the Dominant Religious Force in the Western World in a Few Centuries* (San Francisco: HarperSanFrancisco, 1997), 161–62.

10. Stott, *Message of Acts*, 293.

11. Ibid., 292–93.

12. Meredith G. Kline, *Kingdom Prologue* (South Hamilton, Mass.: Gordon-Conwell Theological Seminary, 1993), 101.

13. I recognize that other human factors were used by God to bring about the astonishing growth of the early church in its first three centuries. There was a cultural crisis in the Greco-Roman worldview, and the worship of the old pagan gods was dying out. Nevertheless, historians now realize how important it was for the influence and spread of the church that it first took root in the urban areas.

14. Richard Fletcher, *The Barbarian Conversion: From Paganism to Christianity* (Berkeley: University of California, 1999).

15. See Harvie Conn, "Christ and the City: Biblical Themes for Building Urban Theology Models," in *Discipling the City*, ed. Roger Greenway (Grand Rapids: Baker, 1979), 222–86. Conn writes (p. 237), "The city is the fulfiller of the paradise of God … This eschatological strand repeatedly ties the future of the city with the original, sinless past of Eden and its restoration in Christ. Even under the curse, man's cultural calling will be maintained." In other words, the garden of Eden, had Adam not fallen, would have developed into the city seen in Revelation 21. It would have been a perfect city under God. In his essay, Conn explains that the city has the same three functions as the garden of God did, namely, it is (1) a place to cultivate the earth and "mine the cultural riches of creation," (2) a place to live in safety and security, and (3) a place to meet God.

16. Gordon J. Wenham, *Genesis 1–15* (Word Biblical Commentary 1a; Nashville: Word, 1987), 61.

17. Gordon Spykman, *Reformational Theology: A New Paradigm for Doing Dogmatics* (Grand Rapids: Eerdmans, 1992), 256.

18. Harvie Conn and Manuel Ortiz, *Urban Ministry: The Kingdom, the City, and the People of God* (Downers Grove, Ill.: InterVarsity, 2001), 87.

THE CALL TO THE CITY

Paul and other Christian missionaries went to great cities because when Christianity was planted there, it spread regionally (cities were the centers of transportation routes); it also spread globally (cities were multiethnic, international centers, and converts took the gospel back to their homeland); and finally it more readily affected the culture (the centers of learning, law, and government were in the cities). As we will see in this chapter, the importance of cities for Christian mission today is, if anything, even greater.

Today, cities are more important than ever before. In 1950, New York and London were the only world cities with metro-area populations of over ten million people. Today, however, there are more than twenty such cities — twelve of which achieved that ranking in the last two decades — with many more to come.[1] All of these new megacities are developing in what was once called the Third World. But why?

In the eighteenth century, a combination of population growth and technology brought rural Europe to its "carrying capacity," creating a surplus population. Virtually all of the land was owned and developed, and so every family had some members who left the family farm, the countryside, and the small towns to make a living elsewhere. As a result, the great cities of Europe (and, in the nineteenth century, America) swelled in size. Many experts now believe that this type of shift has begun to occur in Africa, in Asia, and to a lesser extent in Latin America, where cities are exploding with people from the rural areas. If the urban-to-rural ratio of these populations stabilizes near 75 percent to 25 percent, as it did in Europe and North America, the next three decades will see over half a billion people move into the cities of Africa and Asia alone — in other words, one new Rio de Janeiro (ten million

people) *every two months.*[2] Currently, Western cities such as New York City grow at approximately 125,000 people per year, but cities such as Dhaka and Lagos are growing at a rate of more than half a million per year. By most estimates, we have reached the point where over 50 percent of the world population now lives in cities, compared to around 5 percent two centuries ago.[3]

GLOBALIZATION AND RENAISSANCE

The significance of cities today lies not only in their growing size but also in their growing influence, and this influence is due to the rise of globalization. The technological revolution has led to an unprecedented mobility of people, ideas, and capital. Because of the Internet and other forms of electronic communication, people around the world are more connected than ever before, and Western urban values in particular are spreading everywhere.

What is the effect of this "flattening" of the world due to globalization?[4] First, globalization *connects cities to the world.* Some people predicted that the rise of technology would end up weakening cities, that it would make agglomeration (a cluster of usually disparate elements) obsolete.[5] Social networking and communication online, it was argued, would make it unnecessary to pay the high costs of living in the city. But as Edwin Heathcote has written, "Digital networking has not, as was forecast, led to a decline in the city. Rather, it has led to an urbanization of the rest of the planet."[6] People, especially young people, want to live in cities. The rise of new forms of technology and mobility has not weakened this desire. Instead, it has dramatically expanded the reach and influence of urban culture. This urbanizing influence now extends far beyond the city limits, affecting even the most rural areas of remote countries. Children in Mexico and Romania are becoming more like young adults in Los Angeles and New York City than the adults in their own locales.

Second, globalization *connects cities to cities*. Not only does globalization connect the rest of the world to urban ideas and culture; it also connects cities to one another, enhancing their power and influence.[7] World cities are more connected to others around the world than they are to their own nations. The elites of New York, London, and Tokyo not only work for the same multinational companies, but they also graduate from common educational institutions, take vacations and buy homes in the same places, and share common social and cultural values. They are better able to identify with the urban elites of other nations than with the nonurban citizens of their own countries.

The strong connections among major cities exist not only through the elites, however. Huge, diverse immigrant populations in global cities tie each urban area tightly to scores of other countries. They travel frequently and communicate daily with their homelands. This means, for example, that thousands of residents of New York City are in much closer communication with people in Athens, Manila, Port-au-Prince, Bogota, Hong Kong, and Lagos than they are with the residents of New Jersey and Connecticut. Each global city is a portal to others.

> "Digital networking has not led to a decline in the city. Rather, it has led to an urbanization of the rest of the planet."
> — Edwin Heathcote

These networked world cities are quickly becoming more economically and culturally powerful than their own national governments. Governments are increasingly losing control of the flow of capital and information and have far less influence than the multinational corporations and international financial, social, and technological networks based in global cities. According to the American journalist Neal Peirce, "Great metropolitan regions — not cities, not states, not even the nation states — are starting to emerge as the world's most influential players."[8]

Cities not only grow and mature, but they can also be reborn. Despite the pessimism about Western cities during the late twentieth century, many have regenerated during the 1990s and the first decade of the twenty-first century. During the twenty years from 1970 to 1990, many American cities went into sharp decline. Immigration of blacks from the South to northern cities resulted in white flight, and many poor people were trapped in inner-city ghettos. In the late 1970s and early 1980s protracted recessions diminished tax revenues and drove some cities near or into actual bankruptcy. Meanwhile, urban planning in the mid-twentieth century privileged the suburbs. Whole urban neighborhoods were bulldozed to create expressways that gave suburban residents easy access to center-city jobs. Planners also favored big stores and stadiums with lots of parking, as well as massive housing projects for the poor. All of this led to downtown urban centers that were like ghost towns after dark. The middle class flight to the suburbs took many jobs, leaving the poor poorer and most neighborhoods riddled with crime. Cities hollowed out into "doughnuts," with poor nonwhite centers and affluent white suburbs.

However, since 1990, American cities have experienced an amazing renaissance.[9] During this time, many cities' population declines have begun to reverse. People began to move back into cities, and center cities began to regenerate at their cores. Why? One of the primary reasons is that during this time the U.S. economy experienced a sustained period of growth, which created a great deal of new wealth and new jobs in knowledge sectors. Second, crime went down in cities for the reasons liberals cite (more jobs) and for the reasons conservatives cite (tougher enforcement). Third, a cultural mood developed (which some call postmodern) embracing eclecticism, the mixture of the old and new, asymmetry, messiness and unmanageability, cultural diversity, and the artistic and organic. All of

COMEBACK: MINNEAPOLIS AND MILAN

Edward Glaeser cites Minneapolis, Minnesota, and Milan, Italy, as cities that have reinvented themselves. Between 1950 and 1980, Minneapolis lost 30 percent of its population, and its location and climate hardly made it a great candidate for urban renaissance. Its older way of attracting human capital—touting its riverside location—was no longer of much appeal. Yet since 1980, the population of Minneapolis has continued to grow, and it now has the highest per capita income in the upper Midwest. Why? Minneapolis has reinvented itself as a *center of education*. It is home to the University of Minnesota, and "the city's most striking economic success stories have some link to that school."[10] One example is Medtronic, the world's largest medical technology company.

Milan was a manufacturing giant that was hit by the same forces that led to the decline in the American Rust Belt. Its population fell almost 30 percent from 1970 through 2000. However, Milan reinvented itself, and today three-quarters of its workers are in services, especially finance, but also health and bio-technologies, telecommunications, and, of course, retail and fashion. The population has continued to grow over the past decade.[11]

these are features of city life rather than of suburban culture. Younger adults began to prefer city life and started moving to urban areas in greater numbers. Fourth, changes in immigration law opened the door to an influx of immigrants from non-European nations. Between 1965 and 1970, U.S. immigration doubled. Then, from 1970 to 1990 it doubled again. Most of this immigration wave emptied into America's cities, renewing and diversifying many neighborhoods. It also completely changed the older, gridlocked, binary black-white dynamic of urban politics into a far more complex, multipolar situation, with many ethnicities and nationalities.

As a result, many American cities began to surge. Professionals streamed into center-city neighborhoods, while new ethnic communities developed within older working-class and poor neighborhoods. Sometimes the gentrification process was more destructive and disruptive to the social fabric; in other cases it had a more wholesome effect. The major actors in this renewed upsurge included empty-nester boomers returning to cities, young professionals seeking cities to live and work in, and a wave of immigrants in inner-city neighborhoods and inner suburbs that eventually produced second-generation college graduates who moved into the center city to live and work. These groups joined the gays and artists who have always chosen to live in urban communities.[12]

Edward Glaeser points out that not all cities have succeeded in the past generation — and he points to Detroit, Michigan, and Leipzig, Germany, as examples. But most cities have found the power to reinvent themselves, argues Glaeser, because the essence of what makes a city a city is the bringing of people together to innovate. At one level, this means bringing together the most highly trained and talented people, the "elites." Yet at another level, it means bringing together the most energetic, ambitious, and risk-taking people from among the poor and middle classes of the world. Cities are cauldrons of reengineering and reinvention, and so it should not surprise us to find that they are always reinventing themselves.

Perhaps the most interesting example of contemporary urban reinvention is what has been called the "consumer city." The post–World War II years brought about the rise of suburbanization and the creation of the commuter city. People chose suburban life for its amenities and comforts and commuted into the city only for work and the occasional show. But Vancouver and Los Angeles are two urban areas that reversed the trend. They became *consumer* cities marked by a new phenomenon —

the reverse commuter. Increasingly, these and other cities offer residents a quality of life they could not find elsewhere in the region — a dizzying variety of artistic, educational, cultural, and entertainment events and venues, but also (now) safe streets, good schools, and excellent public transportation. Many people now move to London, New York, and Paris and are willing to pay a premium to live in the center of the city, even if their jobs take them out of the core of the city each day.[13]

THE FUTURE OF CITIES

Few people now believe we will see a significant decline in the population growth and importance of global cities, at least in the foreseeable future. The growth trends and culture shifts are on too strong a trajectory. However, the Great Recession and hard economic times in the United States and Europe mean that city governments in these countries are being forced to make deep, painful cuts to their budgets, while the private sector faces the prospect of years of high unemployment. The gaps in social service offerings are likely to widen in many cities. These changes will certainly have an impact on the quality of life in cities.[14]

So will Western cities return to the economic and population decline they experienced in the 1970s and 1980s? Several trends are likely to help many cities in the West continue flourishing, at least for the foreseeable future. First, the world will continue to globalize — and globalization is a boon to cities that connect to it. More cities will imitate the biggest and most established cities in the West — New York, Los Angeles, and London — whose strong international connections and influences will help to keep real estate values up and provide a constant source of jobs (regardless of how national economies are faring). As a result, most globalizing cities should be able to remain economically stable.

Second, current urban planning in Western cities has returned to the classic urban form — compact, public transit – oriented, and walkable, mixed-use development (with residences, businesses, retail outlets, educational and cultural institutions, and entertainment venues situated together). The em-

phasis will be on developing neighborhood schools, "complete" streets with sidewalks for pedestrians, and lanes for bicyclists. This renewed emphasis on older forms is sometimes called "New Urbanism" or "Smart Growth," and there are many factors driving this trend. One relates to environmental concerns. Suburban and rural dwellers consume far more energy — electricity, fossil fuels, and other forms — than urban residents.[15] The increasingly urgent search for energy sustainability will continue to press societies to urbanize. Cities, therefore, will remain a very attractive alternative to the suburbs as a social arrangement.

Third, immigration laws have not significantly changed (as of this writing), and so it is likely that the United States will continue to receive immigrants from around the world. Though some trends have seen immigrants moving straight into the suburbs, the structure of city life continues to provide most new immigrants with the essential support resources they need to successfully transition into a new society. Cities today will compete for immigrants, knowing that the urban areas that receive the most immigration will be best positioned for future success.

THERE REALLY IS NO CHOICE

Al Mohler, president of The Southern Baptist Theological Seminary, read the 2010 Special Report by *Financial Times* titled "The Future of Cities" and responded with strong language:

This much is clear—the cities are where the people are. In the course of less than 300 years, our world will have shifted from one in which only 3 percent of people live in cities, to one in which 80 percent are resident in urban areas.

If the Christian church does not learn new modes of urban ministry, we will find ourselves on the outside looking in. The Gospel of Jesus Christ must call a new generation of committed Christians into these teeming cities. As these new numbers make clear, there really is no choice.[16]

Fourth, one of the greatest fears about cities — that high, life-threatening crime is inevitable in very large urban areas — is fast eroding. Led by New York City, many cities in North America have seen startling drops in crime over the past two decades; and this is one of the main drivers of economic and population growth in cities. The decline in crime is often attributed entirely to better police practices, as Mayor Michael Bloomberg of New York recently

---

All current signs lead us to believe that the world order of the twenty-first century will be global, multicultural, and urban.

---

claimed.[17] But criminologists have shown that policing can only account for part of the decline, and that crime only falls off drastically when a variety of factors converge, many of which are impossible to measure directly.[18] These may include the strengthening of "civil society" — in the flourishing of voluntary associations such as stronger parent-teacher alliances, growth in religious institutions, growth in various nonprofit agencies, and greater public-private cooperatives.[19]

Fifth, as far as I can tell, the postmodern mood that leads many young adults to prefer city life to suburban life will continue. This trend is difficult to quantify or fully explain, but the appeal of city life for young people remains quite strong, and the presence of youthful energy and creativity will continue to sustain the growth and strength of cities. According to the *Wall Street Journal* and *The Atlantic*, approximately 32 percent of Americans in the Millennial generation live in cities — and 88 percent of them want to.[20]

Some of the most troubled cities, such as Detroit, will need to make drastic changes, shrinking their urban footprint and redesigning into smaller municipalities. But this is unlikely to become the norm in the United States. I believe globalization and the current cultural mood will continue to make cities highly desirable destinations for ambitious and innovative people, and this will be a decisive factor in continuing the growth and dominance of urban culture.

Now, more than ever, cities set the course of society and life as a whole, even in areas of the world, such as Europe and North America, where cities are not growing as rapidly.[21] All current signs lead us to believe that the world order of the twenty-first century will be global, multicultural, and urban.

THE CHALLENGE OF MINISTRY IN CITIES

The massive growth and influence of cities in our time confront Christian mission with an enormous challenge. The first problem is one of sheer scale and economics. It is critical that we have Christians and churches wherever there are people, but the people of the world are now moving into the great cities of the world many times faster than the church is. Christian communication and ministry must always be translated into every new language and context, but the Christian church is not responding fast enough to keep up with the rapid population growth in cities.

There are five million new people moving into the cities of the developing world every month — roughly the size of the metropolitan areas of Philadelphia or San Francisco. Think of that — how many churches ought there to be in a city the size of Philadelphia? Even if there were one church for every five thousand people — which is five times fewer than the United States average[22] — this means we should be planting a thousand urban churches in the world every month.

But the challenge is not just numerical; it is also conceptual and methodological. Our very models for ministry must become increasingly urbanized. U.S. missions agencies are finding that more and more they must send their workers to live and minister in the growing cities. But seldom are these Americans experienced at life or ministry in the city. A couple of years ago, I met with American missionaries who had been sent to one of the fast-growing megacities of China. They told me their mission agency had assumed that the training they needed had to do with learning the language and understanding Chinese culture. But after a while they realized they knew nothing about living in cities. Each member of their team had grown up in small towns in southern and midwestern areas of the United States. They struggled more with urban life than with life in China per se. And they also came to see that the people they were trying to reach were more like people living in Los Angeles and Manhattan than like those in the Chinese countryside. The leader of the team told me, "Only the language training we received was helpful. We were given no training in how to live in cities and how to reach urban people, and as a result we've been ineffective."

Urbanization is not only transforming how we in the West do mission overseas; it is also transforming the mission landscape in the West itself. Waves of immigration from the Southern and Eastern Hemispheres are coming to the cities of North America and Europe. Many of these immigrants come from parts of the world where belief in orthodox, supernatural Christianity is on the rise. As a result, thousands of new churches are being planted by non-Westerners in the formerly secular cities of London, Paris, and New York.[23] In fact, most of the largest, well-attended churches in London and Paris are led by Africans, and in New York City we have seen hundreds of new churches started by Christians from Asia, Latin America, the Caribbean, and Africa. At first, these new Christian churches remain somewhat isolated from the broader society, evangelizing and growing within ethnic enclaves. But as the children of these Christians become educated in national universities and move into the center city, they will begin to wield greater power and influence in areas of finance, media, and culture. Anglo elites have begun inviting many of these young nonwhites into the upper echelons of business and government, not realizing that a large percentage of them are Christians.[24]

Globalization and urbanization are removing the very distinction between "home" and "foreign" missions (to use, for a moment, the old terminology).[25] Consider the example of a church I know in the borough of Queens in New York City. This church has planted three daughter churches — one in New York's neighboring College Point, one in New York's neighboring Bronx, and one in the "neighboring" Philippines. They had reached so many Filipino immigrants in their own neighborhood that these new Christians wanted to plant a daughter church among their friends and relatives in their country of origin. So they sent a large group of people out from New York City to plant a new church. This is not an isolated case. Every major city is now a portal for reaching the nations of the world. In other words, one of the very best ways to reach the far parts of the world is to reach your own city![26]

Now consider another example. We planted Redeemer Presbyterian Church in the middle of New York City — in central Manhattan. Within a few years, we had planted daughter churches in Westchester County, New York, and New Jersey (the two principal "bedroom communities" of the city). If we had originally located in any particular suburb, however, we would never have been able in so short a time to plant churches in Manhattan or in the other suburbs. Why not? You can't reach the city from the suburbs, but you can reach the suburbs from the city. Cities are like a giant heart — drawing people in and then sending them out. Students come to cities to attend school, and then they graduate and move out. Singles meet in the city, get married, and move out to the suburbs when children are born. Immigrants come to the city and live in ethnic

---

The people of the world are now moving into the great cities of the world many times faster than the church is.

---

enclaves, but as they amass assets and become more established in their new country, they move outward to gain additional space for their growing families. In each case, the movement is from the center outward. As a result, a church that thrives in the city will create a community whose members will spread naturally throughout the adjoining region and into other great cities. In other words,

ONE OF HISTORY'S GREATEST OPPORTUNITIES

Cities can have a major impact on reaching hard-to-reach peoples with the gospel. This is the belief of missionary-theologian Roger Greenway:

> It may be helpful to those who harbor misgivings about cities ... to reflect on the fact that urbanization as a present fact of life for most of the human family is a reality under the providential control of God. In Acts 17:26–27, the apostle Paul observes, "He determined the times set for them and the exact places where they should live. God did this so men would seek him and perhaps reach out for him and find him." Viewed in light of these verses, city growth is not something to be perceived as entirely the work of the devil, but as part of God's providential plan in history. God's redemptive purpose behind urban growth is that "men should seek him and reach out for him"...
>
> Pressed together in metropolises, the races, tribes, and diverse people groups are geographically more accessible than ever before. In some cases the processes of change that new urbanites pass through make them more receptive to the gospel. If this is the case, world urbanization should be viewed in an eschatological as well as missionary framework. God in our time is moving climactically through a variety of social, political, and economic factors to bring earth's peoples into closer contact with one another, into greater interaction and interdependence, and into earshot of the gospel. By this movement God carries forward his redemptive purposes in history. A sign of our time is the city. Through worldwide migration to the city God may be setting the stage for Christian mission's greatest and perhaps final hour.[27]

one of the best ways to reach a region and country is to reach your own city!

THE OPPORTUNITY OF MINISTRY IN CITIES

The growth in size and influence of cities today presents the greatest possible challenge for the church. Never before has it been so important to learn how to do effective ministry in cities, and yet, by and large, evangelical Christianity in the United States is still nonurban.

Along with these challenges comes a range of unique opportunities. I see four important groups of people who must be reached to fulfill the mission of the church, and each of them can best be reached in the cities.

If the church in the West remains, for the most part, in the suburbs of Middle America and neglects the great cities, it risks losing an entire generation of American society's leaders.

---

1. The younger generation. The prospects for advancement, the climate of constant innovation and change, the coming together of diverse influences and people — all of these appeal to young adults. In the United States and Europe, the young disproportionately want to live in cities, and for the highly ambitious, the numbers are even higher. In a *New York Times* op-ed column, "I Dream of Denver," David Brooks looks at Pew Research Center data that shows the sharp difference between younger Americans and older Americans as to their preference for cities:

> *Cities remain attractive to the young. Forty-five percent of Americans between the ages of eighteen and thirty-four would like to live in New York City. But cities are profoundly unattractive to people with families and to the elderly. Only 14 percent of Americans thirty-five and older are interested in living in New York City. Only 8 percent of people over sixty-five are drawn to Los Angeles.[28]*

This means, of course, that if the church in the West remains, for the most part, in the suburbs of Middle America and neglects the great cities, it risks losing an entire generation of American society's leaders.

One of the reasons cities are filled with young adults is that they are also usually filled with students. In university towns it is obvious to the casual observer that students are an important part of the demographic. In large cities, however, there are often enormous numbers of undergraduate and graduate students, but the size and diversity of the urban population make college students less visible. Yet students constitute an extremely important mission field, and urban students have far more local job opportunities available to them after graduation than do those who go to school in "college towns." As a result, college students in cities who are won to the faith are a significant source of future leaders for urban churches.

2. The "cultural elites." The second group is made up of those who have a disproportionate influence on how human life is lived in a society because they exert power in business, publishing, the media, the academy, and the arts. These people live or spend much of their time in city centers. Since cities now influence the culture and values of the world more than ever, the single most effective way for Christians to influence the culture of a nation is to have large numbers of them stay in cities and simply "be the church" there. Also, for all the reasons noted above, ministry that is effective in a world city travels well. Ministry in rural areas of a country may have little transferability to rural areas in other countries. But ministry forms that are effective in one center city are likely to have wide appeal to other center cities, especially with the younger generation.

Some Christians may complain, "We are losing the culture wars." This comment comes from the fact that relatively small groups living disproportionately in cities exert far more cultural influence than evangelical Christians, who live disproportionately outside of cities. Every time I exit the 42nd Street subway station in Manhattan, I pass Viacom, the parent company of MTV. Few institutions have had a greater cultural impact on an entire genera-

tion than MTV. I once read that years of Communist rule had not been able to erode the distinct ethnic identity of the Hungarian minority in Romania. Now, however, a global youth culture is turning Hungarian youth away from their cultural roots. Global consumer youth culture is pumped from Manhattan and Hollywood into the digital devices of kids all around the world. Fifteen-year-olds in rural Mexico are now more "urban" in their sensibilities than their parents are. If churches are to have any influence on the people who create institutions like MTV, they will have to live and minister in the same places where these people live — in the city.

3. Accessible "unreached" people groups. Many people speak about the importance of engaging in mission to the hard-to-reach religious and cultural groups, people who live in remote places or in nations that forbid Christian mission work. But the currents of history are now sweeping many of these formerly unreachable people into cities as rural economies fail to sustain old ways of life.

Millions of these newcomers in the burgeoning cities of the world are more open to the Christian faith than they were in their original context. Most have been uprooted from their familiar, traditional setting and have left behind the thicker kinship and tribal networks they once relied on, and most cities in the developing world often have "next to nothing in working government services."[29] These newcomers need help and support to face the moral, economic, emotional, and spiritual pressures of city life, and this is an opportunity for the church to serve them with supportive community, a new spiritual family, and a liberating gospel message. Immigrants to urban areas have many reasons to begin attending churches, reasons that they did not have in their former, rural settings. "Rich pickings await any groups who can meet these needs of these new urbanites, anyone who can at once feed the body and nourish the soul."[31]

But there is yet another way in which cities make formerly hard-to-reach peoples accessible. As I noted earlier, the urban mentality is spreading around the world as technology connects young generations to urbanized, global hyperculture.

MOVING TO THE CITY

In *Two Cities, Two Loves*, James Montgomery Boice considered the 10 percent ratio given in Nehemiah 11:1 for repopulating Jerusalem and suggested that in America, which is less agricultural, a proportional ratio should be even higher. His point was that if more of the nation's Christians deliberately moved into the largest cities and there lived out a life of love, truth, and servanthood, the culture would be fundamentally changed.[30]

Many young people, even those living in remote places, are becoming globalized semi-Westerners, while their parents remain rooted in traditional ways of thinking. And so ministry and gospel communications that connect well with urban residents are also increasingly relevant and effective with young nonurban dwellers.

4. The poor. A fourth group of people who can and must be reached in cities is the poor. Some have estimated that one-third of the people representing the new growth in cities in the developing world will live in shantytowns. A great majority of the world's poor live in cities, and there is an important connection between reaching the urban elites and serving the poor of your city. First, an urban church's work among the poor will be a significant mark of its validity. It is one of the "good deeds" that Scripture says will lead pagans to glorify God (Matt 5:16; 1 Pet 2:12). Similarly, once cultural elites are won to Christ, discipling them includes reorienting them to spend their wealth and power on the needs of the poor and the city instead of on themselves. In other words, an urban church does not choose between ministry to the poor and ministry to the professional class. We need the economic and cultural resources of the elites to help the poor, and our commitment to the poor is a testimony to the cultural elites, supporting the validity of our message.

We can be confident that the cities of the world will continue to grow in significance and power. Because of this, they remain just as strategic — if not more so — than they were in the days of Paul and the early church when Christian mission was predominantly urban. I would argue that there is nothing more critical for the evangelical church today than to emphasize and support urban ministry.

The need is great, as is the cost — ministry in city centers is considerably more expensive on a per capita basis than it is away from the urban core. But the church can no longer ignore the profound and irreversible changes occurring in the world today. If Christians want to reach the unreached, we must go to the cities. To reach the rising generations, we must go to the cities. To have any impact for Christ on the creation of culture, we must go to the cities. To serve the poor, we must go to the cities.

Many people who are not naturally comfortable in the city will have to follow the example of Abraham. Abraham was called to leave his familiar culture and become a pilgrim, seeking the city of God (Gen 12:1 – 4; Heb 11:8 – 10). And while Christians should not deliberately seek difficulty for its own sake, can we not follow the example of the incarnate Christ, who did not live in places where he was comfortable but went where he was useful (Matt 8:20; John 4:34; Rom 15:3)? Can we not face difficulty for *his* sake (cf. Heb 11:26), embracing both the difficulties and the riches of city living?

1. Where have you witnessed some of the things discussed in this chapter (globalization, gentrification, city renaissance, reverse commuting, postmodernism, etc.) in the life of your nearest city? How do they affect life in that city? How do they affect ministry in that city?

2. If our future will be largely an urban culture, what changes should the church be making today to prepare and adapt?

3. One significant trend discussed in this chapter is the influx of Christian immigrant populations and their increasing access to elite levels of business and society. How do you believe their contributions will shape the future of your ministry?

4. Which of the following city-prone groups do you feel most passionate to reach: the younger generation, the "cultural elites," accessible "unreached" people groups, or the poor? Is that group present in your setting right now? How is urbanization affecting them? Take a moment to reflect on what it would be like to minister meaningfully to the group you have identified.

CHAPTER 13 — THE CALL TO THE CITY {pages 154–63}

1. This is true whether one takes a stricter view of population within legal "city limits" (see www.worldatlas.com/citypops.htm) or larger "metropolitan areas" (see www.citypopulation.de/world/Agglomerations.html).

2. See Edward Glaeser, *The Triumph of the City: How Our Greatest Invention Makes Us Richer, Smarter, Greener, Healthier, and Happier* (New York: Penguin, 2011), 1. Other statistics in this paragraph (and the preceding one) are taken from the *Economist* article "The Brown Revolution" (May 9, 2002), www.economist.com/node/1120305 (accessed January 24, 2012).

3. A good, up-to-date source of information on cities is the special report issued by *Financial Times* in early 2010 titled "The Future of Cities," www.ft.com/cities (accessed January 24, 2012).

4. See Thomas L. Friedman, *The World Is Flat 3.0: A Brief History of the Twenty-First Century*, rev. ed. (New York: Farrar, Straus and Giroux, 2007).

5. See comments on the effects of agglomeration in chapter 14.

6. Edwin Heathcote, "From Megacity to Metacity," *Financial Times* (April 6, 2010), www.ft.com/intl/cms/s/0/e388a076-38d6-11df-9998-00144feabdc0.html#axzz1kNrFC7jH (accessed January 24, 2012).

7. In a photo essay on the website of Foreign Policy, noted urban sociologist Saskia Sassen lists the most influential city-networks in the world: (1) New York – Washington, D.C. – Chicago, (2) Beijing – Hong Kong, (3) Frankfurt – Berlin, (4) Istanbul – Ankara, (5) Brasilia – Rio de Janeiro – Sao Paulo. Each network combines the strengths of finance, government, and the creative arts; see www.foreignpolicy.com/articles/2011/11/28/16_global_cities_to_watch? (accessed January 24, 2012).

8. Neal Peirce, "The 'Citistates' Are on the Rise, and the Competition Is Fierce," *Philadelphia Inquirer* (July 26, 1993), A11, http://articles.philly.com/1993-07-26/news/25975949_1_citistate-nation-states-world-population (accessed January 24, 2012).

9. The dynamics outlined in this section are especially pronounced in American cities, but they characterize many European cities as well.

10. Glaeser, *Triumph of the City*, 236.

11. Ibid., 237 – 38.

12. Redeemer Presbyterian Church in New York City came into existence at the very beginning of this renaissance — in 1989. At that time, moving into the center city to begin a church seemed to be a fool's errand. The year we moved to New York City, a highly publicized poll revealed that most of the residents of NYC would move away if they could. Indeed, in the 1970s and into the 1980s, nearly everyone was trying to leave cities — well-off and poor, white, black, and immigrant. Those were bad times! Yet, within a few years of our founding, I began to get calls from churches, denominations, and leaders who had begun to notice the renaissance in nearby cities. They realized it was time to plant churches to reach the new residential communities that were growing in cities.

13. Ibid., 131 – 32, 238 – 41, 259 – 60.

14. See Ariella Cohen, "Cities in Crisis," *Next American City* (Spring 2009), http://americancity.org/magazine/article/cities-in-crisis/ (accessed January 24, 2012).

15. See David Owen, *Green Metropolis: Why Living Smaller, Living Closer, and Driving Less Are the Keys to Sustainability* (New York: Riverhead, 2009). For a shorter survey, see "Is There Anything Greener than Blacktop?" in Glaeser, *Triumph of the City*, 199.

16. Albert Mohler, "From Megacity to 'Metacity' — The Shape of the Future," AlbertMohler.com (April 22, 2010), www.albertmohler.com/2010/04/22/from-megacity-to-metacity-the-shape-of-the-future/ (accessed January 24, 2012).

17. "In the absence of evidence that a reduction or increase in crime can be tied to economic or environmental variables, Mr. Bloomberg said he concluded the success is due to 'a better police department than ever before.' 'We have looked for every kind of relationship and correlation to the weather, the economy, or whatever,' he said. 'It's not there' (Tamer El-Ghobashy, "Mayor Touts 'Safest Decade,' " *Wall Street Journal* (December 29, 2011), http://online.wsj.com/article/SB100014240529702047202045771270921223640490.html.

18. In the *Wall Street Journal* article "Mayor Touts 'Safest Decade,' " James Alan Fox, a professor of criminology, states that policing is just one of several factors that contribute to precipitous crime reductions. "There's no one reason why crime falls." Fox cites, in addition to better policing, an aging population, an increase in incarceration, and the stabilizing of illegal drug markets. But Franklin Zimring, in *The City That Became Safe*, states that New York City's crime reduction happened despite no significant changes in the population age or incarceration or even illegal drug use. He shows that many of the reasons for precipitous crime reduction are yet unidentified or hard to measure. He does conclude, however, that the last twenty years proves that crime is not a necessary fact of life in major cities.

19. See Peter Berger and Richard John Neuhaus, *To Empower People: From State to Civil Society* (Washington, D.C.: American Enterprise Institute, 1985).

20. S. Mitra Kalita and Robbie Whelan, "No McMansions for Millennials," *Wall Street Journal* (January 13, 2011), http://blogs.wsj.com/developments/2011/01/13/no-mcmansions-for-millennials/; Jordan Weissmann, "Why Don't Young Americans Buy Cars?" *The Atlantic* (March 25, 2012), www.theatlantic.com/business/archive/2012/03/why-dont-young-americans-buy-cars/255001/#.T3H8uIuSBoQ.twitter (accessed April 5, 2012).

21. See Harvie Conn, *The American City and the Evangelical Church* (Grand Rapids: Baker, 1994), 181–82.

22. We estimate there are 322,000 Christian churches for a United States population of 311 million — a bit more than one church for every 1,000 residents (see the website of the Hartford Institute for Religious Research, http://hirr.hartsem.edu/research/fastfacts/fast_facts.html). The average size of a congregation in the U.S. is 75, which means that if there is one church for every 1,000 residents in a city, 7.5 percent of the population will be going to church. Note that these are median figures; actual numbers vary greatly from region to region.

23. See Philip Jenkins, *The Next Christendom: The Coming of Global Christianity*, rev. ed. (New York: Oxford University Press, 2007); idem, *The New Faces of Christianity: Believing the Bible in the Global South* (New York: Oxford University Press, 2008); Lamin Sanneh, *Whose Religion Is Christianity? The Gospel beyond the West* (Grand Rapids: Eerdmans, 2003).

24. These statements are based on numerous examples I have witnessed firsthand in New York City over the past twenty years.

25. See Mark Galli's interview of Bob Roberts, "Glocal Church Ministry," *Christianity Today* 51.7 (July 2007), www.christianitytoday.com/ct/2007/july/30.42.html (accessed January 24, 2012).

26. It should be said that this is not the only way to reach out to the world. There is still a need for Christians in every country to consider the call to relocate to distant lands to accomplish the global mission of the church. To my surprise, in recent years I have seen that domestic urban church planting has almost become romanticized among young evangelicals in the same way overseas missions was romanticized among former generations. We should avoid all rose-colored idealizations. My point is that cities — at home and abroad — are far more important now to the accomplishment of the world mission of the church than they were fifty years ago.

27. Roger Greenway, "World Urbanization and Missiological Education," in *Missiological Education for the Twenty-First Century: The Book, the Circle, and the Sandals*, ed. J. Dudley Woodberry, Charles Van Engen, and Edgar J. Elliston (Maryknoll, N.Y.: Orbis, 1996), 145–46.

28. David Brooks, "I Dream of Denver," *New York Times* (February 16, 2009), www.nytimes.com/2009/02/17/opinion/17brooks.html (accessed January 24, 2012).

29. Jenkins, *Next Christendom*, 93.

30. See James Montgomery Boice, *Two Cities, Two Loves: Christian Responsibility in a Crumbling Culture* (Downers Grove, Ill.: InterVarsity, 1996), 165–77.

31. Ibid., 94.

THE GOSPEL FOR THE CITY

I have made as strenuous a case as I can that the city is one of the highest priorities for Christian life and mission in the twenty-first century. Now I want to press even further. These chapters on City Vision may have given you the idea that I think all Christians should move into cities and serve there. To be clear, this is *not* what I am saying. I believe there must be Christians and churches everywhere there are people. In one sense, there are no "little" places or people.[1] God loves to use unimportant people (1 Cor 1:26 – 31) and unlikely places (John 1:46) to do his work. Jesus wasn't from Rome or even Jerusalem but was born in Bethlehem and raised in Nazareth — perhaps to make this very point. We have been told that now something like 50 percent of the world's population live in cities — but this means that half the population does *not* live in urban areas, and therefore we must not discourage or devalue gospel ministry in the hundreds of thousands of towns and villages on earth. And ministry in small towns may not change a country, but it surely can have a major impact in its region.[2]

And yet a thought experiment may be illuminating here. Imagine you are in charge of establishing new churches in two different towns — one has a hundred residents, while the other has ten thousand residents. Imagine also that you have only four church planters. Where would you send them? Regardless of philosophy, I doubt anyone would send two church planters to each town on the premise that all places are equally important in ministry. It simply would not be good stewardship of God's human resources to send two pastors to a town with only a hundred residents. It is good stewardship, though, to insist that we should increase our attention and emphasis on urban ministry in a day when nonurban areas typically have more churches than cities and when

cities are increasingly exerting more influence on how human life is lived in the world.

So I am not saying that all Christians should pack up and go to live and minister in urban areas. What I *am* saying is that the cities of the world are grievously underserved by the church because, in general, the people of the world are moving into cities faster than churches are. And I am seeking to use all the biblical, sociological, missiological, ecclesial, and rhetorical resources at my disposal to help the church (particularly in the United States) reorient itself to address this deficit.

But the call to the city doesn't end there. Everywhere in the world is more urban than it was ten or twenty years ago. Wherever you live, work, and serve, the city is coming to you. In a sense, every church can and must become a church for its particular city — whether that city is a great metropolis, a university town, or a village. As a result, I believe you can benefit by allowing yourself and your ministry to be intentionally shaped by the realities and patterns of

---

> Every church can and must become a church for its particular city — whether that city is a great metropolis, a university town, or a village.

---

urban life and culture. In order to accomplish this, we must look first at how the dynamics of the city affect our lives and then consider how churches with City Vision will minister in response to these dynamics.

HOW THE CITY WORKS ON US

By many people's reckoning, the "death of distance" should have led to a decline in cities, but it has not.

If you can learn things over the Internet, the thinking went, why pay big-city prices for housing? But real learning, communication, and community are far more complex than we may care to acknowledge. A great deal of research has shown that face-to-face contact and learning can never be fully replaced by any other kind.

It is no surprise, then, that research shows us that productivity is significantly higher for companies that locate near the geographic center of "inventive activity" in their industry. Why? Proximity to others working in your field enables the infinite number of interactions, many of them informal, that turns neophytes into experts more quickly and helps experts stimulate each other to new insights. Edward Glaeser observes, "Much of the value of a dense work environment comes from unplanned meetings and observing the random doings of the people around you. Video conferencing will never give a promising young worker the ability to learn by observing the day-to-day operations of a successful mentor."[3] Other studies reveal that a high percentage of patent applications cited older patents in the same metropolitan region, so "even in our age of information technology, ideas are often geographically localized."[4]

Urban theorists call this "agglomeration." Agglomeration refers to the economic and social benefits of physically locating near one another.[5] It is not surprising, then, that more movies are produced in Los Angeles and Toronto than in Atlanta, because those cities have far larger pools of skilled laborers — writers, directors, actors, technicians — who can make movies happen. It is not surprising that new innovations in financial services come out of Manhattan or new technologies out of Silicon Valley. Why? Agglomeration. The physical clustering of thousands of people who work in the same field naturally generates new ideas and enterprises. But the benefits of agglomeration are not limited to locating near people who, *like* you, work in the same field. There are benefits to be reaped of living near large groups of people who are *unlike* you but who have skills that supplement yours.

A good case study is the world of the arts. "Artistic movements are often highly localized," even more so than in other fields.[6] Urban scholar Elizabeth Currid interviewed New York City cultural producers (fashion designers, musicians, and fine artists) and gatekeepers (gallery owners, curators, and editors), as well as owners of clubs and venues frequented by these groups, people in the media and sometimes the academy, the directors of foundations that supported the arts, and prosperous businessmen and women who often acted as patrons.[7] Art "happened" when complex interactions occurred among people in these diverse sectors of the arts ecosystem — not typically through business meetings in workplaces but through interactions at social gatherings and spontaneous meetings in informal situations. Currid found that the cultural economy depends on having "artistic and cultural producers densely agglomerated," part of a "clustered production system."[8] When these various classes of persons live in geographical proximity, thousands of enterprise-producing, culture-making, face-to-face interactions take place that could not take place otherwise.[9] As Ryan Avent puts it, "Cities are a lot like a good group of friends: what you're doing isn't nearly as important as the fact that you're doing it together."[10]

How do the dynamics of agglomeration bear on the real life of the average city Christian? First, *the*

FACE-TO-FACE

Two researchers at the University of Michigan gave groups of six students each the rules of a game to play as a team. Some groups were allowed ten minutes of face-to-face interaction to discuss strategy before playing. Other groups were given thirty minutes of electronic interaction before playing the game in the exact same way. The groups that only met electronically before the game did far less well. This and other experiments have helped us to see that "face-to face contact leads to more trust, generosity, and cooperation than any other sort of interaction."[11] Indeed, common sense tells us that we work up to the level of those working around us.

city uniquely links you with many people **like** *you.* The city's challenges and opportunities attract the most talented, ambitious, and restless. So whoever you are, in the city you will encounter people who are far more talented and advanced than you are. Because you are placed among so many like-but-extremely-skilled people in your field, you will be consistently challenged to reach down and do your very best. You feel driven and pressed by the

---

For our own continuing spiritual growth and well-being, we need the city perhaps more than the city needs us.

---

intensity of the place to realize every ounce of your potential. Cities draw and gather together human resources, tapping their potential for cultural development as no other human-life structure can. But sin takes this strength feature of the city — its culture-forming intensity — and turns it into a place tainted by deadly hubris, envy, and burnout. This is what sin does. It is a parasitic perversion of the good. The gospel is needed to resist the dark side of this gift.

Second, *the city uniquely links you with many people* **unlike** *you.* The city attracts society's sub-cultures and minorities, who can band together for mutual support. It is inherently merciful to those with less power, creating safe enclaves for singles, the poor, immigrants, and racial minorities. Because you are placed among such inescapable diversity, you will be consistently challenged in your views and beliefs. You will be confronted with creative, new approaches to thought and practice and must either abandon your traditional ways and beliefs or become far more knowledgeable about and committed to them than you were before. Again, sin takes a strength feature of the city — its culture-forming diversity — and turns it into a place that undermines our prior commitments and worldviews. And again, the gospel is needed to resist the dark side of this gift.

How should Christians respond to these ways that the city challenges us? We must respond with the gospel. And how, exactly, does the gospel help us face these challenges with joy rather than fear? Obviously, it is true that we must bring the gospel to the city and hear the gospel while in the city. But we must also recognize how much *the city itself brings the gospel to us.* The city will challenge us to discover the power of the gospel in new ways. We will find people who seem spiritually and morally hopeless to us. We will think, "*Those* people will never believe in Christ." But a comment such as this is revealing in itself. If salvation is truly by grace, not by virtue and merit, why should we think that *anyone* is less likely than ourselves to be a Christian? Why would anyone's conversion be any greater miracle than our own? The city may force us to discover that we don't really believe in sheer grace, that we really believe God mainly saves nice people — people like us.

In cities we will also meet a lot of people who hold to other religions or to no religion who are wiser, kinder, and more thoughtful than we are, because even after growth in grace, many Christians are weaker people than many non-Christians. When this surprises you, reflect on it. If the gospel of grace is true, why would we think that Christians are a better kind of person than non-Christians? These living examples of common grace may begin to show us that even though we intellectually understand the doctrine of justification by faith alone, functionally we continue to assume that salvation is by moral goodness and works.

Early in Redeemer's ministry, we discovered it was misguided for Christians to feel pity for the city, and it was harmful to think of ourselves as its "savior." We had to humbly learn from and respect our city and its people. Our relationship with them had to be a consciously reciprocal one. We had to be willing to see God's common grace in their lives. We had to learn that we needed them to fill out our own understanding of God and his grace, just as they needed us.

I believe many Christians in the West avoid the city because it is filled with "the other." Because cities are filled with people who are completely unlike us, many Christians find this disorienting. Deep down, we know we don't *like* these people or don't feel safe around them. But see how easily we forget the gospel! After all, in the gospel we learn of a God who came and lived among us, became one of us, and loved us to the death, even though we were wholly other from him. The city humbles us, showing us how little we are actually shaped by the story and pattern of the gospel.

The gospel alone can give us the humility ("I have much to learn from the city"), the confidence ("I have much to give to the city"), and the courage ("I have nothing to fear from the city") to do effective ministry that honors God and blesses others. And in time we will see that, for our own continuing spiritual growth and well-being, we need the city perhaps more than the city needs us.

WHAT SHOULD CHRISTIANS DO ABOUT CITIES?

If this is how the city can change us for the better, what can we do to return the favor?

1. Christians should develop appreciative attitudes toward the city. In obedience to God, Jonah went to the city of Nineveh, but he didn't love it. In the same way, Christians may come to the city out of a sense of duty to God while being filled with great disdain for the density and diversity of the city. But for ministry in cities to be effective, it is critical that Christians appreciate cities. They should love city life and find it energizing.[12] Why is this so important?

First, because so many who live in and have influence in the city do actually *enjoy* living there. If you try to draw them into your church, they will quickly pick up on your negative attitude, which can erect a barrier in their willingness to listen to the gospel. Second, if a church consists primarily of people who dislike urban living, those people won't be staying very long. Your church will be plagued with huge turnover (as if turnover and transience aren't enough of a problem already in the city!).

Preaching and teaching that produce a city-positive church must constantly address the common objections to city living, which include beliefs that city life is "less healthy," too expensive, and

an inferior place to raise families. Two additional objections are especially prevalent. One objection I commonly hear is this: "The country is wholesome; the city is corrupting." Christians should be able to recognize the bad theology (as well as bad history) behind this idea. Liberal humanism of the nineteenth and early twentieth centuries viewed human nature as intrinsically good and virtuous, so they concluded that human problems came from wrong socialization. In other words, we become violent and antisocial because of our environment. They taught that human society — especially urban society — teaches us to be selfish and violent. As we have seen, however, the Bible teaches that the city is simply a magnifying glass for the human heart. It brings out whatever is already inside. In the previous chapter, we examined the city's strengths for culture making, as well as its spiritual dangers. But we must remember that the city itself is not to blame for the evil that humans have sinfully brought into it.

Here is another common objection: "The country inspires; faith dies in the city." While the countryside can indeed inspire, it is quite wrong to say that the urban environment is a harder environment to find and grow in faith. As we noted earlier, many people coming from regions where Christianity is suppressed by the culture hear the gospel for the first time in the great cities where there is more of a "free market" of ideas. Millions of people who are virtually cut off from gospel witness are reachable if they emigrate to cities. Also, many who were raised as nominal Christians come to the cities where they are challenged in new ways and brought to vital, solid faith in the process. I have seen this occur thousands of times during my ministry at Redeemer. The city is, in fact, a spiritual hotbed where people both lose faith and find it in ways that do not happen in more monolithic, less pluralistic settings. This is, yet again, part of the tension of the city we see addressed in the Bible (see chapter 11).

Sometimes the contrast of the countryside and the city is drawn even more starkly. My colleague at Westminster, Harvie Conn, told me about a man who said to him, "God made the country, and man

WENDELL BERRY AND THE "AGRARIAN MIND"

Many people point to the essayist Wendell Berry as a leading light of modern agrarians who seem to make a strong case for rural living over urban living. However, while Berry does laud the life of the farm and the small town, he defines the "agrarian mind" as essentially that which values the *local*:

> The agrarian mind is ... local. It must know on intimate terms the local plants and animals and local soils; it must know local possibilities and impossibilities, opportunities and hazards. It depends and insists on knowing very particular local histories and biographies.[13]

He goes on to speak of the agrarian mind as (1) valuing work not for the money it can command but for what it provides for human flourishing; (2) valuing work that makes things that are concrete, durable, and useful; (3) embracing humility and having little need for growth and wealth; and (4) holding a commitment to a particular place for a lifetime and to conducting one's work, recreation, family life in the same place and within a web of thick, long-term, local personal relationships. Berry contrasts this with an "industrial mind" characterized by pride and a lack of respect and gratitude for nature and limitations and manifesting itself in exploitation and greed.

What this means, I believe, is that a person with an "agrarian" mind can live in a city very well. It is illuminating to compare the seminal work of Jane Jacobs (*The Death and Life of the Great American Cities*) with Berry's work. Jacobs was as committed as Berry to the importance of neighborhood — of local economies in which members of the neighborhood knew each other, had regular dealings with each other, and identified their own interests with the interests of their neighbors.

built the suburbs, but the devil made the city." The theology behind this statement is dubious to say the least. And theologically, it is not a good idea to think of the countryside as intrinsically more pleasing to God. An urban missionary, Bill Krispin, explains why. Bill once said to me, "The country is where there are more plants than people; the city is where there are more people than plants. And since God loves people much more than plants, he loves the city more than the country." I think this is solid theological logic. The apex of creation is, after all, the making of male and female in the image of God (Gen 1:26 – 27). Therefore, cities, which are filled with people, are absolutely crammed full of what God considers the most beautiful sight in his creation. As we have noted before, cities have more "image of God" per square inch than anywhere else, and so we must not idealize the country as somehow a more spiritual place than the city. Even those (like Wendell Berry) who lift up the virtues of rural living outline a form of human community just as achievable in cities as in small towns.

How can you as a church or an individual live out this value if you are not located near a metropolitan area? I believe the best strategy is to include urban ministry in your global missions portfolio. This may mean supporting individual missionaries who serve in cities; an even more effective strategy is to support church-planting ministries in global cities.[15] Another promising trend is the creation of metro-wide partnerships of churches and other agencies to support the holistic work of spreading the gospel throughout the city.

2. Christians should become a dynamic counterculture where they live. It will not be enough for Christians to simply live as individuals in the city, however. They must live as a particular kind of community. In the Bible's tale of two cities, man's city is built on the principle of personal aggrandizement (Gen 11:1 – 4), while "the city of our God ... is beautiful in its loftiness, the joy of the whole earth" (Ps 48:1 – 2). In other words, the urban society God wants is based on *service*, not selfishness. Its purpose is to spread joy from its cultural riches to the whole world. Christians are called to be an *alternate city* within every earthly city, an *alternate human culture* within every human culture — to show how sex, money, and power can be used in nondestructive ways; to show how classes and races that cannot get along outside of Christ can get along in him; and to show how it is possible to cultivate by using the tools of art, education, government, and business to bring hope to people rather than despair or cynicism.

Someone may ask, "Can't Christians be an alternate city out in the suburbs?" Absolutely! This is one of our universal callings as Christians. Yet again, though, the earthly city magnifies the effect of this alternate city and its unique forms of ministry. In racially homogeneous places, it is harder to show in pragmatic ways how the gospel uniquely undermines racial barriers (see Eph 2:11 – 22). In places where few artists live, it is pragmatically harder to show the gospel's unique effect on art. In economically homogeneous places, physically removed from the human poverty that is so pervasive in the world, it is pragmatically harder for Christians to realize how much money they are spending on themselves. What is possible in the suburbs and rural towns comes into sharper focus in the city. The city illustrates in vivid detail the unique community life that is produced as the fruit of the gospel.

3. Christians should be a community radically committed to the good of their city as a whole. It is not enough for Christians to form a culture that merely "counters" the values of the city. We must also commit, with all the resources of our faith and life, to serve sacrificially the good of the whole city, and especially the poor.

It is especially important that Christians not be seduced by the mind-set of the "consumer city" — the city as adult playground. Cities attract young adults with a dizzying variety of amenities and diversions that no suburb or small town can reproduce. Even when holding constant factors such as income, education, marital status, and age, city residents are far more likely to go to a concert, visit a museum, go to the movies, or stop into a local pub than people outside of urban areas.[16] On top of this, urban residents, more than their country cousins,

Jacobs called this "eyes on the street" — people who felt ownership of the environment, were committed to the common welfare, and watched the street, willing to take action if necessary. Both urban neighborhoods and small towns have mixed-land use in which residences, shops, businesses, schools, and so forth were all within walking distance of each other, which leads to more human-scale, local economy.

Jacobs's book was a polemic against the "suburbanization" of the city occurring in the 1960s by planners who were destroying local neighborhoods in order to build large-scale, homogeneous areas of retail, business offices, or residences. The New Urbanism today revels in the very small-scale, walkable, mixed-use communities that Jacobs describes. Political theorist Mark Mitchell writes these interesting words:

> Ultimately, healthy communities will only be realized when individuals commit to a particular place and to particular neighbors in the long-term work of making a place, of recognizing and enjoying the responsibilities and pleasures of membership in a local community. These good things are not the unique provenance of agrarian or rural settings. They can and have been achieved in urban and town settings.[14]

tend to take an unmistakable pride in sophistication and hipness. Christians must not be tempted to come to the city (or at least not to remain in the city) for these motivations. Christians indeed can be enriched by the particular joys of urban life, but ultimately they live in cities to serve.

Christians must work for the peace, security, justice, and prosperity of their neighbors, loving them in word and deed, whether or not they believe the same things we believe. In Jeremiah 29:7, God calls the Jews not just to live in the city but to love it and work for its shalom — its economic, social, and spiritual flourishing. Christians are, indeed, citizens of God's heavenly city, but *these citizens are always the best possible citizens of their earthly city*. They walk in the steps of the One who laid down his life for his opponents.

Christians in cities must become a counterculture for the common good. They must be radically different from the surrounding city, yet radically committed to its benefit. They must minister to the

---

Christians should seek to live in the city, not to use the city to build great churches, but to use the church's resources to seek a great, flourishing city.

---

city out of their distinctive Christian beliefs and identity. We see this balance demonstrated when we examine the early Christian understanding of citizenship. Paul used his Roman citizenship as leverage and defense in the service of his wider missional aims (Acts 16:37 – 38; 22:25 – 29; cf. 21:39; 23:27). He tells the Ephesians that because of the work of the gospel, "You are no longer foreigners and aliens, but *fellow citizens with God's people* and *members of God's household*, built on the foundation of the apostles and prophets, with Christ Jesus himself as the chief cornerstone" (Eph 2:19 – 20, emphasis mine).

And to the church in Philippi, Paul writes, "Our citizenship is in heaven. And we eagerly await a Savior from there, the Lord Jesus Christ, who, by the power that enables him to bring everything under his control, will transform our lowly bodies so that they will be like his glorious body" (Phil 3:20 – 21). Though Roman citizenship was a beneficial badge and indeed carried valuable social status, Paul is clear that Christians are, first and foremost, citizens of heaven.

Joseph presents an interesting Old Testament demonstration of this tension. When he is made prince of the land (Gen 41:39 – 40), he pursues the wealth and good of *Egypt*, just as he had previously done in prison and in Potiphar's house. Through his pursuit of the good of the city, salvation comes to the people of God. This story is especially striking because God puts Joseph in the position to save *the city* from hunger, not just the people of God.

In the end, Christians live not to increase the prosperity of our own tribe and group through power plays and coercion but to serve the good of all the people of the city (regardless of what beliefs others hold). While secularism tends to make people individualistic, and traditional religiosity tends to make people tribal, the gospel should destroy the natural selfishness of the human heart and lead Christians to sacrificial service that benefits the whole city. If Christians seek power and influence, they will arouse fear and hostility. If instead they pursue love and seek to serve, they will be granted a great deal of influence by their neighbors, a free gift given to trusted and trustworthy people.

Christians should seek to live in the city, not to *use* the city to build great churches, but to use the resources of the church to seek a great, flourishing city. We refer to this as a "city growth" model of ministry rather than a strictly "church growth" model. It is the ministry posture that arises out of a Center Church theological vision.

SEVEN FEATURES OF A CHURCH FOR THE CITY

It is infinitely easier to *talk* about living out this posture "on the ground" in our cities than to actually do it. The challenge is to establish churches and other ministries that effectively engage the realities of the cities of the world. The majority of evangelical Protestants who presently control the United States mission apparatus are typically white and nonurban in background. They neither understand nor in most cases enjoy urban life. As I have been arguing, many of the prevailing ministry methods are forged outside of urban areas and then simply imported, with little thought given to the unnecessary barriers this practice erects between urban dwellers and the gospel. Consequently, when ministers go into a city, they often find it especially hard to evangelize and win urban people — and equally difficult to disciple converts and prepare Christians for life in a pluralistic, secular, culturally engaged setting. Just as the Bible needs to be translated into its readers' vernacular, so the gospel needs to be embodied and communicated in ways that are understandable to the residents of a city.

I believe churches that minister in ways that are indigenous and honoring to a city — whatever its size — exhibit seven vital features:

1. respect for urban sensibility
2. unusual sensitivity to cultural differences
3. commitment to neighborhood and justice
4. integration of faith and work
5. bias for complex evangelism
6. preaching that both attracts and challenges urban people
7. commitment to artistry and creativity

We'll unpack each of these characteristics in more detail here, as well as note where several of them are covered more fully in later chapters of the book.

1. Respect for urban sensibility. Our culture is largely invisible to us, which is why it is revelatory to leave one's society and live in a very different culture for a while. This experience enables us to see how much of our thought and behavior is not based on universal common sense but on a particular cultural practice. And it is often easier to see the big cultural differences than the small ones. Christians who move to cities within their own country (or even region) often underestimate the importance of the small cultural differences they have with urbanites. They speak and act in ways that are out of step with urban sensibilities, and if this is pointed out to them, they despise the criticism as snobbishness.

Most American evangelical churches are middle class in their corporate culture. That is, they value privacy, safety, homogeneity, sentimentality, space, order, and control. In contrast, the city is filled with ironic, edgy, diversity-loving people who have a high tolerance for ambiguity and disorder. On the whole, they value intensity and access more than comfort and control. Center-city people appreciate sophistication in communication content and mode, and yet they eschew what they consider slickness, hype, and

excessive polish. Being able to strike these nuanced balances cannot be a matter of performance. Christian leaders and ministers must genuinely belong to the culture so they begin to intuitively understand it.

Center-city culture in particular is filled with well-informed, verbal, creative, and assertive people who do not respond well to authoritative pronouncements. They appreciate thoughtful presentations that are well argued and provide opportunities for communication and feedback. If a church's ministers are unable to function in an urban culture, choosing instead to create a "missionary compound" within the city, they will soon discover they cannot reach out, convert, or incorporate the people who live in their neighborhoods.

2. Unusual sensitivity to cultural differences. Effective leaders in urban ministry are acutely aware of the different people groups within their area. Because cities are dense and diverse, they are always culturally complex. This means not only that different races and socioeconomic classes are in closer physical proximity than in other settings, but that other factors, such as ethnicity, age, vocation, and religion, create a matrix of subcultures. In New York City, for example, older downtown artists (over the age of fifty) are significantly different from younger artists. The Jewish community in New York City is vast and variegated. The cultural differences among African-Americans, Africans, and Afro-Caribbeans are marked, even as they share a broad sense of identity over against white culture. Some groups clash more with particular groups than others (e.g., African-Americans and Koreans in some cities). The gay community is divided between those who want to be more integrated into mainstream culture and those who do not. Asians talk about being "1.0, 1.5, or second generation."

Fruitful urban ministers must first notice these differences and avoid thinking they are inconsequential. Then they must seek to understand these different people respectfully and navigate accordingly in communication and ministry without unnecessarily offending others. In fact, urban ministers should constantly surprise others with how well they understand other cultures. If you are an Anglo man, for example, you should occasionally hear something like, "I didn't think a white man would know about that."

Those raised in culturally homogeneous areas who move to a city soon come to realize how many of their attitudes and habits — which they thought of as simply universal common sense — were deeply tied to their race and class. For instance, Anglo-Americans don't see themselves as making decisions, expressing emotions, handling conflict, scheduling time and events, and communicating in a "white" way — they just think they are doing things the way everybody knows things ought to be done. In an urban setting, people typically become more sensitive to these blind spots. Why? Because they are acquainted with the aspirations, fears, passions, and patterns of several different groups of people through involvement with friends, neighbors, and colleagues who come from these groups. They have personally experienced how members of different ethnic or even vocational groups use an identical word or phrase to mean different things.

No church can be all things to all people. There is no culturally neutral way of doing ministry. The urban church will have to choose practices that reflect the values of *some* cultural group, and in so doing it will communicate in ways that different cultural groups will see and hear differently. As soon as it chooses a language to preach in, or the music it will sing, it is making it easier for some people to participate and more difficult for others.

Nevertheless, the ever-present challenge is to work to make urban ministry as broadly appealing as possible and as inclusive of different cultures as possible. One of the ways to do this is to have a racially diverse set of leaders "up front." When we see someone like ourselves speaking or leading a meeting, we feel welcomed in a hard-to-define way. Another way is to listen long and hard to people in our congregation who feel underrepresented by the way our church does ministry. In the end, we must accept the fact that urban churches will experience recurring complaints of racial insensitivity. Urban ministers live with the constant sense that they are failing to embrace as many kinds of people as they should. But they willingly and gladly embrace the challenge of building racial and cultural diversity in their churches and see these inevitable criticisms as simply one of the necessary costs of urban ministry.

3. Commitment to neighborhood and justice. Urban neighborhoods are highly complex. Even gentrified neighborhoods, full of professionals, may actually be "bipolar." That is, alongside the well-off residents in their expensive apartments, private schools, and various community associations and clubs is often a "shadow neighborhood" filled with many who live in poverty, attend struggling schools, and reside in government housing.

Urban ministers learn how to exegete their neighborhoods to grasp their sociological complexity. They are obsessed with studying and learning about their local communities. (Academic training in urban ethnography, urban demographics, and urban planning can be a great help to a church's lay leaders and staff members.) But faithful churches do not exegete their neighborhoods simply to target people groups, although evangelistic outreach is one of the goals. They are looking for ways to strengthen the

---

Urban churches train their members to be neighbors in the city, not just consumers.

---

health of their neighborhoods, making them safer and more humane places for people to live. This is a way to seek the welfare of the city, in the spirit of Jeremiah 29.

Urban churches train their members to be neighbors in the city, not just consumers. As we have seen, cities attract young professionals by providing something of a "theme park" with thousands of entertainment and cultural options, and many new urban residents tend to view the city as simply a place where they can have fun, develop a résumé, and make friends who will be of help to them in the future. They plan to do this for a few years and then leave. In other words, they are *using* the city rather than living in it as neighbors (as Jesus defines the term in the parable of the Good Samaritan in Luke 10:25 – 37).

In the middle years of the twentieth century, Jane Jacobs wrote the classic *The Death and Life of Great American Cities*. Jacobs's great contribution came in demonstrating the importance of street life for civil society. She observed how foot traffic and street life and a mixture of residences and businesses (viewed negatively by suburban zoners and even many urban planners at the time) were critical for economic vitality, for safety, for healthy human relationships, and for a strong social fabric. Jacobs was a major opponent of large-scale urban projects in the mid-twentieth century, the very projects that

eventually ruined neighborhoods and the street life she had promoted.

Jacobs writes the following:

Looking at city neighborhoods as organs of self-government, I can see evidence that only three kinds of neighborhoods are useful: (1) the city as a whole; (2) street neighborhoods; and (3) districts of large, subcity size (composed of 100,000 people or more in the case of the largest cities).

Each of these kinds of neighborhoods has different functions, but the three supplement each other in complex fashion.[18]

Jacobs explains how each of these is indeed a neighborhood and how each requires the participation of all urban residents to keep the city healthy. In other words, you must know your literal neighbors (your street neighborhood) and have some familiarity with the blocks around your residence (your district). And yet this in itself is not enough. "Ward politics" — in which one neighborhood pits its own good against the good of the other parts of the city — is unwholesome and unhealthy. So it is important for Christians and Christian ministries to find ways to be neighbors to the whole city, not just to their immediate street neighborhood. Failing to engage in the interests of the entire city often results in a lack of involvement in helping the poorest residents of the city. It is equally important that a church not minister just to the whole city while ignoring its local neighborhood. If this happens, a church can become a commuter church that no longer knows how to reach the kind of people who live in their immediate vicinity.

Urban churches, then, should be known in their community as a group of people who are committed to the good of all their neighbors, near and far. It takes this type of holistic commitment from all residents and institutions to maintain a good quality of life in the city, and a church that is not engaged in this manner will (rightly) be perceived by the city as tribal.

4. Integration of faith and work. Traditional evangelical churches tend to emphasize personal piety and rarely help believers understand how to maintain and apply their Christian beliefs and

One "occupational hazard" of urban church planting is having a new church rent its worship space and therefore only *corporately* reside in a particular neighborhood for the few hours during which they rent the space. Often this means, on the one hand, that the neighbors have no idea there is a church meeting in that space; on the other hand, church members feel very little responsibility to "love their neighbors." It is important for churches that rent space to own their neighborhood. Church leaders should therefore be intentional about inhabiting their neighborhood. They should go to local community boards and neighborhood association meetings, as well as contact local government officials and representatives to discover how they can best serve the needs of the neighborhood. This has not been a strength of Redeemer Church in the past, and we are working to change this now that we have moved into our first owned space on the Upper West Side of Manhattan.

practice in the worlds of the arts, business, scholarship, and government. Many churches do not know how to disciple members without essentially pulling them out of their vocations and inviting them to become heavily involved in church activities. In other words, Christian discipleship is interpreted as consisting largely of activities done in the evening or on the weekend.

Many vocations of city dwellers — fashion and the media, the arts and technology, business and finance, politics and public policy — demand great amounts of time and energy. These are typically not forty-hour-a-week jobs. They are jobs that dominate a person's life and thinking, and urban Christians are confronted with ethical and theological issues every day in the workplace. Preaching

and ministry in urban churches must therefore help congregants form networks of believers within their vocational field and assist them in working through the theological, ethical, and practical issues they face in their work.

In addition to the practical issues of how to do their individual work, urban Christians need a broader vision of how Christianity engages and influences culture. As we have discussed, cities are culture-forming incubators, and believers in such places have a significant need for guidance on how Christian faith should express itself in public life. For more on this subject, see part 5 (Cultural Engagement) and part 7 (Integrative Ministry).

5. Bias for complex evangelism. Two kinds of urban churches can grow without evangelism. The first is the ethnic/immigrant church. While many ethnic churches are evangelistic, it is possible for them to grow without conversions, as new immigrants are always looking for connections to their own people in the city. Ethnic churches therefore become informal "community centers" for people of the same race and subculture — and they can grow simply by gathering new immigrants who want to be part of the fellowship. Second, churches in Western center cities can grow without evangelism by meeting the needs of one particular "immigrant subculture" — evangelical Christians — through preaching, music, children's programs, and so forth. In the past, in cities outside of the southern and midwestern United States, there simply was no constituency of "church shoppers" to attract. However, during the urban renaissance of the last fifteen years, this situation has changed, and cities have become desirable destinations for young adults from all over the country. Redeemer Presbyterian Church's experience is a good way to understand this phenomenon.

Redeemer was begun in Manhattan at the end of the 1980s, during the end of an era of urban decline. Crime was high and the city was losing population, and there were few or no Christians moving into New York City from the rest of the country. During the first several years of Redeemer's existence, it grew through aggressive but winsome evangelism.

An evangelistic consciousness permeated the young congregation, and several hundred people came to faith out of nonbelief and nonchurched backgrounds over the first five years.

By the mid-1990s, the urban regeneration had begun, and we noticed that young adults from Christian backgrounds were moving to the cities. By the end of the decade, we found that we could (and did) grow substantially by drawing these folks in and helping them live out their Christian lives in service to the city. This is, of course, a very good and important thing, but it can also mask a lack of evangelism, and in the end, nonevangelistic church growth can't help reach the city in the most profound way. Recognizing this danger, our church has recommitted itself to reigniting our ethos of evangelism.

Not only must an urban church be committed to evangelism; it must be committed to the *complexity* of urban evangelism. There is no "one size fits all" method or message that can be used with all urban residents. For example, it is impossible for a Christian minister in London to share the gospel in exactly the same way with an atheist native Scot or a Muslim from Pakistan — yet they may both be the minister's literal neighbors. Urban evangelism requires immersion in the various cultures' greatest hopes, fears, views, and objections to Christianity. It requires a creative host of different means and venues, and it takes great courage.

6. Preaching that both attracts and challenges urban people. Perhaps the greatest challenge for preachers in urban contexts is the fact that many secular and nonbelieving people may be in the audience. Of course, urban congregations can be as ingrown as any others, but certain dynamics of urban life can more readily make city church gatherings "spiritually mixed" and filled with nonbelievers. Urban centers have higher percentages of single people, and it is far easier for a single Christian to get a single, non-Christian friend to come to a church gathering than it is for a Christian family to get an entire non-Christian family to come. Singles make unilateral decisions (without having to consult others), tend to spend more time out of their homes, and are more open to new experiences. Also,

cities are not "car cultures"; they are pedestrian cultures, and it is not unusual for people to simply walk off the street into church out of curiosity. Finally, cities are places where people come to "make it," are often separated from extended families, and are under a great deal of stress. As a result, urban people are often in a spiritual search mode and can be hungry for human connection and a sense of belonging.

The challenge for the urban preacher is to preach in a way that edifies believers and engages and evangelized nonbelievers at the same time. We will speak more about evangelistic worship in chapter 23. But here are some pointers.

First, be sure to preach sermons that ground moral exhortation in Christ and his work (see the section in chapter 6 titled "Preaching for Renewal"). Show how we live as we should only if we believe in and apply Christ's work of salvation as we should. In this way nonbelievers hear the gospel each week, yet believers have their issues and problems addressed as well.

Second, be very careful to think about your audience's premises. Don't assume, for example, that everyone listening trusts the Bible. So when you make a point from the Bible, it will help to show that some other trusted authority (such as empirical science) agrees with the Bible. Use it to promote trust of the Bible, saying something like, "See, the Bible was telling us centuries ago what science now confirms." That will help convince your hearers of that point so you can move on. By the end of the sermon, of course, you will be appealing only to God's Word, but in the early stages of the sermon you invite nonbelievers along by showing respect for their doubts about the Bible's reliability.

Third, do "apologetic sidebars." Try to devote one of the three or four sermon points mainly to the doubts and concerns of nonbelievers. Keep in your head a list of the ten or so biggest objections people have to Christianity. More often than not, the particular Scripture text has some way to address them. Always treat people's typical doubts about Christianity with respect. Jude reminds us to "be merciful to those who doubt" (Jude 22). Never give the impression that "all intelligent people think like I do." Don't hesitate to say, "I know this Christian doctrine may sound outrageous, but would you consider this …?"

Fourth, address different groups directly, showing that you know they are there, as though you are dialoguing with them: "If you are committed to Christ, you may be thinking this — but the text answers that fear," or "If you are not a Christian or not sure what you believe, then you surely must think this is narrow-minded — but the text says this, which speaks to this very issue."

Fifth, consider demeanor. The young secularists of New York City are extremely sensitive to anything that smacks of artifice to them. Anything that is too polished, too controlled, too canned will seem like salesmanship. They will be turned off if they hear a preacher use noninclusive gender language, make cynical remarks about other religions, adopt a tone of voice they consider forced or inauthentic, or use insider evangelical tribal jargon. In particular, they will feel "beaten up" if a pastor yells at them. The kind of preaching that sounds passionate in the heartland may sound like a dangerous rant in certain subcultures in the city.

Sixth, show a deep acquaintance with the same books, magazines, blogs, movies, and plays — as well as the daily life experiences — that your audience knows. Mention them and interpret them in light of Scripture. But be sure to read and experience urban life across a spectrum of opinion. There is nothing more truly urban than showing you know, appreciate, and digest a great diversity of human opinion. During my first years in New York, I regularly read *The New Yorker* (sophisticated secular), *The Atlantic* (eclectic), *The Nation* (older, left-wing secular), *The Weekly Standard* (conservative but erudite), *The New Republic* (eclectic and erudite), *Utne Reader* (New Age alternative), *Wired* (Silicon Valley libertarian), *First Things* (conservative Catholic). As I read, I imagine dialogues about Christianity with the writers. I almost never read a magazine without getting a scrap of a preaching idea.

7. Commitment to artistry and creativity. According to the United States census, between 1970 and 1990 the number of people describing themselves as "artist" more than doubled, from 737,000 to 1.7 million. Since 1990, the number of artists continued to grow another 16 percent to nearly two million. Professional artists live disproportionately in major urban areas, and so the arts are held in high regard in the city, while in nonurban areas little direct attention is typically given to them. Urban churches must be aware of this. First, they should have high standards for artistic skill in their worship and ministries. If you do not have such

---

By his grace, Jesus lost the city-that-was, so we could become citizens of the city-to-come, making us salt and light in the city-that-is.

---

standards, your church will feel culturally remote to the average urban dweller who is surrounded by artistic excellence even on the streets where talented artists sing and perform.

Second, city churches should think of artists not simply as persons with skills to use. They must connect to them as worshipers and hearers, communicating that they are valued for both their work and their presence in the community. This can be done in a variety of ways. One way includes being sensitive to your own region's or city's particular art history (e.g., Nashville is a music center; New England and the Midwest have many writers; New Mexico is a center for visual artists). Take time to listen to the artists and musicians in your church to understand something about the nature of the local artistic community and how the creative process works. Do your best to work with local artists and musicians rather than flying in your favorite artists long-distance for concerts or shows. When you make use of artists' gifts, take their advice on how the music and the art should be done; don't simply give orders to them.

God has given us the city for his purposes, and even though sin has harmed it, we should use the resources of the gospel to repair broken cities. Jesus himself went to the city and was crucified "outside the city gate" (Heb 13:12), a biblical metaphor for forsakenness. By his grace, Jesus lost the city-that-was, so we could become citizens of the city-to-come (Heb 11:10; 12:22), making us salt and light in the city-that-is (Matt 5:13 – 16).

So we urge *all* the people of God to recognize and embrace the strategic intensity of cities — and therefore to respond to the urgent call to be *in the city* and *for the city* from every coordinate on the globe. City Vision recognizes God's creational intentions for cities and calls the people of God to be the city of God within the city of man.

QUESTIONS FOR DISCUSSION AND REFLECTION

1. If you are not located in a city, how might City Vision shape and improve the fruitfulness of your current ministry?

2. How is agglomeration evident around you? Which types of trades, skills, inventors, or culture makers are concentrated most highly in your area? In what ways can your ministry seek face-to-face opportunities to minister to and through this population — that is, to become an "agglomerizing" church?

3. Keller writes, "The city itself brings the gospel to us. The city will challenge us to discover the power of the gospel in new ways." How does this chapter suggest this happens? How have you experienced this?

4. Which of the seven features of a church for the city does your church currently exhibit? How might those outside your community answer this question?

CHAPTER 14 — THE GOSPEL FOR THE CITY {pages 166–79}

1. I am thinking of a sermon by Francis A. Schaeffer titled "No Little People, No Little Places," in *No Little People: Sixteen Sermons for the Twentieth Century* (Downers Grove, Ill.: InterVarsity, 1974); see www.sbts.edu/resources/files/2010/02/sbjt_062_schaeffer.pdf (accessed January 24, 2012).
2. Thanks to Richard Coekin for convincingly emphasizing this point to me.
3. Ibid., 36.
4. Ibid.
5. For a thorough but highly technical study of this subject, see Edward L. Glaeser, *Cities, Agglomeration, and Spatial Equilibrium* (New York: Oxford University Press, 2008).
6. Ibid., 1.
7. See Elizabeth Currid, "How Art and Culture Happen in New York: Implications for Urban Economic Development," *Journal of the American Planning Association* 73:4 (Autumn 2007): 454–67.
8. Ibid., 454.
9. Ibid.
10. Ryan Avent, *The Gated City. How America Made Its Most Productive Places Ever Less Accessible* (Amazon Digital Services. Kindle Single, 2011)
11. Edward Glaeser, *The Triumph of the City: How Our Greatest Invention Makes Us Richer, Smarter, Greener, Healthier, and Happier* (New York: Penguin, 2011), 35.
12. Some have pointed out to me that when Jonah was rebuked for not "loving the city" as God did (Jonah 4:10–11), he was being challenged to love the *people* of the city — not "city living" or the city as social structure. And this certainly is true for the Jonah text. Nevertheless, as we have shown in the chapter "The Tension of the City," the Bible *does* see the city as a positive social arrangement, and many Bible scholars (e.g., Henri Blocher, Meredith Kline) even argue that the Bible sees the city as God's creation. Speaking practically, Christians who want to be fruitful in cities must have at least a positive appreciation for the strengths and advantages of city life as outlined in this part of the book.
13. Wendell Berry, *Citizenship Papers* (Berkeley, Calif.: Counterpoint, 2004), 116.
14. Mark T. Mitchell, "Wendell Berry and the New Urbanism: Agrarian Remedies, Urban Prospects," *Front Porch Republic* (March 20, 2011), www.frontporchrepublic.com/2011/03/wendell-berrys-new-urbanism-agrarian-remedies-urban-prospects/ (accessed January 24, 2012).
15. Full disclosure: global city church planting is one of my greatest passions. It is the primary focus of our affiliated global missions agency, Redeemer City to City (visit www.redeemercitytocity.com).
16. Glaeser, *Triumph of the City*, 126. See also p. 259, where Glaeser carefully critiques the view of Richard Florida, namely, that cities flourish when they attract the young and hip, artists, the avant-garde, and people who have alternative lifestyles. Glaeser believes that cities should instead concentrate on "core public services" — safe streets, good schools, and so on.
17. See Edmund Clowney, *The Church* (Downers Grove, Ill.: InterVarsity, 1995).
18. Jane Jacobs, *The Death and Life of Great American Cities* (New York: Vintage, 1961), 117.

chapter 15

THE CULTURAL CRISIS OF THE CHURCH

The contemporary American church is pulsing with intramural debates. Within the church today we see battles over the authority of the Bible, justification by faith, the atonement, gender roles in the family and the church, ways to conduct worship, and methods for evangelism, as well as innumerable disputes over the nature and ministries of the church. Then we have the more academic debates about the meaning of the kingdom of God, the character of God (e.g., "open theism" and "the social Trinity"), the "new perspective on Paul," the goals of the mission of the church, and questions surrounding issues of epistemology and the nature of truth.

On the surface these look like a diverse array of doctrinal disputes. But more often than not, lurking beneath these issues is the question of how Christians should relate to the culture around us. Some believe that the church's message is becoming incomprehensible to outsiders and therefore we should increasingly adapt it to the culture; while others believe that the church is already too influenced by the culture and we need to be more confrontational toward contemporary societal trends. Most church leaders are somewhere in the middle, but they can't agree on where we should confront or where we should adapt. As a result, the church is fragmenting even beyond its old divisions of denominational and theological traditions. Within each of the bodies of Baptists, Presbyterians, Anglicans, Lutherans, Methodists, and Pentecostals lie deep divisions over how to engage culture. In fact, there may be no more divisive issue in the contemporary American church today.

What has triggered this conflict?

CULTURE SHIFT

In the early part of the twentieth century, the fundamentalist-modernist controversy left much

of the United States' educational and cultural establishment in liberal and secular hands, and conservative Christians in America responded by creating a massive network of their own agencies — colleges, periodicals, publishing companies, radio and television networks, and so on.[1] Nevertheless, the major cultural institutions of North America, although they rejected traditional Christian doctrine, continued to inculcate broadly Christian moral values. Most people in society continued to have views largely congruent with Christian teaching on respect for authority, sexual morality, caution about debt and materialism, and emphasis on modesty, personal responsibility, and family. Until the middle of the twentieth century, therefore, most conservative Christians in Western societies felt basically at home in their own cultures.

Sometime in the middle of the twentieth century, however, Western culture began to change rather dramatically. In Great Britain and Europe, church attendance fell precipitously after World War II.[2] And in the United States, while church attendance and religious observance rose initially after the war, by the late 1960s a major cultural shift was afoot. In their book *American Grace*, Robert Putnam and David Campbell call this a "shock" to American society's connection to Christianity and the church.[3] A "basic shift of mood" and crisis of confidence occurred, with regard not only to older ideals of patriotism and national pride but also to traditional moral values — particularly sexual mores. The very idea of moral authority began to be questioned.

In the United States, this new mood erupted with a vengeance and was widely transmitted through the youth culture of the 1960s. Popular music questioned all moral authority. Hollywood and television somewhat more slowly began to adopt the same tone. Two famous Westerns that came out in 1969 — *True Grit* and *Butch Cassidy and the Sundance Kid* — represented the two clashing worldviews. The former expressed a traditional view of virtue, while the latter subverted traditional understandings of good, evil, and moral authority. In 1952, 75 percent of Americans said that religion was "very important to them personally," but less than half of that percentage said so by the mid-1970s. Church attendance dropped from approximately 50 percent of the population in 1958 to about 40 percent in 1969, the fastest decline ever recorded in such a short span of time. Even more striking was the decline in church attendance among people in their twenties. In 1957, 51 percent of the members of that age group attended church; by 1971, that number had fallen to 28 percent.[5]

Most noticeable to Christians, however, was how the main public and cultural institutions of the country no longer supported basic Judeo-Christian beliefs about life and morality.[6] Before these changes, Americans were largely "Christianized" in their thinking. They usually believed in a personal God, in the existence of heaven and hell, and in the concept of moral authority and judgment, and they generally had a basic grasp of Christian ethics. A gospel presentation could assume and build on all these things in seeking to convict them of sin and the need for the redemption of Christ. Now, for more and more Americans, all these ideas were weakening or absent. The gospel message was not simply being rejected; it was becoming incomprehensible and increasingly hated. The world that Christians in the West had known — where the culture tilted in the direction of traditional Christianity — no longer existed. The culture had become a problem the church could no longer ignore.

Here is a personal case study illustrating this shift. My own parents — born in the 1920s — were evangelical Christians, while my wife's parents, who were born during the same decade and in the same U.S. state of Pennsylvania, were not. Yet if you had asked the four of them what they believed about the morality of sex outside of marriage, homosexuality, and abortion — or about almost any economic or ethical issue, such as going into debt or national pride and patriotism — you would have heard almost identical answers. Why? That era had cultural consensus about basic moral convictions. Yes, evangelicals often opposed smoking, drinking, profanity, and going to most movies — and those would not have been mainstream views. Nevertheless, evangelical churches could assume that the institutions of the culture went a long way toward giving citizens the basic "mental furniture" for understanding a gospel presentation. In the 1940s, a Christian minister could say to almost any young adult in the country, "Be good!" and they would know what he was talking about. By the late 1970s, if you said, "Be good!" the answer would be, "What's your definition of good? I might have a different one. And who are you to impose your view on me?"

Before this shift, nonbelievers did need to be persuaded of many doctrines in order to become

Christians. They needed to understand that God was more holy than they had thought, but there was no need to convince them that God existed or that he got angry at disobedience. They needed to see they were more alienated from God than they thought, but there was no need to convince them that there is such a thing as sin or that there were moral, transcultural absolutes. People did need to see exactly what Jesus had done to save them, but there was less need to establish that Jesus lived and that he did the things the Bible said he did. People needed to learn that salvation was not by works but by faith; but virtually everyone had at least some idea of "salvation" and some type of belief in an afterlife. Finally, people needed to have the difference between faith and works explained to them, and how they had been relying on their works. They would often say to the gospel presenter, "Oh, I didn't realize that! How can I get it right?"[7]

In short, evangelicals could count on their listeners to at least be mentally able to understand the message of the Christian faith — a message largely seen as credible and positive. Their job was to convict people of their personal need for Christ and rely on the power of the Holy Spirit to urge them

---

The world that Christians in the West had known — where the culture tilted in the direction of traditional Christianity — no longer existed.

---

to make a personal commitment to Christ. Gospel presentations could be kept rather simple, stressing the importance of repentance and faith, without the enormous work of having to establish the very existence and character of the biblical God or the other parts of the basic framework of the Christian understanding of reality. In addition, it wasn't too difficult to bring people into church. It was generally understood that being part of a church was a good thing. In fact, those who wanted to be respected members of a local community understood that lo-

THE CAUSES OF SHIFTS AWAY FROM TRADITIONAL CULTURE

Some explain the shift in Western culture away from traditional moral values by looking at intellectual history. They point, for example, to the way *Enlightenment philosophies* have worked themselves out through our societies. The basic principle of the Enlightenment was a new approach to knowledge. The individual was not to trust tradition, custom, or morals. Nothing was to be taken on authority — everything had to be proved to one's own reason.[8]

Others point to the rise of *Romanticism*, which was itself a reaction to the emphasis on science and reason. Romanticism stressed feeling and experience over reason but was just as radically individualistic and just as hostile to inherited tradition, moral values, and religious faith as was the rationalistic side of the Enlightenment.

Still others argue that it isn't so much that intellectual beliefs shape social patterns but that *new social realities* affect belief. For example, some claim that capitalism corrodes traditional values, pointing to technological advances such as air travel, television, contraception, and the Internet as innovations that have undermined moral values and traditional communities in favor of individual freedom and choice.

cal church attendance would be part of the package.[9]

However, as the main cultural institutions stopped supporting Christianity, many Christians felt seriously out of place in their own society. In particular, younger adults became confused, resistant, and hostile to classic presentations of the gospel.[10] By the mid-1990s there was a growing sense that the conservative churches of the U.S. were fast losing contact with culture and society, despite the fact that in the late 1970s and early 80s the seeker-church movement had sought to make the church more appealing to contemporary people. The extensive study by Robert Putnam and David Campbell has shown this perception to be correct. While the mainline churches had begun their decline earlier, conservative churches were now in decline as well.

The reasons for this culture shift continue to be a subject of much debate, but one thing is certain: it became increasingly harder for evangelical Christians to be indifferent to culture.

THE STANCE OF PIETISM

How did most of the evangelical church in the United States relate to culture during the greater part of the twentieth century? The basic stance was to ignore culture and put all stress on conversions and on the spiritual growth of individuals. This was not, at its core, a particular model for relating Christ to culture. Some would say this was a form of cultural withdrawal or hostility, but I argue that this was not so much a negative view of human culture as one of indifference. Culture simply was not an issue. Too much attention to it was seen as a distraction. Young Christians had ministers and missionaries — not artists or business leaders — lifted before them as the ideals, not because involvement in culture was bad; it just wasn't the important thing. All were encouraged to enter full-time Christian ministry in order to evangelize the world.

Of course, in another sense this *was* a model for engaging culture, because this view often included a statement like this: "Yes, this society is not all that it ought to be. But the way to change the world is to change hearts one at a time through evangelism and discipleship. If we had enough real Christians in the world, society would be more just and moral."

I will call this approach "pietism." The word derives from a seventeenth-century movement within the church in German-speaking central Europe, in which the emphasis moved from doctrinal precision to spiritual experience, from clergy-led efforts to lay ministry, and from efforts to reform the intellectual and social order to emphasis on evangelistic mission and personal discipleship.[12] Mark Noll argues that German pietism was one of the main sources (though not the only one) of contemporary English-speaking evangelicalism. Other sources included Puritanism and the revivalist Anglicanism of Wesley and Whitefield. These various strains or roots were not identical in their attitude toward culture. German pietism was greatly submissive to the state and culture, while much of Puritanism was not. So when American fundamentalism went into a more pietistic mode in the first half of the twentieth century, it was drawing more on one of its historic roots than on others.[13]

However, over the past fifteen years, many American evangelical Christians have abandoned the pietistic stance. Because of the (relatively abrupt) shifts in the West toward a post-Christian culture, many Christians were shaken out of their indifference. It became less possible for them to view the main cultural institutions as a favorable or even a benign force. They felt they needed to think about culture at the very least — and then to fight it, reclaim it, adapt to it, or deliberately withdraw from it.

Yet even if our social realities had not changed, there are several serious flaws in the pietistic indifference to culture. First, many have promoted the pietistic stance by arguing that increasing the numbers of Christians will somehow improve or change a society. But as James Hunter convincingly argues, numbers do not always equate to influence. Even if 80 percent of the population of a country are Christian believers, they will have almost no cultural influence if the Christians do not live in cultural centers and work in culture-forging fields such as academia, publishing, media, entertainment, and the arts.[14] The assumption that society will improve simply by more Christian believers being present is no longer valid. If you care about having an influence on society, evangelism is not enough.

Others who adopt a pietistic stance have argued that it is not a proper goal for Christians to try to improve culture at all, even indirectly. The nineteenth-century evangelist Dwight Moody was reputed to have said, "I look upon this world as a wrecked vessel. God has given me a lifeboat and said to me, 'Moody, save all you can.'"[15] This is a classic depiction of the pietistic mind-set. The argument is this: Who needs to engage culture when people are spiritually lost and dying? What should matter is evangelism and personal discipleship.

But this view is naive about culture's role in *preparing people for evangelism*. A pastor once explained to me how he became aware of this truth. He told me that for years he had encouraged the best and brightest in his church to enter full-time Christian ministry, not to enter secular vocations. Yet as the decades went by, he noticed that more

SYMBOLIC CAPITAL

In his book *To Change the World*, James D. Hunter argues that there are a large number of evangelical Christians in the United States, but they are having far less of an impact on how human life is lived in our society than much smaller groups of people who have a greater presence in urban, academic, and cultural centers. As Hunter points out, culture operates along lines of "symbolic capital." If you teach sociology at Harvard, you have much more of this "capital" than you do if you teach sociology at a community college in Nebraska. Your voice will be heard more clearly by more people — doors will open for you to make your arguments and promote your views. Your views will be taken more seriously.

Today, while orthodox Christians make up, say, 30 percent of the U.S. population, they occupy only a tiny percentage of the positions of influence in cultural institutions and urban centers, which for the other 70 percent leads to little or no practical impact on how human life is lived in society.

and more people were not merely disagreeing with his gospel message; they couldn't even grasp the basic concepts of right and wrong, sin and grace. He confided, "I realized if all Christians only evangelize — if no Christians write novels or make movies or work in the culture at all — pretty soon the most basic concepts of Christianity will be so alien that no one will even understand me when I preach." It could be argued that this has indeed already happened. The culture's shift has exposed the significant problems with the pietistic stance of indifference toward culture.

The pietistic stance is also naive about culture's role in the process of *discipleship*. The reality is that if the church does not think much about culture — about what parts are good, bad, or indifferent according to the Bible — its members will begin to uncritically imbibe the values of the culture. They will become assimilated to culture, despite intentions to the contrary. Culture is complex, subtle, and inescapable, as we have seen in our treatment of contextualization. And if we are not *deliberately* thinking about our culture, we will simply be conformed to it without ever knowing it is happening. An interesting example is how churches in the evangelistic, pietistic tradition have readily adopted "seeker oriented" models of ministry that use modern techniques of marketing and promotion without thinking about whether the very techniques themselves import the cultural values of consumerism and individualism.

If we are not *deliberately* thinking about our culture, we will be conformed to it without ever knowing it is happening.

THE EMERGENCE OF MODELS

The movement away from the pietistic stance toward culture had humble beginnings. In the 1940s, a small handful of young men from fundamentalist churches began to pursue PhDs at Harvard and Boston Universities.[16] One of them, Carl F. H. Henry, recognized that while the culture still appeared to be largely based on Christianity, Christian morality was impossible to maintain over the long term in a society without Christian doctrine. In his seminal work *The Uneasy Conscience of Modern Fundamentalism*, he called Bible-believing Protestants to reenter major cultural institutions and engage as Christians "from a Christian worldview" in the public arena of scholarship, law, and art.[17] Twenty years later, Francis Schaeffer, who called Christians to relate to culture in this way, became the first popular figure to gain traction with an entire generation of evangelicals. He gave Christian perspectives on existentialism, the movies of Fellini and Bergman, the lyrics of Led Zeppelin, and the art of Jackson Pollack in an era when "Christian college students were not even allowed to go to Disney movies."[18]

As the pietistic stance faded, evangelicals began to search for models for relating Christ to culture, something they felt they hadn't needed previously.[19] One of the first alternatives that emerged out of the decline of the pietistic stance had its roots in the idea of "Christian worldview," especially as formulated by Abraham Kuyper of the Netherlands. Kuyper's views were perhaps most seminally expressed in "Sphere Sovereignty," the address he delivered at the opening of the Free University of Amsterdam in 1880. In his lecture, he argued that in the university, medicine, law, the natural sciences, and art would be studied and conducted on the basis of Christian principles, which had to be brought to bear on "every department, in every discipline, and with every investigator." "No single piece of our mental world is to be hermetically sealed off from the rest," he asserted, and then famously added, "there is not a square inch in the whole domain of our human existence over which Christ, who is Sovereign over *all*, does not cry: 'Mine!' "[20] All human activity and production are done for some end, with some vision, on the basis of some understanding of ultimate reality and the meaning of life — and this understanding will affect how the activity and production are carried out. Therefore, cultural production is something Christians should do, and they should do it in a way that accords with the glory of God. In other words, they should fully engage culture.[21]

In North America, this Kuyperian view of cultural engagement was first promoted by thinkers and institutions associated with certain strains of Reformed theology and has been dubbed "neo-Calvinism."[22] This movement called Christians to engage and change culture by carrying out their vocations from a distinctively Christian worldview. However, by the middle of the twentieth century, writers such as Gordon Clark, Carl F. H. Henry, and especially Francis Schaeffer had popularized the idea of worldview among American evangelicals, so that today the idea of Christian worldview as a basis for cultural engagement is widespread.[23] Through the writings of Schaeffer, James W. Sire, and authors of a host of other popular-level books and curriculum, the concept has spread broadly. It is fair to say it is a staple of Sunday school courses and youth ministry programs in the evangelical churches of North America. Joel Carpenter, in a paper delivered at Harvard Kennedy School, argued that the Kuyperian tradition of worldview has essentially captured most of evangelical higher education in North America.[24]

The original proponents of Kuyperian worldview engagement tended to be liberal in their politics — favoring European-style centralized economies and an expansive government with emphasis on justice and rights for minorities. However, another "wing" of Christian worldview proponents emerged in the 1970s and 1980s in the United States — the Religious Right. Many fundamentalist Christians such as Jerry Falwell, who had visibly championed the pietistic stance, abandoned it. Falwell and others came to believe that American culture was fast abandoning its moral values, and so he led conservative Christians to become a political force within the Republican Party.[25] The Religious Right made heavy use of the concept of worldview, as well as the notion of "transforming culture," but connected these ideas directly to political action in support of conservative policies. The expansive secularist state was seen to be an enemy that should be shrunk, and not only because it promoted abortion and homosexuality.[26] Conservative political philosophy believed that taxes should be low, the state shrunk to favor the private sector and the individual, and the military expanded. Those on the Religious Right often justified the entire conservative agenda on the basis of a biblical worldview. The movement claimed we needed political leaders who governed from a Christian worldview, which was defined largely as limited government, lower taxes, stronger military, and opposition to abortion and homosexuality.

A second response to the culture shift ascended around the same time as the Religious Right — the growth of the "seeker church" movement. Led by Willow Creek Community Church in the Chicago suburbs, the movement began in the late 1970s and grew to prominence in the 1980s.[27] One of the roots of this movement is the church growth trend that grew out of the thinking of missiologist Donald McGavran, who taught that non-Christians should not be asked to hurdle major cultural barriers in order to become believers. With this principle in mind, the seeker church movement detected the culture shift and recognized that Christianity was becoming increasingly culturally alien to nonbelievers. Its recommended solution was not "church as usual" (as with those who held on to the pietistic stance); nor was it "politics with a vengeance" (as with the Religious Right). Instead, this movement spoke frequently of the church's *irrelevance* and sought to "reinvent church" — principally by adapting sophisticated marketing and product development techniques from the business world — so it would appeal to secular, unchurched people.[28]

These two responses indeed represented major changes from the pietistic stance that essentially ignored or denounced culture. The Religious Right sought to aggressively change culture, while the

POLITICS, NEO-CALVINISTS, AND THE RELIGIOUS RIGHT

One of the keys to the political difference between the neo-Calvinists and the Religious Right has to do with differing interpretations regarding what Romans 13:3–4 teaches about the role of the state. Neo-Calvinists understand the text as teaching that the government has *two* basic functions: to administer justice by punishing wrongdoers and to promote the public welfare by providing for the basic material needs of people, particularly the weak and poor members of society.[29]

Those on the right counter that Romans 13:3–4 teaches only the first of these two functions—that the state is an enforcer of the law; it should essentially provide police and a legal system and a military defense, and that is all.[30]

seeker church movement called Christians to become relevant to it. It was not long, however, before Christians began to respond not only to the culture shift but also to these "responses." By the late 1990s, a new trend among young evangelicals appeared, known as "the emerging church."[31] The emerging church was yet another response to the ongoing cultural shift. Book after book was published, announcing the "death of Christendom"

and "the death of modernity." Lesslie Newbigin had called on the churches of the West to have a "missionary encounter with Western culture,"[33] and by the end of the 1990s, a group of scholars had produced a book based on Newbigin's basic insights titled *Missional Church*.[34] "Missional church" and "emerging church" became shorthand terms that described a new way of engaging culture.

But what is this new way? In reality, it is several different ways. Many young evangelical leaders agreed that both the Religious Right and the marketing techniques of the seeker church movement had failed to relate to culture rightly. They saw the Religious Right as evidence that the church had been taken captive by a naive loyalty to Americanism and free-market capitalism rather than to a truly biblical way of thinking and living. Others rejected the seeker church movement, perceiving it as a sellout to individualism and consumerism. To many Christians, both groups had become captive to Western, modern, Enlightenment culture. In response, those involved in the missional/emerging church emphasized doing justice and rendering service in the broader human community — something that neither the Religious Right nor the seeker church (much less the older pietistic churches) had emphasized. Emerging church leaders also emphasized (as Francis Schaeffer did in his early years) involvement in culture making and the goodness of secular vocation. The movement's third emphasis was on spiritual formation and contemplative spirituality, often deploying spiritual disciplines that have historically been associated with Roman Catholicism and Eastern Orthodoxy.[35] These were offered as an alternative to the pro-consumerist seeker movement.[36]

However, the missional/emerging church has quickly fractured into numerous, semi-identifiable streams. Interestingly, much of the fragmentation is over the question of how to relate Christianity to culture. Emerging church proponents know what they *don't* want — the cultural obliviousness of pietism, the triumphalism of the Religious Right, and the lack of reflection and depth of most seeker churches. Yet they have not agreed on what the

THE "TWO KINGDOMS" AND TRANSFORMATIONIST MODELS

The debate within Reformed circles between those who advocate a Kuyperian perspective of cultural transformation and those who propose what is known as the "Two Kingdoms" view is well summarized by Dan Strange.[32] Strange calls the two camps the "Common Kingdom" model (we will refer to this as the "Two Kingdoms" view) and the "Confessional Kingdom" model (we will refer to this as the Transformationist or neo-Calvinist view). Strange lists the proponents of the "Two Kingdoms" model as Meredith Kline, Michael Horton, Daryl Hart, Stephen Grabill, Ken Myers, and David VanDrunen. He lists the thinkers of the Transformationist model to be Cornelius Van Til, Vern Poythress, Peter Leithart, and John Frame.

In the following chapters, we'll unpack both of these models for relating to culture. At this point, I emphasize that while this controversy involves a relatively small number of authors and readers, it is well worth our attention because the Reformed evangelical world, though numerically small, has an outsized impact on the broader evangelical community through its educational institutions and publications, and because it is a window into the kind of debates over culture now dividing conservative Christians within a variety of traditions and denominations throughout the world.

ideal model for relating to culture *should* be. Some of the churches in the emerging movement have been criticized as little more than seeker churches adapted to the more ironic sensibilities of younger generations. Others in the emerging stream have opted for a "neo-Anabaptist" perspective heavily influenced by such writers as Stanley Hauerwas and John Howard Yoder.

My main aim in examining the models is to suggest that the way forward on how to best engage culture is a careful *balance* among several polarities.

The dissension over different models continues through heated intramural debates within denominations and traditions. One example is within the community of conservative Reformed churches in which the Kuyperian "cultural transformation" point of view has reigned for decades. In recent years, a sharply different point of view has been advanced, often called the "Two Kingdoms" model for relating Christ to culture. Against the Kuyperian perspective, this group argues that "kingdom work" does *not* include transforming and redeeming culture, but only building up the church. In addition, those who hold to the Two Kingdoms model believe that Christians should live in the world as equal citizens with everyone else, appealing to commonly held intuitions about decency, right and wrong, and good order. In other words, Christians should not try to transform the culture to reflect Christian standards or beliefs.

What do we see today? Many of the historic models for relating Christ to culture are being rediscovered, tried, revised, and argued over. In the next chapter, we'll take a closer look at the most prominent current forms of these models. Usually I find it unhelpful to spend too much time critiquing the views of others; it is often better to move on quickly to constructing a positive plan for action. But in this instance I believe that thoughtful, compact critiques of the main streams of thinking and practice in the area of Christianity and culture will be helpful to you as a practitioner. Many find that seeing the models laid out side by side helps them both better situate and understand their own influences and "decode" the positions of those with whom they disagree.

In the end, my main aim in examining the models is to suggest that the way forward on how to best engage culture is a careful *balance* among several polarities. I believe the models we'll be examining each have a firm grasp of a particular important truth, yet they tend to downplay other important truths. As a result, in its purest form, each model is biblically imbalanced, finding itself on the edge of a precipice that we must take care not to plunge over — and none of them are, as D. A. Carson puts it, "compelling as a total explanation or an unambiguous mandate."[37] So in search of a more balanced approach, let's turn to the current landscape of models for relating Christianity to culture.

QUESTIONS FOR DISCUSSION AND REFLECTION

1. Keller writes, "The contemporary American church is pulsing with intramural debates." Take a few minutes to list some of the deepest controversies that have taken up time and provoked debate within your own theological community or denomination. Which of these can be clearly attributed to culture shift and your community's views on Christ and culture?

2. Several causes are given for the shift in our culture away from traditional moral values (the rejection of authority, radical individualism, technological advances, etc.). Regardless of the cause, the gospel message has now become "increasingly incomprehensible" to people. How have you experienced this challenge as you communicate the gospel in your own cultural context? What aspects of the gospel do you find are most difficult for people to grasp?

3. Those who promote pietism argue that:
   - the way to change the world is to change hearts one at a time through evangelism and discipleship
   - increasing the numbers of Christians will somehow improve or change a society
   - it is not a proper goal for Christians to try to improve culture at all, even indirectly

   After reading this chapter, how would you respond to each of these objections? What are the strengths and weaknesses of the pietistic stance toward culture?

4. Which of the various religious responses to the culture shift described in this chapter (i.e. Religious Right, seeker church, emerging/missional church, etc.) have you been involved with? Did the historical overview in this chapter match your own experience?

CHAPTER 15 — THE CULTURAL CRISIS OF THE CHURCH *(pages 181–90)*

1. This story is told well in Joel A. Carpenter, *Revive Us Again: The Reawakening of American Fundamentalism* (New York: Oxford University Press, 1999).
2. A strong reaction against traditional cultural values in general and Christianity in particular came to Britain and Europe more quickly after World War II than it did in the United States. It may be that the culture shift happened faster in Europe than in the U.S. because evangelical Christianity in the U.S. is populist — appealing to the masses — while evangelicalism in the UK is not (see Alister Chapman, "The Educated Evangelicalism of John Stott," http://blogs.westmont.edu/magazine/2009/11/09/the-educated-evangelicalism-of-john-stott/ [accessed January 30, 2012]). In other words, the broad appeal of populist evangelical Christianity among the poor and working classes has probably served to keep American society more traditional. Some observers believe this may be changing, however (see, e.g., Robert D. Putnam and David E. Campbell, *American Grace: How Religion Divides and Unites Us* [New York: Simon and Schuster, 2010]).
3. This social shift actually happened in two stages, according to Putnam and Campbell. In the 1960s, many in the mainline Protestant churches identified with the ideas of 1960s counterculture, which led to a backlash so that many Americans during the late 1970s through the early 1990s moved from mainline churches into more evangelical and conservative churches and swelled their ranks. This helped fuel the rise of the Christian Right, which vigorously opposed the views of 1960s radicals. However, according to Putnam and Campbell, just as mainline churches became associated with the extreme Left, so the evangelical church by the 1990s had come to be identified with the hard political Right, thus causing a similar move away from the conservative church and its values, particularly by those under the age of thirty-five. Meanwhile, many of the young 1960s radicals had completed their "long march through the major cultural institutions," especially the American academy, and the entertainment/media world. The result is that United States society — in particular in its large cities and on the coasts — has finally begun to approximate Europe and Canada in the disdain with which Christian doctrine and Christian morality is held in the public culture (see Putnam and Campbell, *American Grace*, 91–133).
4. Quoted in Barry Hankins, *Francis Schaeffer and the Shaping of Evangelical America* (Grand Rapids: Eerdmans, 2008), 42.
5. Figures cited in Putnam and Campbell, *American Grace*, 97–99.
6. For example, in the 1950s, the movie studio producing Cecil B. DeMille's *The Ten Commandments* sent monuments of the biblical Ten Commandments to hundreds of public buildings — parks, courthouses, etc. These monuments were accepted and set up everywhere, and no one even raised an eyebrow. In the last twenty years, of course, such monuments are the subject of intense litigation and debate.
7. The preceding paragraphs are based on my own experience of doing personal evangelism in the homes of a small town in Virginia during the late 1970s and early 1980s. There the population had been "Christianized" by the culture, as had been done in the West for centuries, though few people understood the gospel or had a vibrant personal faith.
8. See Peter Gay, *The Enlightenment: The Rise of Modern Paganism*, vol. 1 (New York: Norton, 1995); idem, *The Enlightenment: The Science of Freedom*, vol. 2 (New York: Norton, 1996).
9. I once heard a lecture by the management pioneer Peter Drucker. He told how surprised he was when he moved to the New York City area in the 1950s (to teach at New York University) and tried to take out a mortgage in order to buy a house. At the bank he was asked if he went to church or synagogue. He was surprised to be asked this (Drucker was from Austria) and asked why it was relevant. He was told something along the lines of, "Why would we trust a man who didn't go to church or synagogue?"
10. See Putnam and Campbell, *American Grace*, 124–25.
11. Ibid., 125.
12. See Philip Jacob Spener, *Pia Desideria*, trans. Theodore G. Tappert (Minneapolis: Fortress, 1964).
13. Mark Noll, *The Rise of Evangelicalism: The Age of Edwards, Whitefield and the Wesleys* (Downers Grove, Ill.: InterVarsity, 2003), 60–65.
14. See James D. Hunter, *To Change the World: The Irony, Tragedy, and Possibility of Christianity in the Late Modern World* (New York: Oxford University Press, 2010), 90.
15. Quoted in William McLoughlin, *Modern Revivalism: Charles Grandison Finney to Billy Graham* (Eugene, Ore.: Wipf & Stock, 2005), 257.
16. The story is told in Owen D. Strachan, "Reenchanting the Evangelical Mind: Park Street Church's Harold Ockenga, the Boston Scholars, and the Mid-Century Intellectual Surge" (unpublished PhD diss., Trinity Evangelical Divinity School, 2011).
17. Carl F. H. Henry, *The Uneasy Conscience of Modern Fundamentalism* (Grand Rapids: Eerdmans, 1947).

18. See Hankins, *Francis Schaeffer*, 63. Hankins helpfully shows that Schaeffer's legacy was twofold. When he was in Europe (in the 1950s and 1960s), Schaeffer popularized to a generation of younger evangelicals the ideas of worldview and of moving out into public culture to speak and work in a society-influencing, distinctively Christian manner (see Hankins's ch. 5: "Progressive Prophet of Culture"). Later, when he returned to the United States (in the 1970s and 1980s), he laid the foundation for the Christian Right (see Hankins's ch. 8: "A Manifesto for Christian Right Activism"). In other words, Schaeffer was what we will later call a "Transformationist," operating at different stages in his life as neo-Calvinist thinker and Christian Right activist.

19. I would not call the pietistic stance a model for relating Christ to culture. It would be clearer to see it as the *absence* of a Christ and culture model, or even an "anti-model." Even Christ and culture models that advise deliberate withdrawal have particular (negative) views of human culture derived from reflection on Scripture and culture. The pietistic stance is more of a mind-set that ignores culture or sees it as mainly irrelevant.

20. Abraham Kuyper, "Sphere Sovereignty," in *Abraham Kuyper: A Centennial Reader*, ed. James D. Bratt (Grand Rapids: Eerdmans, 1998), 488. The entire address is found on pp. 463 – 90.

21. In his essay "Common Grace in Science," Kuyper wrote, "A thought of God forms the core of the essence of things; God's thinking prescribes their form of existence, their appearance, their law for life, their destiny." He likens this to a pocket watch. A child may see "the golden case, the face, and the moving hands" but will understand neither what lies within the watch to make it tick nor the purpose of the ticking — not just to make sounds but also to measure time. Until you know what a watch is for, you don't understand it, and you can't evaluate whether it is a good or bad watch. Kuyper then says that the non-Christian looks at the world the way a child looks at a watch. Only the person with the Word of God knows why things are and why they operate in the world as they do. What then is education and work done from a Christian worldview? It is to use "an ability imparted to man to unwrap the thoughts of God that lie embodied in creation" (Bratt, *Abraham Kuyper: A Centennial Reader*, 444).

22. The thinkers usually associated with neo-Calvinism include Abraham Kuyper, Herman Dooyeweerd, Herman Bavinck, Albert Wolters, Richard Mouw, Alvin Plantinga, Nicholas Wolterstorff, Cornelius Plantinga, George Marsden, Evan Runner, Calvin Seerveld, Craig Bartholomew, Michael Goheen, and James Skillen. Institutions include Calvin College and Calvin Theological Seminary in Grand Rapids, Michigan; Dordt College in Sioux Center, Iowa; the CCO (Coalition for Christian Outreach) and its annual Jubilee Conference; Redeemer University College in Ancaster, Ontario, Canada; the Institute for Christian Studies in Toronto, Ontario, Canada; the Center for Public Justice in Washington, D.C.; and Trinity Christian College in Palos Heights, Illinois. For an introductory sketch of the movement, see Derek Melleby, "Neo-Calvinism 101," www.vanguardchurch.com/neo-calvinism_101.htm (accessed January 30, 2012).

23. For a comprehensive but accessible survey, see David K. Naugle, *Worldview: The History of a Concept* (Grand Rapids: Eerdmans, 2002). Naugle lists those who pioneered the concept with Protestant evangelicals: Abraham Kuyper, Gordon Clark, Carl F. H. Henry, and Francis Schaeffer. For a brief, helpful introduction to the concept, see James W. Sire, *Naming the Elephant: Worldview as a Concept* (Downers Grove, Ill.: InterVarsity, 2004), and his classic, *The Universe Next Door: A Basic Worldview Catalog*, 5th ed. (Downers Grove, Ill.: InterVarsity, 2009).

24. Carpenter ("The Perils of Prosperity: Neo-Calvinism and the Future of Religious Colleges," in *The Future of Religious Colleges*, ed. Paul J. Dovre [Grand Rapids: Eerdmans, 2002], 183) points out that older bases for Christian higher education — "such as the Renaissance Christian humanism practiced at the early Harvard, or the Scottish Enlightenment's Common Sense philosophy, as propagated for a century out of Princeton, have largely disappeared from the American scene."

25. In the last part of his life, Francis Schaeffer, who originally promoted worldview as an inspiration for Christians to enter the arts, the academy, business, and the media, lent his support to Falwell and the growth of the Christian Right (see Hankin, *Francis Schaeffer*, 200 – 204). Kuyper's contemporary legacy is therefore quite politically mixed. On the one hand, the movement of neo-Calvinism based on Kuyper's thought is marked by thinkers whose political views tend to be centrist or center-left. On the other hand, Kuyper has been the hero of the Religious Right and to some degree to the followers of Rousas Rushdoony and those in the camp called Christian Reconstructionism or theonomy.

26. Ronald Reagan, in his presidential inaugural address, January 20, 1981, famously said, "Government is not the solution to our problem; government is the problem."

27. Lynne and Bill Hybels wrote an "autobiography" of Willow Creek under the title *Rediscovering Church: The Story and Vision of Willow Creek Community Church* (Grand Rapids: Zondervan, 1997).

28. G. A. Pritchard (*Willow Creek Seeker Services: Evaluating a New Way of Doing Church* [Grand Rapids: Baker, 1995]) wrote an early critique of Willow Creek. Pritchard found that seeker services drew a greater percentage of believers than seekers. Kimon Sargeant (*Seeker Churches: Promoting Traditional Religion in a Nontraditional Way* [New Brunswick, N.J.: Rutgers University Press, 2000]) provided another critique of the seeker movement. Sargeant and others argue that by adapting ministry to techniques drawn from the secular business and therapy worlds, churches unwittingly bring in the underlying values embodied in those techniques and subtly change the Christian message.

29. See H. Henry Meeter, *The Basic Ideas of Calvinism* (Grand Rapids: Baker, 1990), 104 – 5.

30. See Gary North, ed., *Theonomy: An Informed Response* (Tyler, Tex.: Institute for Christian Economics, 1991), 96 – 123, 249 – 73.

31. So much has been written about the emerging church that I won't even try to compile a bibliographic footnote!

32. Dan Strange, "Not Ashamed! The Sufficiency of Scripture for Public Theology," *Themelios* 36.2 (July 2011): 238 – 60, http://tgc-documents.s3.amazonaws.com/journal-issues/36.2/Themelios_36.2.pdf (accessed January 30, 2012).

33. See Lesslie Newbigin, "Can the West Be Converted?" *Princeton Seminary Bulletin* 6.1 (1985): 25 – 37, www.newbigin.net/assets/pdf/85cwbc.pdf (accessed January 30, 2012). We will treat Newbigin and the "missional" conversation in greater detail in part 6.

34. Darrell L. Guder, ed., *Missional Church: A Vision for the Sending of the Church in North America* (Grand Rapids: Eerdmans, 1998).

35. The forerunners of this stream of influence were Richard Foster, *A Celebration of Discipline: The Path to Spiritual Growth*, 3rd ed. (New York: HarperCollins, 1988); and Dallas Willard, *The Spirit of the Disciplines: Understanding How God Changes Lives* (New York: HarperCollins, 1988).

36. See Kent Carlson and Mike Lueken, *Renovation of the Church: What Happens When a Seeker Church Discovers Spiritual Formation* (Downers Grove, Ill.: InterVarsity, 2011).

37. D. A. Carson, *Christ and Culture Revisited* (Grand Rapids: Eerdmans, 2008), 224.

chapter 16

THE CULTURAL RESPONSES OF THE CHURCH

In response to the cultural crisis that has shaken so many evangelicals out of their pietistic stance, Christians (particularly in the United States) have been answering the question of how to relate to culture in four basic ways, which I will call the Transformationist model, the Relevance model, the Counterculturalist model, and the Two Kingdoms model.[1] In the previous chapter, we sketched out the historical emergence of these views and some of their animating ideas, and in the following chapters we will address them in greater detail. I believe that setting out these four basic categories is a clarifying and important preparation to developing a Center Church vision for cultural engagement.

DIFFERENCES AMONG NIEBUHR'S MODELS

Niebuhr understood his first two models to be extreme opposites — "Christ against culture" sees culture most negatively, as an expression of human fallenness, while "Christ of culture" sees it most positively, as an expression of God's gracious activity. The other three models — "Christ above culture," "Christ and culture in paradox," and "Christ transforming culture" — are positions between the two extremes, with "Christ above culture" having the most positive view of culture of these three.

Perhaps an illustration can help us distinguish the differences among the models within Niebuhr's framework. Think of a particular cultural product — say, a computer. The "Christ against culture" person may refuse to use it because it undermines human community. The

THE PROBLEM WITH MODELS

Over the last three decades, the alternatives that have emerged to the pietistic stance roughly resemble many of the models laid out in H. Richard Niebuhr's classic book *Christ and Culture.*[2] Niebuhr lays out five basic ways of relating Christ to culture:

1. **Christ against culture:** a *withdrawal* model of removing oneself from the culture into the community of the church
2. **Christ of culture:** an *accommodationist* model that recognizes God at work in the culture and looks for ways to affirm this
3. **Christ above culture:** a *synthetic* model that advocates supplementing and building on the good in the culture with Christ
4. **Christ and culture in paradox:** a *dualistic* model that views Christians as citizens of two different realms, one sacred and one secular
5. **Christ transforming culture:** a *conversionist* model that seeks to transform every part of culture with Christ

Niebuhr considered the first model far too naive about the power of redemption and our escape from the effects of original sin. But he considered the second model far too untroubled by the cultural status quo and the ongoing reality of sin. He saw the third model as being at the same time too sanguine about both culture *and* Christ, lacking a sense of the importance of divine judgment, while he saw the fourth model as too pessimistic about the possibility for cultural improvement. Of all the models, Niebuhr considered the last model to be the most balanced — neither as pessimistic about culture as the sectarians and dualists nor as naively optimistic as the accommodationists and synthesists.

Still, even though Niebuhr presented these five models as distinct ways of understanding the relationship between Christ and culture, he acknowl-edged the "artificiality" of talking about models. He wrote, "When one returns from the hypothetical scheme to the rich complexity of individual events, it is evident at once that no person or group ever conforms completely to a type."[3] Niebuhr admitted that the sketching of models and categories has its pitfalls, namely, that some people conform well to a type, but many others do not.

Why use models at all then? I believe there are two reasons. The first one Niebuhr himself states: "The method of typology . . . has the advantage of calling to attention the continuity and significance of the great *motifs* that appear and reappear in the long wrestling of Christians with their enduring problem. Hence it also helps us to gain orientation as we in our own time seek to answer the question of Christ and culture."[4] In other words, each of the models has running through it a motif or guiding biblical truth that helps Christians relate to culture. Each model collects people and groups who have stressed that motif, and by doing so, it helps us see the importance of that particular principle.

The second way the use of models helps us is by their very inadequacy. Many people and groups do not fit into any one category because they sense (rightly) that no one model can do justice to all of the important biblical themes. Within each model, then, there will be some who will be better at incorporating insights from other models, and some who conform exclusively to a type. So the fact

---

> Why use models at all? Because each of
> the models has running through it a
> motif or guiding biblical truth that
> helps Christians relate to culture.

---

that models often fail as descriptors is instructive in itself.[5] Through their limitations, models encourage church leaders to avoid extremes and imbalances and to learn from all the motifs and categories.

We can't make sense of what people do without

"Christ of culture" person will adopt it fully, assured that it is something God has brought about. The "Christ above culture" person will also adopt it but only use it for the purposes of evangelism and Christian teaching. The "Christ and culture in paradox" person will use the computer with some wariness and take great care not to indulge too deeply. Finally, the "Christ transforming culture" person will study the effects of computers on human relationships, communities, and character and then develop particular ways to use comput-ers that do not undermine but instead support human flourishing as the Bible defines it.

Since I adapted this illustration from an article written for students on the website of Calvin College, some readers may rightly discern a Transformationist slant in this illustration.[6] Still, it is helpful.

relating them to others and noticing continuities and contrasts. This is the nature of modeling. Nev-ertheless, none of us like to be put into a category. Though I will show there are a variety of positions even within a particular model, some readers will still feel pigeonholed and should keep in mind that I am going to be expounding the sharpest and clearest versions of these positions. I realize that not everyone who identifies with a movement holds all its views in precisely the same way, and so I will necessarily have to flirt with overgeneralization. Yet if church and culture truly is the issue below the waterline of many of our struggles as the church, I believe it is critical to make and study maps of this particular landscape.

THE TRANSFORMATIONIST MODEL

The first model for cultural engagement is the Transformationist model, which engages culture largely through an emphasis on Christians pursu-ing their vocations from a Christian worldview and thereby changing culture. Since the lordship

NIEBUHR AND SUBSEQUENT MODELS

Niebuhr's work has been subjected to innumerable critiques. One set of critiques comes from proponents of particular views who believe Niebuhr caricatures them. Another critique is that Niebuhr assumes the "Constantinian settlement," namely, that Christianity will be a society's established faith in some way. This is true to some extent, as Niebuhr does assume an identification of the majority of the citizenry with mainline Protestantism. Critics charge that if you assume that the era of "Christendom" is over, you have to redo all the categories—and you come up with those who hold that Christendom was a good idea (formal state or informal coercive social power as ways to promote the Christian faith) and those who do not.[7] Others have argued that each of the five models have at least two approaches—a healthy and an unhealthy one. Still others say that Niebuhr's work assumes monolithic, nonpluralistic cultures and is therefore less relevant today.

In D. A. Carson's book-length biblical critique of Niebuhr, he concludes that the second model ("Christ of culture") is wrong and unbiblical, and that all of the rest of the models have biblical warrant and may be valid for a particular time and setting, but none can be said to do justice to all the biblical themes and teachings about culture.[8]

Despite the withering criticism, most of the alternative approaches to culture that are proposed and promoted today correspond generally to Niebuhr's categories. It won't be hard to see the relationship of the four approaches I am identifying to the historic models of Niebuhr's *Christ and Culture*. They are not identical, and yet the four models presented in this chapter correspond roughly to Niebuhr's "Christ transforming culture" (Trans-

of Christ should be brought to bear on *every* area of life—economics and business, government and politics, literature and art, journalism and the media, science and law and education—Christians should be laboring to transform culture, to (literally) change the world. As we said earlier, this model is heavily indebted to the work and thought of the Dutch theologian and political leader Abraham Kuyper.

Kuyper contributed two fundamental insights to this debate. First, in every sphere of life Christians are to think and act distinctively *as* Christians. They do so because all cultural behavior presupposes a set of (at least implicit) religious beliefs. Everyone worships and is moved by some ultimate concern, and whatever this concern is will shape their cultural products. Kuyper's second basic insight is this: "Christians should articulate their way of thinking, speaking, and acting ... in the course of interacting with non-Christians in our shared human practices and institutions."[9] In other words, if as a Christian I am conscious of my Christian beliefs as I am living and working, these beliefs will affect everything I do in life. My culture making will move a society in a particular direction, and consequently I will be changing culture.

Though I am labeling as Transformationist those who center their engagement with culture on Kuyper's two key insights, it is important to note that the particular modes of application and implementation differ significantly among the various camps within this model. As we mentioned earlier, one of the groups is the Religious or Christian Right, who see cultural change effected primarily through political and issue-based activism. The language of the Religious Right includes calls for believers to penetrate cultural institutions, work out of a Christian worldview, and transform the culture in the name of Christ. The early architects of the movement (such as Francis Schaeffer, Chuck Colson, and others) based much of their work on Kuyper's insights. A 2008 article in *Perspectives*, a journal of politically progressive Calvinists, even lamented that the basic ideas of Kuyper—someone whom progressive neo-Calvinists consider their intellectual hero — had now become the basis for much of the Christian Right in the United States.[10] The Christian Right, of course, believes that a consistent biblical worldview leads to a conservative political philosophy.

Many have also pointed out the connections between Kuyper and a much smaller movement known as Christian Reconstructionism or theonomy.[11] This movement is based on the writings of Rousas Rushdoony, who advocated basing the modern state on biblical law, including much of the "civil law" portion of the Mosaic legislation.[12] Those in this camp envision a repristinated Christendom in which the government overtly supports the Christian faith and provides only limited tolerance for members of other faiths. Rushdoony often spoke of the "heresy of democracy."[13] Others outside of the United States have also made a case for a "confessionally Christian state."[14]

The original group in North America that invoked Kuyper for cultural engagement was comprised of neo-Calvinists. Yet this group differs sharply from the Christian Right and the Reconstructionists in several ways, most noticeably in their *politics*. The Christian Right is politically conservative, seeing low taxes and deregulated business as proper expressions of the biblical principles of individual freedom and private property. The neo-Calvinists, however, are center-left in their politics, seeing a progressive tax structure, strong labor unions, and

---

The Transformationist model engages culture largely through an emphasis on Christians pursuing their vocations from a Christian worldview and thereby changing culture.

---

more centralized economies as appropriate political expressions of the biblical principles of justice. And while those in the Christian Reconstructionist camp have taught that the civil government should be explicitly committed to biblical truth and standards, the neo-Calvinists speak instead of

formationist), "Christ of culture" and "Christ above culture" (Relevance), "Christ against culture" (Counterculturalist), and "Christ and culture in paradox" (Two Kingdoms).

James Hunter (*To Change the World: The Irony, Tragedy, and Possibility of Christianity in Late Modernity* [New York: Oxford University Press], 2010) critiques three of Niebuhr's models under the titles "Defensive Against" (Transformationist), "Relevant To" (Relevance), and "Purity From" (Counterculturalist). His critiques are helpful for better understanding the strengths and weaknesses of Niebuhr's original models.

"principled pluralism" — the belief that Christians in government should seek principles of justice that can be recognized as such by nonbelievers because of natural revelation or common grace, and yet these principles clearly align with biblical principles as well.[15]

A second difference among the groups within the Transformationist model is in their overall strategy for *engagement*. The Christian Right typically seeks cultural change through targeted political activism against abortion and same-sex marriage and for the promotion of the family and traditional values. The strategy of the neo-Calvinists has focused primarily on education. A large network of Christian schools and colleges endeavor to produce students who "think Christianly" within every academic discipline and work in every field out of a Christian worldview. This view has influenced other evangelical colleges, publishing houses, and even a parachurch campus ministry — CCO (formerly Coalition for Christian Outreach).[16]

A third difference is *theological*. One of the main differences between the neo-Calvinists and the Religious Right has to do with neo-Calvinists' belief that Christians do not rely on the Bible alone when seeking guidance regarding business, art, and vocation. They teach that we can discern many of

God's intentions for our life in the world by looking at creation, at "general revelation."[18] In other words, while neo-Calvinists believe there is a distinctively Christian way to carry out our cultural activity, they believe non-Christians can intuitively discern much of how God wants humans to live in culture. I believe this view helps neo-Calvinists make common cause with nonbelievers and adopt a far less combative stance in the public sphere.

Though we see clear differences among the various camps in the Transformationist model, all people working within this model share several commonalities.

1. They view "secular" work as an important way to serve Christ and his kingdom, just as is ministry within the church. They understand Christ's saving purposes as including not only individual salvation but also the renewal of the material world. Therefore, Christians should not only build up the church through Word and Sacrament but also work to restore and renew creation.

Theologian Herman Bavinck taught that God's saving grace "does not remain outside or above or beside nature but rather ... wholly renews it."[19] Theologian Geerhardus Vos, following Bavinck, sees the kingdom of God operating in the world in two ways: first, *within the church* as it ministers in Word and sacrament, and second, when Christians live lives *in society* to God's glory. Vos writes, "There is a sphere of science, a sphere of art, a sphere of the family and of the state, a sphere of commerce and industry. Whenever one of these spheres comes under the controlling influence of the principle of the divine supremacy and glory, and this outwardly reveals itself, there we can truly say that the kingdom of God has become manifest."[20]

2. Even more than the other models we will examine shortly, Transformationists celebrate and assign high value to Christians who excel in their work and enter spheres of influence within business, the media, government and politics, the academy, and the arts.[21] This is due, I think, to the fact that Transformationists truly believe secular vocations are an authentic way of bearing witness to Christ's kingdom. In addition, those who embrace this model are more likely to see the importance of human institutions for shaping culture and therefore stress the importance of Christians living and working in them.[22]

3. All those in this category believe that the main problem with society is a secularism that has disingenuously demanded a "naked public square." In the name of tolerance and neutrality, secularist elites have imposed a particular worldview on society, forbidding believers from striving to see their beliefs and values reflected in culture. The assumption behind this is that Christians have been passive or that they have fallen into "dualism" — keeping their

faith and beliefs strictly private and not letting them influence and change the way they live in public life. As I will show later, I believe this is largely a correct assessment and an important plank in the development of a faithfully biblical approach to culture.

PROBLEMS WITH THE TRANSFORMATIONIST MODEL

We can identify several significant problems with the Transformationist model, but I will begin by noting the movement of self-correction already going on within this model, especially within the neo-Calvinist part of the spectrum, and so my critique largely conforms to what members of the movement themselves are saying.[23]

1. The conception of "worldview" in Transformationism is too cognitive. The idea of "biblical presuppositions" is often understood as purely a matter of bullet-point beliefs and propositions. James K. A. Smith has written a book-length criticism of this aspect of "Christian worldview" movement titled *Desiring the Kingdom*.[24] Smith, a Calvin College professor, doesn't deny that ultimately everyone has a worldview. But he argues that a person's worldview is not *merely* a set of doctrinal and philosophical beliefs completely formed by reason and information. A worldview is also comprised of a set of hopes and loves — "tacit knowledge" and heart attitudes — that are not all adopted consciously and deliberately. They are more the result of experience, community life, and liturgy (or daily practices).

2. Transformationism is often marked by "an underappreciation for the church ... For [Transformationists], the implication is that the 'real action' is outside the church, not the church itself."[25] What really gets many Transformationists excited is not building up the church but penetrating the bastions of cultural influence for Christ. The problem here is twofold. First, just as pietism tended to lift up full-time ministry and denigrate secular vocations, Transformationism can lead to the opposite extreme. Much of the excitement and creative energy ends up focusing on cosmic or social redemption rather than on bringing about personal conversion through evangelism and discipleship. Second, as James K. A. Smith points out, worldview formation happens not just through education and argument (the neo-Calvinist emphasis) or mainly through politics (the Christian Right approach). Rather, it derives from the narratives we embrace, especially those that give us a compelling picture of human flourishing that captures our hearts and imaginations. These narratives are presented to us, not mainly in classrooms, but through the stories we absorb from various sources.[26] Smith insists, therefore, that the liturgy and practices of church communities are critical for the formation of worldview. This is an important corrective — it balances the Kuyperian emphasis on penetrating the cultural institutions with the Counterculturalists' stress on the importance of Christians belonging to "thick" Christian communities (we will look at this in more detail shortly).

3. Transformationism tends to be triumphalistic, self-righteous, and overconfident in its ability to both understand God's will for society and bring it about. One writer refers to a "hubris that one has both access to the power to get at the root of the problem and then the wisdom to know how to better the structures of society with insights from the gospel."[27] Part of this tendency to hubris is an overconfidence that we can glean from Scripture easily applied principles for economics, art, and government.[28] Neo-Calvinist philosopher Richard Mouw has joked that neo-Calvinists "seem to have an unusual facility for finding detailed cultural guidance in the biblical record."[29] This could readily be said of the Christian Right and the theonomists as well. The danger is that we may be tempted to think we can envision virtually an entire Christian

---

THE MESSAGE GETS THROUGH

Neo-Calvinist Al Wolters writes, "In spite of human perversity, some of God's message in creation gets through [to non-Christians] ... Even without God's explicit verbal positivization of the creational norms for justice and faithfulness, stewardship and respect, people have an intuitive sense of normative standards for conduct."[30]

James Hunter's claim that political activism does not typically lead cultural change is supported by an interesting finding in Robert Putnam and David Campbell's *American Grace.* Today's young adults are surprisingly united in saying that one reason they have turned from the church is the antihomosexual activism of the Religious Right. So why are young adults much more liberal in their views regarding homosexuality, so liberal, in fact, that they find the traditional Christian position on sex to be offensive and harmful? Putnam and Campbell, among other reasons, say "TV and the movies normalized homosexuality during this period."[31] In other words, while some Christians were hoping that legislation would change people's attitudes, it was pop culture, the academic institutions, the arts, and the media that were shaping the popular mind. Public policy is only now beginning to follow suit.

Since James Hunter is seeking to correct an imbalance — an overreliance on politics and activism for cultural change — he could be read as proposing that believers should not be involved in politics or government. This is not what he is doing. Christians have a high calling to represent Christ in *all* vocations — in the public sphere as well as in the church.

culture. This is a failure to discern the Bible's redemptive historical story line. There is no book of Leviticus in the New Testament dictating what to eat, what to wear, or how to regulate a host of cultural practices. While there are important biblical values and principles that give guidance to Christians in business or public service — particularly a Christian vision of human flourishing — there are no detailed biblical plans for running a company or a government. In addition, Transformationists

can be overconfident about their ability to create cultural change. Slogans such as "taking back the culture" and the very phrase "transforming culture" itself lead to expectations that Christians can bring about sweeping changes. But as James Hunter masterfully shows, human culture is extraordinarily complex and not controllable by any one means. All changes that Christians can produce will be incremental.[32]

4. Transformationism has often put too much stock in politics as a way to change culture.[33] Hunter points out that government/politics is only one set of institutions in the cultural matrix, and he argues that the Religious Right, at least, has overestimated the influence of this institution. In general, he argues, politics is "downstream" from the true sources of cultural change, which tend to flow in a nonlinear fashion from new ideas produced in the "cultural centers" — the academy, the arts, the media companies, and the cities. Scholars generate new theories, some of which win the field and begin to hold sway. People influenced by the theories begin to act on them in other cultural institutions — teaching in schools, publishing books, producing plays and movies, using the narrative to cover the news — and slowly public opinion begins to shift. On the basis of this public opinion, laws begin to be passed.

An illustration is sexual harassment laws. Imagine trying to get harassment laws passed anywhere in America in 1910; it would have been impossible. A sea change had to come in our thinking about sex, gender roles, and human rights through all the various cultural institutions — all before laws could be introduced. Politics helps to cement cultural changes, but it typically does not lead them.

5. Transformationists often don't recognize the dangers of power.[34] As James Hunter points out, it is impossible for Christians to avoid the exercise of power in society.[35] Yet just as the pietistic stance underestimates the importance of human institutions, the activism of the Transformationist model often underestimates the danger of Christians becoming too absorbed in seeking and exercising power. Some Transformationists seem to think they cannot initiate any cultural changes unless

Christians as a bloc gain political clout, but there are numerous examples of how the church loses its vitality when Christianity and the state are too closely wedded.[36] Miroslav Volf writes, "Christian communities [should be] more comfortable with being just one of many players, so that from whatever place they find themselves — on the margins, at the center, or anywhere in between — they can promote human flourishing and the common good."[37] Volf speaks of two "malfunctions" that a religious faith can exhibit in its relationship with culture. One he calls "idleness," and the other "coerciveness." Idleness — cultural withdrawal and passivity — is not a temptation for Transformationists, but coerciveness can be. Volf argues convincingly that Christianity, when true to its biblical self, is not a coercive faith. A proper understanding of the gospel, of the cross, and of Christian ethics would make it impossible for Christians to use power to oppress.[38] But it is not at all impossible to lose sight of these realities and to use power coercively in Christ's name. The Afrikaner supporters of Abraham Kuyper, for example, did so when justifying the brutal policies of apartheid in order to maintain a "Christian culture."[39] By setting our sights on gaining and retaining political influence, it is possible to miss the biblical themes of how God regularly works among the weak and the marginal and of how any truly Christian society must promote *shalom* – peace and justice for every citizen. One of the more worrisome aspects of the Religious Right to this point has been the apparent absence of concern for the poor.

THE RELEVANCE MODEL

The second contemporary model of cultural engagement we will call the Relevance model.[40] As with the Transformationist model, very different groups operate within it, and the spectrum here is even broader than that within the other categories. Indeed, many of these groups are pointedly critical of one another, and would cringe at the word *relevant* as a description of their ministry. Nevertheless, I think the word helps us identify a common thread connecting all of these movements and writers.

In H. Richard Niebuhr's scheme, his second and third models are the most positive toward culture.

Niebuhr describes those of the second type — "the Christ of culture" — as being "equally at home" within the church and out in the culture.[41] This model sees Christianity as being fundamentally compatible with the surrounding culture. Those who embrace this model believe that God is at work redemptively within cultural movements that have nothing explicitly to do with Christianity. It sees Christ at work in all "movements in philosophy toward the assertion of the world's unity and order, movements in morals toward self-denial and the care for the common good, [and] political concerns for justice."[42] It is not just that these things are good in some general way — they are the work of God's Spirit. For Niebuhr, liberal theology was an example of this model. Liberal churches do not believe in an infallible Bible, an historical incarnation, an atoning sacrifice on the cross, or a literal resurrection. They reject any "once for all-ness" regarding Christian doctrine and salvation. They see God continually revealing new things and doing new things in history and culture.[43]

Another more recent expression of this approach is liberation theology, which grew out of the Roman Catholic Church in Latin America in the late twentieth century.[44] Liberation theology understood sin and salvation in radically corporate categories, so that Christian salvation is equated with liberation from unjust economic, political, and social conditions. Liberation theology fits the "Christ of culture" pattern because it sees movements of political liberation from oppression as God's work in the world — a work that the church should join. And so liberation theology "[obliterates] the distinction between the church and the world by identifying the purpose of God with the present historical situation."[45]

Niebuhr's third model is "Christ above culture" (also called the synthesist position). This approach has a stronger view of "the universality and radical nature of sin" than the second model, but nevertheless continues to have a very positive view of culture. The synthesists tend to be "both-and" people who feel no need to rethink and remake cultural products but rather to adopt them and supplement them with Christian faith. This model seeks to "build from culture to Christ."[46] Niebuhr names as the prime example of this model Thomas Aquinas, who sought to "synthesize the ethics of culture with the ethics of the gospel" rather than "transform" the ethics of culture with the gospel.[47]

The animating idea behind these approaches is that God's Spirit is at work in the culture to further his kingdom; therefore Christians should view culture as their ally and join with God to do good.[48] The primary way to engage culture, then, is for

---

The animating idea behind the Relevance model is that God's Spirit is at work in the culture to further his kingdom.

---

the church to adapt to new realities and connect to what God is doing in the world. Christians and churches that emphasize these ideas — those who embrace the Relevance model — share several common characteristics.

1. In general, they are optimistic about cultural trends and feel less need to reflect on them, exercise discernment, and respond to them in discriminating ways. Even one of the milder forms of the Relevance model — the seeker church movement — is much more sanguine about both modern capitalism and psychology than other models, and so it borrows heavily from the worlds of business and therapy without giving a great deal of thought to whether such methods import an underlying worldview and so reshape Christian ministry in the world's likeness.

2. People operating within this model put great emphasis on the "common good" and "human flourishing." They emphasize the modern church's failure to care about inequality, injustice, and suffering in the world. They call the church to work for justice in society, and they declare that only when it does so will it regain the credibility to speak to society about God. They see God at work outside the church, moving history toward greater recon-

ciliation of individuals, races, and nations through various movements of liberation. Christians are to join in what is already happening — efforts to work against hunger, improve social conditions, and fight for human rights.

3. Those who hold to this model seldom speak of a Christian worldview. The very concept of "worldview" assumes a much greater gap or antithesis between Christian truth and human culture than this (more optimistic) model sees. Perhaps another reason Relevants do not talk much about worldview is that so many of them are sharply critical of the Religious Right. They intentionally avoid the negative rhetoric of "dying" or "declining" culture — or of "losing" or "winning" the culture — that characterizes that particular movement.

4. Relevants seek to engage culture by reinventing the church's ministry to be more relevant to the needs and sensibilities of people in the culture and more committed to the service and good of the whole human community. While not condoning immorality and relativism, they locate the main problem in the church's incomprehensibility to the minds and hearts of secular people and its irrelevance to the problems of society. The church has lost touch with the people and the times, this group observes. It has failed to adapt to cultural changes. While others think Christians have become too assimilated to the world around them, this group assumes that, on the contrary, Christians are too withdrawn into their own subcultures, too hostile and condemning of nonbelievers, and too disconnected from them.

5. Adherents of this model make little distinction between how individual Christians should act in the world and how the institutional church should function. Every other model makes more of this difference, speaking of different "spheres" or "kingdoms," arguing that — no matter what individual Christians may do — there are some inappropriate ways for the organized church to engage culture. Relevants, however, issue a blanket call for the church to become deeply involved in the struggle for social justice. The mainline Protestant churches have for years seen their denominational agencies

actively lobbying for legislation and engaging in direct political action. Many of the emerging churches also sense a mandate to become directly involved in justice issues in their locale without calling for any discriminating reflection on how politically involved they should be as an institutional body.

Whom, then, do we place within this category?

At one end of the spectrum, I put many of the older evangelical megachurches. Robert Schuller, a pioneer of the megachurch movement, was extremely open about how he applied the techniques of business and therapy to church ministry. In his book *Your Church Has Real Possibilities*, he lists "seven principles of successful retailing" and insists that any church that wants to grow must apply them directly to the church's ministry, including "excess parking."[49] Unfortunately, Schuller was just as open about reshaping doctrine along the lines of contemporary psychology, proposing that sin be redefined as a lack of self-esteem.[50] More doctrinally orthodox leaders such as Rick Warren and Bill Hybels have deliberately sought to be explicit about sin and judgment.[51] Nevertheless, churches that we could characterize as being in the seeker church movement still rather heavily rely on techniques of business, marketing, technology, and product development; have a strong emphasis on self-fulfillment and the practical benefits of faith to individuals; and use a language sometimes light on theological particulars.[52] They speak often about the need for the church to be "relevant" but little about Christian worldview or thinking out how to integrate one's faith with one's work and vocation.

Further along the spectrum, into the middle of this model, I would put many of the newer emerging churches, particularly those inspired by the old Emergent Village organization led by Brian McLaren and Tony Jones.[53] The emerging church strongly rejected the boomer-led megachurches as market driven, "canned," and "consumerist." They especially criticized the individualistic cast of these ministries and (at least in the 1970s and 1980s) their relative lack of involvement in care for the poor and in the struggle for justice in society. And yet their critiques have been more grounded in cultural analysis than in biblical and theological exegesis. That is, the main operating principle of the emerging church is its choice to adapt to the postmodern shift rather than to confront it.[54] An influential text that embodies this understanding of the church and mission is *Missional Church*, edited by Darrell Gruder.[55] This book is a compendium of contributions that do not agree on all points. Some are more in line with the "Counterculturalist" model discussed below. But they agree on a couple of basic points, namely, that the kingdom of God is primarily a new social order of peace and justice that God is bringing about now in the world, and that the church's calling is to bear witness to it. The job of the church, in this view, is to discover what God is doing out in the world and to get involved with it.[56]

Finally, at the other extreme of the spectrum within this model, we might place those in mainline, liberationist theology groups. While many in the emerging church seek to blend doing justice with doing evangelism, many believe that doing justice essentially *is* doing evangelism. In this view, the gospel is the good news of the coming kingdom of peace and justice, and so, rather than calling for individual conversions, they invite individuals to join the church in order to work for justice. By the middle of the twentieth century, the World Council of Churches had interpreted the *missio Dei* — the mission of God — as God already at work in the world redeeming the whole creation by setting up a new social order of economic justice and human rights. It is not, they said, that the church has a mission and God blesses it, but that God has a mission already out in the world and the church must join it. "The world sets the agenda for the church" was their slogan.[57]

PROBLEMS WITH THE RELEVANCE MODEL

As with the Transformationist model, we can identify several significant problems with the Relevance model.

1. By adapting so heavily and readily to the culture, such churches are quickly seen as dated whenever the culture shifts or changes. The most visible case study is the fast decline of the mainline Protestant denominations. Ironically, it was their very adaptation to culture — their efforts to become relevant — that led mainline Protestantism to a place where it is now considered to be irrelevant and out of touch with the culture. Because they have removed the supernatural element and downplayed doctrinal beliefs, mainline churches appear to most people to be no different from any other social service institution. When a church becomes an organization that only offers social services, counseling, and other community activities, the questions many ask are, "Why does it exist? Why do we need this institution when it is doing, often somewhat amateurishly, what so many secular institutions are doing more effectively?" Many churches, in the name of adapting to the culture, have lost their distinctives and, consequently, the cultural power of Christianity.[58]

Even those in this category who are not theologically experimental — such as the evangelical seeker churches and many in the emerging church — place a heavy emphasis on adapting *methods* to new cultural realities. This often means such ministries look dated very quickly, unlike those in liturgical and traditional churches. Robert Schuller's church heavily adapted to the World War II generation and began graying by the 1980s, and the same is true of many seeker churches today.

2. A second critique has to do with the attitude this stance takes toward doctrine. Earlier, we discussed the need for contextualization, emphasizing that true contextualization begins with Scripture as a normative, nonnegotiable truth. But in this model — especially in its extreme forms — culture becomes normative over Scripture. Of all the models, this one most often downplays the need for both theological precision and the insights of Christian tradition. More than any other model, this approach encourages us to minimize or reengineer traditional doctrines in order to adapt to new cultural realities. Many young Christian leaders are moving in this direction, even though they are aware of the mistakes of the older liberal churches. Some raised in evangelical circles now call themselves "post-evangelical." They say they believe the ancient, orthodox creeds of the church, but beyond

that, they do not wish to debate doctrine. They argue, for example, that the traditional evangelical belief in the inerrancy of the Bible is "rationalistic" and that the classic doctrines of substitutionary atonement and forensic justification are "individualistic." They are reluctant to speak of any doctrinal boundaries, of any inviolable beliefs that cannot be compromised.

3. Most of the different groups in the Relevance model share a significant emphasis on doing justice, on caring for the environment, and on carrying out various forms of social service. When these concerns are emphasized, evangelism and conversion may still be acknowledged and tacitly affirmed, but sometimes as no more than lip service. **The main energy behind churches that follow this model is often directed not toward the teaching of the gospel and seeking conversions but toward producing art, doing service projects, or seeking justice.** Churches that lose their commitment and skill for vigorous evangelism will not only neglect their primary calling, but will inevitably fail to reproduce themselves. It takes new converts and changed lives for churches to truly be of service to the community.

While the second and third criticisms are more appropriate to churches at the liberal end of the spectrum, the evangelical megachurches are open to the criticism that by overly adapting to methods of secular management and therapy, the church has been diluted into a dispenser of spiritual goods and services and turned its members into an audience of consumers. Traditional churches — with their emphasis on theological training, catechesis, and liturgical and ecclesiastical practices — produced real character and ethical change, but this kind of spiritual formation often does not occur in the typical evangelical megachurch.[59]

4. It is especially in this model that the distinctiveness of the Christian church begins to get blurry. Traditionally, the church has been seen as the only institution that ministers the Word and the sacraments; that determines what is the true, biblical preaching of the Word; and that brings people into a community governed and disciplined by called and authorized leaders. In the Relevance model, however, the importance of such distinct ministry fades. What matters is not what happens inside the church, but out in the world. If, as some propose, God's mission advances through historical processes moving toward increasing economic justice and social equality, this "removes the church from the equation of how God works in the world."[60]

THE COUNTERCULTURALIST MODEL

The third of our four models is what we will call the Counterculturalist model. I've given it this name because those within this model place their emphasis on the church as a *contrast society* to the world. And while other models of cultural engagement speak about the important concept of the kingdom of God, this model strongly emphasizes that the kingdom is manifest primarily as a church community in *opposition* to the kingdom of this world.

1. Those operating in this model do *not* see God working redemptively through cultural movements outside the church. Even the pietistic stance held hope that enough evangelistic work would eventually reform society, but this model does not agree. Human society will be what it has always been — the realm of "empire," of "the powers," of capitalistic markets, oppressive governments, and other social systems that crush people in order to increase the power of their leaders. Those in the Counterculturalist camp use the term *empire* to deliberately underscore how, even in a world of democracy and pluralism, oppression continues. They bluntly declare that we should not expect to see lasting improvements in society and harbor little hope that the culture can be transformed along Christian lines.[61] Their emphasis is on the dissimilarity between the kingdom of this world — a set of systems based on power and human glory — and Christ's kingdom, a community based on love, service, and the surrender of power. As Stanley Hauerwas and William Willimon have written, "The world, for all its beauty, is hostile to the truth."[62]

2. This model calls the church to avoid concentrating on the culture, looking for ways to become relevant to it, reach it, or transform it. In fact, the church should not be focusing on the world at all. If there is a cultural crisis today, they say, it is because the culture has invaded the church, and that consequently *the church is not truly being the church.* The church is to be a counterculture, an alternate human society that is a sign of the kingdom to the world. It should not try to turn the world into Christ's kingdom. Rather, the best thing the church can do for the world is to exhibit Christ's kingdom to it, largely through the justice and peace of its community.

The Counterculturalist model places its emphasis on the church as a *contrast society* to the world.

---

3. This model levels sharp criticisms against the conservative evangelical church (particularly the Christian Right), the liberal mainline church, and the new evangelical megachurch. In their view, virtually all branches of the church in the West today have been corrupted by the "Constantinian error" of seeking to reform the world to be like the church. Counterculturalists predict that when Christians try to make the world more like the church, they succeed only in making the church like the world. Invariably, our attempts to influence or transform culture will become corrupted by power and dominated by the political economy of capitalism and liberal democracy. When this happens, the church will have prostituted itself and will no longer have anything of value to share with the world.

Those who adopt the Counterculturalist model look at the liberal mainline Protestants and note how they have become the "Democrat Party at prayer." They look at the Religious Right and see much the same thing — the "Republican Party at prayer." They believe that politicization — on both sides of the political spectrum — has alienated much of the populace and weakened the church's witness. Those who follow this model also criticize the evangelical megachurches as they try to be relevant and meet felt needs. This, they point out, only turns the church into a consumerist mall of services that reflects the reigning spirit of the world — the spirit of self-absorbed market capitalism. By simply giving people what they want, churches fail to confront the innate selfishness and individualism being nurtured by modern capitalism.

4. Counterculturalists insist that instead of trying to change the culture through this consumeristic narrative, the church needs to follow Christ "outside the camp" and identify with the poor and the marginalized. It needs to have thick, rich, liturgical worship that shapes Christians into a new society. The church does not "advance," "build," or "bring" the kingdom; it is to be a *sign* of the future kingdom to the world as it seeks to be a new human society ordered on the basis of God's law and salvation. Real Christianity, says the Counterculturalist thinker, is a life of simplicity, of material self-denial for the sake of charity, justice, and community. It means decreasing both geographical mobility (committing to a local church and a neighborhood) and social mobility (giving away large amounts of your income to those in need).

Who are the Counterculturalists? James Hunter has observed that of all the current Christian models for relating Christianity to culture, this approach has the most intellectual firepower behind it. Many Counterculturalists are scholars/writers who teach at or are associated with Duke University Divinity School, including Stanley Hauerwas, William Willimon, and Richard Hays. They are mainline Protestants dubbed by some as "neo-Anabaptists," who draw inspiration not so much from the magisterial Reformation (Lutheran and Calvinist) but the Radical Reformation of sixteenth-century Europe. The Radical Reformers demanded a sharp distinction between church and state, were often pacifists who refused to serve in the military, formed tight communities that were virtually or literally communes, and called on believers to avoid political entanglements.[63] In addition there are the actual Anabaptists — the churches that have descended directly from the original Anabaptist churches, especially the Mennonites and the contemporary Amish and Hutterites. John Howard Yoder's book

The Politics of Jesus is an important guide to those who follow this model.[64] Another scholarly movement in this category is the "Radical Orthodoxy" of John Millbank and Graham Ward.[65]

Many who have been placed in the broad category of the emerging church also fall into this category, including evangelical thinkers such as David Fitch and Shane Claiborne. Claiborne is the most prominent member of a movement called the "new monastics." Like others influenced by the Anabaptists, they severely criticize capitalism and "empire."[66] They emphasize strong multiracial, cross-class Christian community; a simple lifestyle; practical engagement with the poor; contemplative spirituality; and a prophetic stance against big corporations, the military, and consumer capitalism. The new monastics, though eschewing the idea of cultural transformation, tend to support liberal political policies, which puts them at loggerheads with the Religious Right and, typically, with evangelicals who remain in the pietistic stance. This also marks them out as different from seeker church leaders such as Bill Hybels and Rick Warren, who have tended to be more centrist or apolitical.[67]

The first two models we've examined (the Transformationists and Relevants) have typically contained a diversity of groups and thinkers whose practices and rhetoric differ quite widely. This is less true in this model. Of course, one could place the Amish at one end of the spectrum, representing those who take the spirit of a "counterculture" as literally as possible. In the middle of the spectrum are the new monastics, who live more within the mainstream culture than do the Amish but still create intentional communities and often live together in urban neighborhoods in direct contact with the poor. At the other end of the spectrum are those whose churches are not literally communal but whose theology is driven by the themes and motifs of the Counterculturalist model.

PROBLEMS WITH THE COUNTERCULTURALIST MODEL

As with the Transformationist and Relevance models, we can identify a number of significant problems with the Counterculturalist model.

1. Critics of the Counterculturalist model charge that it is more pessimistic about the prospect of social change than is warranted.

To use a justly famous example, didn't Wilberforce accomplish a true and good social change when he and his allies worked to abolish slavery in the British Empire?[68] Was that an illegitimate project? It seems so, according to this model. A much subtler yet powerful example is the Christianization of Europe. Christianity permanently altered the old honor-based European cultures in which pride was valued rather than humility, dominance rather than service, courage rather than peaceableness, glory more than modesty, loyalty to one's own tribe rather than equal respect for all individuals. Even though there is today some slippage in Western society back toward that pagan worldview, today's secular Europeans are still influenced far more by the Christian ethic than by the old pagan ones. And, by and large, Western societies are more humane places to live because of it. In other words, Christianity transformed a pagan culture.

The Counterculturalist model rightly warns us against triumphalism. But assuming we are willing to leave behind our utopian dreams of creating a Christian society or a "redeemed culture," history teaches us that it is indeed possible to improve and even transform some social structures. D. A. Carson writes the following:

> Sometimes a disease can be knocked out; sometimes sex traffic can be considerably reduced; sometimes slavery can be abolished in a region; sometimes more equitable laws can foster justice and reduce corruption … Yet in these and countless other ways cultural change is possible. More importantly, doing good to the city, doing good to all people (even if we have special responsibility for the household of faith), is part of our responsibility as God's redeemed people.[69]

2. The Counterculturalist model tends to demonize modern business, capital markets, and government.

There is a constant critique of capitalism (in almost all its forms) and a depiction of most businesspeople as greedy and materialistic. Also, its pacifism often goes beyond the simple refusal to engage in taking life in combat to the depic-

DIFFERENCES AMONG COUNTERCULTURALISTS

The Counterculturalist model is far from monolithic. At the popular level, much of the rhetoric of younger leaders and new churches inspired by this model sounds almost *anti-cultural*, as if *human* culture is something to be replaced with a *pure Christian* one. Most thoughtful thinkers in this category, however, do believe in some measure of necessary contextualization, but of all the "models of contextualization" laid out by Stephen Bevans in his helpful text *Models of Contextual Theology*, his Countercultural model is the most confrontive of and the least adaptive to present cultural realities.[70]

Bevans outlines five models of contextualization, moving from the most positive toward the surrounding culture to the most negative. They are, in that order, called the "Anthropological," "Praxis," "Synthetic," "Translation," and "Countercultural" models. The last is associated with Hauerwas, Yoder, and Newbigin. Bevans argues that the Countercultural model gets the reputation for being nothing more than "culture bashing," but that thinkers such as George Hunsberger and Lesslie Newbigin, while highly critical of Western culture, nonetheless still believe the gospel must be "clothed in symbols which are meaningful" to the culture we are trying to reach.[71]

tion of all human government as inherently violent. This view discourages Christians from getting involved in the business world (except for small entrepreneurial ventures with high social consciousness) or in politics (except at local levels in order to change neighborhood dynamics). James Hunter argues that, ironically, the Counterculturalists have in many ways been unintentionally shaped by late modern Western culture. In particular he refers to the movement's "neo-Nietzschean politics," which fuels resentment against power rather than appealing to truth, persuasion, and reasoned discourse. Hunter shows how, despite Counterculturalists' claim to eschew power and politics, this may be the most profoundly political of all the models:

> *In some respects, neo-Anabaptists politicize their engagement with the world even more than the Right and the Left because they cast their oppositions to the State, global capitalism and other powers in eschatological terms. To literally demonize such powers as the State and the market as they do means that they draw much of their identity and purpose in the here and now through their cosmic struggle with them … Their identity depends on the State and other powers being corrupt.*[72]

Hunter then quotes Charles Matthewes as saying that neo-Anabaptists have a "passive-aggressive ecclesiology." That is, while claiming to refuse to be sullied by politics, they use the language of politics as much or more than any model, and while professing to avoid power, they use power language to demonize their opponents.

3. The Counterculturalist movement fails to give sufficient weight to the inevitability of contextualization, of a Christian community necessarily relating and adapting to the surrounding culture. As one writer observed, "The idea that the church can sustain itself as a discrete culture reflecting Christian values, isolating itself from the competing values of the secular world, is a problematic premise."[73] For example, Chinese Christians will certainly be shaped profoundly by their Christian faith. The current culture in China is the result of several traditions and worldviews — Confucianism, animism, and secular materialism. Christianity will certainly affect believers' "Chinese-ness." And yet, Chinese Christians are still Chinese. Think next of Finland. Finnish culture is the result of both Lutheranism and secularism. Orthodox Christians there will be quite different from much of Finnish culture and yet will still be Christian Finns, not Christian Americans or Christian Chinese. Their Christian Finnish-ness is not identical to Christian Chinese-ness. A pan-European/African multiethnic congregation in urban Germany will be different yet again.

Not only will Christians unavoidably be influenced by culture; they will unavoidably change the culture. All communities and individuals do, to some extent, shape the culture around them simply by living their lives. To give a specific example, when a group of new monastic, middle-class Christians moves into a poor community to serve it, they change it culturally by their very arrival. Their presence in the neighborhood changes property values, as well as the various flows of social, financial, and human capital in and out of the neighborhood. We can't avoid changing the culture. Speaking more generally, the way Christians choose to spend their time and money and how they do their work in the world will all necessarily be shaped by their Christian beliefs and priorities. These will in turn have an impact on how other people live their lives. James Hunter has noted that the separatism of the neo-Anabaptists stems in part from their almost wholly negative view of social power as evil. But everyone has social power, argues Hunter. So in the end, Counterculturalists are more involved in culture than their model admits.

4. A fourth criticism focuses on doctrine. Many in both the contemporary and the classic Anabaptist traditions are happy to affirm general evangelical statements of doctrine such as the Lausanne Covenant. However, because Anabaptist theology stresses the horizontal aspects of sin (e.g., abusing creation, violence in human relationships) and sometimes places less emphasis on the vertical (e.g., offending the holiness of God) in its understanding of Christ's work, **it tends to downplay the doctrines of justification and substitutionary atonement.** Often the primary understanding of the atonement is a form of *Christus Victor*, in which Christ defeats the powers on the cross. Some Anabaptist theologians strongly reject the notion of propitiation (that the cross satisfied the wrath of God) as a "violent" theory of the atonement.

5. Perhaps unintentionally, this model may undermine a church's emphasis and skill at evangelism — even more than the Relevance

model may. The Counterculturalist advocates understand the Christian community itself — its unity and social patterns — as being *the* way of proclaiming the gospel to the world. They believe that "belonging precedes believing" and that evangelism consists of drawing people into an attractive community of love that is promoting justice in the world. This often means, practically, that the church puts little or no thought into how to clearly communicate verbally the gospel message in calling individuals to repentance. As we observed earlier, any element within a model that cuts off the motivation for vigorous evangelism can undermine the entire model. Without a steady stream of new converts and changed lives, the vitality and vision of the model cannot be fully realized.

THE TWO KINGDOMS MODEL

Of the four models I am sketching, this final one — the Two Kingdoms model of cultural engagement — may well be the least-known among evangelical Christians in the United States. However, in its Lutheran form it has a long and venerable pedigree, as well as a place in Niebuhr's catalog of models (as "Christ and culture in paradox"). More recently, a number of conservative Reformed writers have undertaken a fresh articulation of this approach, claiming that it is the view John Calvin took of the relationship of Christ to culture and vigorously arguing for it on principles of Reformed theology, particularly as a counterpoint to the neo-Calvinist Transformationalists who follow Kuyper.[74]

The name "Two Kingdoms" comes from the core teaching that God rules all of creation, but he does so in two distinct ways. First, there is the "common kingdom" (often called the earthly or even "left-hand" kingdom) established through the covenant with Noah in Genesis 9.[75] In this realm, all human beings are members, and people know right and wrong through natural revelation or common grace. According to Romans 1:18 – 32 and 2:14 – 15, the light of nature and the human conscience give all human beings intuitions about God's standards of behavior, as well as wisdom and insight so that sin in the world is restrained. For example, even if someone does not believe the biblical teaching that God made man in his own image, nevertheless the sacredness and dignity of every human being can be known intuitively without belief in the Bible. Christians should be willing to work alongside non-Christian neighbors as co-citizens, sustained in their life together by God's common grace. Believers do not try to impose biblical standards on a society but instead appeal to common understandings of

---

"Two Kingdoms" comes from the teaching that God rules all of creation through the "common kingdom" in which all people operate by natural revelation and the "redemptive kingdom" in which Christians are ruled by special revelation.

---

the good, the true, and the beautiful shared by all people. We love and serve our neighbors in this common kingdom.

In addition to the common or earthly kingdom, there is the "redemptive kingdom" (sometimes called the "right-hand kingdom"), established with Abraham in Genesis 12. Only Christians are members of this kingdom, and they are ruled not through common grace and natural revelation but through the special revelation of God's Word. They are nurtured within the church by means of preaching and the sacraments. In this view, building up the church — evangelism, discipleship, Christian community — is the only truly redemptive "kingdom work."

This twofold framework for the nature of God's rule is the animating principle of this model. Two Kingdoms advocates believe the main problem today is the confusion of these two kingdoms, whether by the liberal church striving for relevance or by newer conservatives trying to transform culture. From this conviction flow the following features of the Two Kingdoms model for relating Christ to culture.

1. Two Kingdoms proponents, unlike those in the Counterculturalist model (or those who take the pietistic stance), place a high value on Christians

pursuing their work in "secular" vocations. We must not think we can only serve God within the church. All work is a way to serve God and our neighbor.

2. The Two Kingdoms model differs significantly from the Transformationists in their counsel on *how* Christians should do their work in the world. While Christian work in the common kingdom has dignity and usefulness, Two Kingdoms advocates tell believers they are not to look for "uniquely 'Christian' ways of doing ordinary tasks."[77] A word that is conspicuously absent from Two Kingdoms discourse on secular work is the term *worldview*. As co-citizens in the common kingdom, Christians do not have unique ideas of the common good and human flourishing that non-Christians cannot intuitively know. There is no distinctively Christian civilization. Thus, according to the Two Kingdoms model, believers are not creating *distinctively* Christian culture.[78] They should not try to change

culture so that it reflects Christian beliefs, nor should they think they are to "heal" creation. God's ruling power in the common kingdom is only to restrain evil — not to improve the culture by diminishing the effects of sin on human society. All that occurs in this realm is "temporal, provisional, and bound to pass away" — "not matters of any ultimate or spiritual importance."[79] When Christians are doing their work in the world, they are serving God and their neighbors, but they are not restoring creation or moving culture into a more Christian direction. Here Two Kingdoms thinkers join with the Counterculturalists in their criticism of Transformationism. The job of the church, they say, is not to change society but to simply be the church. There is no warrant for us to seek to create a Christian society.

3. Two Kingdoms proponents part ways not only with Transformationists but also with Counterculturalists over their view of human government and the general world of commerce. While Transformationists see the secular state as a huge problem, and Counterculturalists see it as a seat of violence and empire, the Two Kingdoms model sees a secular, neutral state as exactly what God wants, *not* a state coercively imposing religious values.[80] The Two Kingdoms view generally says the same thing about commerce and capital markets. These are not demonic (as the Counterculturalist says) or so fallen that they need to be redeemed (as the Transformationist says). They are spaces of common grace where Christians should pursue their callings with skillfulness and joy. Christians should not feel guilt and "unbiblical pressure" to establish Christian theories or practices of business or government.[81]

4. As a direct implication of everything we have said, Two Kingdoms advocates are very guarded about how much improvement, if any, Christians can expect to see in culture. They counsel us to avoid not only triumphalism but also great optimism. The Two Kingdoms model "demands limited and sober expectations ... The [common] kingdom, regulated by natural law, is severely limited in what it can attain."[82] As we have noted, God's common kingdom is predominantly a force for restraining

disorder, not for building a new order. As Van-Drunen argues, everything here on earth except for our souls and resurrection bodies is going to be destroyed. Nothing we do in the common kingdom, therefore, is of lasting importance. In the end, we should not expect too much out of this life — we should set all our hopes fully on the future hope of Christ's final salvation and return.

Is there a spectrum within this model, as we have seen to one degree or another in the others? Yes, there is. First, there is a distinction between the traditional Lutheran understanding of the Two Kingdoms and the recent version being promoted by conservative Reformed authors. Luther did not see the Two Kingdoms as the realm of the world and the church, but as the realm of the physical and the spiritual. For Luther, then, the visible, institutional church was actually part of the "temporal" kingdom in which even church government was ordered with a form of law, while the invisible church was the mystical communion of saints who live together under grace and in freedom.[83] Luther — and Lutheranism — did not believe, then, in as radical a disjunction between church and state as is set forth by contemporary Reformed Two Kingdoms advocates. Luther and Calvin called on kings and nobles to make Protestant reform the law of their lands.

There is also something of a spectrum within the Reformed Two Kingdoms camp. As we have seen, proponents of the Two Kingdoms view by and large resist the Transformationist idea that our worldview makes believers' work in the world profoundly different from that of nonbelievers. Two Kingdoms authors say that by means of common grace, not the Bible, God lets believers and nonbelievers know what they need to know to fulfill vocations in the world. Typical of this perspective is T. David Gordon, writing in *Modern Reformation*, where he strenuously argues that Christians out in the world do *not* do their work differently than nonbelievers do.[84] In his writings, Gordon insists that Christians do not labor in a "distinctively Christian" manner, nor do they seek to change the world or society.[85] David VanDrunen chimes in with this observation: "Generally speak-ing, believers are not to seek an objectively unique Christian way of pursuing cultural activities."[86]

However, Michael Horton, a prominent Two Kingdoms theologian and an editor of *Modern Reformation*, has taught that Christians *should* "pursue their vocation in a 'distinctively Christian' way."[87] This is a real difference, based perhaps on somewhat different views of the power of common grace or the purpose of Scripture, and yet with regard to Christian worldview, both thinkers are much more like each other than they are like Transformationists.[88] While Horton studiously avoids the term *worldview*, he has written that the form of Christians' work in the world *is* distinct from that of non-Christians, and that, while the institutional church should not be aiming to change the world, individual believers should be "salt" and should seek to reform society. He writes the following:

> The biblical drama, doctrines, and doxology yield a discipleship in the world that does indeed transform. It never transforms the kingdoms of this age into the kingdom of Christ (for that we await the King's bodily return); however, it does touch the lives of ordinary people every day through ordinary relationships. Not everyone is a William Wilberforce, but we can be glad that he was shaped by the faithful ministry of the Anglican Calvinist John Newton and committed his life to the extirpation of the slave trade.[89]

THE CREATION MANDATE

Two Kingdoms authors part ways with neo-Calvinists over the "creation mandate" of Genesis 1 and 2. Neo-Calvinists see God as giving Adam (and therefore all human beings) a mandate to create culture, to do work and develop the creation (see Gen 1:26 – 28; 2:15). Yet Two Kingdoms authors insist that the work God gave to Adam — to guard and cultivate the garden — has been fulfilled by Christ, and therefore "Christian" cultural endeavors should *not* be understood as getting back to Adam's original task.

In the final chapter of *Living in God's Two Kingdoms*, "Education, Vocation, and Politics," David VanDrunen first says "there are many unique things about Christians' cultural activity," but then he explains that the main way they are distinct is "subjectively," that is, in their motivation to do things wholeheartedly for the Lord (pp. 167–68). When he asks if Christian work is "objectively" distinctive — that is, distinctive in its actual form or content, not just in motivation — he answers in the negative. He then reiterates what he has stated in the rest of his book — that the normative standards for cultural activity are not *distinctively* Christian; they are common grace norms available to all.

Later, in the context of a discussion of education, VanDrunen bluntly states that "neither the church nor the family ... has competence to impart a comprehensively detailed world and life view." If the modifier "comprehensively detailed" is strong enough, it is unlikely that any neo-Calvinist would disagree with VanDrunen. No one who advocates a Transformationist perspective believes there is a New Testament version of the book of Leviticus that dictates the Christian way to eat and dress. But in the context, VanDrunen hints that when a school or family tries to teach children a worldview, they are usurping the place of the minister, who is to teach the Bible to the youth inside the church (pp. 177–78.)[90]

As we have seen, this is different in content and in spirit from what many other Two Kingdoms advocates have written. It gives more weight to the concept of worldview (without using the word), to the idea that the culture is fallen and distorted by sin, and to the hope that cultural reform is desirable and possible.

PROBLEMS WITH THE TWO KINGDOMS MODEL

Several problems have been cited with the Two Kingdoms model.[91]

1. The Two Kingdoms model gives more weight and credit to the function of common grace than the Bible does. Two Kingdoms authors insist that Christians do not need to bring their understanding of the Bible and the gospel to bear on public life in order to strengthen it, because society is and can be kept healthy through the light of natural revelation given by God to all people. While this rightly highlights what the Bible says about the existence of common grace, it does not do equal justice to the biblical teaching that human beings suppress the truth they have (Rom 1:18–32) and therefore do *not* read natural revelation rightly. When John Calvin speaks of natural revelation in his *Institutes*, he strikes the balance perfectly. He writes the following:

> Let that admirable light of truth shining in [secular writers] teach us that the mind of man, though fallen and perverted from its wholeness, is nevertheless clothed and ornamented with God's excellent gifts. If we regard the Spirit of God as the sole fountain of truth, we shall neither reject the truth itself, nor despise it wherever it shall appear, unless we wish to dishonor the Spirit of God ... Those men whom Scripture (1 Cor 2:14) calls "natural men" were, indeed, sharp and penetrating in their investigation of inferior things. Let us, accordingly, learn by their example how many gifts the Lord left to human nature even after it was despoiled of its true good.[92]

And yet, just before this passage Calvin writes that while it is true that "in man's perverted and degenerate nature some sparks still gleam ... [the light is nonetheless] choked with dense ignorance, so that it cannot come forth effectively ... [His] mind, because of its dullness ... betrays how incapable it is of seeking and finding truth."[93] Two Kingdoms advocates have often written as if natural law and common grace are enough to guide human beings — without the light of the Bible — to build a society that is peaceful and prosperous, one that fits human nature and destiny. But this seems to go beyond what the Bible teaches, namely, that human beings usually distort, suppress, and deny the natural revelation of God.

2. Much of the social good that Two Kingdoms people attribute to natural revelation is really the fruit of the introduction of Christian teaching — of special revelation, if you will — into world cultures. For example, Nicholas Wolterstorff has argued that the very idea of human rights came out of Christian teaching on the image of God. It did not develop, and perhaps could not have developed, out of other views of human nature.[94] Now, for highly complex reasons, the idea of human rights has gone global. Samuel Moyn has recently argued that human rights have filled the enormous vacuum left by the collapse of revolutionary socialism, as well as most other credible frameworks for grounding moral values and justice.[95] But we should still ask, "Where did the idea of human rights come from?" Since so many secular people support it, does this mean it is a product of natural revelation? No — it is the product of various factors. The world has been exposed to biblical teaching and has taken this insight of special revelation and given it a more universal, non-Christian meaning. But the basic ideas of inherent human dignity, the importance of forgiveness rather than vengeance, the importance of philanthropy and charity — all of these grew out of Christian civilization, for they were virtually absent in Western pagan and Eastern civilizations.[96] They now seem to have become permanent fixtures of contemporary Western life, even though the original basis for them, the Christian faith, has been largely abandoned by the culture.

Is it right, then, to strictly say that culture is ordered by natural revelation and hold that the Bible should not be brought to bear on public life? As Dan Strange observes, quoting Peter Leithart, the real condition in most Western societies is one of "middle grace"[97] — a complex interaction of concepts introduced from the Bible that get traction broadly for a host of other reasons, which we could eventually come to see as common grace.

A famous example is the abolitionist movement, led by evangelical Christians such as William Wilberforce and others. Christian leaders of the movement were inspired by views of human nature taken from the special revelation of the Bible. And yet they would have never been successful in their endeavors unless many non-Christian people had found the call to abolish slavery resonating in their hearts and consciences as well — the product of common grace. The question is whether non-Christian religions and people could have originally produced the idea that slavery per se is wrong. Historically, this idea grew out of Christian reflection on the idea of the *imago Dei*.[98] In other words, slavery could not have been abolished without common grace, but it would never have been abolished with *only* common grace.

3. The Two Kingdoms model implies or teaches that it is possible for human life to be conducted on a religiously neutral basis. This model wants the state to be secular and neutral. It denies the need for a Christian perspective on law, government, economics, and art. But it can be argued that the secular state is not only an undesirable goal. In the end, it is an impossibility. A secular state is really a myth — a disingenuous product of the Enlightenment.[99] As we observed in the chapters on contextualization, our practices are unavoidably grounded in fundamental beliefs about right and wrong, human nature and destiny, the meaning of life, what is wrong with human society, and what will fix it. All of these working assumptions are based on nonprovable faith assumptions about human nature and spiritual reality. Michael Sandel, who teaches a popular course on justice at Harvard University, states that all theories of justice are "inescapably judgmental." He goes on to observe that you cannot hold a position on financial bailouts, surrogate motherhood, same-sex marriage, affirmative action, or CEO pay without assuming some underlying beliefs about "the right way to value things." For example, when one person says women should have the right to choose an abortion while another says women shouldn't have that choice, each is valuing things differently — a valuation

In his history classes, C. John Sommerville used to demonstrate to students how thoroughly Christianized they were, even those who were atheistic or antireligious. He would list the values of shame-and-honor cultures (like those of pagan northern Europe before the advent of Christian missionaries) and include values like pride, a strict ethic of revenge, the instilling of fear, the supreme importance of one's reputation and name, and loyalty to one's tribe. Then he would list corresponding Christian values, which had been hitherto unknown to the pagans of Europe — things like humility, forgiveness, peaceableness, and service to others, along with an equal respect for the dignity of all people made in God's image.[100] Many of Sommerville's most antireligious students were surprised to learn just how deeply they had been influenced by ways of thinking and living that had grown out of biblical ideas and been passed on to them through complex social and cultural processes.

His point was that much of what is good and unique about Western civilization is actually "borrowed capital" from a Christian faith, even though the supernatural elements of the faith have been otherwise neglected of late in the public sphere.

do dentistry from a Christian worldview?" The fact that Christians and non-Christian dentists fill cavities in the same way shows that indeed we do share common intuitions about life and our common humanity in the *imago Dei*. And Two Kingdoms advocates are correct that the Bible is not a comprehensive handbook for running a business or doing plumbing. We quoted Two Kingdoms theologian T. David Gordon in a footnote earlier in this chapter: "The Bible is sufficient to guide the human-as-covenanter" — that is, as a Christian living in the covenant community — "but *not* sufficient to guide the human-as-mechanic, the human-as-physician, the human-as-businessman, the human-as-parent [or spouse] ... or the human-as-legislator."[102] Michael Horton has likewise written, "There is no difference between Christians and non-Christians with respect to their vocations ... If Christians as well as non-Christians participate in the common curse and common grace of this age in secular affairs, then there is no 'Christian politics' or 'Christian art' or 'Christian literature,' any more than there is 'Christian plumbing.' "[103]

The critics' response is that the Bible doesn't give a comprehensive handbook for *anything*, not even for being the church or living a Christian life. Gordon is right to say that the Bible does not give us all we need to know to be good parents or spouses. It leaves many details up to us — but what it does tell us is profound and powerful and makes Christian marriages different from those based on other worldviews and philosophies of life. The Bible speaks to an enormous range of cultural, political, economic, and ethical issues that have a marked impact on every area of life. Historian John Sommerville argues that Western society's most pervasive ideas — such as the teachings that forgiveness and service are more admirable than saving face and revenge — have deeply biblical roots that are very different from the shame-and-honor cultures in the pre-Christian Western Hemisphere (see sidebar on "Borrowed Capital"). Theologian Michael Allen reminds us that "Christian faith has [necessarily] cultural implications."[104] Many have argued that the very rise of modern science could

always based on moral beliefs that are not scientifically based. These implicit assumptions are acts of faith, and therefore there can ultimately be no neutral, secular state. All cultures and governments will be animated by certain of these acts of faith and not by others.[101]

Sometimes Two Kingdoms advocates will ask advocates of the Transformationist model, "What is the Christian form of auto repair? How should we

have only occurred in a society in which the biblical view of a sole, all-powerful, and personal Creator was prevalent.[105] It seems naive to claim that Christian faith does not unavoidably shape culture in deep ways.

The issue of slavery provides an interesting example of how Christianity changes culture. While Christians are usually criticized for having waited so long to abolish slavery, Miroslav Volf points out how even in the New Testament the gospel was sounding its death knell. Paul told Philemon, a Christian slave owner, to receive and treat his slave Onesimus as a "beloved brother" not only "in the Lord" but "in the flesh" (Phlm 16 ESV). New Testament scholar Douglas Moo explains that Paul used the phrase "in the flesh" to refer to "that aspect of human life that is bound by earthly oriented interests (cf. NJB, 'on the natural plane')."[106] So Moo concludes that although Onesimus will technically remain Philemon's slave for the time being, "Paul is saying in effect, 'Your relationship with Onesimus will no longer be dictated by your legal relationship (master-slave) but by your spiritual relationship (brothers).'"[107] This is to so transform the use of power within the relationship that, as Volf states, "Slavery has been abolished even if its outer institutional shell remains as an oppressive reality."[108]

As we reflect on these examples, we see that while the New Testament may not give believers direct calls to *transform society*, the gospel faith of Christians clearly had immediate and far-reaching impact on social and economic relationships, and not only strictly within the church. Indeed, then, Christian faith touches on and affects *all of life*, and to claim otherwise is to be less than fully faithful to the biblical or historical record.

4. The Two Kingdoms model produces a form of "social quietism." According to the Two Kingdoms approach, Christians should not be overconfident of our ability to improve or move the world to a greater reflection of Christian values. This approach, while it neutralizes the triumphalism of some elements of the Christian Right, can lead to the opposite error. As Kevin DeYoung states, this model shows an "unwillingness to boldly call

THE TWO KINGDOMS AND LUTHERAN THEOLOGY

Lutheran theology has historically promoted the Two Kingdoms understanding of how to relate Christ to culture. D. A. Carson quotes Robert Benne, a Lutheran theologian who is critical of aspects of his own tradition:

> Were this version of Lutheran theology taken to its logical conclusion it would deprive the gospel of any intellectual content and the [civil] law of any moral content. The biblical narrative and theological reflection on it would not be given any epistemological status to engage secular learning. It would champion a form of Lutheran quietism in the realm of education. Much as German Lutherans in the 1930s separated the two kingdoms (government under law separated from Christianity under the gospel) and allowed the Nazi movement to go unchecked by appeal to the intellectual and moral content of the Christian vision, so this approach would allow modern secular learning to go unchallenged by that vision.[109]

Christians to work for positive change in their communities and believe that change is possible."[110] Michael Allen points to the uncomfortable case of the mid-nineteenth-century Southern Presbyterian Church in the United States and its doctrine of the "spirituality of the church." In his 1859 "Address to All the Churches of Christ," J. H. Thornwell laid out a classic Two Kingdoms view, insisting that "the provinces of church and state are perfectly distinct, and the one has no right to usurp the jurisdiction of the other ... The state looks to the visible and the outward; the church is concerned for the invisible and inward ... The power of the church is exclusively spiritual."[111] He goes on to defend the refusal of the Southern church to condemn slavery. Allen argues that the "spirituality of the church" teaching continued to affect Southern churches even into the civil rights era, where "many leaders and congregations objected to denominational support of social and political goals."[112]

5. The Two Kingdoms view contributes to too great a hierarchy between clergy and laypeople. While many adherents of the Two Kingdoms model encourage Christians to excel in their vocations and see them as a way to serve God, they do not view such work as "kingdom work."[113] The Two Kingdoms churches will in the end, then, be less celebrative of Christians in secular vocations than will the Transformationists. Not only that, but often within the church itself, the Two Kingdoms emphasis on the ordained ministry of the Word and sacrament can lead to "an exaggerated distinction between laity and church officers (e.g., evangelism is the responsibility of elders and pastors not of the regular church members.)"[114]

COMING TOGETHER ON CULTURE?

In late 2011, I wrote a blog post titled *Coming Together on Culture*. I noted that despite the division over Christ and culture in the Christian church today, I perceived that a percentage of people in each camp were listening to the critiques and were incrementally (and almost secretly) making revisions that moved them closer toward the other camps and positions.

In my blog post, I summarized the Transformationist and Two Kingdoms views, arguing that while each model had some imbalances, many were recognizing them and incorporating insights from various models:

Transformationism is seen as too triumphalistic, coercive, naive about sin, and often self-righteous. It does not appreciate sufficiently God's common grace given to all people. It may not prepare Christians well to make common cause with nonbelievers for the common good, or to appreciate the goodness of all work, even the most "menial" kind. It is criticized for putting too much emphasis on the intellect — on thinking out your philosophical worldview — and not enough on the piety of the heart and the reordering of our loves. It is critiqued for putting too much hope in and emphasis on Christians taking political power ...

The Two Kingdoms approach is seen as too pessimistic about the possibility of social change. Paradoxically, many holding this position are also too naive and optimistic about the role of common grace in the world. They argue that Christians can work beside nonbelievers on the basis of common moral intuitions given to all by natural revelation ... The Two Kingdoms approach gives too little weight to the fact that every culture is filled with idols, that sin distorts everything, that there can be no final neutrality, and that we need Scripture and the gospel, not just natural revelation, to guide us in our work in the world.[115]

The post generated some resistance. Michael Goheen, a noted author from the Kuyperian movement, countered that he and coauthor Craig Bartholomew (along with others), while solidly in the Transformationist camp, had "appropriated the work of Newbigin and would espouse a more missional Kuyperianism. That is, social engagement is not first of all to change society — that may happen but ... the goal ... is to witness to the lordship of Christ over all areas of public life and to love our neighbor as we struggle against dehumanizing idolatry."[116] Meanwhile, Michael Horton, a prominent Two Kingdoms theologian, wrote a post in response to mine, similarly objecting to the depiction of the Two Kingdoms position. Although six years

---

A percentage of people in each camp is listening to the critiques and is incrementally making revisions that move them closer toward the other camps and positions.

---

ago he had written, "There is no difference between Christians and non-Christians with respect to their vocations" and "there is no 'Christian politics' or 'Christian art' or 'Christian literature,' any more than there is 'Christian plumbing,'"[117] he now wrote, "Nothing in the 2K [Two Kingdoms] view entails that 'Christians do not, then, pursue their vocation in a "distinctively Christian way"' or 'that neither the church nor individual Christians should be in the business of changing the world or society,'" and he added that Christian-led social reforms were good things.[118]

These two writers, however, despite their valid concerns about caricature, provide evidence that indeed there may be a "coming together on culture" among Christians. Mike Goheen's emphasis, still clearly within a Kuyperian model, has incorporated insights and critiques from other sources. And while many Two Kingdoms proponents indeed deny that (apart from their inner motivations) Christians do their work in a distinctive way or that they should be involved in trying to change society, Michael Horton's comments show an admirable facility to learn from the strengths and the critiques of other views. In the hope that I can contribute to this growing convergence, I turn now to some admirable examples of balance with regard to this issue, followed by an analysis of how the four models can relate more appreciatively to the insights of the others.

QUESTIONS FOR DISCUSSION AND REFLECTION

1. This chapter summarizes four models of cultural response:

   - Transformationist model
   - Relevance model
   - Counterculturalist model
   - Two Kingdoms model

   Which of the four models most closely represents your own? Which models were you unfamiliar with? Which critiques did you particularly resonate with, and which (if any) did you find yourself objecting to?

2. Keller writes, "The fact that models often fail as descriptors is instructive in itself." Models are often inadequate, particularly when we are looking at the sharpest and clearest version of a position. Yet their very inadequacy can help us by revealing the limitations of a particular view and encouraging us to avoid extremes. With this in mind, how would you summarize the greatest strength of each model? What do you believe is the biggest problem or weakness with each model?

3. Take some time to identify the various streams of theology that have shaped your thinking about the gospel and culture, noting the authors, mentors, traditions, articles, conferences, personal experiences, and biases that have influenced you. Has a particular stream of thought dominated your thinking about the church and culture, or have you been influenced by multiple streams? Which ones? Who were the key voices that shaped your practice into what it is today?

CHAPTER 16 — THE CULTURAL RESPONSES OF THE CHURCH {pages 194–217}

1. I know many of my readers are not ministering in the United States. However, because of its reach, the U.S. church's struggles have ripple effects everywhere. Those ministering in other countries may uncritically adopt materials forged in the United States because they don't know the background debates and perspectives the material represents. So I hope this description helps readers understand not only the U.S. situation but their own as well. For example, while there is no exact analogy to the Religious Right in the UK, other forms of the "Transformationist" category are present. I expect, therefore, that most of this chapter will be of some help to those who minister in cities around the world.

2. H. Richard Niebuhr, *Christ and Culture* (New York: Harper, 1956). This summary is based on that of George Hunsinger as outlined in R. Michael Allen, *Reformed Theology* (Edinburgh: T&T Clark, 2010), 168.

3. Niebuhr, *Christ and Culture*, 44.

4. Ibid.

5. Indeed, I'll go so far as to say that whenever a thinker (such as Newbigin) doesn't fit well into one model, it is a sign of strength.

6. See Timothy Keller, "Niebuhr's Christ and Culture," www.calvin.edu/academic/rit/webBook/chapter7/niebuhrTech.htm (accessed January 31, 2012).

7. See Craig A. Carter, *Rethinking Christ and Culture: A Post-Christendom Perspective* (Grand Rapids: Baker, 2007).

8. See D. A. Carson, *Christ and Culture Revisited* (Grand Rapids: Eerdmans, 2008).

9. Nicholas Wolterstorff, "In Reply," *Perspectives: A Journal of Reformed Thought* (February 2008), www.rca.org/page.aspx?pid=3772 (accessed January 31, 2012).

10. Steve Mathonnet-VanderWell, "Reformed Intramurals: What Neo-Calvinists Get Wrong," in *Perspectives* (February 2008), www.rca.org/page.aspx?pid=3771 (accessed January 31, 2012). *Perspectives* was previously titled *The Reformed Journal*, and in the 1970s and 1980s it was the main forum for Kuyperian neo-Calvinist writers such as Nicholas Wolterstorff, Alvin Plantinga, Richard Mouw, George Marsden, and others. See Barry Hankins, *Francis Schaeffer and the Shaping of Evangelical America* (Grand Rapids: Eerdmans, 2008), which shows the links between Kuyper, Schaeffer, and Colson (pp. 121, 139) and Schaeffer's role in the early formation of the Christian Right (pp. 192 – 227).

11. See Jeff Sharlet, *The Family: The Secret Fundamentalism at the Heart of American Power* (New York: HarperCollins, 2008), 342 – 50, 429; see also Hankins, *Francis Schaeffer*, 192 – 227, for the connections between the thought of Rousas Rushdoony, John Whitehead, and Francis Schaeffer as it helped influence the beginnings of the Christian Right.

12. See Rousas John Rushdoony, *The Institutes of Biblical Law* (Phillipsburg, N.J.: Presbyterian & Reformed, 1990); Gary North and Gary DeMar, *Christian Reconstructionism: What It Is, What It Isn't* (Tyler, Tex.: Institute for Christian Economics, 1991). Reconstructionists have not called for a Christian minority to take power and impose biblical moral law on the majority but instead believe that Christianity will grow among the population in the future until there is a Christian consensus, and then biblical law — including execution for idolatry, adultery, homosexuality, etc. — will be put into effect.

13. Rushdoony, *Institutes of Biblical Law*, 100, 214, 747.

14. See David Field, "Samuel Rutherford and the Confessionally Christian State," http://davidpfield.com/other/RutherfordCCS.pdf (accessed January 31, 2012).

15. For a conservative Transformationist critique of the neo-Calvinist idea of "principled pluralism," see Field, "Samuel Rutherford and the Confessionally Christian State," 27 – 32.

16. This is, of course, a generalized statement. There are those within the Christian Right who use an educational strategy. Chuck Colson employs a predominantly educational strategy — worldview education — for cultural transformation, though clear political overtones often come through in his training and publications. And, by the same token, I understand there have been political movements, particularly within Canada, associated with neo-Calvinism.

17. Wolterstorff, "In Reply."

18. See Albert M. Wolters, *Creation Regained: Biblical Basics for a Reformational Worldview*, 2nd ed. (Grand Rapids: Eerdmans, 2005), 27 – 39.

19. Herman Bavinck, "Common Grace," trans. R. C. Van Leeuwen, *Calvin Theological Journal* 24 (1989): 59 – 60, 61.

20. Geerhardus Vos, *The Teaching of Jesus Concerning the Kingdom of God and the Church* (Eugene, Ore.: Wipf & Stock, 1998), 163. As soon as he says this, however, Vos goes on to make it clear that this does not mean the institutional church should have political power or control society through the state. Rather, the kingdom of God manifests itself in society outside the church as regenerate individual Christians do their work and live their lives to God's glory. Here he honors the important "sphere sovereignty" teaching of Kuyper. Vos defines the kingdom in this way: "The kingdom means the renewal of the world through the introduction of supernatural forces" (p. 192). By this he means it is not just a subjective experience of God in the heart, but the power of God that has come into the world through a great series of "objective … facts and transactions" purposed to eventually overcome all sin, evil, suffering, and death in the world.

21. While many who hold to the Two Kingdoms model encourage Christians to excel in their vocations and see this as serving God in general, most strongly disagree that such work is *kingdom* work or that it furthers Christ's saving purposes. So, ultimately, I believe "Two Kingdoms" will in practice be less celebrative of Christians in secular vocations than will the Transformationists.

22. For a good, brief overview of the importance of institutions, see Hugh Heclo, *On Thinking Institutionally* (Boulder, Colo.: Paradigm, 2008).

23. For a book that provides something of this kind of self-examination and correction for the Christian Right, see Michael Gerson and Peter Wehner, *City of Man: Religion and Politics in a New Era* (Chicago: Moody, 2010). Gerson and Wehner are political conservatives who are critical of the Religious Right, warning of the danger of identifying the City of God with any particular political agenda. The book calls Christian readers to a much more measured and chastened — but still moderately conservative — political engagement.

24. James K. A. Smith, *Desiring the Kingdom: Worship, Worldview, and Cultural Formation* (Grand Rapids: Baker, 2009). Smith, citing Canadian philosopher Charles Taylor, proposes that the term "social imaginaries" would be a better term than "worldviews."

25. Mathonnet-VanderWell, "Reformed Intramurals." This article lists a series of criticisms of Transformationism from within the neo-Calvinist movement.

26. I do not have room here to review Smith's important book. In brief, I believe his thesis is largely correct, especially in his dependence on Augustine, who argues that worldviews are the product of "the order of our loves," not merely our doctrine. However, I think the book tends to buy too deeply into Aristotle over Plato. Plato taught that right action follows from right thinking — "as we think so we are," while Aristotle taught that right thinking follows from right action and behavior — "we become what we do." I think Christians should be careful not to lift up either thinking or behavior as the key. An overly Platonic view will indeed see teaching and preaching as the main way we change lives, while an overly Aristotelian view will tend to see liturgy and the sacraments as the main way. But the key is the heart. The heart's commitments are changed through repentance — which involves both thinking and behavior. As Thomas Cranmer taught us to pray, "Grant ... that our hearts, and all our members, being mortified from all worldly and carnal lusts, may in all things obey thy blessed will; through the same thy son Jesus Christ our Lord" (C. Frederick Barbee and Paul F. M. Zahl, *The Collects of Thomas Cranmer* [Grand Rapids: Eerdmans, 1999], 12).

27. Mathonnet-VanderWell, "Reformed Intramurals."

28. "The Christian way to eat your peas," as one anti-Transformationist wag once put it to me.

29. Quoted in Mathonnet-VanderWell, "Reformed Intramurals."

30. Wolters, *Creation Regained*, 28 – 29.

31. Robert D. Putnam and David E. Campbell, *American Grace: How Religion Divides and Unites Us* (New York: Simon and Schuster, 2010), 128.

32. See James D. Hunter, *To Change the World: The Irony, Tragedy, and Possibility of Christianity in the Late Modern World* (New York: Oxford University Press, 2010), 3 – 98.

33. Ibid.

34. As we will see, while many Counterculturalists are too afraid of exercising power in society, many Transformationists are not afraid enough.

35. Hunter, *To Change the World*, 35.

36. See D. A. Carson, *Christ and Culture Revisited* (Grand Rapids: Eerdmans, 2008), 145 – 204. For a defense of Christendom, see Peter Leithart, *Defending Constantine: The Twilight of an Empire and the Dawn of Christendom* (Downers Grove, Ill.: InterVarsity, 2010). For a strong critique of Christendom — and how wielding political power corrupts the church — see the works of John Howard Yoder.

37. Miroslav Volf, *A Public Faith: How Followers of Christ Should Serve the Common Good* (Grand Rapids: Baker, 2011), 79.

38. Ibid., 17 – 21, 37 – 54.

39. See Mathonnet-VanderWell, "Reformed Intramurals."

40. Here I remain close to the terminology of James Hunter, who names this approach "Relevant To."

41. H. Richard Niebuhr, *Christ and Culture* (New York: Harper, 1956), 80.

42. Ibid., 106.

43. See ibid., 84, 90.

44. See the movement's most seminal book, written by the Peruvian priest Gustavo Gutierrez (*A Theology of Liberation: History, Politics and Salvation* [Maryknoll, N.Y.: Orbis, 1971]).

45. Harvie Conn, "The Mission of the Church," in *Evangelicals and Liberation*, ed. Carl Amerding (Phillipsburg, N.J.: Presbyterian & Reformed, 1977), 81. Conn brilliantly points out that liberation theology is indeed too "worldly" — too willing to "baptize" historical/cultural trends as the redemptive work of God. But, he argues, conservative evangelicals who accept an unjust social status quo (and enjoy its benefits) instead of fighting against it are ironically doing just what the liberationists are doing, though in reverse. They are baptizing the historical/cultural order as God's work. Conn writes (p. 82), "In spite of the apparent differences between the revolutionary and the conservative, there is basically one essential

agreement — both identify the purpose of God with the present historical situation. In one there is conformity to the status quo; in the other a conformity with the revolution."

46. This is the way George Hunsinger summarizes this model. Hunsinger's useful summary of Niebuhr's models is found in R. Michael Allen, *Reformed Theology* (Edinburgh: T&T Clark, 2010), 168. Hunsinger adds that Niebuhr found the "Christ above culture" model "at one and the same time too credulous about culture and too conciliatory about Christ, lacking an adequate sense of divine judgment."

47. Niebuhr, *Christ and Culture*, 130; see D. A. Carson's treatment of the "Christ above culture" pattern in *Christ and Culture Revisited*, 20 – 22.

48. While the Two Kingdoms also has a positive view of God's activity in the world, it makes a very sharp distinction between what God does in the world and in the church; it would never say that God's work in the world, apart from the church and the preaching of the Word, is redemptive or something the church must adapt to and join with.

49. Robert Schuller, *Your Church Has Real Possibilities* (Glendale, Calif.: Regal, 1975).

50. Robert Schuller, *Self-Esteem: The New Reformation* (Waco, Tex.: Word, 1982), 14.

51. Bill Hybels and Rick Warren are friends of mine, and I can vouch for the fact that, despite a deluge of withering criticism of their churches from across the spectrum, they have not simply recoiled or responded harshly. They have listened to their critics, even the severest, with humility and appreciation and have continually made adjustments to their ministries. For example, see the self-critique by Bill Hybels and Greg Hawkins, *Reveal: Where Are You?* (South Barrington, Ill.: Willow Creek Association, 2007).

52. Gary Pritchard's PhD dissertation provided one of the first major critiques of the seeker church movement. A popular version of his Northwestern University doctoral thesis was published later as *Willow Creek Seeker Services: Evaluating a New Way of Doing Church* (Grand Rapids: Baker, 1996).

53. As we will see below, many emerging churches fit better into the Counterculturalist model than they do into this one.

54. Ultimately, this is the same path that seeker churches and liberal churches follow; they are simply adapting to a different dominant culture.

55. Darrell L. Guder, ed., *Missional Church: A Vision for the Sending of the Church in North America* (Grand Rapids: Eerdmans, 1998).

56. See ibid.

57. See J. C. Hoekendijk, *The Church Inside Out* (Philadelphia: Westminster, 1967), 19 – 20. See *The Church for Others and the Church for the World: A Quest for Structures for Missionary Congregations* (Geneva: World Council of Churches, 1967). For a good discussion of the recent history of the *missio Dei* concept and of how it grew out of new theological understandings of the Trinity and the kingdom of God, see Craig Van Gelder and Dwight J. Zscheile, *The Missional Church in Perspective: Mapping Trends and Shaping the Conversation* (Grand Rapids: Baker, 2011), 17 – 40. We address the missional church in detail in part 6.

58. This effect was predicted by J. Gresham Machen in *Christianity and Liberalism* (Grand Rapids: Eerdmans, 1923).

59. See Kent Carlson and Mike Luekin, *Renovation of the Church: What Happens When a Seeker Church Discovers Spiritual Formation* (Downers Grove, Ill.: InterVarsity, 2011).

60. Van Gelder and Zscheile, *Missional Church in Perspective*, 70.

61. As we will see, the Two Kingdoms model also teaches that Christians should not try to transform culture along Christian lines, but it is much more sanguine about society as a whole and about the goodness of Christian participation in secular callings.

62. Stanley Hauerwas and William Willimon, *Resident Aliens: Life in the Christian Colony* (Nashville: Abingdon, 1989), 47.

63. James Hunter calls adherents of this model "Neo-Anabaptists" and gives a particularly insightful critique in *To Change the World: The Irony, Tragedy, and Possibility of Christianity in the Late Modern World* (New York: Oxford University Press, 2010), 150 – 66.

64. John Howard Yoder, *The Politics of Jesus* (Grand Rapids: Eerdmans, 1972).

65. Radical Orthodoxy at first glance may seem to have little to do with Anabaptists, since it is a contemporary movement of largely High Church Anglicans. Yet it levels a similar critique at modern secular thought and culture as that offered by Hauerwas (see James K. A. Smith, *Radical Orthodoxy: Mapping a Post-Secular Theology* [Grand Rapids: Baker, 2004]).

66. See Shane Claiborne, *Jesus for President: Politics for Ordinary Radicals* (Grand Rapids: Zondervan, 2008). Claiborne is known for his "litany of resistance": "With governments that kill ... we will not comply. With the theology of empire ... we will not comply. With the hoarding of riches ... we will not comply. To the peace that is not like Rome's ... we pledge allegiance" (quoted in Ron Cole, "The Subversive Alternative Language of the Kingdom ..." [October 11, 2007], http://thewearypilgrim.typepad.com/the_weary_pilgrim/2007/10/the-subversive-.html [accessed February 1, 2012]).

67. For more on the new monasticism, see Jonathan Wilson, *Living Faithfully in a Fragmented World: Lessons for the Church from MacIntyre's After Virtue* (Harrisburg, Pa.: Trinity Press, 1998); Shane Claiborne, *The Irresistible Revolution: Living as an Ordinary Radical* (Grand Rapids: Zondervan, 2006); Jonathan Wilson-

Hartgrove, *New Monasticism: What It Has to Say to Today's Church* (Grand Rapids: Brazos, 2008).

68. It is worth observing that Wilberforce, who himself could be put in the "Christ transforming culture" model, was nonetheless helped immensely by Quakers and other Protestants from an Anabaptist tradition on how to relate to culture.

69. Carson, *Christ and Culture Revisited*, 218.

70. See Stephen B. Bevans, *Models of Contextual Theology*, rev. ed. (Maryknoll, N.Y.: Orbis, 2004), 32, 119.

71. Ibid., 119, 175 n.8.

72. Hunter, *To Change the World*, 164.

73. Van Gelder and Zscheile, *Missional Church in Perspective*, 142.

74. David VanDrunen (*Living in God's Two Kingdoms: A Biblical Vision for Christianity and Culture* [Wheaton, Ill.: Crossway, 2010] provides an accessible exposition of the Two Kingdoms model from the perspective of Reformed covenant theology. For summaries of the positions and arguments on both sides of this controversy within the conservative Reformed world (particularly in the U.S.), see the article by British scholar Dan Strange, "Not Ashamed! The Sufficiency of Scripture for Public Theology," *Themelios* 36.2 (July 2011): 238 – 60, http://tgc-documents.s3.amazonaws.com/journal-issues/36.2/Themelios_36.2.pdf (accessed January 30, 2012).

75. See VanDrunen, *Living in God's Two Kingdoms*, 75 – 76.

76. Martin Luther, "Commentary on Psalm 147," in *Luther's Works: Selected Psalms III*, vol. 14, ed. Jaroslav Pelikan (St. Louis, Mo.: Concordia, 1958), 114 – 15.

77. VanDrunen, *Living in God's Two Kingdoms*, 27.

78. Ibid., 62.

79. Quoting VanDrunen, *Living in God's Two Kingdoms*, 26, and Strange, "Not Ashamed!" 244, respectively.

80. See Strange, "Not Ashamed!" 245. "[For the Two Kingdoms view] the secular state is … one of the triumphs of the West."

81. VanDrunen, *Living in God's Two Kingdoms*, 27.

82. David VanDrunen, *A Biblical Case for Natural Law* (Grand Rapids: Acton Institute, 2006), 40.

83. See William Wright, *Martin Luther's Understanding of God's Two Kingdoms* (Grand Rapids: Baker, 2010).

84. T. David Gordon, "The Insufficiency of Scripture," *Modern Reformation* 11 (January – February 2002): 19. Gordon writes, "The Bible is sufficient to guide the human-as-covenanter, but not sufficient to guide the human-as-mechanic, the human-as-physician, the human-as-businessman, the human-as-parent, the human-as-husband, the human-as-wife, or the human-as-legislator." See also his response brought about by criticism of his original article ("Response from T. David Gordon," *Modern Reformation* 11 [May – June 2002]: 46).

85. See Gordon, "Insufficiency of Scripture," 11. I am also basing this statement on hundreds of comments and posts on Two Kingdoms websites.

86. VanDrunen, *Living in God's Two Kingdoms*, 168.

87. See Michael Horton, "Christ and Culture Once More," White Horse Inn Blog (December 17, 2011), www.whitehorseinn.org/blog/2011/12/17/christ-and-culture-once-more/ (accessed February 2, 2012).

88. Here is another example of differences within a model or category. Many proponents of the Two Kingdoms approach teach that this material world will burn up completely, and so nothing we do here — other than the spiritual work of evangelism and building up the church — will transfer over into the new heaven and new earth. However, Michael Horton (*The Christian Faith: A Systematic Theology for Pilgrims on the Way* [Grand Rapids: Zondervan, 2011], 348, 989 – 90) seems to follow Herman Bavinck and others in saying that this material world will not be completely annihilated and replaced by a new one, but rather the present one will be "transitioned" and renewed, along with our bodies. David Van-Drunen (*Living in God's Two Kingdoms*, 65 – 66) takes the position that our bodies will be resurrected and renewed, but nothing else in creation will be renewed — it will all be burned up and replaced.

89. Horton, "Christ and Culture Once More," White Horse Inn Blog (December 17, 2011). Horton's blog post was written in response to my post on Christ and culture in which I had summarized the Two Kingdoms position. Horton states (quoting my post), "Nothing in the 2K [Two Kingdoms] view entails that 'Christians do not, then, pursue their vocation in a distinctively Christian way' or 'that neither the church nor individual Christians should be in the business of changing the world or society.'" As I've shown, many Two Kingdoms proponents — including VanDrunen — say the opposite. Horton also writes that, while the church as an institution should not be trying to reform society, Christian individuals should be (as "salt") and can be part of major movements such as the abolition of slavery.

90. VanDrunen, *Living in God's Two Kingdoms*, 167 – 68, 177 – 78.

91. A good place to start for a Two Kingdoms critique is Daniel Strange, "Not Ashamed!" 238 – 60. While Strange focuses on recent exchanges within the Reformed world, the broad outlines of his summaries and criticisms hold for the broader conversation between models as well. For a general critique of the Two Kingdoms model, both Lutheran and Reformed, see Carson, *Christ and Culture Revisited*, 210 – 18.

92. John Calvin, *Institutes of the Christian Religion*, ed. John T. McNeill (Philadelphia: Westminster, 1960), 1:273 – 75.

93. Ibid., 1:270 – 71.

94. See Nicholas Wolterstorff, *Justice: Rights and Wrongs* (Princeton, N.J.: Princeton University Press, 2008), 44 – 64; see also Brian Tierney, *The Idea of Natural Rights: Studies on Natural Rights, Natural Law, and Church Law 1150 to 1625* (Grand Rapids: Eerdmans, 1997). In chapter 1, Wolterstorff points out that before the Christian idea of *imago Dei*, no society thought of every single human being as equal in dignity and worth. Human beings were judged by various "capacities," and any group that lacked, say, rationality or some other virtue was considered worthy of being slaves. Even Aristotle said some people were born to be slaves.

95. See Samuel Moyn, *The Last Utopia: Human Rights in History* (Cambridge, Mass.: Harvard University Press, 2010).

96. See David Bentley Hart, *Atheist Delusions: The Christian Revolution and Its Fashionable Enemies* (New Haven, Conn.: Yale University Press, 2009). Hart makes a case for these and many other "givens" of modern life coming from biblical understandings of things.

97. Quoted in Strange, "Not Ashamed!" 255 – 56.

98. See Rodney Stark, *For the Glory of God: How Monotheism Led to Reformations, Science, Witch-Hunts, and the End of Slavery* (Princeton, N.J.: Princeton University Press, 2004), 291 – 366.

99. See Strange, "Not Ashamed!" 248.

100. See C. John Sommerville, The Decline of the Secular University (New York: Oxford University Press, 2007), 69 – 70.

101. Michael Sandel, *Justice: What's the Right Thing to Do?* (New York: Farrar, Straus, and Giroux, 2009), 261.

102. Gordon, "Insufficiency of Scripture," 19.

103. Michael S. Horton, "How the Kingdom Comes," *Christianity Today* 50.1 (January 2006): 42, www.christianvisionproject.com/2006/01/how_the_kingdom_comes.html (accessed February 2, 2012).

104. Allen, *Reformed Theology*, 174. For example, justification by faith alone undergirds ethnic harmony within the people of God (see Gal 2 – 3). Similarly, the doctrine of Christ's resurrection threatens to undo various economic and political practices that developed around idol worship in Asia Minor (Acts 17; 19).

105. See Stark, *To the Glory of God*; Diogenes Allen, *Christian Belief in a Postmodern World: The Full Wealth of Conviction* (Philadelphia: Westminster, 1989).

106. Douglas Moo, *The Letters to the Colossians and to Philemon* (Pillar New Testament Commentary; Grand Rapids: Eerdmans, 2008), 422.

107. Ibid.

108. Volf, *A Public Faith*, 92.

109. Quoted in Carson, *Christ and Culture Revisited*, 212.

110. Kevin DeYoung, "Two Kingdom Theology and Neo-Kuyperians," http://thegospelcoalition.org/blogs/kevindeyoung/2009/08/14/two-kingdom-theology-and-neo-kuyperians/ (accessed February 6, 2012).

111. Quoted in Allen, *Reformed Theology*, 170 – 71.

112. Ibid., 172.

113. See p. 229 for Geerhardus Vos's argument that this is not the case, that laypeople doing work that honors Christ in the world is a sign of God's redemptive kingdom. David VanDrunen (*Living in God's Two Kingdoms*, 190) comments, "The gospel ministry is not just one profession among many. The Lord Jesus and his apostles never lamented the lack of good engineers or gave instructions for training electricians, but Christ did say, 'The harvest is plentiful, but the laborers are few.'" VanDrunen goes on to make clear he believes that when Jesus speaks of "laborers," he is referring to ordained ministers.

114. DeYoung, "Two Kingdom Theology and Neo-Kuyperians."

115. Tim Keller, "Coming Together on Culture, Part 1: Theological Issues," http://redeemercitytocity.com/blog/view.jsp?Blog_param=400 (accessed February 6, 2012).

116. Ibid. See Mike Goheen's comment on the blog.

117. Horton, "How the Kingdom Comes."

118. Horton, "Christ and Culture Once More."

WHY ALL THE MODELS ARE RIGHT … AND WRONG

Earlier, we acknowledged the fact that dividing people into broad categories, or models, always has pitfalls. Some people conform well to the type, while others do not. Within a given model, we can find areas of pointed disagreement. And as we've seen in the case of the Christ and culture issue, people change; thoughtful proponents of certain models are always open to having their views tempered and enriched by insights from the others. We see also a growing body of work that appreciates and criticizes the various Christ and culture models and calls for a nuanced and balanced approach. I have cited several of these already — by Miroslav Volf, D. A. Carson, James Hunter, and Dan Strange.[1] Perhaps the best reason for hope in a balanced Christ and culture model is the example of individuals whose thought and practice defy being contained within a single model.

Lesslie Newbigin, for instance, is often cited by Transformationists, Counterculturalists, and Relevants, even though they may not share all his doctrinal views. Counterculturalists respond to his stress on the church community itself as "the hermeneutic of the gospel,"[2] while Transformationists appreciate his emphasis on training Christians to integrate their faith with their work and influence culture.[3] For nearly everyone thinking about culture, Newbigin's analysis of the post-Christian character of the West is seminal. Most startling of all, Newbigin argues for the possibility of a government that is overtly based on Christian values. He contends that the logic of the cross should lead such a government to be noncoercive toward minorities, committed to the common good of all, and therefore could still allow a pluralistic society to flourish. It is an explicitly Christian political vision that does not sound quite like Christian Reconstructionism, with its claim that democracy is a "heresy," or like the principled pluralism of neo-Calvinism.[4]

Another hard-to-classify thinker is Jim Wallis, the author of *God's Politics.*[5] Wallis is a strong supporter of leaders of the new monasticism (part of what we are calling the Counterculturalist model). He wrote the foreword to Shane Claiborne's manifesto, *The Irresistible Revolution*, and yet he also calls Christians to invest in electoral politics, causing James K. A. Smith to ask whether Wallis promotes a "Constantinianism of the left."[6] He writes that Wallis focuses on " 'people of faith' getting out the vote, lobbying congress, and doing everything they can to marshal the political process to effect prophetic justice." Wallis might be classified, then, as someone in the Relevance model, like mainline Protestants, or perhaps as a Counterculturalist. It is hard to say.

Yet another prominent example of a theologian who inspires reflection across the categories is N. T. Wright. Counterculturalists appreciate his reworking of the doctrine of justification so that salvation is not so much a matter of individual conversion as it is becoming part of a new community.[7] But Wright is not a Counterculturalist. He calls Christians to engage directly with the culture, suggesting that "through the hard work of prayer, persuasion, and political action, it is possible to make governments … see that there is a different approach than unremitting violence." This he calls "restorative justice" and cites the example of Desmond Tutu in South Africa. He goes on to speak of calling governing authorities to keep in check those who through greed and force would otherwise exploit the poor and weak.[8] In this he sounds somewhat like the liberal political side of the Relevance model.

Wright sometimes sounds like a neo-Calvinist when he calls Christians to "advance the healing of the world" with "art, music, literature, dance, the-ater, and many other expressions of human delight and wisdom," and urges artists to "join forces with those who work for justice."[9] He concludes *Simply Christian* this way:

> We are called to be part of God's new creation, called to be agents of that new creation here and now. We are called to model and display that new creation in symphonies and family life, in restorative justice and poetry, in holiness and service to the poor, in politics and painting.[10]

FINDING A WAY FORWARD

As we consider the various models and see think-ers who have learned from models other than their own, and as we witness those who have seemed to transcend or incorporate several models, how do we situate ourselves in the debate? How do we make choices about the proper way for Christians to relate to culture?

As we have seen, each of the four models has biblical support, and each effectively responds to a key problem the church faces in relating to culture. For example, is the lack of vibrant, courageous, effective evangelism a major problem that needs to be addressed? Certainly. But what about the failure of Christians to live out their worldview in the institutions of culture? Isn't it a major problem that Christians are vastly underrepresented in many sectors of the cultural economy? Absolutely. In the visual arts, literature and poetry, theater and dance, academic and legal philosophy, academic think tanks, major research universities, leading opin-ion magazines and journals, high-end journalism, most major foundations, public television, film, and high-end advertising agencies — there are few or no recognizably Christian voices.

And have we seen the church faithfully standing up for justice on behalf of those in need? Large seg-ments of the Bible-believing church in the United States once supported the institution of slav-ery — supported by (flawed) biblical exegesis. This mistaken accommodation to cultural values led to an enormous loss of credibility for the church.[11] And this wasn't just a onetime event either. In the twentieth century, large segments of the church also supported segregation.

Yet we could also argue that the greatest problem for the church today is our inability to connect with nonbelievers in a way that they understand. Isn't it a major issue that the evangelical church exists as a subcultural cul-de-sac, unable to speak the gospel intelligibly to most Americans, and is perceived to be concerned only with increasing its own power rather than with the common good? Of course it is. Early Christian bishops in the Roman Empire, by contrast, were so well-known for identifying with the poor and weak that eventually, though part of a minority religion, they were seen to have the right to speak for the local community as a whole. Caring for the poor and the weak became, ironically, a major reason for the cultural influence the church eventu-ally came to wield. If the church does not identify with the marginalized, it will itself be marginalized. This is God's poetic justice.

But perhaps the heart of the problem is our com-munal "thinness," the lack of distinctiveness in our own Christian communities. Isn't the church's real challenge today not only the views we hold but also our failure to practice a distinctly different way of life? Some evangelical Christians may refrain from drinking alcohol, but they are still as individualistic and consumeristic, as materialistic and obsessed with power pursuits, as everyone else. This is an enormous problem for our witness in the world.

Perhaps the problem, then, is in the ways we have repeatedly attempted to wield political clout and forcefully bring back a Christian-dominated soci-ety. Have our goals been misplaced? Have we been compromised by our focus on securing power and control through political means? Many, including sociologists Robert Putnam and David Campbell, have argued convincingly that this focus — this idol — is a real problem for the church today.

In short, the answer to all of these questions is *yes*. When we look at each of these models from some distance, it is clear that they all identify a real problem with the church and its witness in the culture. So it is not hard to see why each model has committed adherents. Each one is on to something — an essential truth about the relationship of the gospel to culture — that is extremely important. And yet none of them, taken alone, give us the full picture. None of them have been able to win the field. The core diagnoses of each model are correct and essential, yet incomplete. As a result, the core prescriptions are admirable and necessary, yet unbalanced. Is there a way forward?

TWO QUESTIONS ABOUT CULTURE

I believe most of these concerns can be reduced to two fundamental questions. The first question deals with our attitude toward cultural change: *Should we be pessimistic or optimistic about the possibility for cultural change?* The second question exposes our understanding of the nature of culture itself and speaks to its potential for redemption: *Is the current culture redeemable and good, or fundamentally fallen?* Our answers to these questions reveal our alignments with biblical emphases as well as our imbalances.

CULTURAL CHANGE: PESSIMISTIC OR OPTIMISTIC?

James Hunter argues that culture changes mainly (though not exclusively) from the top down rather than from the grassroots up.[12] Cultural changes tend to flow out of urban and academic centers. But these changes are typically not initiated by the innermost elites with the highest positions of prestige, for they have a vested interest in the status quo. Nor are they started by grassroots people at the periphery of cultural power, for they are often powerless to effect lasting change, being altogether shut out of institutions and cultural sectors that shape social life and thought. Instead, it is the "outer elites" — usually young men and women who are either low on the ladder of the highest-prestige institutions, or in the less influential or newer institutions — who initiate these changes.[13] In addition, the culture changes more readily when networks of common cause overlap different cultural fields, when the networks that initiate a change include people from the worlds of business, the academy, the arts, the church, and multiple other disciplines, all working together. Still, this is never a simplistic process or formula for effecting change. Because culture is a product of history, not merely of ideas, it has a kind of erratic inertia. It doesn't change easily or without a fight.[14] But it can, in the end, be changed.

This complex and rich understanding of cultural change throws a new light on each model. Each model has a tendency, especially among some of its more strident proponents, to be either *too optimistic* or *too pessimistic* about culture change. And within the groups that tend toward optimism, they tend to be too limited in their understanding of how culture can be changed. Some see the importance of arguing

---

Each model contains an essential truth about the relationship of the gospel to culture. And yet none of them, taken alone, give us the full picture.

---

for truth claims, while others put more emphasis on the importance of communities and of historical processes — but any one of these can be the crucial factor in a culture shift. All of them can play a part, and none of the current models give equal or adequate weight to them all.

CULTURE: REDEEMABLE, OR FUNDAMENTALLY FALLEN?

D. A. Carson helps address the second question about the nature of culture when he points out how each of the models for cultural engagement fails to do justice to the fullness of the biblical story line or "metanarrative" — the great turning points and stages in the history of God's redemption: (1) creation, (2) the fall into sin, (3) redemption first through Israel and the law, then through Christ and the new covenant, and finally (4) heaven, hell, and the restoration of all things.[15] The Two Kingdoms model puts emphasis on the goodness of the material *creation*, the strength of the image of God in all human beings, and God's common grace to all people. Transformationists put greater emphasis on the pervasive effects of the *fall* into sin on all of life, on the antithesis between belief and unbelief, and on the idols at the heart of every culture. Counterculturalists stress the form of God's *redemption* throughout history, namely, by calling out and creating a new people, a new humanity, that exhibits to the world what life under Christ can and should look like. Finally, many of those in the Relevance category put great weight on God's *restoration* of

---

Each model tends to overlook the implications of the points on the biblical story line other than the one around which it finds its center of gravity.

---

this creation, on the healing of the nations, and on the resurrection from the dead.

All of these points on the biblical story line are covered well by the sum of the four models, and the implications of each point of the story line for relating Christ to culture are being faithfully thought out and applied. The problem, however, is that each model tends to overlook the implications of the points on the story line other than the one around which it finds its center of gravity. Two Kingdoms people are criticized for being naive about how people truly need the Scripture and the gospel, not just general revelation, to guide their work in the world. Transformationists are charged with being combative and triumphalistic, unable to appreciate the work and contributions of nonbelievers. Counterculturalists are said by critics to make such a sharp distinction between the world and the church that they end up missing some of the implications of both creation and fall — they underestimate the levels of sinfulness inside the church and of common grace at work in the world. The reality of sin that remains in believers means that the church is never nearly as good and distinctive as its right beliefs should make it; common grace in nonbelievers means that the world is never as bad as its wrong beliefs should make it. Finally, those in the Relevance category are often criticized for forgetting that the kingdom of God in the world is *both* "already" *and* "not yet." God is going to restore the creation, but he has not done it yet. To overlook the intransigence and darkness of human culture is to fail to take seriously enough the doctrine of the fall. To put more emphasis on serving the common good than on evangelizing the lost is to forget the "particularity" of redemption, of God's calling a people to himself. "In short," Carson concludes, "it appears that some, and perhaps all, of [these models] need to be trimmed in some way by reflection on the broader realities of biblical-theological developments."[16]

BIBLICAL-THEOLOGICAL RESOURCES

To move forward, we must seek theological balance, and by this I do not mean some midpoint between liberal and orthodox theology. Rather, D. A. Carson speaks of allowing the various points of biblical theology to "control our thinking *simultaneously and all the time*."[17] To flesh this out, we'll briefly survey the basic theological ideas that have special relevance for Christian cultural engagement and give initial direction about the specific balance we need to maintain in each area.[18]

CREATION

The doctrine of creation tells us, first of all, that the material world is important. Unlike other ancient creation accounts, the earth is not the result of a power struggle between deities, but is a work of art and love by one Creator. A major part of God's work is his delight in continuing to sustain and cultivate creation (Pss 65:9 – 13; 145:21; 147:15 – 20). If God himself does both of these things — if he both cultivates and sustains the material creation *and* saves souls with his truth — how can one say that an artist or banker is engaged in "secular" work and that only professional ministers are doing "the Lord's work"?

In the Genesis creation account, Adam and Eve are called to be fruitful and multiply, to have dominion (Gen 1:26 – 28). Michael Allen writes, "Sandwiched as it is between divine declarations of creation's goodness, this calling suggests that familial, social, political, and economic activities are part of God's good intentions for the world."[19] The garden is given to human beings to care for and cultivate

(Gen 2:15). A gardener does not merely leave a plot of ground as it is but rearranges the raw material so it produces things necessary for human flourishing, whether food, other materials for goods, or simply beautiful foliage. Ultimately, all human work and cultural activity represent this kind of gardening.

FALL

Michael Allen observes, "Death and sin limit the potential of culture, inasmuch as they skew the desires and abilities of cultural agents, who now pursue the wrong rather than the good."[20] Genesis 3:17 – 19 describes God's curse that falls after Adam and Eve sin. The text shows us that sin infects and affects every part of life. In a suggestive passage, Francis Schaeffer summarizes it this way:

> We should be looking now, on the basis of the work of Christ, for substantial healing in every area affected by the fall . . .
>
> Man was divided from God, first; and then, ever since the fall, man is separated from himself. These are the psychological divisions . . .
>
> The next division is that man is divided from other men; these are the sociological divisions. And then man is divided from nature, and nature is divided from nature . . . One day, when Christ comes back, there is going to be a complete healing of all of them.[21]

So sin affects everything — not just hearts, but entire cultures, every area of life. The doctrine of sin cuts two ways. On the one hand, it means we must not think we can escape from sin and its effects by withdrawing into our countercultures; nor, on the other hand, can we forget that sin infects the way all work and culture making are done or that idols are at the core of every culture. Thus, under the category of "fall" we must take into account the complementary truths of God's curse and his common grace (see sidebar on "The Antithesis"). Any goodness in the world — any wisdom or virtue — is an undeserved gift from God (Jas 1:17). Common grace is not special or saving grace; it is a restraining force that allows good things to come in and through people who do not know Christ's salvation.

A particularly important passage for this doctrine

THE ANTITHESIS

Daniel Strange, in his essay "Not Ashamed!" writes the following:

> Under "Fall" we must reckon anthropologically with the complementary truths of the "antithesis," common grace, and the image of God. The "antithesis" is God's judicial curse sovereignly inflicted on humanity in Genesis 3:15 and which from then until now puts enmity between followers of God and followers of Satan at all levels, intellectual and moral, individual and societal. The antithesis is *principally* "the diametrical opposition between belief and unbelief and therefore between belief and any compromise of revealed truth" [quoting John Frame]. The Bible presents this stark contrast between belief and unbelief in many ways: light and dark, death and life, those who are blind and those who can see, covenant keepers and covenant breakers, those in Adam and those in Christ. I stress *principially* because as well as affirming the truth of the antithesis we must also affirm two other biblical truths. First, as believers we know in practice that a version of the antithesis still runs through our own hearts as we daily deal with our indwelling sin, sin which is a contradiction according to who we are in Christ. Second, we note an analogous inconsistency in the unbeliever.[22]

---

is God's blessing of Noah in Genesis 8 – 9, where God promises to bless and sustain the creation through means *besides* his redeemed people.[23] John Murray writes that common grace is "every favour of whatever kind or degree, falling short of salvation, which this undeserving and sin-cursed world enjoys at the hand of God."[24]

This biblical understanding of our fallenness — cursed yet still sustained by non-salvific grace — is crucial for relating Christ to culture. The

CULTURAL MODELS AND ESCHATOLOGY

In *Reformed Theology*, Michael Allen suggests that eschatology — how you think about the last things — will have an impact on your Christ and culture model. Premillennialists are the most pessimistic about cultural change, postmillennialists are the most optimistic, and amillennialists hold a variety of stances.

An aspect of eschatology is one's belief in how much, if any, continuity there will be between this world and the next. Second Peter 3:10–12 and Revelation 21:1 state that the physical elements of this earth will melt and be destroyed by fire, but Romans 8:19–22 speaks about nature being liberated from its bondage to decay and about our bodies being "redeemed." Taking these two sets of texts together leads us to affirm that some of this present life and world survives and is renewed and that some of it is destroyed.

world is inherently good and sustained by common grace — yet it is cursed. Christians are redeemed and saved — yet they are still filled with remaining sin. The battle line between God and idols not only runs through the world; it runs through the heart of every believer. So the work and cultural productions of Christians and non-Christians will have both idolatrous and God-honoring elements in them. Cultural products should not be judged as "good if Christians make them" and "bad if non-Christians make them." Each should be evaluated on its own merits as to whether it serves God or an idol.

Against this background doctrine of the fall we remember Jesus' call to his disciples to be "salt of the earth" (Matt 5:13). Salt kept meat renewed so that it did not go bad. The salt metaphor does indeed call Christians to go out and be involved with the world — salt cannot do its work unless it is distributed. Christians are to penetrate all the arenas of

society. But being salt means having a restraining influence on a society's natural tendencies to decline and fall apart. While social engagement is necessary and can be fruitful, we should not usually expect to see grand social transformations.

So while the doctrine of creation shows us the goodness of work and of so-called secular callings and gives us a vision for culture building, the doctrine of the fall warns us against utopianism and triumphalism.

REDEMPTION AND RESTORATION

The coming of Christ — his incarnation, life, death, resurrection, and ascension — holds great significance for cultural engagement. One of the most important aspects of the Christian understanding of Christ's salvation is that it comes in stages. As Francis Schaeffer has pointed out, sin has ruined and defaced every aspect of life, and so Christ's salvation must also renew every aspect of life — it must eventually free us totally from the curse on sin. As Isaac Watts wrote, "He comes to make his blessings flow *far as the curse is found*."[25]

And yet Christ's saving and ruling power, often spoken of under the heading of "the kingdom of God," comes to us in two great stages. As Geerhardus Vos has observed, the kingdom of God is "the realm of God's saving grace," which is entered now through the new birth and faith in Christ (John 3:3, 5; Col 1:13).[26] In this sense, the kingdom of God is already here (Matt 12:28; Luke 17:21; 21:31). But the kingdom is also, according to Vos, a realm of "righteousness and justice and blessing." It is a new social order (1 Pet 2:9) that shows itself especially in the church. The Psalms vividly tell us that God's ruling power will heal not only human social problems but also nature itself, which is currently subject to decay (Rom 8:20–25). Psalms 72, 96, and 97 tell us that under the true king, grain will grow on the tops of mountains (Ps 72:16), and the fields, flowers, rocks, and trees will sing for joy (Ps 96:11–13). Herman Bavinck has noted that grace does not remove or replace but rather restores nature. Grace does not do away with thinking and speaking, art and science, theater and literature, business and economics; it remakes and restores what is amiss.[27]

To use Francis Schaeffer's terminology, the spiritual alienation between God and humanity is removed when we believe; we are justified and adopted into his family. But the psychological, social, cultural, and physical effects of sin are still with us. We can expect to see some healing now, yet full healing and removal of those results await the last day. So the kingdom of God, though "already" truly here, is "not yet" fully here (Matt 5:12, 20; 6:33; 7:21; 18:3; 19:23 – 24).[28]

Schaeffer suggests we can expect to see "substantial" healing now throughout the created order — but what does this really mean? Just how "already" and how "not yet" is the kingdom? Michael Allen puts it pointedly: "The real issue in the relationship of Christianity and culture, therefore, is ... in what time and at what pace will these things happen?"[29]

Closely related to the question of *when* we see the fruit of the inaugurated kingdom is the question of the relationship between the church and the kingdom. Sometimes the Bible talks about the kingdom as though it operates inside the realm of the church alone; at other times it speaks as if it is outside the church, incorporating the entire world.[30] Just as the biblical teaching on our fallenness gives us complementary truths that we must resolve to hold in balance — the curse and common grace — so too does the biblical teaching on Christ's redemption. His saving power is already at work, but not yet fully here. This saving power is at work in the gathered church, but it is not exclusive to the church. Here again we see why the different models are correct — and yet how easily they can become reductionistic and unbalanced. We should expect healing from sin in all areas of life — private *and* public, within the church *and* out in culture. We must see the gathered church as the great vehicle for this restoration — and yet individual Christians out in the world can be said to be representatives of the kingdom as well. We cannot separate our spiritual or church life from our secular or cultural life. Every part of our life — vocational, civic, familial, recreational, material, sexual, financial, political — is to be presented as a "living sacrifice" to God (Rom 12:1 – 2).

THE GOSPEL AND THE KINGDOM

It is evident that one of the main reasons for many of the divergent approaches to cultural engagement — among many aspects of ministry today — is the differing views of the nature of the kingdom. I recommend an older work that provides unusual balance and biblical insight — Geerhardus Vos's *The Teaching of Jesus Concerning the Kingdom of God and the Church*.[31]

Vos summarizes his exegesis and findings in a final chapter titled "Recapitulation." There he states that the kingdom of God "means the renewal of the world through the introduction of supernatural forces." For Vos, the kingdom is not just a subjective experience of God in the heart, but the power of God come into the world through a series of "objective facts and transactions" purposed to eventually overcome all sin, evil, suffering, and death in the world.

Vos helpfully observes in the Bible three aspects of the kingdom that must be kept together. First, it is *the realm of God's saving grace*. Because salvation is by grace, not works, God is King and Sovereign of our salvation. Second, it is *the realm of righteousness and justice*. A kingdom always operates according to the norms of the King. So the kingdom of God is a new way of living and a new set of relationships and social arrangements. Third, it is *the realm of blessing and joy*. God's future power, which will renew all creation, is present in our lives now.

Vos teaches that the kingdom of God mainly operates through the church, but that it also operates through Christians who integrate their faith and their work.

> Undoubtedly the kingship of God, as his recognized and applied supremacy, is intended to pervade and control the whole of human life

in all its forms of existence. This the parable of the leaven [Matt 13:33] plainly teaches. These various forms of human life have each their own sphere in which they work and embody themselves. There is a sphere of science, a sphere of art, a sphere of the family and of the state, a sphere of commerce and industry. Whenever one of these spheres comes under the controlling influence of the principle of the divine supremacy and glory, and this outwardly reveals itself, there we can truly say that the kingdom of God has become manifest.[32]

Vos immediately makes it clear, however, that the institutional church should not have political power or control society through the state.

So Vos states, in summary, that (1) the main way to see the kingdom forces of God at work is in the institutional church, whose main job is to minister through the Word and sacrament to win people and disciple them in Christ, and (2) when Christians are living in society to God's glory, this, too, is a manifestation of the kingdom of God.

Without this rare balance, there is a tendency to see the kingdom as either strictly spiritual and operating within the church or mainly social and operating in the liberation movements out in the world. Vos's biblical balance will enable us to avoid imbalances in the cultural engagement and missional church debates in particular. I recommend reading his book carefully and in its entirety.

THE LANDSCAPE OF CHRISTIAN CULTURAL ENGAGEMENT

What do we learn from this brief survey? The word *balance* thrusts itself on us yet again. The biblical material calls for a balance not of compromises but of "being controlled simultaneously and all the time" by all of the teaching in Scripture. A survey of the various Christ and culture models demonstrates precisely what D. A. Carson suggests — that indeed each of them fails to be controlled by all the biblical teaching *all the time*. Do those within the Two Kingdoms model do justice to the cultural mandate, the pervasive nature of idolatry, the insufficiency of natural revelation, and the reality of the kingdom outside the church? Does the Transformationist model do full justice to the "not yet-ness" of the kingdom, to how much Christians participate with all humans in the common curse and common grace, or the lack of clear calls to "take the culture" in the New Testament? Do those in the Relevance model do justice to the depth and pervasiveness of idolatry in all hearts and cultural products, the particularity and offense of the gospel, and, again, to the not yet-ness of the kingdom? Do the Counterculturalists do justice to the "already" nature of the kingdom or to their participation with the rest of the world in common curse and common grace? I think the answer to all these questions is, "Not sufficiently."

> The biblical material calls for a balance not of compromises but of "being controlled simultaneously and all the time" by all of the teaching in Scripture.

I have been making the case that each model is biblically unbalanced. That is, each has a pivotal theme that is true but insufficient, and the more we reductionistically apply that theme to cultural engagement without reference to other themes in the Bible, the more unbalanced the theological vision and the less fruitful the work. To visually represent this, I have created a illustration in which the four models are graphed against two axes. The vertical axis represents the *nature* of our cultural world ("Is the current culture redeemable and good, or fundamentally fallen?"). At the top is the belief that the world is full of strong common grace, that

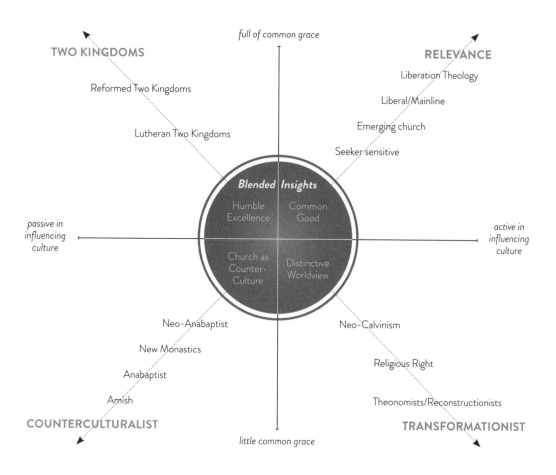

full of common grace

TWO KINGDOMS

Reformed Two Kingdoms

Lutheran Two Kingdoms

RELEVANCE

Liberation Theology

Liberal/Mainline

Emerging church

Seeker-sensitive

passive in
influencing
culture

active in
influencing
culture

Blended Insights

Humble
Excellence

Common
Good

Church as
Counter-
Culture

Distinctive
Worldview

Neo-Anabaptist

New Monastics

Anabaptist

Amish

COUNTERCULTURALIST

Neo-Calvinism

Religious Right

Theonomists/Reconstructionists

TRANSFORMATIONIST

little common grace

nonbelievers can readily understand natural revelation, and that God is at work in many ways in the world. At the bottom of the spectrum is the belief that the world is a dark and evil place, that God's natural revelation is hard to read, and that God's activity happens in and through the church alone. The horizontal axis represents the spectrum of views on our attitude toward cultural *change* ("Should we be pessimistic or optimistic about cultural change?"). On the left end of the spectrum is the belief that we should not actively try to change culture; on the right hand is the belief that we should be active in culture and optimistic about our efforts to change it.

The Transformationist and Countercultural-

ist models are in the bottom half of the diagram because they share a lack of faith in common grace and a conviction of a radical antithesis between the world and the values of God's kingdom. As a result, they emphasize the need for a strong, prophetic critique of the idols of the culture. The Two Kingdoms and Relevance models are on the top because they are much more positive about finding common ground with nonbelievers in the culture.

The Two Kingdoms and Counterculturalist models are on the left because they both believe that strong Christian attempts to "engage" and "transform" lead to syncretism and compromise. Both call Christians to simply "be the church" rather than seek to change the culture. Meanwhile, the Relevants and Transformationists are on the right because they both spend much time reflecting on culture and enthusiastically calling Christians to become involved in culture in order to influence it for Christ. Each of the models on the right criticizes the two on the left for dualism and withdrawal.

If we ended this discussion here, it might lead to the conclusion that we can simply combine all the best of the models, leave out the extremes, and find ourselves with a perfectly balanced and faithful "über-model" that all of us should follow. To conclude this would be simplistic and incorrect. In my final chapter on this subject, I will lay out guiding principles for being faithful, balanced, and skillful in relating Christianity to culture in a fast-changing world — regardless of which model most shapes our own practice.

QUESTIONS FOR DISCUSSION AND REFLECTION

1. Keller writes, "Some people conform well to the type, while others do not. Within a given model, we can find areas of pointed disagreement … Thoughtful proponents of certain models are always open to having their views tempered and enriched by insights from the others." What in this chapter challenged or provoked you? What did you find helpful? What did you disagree with?

2. This chapter provides two fundamental questions about culture to consider:

   • Should we be pessimistic or optimistic about the possibility for cultural change?
   • Is the current culture redeemable and good, or fundamentally fallen?

   How would you answer each of these two questions? On a scale from 0 to 10 (0 = not at all, and 10 = highly), how optimistic are you about the ability of believers to change culture? On the same scale, how redeemable do you believe culture to be? Do you find yourself leaning in one direction or the other on each question? If so, why?

   Possibility for Cultural Change

   Pessimistic   Optimistic

   0 1 2 3 4 5 6 7 8 9 10

   Nature of Culture

   Fundamentally fallen   Redeemable and good

   0 1 2 3 4 5 6 7 8 9 10

3. D. A. Carson speaks of allowing the various points of biblical theology to "control our thinking simultaneously and all the time." How do the elements of the biblical story line affect your understanding and practice of cultural engagement?

   • creation
   • the fall
   • redemption and restoration

4. Examine the illustration representing the Center Church model of cultural engagement. Where would you place yourself on this illustration? Where would you place each of your ministry colleagues and leaders? How can the different emphases within your team help to create a balanced, faithful perspective on cultural engagement?

CHAPTER 17 — WHY ALL THE MODELS ARE RIGHT … AND WRONG {pages 223–32}

1. See especially Daniel Strange, "Evangelical Public Theology? What on Earth? Why on Earth? How on Earth?" in *A Higher Throne: Evangelicals and Public Theology*, ed. Chris Green (Nottingham, UK: InterVarsity, 2008).

2. Lesslie Newbigin, *The Gospel in a Pluralist Society* (Grand Rapids: Eerdmans, 1989), 222 – 33.

3. Lesslie Newbigin, *Foolishness to the Greeks* (Grand Rapids: Eerdmans, 1986), 143 – 44. Here Newbigin cites Herman Dooyeweerd and seems conversant with and supportive of themes associated with neo-Calvinism.

4. See Lesslie Newbigin, Lamin Sanneh, Jenny Taylor, *Faith and Power: Christianity and Islam in "Secular" Britain* (London: SPCK, 1998), 20 – 24, 144 – 61. The father of Christian Reconstructionism, Rousas Rushdoony, calls democracy a "heresy" (*The Institutes of Biblical Law* [Phillipsburg, N.J.: Presbyterian & Reformed, 1980]), 100, 214, 747.

5. Jim Wallis, *God's Politics: Why the Right Gets It Wrong and the Left Doesn't Get It* (SanFrancisco: HarperSanFrancisco, 2005).

6. See James K. A. Smith, "Constantinianism of the Left?" http://forsclavigera.blogspot.com/2005/05/constantinianism-of-left.html (accessed February 6, 2012).

7. N. T. Wright, *What Saint Paul Really Said* (Grand Rapids: Eerdmans, 1997). Wright argues (p. 119) that justification isn't "so much about soteriology as about ecclesiology; not so much about salvation as about the church." He writes, "The gospel creates, not a bunch of individual Christians, but a community. If you take the old route of putting justification, in its traditional meaning, at the centre of your theology, you will always be in danger of sustaining some sort of individualism" (pp. 157 – 58). In part 6 ("Missional Community"), I explain why I think this kind of reengineering of the classic gospel is problematic.

8. N. T. Wright, *Simply Christian: Why Christianity Makes Sense* (San Francisco: HarperSanFrancisco, 2006), 226.

9. Ibid., 235 – 36.

10. Ibid. See Wright's articulation of a "Christian worldview" using the traditional neo-Calvinist categories of creation-fall-redemption-restoration (*The New Testament and the People of God* [Minneapolis: Fortress, 1992], 132).

11. See Mark Noll, *The Civil War as a Theological Crisis* (Chapel Hill: University of North Carolina Press, 2006).

12. James D. Hunter, *To Change the World: The Irony, Tragedy, and Possibility of Christianity in the Late Modern World* (New York: Oxford University Press, 2010), 41 – 42.

13. Ibid., 42 – 43.

14. Ibid., 37 – 38, 43 – 44.

15. See D. A. Carson, *Christ and Culture Revisited*, (Grand Rapids: Eerdmans, 2008), 44 – 58.

16. Ibid., 60.

17. Ibid., 59, emphasis his.

18. Another, shorter survey of these biblical-theological points is found in R. Michael Allen, *Reformed Theology* (Edinburgh: T&T Clark, 2010), 157 – 69.

19. Ibid., 159.

20. Ibid., 160.

21. Francis A. Schaeffer, *Pollution and the Death of Man: The Christian View of Ecology* (Wheaton, Ill.: Tyndale House, 1970), 65-66. Schaeffer expands on this idea of substantial healing from the results of sin in *True Spirituality* (Wheaton, Ill.: Tyndale House, 1971).

22. Daniel Strange, "Not Ashamed!" *Themelios* 36.2 (July 2011): 65, http://tgc-documents.s3.amazonaws.com/journal-issues/36.2/Themelios_36.2.pdf (accessed January 30, 2012).

23. For a short but comprehensive list of biblical examples of common grace, see Allen, *Reformed Theology*, 162.

24. John Murray, *Collected Writings of John Murray* (Edinburgh: Banner of Truth, 1977), 2:96.

25. Isaac Watts, "Joy to the World," emphasis mine.

26. For Vos's view, see sidebar on "The Gospel and the Kingdom" on pp. 229 – 30.

27. See, e.g., Herman Bavinck, *Reformed Dogmatics, Volume 2: God and Creation*, ed. J. Bolt (Grand Rapids: Baker, 2004). The editor writes that "the teaching that 'grace restores nature' is seen as one of the key elements in Bavinck's theology" (p. 19).

28. A good summary of the teaching on the "present (yet) coming kingdom" is found in Bavinck, *Reformed Dogmatics, Volume 3: Sin and Salvation in Christ*, ed. J. Bolt (Grand Rapids: Baker, 2006).

29. Allen, *Reformed Theology*, 164; see Douglas Moo, "Nature in the New Creation: New Testament Eschatology and the Environment," *Journal of the Evangelical Theological Society* 49 (2006): 449 – 88.

30. See D. A. Carson, *The God Who Is There: Finding Your Place in God's Story* (Grand Rapids: Baker, 2010), 82. Some people read the parable of the weeds in Matthew 13 as being about true and false Christians within the church, but in the parable the kingdom is a field, and in Jesus' explanation he says, "the field is the world" (v. 38), not the church. Louis Berkhof (*Systematic Theology* [Grand Rapids: Eerdmans, 1996], 570) writes, "The visible church may certainly be said to belong to the kingdom, to be a part of the kingdom, and even to be the most important visible embodiment of the forces of the kingdom . . . [But] the kingdom may be said to be a broader concept than the church, because it aims at nothing less than the complete control of all the manifestations of life. It represents the dominion of God in every sphere of human endeavor." Berkhof represents the views of Abraham Kuyper, Herman Bavinck, and Geerhardus Vos as well.

31. Geerhardus Vos, *The Teaching of Jesus Concerning the Kingdom of God and the Church* (Eugene, Ore.: Wipf & Stock, 1998).

32. Ibid., 162 – 63.

CULTURAL ENGAGEMENT THROUGH BLENDED INSIGHTS

As we have seen, the cultural situation in the West has forced every minister to adopt some model of relating Christ to culture. Many ministers, I believe, are largely unaware of the presuppositions, historical roots, or weaknesses of their model, or of the biblical merits of other models. Yet if you've come this far, I hope no one can say this of you. Nevertheless, you are still operating from within your own model. You have a personal history, temperament, church tradition, and ministry context that leads you to emphasize certain ways of relating to culture. In this chapter, I will offer practical counsel on how to operate faithfully and skillfully within the model you inhabit.

SEEK THE CENTER

The first principle is that *proponents of each model should do their best to discern and incorporate the insights of the other models.* Referring again to the illustration on page 231, each of us should "seek the center" — i.e., to seek to face and operate close to the illustration's center. The main way to do this is to appreciate the seminal insights of each model, so we'll summarize them again here.

The Relevants are especially inspired by the coming shalom and restoration of all things. They emphasize the importance of a church that exists for others, *doing sacrificial service for the common good.* If the Christian faith is to have any impact on culture, the time must come when it is widely known that secularism tends to make people selfish, while general religion and traditional morality make people tribal (concerned mainly for their own), but the Christian gospel turns people away from both their selfishness and their self-righteousness to serve others in the way that Jesus gave himself for his enemies. Just as Israel was told to "seek the

peace and prosperity" of the great pagan city of Babylon (Jer 29:7), so Christians should be well-known as people who seek to serve people — whether they embrace Christianity or not.[1]

The Transformationists have a keen sense of the effects of the fall on human culture; their main focus is on *thinking and living in all areas of life in a distinctively Christian manner.* Most of our churches' discipleship models operate by drawing laypeople out of the world and into the life of the church — which can be unhelpful. D. Michael Lindsay's *Faith in the Halls of Power* shows that Christians who are deeply involved in cultural centers and institutions feel largely unappreciated by and alienated from the church.[2] Few churches actively support people to follow Christ in both their private and public lives, but the Transformationists are filling this gap.

The Counterculturalists point to God's redemptive strategy of calling out a distinct people for himself; their lead theme calls the church *to be a contrast community and sign of the future kingdom,* if we are to have any witness to the world. Those who advocate this model rightly argue that Christians who work as individuals dispersed within cultural institutions cannot give the world a Christian vision of human flourishing in the same way that a community can. The church can provide the best setting for shaping a Christian's worldview for work in the world.[3]

Those holding the Two Kingdoms view revel in the goodness of creation; their basic idea centers on the dignity of secular vocation and the importance of doing this work in a way *marked by an excellence that all can see.*[4] The distinctiveness of Christian work will have little impact, directly or indirectly, unless it is accompanied by excellence. Martin Luther is reported to have been asked, "How can I be a Christian shoemaker?" and to have answered, "Make excellent shoes for an excellent price" — in other words, be the best shoemaker you can be. The very act of honest work, even in its simplest forms, even when it is difficult to do out of a discernibly Christian worldview, is a wondrous good in and of itself. And therefore farming, police work, and other vocations in which we serve the common good are vehicles for God's love and care to the degree that they are done *very well* — with utmost skill and honesty.

These are the driving themes of the models. Each is represented as a line radiating out from the center of the grid. The farther you are from the center, the more you hold a particular model's theme reductionistically, with little regard for the insights of others, and therefore stand in great danger of failing to honor all of the biblical themes at the same time — creation, fall, redemption, and restoration. The center of the diagram, near the meeting of the axes, represents a place where there is a greater reliance on the whole cloth of biblical themes — marked by an effort to hold together the realities of creation and fall, natural revelation and special revelation, curse and common grace, the "already but not yet," continuity and discontinuity, sin and grace. The closer you are to the center of the grid, the more you hold your theme in balance with the other themes. This is a Center Church model for cultural engagement in which we seek to avoid the imbalances of triumphalism or withdrawal in the existing models and are equally loath to commit either cultural compromise or cultural withdrawal. A Center Church approach seeks to blend the cultural and biblical insights of all the models into our actual practice and ministry.[5]

For example, the Two Kingdoms model rightly lifts up the dignity and divine significance of *all* work done by all people. Regardless of who is doing it, any work done with excellence and skill that serves other people and the common good should be appreciated and celebrated by Christians. However, the Transformationist model points out the idolatries animating our lives, including our work, and therefore values work done from a distinctly Christian understanding of human flourishing. To

combine both of these attitudes enables Christians to be both humble and appreciative of nonbelieving colleagues and yet not satisfied with doing work according to the reigning standards and philosophies in their field.

Miroslav Volf titles a section of his book *A Public Faith* "Two Noes and One Yes." This means, first, saying no to what he calls "total transformation" — to a goal of transforming the whole culture we inhabit. What Christians build culturally is not like

---

A Center Church approach seeks to blend the cultural and biblical insights of all the models into our actual practice and ministry.

---

the modern cities (Brasilia is the best example) that are built from scratch. It is like rehabilitating an existing city while living in it.[6] It means, second, saying no to what he calls "accommodation." Finally, we say yes to "engagement," which Volf describes as "expressing the middle between abandoning and dominating the culture ... what it might mean to assert one's difference while remaining within it," of "leaving without departing."[7]

Volf continues to spell this out by describing three stances that Christians can take to a particular element of culture. They can (1) adopt it as something acceptable, (2) take up the element but transform it from within, or (3) reject it and even work to abolish it in a society for the good of all.[8] By locating a large part of Christian difference in the unique biblical understanding of human nature and human thriving, Volf bridges a gap between the Transformationists and the Relevants. He makes shalom a critical goal of our culture making, yet insists that the common good be given biblical definition and content.[9]

I believe each model has at its core a unique insight about the world and a fundamental truth from the Bible that any professing Christian must acknowledge. And therefore, those within each model should seek in humility to find the genius and wisdom of the other approaches to better honor God's Word and his will.

KNOW THE SEASON

So we should learn from all of the models, but does this mean the ideal position is one that does not fit into any of the models, that straddles the lines perfectly and balances all the insights and emphases of the models in perfect symmetry? I don't believe so, for two reasons.

First, H. Richard Niebuhr believed that Christianity's relationship to a culture went through a cycle.[10] He pointed to three stages of a historical cycle and how they follow one another.[11]

1. In the beginning, we have what Niebuhr calls the "converted church" in which the church and culture are sharply dissimilar and at deep odds with each other. The church is alien to the world. In this situation, the church emphasizes its distinction from the world and has strong standards for baptism and a high level of accountability within the community for Christian practice. It also engages in aggressive evangelism.

2. Next comes an "allied church" stage in which the church "enters into inevitable alliance with converted emperors and governors, philosophers and artists, merchants and entrepreneurs, and begins to live at peace in the culture they [these influential culture makers] produce under the stimulus of their faith." During this stage the church becomes far less rigorous in discerning signs of repentance and faith. Many people come into the church simply out of cultural pressure. The difference between the church and the world diminishes to near zero. At some point the culture itself begins to drift from its Christian roots because the church is no longer a spiritually dynamic force. Rather than the church shaping the culture, the culture shapes the church.

3. What happens then? A stage of renewal: "Only a new withdrawal [into the church as a contrast community] followed by a new aggression [of evangelism] can then save the church and restore to it the salt with which to savor society."

Niebuhr wrote in 1935 that this cycle has happened three times, and he was thinking of Western civiliza-

tion when he laid out his stages.[12] Of course, to talk of three stages falls short of the complex reality. For example, Niebuhr is right that Christianity became corrupt, declined, and managed to come back. But did the reformers in the past face the hostile secularism of the modern West? I don't believe so; it is clear that to reengage a post-Christian society is not at all the same as evangelizing a pre-Christian society.

Here is one example. The pagans of the first and second century were astonished at the Christians' compassion for the sick and the poor. David Bentley Hart explains that Christians essentially invented orphanages and hospitals — no one had ever thought of them. Nicholas Wolterstorff makes the case that the idea of human rights came from Christian reflection on the *imago Dei*.[13] Christian compassion was therefore unique, attractive, and compelling to pre-Christian pagans. In our post-Christian society, this approach to human rights and commitment to compassion have been preserved, and therefore Christians' compassion and championing of human rights have a less dramatic effect on nonbelievers today. Indeed, because Christianized, European America committed genocide against Native Americans and allowed and promoted the African slave trade, the Christian faith is given little credit for the massive good that it has done for Western culture. Addressing post-Christian pagans is not at all the same as addressing pre-Christian pagans.

I want to adapt Niebuhr's proposal and suggest four seasons in the cycle of the church's relationship to a culture.

1. *Winter* describes a church that is not only in a hostile relationship to a pre-Christian culture but is gaining little traction; is seeing little distinctive, vital Christian life and community; and is seeing no evangelistic fruit. In many cultures today, the church is embattled and spiritually weak.
2. *Spring* is a situation in which the church is embattled, even persecuted by a pre-Christian culture, but it is growing (e.g., as in China).
3. *Summer* is what Niebuhr described as an "allied church," where the church is highly regarded by

the public and where we find so many Christians in the centers of cultural production that Christians feel at home in the culture.

4. *Autumn* is where we find ourselves in the West today, becoming increasingly marginalized in a post-Christian culture and looking for new ways to both strengthen our distinctiveness and reach out winsomely.

At first glance, it seems that the Counterculturalist is most appropriate for "winter" (when there is a need to recover and nurture real Christianity); the Transformationist for "spring" (when cultural institutions are increasingly filled with Christians who need to be discipled for culture making); the Two Kingdoms for "summer" (when there is widespread cultural consensus on what human flourishing looks like); and the Relevance model for "autumn" (when many are still open to the gospel, but people are also beginning to question the relevance of faith for life).

This lineup is still too simplistic, however. For example, the American South and Sweden are both parts of post-Christian Western culture, but huge differences exist between them. In many parts of the American South, the church still has a great deal of public influence and positive regard — it's still summer there. In addition, the models in their most unbalanced forms are never fully fruitful in any time or place. So for example, many champion the Counterculturalist model as the proper response to a post-Christian culture. It is often pointed out that the original monastic orders saved Christian civilization and evangelized pagan Europe. But is the new monasticism as effective and aggressive in its personal evangelism as were the original monastics? Many in the Counterculturalist model are in such a pitched reaction against the individualism of seeker churches and church growth movements that the message "you must be born again" is lost.[14] Instead, they say, we should simply be a loving community that carries out justice and seeks peace. Often those with a Two Kingdoms mind-set place an emphasis on evangelism and discipleship, which, as we have seen, is especially crucial for a season in which the church is marginal within a culture.[15]

So there are no simple answers to the question, "What season is it?" Yet it is a question that we must ask. If all these models in their balanced formulation have biblical warrant, where will we situate ourselves? The answer is not simply an attempt to hit on the perfect balance between all four all of the time. As we have seen, each model has a "tool kit" of biblical themes and approaches, and our present cultural season helps us better understand which tools we need to take out of the kit and use.[16]

FOLLOW YOUR CONVICTIONS

The second reason we cannot simply call for a perfect union of all of the models is that each one tends to attract people on the basis of their different ministry gifts and callings. As the apostle Paul has famously told us, while all Christians must have all the Spirit's "fruit" (or character virtues), no Christian has all of the Spirit's gifts. Paul indicates in such places as 1 Corinthians 12 – 14; Ephesians 4; and Romans 12 that God gives each Christian one (or perhaps more) spiritual gift that equips him or her to serve others in the name of Christ. So the model we embrace will likely be influenced by the temperament and spiritual gifts we possess. How, then, do we discern what our spiritual gifts are?

Why do each of us tend to feel most comfortable with one of these models? My view is that it has to do largely with our gifts and calling.

As a pastor helping people answer this question over the years, I have noticed that people's differing gifts are often revealed by the different human needs with which they resonate. Evangelizing is a duty of a Christian, as is helping the poor. But these ministries are also gifts — some people are especially gifted to do evangelism, and others to show mercy to those in need.[17] I often encountered people in my church who pressed me about particular ways that our church was failing in ministry. Some were passionate about evangelism; some were insistent we reach out to the needy; others bewailed how disorganized we were whenever we tried to do evangelism or mercy! I came to realize that some had the gift of evangelism, some of mercy, and some of administration, and their gifts made them particularly sensitive to certain kinds of problems. As their pastor, I needed to warn them that their gifts were giving them a bit of tunnel vision, but mainly I needed to train and release them into the area of ministry the Spirit was calling them through the distribution of his gifts.

I believe something similar (and related) is happening when it comes to these models of Christ and culture. As I read books by people who have thought through these matters, it seems that virtually no one can be neutral, unbiased, and uncommitted to a particular model. I have quoted from the works of Daniel Strange, Miroslav Volf, James Hunter, and many others — but as balanced and nuanced as these writers are, they usually show they are most comfortable with one particular model and most conversant with one model's set of tools. Michael Goheen has done deep reading for years in the "missional" writings of David Bosch, Lesslie Newbigin, and others; has incorporated much of what we call Counterculturalist thinking; and yet considers himself a Kuyperian.[18] Kevin DeYoung wrote a blog post in which he critiqued both the Transformationist and the Two Kingdoms models. He drew this conclusion:

> Perhaps there is — I can't believe I'm going to say it — a middle ground. I say, let's not lose the heart of the gospel, divine self-satisfaction through self-substitution. And let's not apologize for challenging Christians to show this same kind of dying love to others. Let's not be embarrassed by the doctrine of hell and the necessity of repentance and regeneration. And let's not be afraid to do good to all people, especially to the household of faith. Let's work against the injustices and suffering in our day, and let's be realistic that the poor, as Jesus said, will always be among us. Bottom line: let's work for change where God calls us and gifts us, but let's not forget that the Great Commission is go into the world and make disciples, not go into the world and build the kingdom.[19]

Nevertheless, DeYoung wishes to identify most with what he calls the "careful two kingdoms theology."[20]

CASE STUDY: WILLIAM STUNTZ

A good case study of Christian cultural engagement and impact is the late William Stuntz, formerly professor of criminal law at Harvard Law School. Though he was an evangelical Christian and conservative Republican who was open about his faith and politics, when he died of cancer at the age of fifty-two, *The New York Times* paid him a remarkable tribute with a full op-ed piece on its editorial main page by Lincoln Caplan.[21] It said that his scholarship in the area of criminal law was so strong that he had refuted the other thinkers and had a "profound" influence on the field. One of his accomplishments, according to the writer, was the incorporation of mercy to the marginalized without undermining rule of law. And yet the writer recognized that his arguments were not just skillful, but grounded in his Christian beliefs. While "literally defining the field," Caplan wrote, "he was living his faith." The piece also pointed to his inspiring example as he dealt courageously with cancer and faced his impending death with grace.

Here we see a man who definitely engaged and influenced the culture, brought his faith and its distinctive worldview to bear on the field of law, did it with undeniable excellence, and showed compassion for the poor within his theories of justice. In spite of the fact that he worked in places that largely disdained the Christian faith, the combination of his clear commitment to the common good, the integration of his faith with his scholarship, and his undeniable skill and excellence combined to make a real difference.

Another important observation in the case of William Stuntz is that he did his work first at the University of Virginia and later at Harvard, two major institutions with a lot of "symbolic" or cultural capital (see sidebar on "Symbolic Capital" on p. 185). Many Christians share with many Americans an anti-institutional bias, and therefore they grossly underestimate the power of institutions to shape culture. Hugh Heclo's little book *On Thinking Institutionally* can go a long way toward correcting this mistake.[22] Here the Counterculturalist model serves us poorly, since it tends to see all worldly institutions as part of "empire" and no place for Christians to serve. However, in the case of William Stuntz, Christian excellence was available for all to see precisely because he functioned in one of the main public cultural institutions. All of the biblical warnings against pride, love of wealth, and hunger for power must be kept in mind, and not all cultural change automatically flows from elite circles at the very top.[23] But Christians should still seek to be a faithful presence in the major cultural institutions.[24]

Why do each of us tend to feel most comfortable with one of these models? My view is that it has to do largely with our gifts and calling. There is little doubt that people with gifts and a personal calling to serve the poor tend to be attracted to forms of the Relevance or Counterculturalist models. People with the greatest passion for evangelism will tend to appreciate the Two Kingdoms or perhaps the Transformationist model. Many have charged Transformationism with being the Christ and culture model that only college-educated people with an intellectual or academic bent can love or even understand. All of these observations are correct to some degree.

So what does this mean? I believe it indicates we should inhabit the model that fits our convictions, whose "tool kit" best fits our gifts. Once we know

our model, we should be able, depending on the cultural seasons and context, to use tools from the other kits. On this point, Andy Crouch's distinction between postures and gestures is a vivid and elegant way to express this flexibility. Crouch sees our basic model or stance toward culture to be a "posture" — our "unconscious default position" — but a "gesture" is an ad hoc move that briefly seems to come out of another model. A person whose posture is highly antagonistic to culture in general might still in a gesture accept some particular cultural trend, while a person whose posture toward culture is mainly friendly may still in a gesture feel a particular cultural element must be completely condemned.[25]

REMEMBER THE DIFFERENCE BETWEEN *ORGANIZED* AND *ORGANIC*

One of the greatest points of tension between the models is in the way they understand the *mission* of the church (which will be addressed in the next section). The traditional understanding of the Great Commission is that the church has been given the mandate to go into all the world to preach the gospel in order to make disciples of men and women from all nations.[26] But three of the four models seem to add significantly to this mission. Many fear that emphasizing mercy and justice, or political and cultural engagement, will displace or at least severely erode the church's capacity for evangelism and discipleship. In reaction to this emphasis, many are adopting a Two Kingdoms model, which clearly insists that the mission of the church is only and strictly to preach the Word, evangelize, and make disciples. While warnings about the "social gospel" are warranted, I believe we must still come to grips with the Bible's call to the Christian community to do justice and love mercy. But how?

At this point it is important to remind ourselves of the critical distinction between the "church institutional" and the "church organic." Abraham Kuyper taught that the church institutional was the gathered church, organized under its officers and ministers. It is called to do "Word and sacrament" — to preach the gospel, baptize, and make disciples. This he distinguished from the church organic, referring to all Christians living in the world who have been discipled and equipped to bring the gospel to bear on all of life. We should not think of Christians out in the world as merely distinct and detached individuals. They are the body of Christ, the church. As Christians in the world, they are still to think and work together, banding together in creative forms, being the church organic that the church institutional has discipled them to be. Theologian John Bolt writes the following:

> In Kuyper's view, Christians who go out into their various vocations do so neither as direct emissaries of the institutional church nor as mere individual believers ... Christian social, cultural, and political action does not flow directly from structures and authorities of the church, but comes to expression organically in the various spheres of life as believers live out the faith and spirituality that develops and is nurtured in the church's worship and discipline.[27]

Michael Allen points out that H. Richard Niebuhr himself failed to distinguish between the rights and responsibilities of the Christian and those of the church, and this oversight has been deadly to mainline churches. Allen contrasts the mistake of the "spirituality of the church" doctrine that led to the Southern U.S. churches' support of slavery with the opposite error of mainline Protestant denominations that have become deeply and institutionally involved in politics. "One story shows a church that will not address any social ills, even the evils of chattel slavery, while the other tale portrays a church speaking authoritatively, even lobbying, with regard to very detailed political action plans."[28] Kuyper's distinction solves this dilemma well. A church that is educating and discipling people to do justice in the public sphere will have to be sensitive to social issues and ills in its teaching and preaching, and yet it will not make the fatal mistake of becoming a lobbying group and losing sight of its main mission.[29]

This distinction helps to bridge the gaps between the Christ and culture models. If it is maintained, then those becoming enamored with justice and cultural engagement will avoid falling into the error of the older mainline churches that lost their vision for evangelism and discipleship. On the other hand, faithful churches concerned to maintain the mission of the church as disciple making will disciple people to evangelize — but also to engage culture and do justice.

ACT, DON'T REACT

I've become convinced that one of the reasons we have not seen more balanced cultural engagement "near the center" is that many of us are not choosing our Christ and culture model in the right way. Instead of looking at Scripture, the culture, and our own gifts and calling, we tend to form our views in visceral reactions to the behavior of other Christians. In other words, we stand here and not there because *those* people are there and not here. While it is true that all of these models draw on older antecedents and patterns that have been in the church for centuries, there is a tendency for their contemporary versions to be defined in reaction and hostility to one another. The various groups are like large tectonic plates along which major and minor

---

While it is true that all of these models draw on older patterns that have been in the church for centuries, their contemporary versions tend to be defined in reaction and hostility to one another.

---

eruptions and quakes happen constantly. Each camp is calling the church to do different things, and they regularly attack one another for the ways they emphasize their differences. Indeed, they can most easily raise money from donors by depicting themselves as the faithful antidote to the other groups.

This tendency — to react rather than act — lies behind the reductionistic impulse at the extreme of each model, an impulse that becomes self-defeating in the end, leading to imbalance and unfaithfulness to the full biblical witness. So what should we do about this problem? I end with some practical exhortations.

1. Avoid arrogance. It is extremely easy to believe that the culture model that has helped you the most is the best one for everyone. It is especially easy to feel superior if you compare the strengths of your favorite model with the weaknesses of the others. Don't do that. Do not think that your particular tradition is "the new thing God is doing" and all the others are fading away. A balanced assessment shows that none of these particular traditions are dying. Each has serious weaknesses but also great strengths.

2. Avoid blame. If you have grown by adopting another culture model, you may feel angry or betrayed by the former one. You may have had good or bad personal experiences at the hands of cultural elites, which may have influenced you unduly. You may blame a certain model for all the troubles of the church because rabid proponents hurt the last congregation of which you were a member. Forgive, and look for places where you can repent. Try to remove the personal histories as you think about culture. Look at the Bible, the cultural moment, and your gifts.

3. Avoid frustration. If you are in a church or denomination that does not share the cultural model you feel is best, it can have a radicalizing effect on you. Opposition can push you into more extreme forms of your position. Don't let conflict make you too rigid a proponent for your approach.

4. Avoid naïveté. Some people say "a plague on all your houses" and insist that one church transcend all models or incorporate them all. Because every church and Christian has history, a temperament, and a unique take on various theological issues, every church and Christian will be situated in some tradition and model. It is inescapable. The gospel should give us the humility both to appreciate other models and to acknowledge that we have a model of our own. So enjoy the strengths of your position, admit the weaknesses, and borrow like crazy from the strengths of the others.

1. Keller writes, "If all these models in their balanced formulation have biblical warrant, where will we situate ourselves? The answer is not simply an attempt to hit on the perfect balance between all four all of the time." We must also learn to discern the current "season" in the cycle of the church's relationship to a culture.

   - *Winter* — a church that is hostile to culture, seeing little fruit; embattled and spiritually weak.
   - *Spring* — a church that is embattled, possibly persecuted by the culture, but is seeing growth.
   - *Summer* — an "allied" church, highly regarded by the culture with Christians in the centers of cultural production.
   - *Autumn* — a church that is increasingly marginalized in a post-Christian culture, looking for new ways to reach out winsomely.

   In which of these four seasons do you and your ministry peers find yourself right now? To which signs or factors can you point as proof? Does this change when you consider your context nationally or regionally? How is this current season of cultural engagement different from that of the previous generation of church leaders?

2. Andy Crouch's distinction between postures and gestures is "a vivid and elegant way to express this flexibility" needed for balanced cultural engagement. Crouch sees our basic model or stance toward culture to be a "posture" — our "unconscious default position" — but a "gesture" is an ad hoc move that briefly seems to come out of another model. Can you cite an instance when you embraced a gesture that didn't match your typical posture? What were the reasons that led you to do this?

3. What do you think of the distinction between the role of the church as an organized institution and the church as an organic body of individual believers? How does this distinction aid in thinking about cultural engagement and the mission of the church? Do you believe it is a biblical distinction?

4. Keller writes, "Many of us are not choosing our Christ and culture model in the right way. Instead of looking at Scripture, the culture, and our own gifts and calling, we tend to form our views in visceral reactions to the behavior of other Christians." This chapter closes with four practical suggestions.

   - Avoid arrogance.
   - Avoid blame.
   - Avoid frustration.
   - Avoid naïveté.

   How can you seek to avoid reacting to the extremes of other models? Which of these four concerns is most relevant to you?

CHAPTER 18 — CULTURAL ENGAGEMENT THROUGH BLENDED INSIGHTS *(pages 235–43)*

1. For more on this subject see Tim Keller, *Generous Justice: How God's Grace Makes Us Just* (New York: Dutton, 2010).
2. D. Michael Lindsay, *Faith in the Halls of Power: How Evangelicals Joined the American Elite* (New York: Oxford University Press, 2007).
3. See James K. A. Smith, *Desiring the Kingdom: Worship, Worldview, and Cultural Formation* (Grand Rapids: Baker, 2009). Smith believes that liturgy, corporate worship, and community practices such as radical hospitality, forgiveness and reconciliation, and shared resources within a common life are far more powerful for shaping a Christian worldview than classes about worldviews. Christians will only be equipped to integrate faith and work and to operate out of a Christian worldview if they are deeply involved and embedded in a strong and "thick" Christian community.
4. Michael Horton ("How the Kingdom Comes," *Christianity Today* 50.1 [January 2006]: 42, www.christianvisionproject.com/2006/01/how_the_kingdom_comes.html) writes, "There are no calls in the New Testament either to withdraw into a private ghetto or to 'take back' the realms of cultural and political activity. Rather, we find exhortations, like Paul's, to the inauspicious yet crucial task of loving and serving our neighbors with excellence."
5. I consider my Center Church model of "blended insights" to be essentially the same approach as James Hunter's "faithful presence" described in *To Change the World* (New York: Oxford University Press, 2010).
6. Miroslav Volf, *A Public Faith: How Followers of Christ Should Serve the Common Good* (Grand Rapids: Baker, 2011), 93 – 94.
7. Ibid., 90 – 91.
8. Ibid., 91 – 92. Volf (p. 158 n.1) observes that his approach has affinities with the approach of James Hunter.
9. See ibid., ch. 4, "Human Flourishing," 55 – 74.
10. Thanks to Dr. Michael Wittmer for leading me to this essay by Niebuhr and proposing that the spiritual health of our culture may influence the Christ and culture model we choose.
11. See H. Richard Niebuhr, "Toward the Independence of the Church," in *The Church Against the World*, ed. H. Richard Niebuhr, Wilhelm Pauck, and Francis P. Miller (Chicago: Willett, 1935), www.religion-online.org/showchapter.asp?title=412&C=194 (accessed February 7, 2012).
12. Niebuhr was evidently thinking that the first cycle occurred when the early church grew until it became a virtual state religion under Constantine and later had to be renewed by the rise of monasticism. The second cycle took place when the monastic orders evangelized pagan Europe, which led to the corruption of the medieval church, which had to be renewed by the Protestant Reformation. The third cycle was the rise of Protestant and Catholic Christendom in Europe and North America and then the current decline under the rise of secularism. The right "renewal" mode is still being debated.
13. David Bentley Hart, *Atheist Delusions: The Christian Revolution and Its Fashionable Enemies* (New Haven, Conn.: Yale University Press, 2009); Nicholas Wolterstorff, *Justice: Rights and Wrongs* (Princeton, N.J.: Princeton University Press, 2007).
14. See part 6 of this book on Missional Community.
15. See, e.g., Kevin DeYoung and Greg Gilbert, *What Is the Mission of the Church? Making Sense of Social Justice, Shalom, and the Great Commission* (Wheaton, Ill.: Crossway, 2011). DeYoung and Gilbert take what seems to be a moderately Two Kingdoms approach to culture. They rightly warn that some of the other models — like Transformationism, the liberal end of what we are calling the Relevance model, and the neo-Anabaptists undermine a strong emphasis on ecclesiastical evangelism.
16. Thanks to Michael Wittmer for the concept of each model as a tool kit.
17. Ephesians 4:11 speaks of God giving some the gift and calling of "evangelist," and Romans 12:7 – 8 speaks of the gifts of serving (*diakonia*) and mercy. First Peter 4:11 mentions "speaking" gifts and "serving" gifts, which many commentators believe refers to categories of gifts — gifts that have to do with preaching and teaching and gifts that have to do with deeds, administration, and service.
18. See Michael Goheen, *As the Father Sent Me, I Am Sending You: Lesslie Newbigin's Missionary Ecclesiology* (Zoetermeer, Netherlands: Boekencentrum, 2000), for an argument that the missional ecclesiology of Newbigin is not incompatible with a Kuyperian understanding. See Michael Goheen and Craig Bartholomew, *Living at the Crossroads: An Introduction to Christian Worldview* (Grand Rapids: Baker, 2008), for an excellent, accessible presentation of a Transformationist approach that is shorn of triumphalism and lifts up the importance of the church as contrast community.
19. Kevin DeYoung, "Two Kingdom Theology and Neo-Kuyperians," http://thegospelcoalition.org/blogs/kevindeyoung/2009/08/14/two-kingdom-theology-and-neo-kuyperians/ (accessed February 8, 2012).
20. Kevin DeYoung, "You Can Get There from Here," http://thegospelcoalition.org/blogs/kevindeyoung/2011/12/22/you-can-get-there-from-here/
21. Lincoln Caplan, "William Stuntz," *New York Times* (March 23, 2011), www.nytimes.com/2011/03/24/opinion/24thu4.html (accessed February 8, 2012).
22. Hugh Heclo, *On Thinking Institutionally* (Boulder, Colo.: Paradigm, 2008).

23. See James Hunter's observation (*To Change the World*, 42 – 43) that cutting-edge cultural changes often flow not from the very top of cultural power or from the grassroots but from the "outer elites," men and women (often, but not always, young) who are within the institutions and arenas of cultural influence but not at the very center.

24. As I argue in earlier chapters, one of the main ways Christians can draw closer to the centers of cultural influence is by living their lives and pursuing their vocations in the great cities of the world.

25. See Andy Crouch, *Culture Making: Recovering Our Creative Calling* (Downers Grove, Ill.: InterVarsity, 2008), 90 – 96. Thanks to Michael Wittmer for reminding me of this chapter in Andy's book.

26. For a good traditional exposition of the Great Commission, see DeYoung and Gilbert, *What Is the Mission of the Church?*, 15 – 66.

27. John Bolt, *A Free Church, A Holy Nation: Abraham Kuyper's American Public Theology* (Grand Rapids: Eerdmans, 2000), 428 – 29.

28. R. Michael Allen, *Reformed Theology* (Edinburgh: T&T Clark, 2010), 174.

29. See ibid., 175.

30. Ibid.

CITY BALANCE

*underadapted
only challenge* ———————————————————— *overadapted
only appreciate*

Center Church ministry is neither undercontextualized nor overcontextualized to the city and the culture. Because the city has potential for both human flourishing and human idolatry, we minister with balance, using the gospel to both appreciate and challenge the culture to be in accord with God's truth.

- Be informed and shaped by all of Scripture all of the time — the parts that are offensive to our personal and cultural sensibilities, as well as those that are more plausible and energizing to us.

- Realize that while no truth can be articulated in a culture-transcending way, the truth does transcend culture.
- Be willing to interact with different cultures in order to come to a more rounded biblical Christianity.
- Have a stance toward the city/culture that includes critical enjoyment and appropriate wariness, for it is a mix of both common grace and sin.
- Confront hearers with an epistemological challenge, a personal challenge, and a proclamation of Christ.

- Employ more than one type of appeal in gospel presentations — logical and existential, short-term and long-term.
- Minister with boldness and confidence as well as with humility and irony, for the gospel creates both in you at the same time.
- Hold to one true gospel, yet learn to creatively adapt it in culturally specific ways.
- Actively engage the city/culture, while avoiding cultural captivity in all its forms (cultural fundamentalism and withdrawal; cultural relativism and syncretism).
- Drill (affirm culture) and blast (confront culture) when you preach and teach.
- Address both "A" beliefs and doctrines and "B" beliefs and doctrines.
- Use a balance of all the atonement grammars (battlefield, marketplace, exile, temple, law court, substitution).
- See cities as a social form with the potential for both God-given purpose and self-centered rebellion against God.
- Live as both residents and foreigners in this world.
- Emphasize the goodness of secular vocation and the importance of building up the church.
- Take a view of cultural engagement that is informed by the whole of the biblical story line so that it is neither too pessimistic nor too optimistic about the possibility for cultural change and so that it affirms the presence of both common grace and pervasive sin in every culture.
- "Seek the center" by incorporating the key biblical insights of each Christ-and-culture model, where there is a greater reliance on the whole cloth of biblical themes — creation and fall, natural and special revelation, curse and common grace, the "already but not yet," continuity and discontinuity, sin and grace.
- Realize that your preferred model for relating the church to culture is the product of external forces (theological commitments) and internal forces (temperament and spiritual gifts).
- Understand the mission of the church in both institutional and organic terms.

MOVEMENT

structured organization
tradition and authority

fluid organism
cooperation and unity

{ *A Center Church is both an organism and an organization. Because the church is both a stable institution with inherited traditions and a dynamic movement of the Holy Spirit, we minister with balance, rooted in our ecclesial tradition yet working cooperatively with the body of Christ to reach our city with the gospel.* }

MOVEMENT

Our goal as Christians and Christian ministers is never simply to build our own tribe. Instead, we seek the peace and prosperity of the city or community in which we are placed, through a gospel movement led by the Holy Spirit. Movements like these do not follow a "bounded-set" approach in which you only work with others who can sign off on nearly all your distinctive beliefs and practices. Rather it follows a "centered-set" orientation in which you work most closely with those who face with you toward the same center. That center is a classic, orthodox understanding of the gospel of Jesus Christ, a common mission to reach and serve your city, and a commitment to have a generous, Christ-focused posture toward people who disagree with you. It's a type of movement that is missional, integrative, and dynamic.

There is an ongoing conversation today about the nature of the church's mission and its relationship to the work of individual Christians in the world. In part 6, **Missional Community**, we look at the history of the discussion, outline what it looks like to be a missional church today, offer some words of caution about the missional conversation, and suggest how churches can practically equip their people in missional living.

In part 7, we examine what it means to have an **Integrative Ministry**. This requires applying a Center Church theological vision to four "ministry fronts." Churches must first seek to *connect people to God* through evangelism and worship. Second, an integrated church will work to *connect people to one another* through community and discipleship. The church should also seek ways of *connecting people to the needs of the city* through mercy and justice ministries. Finally, churches must help *connect people to the culture* through the integration of faith and work.

In part 8, we conclude by discussing what it means to develop **Movement Dynamics** in your church and throughout the city. To faithfully connect the gospel with the culture we will need to develop intentional movements of churches planting new churches that faithfully proclaim God's truth and serve their communities.

chapter 19

THE SEARCH FOR THE MISSIONAL CHURCH

The word *missional* first became popular after the 1998 publication of the book titled *Missional Church* and in the years since it has been adopted and used widely.[1] Many are asking, "How can we really be missional?" An entire generation of younger evangelical leaders has grown up searching for the true missional church as if for the Holy Grail. Seemingly a dozen books come out each year with the word *missional* in their title, but a survey of these books reveals that the word has significantly different meanings and is used in different ways by different authors, organizations, and churches — leading to much confusion about what, exactly, the term *missional* means.

Before the term *missional* exploded throughout the Christian world, it was primarily used in mainline Protestant and ecumenical circles in a manner closely associated with the Latin phrase *missio Dei*. The phrase was originally coined to convey the teaching of Karl Barth about the action of God in the world. According to Lesslie Newbigin, the term *missio Dei* became prominent after the 1952 world mission conference in Willingen, Germany. It was a way of referring to the idea that God is active in the world, working to redeem the entire creation, and that the church's task is to participate in this mission.[2]

In his influential 1991 book *Transforming Mission*, David Bosch explained that the term *missio Dei* was firmly grounded in Trinitarian theology. Bosch noted that in the past, mission was largely viewed as a category of soteriology (as a way to save souls) or as a category of ecclesiology (as a way to expand the church). In contrast, the concept of *missio Dei* implied that mission should be "understood as being derived from the very nature of God … put in the context of the doctrine of the Trinity,

not of ecclesiology or soteriology."[3] The Trinity is, by nature, "sending." The Father sends the Son into the world to save it, and the Father and the Son send the Spirit into the world. And now, said Bosch, the Spirit is sending the church. In short, God does not merely send the church in mission. God already is in mission, and the church must join him. This also means, then, that the church does not simply have a missions department; it should wholly exist to *be* a mission.

At first glance, this seemed to be a strong and sound theology of mission. As time went on, however, it meant the church actually came to be seen as less relevant. Lesslie Newbigin wrote these words in the late 1970s:

> *If God is indeed the true missionary, it was said, our business is to not promote the mission of the church, but to get out into the world, find out "what God is doing in the world," and join forces with him. And "what God is doing" was generally thought to be in the secular rather than in the religious sectors of human life. The effect, of course, was to look for what seemed to be the rising powers and to identify Christians' missionary responsibility with support for a range of political and cultural developments.[4]*

Harvey Cox of Harvard Divinity School wrote, "What God is doing in the world is politics … Theology today must [therefore] be that reflection-in-action by which the church finds out what this politician-God is up to and moves in to work along with him."[5] In many mainline and ecumenical circles, *mission* came to mean working with secular human rights movements or rising left-wing political organizations. The results, Newbigin wrote, were "sometimes bizarre indeed. Even Chairman Mao's 'little red book' became almost a new Bible."[6] Newbigin, who was one of the key people involved in the forming of the World Council of Churches,

Though many evangelicals have appropriated his ideas, Lesslie Newbigin himself never claimed to be an evangelical. He openly repudiated the evangelical doctrine of Scripture and held to the Barthian idea that God's sovereign election of people was not to salvation but only to service. Newbigin, at a number of places in his writing, seems to veer close to universalism.

Nevertheless, as time went on, he became more and more critical of the liberal theology of the WCC. Originally, the WCC was committed to a "Christocentric universalism"; that is, the denominations of the WCC put all other doctrinal differences aside except their common commitment to Christ in order to make the unity of the church prominently visible as part of its mission to the world. After the appointment in 1992 of Konrad Raiser as general secretary of the WCC, the organization moved to a new position in which the only necessary basis for solidarity in mission was commitment to the transformation of society for justice and peace. Raiser defended his approach in *Ecumenism in Transition: A Paradigm Shift for the Ecumenical Movement?* Raiser's approach essentially left Christ out of the Trinity. He argued that the Father's will was for justice, peace, and the restoration of creation, and he sent his Spirit out into the world to accomplish this in all sorts of ways, many or most of them having nothing to do with Christianity or the church.

This was the very thing Newbigin had criticized in *The Open Secret*. Newbigin wrote a scathing review of Raiser's book in which he argued that Christ and his atoning death are central to Christian mission, and that, though "I do not want to endorse all that is done by

became increasingly concerned that the concept of the *missio Dei* left little need for the church. The church could not meet human needs as well as social service agencies could, nor could it change society as well as political parties and organizations could. So in this view, the church became inconsequential.

In *The Open Secret*, Newbigin criticized what he called the "secularization" of mission. He argued that conversions, the growth of the church, and the quality of Christian community were all critical and central to mission. Newbigin looked with favor on the theories of missiologist Donald McGavran, who taught that the purpose of mission was "church growth" in quality and quantity.[7] Nevertheless, Newbigin retained the term *missio Dei* and its original theological concept of a missionary God. He insisted that the church needed to grow through evangelism yet be involved in service and in the struggle for justice in the world as well. Newbigin sought to uphold the basic idea of the *missio Dei*, but he tried to save it from the excesses and distortions of the ecumenical movement.

THE NEWBIGIN-BOSCH RESCUE

Lesslie Newbigin had been a British missionary in India for several decades. When he returned to England in the mid-1970s, he saw the massive decline of the church and Christian influence that had occurred in his absence. At the time he left England, Western society's main cultural institutions still Christianized people, and the churches were easily gathering those who came to their doors through social expectation and custom. Churches in the West had always supported "missions" in overseas non-Christian cultures (such as India). There on the "mission field," churches functioned in a different way than they did in Europe and North America. Churches in India did not merely support missions or even do missions — they *were* missional in every aspect. They could not simply process Christianized people as churches did in the West. Rather, every aspect of their church life — worship, preaching, community life, and discipleship — had to be a form of mission.

For example, on the mission field, visitors to a worship service could not be expected to have any familiarity with Christianity. Therefore the worship and preaching had to address them in ways both comprehensible and challenging. On the mission field, believers lived in a society with radically different values from those they were taught in church. This made "life in the world" very complicated for Christians. Discipleship and training had to equip believers to answer many hostile questions from their neighbors. It also had to spell out Christian personal and corporate behavior patterns that distinguished them and showed society what the kingdom of God was all about. In other words, away from the West, churches did not simply have a missions department; Christians were "in mission" in every aspect of their public and private lives.

When he returned to England, Newbigin discovered that the ground had shifted. The cultural institutions of society were now indifferent or overtly hostile to Christian faith, and the number of people who went to church had plummeted. Western culture was fast becoming a non-Christian society — a "mission field" — but the churches were making little adjustment. While many Christian leaders were bemoaning the cultural changes, Western churches continued to minister as before — creating an environment in which only traditional and conservative

---

Rejecting the common view that the West was becoming a *secular* society without God, Newbigin viewed it as a *pagan* society filled with idols and false gods.

---

people would feel comfortable. They continued to disciple people by focusing on individual skills for their private lives (Bible study and prayer) but failed to train them to live distinctively Christian lives in a secular world — in the public arenas of politics, art, and business. All they preached and practiced assumed they were still in the Christian West, but the Christian West was vanishing.

the churches and movements that bear the name 'evangelical' ... it is a very important fact that these bodies are the ones that are growing and showing increasing breadth of vision in their approach to the whole range of contemporary human problems, while the bodies that hold the doctrinal position represented in this book are largely in decline."[8]

This was a disastrous tactic. Western churches, Newbigin argued, had to put the same kind of thought and effort into reaching their alien, non-Christian culture as the churches in India, China, and the rest of the world did. Over the last twenty-four years of his life, Newbigin argued tirelessly and trenchantly that the church had to come to grips with the fact that it was no longer functioning in "Christendom." Rejecting the common view that the West was becoming a *secular* society without God, Newbigin viewed it as a *pagan* society filled with idols and false gods.[9] He especially criticized the ideology of the European Enlightenment and its idolatrous commitment to the autonomy of human reason that had led to the illusion of neutral, value-free, objective knowledge. This commitment to reason had seduced Western cultural leaders into believing we did not need God or any particular religious faith in order to have a well-ordered, just, and moral society. Critical to the church's mission in the West, he said, was the unmasking of this false god by showing the futility of the "Enlightenment project" — the fruitless effort to find consensus on morality, right and wrong, justice, and human flourishing on the basis of secular reason.

In his books *The Open Secret*, *Foolishness to the Greeks*, and *The Gospel in a Pluralist Society*, Newbigin fleshed out what mission to Western society could look like.[10] It included a public apologetic against the autonomy of human reason that was overtly indebted to Alasdair MacIntyre and Michael Polanyi but that incorporated the approach of Abraham Kuyper and Herman Bavinck as well. It also emphasized equipping believers to integrate their

Newbigin gives his short list of ingredients for a "missionary encounter with Western culture" that includes the following elements:[11]

1. a new apologetic (that takes on the so-called neutrality of secular reason)
2. the teaching of the kingdom of God (that God wants not only to save souls but heal the whole creation)
3. earning the right to be heard through willingness to serve others sacrificially
4. equipping the laity to bring the implications of their faith into their public calling and so transform culture
5. a countercultural church community
6. a unified church that shows the world an overcoming of denominational divisions
7. a global church in which the older Western churches listen to the non-Western churches
8. courage

Compare this list with David Bosch's short list from *Believing in the Future* summarized in this section.

faith and work, changing society as they moved out into their vocations in the world, as well as emphasizing the importance of the Christian church as a "hermeneutic of the gospel." Newbigin believed that the love, justice, and peace that ought to characterize the Christian counterculture were primary ways of bearing witness to God in a pluralistic society. With these last two emphases — the renewal of society and the church as a "contrast" community — Newbigin combines several of the cultural approaches we looked at earlier.

Most important, Newbigin proposed something of a middle way (though he never used that term)

with the *missio Dei*. In his critical review of Konrad Raiser's book defending the approach of the World Council of Churches, he wrote the following:

> *Raiser, of course, is absolutely right to protest against an ecclesiocentric concept of mission, as though the church were the author and the goal of mission. But this whole vision is too much shaped by the ideology of the 1960s with its faith in the secular, and in human power to solve problems. The thesis is heavily marked by a model ... that interprets all situations in terms of the oppressor and the oppressed and that tends to interpret the struggles of the oppressed as the instrument of redemption. This model owed not a little to Marxist thought, and the collapse of Marxism as a world power has created a new situation with which the WCC has to come to terms.[12]*

Newbigin rejected the direct identification of God's redemption with any movement that improves socioeconomic well-being. He rightly said that the idea of defining mission as "what God is doing out in history" too closely draws its origins from the Marxist ideas of class struggle as the meaning of history. But then Newbigin sought to strike a note of balance:

> *The (literally) crucial matter is the centrality of Jesus and his atoning work on the cross, that work by which he has won lordship over the church and the world ...*
>
> *It is one of the most pressing tasks for the immediate future to rediscover a doctrine of redemption that sees the cross not as the banner of the oppressed against the oppressor but as the action of God that brings both judgment and redemption for all who will accept it, yet does not subvert the proper struggle for the measure of justice that is possible in a world of sinful human beings.[13]*

Here Newbigin takes the struggle for justice in the world out from the center of the meaning of redemption. Redemption is first of all the action of God in Christ, and this action calls for a decision. It must be accepted, not rejected.[14] And yet there is still a place for us to struggle for the "measure of justice" in this world.

In his book *Transforming Mission*, David Bosch further develops Newbigin's idea of the *missio Dei*.

In Bosch's examination of Luke's theology of mission, he sees a charge to proclaim Christ and the call for conversion, as well as to show God's concern for justice for the poor. In his *Believing in the Future*, Bosch goes further in spelling out a vision for mission in a post-Christian West. He restates the core idea of the *missio Dei* — that God's mission is to restore creation, and the church is called to participate in this mission. Bosch says that mission is not just "recruitment to our brand of religion; it is alerting people to the universal reign of God."[15] Then he suggests how this may be done. First, he says, we must avoid two opposing errors: (1) trying to re-create a Christian society (the mistake of medieval Christendom) and (2) withdrawal from society into the "spiritual realm" (the mistake of modernity).[16] Second, we must learn how to publicly and prophetically challenge the idol of autonomous reason and its results.[17] Third, we must take pains to make our churches into contrast societies, countercultures that show society what human life looks like free from the idols of race, wealth, sex, power, and individual autonomy.[18] So we contextualize our message in ways that avoid syncretism on the one extreme and irrelevance on the other; we better equip the laity for their public callings; and we cultivate vital, life-shaping worship as the dynamic heart of mission. These steps show the world a countercultural model of society and shape people so that the gospel influences how they live in the world.[19] Finally, we must model to the world as much unity between churches as is practically possible.

An insight animating all of this work is the idea of *the cultural captivity of the church* in the West. Bosch, like Newbigin, is especially critical of Enlightenment rationalism and its various effects in Western culture — materialism, consumerism, individualism, and the breakdown of community. He maintains that the church is too deeply shaped by the spirit of the age, in *both* its conservative and liberal forms. In its liberal form, it has bought uncritically into a secular account of things, de-supernaturalizing the gospel so that the Spirit's work is seen mainly in secular movements of liberation, thus turning the liberal mainline churches into little

more than social service centers where the language of secular rights activists reigns. In its conservative form, it has bought uncritically into the idea of religion as the fulfillment of individual consumer needs, thus turning the conservative church into something like felt-need shopping centers where the language of modern therapy and marketing reigns. People see Christ as a way to self-fulfillment and prosperity, not as a model for radical service to others. Both wings of the Christian church are, then, captive to the reigning idols of Western culture.[20] They are failing to challenge these idols in their preaching and practice.

Because of the influential writings of Newbigin and Bosch, a new, more fully realized understanding of the *missio Dei* was developing by the mid-1990s. It sought to avoid the secularization of mission found in the liberal churches. The overarching narrative was still that God is in mission to renew the whole creation, but the new view stressed the public proclamation of Christ as Lord and Hope of the world and therefore the necessity of both conversion and the growth of the church. This new, rehabilitated view of the *missio Dei* began to capture the attention of many Christians outside of the liberal mainline who were struggling with the question of how to relate to an increasingly post-Christian culture.

THE MISSIONAL CHURCH MOVEMENT TODAY

When *Missional Church* (edited by Darrell Guder) first appeared in 1998, it built on this new understanding of *missio Dei* that had been previously developed by Lesslie Newbigin and David Bosch. The book laid out the same dilemma: the culture was no longer Christianized and now the church was "on the mission field to the modern world," yet the church was captive to the culture of modernity and thus had no real alternative to offer. The church must therefore reform itself and discover new ways to engage culture. But how was this to be done? Again, the answers sounded many of the same themes as Newbigin and Bosch: the church as a contrast community, contextualization of the message, concern not only for church growth but also

What caused Christianity to lose so much influence in the West, especially after World War II? Lesslie Newbigin understands historical patterns as being caused by ideas and intellectual trends working their way out through a society's institutions. He blames the outworking of the eighteenth-century Enlightenment—promoting the sufficiency of individual human reason with no need for faith in God—for a great deal of the shift.

Ross Douthat's book *Bad Religion* provides a somewhat different and illuminating account of the loss of Christendom in the United States after World War II. He attributes the change to five major social catalysts:[21]

1. political polarization between left and right, which took many churches captive (mainline Protestants toward the left, evangelicals toward the right) and weakened credibility

2. the sexual revolution and the birth control pill that fueled it

3. the dawn of globalization and the impression that Christianity was imperialistically Western

4. the enormous growth in the kind of material prosperity that always works against faith

5. the loss of the elites and the academic cultural institutions they control (see ch. 2, "The Locust Years")

I see no reason why Newbigin's history-of-thought approach and Douthat's sociology-of-knowledge approach cannot both be right. A third strain of analysis could easily find the faults within the church itself. As H. Richard Niebuhr points out in his essay "Toward the Independence of the Church," the church becomes weak and even corrupt when it becomes successful in a culture.[25]

for justice. The book's theological commitments were firmly based on the concept of the mission as participation in the purpose of the triune God to redeem creation.[22]

The time for these ideas was ripe, and the term "missional church" became popular in evangelical circles. The evangelical church as a whole was becoming aware of the cultural shift happening around them and the growing ineffectiveness of much of the traditional ministry approach. Some in the mainline church were becoming disenchanted with the emptiness of ecumenical theology, but they were either unable or not interested to join the evangelical movement. Many of these church leaders picked up the basic vision for the missional church in Western culture found in Guder's book.

Many people supplemented the ideas of the *missio Dei* and the missional church with other theological and cultural content, which has led to a dizzying variety of sometimes contradictory definitions of *missional*.

But many people picked up the ideas of the *missio Dei* and the missional church and supplemented them with other theological and cultural content, which has led to a dizzying variety of different and sometimes contradictory definitions of the term *missional*. Craig Van Gelder has written an entire volume just trying to categorize the different approaches and definitions around the idea. He and his colleague Dwight Zscheile have discerned four broad, overlapping "streams" of the missional conversation:

1. Being missional is being *evangelistic*. Some churches (and authors) have simply adopted *missional* as a synonym for being highly committed to evangelism and foreign missions. Like all expressions of being missional, the starting point is how our culture has changed, how outreach requires more ingenuity and diligence than ever, and the assertion that every Christian is a missionary. Those in this category also usually embrace a somewhat more holistic approach to outreach, encouraging various forms of community service. However, the underlying theology is quite traditional. Mission is largely conceived as bringing people into individual salvation through the church. The distinctive ideas of the *missio Dei* — the work of God's Spirit in the world to restore all creation and the cultural captivity of the Western church — are missing.[23]

2. Being missional is being *incarnational*. Another set of voices criticizes the Christendom model of church as "attractional." The attractional model is based on non-Christians coming or being invited into the programs and ministries of the church. They come in to hear the preaching, to participate in programs that minister to their felt needs, or to attend for baptisms, weddings, and funerals. This, it is said, is now an obsolete model (though it still works in more traditional parts of the West and with the shrinking body of "Christianized" non-Christians).

In place of the attractional model, they recommend an incarnational model, where Christians live geographically close to each other, create a thick and rich community among themselves, and then become deeply involved in the civic and corporate life of their neighborhood or city. Church planting in this paradigm does not need to begin with a full-time minister, a core group, and a worship service. Instead, a few Christian families move into a neighborhood and fully participate in its life, discover the needs of the citizens, and begin to meet them in Christ's name. Christian community grows organically, gradually coming to include many of the nonbelievers who labor for peace and justice in the neighborhood. In general, the adoption of this view leads to the proliferation of informal house churches.[24]

3. Being missional is being *contextual*. Some thinkers put more emphasis on the shifts in late modern and postmodern culture, the cultural captivity of the church, and therefore the need to contextualize every part of the church's ministry so it engages this post-Christendom reality. This approach includes aspects of the first two views, as thinkers in this category emphasize being ingeniously evangelistic and incarnational in the com-

For example, why did the mainline and the evangelical church get co-opted by American political parties and lose credibility? Was it not due to a lack of robust, vital orthodoxy within these bodies? For more, see the discussion of Niebuhr's essay and this dynamic in part 5 of this book (pp. 237 – 38). If all these approaches are indeed complementary and their conclusions are on point, Christianity in the West has been the victim of "a perfect storm" of trends, factors, and forces.

munity — but they go further. In this view it is possible to deepen Christian community and be involved in community service and yet still be a subculture that does not really engage post-Christian Western society. To be a truly missional church involves deep reflection on culture and discovering creative ways of communication and church practice that both adapt to culture and challenge it. Those who fall into this category appreciate the incarnational house church model but see it as one good and possible ministry form among many others.

Van Gelder and Zscheile list authors who advance this view, and many of them seem to assume a more traditional evangelical theology than those in the final category.[26] Still, they all accept that the basic measures proposed by Newbigin for a "missionary encounter with Western culture" — a new apologetic, the church as contrast community, holistic outreach, engaging culture through vocations — are correct. In their own works, they seek to flesh out what Newbigin's measures might look like.

4. Being missional is being *reciprocal and communal*. This group of thinkers applauds the emphases of the other three. They are glad to affirm that every Christian is in mission. They support the idea of the church as far more incarnationally involved in the life of its community, and they believe firmly in the importance of contextualization and cultural engagement. They do not, however, believe the others have taken the implications of the *missio*

SELF AND THE FULFILLMENT OF ITS NEEDS

Alan Roxburgh and Scott Boren have more to say about the impact of individualism:

> When we attend to the way people talk about the gospel, it does not take long to discover just how much the focus lies on meeting personal needs. During testimony sessions about mission trips, people explain how it changed them or how it gave them an experience they will never forget. In modernity the purpose of life is to fulfill one's personal destiny, goals, or needs … For moderns, it's almost impossible to read the biblical narrative without assimilating it to the modern categories of the self and the fulfillment of its needs.
>
> In Scripture, mission calls a people into a radically different vision on a journey bigger and other than ourselves. Scripture calls us into the memory of an amazing story … not for ourselves but for the sake of the world. The strangeness of this story is its illogical and irrepressible meaning: find life by losing it; only by leaving the places of security are the purposes of God discovered. The God revealed in Scripture gives himself away for the sake of the world.[27]

Dei far enough. They believe *missio Dei* calls us to a careful reworking of both our theology and practice.

Those who adopt this approach have arrived at two conclusions. First, if God already has a mission, then a church should not do mission by designing methods to draw people into their services. It must be responsive to what God is already doing in the world. Alan Roxburgh, one of the original essayists in *Missional Church*, writes that the one question missional churches ask over and over is this: "What is God up to in this neighborhood?" The missional church listens to people in the community and "becomes open to being surprised by God's purposes."[28]

Rather than simply announcing to the world what it needs to know, the church listens and learns what God is doing and then gets involved.

Second, in order to overcome the Enlightenment's individualism, the church must redefine sin, mission, and salvation in corporate and communal terms. Rather than speaking of sin primarily as an offense against a holy God, sin is seen, in horizontal terms, as the violation of God's shalom in the world through selfishness, violence, injustice, and pride.[29] Rather than speaking of the cross as primarily the place where Jesus satisfied the wrath of God on our sin, Jesus' death is seen as the occasion when the powers of this world fell on Jesus and were defeated.[30] Mission, then, is ultimately not about getting individuals right with God but about incorporating them into a new community that partners with God in redeeming social structures and healing the world.[31]

WHAT DO THESE APPROACHES HAVE IN COMMON?

Many conservative evangelicals reject the term *missional* because of its association with emerging church thinkers such as Brian McLaren, because of its connection to the ecumenical movement and the theology of Karl Barth, or simply because it is such a hard word to define.[32]

I sympathize. But the fact remains that a large number of Christian believers today are on an earnest search for the missional church, regardless of whether or not they use the term. Those who hold to conservative doctrines often inhabit the first category — "missional as evangelistic" — and are now beginning to populate the second and third categories — "missional as incarnational" and "missional as contextual." Those with liberal and mainline church beliefs are also found in the second and third categories but are especially attracted to the fourth category ("missional as reciprocal and communal").[33]

Despite very real and important differences among these four missional streams, I believe they have important things in common. In the remainder of the chapter, I'll summarize the primary areas of consensus and strength in the missional conversation.

First, we have entered a post-Christian or post-Christendom age. For centuries in the Western world, the Christian church had a privileged place, but this is no longer true. Rather than being a force at the center of culture, Christianity has moved to the margins. There is broad recognition that the church had allowed cultural institutions to do a lot of its heavy lifting, infusing people with a broadly Christian way of thinking about things — respect for the Bible, allegiance to the Ten Commandments, commitment to the ethical teachings of the Gospels; belief in a personal God, an afterlife, a judgment day, and moral absolutes. But no longer can we expect people who already have these basic beliefs to simply come to church through social pressure and out of custom. The times have changed.

CULTURAL CAPTIVITY OF THE CHURCH

Second, those in the incarnational, contextual, and communal/reciprocal streams further recognize the cultural captivity of the church and the need to contextualize the gospel message so it is both comprehensible and challenging for those in a pluralistic, late-modern society. Many call for a gospel that escapes cultural captivity by chal-

> To the self-absorbed culture we say, "You must lose yourself — in service to Christ and others — to truly find yourself." To the rationalistic culture we say, "You cannot have the things you want — meaning, dignity, hope, character, shared values, and community — without faith."

lenging the Enlightenment individualism of both secular people and certain members of evangelical churches. Alan Roxburgh and Scott Boren write, "Modernity replaces mission with self-actualization of the expressive, autonomous individual,"[34] and it is this individualism that must be challenged and confronted. Newbigin argues that the church must also unmask the autonomy of human reason. Remember that contextualization means showing

how only in Christ can the baseline narratives of a culture be resolved. To the self-absorbed culture we say, "You must lose yourself — in service to Christ and others — to truly find yourself." To the rationalistic culture we say, "You cannot have the things you want — meaning, dignity, hope, character, shared values, and community — without faith."

SENT OUT TO BE A BLESSING

Third, all those pursuing the missional church also believe that Christian mission is more than just a department of the church, more than just the work

> In Christendom, you could afford to train people solely in prayer, Bible study, and evangelism — skills for their private lives — because they were not facing radically non-Christian values in their public lives.

of trained professionals. The biblical God is by nature a sending God, a missionary God.[35] The Father sends the Son; the Son sends the Spirit and his disciples into the world. Therefore the whole church is in mission; every Christian is in mission. God never calls you in to bless you without also sending you out to be a blessing (Gen 12:1 – 3; cf. 1 Pet 2:9). So a Christian is not a spiritual consumer, coming in to get his or her emotional needs met and then going home. A missional church, then, is one that trains and encourages its people to be in mission as individuals and as a body. All of the voices in the missional conversation agree that the church must not be *only* attractional; it also must equip and send the laity into the world to minister.

One implication of this view is that missional churches must equip laypeople both for evangelistic witness and for public life and vocation. In Christendom, you could afford to train people solely in prayer, Bible study, and evangelism — skills for their private lives — because they were not facing radically non-Christian values in their public lives. In a missional church, all people need theological education to "think Christianly" about everything and to act with Christian distinctiveness. They need to know which cultural practices reflect common grace and should be embraced, which are antithetical to the gospel and must be rejected, and which practices can be adapted or revised.[36]

A CONTRAST COMMUNITY

Finally, most missional thinkers agree that in our Western culture, we must be *a contrast community*, *a counterculture*. The quality, distinctiveness, and beauty of our communal life must be a major part of our witness and mission to the world. Jesus stated that the quality and visibility of Christians' love for each other will show the world that the Father *sent* him (John 17:20 – 21). In other words, our mission cannot go forward without Christians being involved not only in calling people to conversion but also in service to the community and in doing justice.[37] This is part of the balance Newbigin struck. While many in the liberal church redefine evangelism as seeking a more just society and many conservative churches see Christians' work in the world as strictly proclamation and conversion, most missional thinkers agree that the witness of Christians must be in both word and deed.

Part of being this kind of counterculture involves loving the city — its culture and people. Often, churches gather around them people who do not like the city or who do not expect to stay there. This inclination can occur among conservative churches that despise the secular, immoral society around them or with churches comprised largely of expatriates or immigrants from other countries. Such churches are often indifferent or hostile to their own locale, and as a result, most of the long-term residents of the community will feel unwelcome in these churches. A missional church enjoys, cares for, and prays for its city.

Another aspect of this contrast community is unity across church communities and denominations. In Christendom, when "everyone was a Christian," it was perhaps useful for a church to define itself primarily in contrast with other churches. Today, however, it is much more illuminating and helpful for a church to define itself in relationship to the values of the secular culture. If we spend our time bashing and criticizing other kinds of churches, we simply play into the common defeater that all Christians are intolerant. While it is right to align ourselves with denominations that share many of our distinctives, at the local level we should cooperate with, reach out to, and support the other congregations and ministries in our local area. To do so will raise many thorny issues, of course, but our bent should be in the direction of cooperation.

I believe these points of common ground in the missional conversation are sound and generally consistent with a Center Church theological vision. I would use the phrase "missional church" less cautiously and more expansively if these were indeed understood to be the key aspects of the definition.

Still, as fruitful as the search for the missional

WHAT IS A "MISSIONAL" SMALL GROUP?

A missional mind-set can and should pervade every area of the church. For example, let's consider what a missional small group could look like. It is more than just a group of people involved in a specific evangelism program (although that is a good thing). Rather, its members love the city and talk positively about it; they speak in language that is not filled with pious tribal or technical terms and phrases, nor do they use disdainful or combative language. In their Bible study, they apply the gospel to the core concerns and stories of the people in their culture. This is a group obviously interested in and engaged with the literature, art, and thought of the surrounding culture, and they can discuss it appreciatively and yet critically. They exhibit deep concern for the poor, are generous with their money, model purity and respect toward the opposite sex, and show humility toward people of other races and cultures, as well as toward other Christians and churches.

church has been, it has not always taken the church into friendly or helpful territory. Significant and important differences exist among various groupings in the missional conversation. In the next chapter, I'll look at key dangers and imbalances induced by some of the thinkers and practitioners in the missional conversation and suggest some course corrections.

QUESTIONS FOR DISCUSSION AND REFLECTION

1. Keller writes, "The word [*missional*] has significantly different meanings and is used in different ways by different authors, organizations, and churches — leading to much confusion about what, exactly, the term *missional* means." How have you used or defined *missional*? How has this chapter changed or contributed to your understanding of this term?

2. The concept of *missio dei* suggests that "God does not merely send the church in mission. God already is in mission, and the church must join him." What do you believe is the mission of God and what role does the church have in that mission? How would you distinguish between the mission of God and the mission of the church?

3. Of the four understandings of "missional" presented in this chapter, which most closely aligns with your own? What is it about the other understandings that you find objectionable?

4. Four common emphases characterize those who embrace the idea of being missional:

   - acknowledging that we have entered a post-Christian age in the West
   - recognizing the cultural captivity of the church and the need to contextualize the gospel for a pluralistic society
   - affirming that mission is the job of every Christian
   - calling the church to be a contrast community

   What are some of the unique elements of each emphasis that are discussed in this chapter? Which of these resonated most with you as you read about them? Which is the most difficult to persuade others of within your community?

1. Darrell L. Guder, ed., *Missional Church: A Vision for the Sending of the Church in North America* (Grand Rapids: Eerdmans, 1998).
2. Lesslie Newbigin, *The Open Secret: An Introduction to the Theology of Mission*, rev. ed. (Grand Rapids: Eerdmans, 1995), 18.
3. David Bosch, *Transforming Mission: Paradigm Shifts in Theology of Mission* (Maryknoll, N.Y.: Orbis, 1991), 389 – 90 (the quotes in this paragraph are from these pages).
4. Newbigin, *Open Secret*, 18.
5. Harvey Cox, *The Secular City* (New York: Macmillan, 1965), 255.
6. Newbigin, *Open Secret*, 18.
7. Ibid., 121 – 23.
8. Lesslie Newbigin, "Ecumenical Amnesia," in *International Bulletin of Missionary Research* 18.1 (January 1994): 2 – 5, www.newbigin.net/assets/pdf/93reit.pdf (accessed February 15, 2012).
9. In *The Open Secret*, Newbigin writes of "the paganism that was showing its power in the heart of old Christendom" (p. 8).
10. *The Open Secret* (Grand Rapids: Eerdmans, 1978); *Foolishness to the Greeks* (Grand Rapids: Eerdmans, 1986); *The Gospel in a Pluralist Society* (Grand Rapids: Eerdmans, 1991).
11. Lesslie Newbigin, "Can the West Be Converted?" *International Bulletin of Missionary Research* 11.1 (January 1987): 2 – 7.
12. Newbigin, "Ecumenical Amnesia," 4 – 5, www.newbigin.net/assets/pdf/93reit.pdf (accessed February 15, 2012).
13. Ibid.
14. Newbigin's phrase "judgment and redemption for all who will accept it" could be interpreted to mean that all people who accept it receive both conviction of sin (judgment) and the acceptance of grace.
15. David Bosch, *Believing in the Future: Toward a Missiology of Western Culture* (Valley Forge, Pa.: Trinity Press International, 1995), 33.
16. Ibid., 33 – 35.
17. Ibid., 47 – 53.
18. Ibid., 56 – 57.
19. Ibid., 55 – 62. Bosch lists many of these ingredients briefly at the end of the book. He includes addressing ecological issues and listening carefully and respectfully to the theological insights and personal experiences of the churches of the Third World.
20. David Bosch criticized not only the practices of both the liberal and the conservative churches but also their doctrine, particularly their view of Scripture, as being shaped by modernity. For example, in *Transforming Mission* (p. 342), he wrote, "The subject-object dichotomy [of the Enlightenment] meant that, in admittedly very opposite ways, the Bible and, in fact, the Christian faith as such, became objectified. Liberals sovereignly placed themselves above the biblical text, extracting ethical codes from it, while fundamentalists tended to turn the Bible into a fetish and apply it mechanically to every context, particularly as regards the 'Great Commission.'"
21. Ross Douthat, *Bad Religion: How We Became a Nation of Heretics* (New York: Free Press, 2012).
22. The book is a compendium of essays from different authors and so does not speak always with one voice. While Newbigin himself was able to mix Transformationist measures with Counterculturalist measures in his agenda for cultural engagement, many of the contributors to *Missional Church* fell more into one camp or the other. For a good discussion of the book and its message and the differences among the authors, see Craig Van Gelder and Dwight J. Zscheile, *The Missional Church in Perspective: Mapping Trends and Shaping the Conversation* (Grand Rapids: Baker, 2011).
23. Van Gelder and Zscheile call this group "'Discovering' Missional," who "tend to utilize missional language to promote a more traditional understanding of mission" (p. 71), i.e., those who consider "mission" to be primarily an expanding of the church rather than joining with God to renew the creation. (The label is a bit patronizing, since the authors depict them as still discovering the concept but not really understanding it.) They cite Frank Page, *The Nehemiah Factor* (Birmingham, Ala.: New Hope, 2008), and Rick Rusaw and Eric Swanson, *The Externally Focused Church* (Loveland, Colo.: Group, 2004) as examples of this group (see lists of authors on pp. 72 – 74).
24. The seminal text for this approach is Michael Frost and Alan Hirsch, *The Shaping of Things to Come: Innovation and Mission for the 21ˢᵗ-Century Church* (Grand Rapids: Baker, 2004). See also the books and website of David Fitch of Reclaiming the Mission (www.reclaimingthemission.com). I also recommend the books of Tim Chester and Steve Timmis; see esp. *Everyday Church: Mission by Being Good Neighbours* (Nottingham, UK: Inter-Varsity, 2011).
25. H. Richard Niebuhr, "Toward the Independence of the Church," in *The Church Against the World*, ed. H. Richard Niebuhr, Wilhelm Pauck, and Francis P. Miller (Chicago: Willett, 1935), www.religion-online.org/showchapter.asp?title=412&C=194 (accessed February 7, 2012).
26. Van Gelder and Zscheile list Jim Belcher of Deep Church, Dan Kimball, and me, among others (p. 87). I would include Ed Stetzer here as well.

27. Ibid., 59–60.

28. Alan J. Roxburgh and M. Scott Boren, *Introducing the Missional Church: What It Is, Why It Matters, and How to Become One* (Grand Rapids: Baker, 2009), 93. Van Gelder and Zscheile (*Missional Church in Perspective*) state that a missional theology calls the church to "reciprocity, mutuality, and vulnerability" (p. 133); because the Trinity is seen as a nonhierarchical, mutual community of persons, the missional church must have a reciprocal, open, and dynamic relationship to the world (p. 110).

29. For one of many places where this horizontal reworking of sin and redemption is carried out, see N. T. Wright, *Evil and the Justice of God* (Downers Grove, Ill.: InterVarsity, 2006). Wright states, "Evil is the force of anti-creation, anti-life, the force which opposes and seeks to deface and destroy God's good world of space, time, and matter, and above all God's image-bearing human creatures ... [But] it is true, as the Gospel writers have been trying to tell us, that evil at all levels and of all sorts had done its worst and that Jesus ... supremely on the cross had dealt with it, taken its full force, exhausted it" (p. 89).

30. See Wright, *Evil and the Justice of God*. "The New Testament writers report ... the remarkable sign of evil doing its worst and being exhausted. When Jesus suffered, he did not curse, and when he was reviled, he did not revile in return" (pp. 88–89). "The death of Jesus is seen ... as the means whereby evil is ... defeated and its power is exhausted" (p. 136).

31. Van Gelder (*Missional Church in Perspective*), who puts himself in this category, criticizes thinkers who don't embrace the implications in the *missio Dei* of what he calls "the social Trinity." He argues that putting the emphasis on the fact that God is a community of mutual love who is redeeming all of creation will keep us from seeing "individual Christians as the focus of God's redemptive work" and will strengthen "the communal nature of the church as well as the corporate nature of discipleship"(p. 84).

32. Despite the fact that Brian McLaren and others in the Emergent network adopted the term, Alan Roxburgh and Scott Boren (*Introducing the Missional Church*, 47–62) show that the emerging church and the missional church are not the same thing. Indeed, as I will argue, it is possible to properly use the term *missional* without buying into the mainline/ecumenical definition of the *missio Dei*.

   Much of the work of the mainline-oriented missional church thinkers (represented by the "reciprocal and communal" group) seems to have Karl Barth's shadow behind much of it. Barth reworks the doctrine of election so that (in his view) all people are elect in Christ, even those who do not believe, so that all human beings are essentially *simul justus et peccator*. There is much controversy over how Barth's view works itself out in ministry practice, but many who accept it deem it inappropriate to view non-Christians as being under the wrath of God and in need of personal reconciliation. It is not hard to see how this would move the focus of a church's ministry from calling individuals to conversion to building community and healing society.

33. Conservative evangelicals in particular should bear in mind that the theology of Lesslie Newbigin and David Bosch, while not evangelical, may still be appreciated as a reaction and critique of the thoroughly secular theology of many of the churches that make up the World Council of Churches.

34. Roxburgh, *Introducing the Missional Church*, 59.

35. See John R. W. Stott, "The Living God Is a Missionary God," in *You Can Tell the World*, ed. James E. Berney (Downers Grove, Ill.: InterVarsity, 1979), 3–9, www.963missions.com/Stott_TheLivingGod.pdf (first presented at the 1976 Urbana Student Missions Convention).

36. See more on this subject in part 5 ("Cultural Engagement") and in part 7 ("Integrative Ministry"), as well as a full treatment in chapter 21 ("Equipping People for Missional Living").

37. Those who lean toward a conservative theology may say (as I would) that while the mission of the church qua church (the institutional church) is to evangelize and make disciples, individual Christians must be well-known for their sacrificial service to the poor and common good if a society is going to give the gospel a hearing.

CENTERING THE MISSIONAL CHURCH

Though a clear and valuable benefit exists in identifying the common ground of the missional church, the range of differences among various definitions and viewpoints is great, and many aspects of the visions for "missional living" contradict each other. Everyone involved in the missional conversation concludes that others are making significant errors, and I am no different in this regard. As I have observed the ongoing conversation about the missional church and tested many of these ideas as a practitioner, I have three primary concerns with the way some segments of the missional conversation are appropriating the core insights outlined at the end of the previous chapter. We need to learn how to discern and avoid each of these problems if we are to be effective in developing a ministry with a Center Church orientation.

PROBLEM #1: NOT COMPREHENSIVE ENOUGH

First, we examine the branch of the conversation that sees the missional church as simply being evangelistic. I agree that any missional church must be pervasively, intensely evangelistic in the common use of the word — we must call people to personal conversion. However, the typical evangelical gospel presentation is too shallow. It speaks cursorily about a God whom we have sinned against, a Savior who died for our sins, and a call to believe in this Savior. The simplicity of this communication presumes that those listening share the same essential understanding of the words *God* and *sin* as the speaker.

But what if a growing majority of people outside the church live by such a radically different view of life that much of what is now said and done by the Christian community is inexplicable or even deeply offensive to them? What if many listeners hold a profoundly different understanding of the concepts of God, truth, right and wrong, freedom, virtue, and sin? What if their approaches to reality, human nature and destiny, and human community are wholly different from our own?

For decades, this has been the situation facing Christian churches in many areas around the world — places such as India, Iran, and Japan. Evangelism in these environments involves a lengthy process in which nonbelievers have to be invited into a Christian community that bridges the gap between Christian truth and the culture around it. Every part of a church's life — its worship, community, public discourse, preaching, and education — has to assume the presence of nonbelievers from the surrounding culture. The aesthetics of its worship have to reflect the sensibilities of the culture and yet show how Christian belief shapes and is expressed through them. Its preaching and teaching have to show how the hopes of this culture's people can find fulfillment only in Christ. Most of all, such a congregation's believers have to reflect the demographic makeup of the surrounding community, thereby giving non-Christian neighbors attractive and challenging glimpses of what they would look like as Christians.

One reason much of the evangelical church in the United States has not yet experienced the same precipitous decline as the Protestant churches of Europe and Canada is that, unlike these places, the U.S. still includes sizable remnants of Christendom. We have places where the informal public culture (though not the formal public institutions) still stigmatizes non-Christian beliefs and behavior. There is, according to journalist Michael Wolff, a "fundamental schism in American cultural, political, and economic life. There's the quicker-growing, economically vibrant … morally relativist, urban-oriented, culturally adventuresome, sexually polymorphous, and ethnically diverse nation … And there's the small-town, nuclear-family, religiously oriented, white-centric other America, [with] … its diminishing cultural and economic force … two countries."[1]

To reach this growing post-Christendom society in the West will obviously take more than what we ordinarily call an *evangelistic* church; it will take a *missional* church. This church's worship is missional in that it makes sense to nonbelievers in that culture, even while it challenges and shapes Christians with the gospel.[2] Its people are missional in that they are so outwardly focused, so involved in addressing the needs of the local community, that the church is well-known for its compassion. The members of a missional church also know how to

---

The idea that "to be missional is to be evangelistic" is too narrow. A missional church is not *less* than an evangelistic church, but it is much more.

---

contextualize the gospel, carefully challenging yet also appealing to the baseline cultural narratives of the society around them.[3] Finally, because of the attractiveness of its people's character and lives, a missional church will always have some outsiders who are drawn into its community to incubate and explore the Christian faith in its midst.

So the idea that "to be missional is to be evangelistic" is too narrow. A missional church is not *less* than an evangelistic church, but it is much more.

PROBLEM #2: TOO TIED TO A PARTICULAR FORM

A second major problem is the tendency to put too much emphasis on a particular church form. Many who participate in missional church discussions insist that the church should be incarnational rather than attractional.[4] If taken as a broad principle, this is a correct statement. That is, if an attractional church is understood as tribal, as showing

little concern for the broader community, drawing people in from the world and absorbing them into internal church programs that only meet their felt needs rather than equipping them to serve — then a missional church should not be attractional.[5] And if *incarnational* can be defined as a church that listens to its community to learn what its needs are, speaks and interacts with its community with respect, equips and sends its people out to love and serve — then all missional churches should be incarnational.

However, many argue that any church that bases its ministry on bringing people in to a large weekly meeting cannot be missional. David Fitch, a pastor in the missional community Life on the Vine, writes the following about megachurches:

> Mega-church … packages a service to speak a message that they assume can make sense to anonymous guests. Missional assumes the opposite — that people have no language or history by which to understand the words "Jesus is Lord." Therefore we must incarnate/embody the gospel for it to make sense. A packaged entertaining speaker/program every Sunday simply cannot do the job of communicating the gospel in post-Christendom.[6]

Fitch asserts that non-Christians in a post-Christian society will be so completely unable to understand the gospel that any mere verbal presentation of it will not be compelling or understood. In addition, he argues that any church that focuses on a large weekly gathering will by necessity require too much time and money for the church to be missional. For Fitch, to be missional is "to spend most of one's time and ministry outside the four walls of a church building, inhabiting a neighborhood learning who they are, what they do, and where the spiritual/holistic needs are. Its rhythm contradicts the rhythm of an attractional church."[7]

Many believe, along with Fitch, that a missional church cannot take the form of a large church or even of a small traditional church that is centered on a weekly worship and preaching service. Those who hold this view organize either as small house churches (ten to fifty people) with bivocational pastors and leaders or as a network of midsize house churches that gather for larger "attractional" meetings occasionally.

A practical resource for creating a missional church is Mike Breen's *Launching Missional Communities: A Field Guide*.[8] Key attributes of a missional community include:

- **Size.** A missional community is larger than six to twelve persons, the size of a typical small cell group. Small groups tend to be inwardly focused; also, most small groups do not endure for a long time. Instead, missional communities of twenty to fifty persons are more like the size of an extended family. Groupings of this size are said to be "large enough to dare; small enough to care."

- **Focus.** These communities meet regularly for fellowship and mutual edification and also to take responsibility to serve and reach a particular neighborhood or group of people. Examples mentioned in *Launching Missional Communities* include serving a Slovakian gypsy population, Somalian refugees, university students, a wealthy neighborhood, a poor neighborhood, young parents, Iranians (including Muslims), and parents of teenagers.

- **Center of gravity.** "The center of gravity" in this church form is the midsize missional community, *not* the large, weekly worship gathering. Small groups are optional, and large worship gatherings are often episodic or nonexistent. Breen suggests that missional communities meet with others for preaching and celebration in a Sunday large worship gathering "no less than once a month and no more than three times a month."

Michael Frost and Alan Hirsch address this model:

Most of the emerging churches we have been able to uncover are quite intentional about developing smaller communities ... It is also much closer to New Testament ecclesiology and missions practice. The household church unit was the primary unit of missional community in the New Testament. Today whether they meet in homes like the contemporary house church movement or not is irrelevant. What is important is that they tend to be smaller, more diverse, less organized, life-oriented, missional, relational, faith communities, not requiring their own specialized churchy buildings.[9]

I believe this view presents too rigid an understanding of the missional church. I pastored a small church in a small, working-class town for nearly ten years. My church naturally had the kind of characteristics that house churches are seeking to create through intentional planning. Missional communities seek to re-create the *oikos* — the large, extended family of children, grandchildren, relatives, business associates, and neighbors that constituted most churches in the New Testament — and insist that ministry should be informal, relational, and organic.[10]

However, the midsized groups that are gathered into missional communities are not truly *oikoi*. They are usually not related to each other by a variety of blood ties, do not work in the same shops and plants, have not gone to the same schools, and have not belonged to the same clubs and civic organizations — which is how people in a small town know one another. The Christians in my church did not have to find ways to know their geographic neighbors; they were already deeply enmeshed with them. All the believers lived within a few miles of one another and rarely moved out of the area. We ate together, spent lots of time in each other's homes, and were deeply involved in each other's lives apart from Sunday services. And because of these durable and multivalent relationships, a great deal of outreach, pastoral care, fellowship, and community service did indeed happen organically through relationships. In short, small churches in small towns have, in general, the kind of relationships with each other and the surrounding community that missional communities seek to forge.

For more than twenty years, I've led a very large church in Manhattan in which we have significant mobility and turnover and in which people learn, do ministry, and are cared for mainly through large-scale programs. My conclusion? Both churches had seasons of evangelistic fruitfulness. In many cases, the traditional gathered church does tend to draw people "inside the walls" instead of sending

---

No single *form* of church is intrinsically better at growing spiritual fruit, reaching nonbelievers, caring for people, and producing Christ-shaped lives.

---

and supporting Christians out to minister in their networks of relationships. However, in my own experience, my large urban congregation — particularly in its first decade — was, by and large, far more effective than the small church I served in reaching unchurched and non-Christian people. In the final analysis, I don't believe any single *form* of church (small or large, cell group based or midsize community based) is intrinsically better at growing spiritual fruit, reaching nonbelievers, caring for people, and producing Christ-shaped lives. I say "in the final analysis" because each approach to church — the small, organic, simple incarnational church, and the large, organizational, complex attractional church — has vastly different strengths and weaknesses, limitations and capabilities.

Alan Roxburgh, in his role as a consultant, finds that one of the first questions people ask him is this: "Can you show me a missional church model?"[11] They want a specific way of doing church, with a concrete pattern they can emulate. He rejects the very question, and so should we. Look again at the outline of the features of an effective missional church (pp. 256 – 58). Those features can be present or absent within any church model and size. Nearly any type of church may embrace or resist these

features, though in different ways. All kinds are thriving; and all kinds are failing.

So the idea that "the missional church is the smaller house church" is shortsighted.

PROBLEM #3: LOSS OF A CLEAR UNDERSTANDING OF THE GOSPEL

My third and greatest concern is that, while all missional church books use the term *gospel* constantly, it is obvious they do not mean the same thing by the term. This is a very serious problem. It is especially true of those who see being missional primarily in communal/reciprocal terms (though it occurs in the other categories as well).

The final result of God's redeeming work in Christ will be a completely renewed cosmos — a new heaven and a new earth. Therefore we can say that God is out not only to pardon and save our souls but also to heal all the ways sin has ruined the creation. However, some stress this aspect of God's saving program to the virtual exclusion of any attention to individual conversion. The reason is, as we have seen, that many redefine sin and salvation in completely corporate or horizontal terms. In their view, sin is mainly the selfishness, pride, greed, and violence that destroy community and God's creation. Accordingly, Christ's redemption is primarily the defeat of the forces of evil in the world that cause the harm, and the Spirit's application of this redemption is by means of tearing down barriers and moving toward a human society of sharing, egalitarianism, and mutuality. Finally, becoming a Christian is not about being reconciled to God through repentance and faith but about joining the new community that is at work to bring about a world of peace and justice. The classic doctrines regarding sin — as an offense against God's holiness that incurs his righteous wrath, as Christ propitiating God's wrath and taking our punishment as our substitute, and as the "great exchange" of our sin being placed on Jesus and his righteousness being placed on us — are rejected as too individualistic and as a contributing reason for the church's failure to become missional. Of course, as we have observed many

REWORKING THE DOCTRINE OF SALVATION

While we cannot unpack all of the theological assumptions that underlie the reworking of the concept of salvation into corporate terms, one premise, it seems to me, is a *one-dimensional view of the kingdom of God.* According to Geerhardus Vos (see pp. 229–30), the kingdom of God is "the realm of God's saving grace" that is entered by the individual through the new birth. The doctrine that we are justified through faith in Jesus' finished work—not our own—can easily be put in kingdom terms. Jesus is "King" of our salvation—he fully accomplishes it; we contribute nothing. Vos then notes that the kingdom of God is also "a realm of righteousness, justice, and blessing" that has a social-future dimension.

Many today seem to place all the stress on the social dimension of the kingdom, which they pit against the idea of salvation through Christ's imputed righteousness. Another premise is a belief in the social Trinity, a view that puts much more emphasis on the three-ness of God than his unity and stresses God as a nonhierarchical, loving community rather than emphasizing his holiness.[12] Finally, those who do this redefining of the doctrine of salvation often embrace a background belief in the Barthian understanding of all humans as elect in Christ and therefore not under God's judicial wrath.

times in this book, sin has a devastating effect on our corporate life, and Christ's redemption surely will eventually restore creation, but when these traditional doctrines of sin and atonement are discarded, the corporate dimension virtually eliminates the call for individual repentance, faith, and conversion.

It should be acknowledged that the writers in this category continually speak of individual and corporate redemption in such phrases as "not only individual salvation but also" or "more than individual salvation" as a way of indicating that they are not denying or changing traditional evangelism but rather adding to it. But upon reflection, I find that the individual and corporate aspects of salvation, mission, and Christian living are often pitted against one another, and the individual aspect nearly eliminated. These doctrinal shifts result in a very different way of understanding a local church's mission. As mentioned in chapter 5, using the concept of sphere sovereignty, it is best to think of the organized church's primary function as evangelizing and equipping people to be disciples and then sending the "organic church"—Christians at work in the world—to engage culture, do justice, and restore God's shalom. In many expositions of the missional church, this distinction virtually disappears.[13]

Most important, this overly corporate definition of sin and salvation results in a very different way of doing evangelism. Let me give one example. This way of reconceiving sin and redemption (as corporate and horizontal rather than as individual and vertical) was given popular-level expression by Dieter Zander, a pioneer of the emerging church. In an article titled "Abducted by an Alien Gospel," he relates how his aunt shared the gospel with him when he was a child. She said, "If you are lying, you are committing a sin. If you die tonight without having your sins forgiven, you will go to hell." That night, Zander asked Jesus to forgive all his sins and come into his life, and he went to bed sure of eternal life.

After moving as an adult to the San Francisco area, Zander tried talking to a Jewish neighbor about Christianity. What he shared was essentially what he had known of the gospel since childhood: "God loves us, but we've all sinned. God sent Jesus to pay for our sins, and if we trust in Jesus' payment, God will forgive our sins and give us eternal life." But as he spoke, he not only found his gospel presentation ineffective; he found himself thinking, "This just doesn't sound like good *news*."

Going back to Scripture, he came to realize that the heart of Jesus' gospel was "the kingdom of God." And what was this? "The arrival of a different kind of life, under the reign of a present and powerful God who, according to another version of Jesus' good news in Luke 4, was intent upon restoring, healing, redeeming, and reconciling all of creation." Here Zander follows the basic contours of the *missio Dei*. With his new understanding of the kingdom of God as a "different kind of life" and the restoration of all creation, he redesigned his gospel presentation and returned to his Jewish friend:

> *I no longer believe that being a Christian is just a matter of having my sins forgiven … The good news that Jesus announced is that we can live our lives with God — which is the best kind of life that is humanly possible. We don't have to live life alone — taking care of ourselves, being afraid that we don't have what we'll need, being intimidated and controlled by things in our life that we can't seem to change, wondering if there's anything or anyone who can make sense of the whole thing.*
>
> *Jesus' message is, simply, "Turn around and step into a life with God, the kind of life I lived and invite you to live with me."*
>
> *When we accept Jesus' invitation, believe that what he is saying is true, and follow him with our whole life, we experience freedom from past sins and future fears, along with contentment, joy, love, and power today.[14]*

Zander reports that his neighbor responded more positively this time. He concludes his article by saying that we must "bring to people the same message that Jesus brought: the offer of life with God and the invitation to be his coworker in what he is doing in the world."

This article vividly captures how our conception of *missio Dei* will play a significant role in what we actually share with people as the gospel. The gospel of Zander's childhood (let's call it the AG for "alien gospel") was indeed inadequate. First, the AG offers an extremely thin concept of sin. Sin is seen as merely breaking the rules, for which you need

forgiveness. There is no hint of sin as the deep and settled bent of the heart toward self-salvation and idolatry. Because the AG's account of sin is so shallow, listeners do not get the sense either that their sin is deeply unfair, wrong, and offensive to God or that it is profoundly destructive of their own lives. Instead, this view of sin as "rule breaking" leads listeners to see that their only problem is the legal consequences of the sin they face from the Divine

---

Individual and corporate aspects of salvation, mission, and Christian living are often pitted against one another, and the individual aspect nearly eliminated.

Enforcer. Nothing in this presentation shows sin as intrinsically wrong, hateful, destructive, and shameful in itself.

As a result of this thin view of sin, the AG does not really clarify the classic gospel distinction between grace and works, between faith in Christ's saving work and faith in our own saving work. The average hearer of the AG will see themselves as saved, not primarily because of Jesus' death on the cross, but because they are sincerely submitting to God and begging for mercy and resolving to live a better life. Essentially, they do not see themselves as moving from faith in their own moral efforts (whether as secular or religious persons) to faith and rest in Christ's saving work. Rather, they see themselves as moving from living bad lives to living better ones. Their sins are forgiven, and God accepts them *because* they are now living for Jesus — not the other way around.

When we look at Zander's redesign of the gospel (let's call it the KG for "kingdom gospel"), we find that it doesn't actually change this pattern at all. First, there is still no mention of the cross or why it was necessary for Jesus to die. In fact, there is no mention of Jesus' saving work at all. The emphasis is not on Jesus as substitute but on Jesus as a model of living a particular kind of courageous and loving life ("step into … the kind of life I lived and invite you to live with me"). Second, in order to receive both forgiveness of sins and power within, we must "believe that what he is saying is true, and follow him with our whole life." Instead of being invited to believe and rest in the saving work of Christ, there is an invitation to stop living in one way and start living in another. The listener to Zander's gospel can easily conclude the same thing they did when they heard the AG: "If I live in the right way, then I'll be forgiven and accepted."

People who believe they are accepted by God because they lead good lives of sacrificial service will be insecure, unable to take criticism, prone to look down on people who are not "getting it right," and unsure of God's love or of their identity in Christ.

In the end, the AG and the KG are not much different. Both of them tell you that Jesus died for your sins and that you need to receive that forgiveness. So far, so good. But both messages fail to present the offensiveness, depth, and destructiveness of sin, and therefore they miss the "sharp point" of the gospel's spear — the distinction between grace and works, between embracing Jesus as your Savior and merely using him to be your own savior. As we have shown at length earlier in this book, it is understanding and applying this distinction that creates the power for life change. People who believe they are accepted by God because they are leading a traditionally moral, chaste, and good life or because they are living a life of sacrificial service for the needs of the world will be equally insecure, unable to take criticism, prone to look down on people who are not "getting it right," and unsure of God's love or of their identity in Christ. Both are still essentially enslaved to the bonds of works-righteousness. It doesn't matter if it takes a traditional, conservative, moralistic form or a culturally progressive, justice-oriented, kingdom-restoration form.

Evangelicals who describe the gospel as Dieter Zander does will almost always, when asked, profess belief in a traditional understanding of justification by faith. But many others — proponents of the missional church who are outside of the evangelical tradition — have rejected its traditional views of justification and substitutionary atonement. Many will say that talking about the wrath of God and the need for justification simply doesn't work today. Postmodern people, they say, won't find the doctrine of justification by grace compelling because they perceive God, if he exists at all, as someone who accepts them as they are without any need for atonement or radical grace. In the KG presentation, people are called, not to be reconciled to God, but to step out of a life of fear and self-absorption into a life of reliance on God and service to others. You are left with the impression that God has no problem with you — you are just shortchanging yourself by failing to belong to his movement. There is no real barrier to be overcome between you and God, other than your reluctance to join his work. I struggle to see how this approach differs in essence from the AG — the classic "salvation by works" way of understanding salvation. It is salvation by a different kind of works. Instead of offering a contextually sensitive starting place for a gospel presentation, it gives us an entirely different definition of salvation altogether, one that is by works rather than by grace.

It naturally follows that this understanding of sin leads to a different understanding of conversion. Traditional Protestantism believed that conversion was more than simply the adoption of a new set of values; it was seen as a radical change in inner identity. The driving motivation of your life was now rooted in grateful wonder and in love for the One who did so much for you. The old motivations of fear and pride were swept away by God's radical grace. But all of this is muted in the kingdom presentation. When someone hears the KG gospel of submitting to Jesus as Lord and joining his kingdom community, how can they sing Charles Wesley's cathartic refrain from "And Can It Be That I Should Gain"?

My chains fell off, my heart was free,
I rose, went forth, and followed Thee.

What chains? Set free from what, exactly? The biblical gospel brings people to see their peril in light of God's holiness while simultaneously becoming aware of the costly and amazing sacrifice of Jesus, who took upon himself the punishment we deserve. If this is muted in our gospel presentations, we also mute that sense of wonder at the astonishing love of Jesus, the one who has rescued us.

D. A. Carson, in a lengthy review article of various authors who share many similarities with the views of Lesslie Newbigin, David Bosch, and Darrell Guder, wrote the following:

> We have repeatedly seen how the "story" of God's advancing kingdom is cast in terms of rescuing human beings and completing creation, or perhaps in terms of defeating the powers of darkness. Not for a moment do I want to reduce or minimize those themes. Yet from what are human beings to be rescued? Their sin, yes; the powers of darkness; yes. But what is striking is the utter absence of any mention of the wrath of God. This is not a minor omission. Section after section of the Bible's story turns on the fact that God's image bearers attract God's righteous wrath. The entire created order is under God's curse because of human sin. Sin is not first and foremost horizontal, social (though of course it is all of that): it is vertical, the defiance of Almighty God. The sin which most consistently is said to bring down God's wrath on the heads of his people or on entire nations is idolatry — the de-godding of God. And it is the overcoming of this most fundamental sin that the cross and resurrection of Jesus achieve. The most urgent need of human beings is to be reconciled to God. That is not to deny that such reconciliation entails reconciliation with other human beings, and transformed living in God's fallen creation, in anticipation of the final transformation at the time of the consummation of all things. But to speak constantly of the advance of the kingdom without tying kingdom themes to the passion narrative, the way the canonical Gospels do, is a terrible reductionism.[15]

Carson's point is vital. There are most definitely corporate and horizontal aspects in both sin and redemption. These biblical concepts are deep, comprehensive, and far-reaching. But if in the effort to bring these horizontal aspects out more clearly we deny the classic doctrines of grace, then the result will be a destructive imbalance. The classic Protestant understanding of the gospel includes the notion that God is holy and we are under his wrath and curse, but that Jesus bore in our place that wrath, curse, and punishment. When we repent and believe in him, we are given both pardon and Christ's righteousness. This electrifying experience of God's grace makes a Christian passionate for doing justice — for pursuing the horizontal aspects of the gospel. A Christian's zeal for justice comes from a transformed identity that flows from a grasp of the gospel — a gospel proclaiming that salvation is by faith alone, not by works.

THE MARKS OF A MISSIONAL CHURCH

Where does this bring us? I am arguing that a church can robustly preach and teach the classic evangelical doctrines and still be missional. That is, it can still have a missionary encounter with Western culture *and* reach and disciple unchurched, nontraditional nonbelievers in our society. How so?

A church can robustly preach and teach the classic evangelical doctrines and still be missional.

---

1. A missional church, if it is to have a missionary encounter with Western culture, will need to confront society's idols and especially address how modernity makes the happiness and self-actualization of the individual into an absolute. One of the manifestations of this idol is materialism — consumerism and greed that lead to injustice. As we have seen, many believe that in order to have this confrontation we must recast the gospel, but as I explained elsewhere at length, the classic messages of substitutionary atonement and forensic justification provide both a strong theological basis and a powerful internal motivation to live more simply and to do justice in the world.[16] Rejecting these doctrines, then, does not aid us in this encounter with

When Lesslie Newbigin spoke of a "missionary encounter" with the West, he included the idea of apologetics — of making a case. Almost all people in the contemporary missional conversation cite Newbigin's call for the church to be a "contrast community," but they generally ignore what he said about engaging people intellectually. Many missional theorists today say that using arguments and reason to persuade people simply will not work in a postmodern situation. Instead, people will be won by the quality of our community and the vividness of our stories. But just as all people are unavoidably emotional beings, they are also unavoidably rational beings. It is obvious that the most forceful enemies of Christianity — the "new atheists" — use reason to undermine the faith, and these arguments are having some effect.

Newbigin believed that Christians need to expose the myth of the modern world — that a person can jettison any faith in God and rest only on science and naturalism, and yet still have meaning in life, a basis for human dignity, moral consensus, hope for the future, strength of character, shared values, and a strong community. A Western cultural apologetic means showing the world that it *cannot* have these things without faith in God.[17]

because hearers will be viscerally offended or simply unable to understand the basic concepts of God, sin, and redemption. This fact does not, however, require a change in the classic Christian doctrines, but rather skillfulness in contextualizing them so our gospel presentations are compelling even to people who are not (yet) fully persuaded by them. Within Christendom, it was possible to simply exhort Christianized people to do what they knew they should do. As I explained at length in part 3, Christian communicators now must enter, challenge, and retell the culture's stories with the gospel. And, as I argued

---

The traditional gospel of salvation by sheer grace gives us both the internal confidence and the humility to do contextualization.

---

there, it is the traditional gospel of salvation by sheer grace that gives us both the internal confidence and the humility to do contextualization.

3. A missional church will affirm that all Christians are people in mission in every area of their lives. We must overcome the clericalism and lay passivity of the Christendom era and recover the Reformation doctrine of "the priesthood of all believers." Again we can see that classic doctrines of salvation do not obscure this critical idea. Its great proponent was Martin Luther, who associated this "ministry egalitarianism" with the doctrine of free justification rather than through works and merit, which can lead to a hierarchical view that ministry is only for the holy and for those removed from the world.[18] To be missional today requires that lay Christians be equipped by their churches to do three things: (1) to be a verbal witness to the gospel in their webs of relationships, (2) to love their neighbors and do justice within their neighborhoods and city, and (3) to integrate their faith with their work in order to engage culture through their vocations. A missional church will be more deeply and practically committed to deeds of compassion and social justice than traditional

Western culture. In fact, nothing challenges and confronts the modern idolization of the "expressive, autonomous individual" like the simple and ancient gospel message that we all are sinners under God's wrath who need to repent and submit to him.

2. A missional church, if it is to reach people in a post-Christian culture, must recognize that most of our more recently formulated and popular gospel presentations will fall on deaf ears

fundamentalist churches and more deeply and practically committed to evangelism and conversion than traditional liberal churches. This kind of church is profoundly counterintuitive to American observers, who are no longer able to categorize (and dismiss) it as liberal or conservative. Only this kind of church has any chance in the non-Christian West. A church that equips its people in this way will not only be something like a lay seminary in discipleship and training; it will also find ways to strongly support the people in their ministering "outside the walls" of the church.[19] This aspect of missional ministry is so important that I am devoting the next chapter to it.

4. A missional church must understand itself as a servant community — a counterculture for the common good. For centuries in the West, churches could limit themselves to specifically "religious" concerns and function as loose fellowships within a wider semi-Christian culture. Now, however, becoming a Christian involves a

---

> This emphasis on deep and countercultural community is not undermined by the classic Reformation doctrines of justification and imputation but rather is enhanced by them.

---

much more radical break with the surrounding non-Christian culture. The church can no longer be an association or a club but is a "thick" alternate human society in which relationships are strong and deep — and in which sex and family, wealth and possessions, racial identity and power, are all used and practiced in godly and distinct ways. However, while the Christian church must be distinct, it must be set within, not be separated from, its surroundings. Its neighbors must see it as a servant society, sacrificially pouring out its time and wealth for the common good of the city.

Here again I would argue that this emphasis on deep and countercultural community is not undermined by the classic Reformation doctrines of

justification and imputation but rather is enhanced by them. No one has argued more compellingly for this than Dietrich Bonhoeffer in his classic *Life Together*.[20] As Bonhoeffer shows, the gospel decenters the ego and clears the way not only for far deeper and more transparent relationships between Christians (helping to make the church a contrast community) but also for humble, servant relationships with people who do not share our beliefs. The sacrificial service of a missional church will show the world,

DISCOURSE IN THE VERNACULAR

In Christendom, there is little difference between the language inside and outside the church. Documents of the early United States Congress, for example, were riddled with allusions to and references from the Bible, and at that time even nonchurchgoers understood theological terms. In a missional church, however, terms must be explained, and we should always assume that nonbelieving people are present. If we speak as if our *whole neighborhood* is present (not just Christians), eventually more and more of our neighbors will find their way in or be invited there.

So missional churches must seek to intentionally avoid tribal jargon, stylized and archaic language for prayer and worship, "we/they" language, disdainful jokes that mock people who hold different political and religious beliefs, and dismissive or disrespectful comments about those who differ with them. Churches seeking to discourse in the vernacular avoid both sentimentality and hype. Instead, their communication should be marked by gentle humor and honest realism about the leaders' and the church's weaknesses and mistakes, yet seasoned with a ground note of joy and hope that never diminishes. And unless all of their speech flows out of truly humble and bold, gospel-changed hearts, it will be seen as nothing more than marketing and spin.

THE CHURCH'S ROLE IN SEEKING JUSTICE

I have argued in *Generous Justice* and elsewhere in this volume that while the mission of the *gathered* (institutional) church is to proclaim the gospel of individual salvation, to win people to Christ and form disciples, yet the will of God for the church *dispersed*— Christians living in the world—is to minister in both word and deed, to do evangelism and to do justice. If the latter does not minister in both word and deed, no one will listen to the gospel preached by the former.

So in the end, the missional church sends its people out as agents of justice in the world. However, we need to be more careful than those who see social reform as the church's job—a view that usually leads to the politicization of the church in which it becomes identified with particular political parties and causes. Ross Douthat argues that this error has contributed to the decline of orthodox Christianity.[21]

themselves "contextual"—that is, culturally like yet spiritually unlike the people in the surrounding neighborhood and culture.[23] A missional church, then, does not depend on an evangelism program or department to do outreach. Almost all parts of the church's life must be ready to respond to the presence of people who do not yet believe.

6. A missional church should practice Christian unity on the local level as much as possible. In the heyday of Christendom, churches received definition by contrasting themselves with (and constantly criticizing) other denominations and traditions. Today we should define ourselves more by contrasting ourselves with the world and our surrounding culture. The world must see churches avoiding unnecessary divisions.[24]

Six Marks of a Missional Church
1. The church must confront society's idols.
2. The church must contextualize skillfully and communicate in the vernacular.
3. The church must equip people in mission in every area of their lives.
4. The church must be a counterculture for the common good.
5. The church must itself be contextualized and should expect nonbelievers, inquirers, and seekers to be involved in most aspects of the church's life and ministry.
6. The church must practice unity.

then, a "third way" between the individualistic self-absorption that secularism can breed and the tribal self-righteousness that religion can breed.

5. A missional church must be, in a sense, "porous." That is, it should expect nonbelievers, inquirers, and seekers to be involved in most aspects of the church's life and ministry—in worship, small and midsize groups, and service projects in the neighborhood. A missional church knows how to welcome doubters and graciously include them as much as possible in community so they can see the gospel fleshed out in life and process the gospel message through numerous personal interactions.[22] This will only happen if all of the above ingredients are in place and if believers inside the church are

These six marks of a missional church can exist in both large and small churches of various forms and are strengthened, not weakened, by a clear grasp of the understanding of the gospel that was recaptured by the Protestant Reformers. Most of these marks have been or will be expanded on in other parts of this volume. There is one, however, that I think is the most practical single way a church can implement a missional mind-set—*training and equipping the people of the church for ministry*. We will focus our attention on that priority in the next chapter.

QUESTIONS FOR DISCUSSION AND REFLECTION

1. Do you agree with this chapter's assertion that no "single *form* of church … is intrinsically better at growing spiritual fruit, reaching nonbelievers, caring for people, and producing Christ-shaped lives?" Be honest about your own biases — which form is most popular in your context? Why? How might this form be adapted to be more missional?

2. Consider Dieter Zander's story in which he compares the "alien gospel" and the "kingdom gospel." How are these two gospels similar to one another? How does the biblical gospel differ from both of them?

3. Keller writes, "The classic Protestant understanding of the gospel includes the notion that God is holy and we are under his wrath and curse, but that Jesus bore in our place that wrath, curse, and punishment. When we repent and believe in him, we are given both pardon and Christ's righteousness. This electrifying experience of God's grace makes a Christian passionate for doing justice — for pursuing the horizontal aspects of the gospel." Which do you tend to emphasize more in your preaching and teaching, the horizontal or the vertical? How are these two aspects of the gospel connected?

4. Six marks of a missional church are presented in this chapter. A missional church should:

   - confront society's idols and address how modernity makes the desires of the individual into an absolute
   - contextualize skillfully and discourse in the vernacular, recognizing that many people are simply unable to understand the basic concepts of God, sin, and redemption
   - recognize that all Christians are people in mission in every area of their lives
   - understand itself as a servant community — a counterculture for the common good
   - be contextualized and expect nonbelievers, inquirers, and seekers to be involved in most aspects of the church's life and ministry
   - practice Christian unity on the local level as much as possible

   For each of these marks, what unique challenges and opportunities does it provide for communicating the gospel? Which of these does your church need to focus on right now?

CHAPTER 20 — CENTERING THE MISSIONAL CHURCH *(pages 264–75)*

1. Michael Wolff, "The Party Line," *New York* (February 26, 2001), http://nymag.com/nymetro/news/media/columns/medialife/4407/index1.html (accessed February 17, 2012).
2. See chapter 23 for an extended discussion of "evangelistic worship."
3. See part 3 ("Gospel Contextualization") for an extended discussion of what a contextualized gospel message looks like.
4. A number of good theological and practical objections can be raised to habitually using the word *incarnational* to describe ministry. However, for our purposes here, we will accept the practice and the main definition given because the term is widely used in missional church discussions.
5. Alan Roxburgh and Scott Boren (*Introducing the Missional Church: What It Is, Why It Matters, and How to Become One* [Grand Rapids: Baker, 2009], 69) define an "attractional" church this way: "One of the ways the basic story of the gospel has been compromised is that it has become all about us and how God is supposed to meet our needs, and we have created attractional churches that are about how God does just that."
6. David Fitch, "What Is Missional? Can a Mega-Church Be Missional?" www.reclaimingthemission.com/what-is-missional-can-a-mega-church-be-missional/ (accessed February 17, 2012).
7. Ibid.
8. Mike Breen and Alex Absalom, *Launching Missional Communities: A Field Guide* (Pawleys Island, S.C.: 3DM, 2010).
9. Michael Frost and Alan Hirsch, *The Shaping of Things to Come: Innovation and Mission for the 21st-Century Church* (Grand Rapids: Baker, 2004), 211.
10. See Frost and Hirsch, *The Shaping of Things to Come*, 210–24.
11. Roxburgh and Boren, *Introducing the Missional Church*, 21.
12. See Leanne Van Dyk, "The Church's Proclamation as a Participation in God's Mission," in *Trinitarian Theology for the Church: Scripture, Community, Worship*, ed. Daniel J. Treier and David Lauber (Downers Grove, Ill.: InterVarsity, 2009), 225–36; see also Mark Husbands, "The Trinity Is *Not* Our Social Program," in the same volume (pp. 120–41), where he critiques the social Trinity emphasis.
13. For example, Darrell Guder (*Missional Church* [Grand Rapids: Eerdmans, 1998]) reasons that if God's purpose in mission is to "restore and heal creation" (p. 4), then the idea of salvation means bringing the reign of God to bear on communities and organizations. He writes, "For a bank, it might mean granting loans in formerly redlined neighborhoods. For a public school, it might mean instituting peer mediation training among students" (p. 136).
14. Dieter Zander, "Abducted by an Alien Gospel," www.baskettcase.com/blog/2006/11/01/abducted-by-an-alien-gospel/ (accessed February 17, 2012).
15. D. A. Carson, "Three Books on the Bible: A Critical Review," www.reformation21.org/shelf-life/three-books-on-the-bible-a-critical-review.php (accessed February 17, 2012).
16. Timothy Keller, *Generous Justice: How God's Grace Makes Us Just* (New York: Dutton, 2010), esp. 92–108.
17. See Lesslie Newbigin, *The Gospel in a Pluralist Society* (Grand Rapids: Eerdmans, 1989), 1–65.
18. While Luther expounds on this concept in many places, the two seminal works are "To the Christian Nobility of the German Nation" and "The Babylonian Captivity of the Church." These two are joined to "The Freedom of a Christian" in Martin Luther, *Three Treatises* (Minneapolis: Fortress, 1970). For an early modern evangelical effort to recapture the importance of lay ministry, see John R. W. Stott, *One People* (Downers Grove, Ill.: InterVarsity, 1968).
19. For a case that every lay Christian is to minister the Word — that is, evangelize and disciple from the Bible — see Colin Marshall and Tony Payne, *The Trellis and the Vine: The Ministry Mind-Shift That Changes Everything* (Kingsford, Australia: Matthias Media, 2009), 41–60. For resources containing ideas on how to release laypeople to deepen relationships in their neighborhood to do service and witness, see Breen and Absalom, *Launching Missional Communities*, and Tim Chester and Steve Timmis, *Everyday Church: Mission by Being Good Neighbours* (Nottingham, UK: Inter-Varsity, 2011). For a brief overview of how to help people integrate their faith and work, see part 7 ("Integrative Ministry") in this volume, and Timothy Keller, *Every Good Endeavor* (New York: Dutton, 2012).
20. Dietrich Bonhoeffer (*Life Together* [New York: Harper & Row, 1954], 23) writes, "All we can say, therefore, is: the community of Christians springs solely from the biblical and Reformation message of the justification of man through grace alone; this alone is the basis of the longing of Christians for one another."
21. Ross Douthat, *Bad Religion: How We Became a Nation of Heretics* (New York: Free Press, 2012), 63ff.
22. See section on "Missional Evangelism through Mini-Decisions" on pp. 281–82.
23. See section on "Believers with Relational Integrity" on pp. 282–85.
24. See part 8 (Movement Dynamics).

EQUIPPING PEOPLE FOR MISSIONAL LIVING

Until now, we've spent most of our time trying to understand the missional conversation, discerning some of its commonalities and strengths as well as its errors and pitfalls. One recurring theme is the importance of equipping and involving the laity in ministry. Under Christendom, people simply came to the church to receive the ministrations of the professional clergy. We can no longer assume that people will come. This should not be taken to imply that the ordained ministry is obsolete — by no means! It is the responsibility of the ordained leadership to build up the church and its members through the ministry of the Word and sacraments. However, one critical focus of that ministry must now be the discipling of the laity for ministry in the world. This is one of the most practical ways a church can appropriate the insights of the missional conversation, moving toward a centered, balanced approach to ministry.

We find an example of this idea in an interview conducted with Eddie Gibbs and Ryan Bolger of Fuller Seminary. When asked, "What are the marks of churches (people) that live missionally?" Bolger provides a helpful and practical answer: "They no longer see the church service as the primary connecting point with those outside the community. Connecting with those outside happens within the culture, by insiders to that culture who express the gospel through how they live."[1]

The rest of this chapter will propose different ways and means for equipping and encouraging the laity to engage in ministry "within the culture." I give special emphasis to the lay ministry of the Word — the building up of believers and the evangelizing of nonbelievers through preaching and teaching — though in part 7, I will point to some other ways that Christians can do ministry in the world, including the practice of justice and the integration of faith and work.

"INFORMAL MISSIONARIES"

There has always been a strong tendency, as John Stott says, for Christians to "withdraw into a kind of closed, evangelical, monastic community."[2] This is not, of course, how things were in the early church. The Greek word *euangelizō* means "to gospelize," to tell people the good news about what Jesus did for us, and in the book of Acts literally everyone in the early church does it. Not only the apostles (5:42) but every Christian (8:4) did evangelism — and they did so endlessly. Passages such as Romans 15:14; Colossians 3:16; 1 Thessalonians 1:6 – 10; Hebrews 3:13; and 1 John 2:20, 27 indicate that every Christian was expected to evangelize, follow up, nurture, and teach people the Word. This happened relationally — one person bringing the gospel to another within the context of a relationship.

In Michael Green's seminal *Evangelism in the Early Church,* he conveys the conclusion of historians that early Christianity's explosive growth "was in reality accomplished by means of informal missionaries."[3] That is, Christian laypeople — not trained preachers and evangelists — carried on the mission of the church not through formal preaching but informal conversation — "in homes and wine shops, on walks, and around market stalls ... they did it naturally, enthusiastically."[4]

Green quotes pagan writers such as Celsus, who complained with great sarcasm that "we see in private houses ... the most illiterate and bucolic yokels, who would not dare to say anything at all in front of their elders and more intelligent masters. But they get hold of ... any ... who are as ignorant as themselves and say ... 'We know how men ought to live. If your children do as we say, you will be happy yourselves and make your home happy too.' " Green writes, "In fact, of course, it pays the highest compliment to the zeal and dedication of the most ordinary Christians in the subapostolic age. Having found treasure, they meant to share it with others, to the limits of their ability."[6]

Green is careful to point out that not all evangelism in the early church was informal. In his chapter titled "Evangelistic Methods," he speaks of many forms of evangelism that required great training and expertise, including synagogue preaching and open-air preaching, as well as public teaching and "dialogical" evangelism. Early Christian teachers set up academies (schools for instruction in the faith) but also taught science, mathematics, philosophy, and the humanities from a Christian perspective. The great Catechetical School of Alexandria was one, and we know that Justin Martyr started one such school in Rome. Green shows that many non-Christians came to take classes, listen to lectures, and dialogue with teachers. The

original example of this form of evangelism may have been the apostle Paul's lecturing in the public hall of Tyrannus in Ephesus. There he engaged in *dialegomenos* — interactive dialogue with all comers — about the Christian faith daily for two years (Acts 19:9 – 10). Green writes, "The intellectual content of his addresses must have been very stimulating. Here was a man who could hold his own, and presumably make converts, in the course of public debate."[7]

But Green returns to the most important way that Christianity spread — through the extended household (*oikos*) evangelism done informally by Christians. A person's strongest relationships were within the household — with blood relatives, servants, clients, and friends — so when a person became a Christian, it was in the household that he or she would get the most serious hearing.[8] If the head of the household (Greek, *oikos*) became a believer, the entire home became a ministry center in which the gospel was taught to all the household's members and neighbors. We see this in Acts 16:15, 32 – 34 (Lydia's and the jailer's homes in Philippi); Acts 17:5 (Jason's home in Thessalonica); Acts 18:7 (Titius Justus's home in Corinth); Acts 21:8 (Philip's home in Caesarea); and 1 Corinthians 1:16; 16:15 (Stephanas's home in Corinth).

The home could be used for systematic teaching and instruction (Acts 5:42), planned presentations of the gospel to friends and neighbors (Acts 10:22), prayer meetings (Acts 12:12), impromptu evangelistic gatherings (Acts 16:32), follow-up sessions with the inquirers (Acts 18:26), evenings devoted to instruction and prayer (Acts 20:7), and fellowship (Acts 21:7).

If another member of the household became a Christian — the wife, children, or slaves and laborers — then the gospel would spread more indirectly. In his chapter titled "Evangelistic Methods," Green sketches out the different ways the gospel moved through households, depending on who was the first convert.

We also know from the Bible and early historical records that simple friendship was one of the main carriers of the gospel. We see this in John 1 when

Philip passes his knowledge of Jesus on to his friend Nathanael. Green relates how Pantaenus led Clement of Alexandria to Christ, Justin led Tatian, and Octavius led Minucius Felix to Christ — all through friendship, which was taken very seriously by the ancients.[9]

THE LAY MINISTRY DYNAMIC

What does this "every-member gospel ministry" look like in today's world? Here are several examples:

- Jerry is asked by his work colleague Bill how his weekend went. Jerry relates that he went on a men's retreat that provided spiritual resources for forgiving people who have wronged us over the years. When Bill raises his eyebrows and says, "That's interesting," Jerry takes a small plunge and mentions that the thing that helped him most was the idea that even though he has not given God his due, God offers him forgiveness through Jesus.
- Dan and Jill help their two sons, ages five and seven, with Scripture memorization and teach them a simple catechism. They field the boys' questions and help them understand the meaning of the texts they are studying.
- Sally gets to know a young woman named Clara at church. Clara confides that she and her husband are having marriage problems and he isn't willing to go to a counselor. Sally and her husband, Jeff, invite Clara and Sam over for a meal. Sam hits it off with Jeff. Afterward, Clara convinces Sam to meet with Jeff and Sally to talk about their marriage issues. They meet together once a month for four months, studying Ephesians 5 and several other biblical texts on marriage.
- John comes to church with his wife, but he isn't sure what he believes or where he stands on faith. The pastor introduces him to an elder named Tom, who begins meeting with John on occasion to read and discuss a book about basic Christianity. After two meetings, John agrees to study the gospel of Mark with Tom every two or three weeks.
- Jenny begins coming to a small group in the church. She was raised in the church but has so many doubts and questions that her group leader, Beth, begins meeting with her one-on-one. They study Bible passages and read books that address each of her questions, one after the other.
- Ted is a young single lawyer. He knows several other lawyers who go to church with him, though they don't work for his firm. He decides to have a Super Bowl party for several of his non-Christian colleagues and invites two Christian lawyers from church and a couple of other believers as well. The men and women from his workplace hit it off with the lawyers from church. About three months later, one of them shows up in church with one of Ted's friends.
- Jessica meets Teresa, a new believer, at church and invites her to work through a series of six Bible studies for new Christians (on issues such as prayer, Bible reading, the role of the church, understanding the gospel better, etc.).
- Fred has been attending a small group for months. At one point he realizes that he assesses the value of the group strictly on what he gets out of it. He then decides to begin preparing well (studying the passage) and praying for the group. When he comes, he looks for every opportunity to help the Bible study leader by making good contributions and for ways to speak the truth in love so others are encouraged and helped to grow.
- Catherine prays for her friend Megan for months. Megan responds well to two short books on Christian subjects that Catherine has given her. She then invites Megan to an evangelistic event in which Christian truth is presented. On the way home, she fields Megan's questions.
- Joe has a longtime friend from college days named Pete, who is a musician. Pete's performance anxiety is harming his career. Joe has been a sympathetic listener for some time, but finally he bluntly asks Pete to explore the

Christian faith with him. "I think maybe it's the only thing that will help you overcome your problem." Pete is taken aback, but after a while, he expresses interest, mainly out of desperation. Joe warns him, "If Christianity is going to be any help, it will only be if you come to the belief that it is not just helpful but *true*." Pete doesn't want to go to any Christian gatherings, so they start studying the Bible together and listening to sermons and lectures and discussing them.

- Kerrie and two other Christian friends are moms who have young kids. They decide to start a daytime moms' group and invite non-Christian friends. For about a year, the group grows to include a similar number of Christians and nonbelievers. The conversations are general and freewheeling — covering spiritual, social, marriage, parenting, and personal issues. As time goes on, several of the nonbelievers begin to go to church with the believers and cross over into faith. After three years, the group is a Christian Bible study but still open and inclusive toward a few nonbelievers who come regularly.

- Jim and Cynthia are both artists who are involved in a citywide Christian artists' fellowship based in their local church. The fellowship typically includes a discussion of the relationship of faith to art that assumes a Christian belief, but the artists have four events a year that will be either a gallery showing or a book event in which a credible working artist talks to a general audience about how their faith relates to their art. Jim and Cynthia are diligent in bringing non-Christian artists or art appreciators to these events.

- Greg comes to faith in Christ through a skeptics/seeker group hosted by a church. When the date for his baptism is set, he invites a number of non-Christian friends to the service and then takes them out for lunch and discusses the whole event. One friend is very moved by the experience, and Greg invites him to come back. Eventually, the friend begins coming to his small group with him.[10]

We can make several observations about these examples. First, it should be clear that we are not just talking about evangelism in the traditional sense here. Some of these examples show instances of encouraging and building up new believers; some point to ways of spurring Christians on to greater growth in Christ; others depict situations of helping believers address particular problems in their lives. And yet the basic form of this every-member gospel ministry is the same:

- **Organic.** It happens spontaneously, outside of the church's organized programs (even though it occasionally makes use of formal programs).
- **Relational.** It is done in the context of informal personal relationships.
- **Word deploying.** It prayerfully brings the Bible and gospel into connection with people's lives.
- **Active, not passive.** Each person assumes personal responsibility for being a producer rather than just a consumer of ministry; for example, even though Fred continues to come to the small group as he always has, his mind-set has changed.

Traditional evangelism is only one piece of this every-member gospel ministry, and it is often not the largest piece. Still, as lay ministry grows in a congregation, so, too, will the amount of evangelism.

Second, notice we are talking about lay *ministry*, not necessarily lay *leadership*. Often ministers talk about lay ministers and lay leaders as if they are the same thing. But this may betray too much attractional church thinking. By lay leaders, I mean volunteers who lead and run church programs. Being a lay leader can be time-consuming and may even make lay ministry more difficult for a season. Lay leadership usually requires some level of leadership and organizational ability, while lay ministry does not. Lay leaders are extremely important to lay ministry — overworking lay leaders can kill lay ministry in a church — but they are not the same thing. Lay ministers are people who actively bring their Christian example and faith into the lives of their neighbors, friends, colleagues, and community.

My experience has been that when at least 20 to 25 percent of a church's people are engaged in this kind of organic, relational gospel ministry, it creates a powerful dynamism that infuses the whole church and greatly extends the church's ability to edify and evangelize. Lay ministers counsel, encourage, instruct, disciple, and witness with both Christian and non-Christian individuals. They involve themselves in the lives of others so

---

Lay ministers are people who actively bring their Christian example and faith into the lives of their neighbors, friends, colleagues, and community.

---

they might come to faith or grow in grace. Then a certain percentage of the people served by these lay ministers come into the lay ministry community as well, and the church grows in quality and quantity. Because they are being equipped and supported by the church's leaders, those involved in lay ministry tend to feel a healthy sense of ownership of the church. They think of it as "our church," not "their church" (referring to the ordained leaders and staff). They freely and generously give of their time, talent, and treasure.

This is the tide that lifts every boat in ministry. Without Christian education and counseling, without formal and informal diaconal work, without the preaching of the Word and administration of the sacraments, without support for family life, without the management and stewardship of resources, without church government and discipline, laypeople will not be built up into lay ministers. But if lay ministry is happening all through and around the church, it grows each of these other functions in quality and quantity. Where do the human resources and even the financial resources come from to do *all* of the work of the church? They come from every-member gospel ministry.

MISSIONAL EVANGELISM THROUGH MINI-DECISIONS

Notice another assumption behind the examples of lay ministry given here: many people process from

unbelief to faith through "mini-decisions."

We hold to the classic teaching about the nature of the gospel: to be a Christian is to be united with Christ by faith so that the merits of his saving work become ours and his Spirit enters us and begins to change us into Christ's likeness. You either are a Christian or you are not — you either are united to him by faith or you are not — because being a Christian is, first of all, a "standing" with God. However, we also acknowledge that coming to this point of uniting to Christ by faith often works as a process, not only as an event. It can occur through a series of small decisions or thoughts that bring a person closer and closer to the point of saving faith. In a post-Christendom setting, more often than not, this is the case. People simply do not have the necessary background knowledge to hear a gospel address and immediately understand who God is, what sin is, who Jesus is, and what repentance and faith are in a way that enables them to make an intelligent commitment. They often have far too many objections and beliefs for the gospel to be readily plausible to them.

Therefore, most people in the West need to be welcomed into community long enough for them to hear multiple expressions of the gospel — both formal and informal — from individuals and teachers. As this happens in community, nonbelievers come to understand the character of God, sin, and grace. Many of their objections are answered through this process. Because they are "on the inside" and involved in ongoing relationships with Christians, they can imagine themselves as Christians and see how the faith fleshes out in real life.

The process often looks something like this:

1. Awareness: "I see it." They begin to clear the ground of stereotypes and learn to distinguish the gospel from legalism or liberalism, the core from the peripheral. They make mini-decisions like these:

- "She's religious but surprisingly open-minded."
- "You *can* be a Christian and be intelligent!"
- "The Bible isn't so hard to understand after all."
- "A lot of things the Bible says really fit me."
- "I see the difference between Christianity and just being moral."

2. Relevance: "I need it." They begin to see the slavery of both religion and irreligion and are shown the transforming power of how the gospel works. Examples of mini-decisions here are as follows:

- "There must be some advantages to being a Christian."
- "An awful lot of very normal people really like this church!"
- "It would really help if I could believe like she does."
- "Jesus seems to be the key. I wonder who he was."

3. Credibility: "I need it because it's true." This is a reversal of the modern view that states, "It's true if I need it." If people fail to see the reasonableness of the gospel, they will lack the endurance to persevere when their faith is challenged. Examples of mini-decisions include thoughts like these:

- "I see that the Bible is historically reliable."
- "You really can't use science to disprove the supernatural."
- "There really were eyewitnesses to the resurrection."
- "Jesus really *is* God."
- "I see now why Jesus had to die — it is the only way."

4. Trial: "I see what it would be like." They are involved in some form of group life, in some type of service ministry, and are effectively trying Christianity on, often talking like a Christian — even defending the faith at times.

5. Commitment: "I take it." This may be the point of genuine conversion, or sometimes a person will realize that conversion has already happened, and they just didn't grasp it at the time. Examples of mini-decisions include these:

- "I am a sinner."
- "I need a Savior."
- "Though there are a lot of costs, I really must do what Jesus says."
- "I will believe in Jesus and live for him."

6. Reinforcement: "Now I get it." Typically, this is the place where the penny drops and the gospel becomes even clearer and more real.

CREATING A LAY MINISTRY DYNAMIC

A spiritual dynamic cannot really be created or controlled, but just as we need air, heat, and fuel to have a fire, certain environmental factors must be present for this lay ministry dynamic to occur. At least three factors must be in place: believers with relational integrity, pastoral support, and safe venues.

> We will have an impact for the gospel if we are *like* those around us yet profoundly *unlike* them at the same time, all the while remaining very visible and *engaged*.

BELIEVERS WITH RELATIONAL INTEGRITY

A message is contextualized if (1) it is adapted into a new language or culture so it is understandable and yet (2) it maintains its character and original meaning in its former language/culture. Here I'm proposing that Christians *themselves* must be contextualized "letters of the gospel" (see 2 Cor 3:1 – 13). In other words, we will have an impact for the gospel if we are *like* those around us yet profoundly different and *unlike* them at the same time, all the while remaining very visible and *engaged*.

So, first of all, Christians must be like their neighbors in the food they eat and clothes they wear, their dialect, general appearance, work life, recreational and cultural activities, and civic engagement. They participate fully in life with their neighbors. Christians should also be like their neighbors with regard to excellence. That is, Christians should be very good at what others want to be good at. They should be skillful, diligent, resourceful, and disciplined. In short, Christians in a particular community should — at first glance — look reassuringly *similar* to the other people in the neighborhood. This opens up nonbelievers to any discussion of faith, because they recognize the believers as people who live in and understand their world. It also, eventually, gives them a glimpse of what they could look like if they became believers. It means it would be good if a nonbelieving young man on Wall Street could meet Christians in the financial world, not only those who are his age but also those who are older and more accomplished, or if an older female artist could meet Christian women who are artists of her own generation as well as others who are not.

Second, Christians must be also unlike their neighbors. In key ways, the early Christians were startlingly different from their neighbors; it should be no different for us today. Christians should be marked by *integrity*. Believers must be known for being scrupulously honest, transparent, and fair. Followers of Christ should also be marked by *generosity*. If employers, they should take less personal profit so customers and employees have more pay. As citizens, they should be philanthropic and generous with their time and with the money they donate for the needy. They should consider living below their potential lifestyle level. Believers should also be known for their *hospitality*, welcoming others into their homes, especially neighbors and people with needs. They should be marked by *sympathy* and avoid being known as self-serving or even ruthless in business or personal dealings. They should be marked by an unusual willingness to *forgive* and seek reconciliation, not by a vengeful or spiteful spirit.

In addition to these character qualities, Christians should be marked by clear countercultural values and practices. Believers should practice *chastity* and live consistently in light of the biblical sexual ethic. Those outside the church know this ethic — no sex outside of marriage — and any inconsistency in this area can destroy a believer's credibility as a Christian. Today, few people apart from those with strong Christian convictions live this way. Outsiders and non-Christians in the community will also notice how you respond to *adversity*. Being calm in the face of failure and disappointment is crucial to your Christian witness. Finally, they will notice if you are seeking *equity* — if you are committed to the common good of the community. Francis Schaeffer gives an example of what these countercultural values look like:

The Bible does clearly teach the right of property, but both the Old Testament and the New Testament put a tremendous stress on the compassionate use of that property. If at each place where the employer was a Bible-believing Christian the world could see that less profit was being taken so that the workers would have appreciably more than the "going rate" of pay, the gospel would have been better proclaimed throughout the whole world than if the profits were the same as the world took and then large endowments were given to Christian schools, missions, and other projects. This is not to minimize the centrality of preaching the gospel to the whole world, nor to minimize missions; it is to say that the other is also a way to proclaim the good news. [11]

In addition to being *like* others and *unlike* others, Christians should also be *engaged* with others.[12] Mission for a contextualized believer is a matter of everyday life — of developing nonsuperficial relationships with their neighbors, colleagues, and others in the city.

Here are some practical, simple ways to do this:

Engaging neighbors

- Take regular walks in your neighborhood to meet others who are out and about. Keep a regular schedule. Go to the same places at the same time for groceries, haircuts, coffee, shopping. This is one of the main ways you get to know those who live geographically near.
- Find ways to get to know others in your building or neighborhood — through a common laundry area, at resident meetings, and in numerous other ways.
- Find an avocation or hobby you can do with others in the city. For example, don't form a Christian backpacking club; join an existing one.
- Look for ways to play organized amateur sports in the city.
- Volunteer alongside other neighborhood residents at nonprofits and with other programs.
- If you have children, be involved at the school and get to know other parents.
- Participate in city events — fund-raisers, festivals, cleanups, summer shows, concerts, etc.

- Serve in your neighborhood. Visit the community board meeting. Pick up litter regularly. Get involved in neighborhood associations. Find individual neighbors (especially elderly ones) and find ways of serving them.
- Be hospitable to neighbors — when and where appropriate, invite them over for a meal or a movie, etc.

Engaging colleagues, coworkers, and friends

- Do recreational activities with them — watch sports (live or on TV at home or in a nightspot); go to a theater show, museum exhibit, art gallery exhibit, etc.
- Invite them to join a sports league with you.
- Invite them to work out with you at a gym.
- Put together a movie night.
- Go out of your way to eat with them as often as possible. Invite people over for a meal in your apartment or home or just invite them out to try a new restaurant.
- Plan trips or outings — a trip to a beach, a historical site, etc.
- If the person has a skill or interest, ask them (sincerely!) to educate you.
- Organize a discussion group on something — politics, books, etc., inviting mainly non-Christians.

Part of being engaged is to be willing to identify as a believer. Engaging relationally without doing so could be called "the blend-in approach." Many Christians live in a social world of non-Christians but don't think much about their friends' spiritual needs, nor do they identify themselves as believers to their friends. Their basic drive is to be accepted, to avoid being perceived as different — but this approach fails to integrate a person's faith with his or her relationships in the world.

The opposite can be true as well. It is certainly possible for a person to identify as a believer without engaging relationally outside the church. These are Christians who are aware of people's lostness and may get involved in conversations about faith, but their relationships with non-Christians are largely

superficial. We could call this "the Christian bubble approach." In this case, believers fill all of their significant relationships outside of work with other Christians and their time with Christian activities. They have not sought opportunities to learn from nonbelievers, appreciate them, affirm them, and serve them — so regardless of what these Christians believe, those outside the church do not know they care about them.

Forty years ago, most of us knew gay people, but we didn't *know* we did because everybody was carefully quiet about it. As a result, it was possible to believe stereotypes about them. Today most young people know someone who is gay, and so it is harder to believe stereotypes or generalizations about them. I suspect most urban skeptics I talk to today do have Christian friends, but they don't know it, because we are more afraid these days of being publicly identified as believers. In this sense, many Christians today are like gay people were forty years ago — so it is quite natural for people to believe caricatures and stereotypes of Christians because the believers they actually know are not identifying themselves. Skeptics need more than an argument in order to believe; they need to observe intelligent, admirable fellow human beings and see that a big part of what makes them this way is their faith. Having a Christian friend you admire makes the faith far more credible.

These three factors — *like, unlike,* and *engaged* — make up the foundation of what I call Christian relational integrity. Christians have relational integrity when they are integrated into the relational life of the city and when their faith is integrated into all parts of their lives. Why is Christian relational integrity important for evangelism and mission? Many churches think of evangelism almost strictly in terms of information transmission. But this is a mistake. Christian Smith's book on young adult religion in the United States looks at the important minority of young adults who become much more religious during their twenties. The factors associated with such conversions are primarily significant personal relationships.[13]

Alan Kreider observes that early Christianity

grew explosively — 40 percent per decade for nearly three centuries — in a very hostile environment:

> The early Christians did not engage in public preaching; it was too dangerous. There are practically no evangelists or missionaries whose names we know ... The early Christians had no mission boards. They did not write treatises about evangelism ... After Nero's persecution in the mid-first century, the churches in the Roman Empire closed their worship services to visitors. Deacons stood at the churches' doors, serving as bouncers, checking to see that no unbaptized person, no "lying informer," could come in ...
>
> And yet the church was growing. Officially it was a superstitio. Prominent people scorned it. Neighbors discriminated against the Christians in countless petty ways. Periodically the church was subjected to pogroms ... It was hard to be a Christian ... And still the church grew. Why?[14]

This striking way of laying out the early church's social situation forces us to realize that the church must have grown because it was *attractive*. Kreider writes, "People were fascinated by it, drawn to it as to a magnet." He goes on to make a strong historical case that Christians' *lives* — their concern for the weak and the poor, their integrity in the face of persecution, their economic sharing, their sacrificial love even for their enemies, and the high quality of their common life together — attracted nonbelievers to the gospel. Once nonbelievers were attracted to the community by the lives of Christians, they became open to talking about the gospel truths that were the source of this kind of life.

Urban people today do not face the same kind of life-threatening dangers that they did in the Greco-Roman world — plagues, social chaos, and violence. In that environment, being in a loving community could literally mean the difference between life and death. But urban residents today still face many things that Christianity can address. They lack the hope in future progress and prosperity that past generations of secular people have had. They face a lonelier and more competitive environment than other generations have faced. The quality of our lives — marked by evident hope, love, poise, and integrity — has always been the necessary precondi-

tion for evangelism. But this has never been more necessary than it is today.[15]

Why is there so little relational integrity among believers? The answer is largely — though not wholly — motivational. People who are in the blend-in mode often lack courage. They are (rightly) concerned about losing influence, being persecuted in behind-the-scenes ways, or being penalized professionally. On the other hand, those who are in the bubble mode are unwilling to make the emotional, social, or even financial and physical investment in

---

Once nonbelievers were attracted to the community by the lives of Christians, they became open to talking about the gospel truths that were the source of this kind of life.

---

the people around them. Surprisingly, the Internet contributes to much of this. Technology now makes it possible for a person to move to a city and remain in touch with their Christian friends and family in other places, while unintentionally making it easier to ignore the people who are physically living around us. This can contribute to our reluctance to invest emotionally in people.

But this lack of motivation is not the only reason we fail to see laypeople doing evangelistic outreach. Many are highly motivated but still feel handcuffed by a lack of skill and know-how. They find that the questions their non-Christian friends ask about the faith very quickly stump them or even shake their own faith. They feel they can't talk about the Christian faith with any kind of attractive force. This lack of skill and knowledge accentuates their lack of courage (they are afraid of being stumped) and even affects their compassion for others (they feel as though they won't be of any real help). This leads us to consider the second necessary factor for effective lay ministry.

PASTORAL SUPPORT

There is a way to pastor that promotes this every-member gospel ministry, just as there is a way to pastor that kills it. Whatever else they do, pastors and other church leaders must be aware of the importance of lay ministry and intentional about preparing people for it. They must be personally involved in the lives of lay ministers. The reasons so many Christians lack relational integrity — lack of motivation, lack of compassion, or lack of ability and knowledge — are often overcome through a strong pastoral connection with the lay ministers.

This connection does not come primarily through formal, content-heavy training sessions on "how to share your faith" (though this is vital and can be very helpful; at Redeemer, we are producing such materials to fit an urban environment). Instead, it is formed through informal teaching and support and ongoing advice from pastors and ministry leaders. Pastors must constantly remember to encourage and push laypeople to use their relationships for the ministry of the Word.[16]

It is important for a pastor to model how to both *talk* to people about faith issues and *pray* for them. In my earlier years at Redeemer, I did this in two ways: through the sermons I preached and in the Q&A sessions I held after every morning service. I modeled how to pray for people through regular prayer meetings with leaders in which we prayed for our nonbelieving friends. This modeling instills a sense of courage, compassion, and responsibility in people and encourages them to reach out to their friends.

A pastor and his team must be models of Christian relational integrity for the rest of the congregation. David Stroud, a London church planter, shares how his wife, Philippa, became deeply involved in the local public school while he started a neighborhood watch program on their street. These endeavors got them immersed into the life of the city and brought them into many relationships with their neighbors.[17]

In addition to modeling, it is also important that pastors maintain a practical and simple vision for a relational ministry of the gospel. It should be clear that reaching out to friends and colleagues does not necessarily involve sharing a complete gospel presentation in a single encounter. Despite the fact that this was the stated goal of several evangelism training programs a generation ago, only a small number of laypeople (or even clergy!) can do this

well. Reaching out to a friend is much more natural. These organic ways of reaching out must be constantly lifted up for people.

I summarize below some ways to do this, listed in order of intensity. Pastors should equip the people in their church to do all of these, pointing out that most of these behaviors require little more than some honesty and courage. Many of these are drawn from the case studies I gave earlier in this chapter.

1. One-on-one — informal
- Let others know of your Christian faith by simply mentioning church attendance or Christian beliefs in casual conversation.
- Ask questions about other people's beliefs and experiences with faith and church and simply listen appreciatively and sympathetically.
- Listen sympathetically to someone's challenges and mention that you will pray regularly for them.
- Share a difficult personal issue that you have and be sure to mention that your faith helps you by giving you strength and granting you forgiveness, etc.
- Share your spiritual narrative — a brief testimony of your Christian experience.

2. One-on-one — planned/intentional
- Offer someone a book or audio recording about Christian issues and invite them to discuss their reactions.
- Initiate a discussion about a friend's biggest problems with or objections to Christianity. Listen respectfully and give them some things to read and discuss.
- Regularly read a part of the Bible together — preferably one of the Gospels — to discuss the character of Jesus.

3. Provide an experience of Christian community
- Invite friends to situations or activities where they meet believers but where there is no direct Christian event or communication.
- Invite friends to venues where they hear the

gospel communicated and discussed — one-time event, such as an open forum; fellowship group; worship service; group meeting for inquirers, such as book club, seeker group, etc.

4. Share your faith
• Share the basics of the Christian faith with your friend, laying out how to become a Christian and inviting them to make a commitment.

It is important for pastors or elders to be readily available to field questions about issues that church members encounter in discussions with their friends. When a non-Christian asks a question such as, "Why does God allow such evil and suffering?" your people need quick turnaround with help on how to respond. A pastor can also provide free or low-cost materials that Christians can share with their friends. For example, if a Christian is sharing how Christianity helped them face a problem, they could give their friend a book or an audio or video selection that conveys the truth they found helpful. Every believer should have access to half a dozen compelling pieces of content on different subjects that they can give to someone after talking about an issue. This, of course, includes the offer to read and study the Bible together. Along the way, a pastor should try to meet regularly with lay ministers to talk about what is happening in their relationships. This has two purposes. On the one hand, it is a time to celebrate and encourage one another; on the other hand, it is a time to hold one another accountable to think about these relationships with a ministry mind-set that commits to reaching out and opening up to people.[18]

Perhaps most important, a pastor must work in a variety of ways to lay a theological motivational groundwork for lay evangelism using the gospel itself. This must be done in all kinds of venues — teaching, preaching, and personal pastoral support. What does this gospel groundwork look like? It means teaching people that the gospel gives you *humility*. As people come to understand the radical gospel analysis — that both "good" and "bad" people are equally lost and can only be saved by grace — it becomes impossible to be proud and condescending toward others without denying the gospel

itself. Moralistic Christians do evangelism with the attitude, "I'm right; they're wrong — and I enjoy telling people about it." Nothing could be less attractive or more oblivious to the spirit of the message itself. The gospel, by contrast, leads us to look at non-Christians and know that they may very well be better people than we are. I can look at my Hindu neighbor and realize he may be a much better father to his children than I have ever been. The gospel gives us the foundation of a humble appreciation of others on which winsome relationships can be built.

The pastor can also show people how the gospel gives us hope for non-Christians. It is easy to look at some people and say, "They will never become Christians." But when we grasp the gospel, we know that there is no such thing as a typical Christian. No person is more promising material for Christianity than another. Salvation is an undeserved gift. So there is hope for anyone, no matter how far from God they may seem to be. The attitude of your heart should instead be this: "Me, a Christian? Who would have ever thought that someone like me would be a Christian and a child of God? But that is what I am! It's a wonder and a miracle." This attitude leads us to have expectant hope as we think of anyone else.

Finally, we must explain how the gospel gives us courage for evangelism. One of the reasons we shy away from talking about Jesus and the gospel is that we are afraid. We get our sense of value from what people think of us. We want to appear cool or sophisticated or progressive, or we want to look respectable, so we are careful to mind our own business. Sadly, when we think this way, how God regards us is not important enough to us. But the gospel keeps us from being tied to our reputation. When we know that salvation is by grace alone, we know that people come to faith only if God opens their hearts. No amount of brilliance or overpowering reason will serve to bring someone to faith. Therefore, we don't have to worry about our lack of knowledge. It is God's grace that opens hearts, not our eloquence.

If your lay ministers are ineffective in reaching out to others because they are turned off by certain kinds of people or because they lack the hope or courage to talk to others about Jesus, they may not need another book or a course on evangelism. You may just need to help them get back to the foundation — the gospel — and allow the message of God's gracious, undeserved, merciful love for sinners to work itself into their hearts in new ways. I believe the single most important way for pastors or church leaders to turn passive laypeople into courageous and gracious lay ministers is through their own evident godliness.

> The single most important way for pastors or church leaders to turn passive laypeople into courageous and gracious lay ministers is through their own evident godliness.

A pastor should be marked by humility, love, joy, and wisdom that is visible and attracts people to trust and learn from them. As a pastor, you may not be the best preacher, but if you are filled with God's love, joy, and wisdom, you won't be boring! You may not be the most skillful organizer or charismatic leader, but if your holiness is evident, people will follow you. This means, at the very least, that a dynamic, disciplined, and rich prayer life is not only important in the abstract and personal sense; it may be the most practical thing you can do for your ministry.

SAFE VENUES

It is certainly possible to have an evangelistic dynamic built strictly on relational, informal outreach by laypeople. Nevertheless, laypeople are often encouraged and instructed in their ministry if a church provides a varied set of events, gatherings, and meetings in which nonbelievers are exposed more directly to both Christians and to the gospel. Such settings must avoid two common dangers: *confusing* the newcomer (assuming a particular theological or ecclesiastical background) or *offending* the newcomer (putting unnecessary stumbling blocks in front of them). I daresay that most well-intentioned "outreach" events I witnessed over the years have fallen into one or both of these errors. Use your in-

genuity to imagine a variety of meetings and places where people without faith can, through a winsome approach, be stimulated to consider the claims of the Christian gospel. Here are some examples.[19]

- A one-off event, such as an open forum. At Redeemer, these have typically been artistic forums (such as "Excerpts from *Porgy and Bess*," "Coltrane Night," or a Bach Wedding Cantata), followed by a lecture that offers a Christian perspective on the art, with a time for questions and answers.
- A gathering in a small public venue with a brief talk and Q&A on a single topic that addresses problems people have with Christian faith. At Redeemer, we call these "Christianity Uncorked" events.
- A small group that is just beginning to form. When groups are relatively new and the dynamics are still "wet cement," they can better embrace and draw in people who are exploring Christianity.
- A worship service that — through its preaching, music, and liturgy — is comprehensible to non-Christians.
- A group of Christians that meets for four weeks; each week, each member asks one non-Christian friend a question about their religious beliefs for the purpose of listening to (not debating) other religious beliefs and objections to Christianity.
- A group mainly for non-Christians that meets regularly. *Less intense*: a book club focused on reading fiction books by C. S. Lewis, Flannery O'Connor, J. R. R. Tolkien, G. K. Chesterton, Fyodor Dostoyevsky, etc., that get at Christian themes, or even reading books by non-Christians and talking about the faith perspectives and worldviews they represent. *More intense*: Eight-week "seeker groups" that meet to study a book. Some people may respond well to frank discussions about common "defeaters" of Christianity,[20] while others may prefer to explore the life of Jesus through reading one of the Gospels or using a book such as *King's Cross*.[21]

- Onetime "salons" in which Christians bring non-Christian friends to hear an informal presentation by a Christian speaker on a topic, followed by a discussion.
- Worship "after meetings." Examples include a Q&A session after the church service with the preacher of the day, where any questions are allowed, though usually the topic of the message is covered; an apologetics class (five to seven weeks) that makes a case for the truth of Christianity; or a seven-week class covering basic Christian beliefs and Christian living, oriented to new believers but open to attendance by seekers.
- Affinity-based outreach. Campus ministries, vocational (industry-based) ministries, and men's or women's gatherings can have an evangelistic/apologetics aspect in their regular meetings and may hold outreach events at neutral venues, similar to the ones described above.

Evangelism should be natural, not dictated by a set of bullet points and agenda items that we enter into a conversation hoping to cover. Friends share their hearts with each other and do what's best for each other. Evangelism will come organically in friendship if we don't let our pride, fears, and pessimism cause us to hide our faith and heart. We must help our people naturally talk to their friends about how they see reality. The more these gospel dynamics are present in their lives, the more they will draw in new people like a magnet (Acts 2:47) and help them find faith in the most credible, natural, and fruitful way.

In general, simply bringing nonbelievers into the Christian community at any point is safe if the whole community is very warm and accepting toward those without faith, if the community is not culturally alien, if the community is shepherded by pastors who make lay ministry a priority, and if the church is doing balanced and integrative ministry. It is to this last subject that we turn our attention in part 7.

QUESTIONS FOR DISCUSSION AND REFLECTION

1. Read through the various examples of every-member gospel ministry. Which of these situations sound similar to something you have done personally? Which of them spark creative ideas for sharing your faith, as well as for leading others to do so? What could your team do to become more intentional in this type of gospel ministry? Can you add to the list other examples you have seen in your community?

2. What do you think of the idea that people may need to be "welcomed into community long enough for them to hear multiple expressions of the gospel — both formal and informal — from individuals and teachers" before coming to faith? What might keep a nonbeliever from being involved in your community? What are you doing to welcome nonbelievers into your community of faith?

3. This chapter presents the idea of believers having "Christian relational integrity." This means they have an impact for the gospel on the people around them if they are *like* those around them, yet profoundly different and *unlike* them, all the while remaining very visible and *engaged*. What do you think it means to be *like, unlike,* and *engaged with* your community? How do you think your team members are doing in each of these areas? How would you rate your church in the area of relational integrity?

4. Which of the various ideas for providing safe venues do you currently practice in your ministry? How "safe" would an unbeliever rate the venues you provide? What single safe venue would you like to prototype?

CHAPTER 21 — EQUIPPING PEOPLE FOR MISSIONAL LIVING *(pages 277-89)*

1. Ryan Bolger, "Marks of a Missional Church," http://thebolgblog.typepad.com/thebolgblog/2006/01/marks_of_a_miss.html (accessed February 17, 2012).
2. John Stott, *Motives and Methods in Evangelism* (Leicester, UK: Inter-Varsity, 1962), 14.
3. Michael Green, *Evangelism in the Early Church*, rev. ed. (Grand Rapids: Eerdmans, 2003), 243, quoting Adolph Harnack.
4. Ibid.
5. Ibid., 342 – 46.
6. Ibid., 244.
7. Ibid., 315.
8. Ibid., 318 – 38.
9. Ibid., 339.
10. Many of these examples are adapted from the ones found in Colin Marshall and Tony Payne, *The Trellis and the Vine* (Kingsford, Australia: Matthias Media, 2009), 54 – 56. I've added some new examples and contextualized the ones found in the book.
11. Francis Schaeffer, *2 Contents, 2 Realities* (Downers Grove, Ill.: InterVarsity, 1975), 31 – 32.
12. For several good ideas on engagement, see Tim Chester and Steve Timmis, *Everyday Church: Mission by Being Good Neighbours* (Nottingham, UK: Inter-Varsity, 2011), ch. 4 ("Everyday Mission").
13. See Christian Smith, *Souls in Transition: The Religious and Spiritual Lives of Emerging Adults* (New York: Oxford University Press, 2009), 209.
14. Alan Kreider, " 'They Alone Know the Right Way to Live': The Early Church and Evangelism," in *Ancient Faith for the Church's Future*, ed. Mark Husbands and Jeffrey P. Greenman (Downers Grove, Ill.: Inter-Varsity, 2008), 169 – 70.
15. Two other must-read books about the early Christians and their witness through lay ministry are Green, *Evangelism in the Early Church*, and Rodney Stark, *The Rise of Christianity* (New York: HarperCollins, 1990).
16. For excellent, easily remembered outlines to give to laypeople for informal pastoral care and evangelism, see Chester and Timmis, *Everyday Church*, ch. 3 ("Everyday Pastoral Care") and ch. 5 ("Everyday Evangelism").
17. See David Stroud, *Planting Churches, Changing Communities* (Milton Keynes, UK: Authentic Media, 2009), 172.
18. For practical suggestions on how to do this, see Marshall and Payne, *The Trellis and the Vine*, ch. 9 ("Multiplying Gospel Growth through Training Coworkers").
19. For a comprehensive treatment and list of evangelistic venues, see Michael Green, *Evangelism through the Local Church* (Nashville: Nelson, 1992). Though dated, it is the most complete guide to the subject of its title.
20. See Timothy Keller, *The Reason for God Study Guide and DVD: Conversations on Faith and Life* (Grand Rapids: Zondervan, 2010).
21. See Timothy Keller, *King's Cross* (New York: Dutton, 2011).

chapter 22

THE BALANCE OF MINISTRY FRONTS

Churches driven by a Center Church theological vision will pursue an integrative, balanced ministry. Because the gospel not only converts nonbelievers but also builds up believers, the church should not have to choose evangelism over discipleship. Because the gospel is presented to the world not only through word but also through deed and community, we should not choose between teaching and carrying out practical ministry to address people's needs. Because the gospel renews not only individuals but also communities and culture, the church should disciple its people to seek personal conversion, deep Christian community, social justice, and cultural renewal in the city. These ministry areas should not be seen as independent or optional but as interdependent and fully biblical.

The reality is that very few churches furnish all of these "ministry fronts" with balanced resources and attention. Many churches are committed to evangelism, church growth, and church planting. Some put all the stress on fellowship and community. Others are radically committed to the poor and issues of social justice. Still others make much of the importance of culture and the arts. But seldom are these traits combined. Indeed, it is normal to find the leaders of these various ministries resisting or even resenting the other ministry emphases. Those working with the poor think "integrating faith and work" is elitist. Those stressing community, discipleship, and holiness often think that emphasizing church growth produces spiritual shallowness.

But engaging on all of these fronts is required by the nature of the gospel. The experience of grace inspires evangelism as well as intimate, glorious worship of the God who saved us. It creates the new transparency and openness that make deep fellow-

ship possible. The grace orientation of the gospel humbles us and gives us a new passion for justice. And the nature of the gospel helps us discern idolatry in ourselves and in our culture that distorts the way we do our work and live our lives in society.

What's more, engaging on all these fronts is required by the nature of our culture. Ministry in which Christians sacrificially serve the common good of the city is not only biblical but a necessary context for any convincing evangelistic call to believe in Jesus. After all, why should the people of the city listen to us if we are perceived to be out simply to increase the size and power of our own tribe? Or consider cultural engagement. In a previous chapter we said that culture cannot be changed simply through people trying to integrate their faith with their work *or* simply through lots of conversions. It must be both. There must be an increasing

---

Engaging on all of these fronts is required by the nature of the gospel; what's more, it is required by the nature of our culture.

---

number of Christians who are shaped by the gospel through a deep experience of Christian community and who are known for their commitment to the poor. It is only as we do all of these ministries at once that any of them will be most effective. Success on any one front depends on success in the other fronts of ministry. The truth is that if we don't make a strong effort to do *all* of these in some way at once, we won't actually do *any* of them well at all. In other words, Center Church ministry must be *integrative*.

BREAKING THE LIBERAL/CONSERVATIVE PARADIGM

Many people have a driving impulse to place every church somewhere on the ideological spectrum from liberal/left wing to conservative/right wing. But the gospel makes a church impossible to categorize in this way, for it brings both deep, powerful changes that convert people from their sin and deep, powerful social changes as well. It defies the values of our hearts (selfishness and idolatry) and of the world (power, status, recognition, wealth). The gospel pattern is triumph through weakness, wealth through poverty, power through service. Grasping this changes our attitude toward the poor, our own status, and our wealth and careers. Rather than emphasizing *mainly* evangelism (as conservative churches do) or *mainly* social justice (as liberal churches do), we intentionally set out to give a very high emphasis to both — employing a holistic approach that connects the people in our church to the city through both evangelistic proclamation and ministries of justice and mercy. A gospel-centered church should combine the "zeals" that are not typically seen together in the same church.

Only if we produce thousands of new church communities that regularly win secular people to Christ, seek the common good of the whole city (especially the poor), and disciple thousands of Christians to write plays, advance science, do creative journalism, begin effective and productive new businesses, use their money for others, and produce cutting-edge scholarship and literature will we actually be doing all the things the Bible tells us that Christians should be doing! This is how we will begin to see our cities comprehensively influenced for Christ.

BALANCING THE BIBLE'S METAPHORS FOR THE CHURCH

In an important article, Edmund Clowney demonstrates that there are literally dozens of metaphors used by the Bible to describe the church.[1] The church is called "a chosen people ... a holy nation" (1 Pet 2:9) — literally, a distinct ethnic so changed by our encounter with Christ that we are more like one another than like others in our own particular races and societies. The church is also a "family" in which other Christians are my brothers, sisters, mothers, and fathers (Matt 12:49 – 50; 1 Tim 5:1 – 2; 1 John 3:14 – 18). The church is called "the body of Christ" (1 Cor 12:12 – 27) suggesting that all of us, like parts of a human body, have our own different but irreplaceable and interdependent function. These metaphors describe the new connection we have to one another in Christ.

Several metaphors emphasize the unique access we now have to the love and presence of God himself. The church is depicted as the bride of Christ (2 Cor 11:2; Eph 5:32), pointing us to a level of intimacy that goes beyond the deepest of human relationships. It is also referred to as "a royal priesthood" (1 Pet 2:9) and "a holy temple" of God's Spirit, "a spiritual house" (Eph 2:20 – 22; 1 Pet 2:4 – 8).

Other metaphors speak of growth, in both quality and size. The church is "God's field" of crops (1 Cor 3:9), his "harvest" (John 4:35), an "olive tree" (Rom 11:24) and the "branches" on a vine (John 15:5). Along with the references to our role as a priesthood offering sacrifices by sharing and doing good (Heb 13:16) and to our calling to declare God's praises (1 Pet 2:9b), these images speak of how we are to serve God as we connect to the world. And these are only a handful of the eighty-some metaphors used by the Bible to describe the church. Clowney rightly warns against focusing too much on any one of them. All of them must inform our practice of church life, and that poses a great challenge.

Our natural tendency is to prioritize one or two particular metaphors in our understanding of the church and its identity in the world, and neglect others. Cardinal Avery Dulles's book *Models of the Church* points out how, at various places in the history of the church and in particular settings across the range of cultures, this has indeed been the case. Various biblical metaphors of the church have come to dominate Christians' thinking and push out other metaphors, and he lists five church models that tend to emphasize one of the metaphors over all others:[2]

1. The *church as institution* model emphasizes doctrine, theology, and ordained ministerial authority.
2. The *church as mystical communion* points to the church as organic community and fellowship.
3. The *church as sacrament* accents corporate worship.
4. The *church as herald* preeminently does evangelism and preaching.
5. The *church as servant* is a radical community committed to social justice.

Church models are in one sense unavoidable. The spiritual gifts and callings of a congregation's leaders, together with their social context (e.g., university town versus inner-city neighborhood) will necessarily mean every church tends to be naturally better at fulfilling some metaphors and doing some kinds of ministry. Some churches will be better at evangelism, others at teaching and discipleship, others at gathered worship and preaching, others at service to those in need. We know that no one Christian can have all spiritual gifts and carry out all ministries equally well — this is the clear point of 1 Corinthians 12. It can also be argued that no one congregation has all the spiritual gifts (at least not all in proportion) and is therefore unable to do all things equally well. Local churches, just like individual believers, should humbly acknowledge their limitations and recognize that they are just one part of the whole body of Christ in a city, region, or nation.

FOUR MINISTRY FRONTS

None of the metaphors used to describe the church can be ignored — they are all biblical. Every church must seek to be true to *all* of the rich images in Scripture. Yet no church has a perfectly balanced set of gifts and strengths; nor does it have excess leadership or financial capacity! What does it mean, practically, to be faithful to these limitations yet true to all the biblical metaphors?

It means a church should strive to supplement its strong ministries by seeking to do *all* the forms of ministry as skillfully as possible in an integrative way. It should recognize and capitalize on its strengths but never give up seeking to shore up its weak areas, out of respect for all the things that Scripture says a church is and does. It is not unlike the relationship of individual spiritual gifts to Christian duties. For example, the Bible tells all Christians to evangelize and love their poor neighbor. Yet some people have gifts of evangelism (Eph 4:11) and others gifts of mercy and service (Rom 12:7 – 8). So Christian individuals should find ample opportunities to use their gifts but must still take care to do what the Bible says are their duties, even those they do not feel they are very good at.

We must admit the difficulty of this task. In fact, it is one of the hardest balances church leaders have to strike. They must recognize that no church can do all things equally well, and yet they cannot let any functions given to the church "fall off the map." And city churches in particular, because of the complexity of metropolitan society, must be especially careful to engage each area of ministry with as much generous commitment and emphasis as they can.

Instead of speaking about metaphors and models of the church, I prefer to talk about distinct "ministry fronts." These are based on the understanding that the various models and metaphors tend to emphasize particular types of ministry and prioritize them over others. Let me propose four "fronts" to ministry:

1. connecting people to God (through evangelism and worship)
2. connecting people to one another (through community and discipleship)
3. connecting people to the the city (through mercy and justice)
4. connecting people to the culture (through the integration of faith and work)

Of course, very few churches actually engage in all four of these fronts with completely balanced focus and attention. The norm, more often than not, is an atmosphere of competition within the church and between churches, with different ministries vying for resources and attention. But engagement of some kind on all four of these fronts is the only way to honor the full range of the biblical metaphors of the church. This is what I am calling *integrative ministry*.

We have one calling — to sing the praises of God. We declare and demonstrate the glory and goodness of God in diverse ways to different groups of people.

I have not found anyone who has taught the integrative nature of the church's ministry better than Edmund Clowney. In his biblical-theological work on the church, Clowney speaks of the biblical "goals of ministry" as threefold: (1) we are called to minister and serve God through *worship* (Rom 15:8 – 16; 1 Pet 2:9); (2) we are to minister and serve one another through *Christian nurture* (Eph 4:12 – 26); and (3) we are to minister and serve the world through *witness* (Matt 28:18 – 20; Luke 24:28; Acts 5:32). These three goals of ministry show the comprehensive scope of what the church is called to do. We are not called to "specialize" in one of these areas — *only* connecting people to God, to each other, or to the world. We do them all. And Clowney argues that all of these goals are really *one* goal, one fundamental calling and purpose as a church:

> The calling of the church to minister directly to God, to the saints, and to the world is one calling. Paul witnesses to the world of the Gentiles so that they may sing praise to God. Nurture and worship go together too: we sing to God in psalms, hymns, and spiritual songs, but as we do so, we teach and admonish one another (Col 4:16; Eph 5:19). When our hearts are filled with praise to God our very worship becomes a testimony to the world. At Pentecost the disciples praised God in many languages and their praise was a witness to those who heard.[3]

There it is. We have one calling — to sing the praises of God, to declare the excellencies of him who called us out of darkness into his marvelous light (1 Pet 2:9). When we show forth and sing God's praises to the world, we witness. When we show forth and sing God's praises to each other, we build up and disciple. When we show forth and sing God's praises to God in his presence, we worship. We declare and demonstrate the glory and goodness of God in diverse ways to different groups of people. That's why we exist as a church.

THE SPHERES AND ROLES OF THE CHURCH

At this point, it is also helpful to recall something we cited earlier — the distinction made by Abraham Kuyper between the spheres of the institutional church and the organic church. The institutional church is the local church under its officers, while the organic church refers to Christians united in a host of formal and informal associations and organizations, or believers simply working as individuals out in the world. The church, both institutional and organic, must be engaged on all four fronts, either directly or indirectly — and the Kuyperian distinction suggests some differences of role and scope between the two spheres.

The ministry fronts of worship/evangelism and community/discipleship are preeminently the work of the institutional church and its ministers and elders. All individual believers are to be witnesses and to build up other believers. And many parachurch agencies have been very effective in these areas. But the ministry of the local church is the irreplaceable agent for this ministry in the world, for its main task is the ministry of the Word and the sacraments — winning people to faith and building them up as disciples.

When ministering to the economic and material needs of people — the third ministry front of mercy and justice — there is an overlap between the institutional and organic church. The church does the diaconal ministry for people within and immediately around its community. Those in the Reformed tradition believe that the diaconate is a special office within the church dedicated for just this purpose. But there is also the work of economic development and social reform that more systemically tackles the problems of poverty and other societal needs. I believe this type of work is best done by individual Christians or in organizations they form for these specific purposes.[4]

When the institutional church gives attention to cultural engagement — the fourth and final ministry front — it does so primarily by *discipling* a community of believers who work as the church organic. By teaching the Christian doctrine of vocation, the goodness of creation, the importance of culture, and the practice of Sabbath, it should be inspiring and encouraging its members to go into the various channels of culture. It equips its filmmaker members, for example, to be distinctively Christian in their art and work through solid Christian instruction. But in the end, I believe the local church should not form a production company to make feature films.

In the chapters that follow, we will unpack in greater detail what ministry can look like on each of the four fronts, particularly as it integrates with the others. Some of this is merely suggestive, since we obviously cannot set out everything a church should be doing in every area of ministry. Still, I hope it will bring clarity and focus to the mission of the church, along with a much-needed balance in the way we engage in ministry.[5]

QUESTIONS FOR DISCUSSION AND REFLECTION

1. Which of the metaphors of the church given in Scripture (a holy nation, a family, the body of Christ, the bride of Christ, a royal priesthood, the temple of God's Spirit, God's field and harvest, branches on a vine, etc.) do you naturally tend to prioritize? How do these priorities make your church unique?

2. Which of the five models of church described by Avery Dulles most closely align with your own church's model?

   - the "church as institution" model — emphasizes doctrine, theology, and ordained ministerial authority
   - the "church as mystical communion" model — points to the church as organic community and fellowship
   - the "church as sacrament" model — accents corporate worship
   - the "church as herald" model — preeminently does evangelism and preaching
   - the "church as servant" model — a radical community committed to social justice

   How would you describe your church model to others? What would you emphasize?

3. Keller writes, "When the institutional church gives attention to cultural engagement — the fourth and final ministry front — it does so primarily by *discipling* a community of believers who work as the church organic. By teaching the Christian doctrine of vocation, the goodness of creation, the importance of culture, and the practice of Sabbath, it should be inspiring and encouraging its members to go into the various channels of culture." Do you agree with this premise? What are some of the dangers of the institutional church getting directly involved in this work? What are some of the practical ways your church can disciple believers to engage the culture?

CHAPTER 22 — THE BALANCE OF MINISTRY FRONTS *{pages 291–95}*

1. Edmund P. Clowney, "Interpreting the Biblical Models of the Church," in *Biblical Interpretation and the Church*, ed. D. A. Carson (Nashville: Nelson, 1985), 64 – 109.
2. Avery Dulles, *Models of the Church* (Garden City, N.Y.: Image, 1978). I speak more extensively about church models and Dulles's book in the sections on "Church Models and Ministry" and "Church Models and Movements" in chapter 30.
3. Edmund P. Clowney, *Living in Christ's Church* (Philadelphia: Great Commission, 1986), 140.
4. I make the case for this distinction in *Generous Justice: How God's Grace Makes Us Just* (New York: Dutton, 2010, ch. 6).
5. It is important to point out that what follows is not a thoroughgoing theology of worship, community, diaconal ministry, and public discipleship. Nor is it a balanced survey of ministry methods. Rather, it is a set of observations about how each area of ministry interacts with the others. Of course, each of these ministry areas or "fronts" deserves a book-length treatment, which I either have done (e.g., *Generous Justice*), am doing (e.g., *Every Good Endeavor*), or hope to do.

chapter 23

CONNECTING PEOPLE TO GOD

Two generations ago, almost no one was asking, "How shall we worship?" Every church was solidly encased in a particular theological tradition or denomination and worship was done in conformity with the tradition. Today, however, there is a dizzying variety of worship approaches and styles being used, not only in churches across the country (as has always been the case) but even in churches within the same denomination. Sadly, this new diversity has been the cause of much strife and confusion.

Probably the single most common fault line in the "worship wars" has been the conflict between contemporary and traditional worship, which I trace in my chapter in *Worship by the Book*.[1] In countless churches during the 1960s, '70s, and '80s, there was a battle between the WWII generation (who favored traditional hymns, choirs, and instrumentation) and baby boomers (who favored praise songs set to contemporary pop music). By the mid-1990s, this struggle was generally won by the boomers. Today, however, things are much more complicated. Not only are there more than two approaches to worship; there are many dedicated efforts to blend some of them.[2]

Because even the most innovative churches cannot completely reinvent their worship service every week, worship traditions are inevitable. See the chart on the following page for a list of the main ones I observe in the American church today.

Some readers may immediately recoil from the question, "How do we choose a worship form?" because they think it reflects an American consumer mentality that designs or chooses ministry strictly to meet the felt needs of the customer. But while consumerism can indeed be the force behind such a question, the assumptions behind resistance to the question can be just as suspect. Many shy away from considering different worship forms because they simplistically believe there is only one biblically warranted way to do worship. They wrongly assume their own version of Christianity is ahistorical rather than culturally and socially situated. Or they may avoid the question because of the strength of their own tastes. Some people resonate so strongly with certain forms they insist they simply "cannot worship" any other way. But in part 3 (Gospel Contextualization), we saw that all human expressions are to some extent culturally embedded, and this applies to worship as well. While the truths we confess and profess transcend culture, no articulation or embodiment of them can be culture transcending.

Earlier we looked at 1 Corinthians 9:19 – 23, where Paul speaks about adapting for various cultures, becoming "all things to all … that by all possible means I might save some." As we observed, this is not a recipe for relativism. Rather, Paul is reminding us that in every culture there are many things that do not directly contradict Scripture and therefore are neither forbidden nor commanded. In charity and humility, such cultural features should generally be adopted to avoid making the gospel unnecessarily foreign. This is true not only for preaching but also for gathered worship.

Each of us has forms of worship that we believe have solid biblical warrant and that we have seen bear much fruit. Yet we should always admit the degree to which any form of worship reflects cultural and temperamental factors, not merely biblical principles. In this I should speak for myself. I find Reformed and Presbyterian worship to be in accord with God's Word and to be richly satisfying to me. However, this tradition leaves essentially no room

HISTORIC emphasis	CONTEMPORARY emphasis	CONVERGENCE emphasis
Liturgical Emphasis on the physical and the senses; Eucharist is central *High*: Anglican *Moderate*: Lutheran, Episcopal *Lower*: Continental Reformed, Methodist	*Praise and Worship* Emphasis on the emotional; praise music is central *African American*: AME, National Baptist *Classic Pentecostal*: Assemblies of God, Church of God in Christ, Foursquare *Contemporary praise/worship*: Calvary Chapels, Vineyards *Traditional-praise "blend"*: 50/50 worship songs and hymns	*Fusions of Both Form and Music* Emphasis on the mystical; story is central *Liturgical contemporary*: Original form was the "folk Mass" of charismatic Catholics and Anglicans. Now we have a variety of specific liturgical traditions (Anglican, Reformed, etc.) or an amalgamated "Great Tradition" using traditional folk, pop/soft rock, indie rock, jazz, rhythm and blues/gospel, hip-hop, eclectic, and others
Traditional Emphasis on the mental; sermon is central *Free church*: Puritan/Reformed, many independent churches *Body life*: Anabaptist, Quaker, smaller churches, Jesus movement *Revivalist*: Baptist, Methodist	*Seeker-Oriented Worship* Emphasis on the practical; theme is central *Seeker-driven service*: Willow Creek *Seeker-sensitive worship*: Saddleback	

for unpredictability or for public displays of emotion. Why? Presbyterians like to cite the Pauline text about doing all things "in a fitting and orderly way" (1 Cor 14:40), even though this text is embedded in a passage that describes a very un-Presbyterian sounding service. We should admit that, while much of our love for predictability and order comes from a right concern for reverence and decorum in the presence of the King, our particular expression of that reverence is typically strongly northern Euro-

pean and middle-class and often reflects a temperamental bias (maybe even idolatry) regarding control. In short, our preference for a particular way of worship is typically based on a mixture of principle, temperament, and culture.

This gives flexibility, even to those who believe in the "regulative principle" of worship — of whom I am one.[3] That historic view says Christians should not do anything in gathered worship unless there is some warrant for it in the Bible. Yet it makes a distinction between biblical "elements" of worship (e.g., preaching, reading the Word, singing, prayer, baptism and vows) and the "circumstances" — the particular ways in which we do the elements. The Bible does not prescribe or even address innumerable practical considerations. It does not indicate the level of formality and predictability of the service; the length of the service or amount of time devoted to each part; the kinds of harmony, rhythm, or instrumentation of the music; the level of emotional expressiveness; or even the order of worship. There is no equivalent to the book of Leviticus in the New Testament. The Scots Confession of 1560 states, "Not that we think that any policy of order of ceremonies which men have devised can be appointed for all ages, times, and places."[4]

GUIDING PRINCIPLES FOR CONNECTING PEOPLE TO GOD

The Bible, then, leaves us a level of freedom when it comes to many of the practical issues of worship. How do we use this freedom wisely? How can we determine which approach to use? It will be helpful to keep several perspectives in mind as we encourage people to connect to God in worship.

THE NORMATIVE PERSPECTIVE: LOOKING TO THE BIBLE AND THE PAST

First, our *biblical theology* of worship shapes the service. Theoretically, our theology of worship should be a fixed, unchanging thing. In reality, however, our sinful hearts and the richness of Scripture mean that our theology of worship is constantly evolving (toward greater fullness and accuracy, we hope!). It is easy to assume we have *the* balanced understanding of worship, but at any given time, we probably don't. Nevertheless, this is where we begin. We must let our best understanding of what the Word says about worship shape the service we design and use every week.

In addition, a *historical tradition* of worship informs the service. Over the years, Christians have developed a number of historical worship traditions. Tradition is valuable because it connects us to the saints and the church of the past, relying on

the tested wisdom of the generations. Protestants alone have produced (among others) the Lutheran, Anglican, Continental Reformed, Puritan/Free Church, Anabaptist, Revivalist, Pentecostal, and African-American traditions of worship.

A generation or two ago, most evangelicals conducted nonliturgical traditional worship. Then from the early 1970s on, there was a major move toward nonliturgical contemporary worship. But by the 1990s, many were turning again. Concerned with what was perceived as the overly cognitive nature of traditional evangelical worship and the overly sentimental nature of contemporary evangelical worship, many have turned back to even more liturgical forms than the sermon-oriented traditional worship they had abandoned.[5] Many in this movement do not adopt a service from any particular worship tradition but create a pastiche from diverse historic approaches.

Please exercise great care here. As we have said, each worship tradition is rooted in time, place, and culture, and none of them should be seen as an unchangeable absolute. And it is also true that many now-historic traditions were once innovative revisions of an older approach. Recognize, however, that the different worship and spirituality traditions of the church are also grounded in theological differences. So while we cannot say any one of them is the one and only true way, there are some genuine tensions and even contradictions among them. For example, the difference between more sacrament-centered liturgical worship and more Word- or sermon-centered worship is based in large part on different understandings of how God communicates grace, of how spiritual growth occurs, and of the relationship of doctrine and experience. And, as Michael Allen points out, the difference between more emotionally immediate charismatic worship and classic "Word and sacrament" worship is rooted in different views of the relationship of grace and nature. In the former, grace is seen to work more through immediate experience and interruptions of natural laws, while in the latter, "grace perfects nature, rather than ... doing an end-run around it."[6]

WORLD-WINNING WORSHIP

God commanded Israel to invite the nations to join in declaring his glory. The vision of Zion was that it would be the center of world-winning worship (Ps 102:18, 21–22; Isa 2:2–4; 56:6–8). Psalm 105, is a direct command that believers engage in evangelistic worship. The psalmist challenges the people to *"make known among the nations what [the Lord] has done"* (v. 1, emphasis mine). How are they to do this? "Sing to him, sing praise to him; tell of all his wonderful acts" (v. 2). Throughout the Old Testament Scriptures, believers are continually told to sing and to praise God before the nonbelieving nations (see also Pss 47:1; 100:1–5). As God's people praise him, the nations are summoned and called to join in song.

When we turn to the New Testament, we find Peter telling a Gentile church, "You are a chosen people, a royal priesthood, a holy nation, a people belonging to God, that you may declare the praises of him who called you out of darkness into his wonderful light" (1 Pet 2:9). Peter highlights the continuity of God's purposes for his people when he challenges the church to evangelistic worship—the same witness to which Israel was called. But there is a key difference. In the Old Testament, the center of world-winning worship was Mount Zion, but now, wherever we worship Jesus in spirit and in truth (John 4:24), we come to the heavenly Zion (Heb 12:22–24). In other words, the risen Lord now sends his people out singing his praises in mission, calling the nations to join both saints and angels in heavenly doxology. Jesus himself stands in the midst of the redeemed and leads us in the singing of God's praises (Heb 2:12), even as God stands over his redeemed and sings over us in joy (Zeph 3:17).

I believe it is best therefore to examine the Word, draw our theological conclusions, inhabit or be informed by the historic tradition we think most fits our conclusions, and then (however) be open to cultural adaptations and learning from other traditions.[7]

THE SITUATIONAL PERSPECTIVE: CULTURAL AND ECCLESIAL SETTINGS

John Calvin recognized that a worship service is not to be shaped only by theological and historical considerations. He often said that "whatever edifies" should be done: "If we let love be our guide, all will be safe."[8] In other words, it is critical to consider what appeals to the people of our community and our church. Again, let's break this down into two aspects.

First, our *cultural context* shapes the service. Though this idea may be a major source of controversy among some, it is unavoidable nonetheless. We see a strong correlation between approaches to worship and demographic factors such as age, socioeconomic status, and ethnicity. Here are some examples from our own observation in New York City:

- Generally, classical music and liturgy appeal to the educated. "High" cultural forms are those that, by definition, require training to appreciate.
- Generally, contemporary praise/worship approaches are far more likely to bring together a diversity of racial groups.
- Generally, young professional Anglos, especially of the more artistic bent, are highly attracted to the convergence of liturgical/historical with eclectic musical forms.
- Generally, baby boomer families are highly attracted to seeker-sensitive worship and the more ahistorical, sentimental Christian contemporary songs.

As you design your worship, you cannot naively assume you are "just being biblical" about many things that are actually cultural and personal preferences. Think of who is in your community and skew your worship service toward them in all the places where your biblical theology and historic tradition leave you freedom.

Second, keep in mind that our church's *model* and *core values* shape the service. Every church should do worship, evangelism, teaching, community building, and service — but every model relates these elements to one another in different ways. For example, some church models expect to do much of their evangelism in the service; other models do not. Many have pointed out that all worship traditions have slightly different purposes. They are all *worship* — they all aim to honor God by lifting him up, showing everyone his worth, and calling the congregation to give him his due; nevertheless, the different traditions pursue this basic goal in different ways. The traditional/free church approach places more emphasis on *instructing* the worshiper, while the praise/worship approach aims to *exalt and uplift* the worshiper, and the seeker-sensitive approach aims to *uplift* the worshiper while it *evangelizes* the non-Christians present. Our own church model will lead us to either use one of these approaches or mix together various aspects.

THE EXISTENTIAL PERSPECTIVE: TEMPERAMENT AND AFFINITY

Finally, it is necessary to be aware of our own personal affinities — what we as a pastor or worship leader like or dislike in our own experience of worship. The goal should be to play to our own strengths without privileging ourselves over our congregation. On the one hand, far too many ministers create worship services that delight their own hearts but do not connect at all to people who are less theologically and culturally trained. In reply, the ministers maintain that this is "biblical" or "rich" worship, that in our culture people just want to be entertained, that we have to raise people up to a worthy level, not lower ourselves to their level, and so on. But quite often the problem is simply that the minister has created a service that inspires *him* and few others. The apostle Paul warned us not to please ourselves (Rom 15:1 – 3), a temptation we all face when planning worship.

It is easy to use theological arguments to rationalize our personal preferences and tastes. An example is the objection that popular culture is simply not a worthy medium for worship. Those who raise this objection insist that only high culture music should be used, since it takes much more skill to produce and appreciate. But these same critics don't like the idea of jazz services, even though jazz qualifies as high culture and is far more difficult to master and appreciate than rock, gospel, or pop music. More often than not, this reveals that these critics simply *like* classical music and are looking for some theological justification to universalize their own tastes.

At the same time, we can't lead a worship service well in a style that leaves our own hearts cold. Once we are willing to admit that our preferences and tastes are just that, we are still faced with the fact that we can't lead worship unless we are actually engaged in it ourselves. The music and songs must necessarily touch and stir our own hearts. If we have the personality of the contemplative — one who loves quiet and thoughtful reflection — we may have a lot of trouble concentrating on God in a highly charismatic worship service. Ultimately, our own heart's capacities and experiential temperament *must* be a factor in the worship service we choose, design, and use. One of the reasons I put this existential factor third is so that ministers exercise the discipline of consulting the Bible and the people *before* they necessarily consult their own sensibilities.

SEEKER-SENSITIVE VERSUS EVANGELISTIC WORSHIP

In the 1980s, the Willow Creek approach became enormously influential. One of its fundamental premises was the assumption that we cannot reach both Christians and non-Christians in the same gathering. So Willow Creek designed weekend "seeker services." These were not intended to be Christian worship gatherings but were considered outreach events; Christians were encouraged to worship at the midweek services. Ironically, those most hostile to the Willow Creek style of worship usually share the same assumption about worship. They frame the debate like this: "Who is the Sunday service *for* — nonbelievers or God?" Their answer, of course, is that the Sunday worship service is purely for God. They also assume that worship cannot be highly evangelistic. I want to argue that these are false premises.

My thesis is that the weekly worship service can be very effective in evangelism of non-Christians *and* in edification of Christians if it does not aim at either alone but is gospel centered and in the vernacular. Of course, there will be a need for other,

---

The weekly worship service can be very effective in evangelism of non-Christians and in edification of Christians if it is both gospel centered and in the vernacular.

---

more intense experiences of learning, prayer, and community to help Christians to grow into maturity, just as there will be a need for more specifically evangelistic venues and experiences where non-Christians can have their questions and concerns fully addressed. With an awareness of the need for these additional experiences, I believe it is possible for the weekly worship service to be the core of both evangelism and edification.

The biblical basis for evangelistic worship can be developed by a close examination of two key texts: 1 Corinthians 14:24 – 25 and Acts 2. In the 1 Corinthians passage, Paul is addressing the misuse of the gift of tongues. He complains that if nonbelievers enter a worship service and hear people speaking in tongues, they will think the Christians are out of their minds (v. 23). He insists that the Christians should change their behavior so that the worship service will be comprehensible to nonbelievers. If, however, an unlearned one, "someone who does not understand" (an uninitiated inquirer) comes in, and worship is being done unto edification, then the nonbeliever "will be convinced by all that he is a sinner and will be judged by all" (v. 24). How? "The secrets of his heart will be laid bare" (v. 25). This may mean he realizes that the worshipers around him are finding in

God what his heart had been secretly searching for, though in all the wrong ways. It may mean the worship reveals to him how his heart really works. Either way, the result is clear: "So he will fall down and worship God, exclaiming, 'God is really among you!'" (v. 25).

This is a rather remarkable passage. Earlier, in verses 15 – 17, Paul insists that God be worshiped in such a way that it leads to edification. Now he tells us that worship must also be done in such a way that it leads to evangelism. Many of us get distracted from this fact because we are studying this passage to figure out what tongues and prophecy consisted of and whether they continue today. While all of this is debatable, there is at least one unmistakably clear implication of this passage. Virtually every major commentary tells us that in verses 20 – 25, Paul is urging the Corinthian believers to stress prophecy over tongues for two reasons: (1) prophecy edifies believers, and (2) it convicts and converts nonbelievers.[9] In other words, Paul instructs them to stress prophecy over tongues at least in part because it converts people.[10] Why else would he give a detailed description of how a non-Christian comes to conviction in worship?

In Acts 2, we find further compelling evidence for evangelistic worship. When the Spirit falls on those in the upper room, we read that a crowd gathers because they "hear [the disciples] declaring the wonders of God in our own tongues!" (v. 11). As a result, they are curious and interested: "Amazed and perplexed, they asked one another, 'What does this mean?'" (v. 12). Later, they are deeply convicted: "They were cut to the heart and said …, 'Brothers, what shall we do?'" (v. 37). Again we find the church's worship attracting the interest of outsiders. This initial curiosity and interest eventually lead to conviction and conversion; in other words, it is evangelistic.

We must acknowledge some obvious differences between the two situations in Acts 2 and 1 Corinthians 14. First Corinthians 14 pictures conversion happening on the spot (which is certainly possible). But in Acts 2, nonbelievers are first shaken out of their indifference (v. 12), with the actual conversions (vv. 37 – 41) occurring after a later encounter in which Peter explained the gospel (vv. 14 – 36) and showed them how to individually receive Christ (vv. 38 – 39). Others have pointed out that the "tongues" referred to in these two situations

---

It is a false dichotomy to insist we must choose between seeking to please God and being concerned with what unchurched people are thinking about during our worship services.

---

are different. But again, irrespective of what these passages teach about tongues and prophecy, we should not fail to note what they teach us about the purpose of worship and evangelism more broadly. From our survey, we can conclude at least three things:

1. Nonbelievers are expected to be present in Christian worship. In Acts 2, this happens by word-of-mouth excitement. In 1 Corinthians 14, it is more likely the result of a personal invitation from Christian friends. No matter how they arrive at the service, Paul clearly expects that both "unbelievers" and "the unlearned" (literally, "a seeker" or "one who does not understand") will be present in worship (1 Cor 14:23).

2. Nonbelievers should find the praise of Christians to be comprehensible. In Acts 2, this understanding happens by miraculous, divine intervention. In 1 Corinthians 14, it happens by human design and effort. But again, regardless of how this understanding occurs, we must not miss the fact that Paul directly tells a local congregation to adapt its worship because nonbelievers will be present. It is a false dichotomy to insist we must choose between seeking to please God and being concerned with how unchurched people feel or what they might be thinking about during our worship services.

3. Nonbelievers can fall under conviction and be converted through comprehensible worship. As I pointed out earlier, in 1 Corinthians 14,

WELCOMING THE OUTSIDER

Commenting on 1 Corinthians 14:24 – 25, Paul Barnett writes, "Despite all efforts to devise 'programs' for evangelism and outreach, the gathered congregation, in its life and ministry, remains a potent force for gathering in the 'outsider.' Churches and their ministers, however, must ensure that the Word of the Lord is intelligible and powerfully taught so that the visitor will indeed say, 'God is with you.'"[11] Obviously, Barnett is interpreting prophecy as a form of preaching, but our interpretation of this isn't central. Barnett is coming to what I think is an inescapable conclusion that Paul urges the Corinthians to worship in such a way that it edifies them *as it convicts the outsider*.

---

this happens during the service, but in Acts 2, it is supplemented by "after meetings" and follow-up evangelism. God wants the world to overhear us worshiping him. God directs his people not simply to worship but to sing his praises "before the nations." We are called not simply to communicate the gospel *to* nonbelievers; we must also intentionally celebrate the gospel *before* them.

THREE PRACTICAL TASKS FOR EVANGELISTIC WORSHIP

If, as we have seen, it is important to have evangelistic aims in our worship, we are led to a practical question: How do we do it? Let me suggest three practical things churches can do to cultivate evangelistic worship.

2. GET NONBELIEVERS INTO WORSHIP

The numbering here is not a mistake. This task actually comes second, but nearly everyone assumes it comes first! It is quite natural to believe we must get non-Christians into worship before we can begin evangelistic worship. But the reverse is actually true. Non-Christians will not be invited into worship unless the worship is *already* evangelistic. Typically, coming into worship will only happen through personal invitations from Christians. As we read in the Psalms, the "nations" must be directly asked to come. The main stimuli for these invitations are the comprehensibility and quality of the worship experience.

Almost every Christian, if they pay attention, will be able to sense whether a worship experience will be attractive to their non-Christian friends. They may find a particular service wonderfully edifying for *them* and yet know their nonbelieving neighbors would react negatively, and so they wouldn't even consider bringing them along. They do not think they will be impressed or interested. Because this is their expectation, they do nothing about it, and a vicious cycle begins. Pastors see only Christians present, so they lack incentive to make their worship comprehensible to outsiders. But since they fail to make the necessary changes to adapt and contextualize, outsiders never come. The pastors continue to respond to the exclusively Christian audience that gathers, and the cycle continues. Therefore, the best way to get Christians to bring non-Christians to a worship service is to worship *as if* there are dozens of skeptical onlookers. If we worship *as if* they are there, eventually they will be.

1. MAKE WORSHIP COMPREHENSIBLE TO NONBELIEVERS

Contrary to popular belief, our purpose is not to make the nonbeliever "comfortable." After all, in 1 Corinthians 14:24 – 25 and Acts 2:12, 37, a nonbeliever will be "convinced by all that he is a sinner"; "the secrets of his heart will be laid bare"; he will be "amazed and perplexed"; and he will be "cut to the heart"! Our aim is to be *intelligible* to them. We must address their *heart secrets* (1 Cor 14:25), and so we must remember what it is like to *not* believe. How do we do that?

a. Seek to worship and preach in the vernacular. It is impossible to overstate how insular and subcultural our preaching can become. We often make statements that are persuasive and compelling to us, but they are based on all sorts of premises that a secular person does not hold. Preachers often use references, terms, and phrases that mean nothing outside of our Christian tribe. So we must intentionally seek to avoid unnecessary theological or evangelical jargon, carefully explaining the basic theological concepts behind confession of sin, praise, thanksgiving, and so on. In your preaching, always be willing to address the questions that the nonbelieving heart will ask. Speak respectfully and sympathetically to people who have difficulty with Christianity. As you prepare the sermon, imagine a particularly skeptical non-Christian sitting in the chair listening to you. Be sure to add the asides, the qualifiers, and the extra explanations that are necessary to communicate in a way that is comprehensible to them. Listen to everything that is said in the worship service with the ears of someone who has doubts or struggles with belief.

b. Explain the service as you go along. Though there is some danger of pastoral verbosity here that distracts from the worship experience, learn to give one- to two-sentence, nonjargon explanations of each part of the service as it comes. For example, prior to leading a prayer of confession, you might say: "When we confess our sins, we are not groveling in guilt, but we're dealing with our guilt. If we deny our sins, we will never get free from them." It may also be helpful to begin a worship service (as is customary in African-American churches) with a "devotional" — a brief talk that explains the meaning of worship. By doing this, we will continually instruct newcomers in worship.

c. Directly address and welcome nonbelievers. Talk regularly to "those of you who aren't sure you believe this or who aren't sure just what you believe." Give several asides, even trying to express the language of their hearts. Articulate their objections to Christian doctrine and life better than they can do it themselves. Express sincere sympathy for their difficulties, even as you challenge them directly for their selfishness and unbelief. Admonish with tears (literally or figuratively). It is extremely important that the nonbeliever feels we understand them. Always grant whatever degree of merit their objections have.

- "I've tried it before, and it did not work."
- "I don't see how my life could be the result of the plan of a loving God."
- "Christianity is a straitjacket."
- "It can't be wrong if it feels so right."
- "I could never keep it up."
- "I don't feel worthy; I am too bad."
- "I just can't believe."

d. Consider using highly skilled arts in worship. The power of good art draws people to behold it. It enters the soul through the imagination and begins to appeal to the reason. Art makes ideas plausible. The quality of our music, your speech, and even the visual aesthetics in worship will have a marked impact on its evangelistic power, particularly in cultural centers. In many churches, the quality of the music is mediocre or poor, but it does not disturb the faithful. Why? Their faith makes

---

Excellent aesthetics *includes* outsiders, while mediocre aesthetics *excludes*. The low level of artistic quality in many churches guarantees that only insiders will continue to come.

---

the words of the hymn or the song meaningful, despite its lack of artistic expression; what's more, they usually have a personal relationship with the music presenter. But any outsider who comes in as someone unconvinced of the truth and having no relationship to the presenter will likely be bored or irritated by the expression. In other words, excellent aesthetics *includes* outsiders, while mediocre aesthetics *excludes*. The low level of artistic quality in many churches guarantees that only insiders will continue to come. For the non-Christian, the attraction of good art will play a major role in drawing them in.

e. Celebrate deeds of mercy and justice. We live in a time when public esteem of the church is plummeting. For many outsiders and inquirers, the deeds of the church will be far more important than

our words in gaining plausibility (Acts 4:32 – 33). Leaders in most places see "word-only" churches as net costs to their community, organizations of relatively little value. But effective churches will be so involved in deeds of mercy and justice that outsiders will say, "We cannot do without churches like this. This church is channeling so much value into our community that if it were to leave the neighborhood, we would have to raise taxes." Evangelistic worship services should highlight offerings for deed ministry and celebrate by the giving of reports, testimonies, and prayers. It is best that offerings for mercy ministries are received separately from the regular offering; they can be attached (as is traditional) to the celebration of the Lord's Supper. This connection brings before the non-Christian the impact of the gospel on people's hearts (i.e., the gospel makes us generous) and the impact of lives poured out for the world.

f. Present the sacraments so as to make the gospel clear. Baptism, and especially adult baptism, should be given great significance in evangelistic worship. Consider providing an opportunity for the baptized to offer their personal testimony as well as to respond to certain questions. Make the meaning of baptism clear through a moving, joyous, personal charge to the baptized (and to all baptized Christians present). In addition, the Lord's Supper can also become a converting ordinance. If it is explained properly, the nonbeliever will have a specific and visible way to see the difference between walking with Christ and living for oneself. The Lord's Supper confronts every individual with the question, "Are you right with God today? Right now?" There is perhaps no more effective way to help a person take a spiritual inventory. Many seekers in churches in the United States will only realize they are not truly Christians during the "fencing of the table."[12]

g. Preach grace. The one message that both believers and nonbelievers need to hear is that salvation and adoption are by grace alone. If our response to this emphasis on grace-oriented preaching is, "Christians will be bored by all of this," I believe we are revealing a misunderstanding of the gospel. The gospel of free, gracious justification and adoption is not just the way we enter the kingdom; it is also the way we grow into the likeness of Christ. The apostle Paul tells us that it is the original, saving message of "grace alone" that leads to sanctified living:

> For the grace of God that brings salvation has appeared to all men. It teaches us to say "No" to ungodliness and worldly passions, and to live self-controlled, upright and godly lives in this present age, while we wait for the blessed hope — the glorious appearing of our great God and Savior, Jesus Christ.
> Titus 2:11 – 13

Many Christians are defeated and stagnant in their growth because they try to be holy for wrong motives. They say no to temptation by telling themselves:

- "God will get me."
- "People will find out."
- "I'll hate myself in the morning."
- "It will hurt my self-esteem."
- "It will hurt other people."
- "It's against the law, and I'll be caught."
- "It's against my principles."
- "I will look bad."

Some or all of these statements may be true, but the Titus passage tells us they are *inadequate*. Only the grace of God expressed through the logic of the gospel will work.

Therefore, there is one basic message that both Christians and nonbelievers need to hear, again and again: *the gospel of grace*. It can be applied to both groups directly and forcefully. Moralistic sermons will only be applicable to one of the two groups — either Christians or non-Christians. But Christocentric preaching of the gospel grows believers and challenges nonbelievers. Yes, if our Sunday service and the sermon aim primarily at evangelism, eventually we will bore the saints. And if in our preaching we consistently aim primarily at education, we will eventually bore and confuse nonbelievers. But when our worship and preaching aim at praising the God who saves by grace, we will challenge and instruct both believers and nonbelievers.

3. LEAD PEOPLE TO COMMITMENT

We have seen that nonbelievers in worship actually "close with Christ" in two basic ways: some may come to Christ during the service itself (1 Cor 14:24 – 25), while others must be "followed up with" by means of after-service meetings. Let's take a closer look at both ways of leading people to commitment.

It is possible to lead people to a commitment to Christ during the service. One way of inviting people to receive Christ is to make a verbal invitation as the Lord's Supper is being distributed. At our church, we say it this way: "If you are not in a saving relationship with God through Christ today, do not take the bread and the cup, but as they come around, take Christ. Receive him in your heart as those around you receive the food. Then immediately afterward, come up and tell an officer or a pastor about what you've done so we can get you ready to receive the Supper the next time as a child of God." Another way to invite commitment during the service is to give people a time of silence or a period of musical interlude after the sermon. This affords people time to think and process what they have heard and to offer themselves to God in prayer.

In many situations, it is best to invite people to commitment through after-meetings. Acts 2 gives an example. In verses 12 and 13 we are told that some folks mocked after hearing the apostles praise and preach, but others were disturbed and asked, "What does this mean?" Then, we see that Peter very specifically explained the gospel and, in response to the follow-up question "What shall we do?" (v. 37), he explained how to become a Christian. Historically, many preachers have found it effective to offer such meetings to nonbelievers and seekers immediately after evangelistic worship. Convicted seekers have just come from being in the presence of God and are often the most teachable and open at this time. To seek to "get them into a small group" or even to merely return next Sunday is asking a lot. They may also be "amazed and perplexed" (Acts 2:12), and it is best to strike while the iron is hot. This should not be understood as doubting that God is infallibly drawing people to himself (Acts 13:48; 16:14). Knowing the sovereignty of God helps us to relax as we do evangelism, knowing that conversions are not dependent on our eloquence. But it should not lead us to ignore or minimize the truth that God works through secondary causes. The Westminster Confession (5.2 – 3), for example, tells us that God routinely works through normal social and psychological processes. Therefore, inviting people into a follow-up meeting immediately after the worship service can often be more conducive to conserving the fruit of the Word.

After-meetings may take the shape of one or more persons waiting at the front of the auditorium to pray with and talk with seekers who wish to make inquiries right on the spot. Another way is to host a simple Q&A session with the preacher in or near the main auditorium, following the postlude. Or offer one or two classes or small group experiences targeted to specific questions non-Christians ask about the content, relevance, and credibility of the Christian faith. Skilled lay evangelists should be present who can come alongside newcomers, answer spiritual questions, and provide guidance for their next steps.

"WHAT ABOUT DEEPER, MEATIER TEACHING?"

A recurring concern I hear is that evangelistic worship will keep Christians from deeper, meatier types of teaching. Some mean by this that they want theological distinctives spelled out — teaching on how the church's view of certain doctrinal issues differs from that of other churches and denominations. But why should we spend a lot of time preaching about these distinctives when many people present in the service do not believe in (or live as if they do not believe in) the authority of the Bible or the deity of Christ? Don't we want the principal distinctive of the preaching to be the offense and consolation of the gospel to believers and nonbelievers alike? I believe that if we make sure this happens, we will create quite a sharp enough distinction from other churches in our worship.

For example, should a Presbyterian pastor do an extended series of sermons on the case for infant baptism? Apart from the fact that my Baptist friends don't believe that such a case exists (!), this is what I call a Z doctrine, and it is based on X and

A SERMON . . . OR A LECTURE?

The old Puritans (especially Jonathan Edwards) recognized the difference between a sermon and a lecture. The sermon, they said, is more *edifying*—more oriented to the affections and less oriented to detailed cognitive arguments. A major problem among new seminary graduates is that they don't know the difference between a theology paper, a political manifesto, and a sermon. But the congregation certainly does!

I must confess that I used to give lectures in the form of sermons. I explained all the reasons we believed in infant baptism, but I got a lot of "MEGO" looks from people ("My Eyes Glaze Over"). They said to me in effect, "This is surely something I need to work through—but today I need some food for my soul." A lot of pastors who don't understand the ways of the heart very well make their sermons into lectures. Ironically, they may ignore the felt needs of others as a way of meeting their own felt needs. They are personally more comfortable making arguments than healing souls.

Y doctrines — such as the authority of the Bible, the truths of the gospel, and the cost of discipleship. We must preach the whole counsel of God, and when preaching expositionally, we cover and teach what the text teaches. But in general we must stress the X and Y doctrines in our services, continually revisiting them and building on them to explain other truths that may be addressed less often.

It is natural to ask whether this approach is being too timid and is just looking to avoid controversy. But consider this list of the doctrines we hit hard and often in our preaching:

- Jesus is the only way to God (a defense of Christian exclusivism)

- the authority and inerrancy of Scripture
- the Trinity
- propitiation and penal substitution
- imputation
- justification by faith alone
- sanctification by faith alone
- last-day judgment and the reality of hell
- the reality of transcendent moral absolutes
- total depravity and inability to meet moral absolutes
- the orientation of the heart to idolatry
- the sinfulness of any sex outside marriage
- the sovereignty of God over every circumstance, including trouble and suffering

I address each of these topics in sermons regularly. As you can well see, they are not only theologically substantial; they are also controversial. But we are choosing to contend and argue for the basic truths of the faith, of the gospel. I have come to believe that when people clamor for "meaty"

Evangelistic worship is not avoiding the bold proclamation of the truth; rather, it is leading with the offense of the gospel instead of with the truths that are predicated on the gospel.

---

teachings, they are not always asking for in-depth treatments of the doctrines that are central to Christian conviction and life; they want to know more about what separates churches and denominations from each other. As the focus of a worship service (not a lecture) and in a setting designed to include nonbelievers, these types of discussions aren't terribly helpful. So our counsel to people asking the questions is, "Go deeper and learn the details and distinctions in classes, small groups, and in individual relationships with pastors and other Christians" (the lay ministry dynamic at work). Again, this is not avoiding the bold proclamation of the truth; rather, it is leading with the offense of the gospel instead of with the truths that are predicated on the gospel. And then, of course, it is our respon-

sibility to teach the issues in those other settings — without perpetuating the error that we can leave the gospel behind as we do.

We must acknowledge that no approach to preaching, by itself, can be fully adequate for all the training necessary for mature discipleship. Every Christian will need to delve into biblical and theological details that are simply less appropriate for a sermon than for another venue — a class, a lecture, small groups, one-on-one relationships. In this respect, almost every preacher will have someone in their congregation who draws the line between "sermon" and "lecture" further toward the lecture than the preacher does. Some of these will eventually leave to find a church where the preacher draws the line further over so the sermons are more like lectures. I almost always find that these churches have worship services that feel much more like classrooms. They are highly cognitive and contextualized to a northern European cultural style. In many such cases, education is actually squeezing out worship.

So how do we choose a worship form? How do we connect our people to God? We must find a balance between the consumer mentality that seeks only to meet felt needs and our self-centered tendency to assume our own preferences are the only biblically right way to meet God. Instead, we can humbly learn from what the Bible teaches about worship while recognizing that God gives us great freedom in the particulars. As we fill in the blanks for our own worship, we must take into account what the Bible teaches, our own cultural and ecclesial setting, and our own personal temperament and preferences.

In addition, we should intentionally create services in which both evangelism and edification can occur. The weekly worship service can be very effective in evangelism of non-Christians *and* in edification of Christians if it is gospel centered and in the vernacular of the community. In the next chapter, we will turn from the ministry front of connecting people to God to examine how missional churches connect people to one another in that community.

QUESTIONS FOR DISCUSSION AND REFLECTION

1. Which of the five categories of worship traditions most closely matches your own personal style and recent history?

   - *liturgical* — emphasis on the physical
   - *traditional* — emphasis on the mental
   - *praise and worship* — emphasis on the emotional
   - *seeker-oriented* — emphasis on the practical
   - *fusions of both form and music* — emphasis on the mystical

   Have you experienced worship in each of the other traditions? What did you learn from those experiences?

2. Keller writes, "Many now-historic [worship] traditions were once innovative revisions of an older approach." Have you ever researched the history of your tradition's liturgy (or lack thereof)? Against which prior trends was it a reaction? Which beliefs and preferences informed it?

3. Consider the seven suggestions for making worship comprehensible to unbelievers. Which of these are you currently doing? What can you begin to do to make your worship more understandable to outsiders?

4. Do you hear the objection that your church should have "deeper, meatier teaching" in worship? Do you have venues outside the worship service to deal with the "details and distinctions," and do people really hear them there? Can you make your own list of substantial and controversial topics that you "hit hard and often" in your preaching?

CHAPTER 23 — CONNECTING PEOPLE TO GOD *{pages 297–309}*

1. See "Reformed Worship in the Global City," in *Worship by the Book*, ed. D. A. Carson (Grand Rapids: Zondervan, 2002), 193–239.
2. A good, though dated, volume outlining these approaches is Paul Basden, ed., *Exploring the Worship Spectrum: Six Views* (Grand Rapids: Zondervan, 2004).
3. For a good, brief description of the regulative principle of worship, see R. Michael Allen, *Reformed Theology* (Edinburgh: T&T Clark, 2010), 116–21.
4. Scots Confession, www.creeds.net/Scots/c20.htm (accessed February 21, 2012). The Confession goes on to say, "For as ceremonies which men have devised are but temporal, so they may, and ought to be, changed."
5. For a critique of contemporary Christian worship as practiced by many megachurches, see D. H. Williams, "Contemporary Music: The Cultural Medium and the Christian Message," *Christianity Today* 55.6 (June 2011): 46, www.christianitytoday.com/ct/2011/june/culturalmedium.html (accessed February 21, 2012). Williams follows many others in charging that contemporary worship aims directly at the emotions rather than shaping the mind and habits, and that it has been shaped by "consumerist culture … creating a mall-like environment marked by splashiness and simplistic messages." An overlapping but somewhat different critique of evangelical worship is offered by James K. A. Smith, *Desiring the Kingdom: Worship, Worldview, and Cultural Formation* (Grand Rapids: Baker, 2009). Smith is targeting nonliturgical, sermon-oriented worship, which he sees as too oriented to reason and the mind and does not shape the "habits of the heart" as does liturgical worship.
6. Allen, *Reformed Theology*, 133–34.
7. Historic traditions of worship are based on centuries of wisdom and experience, and to rely on one prevents us from having to "reinvent the wheel" every week.
8. John Calvin, *Institutes of the Christian Religion*, ed. John T. McNeill (Philadelphia: Westminster, 1960), 2:1208.
9. See Paul Barnett, *1 Corinthians: Holiness and Hope of a Rescued People* (Fearns, Ross-shire, UK: Christian Focus, 2000); F. F. Bruce, *1 and 2 Corinthians* (Grand Rapids: Eerdmans, 1971); Gordon D. Fee, *The First Epistle to the Corinthians* (Grand Rapids: Eerdmans, 1987); Leon Morris, *1 Corinthians* (Downers Grove, Ill.: InterVarsity, 2008); Anthony C. Thiselton, *The First Epistle to the Corinthians* (Grand Rapids: Eerdmans, 2000).
10. I believe he is saying that tongues only make nonbelievers feel "alien" and judged — but that this kind of judgment does not lead to conversion.
11. Barnett, *1 Corinthians*, 262.
12. "Fencing of the table" refers to instructing those in the worship service that only believers who are committed to forsaking their sins should partake of the Lord's Supper.

CONNECTING PEOPLE TO ONE ANOTHER

The gospel creates community. Because it points us to the One who died for his enemies, it creates relationships of service rather than selfishness. Because it removes both fear and pride, people get along inside the church who could never get along outside. Because it calls us to holiness, the people of God live in loving bonds of mutual accountability and discipline. Thus the gospel creates a human community radically different from any society around it.

Accordingly, the chief way in which we should disciple people (or, if you prefer, to form them spiritually) is through community. Growth in grace, wisdom, and character does not happen primarily in classes and instruction, through large worship gatherings, or even in solitude. Most often, growth happens through deep relationships and in communities where the implications of the gospel are worked out cognitively and worked in practically — in ways no other setting or venue can afford. The essence of becoming a disciple is, to put it colloquially,

---

> The essence of becoming a disciple is, to put it colloquially, becoming like the people we hang out with the most.

---

becoming like the people we hang out with the most. Just as the single most formative experience in our lives is our membership in a nuclear family, so the main way we grow in grace and holiness is through deep involvement in the family of God. Christian community is more than just a supportive fellowship; it is an alternate society. And it is through this alternate human society that God shapes us into who and what we are.

THE FUNCTION OF COMMUNITY

It is natural to think of "community" as a category separate from evangelism and outreach, or from training and discipleship, or from prayer and worship. And of course, we have done this by calling it a distinct ministry front. But to do so can be misleading. Community itself is one of the main ways we *do* outreach and discipleship, and even experience communion with God.

COMMUNITY AND OUR WITNESS

Community shapes the nature of our witness and our engagement in mission. The real secret of fruitful and effective mission in the world is the quality of our community. Exceptional character in individuals cannot prove the reality of Christianity. Atheism, as well as many other religions, can also produce individual heroes of unusual moral greatness. Though such individuals may inspire us, it is all too easy to conclude that these individuals are just that — extraordinary heroes who have set unattainable standards for the rest of us. What atheism and other religions *cannot* produce is the kind of loving community that the gospel produces. In fact, Jesus states that our deep unity is the way the world will know that the Father sent him and has loved us even as the Father has loved him (John 17:23). Jesus says that the main way people will believe that Christians have found the love of God is by seeing the quality of their life together in community.

As we have often seen in this volume, to be faithful and effective, the church must go beyond "fellowship" to embody a counterculture, giving the world an opportunity to see people united in love who could never have been brought together otherwise, and showing the world how sex, money, and power can be used in life-giving ways:

The example of dating. When we think of "sex ethics," we usually think individualistically. What does it mean to follow the biblical sex ethic as a single Christian? It means (1) you should not have sex until you are married, and (2) you should not marry someone who does not share a similar commitment to Christ. But does this exhaust what it means to be a light to the world in the area of sex and relationships?

Jesus urged, "Let your light shine" before the world as a city on a hill—as a counterculture (Matt 5:16). How should Christians *as a community* show the difference Christ makes in the area of sexuality? In our culture, appearance and money are all-important criteria in mate selection. It is certainly true that most churches, even conservative ones, are basically conformed to the world in this area. What if we were a community in which single men didn't date only good-looking women but actually assessed a potential partner's worth primarily on the basis of her character? And what if we were a community in which single women didn't date only prosperous men but actually assessed a potential partner's worth primarily on the basis of his character (cf. 1 Sam 16:7; 1 Pet 3:3–4)?

So it is quite possible to follow the letter of the law in our individual ethics and still miss the importance of showing forth God's glory in our *community's* ways and practices.

The example of career advancement. Jacques Ellul's book *The Technological Society* provides a Christian analysis of the centrality of "technique." Our modern society is highly secular (oriented to the concrete and immediate "now" rather than to spiritual or eternal

- **Sex.** We avoid both secular society's idolization of sex and traditional society's fear of sex. We also exhibit love rather than hostility or fear toward those whose sexual life patterns are different from ours.
- **Money.** We promote a radically generous commitment of time, money, relationships, and living space to social justice and the needs of the poor, the immigrant, and the economically and physically weak. We also must practice economic sharing with one another so "there are no needy persons among us."
- **Power.** We are committed to power sharing and relationship building among races and classes that are alienated outside of the body of Christ. One practical evidence of this is that we need to be as multiethnic a body as possible.

Western believers usually think we show Christlikeness through our individual lives as believers. But it is just as important to exhibit Christlikeness through our *corporate* life together.

COMMUNITY AND OUR CHARACTER

Community shapes the development of our character. In a "classroom relationship," students and teachers have contact with one another primarily at the level of the intellect. The teacher and his students do not live together, eat together, or have much additional contact with one another socially, emotionally, or spiritually. We do not find a classroom relationship between Jesus and his students, nor did his students relate this way with one another. Instead, he created a community of learning and practice in which there was plenty of time to work out truth in discussion, dialogue, and application. This example suggests that we best learn and apply what we are learning in small groups and among friends, not in academic settings alone.

Our character is mainly shaped by our primary social community—the people with whom we eat, play, converse, counsel, and study. We can apply all of the "one another" passages of the Bible to this aspect of Christian community. We are to honor (Rom 12:10), accept (Rom 15:7), bear with (Eph 4:2; Col 3:13), forgive (Eph 4:32; Col 3:13), pray for, and confess sins to one another (James 5:16). We are to cheer and challenge (Heb 3:13), admonish and confront (Rom 15:14; Col 3:16; Gal 6:1 – 6), warn (1 Thess 5:14), and teach one another (Col 3:16). We are to stop gossiping and slandering (Gal 5:15) or being fake (Rom 12:9) with each other. We are to bear burdens (Gal 6:2), share possessions (Acts 4:32), and submit to each other (Eph 5:21). In short, there is no more important means of discipleship — of the formation of Christian character — than deep involvement in the life of the church, the Christian community.

COMMUNITY AND OUR BEHAVIOR

Community shapes our ethics and the spoken and unspoken rules that guide our behavior. Far more of the biblical ethical prescriptions are addressed to us as a community than as individuals. The Ten Commandments were given to Israel at Mount Sinai to form them into an alternate society that would be a light to the nations. The call of Romans 12:1 – 2 to "offer your bodies as living sacrifices" is usually interpreted as a call to individual consecration, but it is actually a demand that we commit ourselves to a corporate body and not live as autonomous individuals any longer. All of Romans 12, in fact, should be read as a description of this new society. In the same way, Jesus' call for his followers to be a "city on a hill" (Matt 5:14) means we must read the entire Sermon on the Mount as a description of this new community, not simply as ethical guidelines for individual believers. Most of the ethical principles or rules in the Bible are not simply codes of behavior for individuals to follow; they are descriptions of a new community that bears the spiritual fruit of love and holiness.

But this should not surprise us. It is really just common sense. Why? Because we all know by experience that it is far harder to live godly lives as individuals. Unless we make ourselves accountable to someone, we will repeatedly slip up and fall away. In addition, many of the ethical prescriptions of the Bible seem maddeningly general — not specific enough to directly address our particular situation. But this is because Jesus expected us to determine how to apply these teachings *as a community*. Take, for example, the numerous warnings against greed

values), and therefore it is rationalistic (placing supreme value on reason) and mechanistic (placing too much faith in the predictability of the physical order). Ellul observes that this modern sensibility shapes everything, including our relationships. Relationships are not an end in themselves but rather a means to further our own interests.

In this environment, we choose to spend time with people who will open doors for us. Our friendships and social relationships are too often based on their usefulness for reaching our economic and social goals. In other words, the people we network with and relate to are not *persons* (subjects) but *objects*. They are means to ends. But the Trinitarian/ Christian view of reality tells us we are not to use others. A Christian counterculture must be a place where relationships are ends in themselves, not means to ends. We are not to gravitate only toward people who are attractive, connected, and powerful.

in the New Testament writings. Unlike adultery, which is clear and obvious, greed is harder to define. Who is to say when we are spending too much money on ourselves? Greed is so insidious that unless we talk with other Christians about it, we will never see it in ourselves. The battle against these sinful habits and idolatrous affections is best worked out in community. Not only can a body of people, pooling their wisdom and experience, come up with culturally appropriate markers and signs of biblical sins such as greed and ruthlessness in business, but the community can more effectively hold itself to live consistently with its beliefs.

COMMUNITY AND GROWING TO KNOW GOD BETTER

Community is the key to true spirituality as we grow to know God by learning to know one another in relationships. In a famous passage, C. S. Lewis

PRACTICAL ADVICE FOR DEVELOPING COMMUNITY

In a city center, building community is the most challenging of the four ministry fronts, largely because of the mobility of the population. City centers are very expensive and difficult places to live. Most people are working enormous hours, and most people see themselves as living there only temporarily. All of this makes it difficult to build community.

The most practical way to build community is by casting a city vision with a positive view of the city, as we discussed in chapter 14 ("The Gospel for the City").

Find ways to encourage Christians to settle down and raise their families in the city (as in Jeremiah 29). Ask people who were going to stay for two years to make it three or four. If people were going to stay only to complete their schooling, ask them to stick around and get their first job in the city.

In addition to the conventional small groups of four to ten people, many city churches will also find that midsize "parish" or "mezzanine" groups are helpful for creating community. These groups usually have twenty to sixty people who live in a neighborhood, work in the same profession, or share a common passion in the city. They eat together regularly and consider how to reach out and serve the surrounding cultural, vocational, or geographic community.

Unless the number of people in midsize and small groups is at least half the number of the people who gather for worship and teaching on Sunday, your church is heading in the direction of being a consumer center rather than a community.

describes a very close friendship between himself, Charles Williams, and Ronald Tolkien (better known as J. R. R. Tolkien). After Charles Williams died, Lewis made this observation:

> In each of my friends there is something that only some other friend can fully bring out. By myself I am not large enough to call the whole man into activity; I want other lights than my own to show all his facets. Now that Charles is dead, I shall never again see Ronald's reaction to a specifically Caroline joke. Far from having more of Ronald, having him "to myself" now that Charles is away, I have less of Ronald. Hence true Friendship is the least jealous of loves. Two friends delight to be joined by a third, and three by a fourth ... We possess each friend not less but more as the number of those with whom we share him increases. In this, Friendship exhibits a glorious "nearness by resemblance" to Heaven ... For every soul, seeing Him in her own way, communicates that unique vision to all the rest. That, says an old author, is why the Seraphim in Isaiah's vision are crying "Holy, Holy, Holy" to one another (Isa 6:3). The more we thus share the Heavenly Bread between us, the more we shall all have.[1]

Lewis's point is that even a human being is too rich and multifaceted a being to be fully known one-on-one. You think you know someone, but you alone can't bring out all that is in a person. You need to see the person with others. And if this is true with another human being, how much more so with the Lord? You can't really know Jesus by yourself.

CHURCHLY PIETY AND "ECCLESIAL REVIVALISM"

Christian community, then, is perhaps the main way that we bear witness to the world, form Christlike character, practice a distinctively Christian style of life, and know God personally. But we must make it clear that we are not speaking merely of informal and individual relationships between Christians but also of membership and participation in the institutional church, gathered under its leaders for the preaching of the Word and the administering of the sacraments of baptism and the Lord's Supper.[2] The preaching of the Word by those gifted, prepared, and authorized by the church to do so, and participation in the Lord's Supper — with all the self-examination and corporate accountability this brings — are critical and irreplaceable ways that Christian community provides witness, spiritual formation, and communion with God.

An old term that summarizes a Christian's life, practice, and spirituality is the word *piety*. For the past 250 years, there has been a steady move away from a focus on churchly piety toward more individualistic, private piety. We discussed this shift in part 2 (Gospel Renewal). Churchly piety puts the emphasis on corporate processes — baptism, submission to the elders and pastors, catechesis in the church's historic confessions, admission to membership, public vows and profession of faith, gathered worship, sitting under the preaching of the Word, regular partaking of the Lord's Supper, and involvement in mission through the church's denominational agencies. Today, however, most evangelical churches stress individualistic piety, which emphasizes private devotions and spiritual disciplines, small group fellowship (with little or no elder oversight), personal witness and service, and participation in many broadly evangelical cooperative ventures.

Historians often trace this shift back to the revivals and awakenings of the eighteenth century and thereafter. As we have said, revivalists believed that it was possible for baptized church members to be unconverted and to be relying on their place in the church for their salvation rather than relying on Christ and his finished work. So they (rightly) called people to self-examination, repentance, and conversion. But when revivalists spoke to people in that way, they weakened (in their minds) the necessity of the church. The revivalist insight led to an overemphasis on direct experience and on self-accreditation. "Who needs the church," many thought, "when I am the judge of whether I'm a Christian or not?" For many, the church became an option, an afterthought, rather than the heart of how Christians live their lives.

Earlier I explained that there are indeed real dangers if revivalistic, individual piety becomes excessive. Historian John Coffey notes that revivalism historically encouraged exchanging

robust theological confessionalism for a doctrinal minimalism; stressed heart experience over formal churchmanship; de-emphasized sacramental routine for crisis decisions; downgraded the ideal of a learned ministry for populist, simplistic preaching; and shed careful theological exegesis in light of the wisdom of the past for naive biblicism.[3] Out of the revivals of the past has come the individualistic piety of the present day.

This is natural, for it is common to go to the opposite extreme in a well-intentioned effort to make a correction. As I said in part 2, I believe that nineteenth-century Princeton Reformed theologians, such as Archibald Alexander and Charles Hodge, took a balanced approach to this issue. On the one hand, they were keenly aware of the dangers of revivalism and stressed the importance of churchly piety. Hodge leveled a sustained critique of Charles Finney's version of revivalism. On the other hand, Hodge was also critical of John Williamson Nevin, who (he believed) overreacted to revivalism in his particular emphasis on the sacraments.[4] As can be seen in Alexander's *Thoughts on Religious Experience* and Hodge's *The Way of Life*, they accepted the basic insights of revivalism, following Jonathan Edwards in his writings on how to discern true spiritual experience; yet they put the church at the center of Christian formation and life.[5]

I have coined the term "ecclesial revivalism" to describe the balance Alexander and Hodge proposed. How can we combine the insights of revivalism with ecclesial practices in the church's ministry today?

1. Preach for conversion yet honor communicant status. One of the ways the Princeton theologians kept the balance can be seen in the way they preached for conversion *and* honored the membership status of believers in the church. Princeton ministers preached that it is possible to mentally subscribe to the doctrines of sin and grace without actually putting heart trust in them and being converted. Conversion, they said, always entails some *heart* conviction of the sin of works-righteousness and some *heart* enjoyment of grace in response to a presentation of the gospel of grace — this is "justifying faith." They directed that Christians should not be admitted to the church, nor baptized children to the Lord's Supper, without an experience of conversion and saving faith. They called existing church members to examine themselves, but they would never declare an individual member unregenerate unless through heresy or moral lapse they came under discipline. If the church had received a person as a member, it was not the place of any individual (other than that person himself) to make a counterdeclaration.

This was an important balance. The Princeton theologians let communicant members know that, under the clear preaching of the gospel, they might come to the conclusion that they had never trusted in Christ savingly but had only been full of "dead works." However, unlike some revivalists, they would never rebaptize a communing member. They would consider such an act too subjective and individualistic. They might say, "You may have a time of spiritual declension and an even greater spiritual renewal sometime in the future. Will you get baptized a third time?" They would direct the person to ground their assurance in both their experience and their participation in the church community and the sacraments. They would say, "You had baptism; now you have an experience of conversion. If you see signs of the fruit of the Spirit growing in you, you can rest assured you are his."

2. Examine candidates for membership. How can we examine people with regard to their Christian experience in such a way that avoids the extremes of formalism and revivalism? Don't insist (1) that everyone has to identify a moment or time in which they were converted, (2) that everyone must have a conversion experience that follows a particular pattern, or (3) that everyone must have a conversion with the same level of experiential and emotional intensity. This is the mistake of overly enthusiastic revivalists. Furthermore, don't look strictly at stated beliefs. Instead, look for gospel beliefs that take "spiritual illumination" to appreciate and grasp. Do they have a view of their sin that goes beyond simply behavior and recognizes idolatry, self-righteousness, and other such sins of heart and motive? Did they have a time in which they realized more clearly that salvation is by Christ's work, not theirs? And look for spiritual "whole-life effect." There should be something more than mere doctrinal subscription and ethical conformity. There should be some sense in the heart of peace and joy. There should be some growth in love. Nevertheless, we should not preclude people who can thoughtfully profess gospel faith and promise gospel living, even if their temperament shows no great emotion. We also must beware of insisting that people of other cultures conform to our patterns.

This balance is seen in the early Princeton theologians with regard to the way in which they treated baptized children within the church. These theologians understood that baptized children were (1) united to the church through the vows of their parents, and therefore accountable to live as Christians, and (2) recipients of God's grace in the life of the family through the sacrament. But they exhorted children to put their faith in Christ and counseled them about what conversion looks like. Archibald Alexander taught that children growing up in the church usually had a series of "religious impressions" over the years, and it was hard to tell which ones were spiritual preparation, which one was conversion, and which ones were deeper growth and commitment. But they described to children the conviction of sin and grace that was necessary for being admitted to the Lord's Supper.[6] They looked for a credible profession of faith, rather than simply admitting any child who completed church instruction.

3. Recover catechesis. In the *Apostolic Tradition*, attributed to Hippolytus, we learn that in the early church, conversion was seen as a journey with several stages. First, seekers were admitted to instruction as catechumens. They were given instruction several times a week in basic Christian worldview and ethics. Second, when inquirers became believers, they became baptismal candidates and were admitted to a new course of instruction leading up to public baptism. They were now seen as believers who had not yet been admitted to the community. The baptismal instruction seems to have emphasized orthodox theology and an understanding of the church and its ministry. Third, after baptism, the new member might receive additional instruction in the practical issues of living and working as a believer in a pagan world.

This ecclesial, corporate approach conceives of spiritual formation as a journey with public, communally celebrated milestones that entail water, food and drink, music, and joy. These milestones are baptism, the Lord's Supper, weddings, and funerals. Unlike modern individualistic ministry models that offer short-term events, intensive classes, and programs, catechesis was much different. It was much more communal, participatory, and physically embodied. The seekers met regularly with one another and with Christian instructors. The baptismal candidates met with one another and Christian teachers and sponsors. Memorization and recitation slowed the process and "drilled in" the theology and practice of the church. It brought about greater life change and more solid assimilation into the church than most contemporary seminars and programs can.

In *Grounded in the Gospel*, Gary Parrett and J. I. Packer urge contemporary Christians to restore catechetical instruction to the life of the church.[7] They argue for training people by using three ancient and biblical summaries — the Apostles' Creed (belief), the Ten Commandments (practice), and the Lord's Prayer (experience). They urge that the process be long-term rather than compressed. They make the case for a process that is not merely formal (classroom instruction) but nonformal and informal. That is, it should incorporate practical experience and include many opportunities for developing personal relationships with mature church members. Most important of all, catechesis incorporates instruction and discipleship with the public worship and life of the whole church. In ancient times, seekers, catechumens, candidates for baptism, and new members were all recognized and prayed for in public worship.

4. Recognize that seekers need process. The success of the Alpha course and other similar courses such as Christianity Explored showed the need for a shift from the mid-twentieth-century's prominent modes of evangelism. Crusade evangelism and various personal evangelism methods (e.g., Campus Crusade's LIFE training, using the Four Laws; Evangelism Explosion) were neither communal nor process oriented. They assumed some background knowledge of the Christian faith. The Alpha course was more in the mode of catechesis and began to show that, as the Western world became more pagan, evangelism had to follow the pattern of the early church. Seekers today need to not only get a body of content but also see Christianity embodied in individuals and a community. They need a long time to ask questions and build up their knowledge of the (now very alien) Christian gospel and worldview. As I argued in the previous chapter, it is possible in most cultures today to make the worship service itself part of this process so nonbelievers find the services to be places where their interest and faith can be nursed and grown.

Seekers today need to not only get a body of content but also see Christianity embodied in individuals and a community.

Indeed, this is vital to merging the revivalist and the ecclesial. Most ecclesial churches do not think of their corporate worship as evangelistic, while most seeker-oriented churches do not think their seeker services can be theologically rich and spiritually edifying to Christians. We need evangelistic sermons that edify, as well as edifying sermons that evangelize. Supplementing the evangelistic worship must be a great variety of groups, events, and processes by which non-Christians can be introduced to the Christian faith.

5. Realize that baptism and reception of members can become much more instructive and a bigger part of worship. Contemporary people will expect brief, intensive procedures they can fit into their fast-changing schedules. Nevertheless, there should at least be a great deal of instruction leading up to any adult baptism. Consider requiring all baptismal candidates to complete a doctrinal course on the Apostles' Creed, the Lord's Prayer, and the Ten Commandments. Also, look for ways that candidates for baptism can be publicly recognized (as in the early church). Seek testimonies of changed lives from new converts who are being instructed and preparing for baptism, even though they haven't yet been baptized. Doing so would highlight to the congregation the importance of the process and also encourage seekers in the congregation to "close with Christ." If your church baptizes infants or has a service of dedication for newborns, consider creating a much more comprehensive process of instructing families in family spiritual formation and discipleship before the rite. In general, we could do a far better job of instructing the congregation on how baptism and membership are milestones in our spiritual journeys.

6. Use the anticipation of the Lord's Supper as a springboard for a season of preparation. A pastoral practice used in some churches that do not have weekly Communion is calling the congregation to brief, focused seasons of preparation. I used to do this at my church in Hopewell, Virginia, where the Lord's Supper was observed only quarterly. For a week or two, as I preached, I asked the church to think about a key area of Christian practice. For example, we might think about our relationships — the need for forgiveness and reconciliation — leading up to Communion Sunday. Everyone was urged to consider whether they should reconcile with anyone in a Matthew 5:23 – 24 or Matthew 18:15 – 17 process. The elders and pastors sometimes would visit the families leading up to the Communion season. Obviously visitation is not always feasible at a large, mobile, urban church, but even this kind of congregation can run classes or have their small groups study a topic and do self-examination regarding specific issues. Sometimes a church can use the period before the Lord's Supper for a time of covenant renewal.

The possibilities are many. But at the end of the day, not many churches combine the power of revivalist preaching and pastoring with ecclesial patterns of church life. Indeed, most people who are strong in one area define themselves over against Christians in the other camp, which makes it harder to incorporate both insights in a healthy way.

THE GOSPEL AND COMMUNITY

Building community is no longer natural or easy under our present cultural conditions. It requires an intentionality greater than that required of our ancestors, and it is uncomfortable for most of us. But our weapon is the gospel itself.

In his classic book *Life Together*, Dietrich Bonhoeffer grounds Christian fellowship solidly in the gospel of justification by faith:

> The Reformers expressed it this way: Our righteousness is an "alien righteousness," a righteousness that comes from outside of us …
>
> God permits [Christians] to meet together and gives them community. Their fellowship is founded solely upon Jesus Christ and this "alien righteousness." All we can say, therefore, is: the community of Christians springs solely from the biblical and Reformation message of the justification of man through grace alone; this alone is the basis of the longing of Christians for one another …
>
> Without Christ we … would not know our brother, nor could we come to him. The way is blocked by our own ego.[8]

How does this work? Our natural condition under sin is to be "glory empty" — starved for significance, honor, and a sense of worth. Sin makes us feel superior and overconfident (because we are trying to prove to ourselves and others that we are significant) and inferior and underconfident (because at a deep level we feel guilty and insecure). Some people's glory emptiness primarily takes the form of bravado and evident pride; for others, it takes the form of self-deprecation and self-loathing. Most of us are wracked by both impulses. Either way, until the gospel changes us, we will use people in relationships. We do not work for the sake of the work; we do not relate for the sake of the person. Rather, we work and relate to bolster our own self-image — to derive it, essentially, from others. Bonhoeffer reminds us that the way to transparency, love, and mutual service is "blocked by our own ego."

But when the gospel changes us, we can begin to relate to others for *their* sakes. It humbles us before anyone, telling us we are sinners saved only by grace. But it also emboldens us before anyone, telling us we are loved and honored by the only eyes in the universe that really count. So we are set free to enjoy people for who they are in themselves, not for how they make us feel about ourselves. Our self-image

---

When we experience Christ's radical grace through repentance and faith, it becomes the foundational event of our lives. Now, when we meet someone from a different culture, race, or social class who has received the same grace, we see someone who has been through the same life-and-death experience.

---

is no longer based on comparisons with others (Gal 5:26; 6:3 – 5). We do not earn our worth through approval *from* people or through power *over* people. We are not overly dependent on the approval of others; nor, on the other hand, are we afraid of commitment and connection to others. The gospel makes us neither self-confident nor self-disdaining but gives us boldness and humility that can increase together.

Strong community is formed by powerful common experiences, as when people survive a flood or fight together in a battle. When they emerge on the other side, this shared experience becomes the basis for a deep, permanent bond that is stronger than blood. The more intense the experience, the more intense the bond. When we experience Christ's radical grace through repentance and faith, it becomes the most intense, foundational event of our lives. Now, when we meet someone from a different culture, race, or social class who has received the same grace, we see someone who has been through the same life-and-death experience. In Christ, we have both spiritually died and been raised to new life (Rom 6:4 – 6; Eph 2:1 – 6). And because of this common experience of rescue, we now share an identity marker even more indelible than the ties

RESOURCES FOR DEVELOPING COMMUNITY

For path-breaking thoughts on how community (especially worship) is related to spiritual formation, worldview instruction, and discipleship, see James K. A. Smith, *Desiring the Kingdom: Worship, Worldview, and Cultural Formation* (Grand Rapids: Baker, 2009).

For practical insights on life in community, see Tim Chester and Steve Timmis, *Total Church* (Nottingham, UK: Inter-Varsity, 2007); idem, *Everyday Church* (Nottingham, UK: Inter-Varsity, 2011); Jonathan Wilson-Hartgrove, *The New Monasticism: What It Has to Say to Today's Church* (Grand Rapids: Brazos, 2008).

For an overview of nine biblical practices for building community, see Timothy Keller, *Gospel in Life Study Guide: Grace Changes Everything* (Grand Rapids: Zondervan, 2010), 59 – 72.

1. affirming one another's strengths, abilities, and gifts
2. affirming one another's equal importance in Christ
3. affirming one another through visible affection
4. sharing one another's space, goods, and time
5. sharing one another's needs and problems
6. sharing one another's beliefs, thinking, and spirituality
7. serving one another through accountability
8. serving one another through forgiveness and reconciliation
9. serving one another's interests rather than our own

that bind us to our family, our race, or our culture.

Peter writes to the church, "As you come to him, the living Stone — rejected by men but chosen by God and precious to him — you also, like living stones, are being built into a spiritual house" (1 Pet 2:4 – 5). Like stones that have been perfectly shaped by the mason, the builder lays each block next to the other, and they interlock into a solid, beautiful temple. When we speak to others who know God's grace, we can recognize that their identity is now rooted more in who they are in Christ than in their family or class. As a result, Christ has created a connection that can surmount the formerly insurmountable barriers to our relationships.

We often think of community as simply one more thing we have to follow in the rules of behavior. "OK, I have to read my Bible, pray, stay sexually pure — *and* I need to go to fellowship." But community is best understood as the way we are to do all that Christ told us to do in the world. Community is more than just the result of the preaching of the gospel; it is itself a declaration and expression of the gospel. It is the demonstration of the good news of freedom in Christ through the evident display of our transformed character and our life together. It is itself part of the good news, for the good news is this: This is what Christ has won for you on the cross — a new life together with the people of God. Once you were alienated from others, but now you have been brought near.

1. Keller writes, "The essence of becoming a disciple is, to put it colloquially, becoming like the people we hang out with the most." Does this describe your own experience? How has the community you belong to uniquely shaped and directed your own growth as a Christian? Who should you hang out with more often?

2. Keller writes, "Exceptional character in individuals cannot prove the reality of Christianity … What atheism and other religions *cannot* produce is the kind of loving community that the gospel produces." Consider your Christian witness as a community. What are some of the ways in which your church community lives and relates to one another in distinctly Christian ways? How are you a witness to the surrounding culture?

3. Keller writes, "Churchly piety puts the emphasis on corporate processes — baptism, submission to the elders and pastors, catechesis in the church's historic confessions … Today, however, most evangelical churches stress individualistic piety, which emphasizes private devotions and spiritual disciplines, small group fellowship (with little or no elder oversight), personal witness and service, and participation in many broadly evangelical cooperative ventures." Which version of piety is more commonplace in your church? Which of the following suggestions for a balanced "ecclesial revivalism" are most helpful to you?

   - Preach for conversion, yet honor communicant status.
   - Develop a way of examining candidates for membership.
   - Recover catechesis so it is communal, participatory, and physically embodied.
   - Recognize that seekers need a process that is both evangelistic and theologically edifying.
   - Use the baptism and reception of members to instruct and disciple.
   - Use the anticipation of the Lord's Supper as a springboard for a season of preparation focused on covenant renewal.

CHAPTER 24 — CONNECTING PEOPLE TO ONE ANOTHER {pages 311–20}

1. C. S. Lewis, *The Four Loves* (New York: Harcourt Brace Jovanovich, 1960), 92–93.
2. I am acutely aware that many readers will not share the same view of baptism and the Lord's Supper I am assuming here by using the word *sacraments* instead of *ordinances*. In general, those who name them "ordinances" believe they are signs and symbols representing the benefits of salvation, while those who describe them as "sacraments" believe that at some level or another they are also "seals" that bring something of the grace signified. Despite these long-standing differences on an important subject, I believe readers across the ecclesiastical spectrum can accept virtually all of what I am saying in this section about the importance of churchly piety.
3. John Coffey, "Lloyd-Jones and the Protestant Past," in *Engaging with Martyn Lloyd-Jones: The Life and Legacy of "the Doctor,"* ed. Andrew Atherstone and David Ceri Jones (Nottingham, UK: Inter-Varsity, 2011), 318. Coffey argues convincingly that, despite the negative results of revivalism, its critics often overplay their hand. Instead of seeing revivalism as a completely novel development, he points out its continuity with elements within the Reformation and Puritanism and critics' tendency to overlook the great achievements of revivalism (see p. 319). For a good but more negative assessment of revivalism, see R. Michael Allen, *Reformed Theology* (Edinburgh: T&T Clark, 2010), 88–94.
4. Nevin, a proponent of what has been called "high church Calvinism," was a student at Princeton under Alexander and Hodge. He appreciated the confessional, ecclesial emphasis but felt it was inconsistent to put such an equal emphasis on conversion and experience. He believed it was subjectivizing Christianity to tell members or baptized children that they should be sure they were converted. For a profile very sympathetic to Nevin, see D. G. Hart, *John Williamson Nevin: High Church Calvinist* (Phillipsburg, N.J.: Presbyterian & Reformed, 2005).
5. See Archibald Alexander, *Thoughts on Religious Experience* (Edinburgh: Banner of Truth, 1967), esp. 59–78; Charles Hodge, *The Way of Life* (Edinburgh: Banner of Truth, 1959).
6. See Alexander, *Thoughts on Religious Experience*, 13–35.
7. Gary A. Parrett and J. I. Packer, *Grounded in the Gospel: Building Believers the Old-Fashioned Way* (Grand Rapids: Baker, 2010); see sidebar on "Catechism in Today's Church" on p. 56.
8. Dietrich Bonhoeffer, *Life Together* (New York: Harper & Row, 1954), 22–23.

CONNECTING PEOPLE TO THE CITY

The gospel does more than connect Christians to one another; it also connects us to those in our cities who do not yet know God and who have needs we can help meet through ministries of justice and mercy. In the West, two sets of ministry concerns — emphasizing word or deed, proclamation or service — have been split off from one another into rival political and denominational factions for nearly a century. "Conservative" ministry stresses the importance of personal morality and approves of calling people to conversion through evangelism and preaching of the gospel; "liberal" ministry stresses social justice and rejects overt calls to convert others. But Jesus calls his disciples to both *gospel messaging* (urging everyone to repent and believe the gospel) and to *gospel neighboring* (sacrificially meeting the needs of those around them, whether they believe or not). The two concerns must always go together. Let's see why.[1]

First, word and deed go together theologically. The resurrection of Jesus shows us that God not only *created* both body and spirit, but that he will also *redeem* both body and spirit. The salvation

---

The church's ministry to the poor makes great sense as a corporate witness to the community of Christ's transforming love.

Jesus will eventually bring in its fullness will include liberation from all of the effects of sin — not only the spiritual effects, but physical and material ones as well. Jesus himself came both preaching the Word *and* healing and feeding. The final kingdom will be one of justice for all. Christians can faithfully proclaim the gospel through both words and deeds

of compassion and justice, serving the material needs of people around us even as we call them to faith in Jesus.

In addition to the theological harmony of these concerns, they also go together practically. In some ways, gospel neighboring *is* gospel messaging. Loving deeds of service to someone, regardless of their race or faith, are always an attractive testimony to the truth and motivational power of the gospel. The church's ministry to the poor makes great sense as a corporate witness to the community of Christ's transforming love and as an important "plausibility structure" for the preaching of the gospel.

BIBLICAL FOUNDATIONS FOR MINISTRIES OF MERCY AND JUSTICE

To examine in greater depth the theological foundations for this type of ministry, let's look at three primary biblical concepts: neighbor, service, and justice.

1. Christians are to love their neighbor. It is typical to think of our neighbors as people of the same social class and means (Luke 14:12). The Old Testament, however, called Israel to recognize the immigrant, the single-parent family, and the poor as neighbors, even if they were from another nation or race (Lev 19:34). In Luke 10:25 – 37, Jesus takes this even further. He says that your neighbor is anyone you come into contact with who lacks resources, even someone from a hated race or another religious faith. Our responsibility to neighbors includes love and justice — two things the Bible closely links. When God says, "Love your neighbor as yourself" (Lev 19:18), he also commands us not to defraud, pervert justice, show partiality to the poor or favoritism to the great, or do anything to endanger our neighbor's life (vv. 13 – 17). According to Jesus, God is a God of justice, and anyone who has a relationship with him will be concerned about justice as well (Luke 18:1–8).

2. Christians are called to serve. The Greek word *diakoneō* denotes humbly providing for the most basic and simple needs through deeds. The root meaning of the word is "to feed someone by waiting on a table." Luke gives the example of Martha preparing a meal for Jesus (Luke 10:40). A group of women disciples followed Jesus and the apostles and provided food and other physical needs, and this ministry is called *diakonia* (Matt 27:55; Luke 8:3). The work of providing daily necessities for the widows in the early church is also referred to as *diakonia* (Acts 6:2). In the upper room, Jesus asks the question, "Who is greater, the one who is at the table or the one who serves [*diakonōn*]?" (Luke 22:27). This question is remarkable because in the value system of the culture of that day, serving others was considered demeaning work. Against this backdrop, Jesus makes the startling statement that Christian greatness is the polar opposite of the values of the world: "I am among you as one who serves (*diakonōn*)" (Luke 22:27). A *diakonos*! A busboy! This is the Christian pattern of greatness and it directly follows the pattern of Christ's work. Our acts of service for others are the evidence that God's love is operative in our lives:

> If anyone has material possessions and sees his brother in need but has no pity on him, how can the love of God be in him? Dear children, let us not love with words or tongue but with actions and in truth.
> *1 John 3:17–18*

3. Christians are instructed to "do justice" or "live justly." Evangelicals tend to translate this phrase (as in Mic 6:8) as "live righteously" and generalize it to mean a broad understanding of Christian obedience to God's Word or simply a commitment to avoiding certain egregious sins. This understanding simply isn't adequate, especially when we study the term as used in the Old Testament.

So what does the Bible mean by doing justice? Old Testament scholar Bruce Waltke defines justice in this startling way: "The righteous (*ṣaddiq*) are willing to disadvantage themselves to advantage the community; the wicked are willing to disadvantage the community to advantage themselves."[2] Most people think of "wickedness" as disobeying the Ten Commandments, as actively breaking the law by lying or committing adultery. And those things are, of course, wicked! But lying and adultery are best understood as the visible tip of the iceberg of wickedness. Below the surface, less visible but no less wicked, are things like not feeding the poor when we have the power to do so, or taking so much income out of the business we own that our employees are paid poorly, or shoveling snow from our own driveway without even thinking to do the same for our elderly neighbors. In all these ways we disadvantage others by advantaging ourselves.

With this understanding, we begin to see that justice is an everyday activity; it is not to be pursued only in courts or legislatures. Living justly means living in constant recognition of the claims of community on us; it means disadvantaging ourselves in order to advantage others. This works itself out in every area of life — in our family and sexual relationships, our jobs and vocations, in our use of wealth and possessions, the rights of citizenship, how we pursue our leisure, how we seek and use corporate profits, how we communicate and present ourselves, and how we form and conduct friendships. It means going well beyond what is legally required of us. A CEO who is willing to say, as Job did, that "justice was my robe" (Job 29:14) cannot think only of his shareholders' profit but must also think of the good of his employees and the community in which the business operates. Many things that managers of a bank can legally do are, according to the Bible, unjust. The Old Testament makes it clear that God's justice means to share food, shelter, and other basic resources with those who have smaller amounts (Isa 58:6–10).

Note that in the Bible, acts that meet basic human needs are not just called acts of *mercy* (see Luke 10:37), which implies compassion for the undeserving; they are considered acts of *justice*, which implies giving people their due. Why? We do not all start out with equal privileges and assets. For

LIMITED RESOURCES FOR THE CHURCH'S MISSION

Church leaders who are unconvinced of the necessity of ministries of mercy often point to the reality of limited resources. "It would simply overwhelm the local church to try to meet the endless economic and material needs of the city," they say. "Besides, there are plenty of agencies doing so, while the church alone calls people to conversion through faith in the gospel. The church should use its limited financial resources almost exclusively on evangelism and the ministry of the Word."

Even church leaders pursuing balanced, integrative ministry have to face this question. So how do we address it? We must first establish that the ministry of the Word is the priority for the local church. The first thing people need to hear when they come to church is "believe in Jesus," not "do justice." Why? Because believing in Jesus meets a more radical human need, and because if they don't believe in Jesus, they won't have the gospel motivation to do justice in the world. So the first priority of the local church under its elders is to make disciples, not to do housing rehabilitation or feed the poor.

However, the church must disciple and support its members so they love their neighbor, integrate their faith into their work, and seek a more just and wholesome society and culture. Therefore, within the church we must experience a great deal of teaching, preaching, and emphasizing how to be Christians in the public sphere and how to be loving servants in our neighborhood. And of course we should have a strong diaconal ministry to meet the economic and material needs of members. So we hold that the institutional church should give priority to Word ministry, but we also teach that Christians must do

example, inner-city children, through no fault of their own, may grow up in an environment extremely detrimental to learning. People may argue over who is primarily at fault in this situation — the parents, the culture, the government, big business, systemic racism, the list goes on. But no one argues it is the child's fault they are in this situation! Everyone would recognize that as far as the children are concerned, their plight is part of the deep injustice of our world — one of the effects of the fall — that we are duty bound to help improve.

It's one thing to want to help remedy injustice; it's another thing to go about it wisely. One of the main reasons this is especially difficult is the unbalanced political ideologies and unbiblical reductionisms that reign in our culture today. Many conservatives are motivated to help the poor solely out of a disposition of mercy — a motivation perhaps rooted in a belief that poverty is almost solely a matter of individual irresponsibility. But this attitude often overlooks the fact that the "haves" are in their position to a great degree because of the uneven distribution of opportunities and resources at birth. As Christians, we know that every material blessing we have is a *gift* from God. If we fail to share the material benefits we have been given or are impatient and harsh with the poor, we are not just guilty of a lack of mercy; we are guilty of injustice. On the other hand, many liberals are motivated to help the poor out of a sense of indignation over aborted justice. But this too misses an important truth, namely, that individual responsibility *does* have a great deal to do with helping people escape from the cycle of poverty.

So conservatives may advocate "compassionate, responsibility-based" solutions that can become paternalistic and even patronizing and are blind to many of the sociocultural factors contributing to the problems of poverty. The liberal orientation against "systemic injustice" can lead to anger, rancor, and division. Both views, ironically, become self-righteous. One tends to blame the poor for everything; the other tends to blame the rich for everything. One approach overemphasizes individual responsibility; the other underemphasizes it.

Christians live justly as a response to grace. At first glance, it does not seem logical that Christ's salvation, which is of sheer grace, should move us to do justice. But the Bible tells us it should. In the Old Testament, God tells the Israelites, "The alien living with you must be treated as one of your native-born. Love him as yourself, for you were aliens in Egypt. I am the LORD your God" (Lev 19:34). The Israelites had been foreigners and oppressed slaves in Egypt. They did not have the ability to free themselves — God liberated them by his grace and power. Now they are to treat all people who have less power or fewer assets as neighbors, demonstrating love and justice to them. So the theological and motivational basis for doing justice is salvation by grace!

At first glance, it does not seem logical that Christ's salvation, which is of sheer grace, should move us to do justice. But the Bible tells us it should.

In James 2:14, the writer states that, while we are saved by faith and not works, real faith in Christ will lead us to deeds of service. And then James shows what these deeds look like:

> Suppose a brother or sister is without clothes and daily food. If one of you says to him, "Go, I wish you well; keep warm and well fed," but does nothing about his physical needs, what good is it? In the same way, faith by itself, if it is not accompanied by action, is dead.

James 2:15 – 17

Read in the context of the entire book of James, we see this is the same reasoning that God used in Leviticus 19:34. A desire to help the poor arises from a heart touched by grace, a heart that has surrendered its feelings of superiority toward any particular class of people.

PRACTICAL APPROACHES FOR MINISTRIES OF MERCY AND JUSTICE

Once we have answered the question of *why* the church should participate in ministries of mercy

both word and deed ministry in the world — and the church should equip them to do so.

What about limited resources? Most of the money that Redeemer members give for mercy ministry (within and beyond the congregation) comes through annual special offerings and designated giving. We take a special offering at Christmas that goes to diaconal ministry within the church. We take another special offering at Easter for Hope for New York, a Christian 501(c)(3) birthed out of Redeemer that does mercy and justice ministry in the city. Other financial contributions to mercy and justice ministry come from our membership through individual gifts.

This works very well. The special offerings are generally new monies above and beyond regular giving. The existence of dynamic and compassionate ministry to the needy elicits generosity that would not come if we failed to give people an opportunity to give as their hearts direct. In fact, I have seen that when people see a church caring about its community in tangible ways, a lot of good-will results, which makes people more willing to give to the regular offerings as well. So we have found that Word ministry and acts of service are not a zero-sum game in terms of the availability of financial resources.

and justice, we must still address the question of *how* it will do so. Within this broad question are dozens of practical questions, and as we begin to debate them, it is important to consider different levels of assistance to the poor and to think about the appropriate role of the church in each.

1. Relief. The first level to consider is *relief* — giving direct aid to meet physical, material, and social needs. Common ways of providing relief are such things as temporary shelters for the homeless, food and clothing services for people in need, medical services, and crisis counseling. A form of relief is direct advocacy in which people in need are given active assistance to receive legal aid, find housing, and gain other kinds of support. But relief programs, when not combined with other types of assistance, will invariably create patterns of dependency.

2. Development. A second type of help is necessary at the level of *development,* bringing a person or community to self-sufficiency. In the Old Testament, when a slave's debt was erased and he was released, God directed that his former master send him out with grain, tools, and resources for a new, self-sufficient economic life (Deut 15:13 – 14). Development for an individual can include education, job creation, and training. But development for a neighborhood or community means reinvesting social and financial capital into a social system — housing development and home ownership, as well as other capital investments.

3. Reform. We can call the broadest level of assistance *reform.* Social reform moves beyond the relief of immediate needs and dependency and seeks to change the social conditions and structures that aggravate or cause the dependency. Job declared that he not only clothed the naked but "broke the fangs of the wicked and snatched the victims from their teeth" (Job 29:17). Moses communicated God's stance against legal systems weighted in favor of the rich and influential (Lev 19:15; Deut 24:17) and systems of lending capital that gouged persons of modest means (Exod 22:25 – 27; Lev 19:35 – 37; 25:37). The prophets denounced unfair wages (Jer 22:13) and corrupt business practices (Amos 8:2, 6). Daniel called a pagan government to account for its lack of mercy to the poor (Dan 4:27). As we read the Bible, we realize that Christians should take a stand in their particular communities as they advocate for better police protection, more just and fair banking practices and zoning practices, and better laws.

But even if we agree these are all essential pursuits for Christians (and they are!), we have not yet answered the question of how the institutional church should be involved. For both theological and practical reasons, I believe the local church should concentrate on the first level of assistance

(relief) and to some degree the second (development). At the second and third levels, in the domains of community development, social reform, and addressing social structures, I think it is generally best for believers to work through associations and organizations rather than directly through the local church.[3]

Why this distinction? One concern is the allocation of scarce financial resources. Many argue that the second and third levels are too expensive and will take financial resources away from the ministry of the Word. I don't see this as an insurmountable problem (see sidebar), but it is true that development and reform efforts tend to require significant sources of funds beyond what can be provided through the operations of a church. Leadership capacity and focus are other scarce resources. The issues of justice and mercy are so complex that the elders and staff of a church likely do not have the skills or time to deal with them properly.

Another reason relates to independence. Many say (and I agree) that these efforts can require too much political activity and enmeshment and may result in the congregation becoming too allied with particular civil magistrates and political parties in ways that can compromise the witness, independence, and authority of the church. In the end, I have seen that most churches in the United States that are deeply involved in caring for the poor have found it wisest to spin off nonprofit corporations to do community development and reform of social structures rather than seek to do them directly through the local congregation under the oversight of the elders.[4]

With these levels of assistance in mind, let's look at several practical issues of philosophy with respect to this aspect of integrative ministry. Often people with the same basic vision will disagree, so you may have to work hard to come to consensus.

1. Level of priority: How much should we help? This kind of ministry is very expensive. How high a priority should it hold in relationship to other ministries? Should a church wait until it has more people and is better established before doing something in this area? The needs are endless, so how can we know what percentage of the church's energy and money should be devoted to it? Here is a place to start. Deed or diaconal ministry — particularly for people inside the church — is prescribed by the Bible in Acts 6:1 – 7 and many other places. So someone in your church should be set apart to meet material and felt needs through deeds. This should be your commitment, regardless of how extensive the ministry becomes.

2. Defining "the poor": Whom should we help? How do we define *need* so we are sure we are serving those we should be serving? How needy must someone be? What if someone in your church says, "We are helping *him*? Why, he's not so bad off!" Here is a guiding idea. Jonathan Edwards applies the principle "love your neighbor as yourself" to this question. You don't wait until you are absolutely destitute before you do something to change your condition; so then you shouldn't help only the absolutely destitute people around you. Don't be too narrow in your definition of "the poor."

3. Conditional or unrestricted: When, and under what conditions, do we help? What should be required of those we help? Anything? Do you require that the persons come to your church or become part of some ministry? Should you work more with members than nonmembers? A guiding thought is Galatians 6:10: "Let us do good to all people, especially to those who belong to the family of believers." This makes it quite clear that we should give priority to brothers and sisters in our church. But it doesn't mean we shouldn't give help to people who are not members but who are in some relationship to our church — either in the immediate neighborhood or in relationships with believers inside.

4. Relief, development, and reform: In what way do we help? I mentioned that justice ministry can consist of helping individuals through simple relief — but it can also mean taking on unjust social systems. Should the church get into politics or stick with feeding the hungry? Keep in mind our discussion above about relief, development, and reform.

Ultimately, it is impossible to separate word and deed ministry because human beings are integrated wholes — body and soul. It is both natural and necessary that ministers of mercy also minister the Word while they are in the process of meeting human needs, and that communicators of the gospel also show compassion with regard to the material needs of the people they are trying

> It is impossible to separate word and deed ministry because human beings are integrated wholes — body and soul.

to reach. An integrative ministry means weaving together word and deed ministry as much as possible. When Jesus raised the dead son of the widow of Nain, he spoke words of comfort (Luke 7:13). After he healed the blind man, he returned with a gospel charge (John 9:35 – 38). These go hand in hand. In Acts 2, explosive growth in numbers (v. 41) leads to radical sharing with the needy (vv. 44 – 45). In Acts 4, economic sharing by people inside the church accompanied the preaching of the resurrection outside the church with great power (vv. 32 – 35). The practical actions of Christians on behalf of people in need demonstrated the truth and power of the gospel. The Roman emperor Julian was an enemy of Christianity, but he admitted that believers' generosity to the poor made it highly attractive:

Why do we not observe that it is their [Christians'] benevolence to strangers ... and the pretended holiness of their lives that have done most to increase atheism [Christianity] ... For it is disgraceful that, when no Jew ever has to beg, and the impious Galilaeans support not only their own poor but ours as well, all men see that our people lack aid from us.[5]

QUESTIONS FOR DISCUSSION AND REFLECTION

1. What does it mean, biblically, to be a *neighbor*, to *serve* others, and to *do justice*? How do our definitions of these terms compare with your own understanding?

2. Discuss the differences between relief, development, and reform. Which of these have you or your church community been involved in? Do you believe the local church should participate in the work of development and reform? Why or why not?

3. Keller writes, "Ultimately, it is impossible to separate word and deed ministry because human beings are integrated wholes — body and soul. It is both natural and necessary that ministers of mercy also minister the Word while they are in the process of meeting human needs, and that communicators of the gospel also show compassion with regard to the material needs of the people they are trying to reach. An integrative ministry means weaving together word and deed ministry as much as possible." How are you and your church seeking to weave together these two aspects of ministry?

CHAPTER 25 — CONNECTING PEOPLE TO THE CITY {pages 322–28}

1. I have written two books on this subject — *Ministries of Mercy: The Call of the Jericho Road*, 2nd ed. (Phillipsburg, N.J.: Presbyterian and Reformed, 1991), and *Generous Justice* (New York: Dutton, 2010). For that reason, this chapter will only sketch out a few basic ideas and principles.
2. Bruce Waltke, *The Book of Proverbs: Chapters 1 – 15* (Grand Rapids: Eerdmans, 2004), 97; see idem, "Righteousness in Proverbs," *Westminster Theological Journal* 70 (2008): 207 – 24.
3. We must be careful not to dogmatically draw lines here. Different social and cultural conditions can affect how directly the church is involved in addressing issues of justice. Looking back, we now applaud the Anglo churches that preached against and worked against the evils of African slavery in America. So, too, the African-American church, under the extreme conditions of slavery and near-slavery, bravely took on all three levels of ministry to the poor, and their work continues to this day.
4. See Keller, *Generous Justice*, ch. 6.
5. Julian (the Apostate), *The Works of the Emperor Julian* (Loeb Classical Library; New York: G. P. Putnam's Sons, 1923), 69, 71.

chapter 26

CONNECTING PEOPLE TO THE CULTURE

In the West during the time of Christendom, the church could afford to limit its discipleship and training of believers to prayer, Bible study, and evangelism because most Christians were not facing non-Christian values at work, in their neighborhoods, or at school. They did not need (or did not think they needed) to reflect deeply about a Christian approach to business, art, politics, the use of community resources, or race relations, to name a few examples. In a missional church today, however, believers are surrounded by a radically non-Christian culture. They require much more preparation and education to "think Christianly" about all of life, public and private, and about how to do their work with Christian distinctiveness.

But even this conviction is countercultural. Our Western cultures continue to cherish the Enlightenment "fact-value distinction," namely, that only things that can be proven scientifically are facts and therefore constitute the only legitimate basis for public work and discourse. Conversely, everything religious, transcendent, or subjective belongs in the sphere of values and should therefore be kept private. The implication for persons of faith is that their religious convictions are not to be brought to bear on their work, whether it is banking, acting, teaching, or policy making. In such an increasingly secular and post-Christian culture, it has become normal for believers to seal off their faith beliefs from the way they work in their vocations. The few who resist usually do so by being outspoken about their personal faith rather than by allowing the gospel to shape the way they actually do art, business, government, media, or scholarship. The church plays an essential role in supporting and encouraging individual Christians as they engage the culture, helping them to work with excellence, distinctiveness, and accountability in their professions.

THE GOSPEL SHAPES OUR WORK

Dualism is a philosophy that separates the spiritual/sacred from the rest of life. It originally had roots in Hellenistic thought, which viewed the material world as bad and the spiritual world as good. The Enlightenment's sharp division between the public world of "objective facts" and a private world of "subjective values" and spirituality is a descendant of dualism (as is the false dichotomy we addressed in the previous chapter regarding "conservative" word ministry and "liberal" deed ministry). These divisions continue to shape the way people understand and express their faith, leading to a widespread form of dualism that sees the church and its activities as good and untainted and the secular world as bad and polluting. In this view, the best way to truly serve God is through direct forms of ministry — teaching, evangelizing, and discipling. Christianity is seen as a means of individual spiritual peace and strength, not as a comprehensive interpretation of reality that pervades everything we do. Over the past few generations, this dualistic approach to ministry and life has effectively removed many Christians from places of cultural service and influence.

A Center Church theological vision promotes the centrality of the gospel as the basis for both ministry in the church and engagement with the culture. As we have tried to show, gospel-centered churches examine all that they do in light of the gospel of grace. But this goes beyond confronting legalistic Christianity to include confronting dualistic Christianity. Why? Because the two are actually related! Legalistic Christianity leads to dualistic Christianity. When people fail to grasp the gospel of grace, they tend toward a Pharisaical obsession with ritual purity or cleanness. If we assume we are saved by the purity and rightness of our lives, we are encouraged to stay within the confines of the church, content to be in relationships and situations where we don't have to deal with nonbelievers and their ideas. In addition, the black-and-white mentality of legalism does not allow for the kinds of flexibility and tolerance for uncertainty that are necessary for deep, thoughtful Christian reflection, creativity, and vocation. For example, while the Bible does tell us a great deal about how the church should operate, it doesn't give explicit details about how to run our businesses in a Christian way. To do so requires

---

Legalistic Christianity leads to dualistic Christianity.

---

engaging with the ideas of the world in a thoughtful manner, which is difficult and threatening — and it is easy to revert to dualism.

The opposite of dualism is worldview Christianity. Christianity is more than simply a set of beliefs I hold so I can achieve salvation for my individual soul. It is also a distinct way of understanding and interpreting everything in the world. It brings a distinct perspective on human nature, right and wrong, justice, beauty, purpose, scientific discovery, technology, and work. If I believe the universe was created, entered, and redeemed by a personal, triune, creator God — rather than believing it happened by accident — then I will necessarily have a distinct view on every one of these fundamental issues. And these perspectives will determine how I live my daily life.

The Bible teaches that *all our work matters to God*. The sixteenth-century Protestant Reformers believed that "secular" work is as valuable and God honoring as Christian ministry. When we use our gifts in work — whether by making clothes, building machines or software, practicing law, tilling fields, mending broken bodies, or nurturing children — we are answering God's call to serve the human community. Our work then, whatever it is, matters greatly to God.

It is equally true to say that *God matters to all our work*. That is, we also believe that the gospel shapes the motives, manner, and methods we use in our work. What, then, is the vision for work held by a church that emphasizes the centrality of the gospel, serves the city, engages the culture, and cultivates a missional community? We do not want Christians to privatize their faith away from their work; nor do we want them to express it in terms of a subculture. Rather we want to see Christians growing in maturity, working in their vocations with both excellence and Christian distinctiveness, seasoning and benefiting the culture in which they live.

Churches must help Christians see how the gospel shapes and informs our work in at least four ways:

1. Our faith changes our *motivation* for work. For professionals and others who are prone to overwork and anxiety, the gospel prevents us from finding our significance and identity in money and success. For working-class people who are prone to captivation to what Paul calls "eyeservice" (Col 3:22 KJV; "their eye is on you," NIV) and drudgery, our faith directs us to "work ... with all [our] heart, as working for the Lord" (Col 3:23).

2. Our faith changes our *conception* of work. A robust theology of creation — and of God's love and care for it — helps us see that even simple tasks such as making a shoe, filling a tooth, and digging a ditch are ways to serve God and build up human community. Our cultural production rearranges the material world in such a way that honors God and promotes human flourishing. A good theology of work resists the modern world's tendency to value only expertise in the pursuits that command more money and power.

3. Our faith provides high *ethics* for Christians in the workplace. Many things are technically legal but biblically immoral and unwise and therefore out of bounds for believers. The ethical norms of the Christian life, grounded in the gospel of grace, should always lead believers to function with an extremely high level of integrity in their work.

4. Our faith gives us the basis for reconceiving the very *way* in which our kind of work is done. Every community works on the basis of a collective map of what is considered most important. If God and his grace are not at the center of a culture, then other things will be substituted as ultimate values. So every vocational field is distorted by idolatry.

THE WORLDVIEW BEHIND YOUR WORK

Are you helping people think about the worldviews behind their work? Encourage them to ask questions like these:

1. What worldviews are predominant in my profession?
2. What are the underlying assumptions about meaning, morality, origin, and destiny?
3. What are the chief fears or threats? What groups or ideas are seen as the enemy?
4. What are the idols? What are the hopes?
5. What is the story line of the culture in which I live?
6. How do those worldviews affect both the form and content of *my* work? How can I work not just with excellence but with Christian distinctiveness?
7. Which parts of the culture's dominant views/theories are basically in line with the gospel and make it possible for me to agree with and use them?
8. Which parts of the dominant views/theories are basically irresolvable without Christ? How can Christ finish the story? In other words, where must I challenge my culture?
9. What opportunities are there in my profession for serving people, serving society as a whole, and witnessing to Christ and the kingdom of God?

Christian medical professionals will soon see that some practices make money for them but don't add value to patients' lives. Christians in marketing will discern accepted patterns of communication that distort reality, manipulate emotions, or play to the worst aspects of the human heart. Christians in business will often discern a bias to seek short-term financial profit at the expense of the company's long-term health or to adopt practices that put financial profit ahead of the good of employees, customers, or others in the community. Christians in the arts live and work in a culture in which narcissistic self-expression can become the ultimate end. And in most vocational fields, believers encounter workplaces in which ruthless, competitive behavior is the norm. A Christian worldview provides believers with ways to interpret the philosophies and practices that dominate their field and bring renewal and reform to them.[1]

HOW THE CHURCH CAN HELP

We must, therefore, reject approaches to work that counsel withdrawal or indifference regarding the culture. Members of such churches are told to either evangelize and disciple through the local church or, at the very least, to send in their tithes so the more committed Christians can please God directly by doing the work of ministry. In these types of churches, there is little to no support or appreciation for the "secular" work of Christians. On the other hand, we must also reject the approach that stresses social justice and cultural involvement but fails to call us to repentance, conversion, and holiness. We want to avoid both simple cultural confrontation and cultural assimilation and instead become an agent for cultural renewal. We want to disciple our people to work in the world out of a Christian worldview.

I believe the church needs to help people work in three specific ways: accountably, distinctively, and excellently.

WORKING ACCOUNTABLY: VOCATION-SPECIFIC SPIRITUAL NURTURE

There is a need to provide the basic "means of grace" — prayer, mutual/peer ministry and accountability, learning in community, shepherding oversight — that both fits the time patterns and addresses the life issues of those in a particular vocation. This will address two common problems. First, the jobs and careers of urbanized culture increasingly do not fit into the traditional "forty hours with weekends off" pattern. They increasingly require travel, have seasonal cycles, and entail many changes of residence, in addition to long and/or changing weekly hours. As a result, many who are moving up in their careers find it difficult to access the normal venues for spiritual nurture — Sunday services and weekly weeknight small groups. So you will need to devise creative ways of providing this nurture, as you reflect on these kinds of questions: Should some groups meet only monthly face-to-face but weekly online? Should some church staff be released to do more frequent one-on-three shepherding and discipleship?

The second dynamic is that each vocation presents many spiritual and moral issues, ethical quandaries, temptations, discouragements, and other questions that particularly confront the Christians in that profession. A good deal of spiritual nurture in the church is very general and only addresses generic or private-world matters. But we spend most of our week in our vocational field, and we need to hear how other Christians have dealt with the same problems we face every day. Some vocations are so demanding that Christians will drop out of them if they fail to receive specific encouragement and support. So Christians in the same profession need to mentor and support each other.[2]

At Redeemer, working accountably takes the form of what we call "vocational fellowships," made up of Christians in the same vocation who band together to minister to one another in the ways mentioned above. Some vocational fellowships consist of periodic gatherings in which people in related professions meet, listen to speakers, and discuss a topic. Others have monthly meetings or weekly small groups. Midsized groups can also be based on vocational commonality rather than on geographic location. For example, you might have a monthly or biweekly meeting of artists. Not only do vocation-specific groups provide accountability and encouragement; they can have an interesting evangelistic edge. Often members of a profession who don't profess to be believers will be attracted toward thoughtful and supportive fellowships of Christians whose work they respect.

WORKING DISTINCTIVELY:
WORLDVIEW DEVELOPMENT AND TRAINING

For many of us, it is obvious we are working for the Lord when we directly use our gifts to convey Chris-

tian messages. But we don't always know how to work *distinctively* for the Lord while going about less obviously Christian cultural and vocational tasks. It is easy for a singer to feel he is using his gifts for Christ as he sings "Every Valley Shall Be Exalted" from Handel's *Messiah*, but how does the gospel make the rest of his work distinctive? Is he just a singer who happens to be a Christian? Or is he a fully Christian singer whose art is shaped by the gospel every day of the week? How will his work be any different from that of a person with radically different beliefs about human nature, God, and the meaning of life? Will the only difference be that he doesn't sleep with his costars or that he only sings religious music? Is career advancement his real motive for what he does, or is he consciously witnessing to the goodness of creation and the meaningfulness of life by the excellence of his art? Will the skill and commitment of his art always testify — even to the most skeptical people — that this world is not an accident, that it is coherent and beautiful, that we were created for a purpose?

The question for the church is this: If we believe that Jesus is Lord in every area of life, how do we train our people in the practice of that lordship?

Similarly, it is easy for an MBA to feel she is using her gifts for Christ as she sits on the board of a charitable nonprofit or serves as a trustee for her church. But how does the gospel make the rest of her work distinctive? Will she have the same view of corporate profits as a person with different beliefs about human nature, God, and the meaning of life? Does she act in all her business dealings with the awareness that every human being is made in the image of God — each person so precious that God has given his Son for them?

The question for the church is this: If we believe that Jesus is Lord in every area of life, how do we train our people in the practice of that lordship? In general, this practice has to arise out of intentional learning communities that bring together three different groups of people: (1) older accomplished Christians in a field, (2) younger arriving Christians in a field, and (3) teachers knowledgeable in the Bible, theology, and church history. These three groups work together to ensure that the right questions are being addressed and to forge answers to those questions that are both biblical and practical. And what kinds of questions will these be? At the very least, these groups should ask three things of every vocation (see sidebar on "The Worldview behind Your Work" on p. 332):

1. What practices in our field are common grace and can be embraced?
2. What practices are antithetical to the gospel and must be rejected?
3. What practices are neutral and can be adapted and revised?

At Redeemer, working distinctively happens in the vocational groups (described below), as well as in the Gotham Fellowship — a program for young adults who are less than five years out of university and working in their first jobs. Those who participate in the program invest heavily in theological training, worldview reflection, and communal spiritual formation.

WORKING EXCELLENTLY: MENTORING AND CULTURAL PRODUCTION

In concert with working accountably and distinctively, Christians must support and help one another to do their work excellently, with diligence and innovation. In some areas this support can be provided through mentoring relationships. Those who are more experienced and accomplished in their field should be moved by the gospel to make themselves available to those who are new in the faith or the field. In other vocational areas, this could even mean cooperative ventures — starting new companies or nonprofits, executing individual artistic projects, initiating a new journal or periodical, creating an art gallery, or starting a volunteer program. This kind of discipleship takes several forms at Redeemer, but one example is the Entrepreneurship Forum

in which the church conducts an annual business plan competition and gives grants to the best plan for a for-profit and nonprofit initiative. Those who present plans must show how the gospel informs the integration of their faith and work.

I place the excellence factor last to remind us that if the first two factors are neglected, the resulting ventures are likely to be poorly conceived. Often we think of "Christian businesses" as those that hire born-again Christians and perhaps have a daily Bible study at the office. It is rare to encounter a business that has thoughtfully worked out its mission and its financial and personnel policies theologically. Many "Christian art" productions are in reality just ways of pulling artists out of the world and into the Christian subculture. In general, cooperation in cultural production should not mean Christians banding together to leave the big, bad world; rather, cooperation involves working together — even with nonbelievers — in order to *serve* the world. This cooperation is not likely to happen until greater numbers of Christians become more willing to embrace a less dualistic understanding of their faith.

As we have seen, Christians make two opposing mistakes in addressing the idols of their vocational field. On the one hand, they may seal off their faith from their work, laboring according to the same values and practices that everyone else uses; on the other hand, they may loudly and clumsily declare their Christian faith to their coworkers, often without showing any grace and wisdom in the way they relate to people on the job. An essential part of the church's integrative ministry is to help believers think through the implications of the gospel for art, business, government, media, entertainment, and scholarship. We have to provide creative ways of delivering spiritual nurture so believers can be *accountable* to other believers and to the faith they profess. We teach that *excellence* in work is a critical means for gaining credibility for our faith; if our work is shoddy, our verbal witness only leads listeners to despise our beliefs. And if Christians live in major cultural centers and do their work in an excellent yet *distinctive* manner, it will ultimately produce a different kind of culture from the one in which we now live.

I am often asked, "Should Christians be involved in shaping culture?" My answer is, "We can't *not* be involved in shaping culture." But I prefer the term "cultural renewal" to "culture shaping" or "cultural transformation." For a possible model, think about the monks in the Middle Ages, who moved out through pagan Europe, inventing and establish-ing academies, universities, and hospitals. They transformed local economies and cared for the weak through these new institutions. They didn't set out to take control of a pagan culture. They let the gospel change how they did their work — which meant they worked for others rather than for themselves. Christians today should strive to be a community that lives out this same kind of dynamic, which will bring the same kind of result.

QUESTIONS FOR DISCUSSION AND REFLECTION

1. In your own ministry context, how have you seen and experienced the effects of dualism? Where have you seen secular institutions retreating from partnership with religious institutions? How has dualism led you to be less integrated in public and in your relationships with others? Where is your church unwittingly retreating from culture and accepting this premise of a private/public dichotomy?

2. If you currently serve in full-time ministry, have you ever worked outside of professional ministry? If so, how does your time in the workforce inform the ways you prepare your congregation for Christ-honoring vocation? If you haven't worked in another vocation, have you ever felt limited in your ability to compellingly argue for biblical ethics and integration at work?

3. This chapter suggests four ways that churches can help Christians see how the gospel informs and shapes their work:

   - Our faith changes our motivation for work.
   - Our faith changes our conception of work.

   - Our faith provides high ethics for Christians in the workplace.
   - Our faith gives us the basis for reconceiving the very way in which our kind of work is done.

   Which of these is most meaningful to you right now? How can you begin to teach and disciple believers to reflect on each of these four ways of relating faith to work?

4. Keller writes, "Each vocation presents many spiritual and moral issues, ethical quandaries, temptations, discouragements, and other questions that particularly confront the Christians in that profession. A good deal of spiritual nurture in the church is very general and only addresses generic or private-world matters. But we spend most of our week in our vocational field, and we need to hear how other Christians have dealt with the same problems we face every day." Think about the various vocations represented in your church and community. How can you begin to encourage and nurture believers to work accountably in their profession?

CHAPTER 26 — CONNECTING PEOPLE TO THE CULTURE *(pages 330–35)*

1. For a full-length treatment of the particular ways in which a gospel-centered worldview applies to work, see Timothy Keller, *Every Good Endeavor: Connecting Your Work to God's Plan for the World* (New York: Dutton, 2012).
2. Of course, we must strike a balance here. In some ways it would be as wrong to segregate Christians by vocation as it would be by race. Suspicion among members of certain professions can be raised, and it is liberating and healthy to build friendships across these kinds of barriers. Some people will not want or need spiritual nurture that is vocation specific. But many others will not otherwise be given the care they need to handle the temptations and quandaries that are unique to their vocation — and so they will abandon either their careers or their beliefs.

chapter 27
MOVEMENTS AND INSTITUTIONS

The missionary enterprise of the nineteenth century offers important insights into the character of effective movements. Early in that century, many of the new churches established by Western missionaries in the non-Western world were locked into unhealthy patterns of dependency. These congregations and denominations had the traditional marks of a true church — the faithful preaching of the Word of God, the right use of the sacraments, and a functioning system of discipline.[1] They held to sound doctrine and included ministers and leaders from the local population, yet they were unable to propagate themselves readily or to support themselves financially. As a result, they remained dependent on Western missionaries and money indefinitely.

An alternate approach to missions — pioneered by John Nevius, Hudson Taylor, Roland Allen, and others — sought to plant churches that were self-sustaining from inception. The goal was establishing congregations that grew naturally, without the artificial "life support" of foreign aid, not only by winning converts effectively within their own cultures but also by attracting and developing new indigenous leaders at such a rate that the churches regularly reproduced themselves. In short, they wanted churches to have a dynamism that made them able to grow from within without needing to be propped up with money and leaders from outside. They wanted these churches to be more than just sound institutions; they wanted them to be vital and dynamic *movements*.

The title of Roland Allen's book, *The Spontaneous Expansion of the Church*, gets at this idea.[2] It evokes the image of spontaneous combustion — combustion without an external ignition source. A church (or group of churches) with movement dynam-

ics generates its own converts, ideas, leaders, and resources from within in order to realize its vision of being the church for its city and culture. Unless the environment is extremely hostile (e.g., heavy persecution, war, economic collapse), the church grows in numbers and in spiritual maturity. In the language of missiologists, such a church is "self-propagating, self-governing, and self-supporting." It will reproduce into other churches that reproduce themselves for the same reasons. The more ideas, leaders, and resources that are pooled and deployed, the more the movement dynamic strengthens and snowballs. As long as the reproducing churches keep a unified vision, the movement can build steam and grow steadily, even exponentially.

A church (or group of churches) with movement dynamics generates its own converts, ideas, leaders, and resources from within in order to realize its vision of being the church for its city and culture.

Churches with no movement dynamics are like a person on a life support machine. I have seen at least three ways in which churches survive without movement dynamics:

1. Some churches have a denominational structure or a missionary structure that subsidizes the church financially.
2. Some churches have a substantial endowment and a building that serves as a community center for the local population. In this situation, there is no need for outside financial or leadership assistance in the near term, but the church

GOD'S SOVEREIGNTY AND CHURCH GROWTH

The subject of church growth can be contro-versial. In the introduction I briefly discussed Paul's metaphor of the church as a garden (1 Cor 3:4–9). In this image, leading a church is like gardening. The garden's growth is determined by at least three factors: (1) the skill and diligence of the gardener, (2) the soil's fertility, and (3) the weather conditions. If skillful ministry is like gardening, and the soil and weather conditions are akin to the sovereignty of God's Spirit, then we see that a lack of church growth cannot be simplisti-cally assumed to be attributable to human failure, nor can it simplistically be excused as God's will. Calvin's classic treatment of God's sovereignty fully affirms the importance of human responsibility.[3]

To generalize, many modern church growth technique books do not give sufficient weight to God's sovereignty, while many anti-church-growth books and voices make excuses for a lack of spiritual vitality in the church. Our point in this chapter is that it is possible for a church to be a doctrinally sound organization but not a dynamic, grow-ing organism. The Bible envisions a church that is both.

does not produce additional resources or dynamism to sustain growth through conver-sions and the spiritual growth of its members. It essentially operates as a well-run business. Finances come from a judiciously managed en-dowment, supplemented by income from rent-als, fees, and a few donations. Many churches sustain themselves as institutions in this way.

3. Some churches have a small, overworked core of people within a larger, stagnant structure.

While the congregation has no movement dynamism, it is propped up from within. That is, a small handful of people give an inordinate amount of time and money to keep a stagnant or declining church going. These individuals may be spiritually vital Christians themselves who cannot spread this vitality to the rest of the church, or they simply may be hardworking people with deep roots in the church, which creates a sacrificial loyalty. This solution is temporary. At some point, the few people who are keeping the church alive through their sacrificial giving grow too tired to continue, and in the absence of an ability to reproduce, the church eventually dies.

HOW MOVEMENTS AND INSTITUTIONS CONTRAST

I am not suggesting simplistically that movements are good and institutions are bad — rather, that organizations should have both institutional char-acteristics and movement dynamics, though there are some tensions and trade-offs in the balance. Institutions promote stable patterns of behavior through rules and policies that change slowly, thereby limiting and shaping people's choices and practices.[4] But this intentional limiting of choices is often a healthy thing. Think for a moment of a grocery store. Customers typically have a good idea of how to check out. They know where to go and where to stand; they know about lines (queues) and about how long to expect to stand in line; and they know what to do when they get to the head of the line. What would it be like if every week the way you pay for your items changed drastically? It would be chaotic. Institutionalization makes it possible for millions of people each day to shop for the things they need in a grocery store. Some of the institu-tional practices are formal (like how to pay), while some of them are informal (like how long people expect to wait in line). If you try to pay for your food at the grocery store with a bar of gold, it just won't work. If customers have to wait for an hour in line, anger will break out. Why? Because "everyone knows" that an hour is too long to wait (at least in a Western country). The grocery store is obligated (informally) to not make you wait that long. If it violates this bond of trust, you probably won't come back. Your expectations and behaviors have been limited, directed, and shaped by this institution. No one could go into a grocery store and shop efficiently if not for institutionalization.

Hugh Heclo defines institutions this way: "Institutions represent inheritances of valued purposes with attendant rules and moral obligations" stewarded by those with authority.[5] This is an abstract, academic description, but it leads us in a helpful direction. Institutions rely on submission to an established authority that preserves the values and purposes of the past. Institutions are necessary and helpful, providing established, reliable systems and frames for accomplishing what needs to be done. Heclo writes, "To live in a culture that turns its back on institutions is equivalent to trying to live in a physical body without a skeleton or hoping to use a language but not its grammar."[6] Institutions bring order to life and establish many of the conditions for human flourishing and civilized society.

Movements, on the other hand, have more to do with the assertion of individual preference and bringing forth the realities of the future. I would define four key characteristics of a movement: vision, sacrifice, flexibility with unity, and spontaneity.

1. First and foremost, movements are marked by a compelling vision. A vision consists of an attractive, vivid, and clear picture of the future that the movement and its leaders are seeking to bring about. A movement states, "If this is where you want to go, come along with us." This picture of the future is accompanied by a strong set of values or beliefs to which the movement is committed. The content of this vision must be expressed so that others can grasp it readily; it must not be so esoteric or difficult that only a handful of people can articulate it.

The content of a vision must be compellingly expressed so that others can learn it and carry it out in their own community without a great deal of centralized control or assistance. So, for example, the transforming concept of the Alcoholics Anonymous "twelve-step group" has been compellingly ex-

pressed and applied in innumerable books. Because of this, a person with a vision for changing lives through such a group can often simply pick up the literature and get started. They won't need anyone's permission or money, and there are many ways to get excellent training. Or, to use a less sanguine example, we could note that one of the reasons al-Qaeda has been effective is that it disseminates its worldview broadly and clearly. People imbibe it and educate themselves with it, and many form terrorist cells that operate without central control or communication. In some cases, they may go to an al-Qaeda training camp to become more effective, but afterward they are largely trusted to work out their own local strategy. The point of these examples is that AA and al-Qaeda are vital, constantly growing movements rather than centralized institutions. This is the reason for their effectiveness and their ability to grow with relatively modest amounts of capital. The key to the success of the vision is its simplicity and availability, often in the form of content that transmits, expounds, and applies the vision.

By contrast, though institutions almost always have a purpose statement written down somewhere (e.g., schools are there to educate, businesses to produce their product, hospitals to heal the sick), the glue that holds the institution together is really its rules, regulations, and procedures. In a movement, a shared vision is what guides the day-to-day choices; in an institution, it is typically the rules and established patterns.

2. The unifying vision in a movement is so compelling that it leads to a culture of sacrificial commitment and intrinsic rewards. Individuals put the vision ahead of their own interests and comfort. In the early days of any movement, the main actors often work without compensation, constantly living in the threat of bankruptcy. The satisfaction of realized goals is their main reward. Some refer to this as "intrinsic" reward — internal, personal fulfillment that comes from knowing you have been instrumental in bringing about so much good. In an institution, however, every position has highly defined rights and privileges, as well as clear compensation and benefits. The main incentive in an institution is centered around these "extrinsic" rewards. Institutional members certainly know there is a job to do, but their work output is balanced carefully against concrete rewards. There is no more practical index of whether your church has movement dynamics than examining whether you have a culture of sacrifice. If the top leaders of the church are the only ones making all the sacrifices, then you don't have a movement culture.

3. Movements are characterized by a stance of generous flexibility toward other organizations and people outside their own membership rolls. Movements make the *what* — the accomplishment of the vision — a higher value than *how* it gets done and *who* gets it done. The vision encourages sacrifice, and members of a movement are willing to make allies, cooperating with anyone who shares an interest in the vision. Institutionalized organizations, on the other hand, are more committed to the importance of inherited practices, right procedures, and accredited persons. They often choose to *not* achieve a result — though it may be strongly desired — if they can't get it done in the prescribed way and with the properly accredited parties.

The spirit of flexibility that we find in a movement means there is a great deal of unity — within the movement as well as in relationship to other organizations. Institutions do not typically encourage this type of unity, even internally. They tend to consist of a set of turf-conscious silos, each more concerned for its own welfare than for the good of the whole. Often, institutions lack organizational unity and may even be hostile toward other organizations.

4. Movements spontaneously produce new ideas and leaders and grow from within. Institutions by their very nature are structured for long-term durability and stability and are prone to resist risky new ideas. But movements are willing to take new risks because the members are already making sacrifices to be part of the work. A movement also tends to attract and reward leaders who produce results. Again, the reason is that accomplishing the vision is so important. Institutions however, because

they value stability and durability, tend to reward leadership according to tenure and the accrual of accepted qualifications and credentials.

Summarizing the important differences between movements and institutions in their strongest forms helps us more clearly see the distinctions (see the table on the next page).

As we see these contrasting characteristics, we begin to better understand why movements are spontaneously generative. A movement is able to generate new ideas because it encourages people to brainstorm and is more willing to experiment and try out new ideas. Movements are "flatter" — less hierarchical and siloed than institutions — and therefore new ideas get traction more quickly. Movements also are better able to generate new leaders because they can attract the most ambitious and creative people. Because they are results oriented, they can quickly identify emerging leaders and promote them. Movements grow faster because their testing of new ideas keeps them adapted to the changes in the environment.

HOW MOVEMENTS AND INSTITUTIONS CONVERGE

Young church leaders can get excited about movements and speak long and loudly against the blindness and deadness of the institutional church.

Maintaining the engine of movement dynamics — a unified vision — necessitates adopting some of the aspects of institutions. The vision becomes a "tradition" that the movement guards and passes on.

Indeed, anyone skimming the left-hand column of the table on the next page knows that too many churches *are* too institutionalized. David Hurst, a Harvard scholar, nicely sums up how movements become institutions — vision becomes strategy, roles become tasks, teams become structure, networks become organizations, and recognition becomes compensation.[7]

INSTITUTION	MOVEMENT
Held together by rules and procedure	Held together by common purpose, vision
A culture of rights and quotas; a balance of responsibilities and rewards	A culture of sacrificial commitment
Emphasis on compensation, "extrinsic" rewards	Emphasis on celebration, "intrinsic" rewards
Changes in policy involve long process, all departments, much resistance and negotiation	Vision comes from charismatic leaders; accepted with loyalty
Decisions made procedurally and slowly	Decisions made relationally and rapidly
Innovations from top down; implemented in department silos	Innovations bubble up from all members; executed by the whole
Feels like a patchwork of turf-conscious mini-agencies or departments	Feels like a unified whole
Values: security, predictability	Values: risk, serendipity
Stable, slow to change	Dynamic, quick to change
Emphasis on tradition, past, and custom; future trends are dreaded and denied	Emphasis on present and future; little emphasis on past
Jobs given to those with accreditation and tenure	Jobs given to those producing best results

Remember, however, that it is wrong to draw too sharp a line between the two forms, or even to pit them against each other so starkly when we look at actual examples. While there are good reasons for Christian movement literature to be highly critical of institutionalism, the impression often left is that all authority, centralized control, and formal processes are bad for ministry. The reality is far more complex. First, though new churches and ministries work hard at remaining informal, noncodified, and noncentralized, institutionalization is unavoidable.

As soon as we make a choice — the creation of a new policy, administrative structure, or consensus of value and belief — and begin carrying it into the future, thus shaping people's routines, expectations, and allowable preferences, we have begun to institutionalize that value or belief.

And some institutionalization is even desirable. As pointed out earlier, a unified vision — held by every member of the movement — is critical to movement dynamics. But this vision cannot change every day, or even every year, or it will create chaos in the movement and retard its growth. Ironically, this means the vision itself requires some codification and control. In other words, maintaining the engine of movement dynamics — a unified vision — necessitates adopting some of the aspects of institutions. The vision becomes, as it were, a "tradition" that the movement guards and passes on.

In addition, we noted that movements rely heavily on the sacrificial commitment of their members, especially when they are just getting started. In this start-up mode, members may max out their credit cards and tap into their savings to get things going. But this way of living is unsustainable. Any vision that is compelling will be a big one, and big visions require long-term effort — an effort that will require, for example, bringing in enough revenue so the founders can pay off their credit cards and eventu-

ally have enough to live on and raise their families. In other words, a movement must eventually settle into a sustainable business model that generates enough resources to cover expenses. If it fails to do this, it will end up burning out the best people and failing to progress toward the vision.

A strong, dynamic movement, then, occupies this difficult space in the center — the place of tension and balance between being a freewheeling organism and a disciplined organization. A movement that refuses to take on some organizational characteristics — authority, tradition, unity of belief, and quality control — will fragment and dissipate. Movements that fail to resist the inevitable tendency toward complete institutionalization will end up losing their vitality and effectiveness. The job of the movement leader is to steer the ship safely between these two perils.

QUESTIONS FOR DISCUSSION AND REFLECTION

1. What would happen if your organization suddenly had to leave its building, was cut off from denominational support structures and deprived of endowments and bank balances, and experienced the loss of its senior leader? Would there be a resilient institution remaining that could pick itself up, start over by the grace of God, and raise up new leaders from within? If not, which of the three types of stagnant structures (subsidized from without, managed by endowment life support, or propped up by a small overworked core) best describes your congregation or organization?

2. This chapter suggests four key characteristics of a movement: vision, sacrifice, flexibility with unity, and spontaneity. How have you experienced these in your own ministry or church setting? In your experience, how do each of these characteristics contribute to the dynamics of the movement?

3. Review the table contrasting institutions with movements. As you consider your own church, what characteristics of a movement do you see? What characteristics of an institution are present? What might you do to encourage additional movement dynamics in your church?

CHAPTER 27 — MOVEMENTS AND INSTITUTIONS *{pages 337–42}*

1. For a simple description of the marks of a genuine church as discerned by the Protestant Reformers, see J. I. Packer, "Word and Sacrament: How a Genuine Church Is Identified," in *Concise Theology* (Wheaton, Ill.: Tyndale House, 2001), 204 – 6. Reformed churches have always named these three marks (Word, sacrament, discipline), though others have argued that church discipline is necessarily involved in a right use of the sacraments, and therefore, they reason, there are properly only two marks of a true church. Whether we break these into two, three, or four line items is not critical as long as all the functions and purposes are recognized. The true church communicates sound biblical doctrine through its teachers and also incorporates people through baptism and the Lord's Supper into a visible covenant community in which its leaders provide wise spiritual oversight.

2. The first to recognize the dependency of the non-Western churches were the British Anglican Henry Venn and the American Congregationalist Rufus Anderson, both of whom urged a model called "indigenization" in which Western missionaries were expected to preach and pastor new churches and eventually raise up indigenous, national leaders and hand the churches over to them. Later, the British Anglican Roland Allen and the American Presbyterian John Nevius urged that this process be started further back and argued that Western missionaries should never act as church planters and sole pastors of non-Western churches. Instead, new converts should be trained and helped to establish churches themselves. Roland Allen wrote *Missionary Methods: St Paul's or Ours?* (London: Robert Scott, 1912) and *The Spontaneous Expansion of the Church, and the Causes Which Hinder It* (London: World Dominion Press, 1927), while Nevius wrote *The Planting and Development of Missionary Churches* (New York: Foreign Mission Library, 1899).

3. John Calvin, *Institutes of the Christian Religion*, ed. John T. McNeill (Philadelphia: Westminster, 1960), 1:197 – 237.

4. Hugh Heclo's great little book *On Thinking Institutionally* (Boulder, Colo.: Paradigm, 2008) lays out the diverse definitions that scholars have given to the idea of institutions.

5. Heclo, *On Thinking Institutionally*, 38.

6. Ibid.

7. David K. Hurst, *Crisis and Renewal* (Cambridge, Mass.: Harvard Business School Press, 2002).

THE CHURCH AS AN ORGANIZED ORGANISM

As we clarify the differences between institutions and movements we must acknowledge that churches are and must be institutions.[1] But they must also be movements. As we have seen over the centuries, churches can meet doctrinal and institutional standards and still lack effectiveness in propagating the faith in their society. At this point it is natural to ask: Is there biblical warrant for being attentive to this distinction and balance between institution and movement? I believe there is. The Scriptures envision churches that are both *organism* and *organization* — or, to put it simply, churches that are organized organisms.

The book of Acts describes the life of the church in organic language. Several times we are told that the church or the number of disciples increased, grew, or spread (4:4; 6:1, 7; 9:31; 16:5). We are also told that the Word of God spread, increased, or grew (6:7; 12:24; 19:20). Acts 19:20 speaks of the Word growing in power, as if the Word of God, the gospel of Christ, has a life and power of its own (cf. Rom 1:16 – 17). Paul speaks of the gospel continually "bearing fruit and growing" (Col 1:6).

The church grows, but it does not grow as other human organizations do — as a business, a sports league, a government agency, or even a viral online movement would grow. The church increases in numbers because the Word of God grows when it reaches listeners in the power of the Spirit (cf. Acts 10 – 11). This biblical language suggests there is an organic, self-propagating, dynamic power operating within the church. In Acts, we see it working essentially on its own, with little institutional support or embodiment — without strategic plans or the command and control of managers and other leaders.

And yet, even though this power operates spontaneously, we see that when the Word of God produces a new church, Paul is always careful to appoint elders — leaders with authority — in every town before leaving it (cf. Acts 14:23). We may be inclined to wonder: How was Paul able to discern so quickly those with leadership ability among the brand-new converts? Wouldn't it have been better to let the new body of believers grow for a couple of

---

From the beginning, the church was both an institution and a movement.

---

years — just meeting together to study and to love and serve each other — before imposing an authority structure on them? Paul's behavior indicates just how important it was for these dynamic, spontaneously growing churches to have an authority structure as a way of ensuring that members would embody the church's apostolically inherited teaching and purpose.

From the beginning, the church was both an institution and a movement. This dual nature of the church is grounded in the work of the Spirit, and it is the Spirit who makes the church simultaneously a vital *organism* and a structured *organization*.[2] One helpful way of understanding this balance is to look at the way the ministry of Jesus is carried out in the church in a general sense through every believer, as well as through specialized roles — a distinction commonly referred to as the *general* and *special* office.

THE GENERAL AND THE SPECIAL OFFICE

Jesus Christ has all the powers and functions of ministry in himself. He has a *prophetic* ministry, speaking the truth and applying it to men and women on behalf of God. Jesus was the ultimate prophet, for he revealed most clearly (both in his words and his life) God's character, saving purposes, and will for our lives. Jesus also has a *priestly* ministry. While a prophet is an advocate for God before people, a priest is an advocate for the people before God's presence, ministering with mercy and sympathy. Jesus was the ultimate priest, for he stood in our place and sacrificially bore our burdens and sin, and he now brings us into God's presence. Finally, Jesus has a *kingly* ministry. He is the ultimate king, ordering the life of his people through his revealed law.

THE GENERAL OFFICE OF BELIEVERS

Every believer, through the Holy Spirit, is to minister to others in these three ways as well.

1. The Bible refers to every believer as a prophet. In Numbers 11:29, Moses states, "I wish that all the LORD's people were prophets," and in Joel 2:28 – 29, this blessing is predicted for the messianic age. In Acts 2:16 – 21, Peter declares that in the church this prophecy is now fulfilled. Every believer is led by the Holy Spirit to discern the truth (1 John 2:20, 27). Each believer is directed to admonish with the word of Christ (Col 3:16), as well as to instruct (Rom 15:14) and encourage other believers (Heb 3:13). Christians are also called to witness to the truth before their nonbelieving friends and neighbors. In Acts 8:4, all of the Christians who "had been scattered" out of Jerusalem "preached the word wherever they went." In 1 Thessalonians 1:8, Paul states that "the Lord's message rang out" from the new converts all over Macedonia and Achaia. Paul exhorted the Corinthian Christians to imitate him in conducting all aspects of life in such a way that people come to salvation (1 Cor 9:19 – 23; 10:31 – 11:1). In Colossians 4:5 – 6, Paul tells all Christians to answer every nonbeliever with wisdom and grace, and in 1 Peter 3:15, Peter charges all believers to give cogent reasons for their faith to non-Christians. Behind all these exhortations is the assumption that the word is dwelling richly in every Christian (Col 3:16). It means that every believer must read, ponder, and love the Word of God, be able to interpret it properly, and be skillful in applying it to their own questions and needs and to those of the people around them.

2. The Bible calls every believer a *priest*— "you are a royal priesthood" (1 Pet 2:9). Just as every believer is a prophet, understanding the word of God now that Jesus has come, so every believer is a priest, having access in the name of Christ, the great High Priest, to the presence of God (Heb 4:14 – 16). Believers, then, have the priestly work of daily offering themselves as living sacrifices (Rom 12:1 – 2) and of offering the sacrifices of deeds of mercy and adoring worship to God (Heb 13:15 – 16). The priesthood of all believers means not only that all are now active participants in joyful public worship (1 Cor 14:26) but also that they have the priestly calling to "do good and to share with others" (Heb 13:16). As prophets, Christians call neighbors to repent, but as priests they do so with sympathy and loving service to address their needs. This is why Jesus calls us to live such lives of goodness and service that outsiders will glorify God (Matt 5:16).[3]

3. The Bible calls every believer a *king.* All believers rule and reign with Christ (Eph 2:6) as kings and priests (Rev 1:5 – 6). Although elders and leaders have the responsibility of church governance and discipline, the "kingship of all believers" means

PROPHETIC WITNESS OF THE BELIEVER

Though John the Baptist was the greatest prophet in history, Jesus makes the startling claim that every single Christian believer is greater in position and calling (Matt 11:11), i.e., that believers are greater prophets than John the Baptist. How can this be? John was greater than other prophets because of his redemptive-historical location — he witnessed to Jesus Christ directly. In the same way, a believer's prophetic witness is greater than the Old Testament prophets or John, because the simplest Christian understands more of the gospel than even John did.

that believers have the right and responsibility to discipline one another. Christians are supposed to confess their sins not only to a minister but to one another, and they are called to pray for one another (Jas 5:16). They are not to rely only on the discipline of elders but are to exhort each other so they don't become hardened by their sin (Heb 3:13). It is the responsibility of not only elders and ministers to discern sound doctrine; all believers must rely on the anointing the Spirit gives them to discern truth (1 John 2:20, 27). The kingly general office is one of

---

The Spirit equips every believer to be a prophet who brings the truth, a priest who sympathetically serves, and a king who calls others into accountable love.

---

the reasons that many denominations have historically given the congregation the right to select its own leaders and officers, with the approval of the existing leaders (Acts 6:1 – 6). In other words, the power of governing the church rests in the people. Though pastors and teachers are uniquely called to build up the body into spiritual maturity (Eph 4:11 – 13), every Christian is called to help build up the body into maturity by "speaking the truth in love" to one another (Eph 4:15). The kingship of every believer also means that every believer has the authority to fight and defeat the world, the flesh, and the devil (cf. Eph 6:11 – 18; Jas 4:7; 1 John 2:27; 4:4; 5:4).

All of these facets of ministry are brought together in 1 Peter 2:9. Here we are told that followers of Christ have been made kings and priests — "a royal priesthood" — that we "may declare the praises of him who called you out of darkness," which is the work of a prophet. The Spirit equips every believer to be a prophet who brings the truth, a priest who sympathetically serves, and a king who calls others into accountable love — even if he or she lacks specialized gifts for office or full-time ministry. This Spirit-equipped calling and gifting of every believer to be a prophet, priest, and king has been called the "general office." This understanding of the general

office helps prevent the church from becoming a top-down, conservative, innovation-allergic bureaucracy. It helps us understand the church as an energetic grassroots movement that produces life-changing and world-changing ministry — all without dependence on the control and planning of a hierarchy of leaders.

THE SPECIAL OFFICE OF MINISTER

The Spirit gives every Christian believer spiritual gifts for ministry (1 Cor 12 – 14) so that service to Christ will constantly arise out of the grassroots of the church. Yet the Spirit also gives gifts and creates "special offices" — roles that carry out a ministry within the church — that sometimes entail authority. The very same Spirit who generates the spontaneous, explosive ministry and growth is also the giver of the gifts of apostle, prophet, and pastor/teacher (Eph 4:11), as well as of governance (Rom 12:8). To be exercised, these gifts must be publicly recognized by the congregation, which requires some kind of organization. There is no way to exercise the gift of governing (Rom 12:8) unless we have an institutional structure — elections, bylaws, ordination, and standards for accreditation. No one can govern without some level of agreement by the whole church about what powers are given to the governors and how these powers are legitimately exercised. So the growth and flourishing of spontaneous ministry depends on some institutional elements being in place.

The special office represents the way Jesus orders and governs his church by the Spirit. Jesus commissions the leaders of the church by assigning them gifts, and so when we select our church's leaders, we are simply recognizing the calling and gifts of the Lord. The distinctive blueprint for your church — the pattern of ministries God desires it to have — is shaped by the gifts assigned to the leaders and members by Jesus himself. Why are some churches particularly effective in reaching some kinds of people more than others? God has given them a particular pattern of gifts and therefore a particular pattern of ministry.

The special office means that the Spirit chooses some people to be leaders and pacesetters for all aspects of the general office. While all Christians should teach and evangelize, the Spirit calls some to be teachers and evangelists (Eph 4:11). All believers should share what they have with the needy, yet the church calls some leaders to be deacons and lead in the ministry of mercy (Acts 6:1 – 6; 1 Tim 3:8 – 13). All Christians should watch over one another and call one another to account (Gal 6:1 – 2; Heb 3:13), and yet every congregation is to have "elders" (Acts 14:23; Titus 1:5) who will look after the people as shepherds care for their sheep (Acts 20:28 – 31; 1 Pet 5:1 – 4). Believers are to submit to the authority of their leaders (1 Thess 5:12; Heb 13:7, 17). When these leaders exercise their gifts, they are also exercising Christ's ministry.

Churches that are solidly grounded in their historic tradition normally have a strong bias for the importance of the special office. They must actively seek to cultivate a greater appreciation for the dynamic and fluid nature of the general office. One way to do this is through the *commissioning of unordained lay leaders and staff* — men and women working alongside traditional ordained leaders. In this way, churches can honor both the dynamic and organizing work of the Spirit.

The Holy Spirit, then, makes the church both an organism and an organization — a cauldron of spontaneously generated spiritual life and ministry, as well as an ordered, structured community with rules and authority. If God only gave gifts to all believers and did not call anyone into a place of authority, the church would be only an organic, spontaneous movement with virtually no institutional structure. If he only gave gifts to "special officers" — ordained ministers — then the church would be exclusively a top-down, command-and-control institution. But God's Spirit creates both the general and the special office — and so we speak of the *ardor* of the Spirit (creating the movement) and the *order* of the Spirit (creating the institution). This dynamic balance of the Spirit's work is what makes the church (in human terms) sustainable.

We see these dynamics vividly come together in 1 Peter 2:4 – 5, where Peter describes Christians as "living stones" in a new temple. Stones in a building

THE HISTORICAL OFFICES OF THE CHURCH

Historically, Protestant churches have gone back and forth on how many biblical special offices there are. John Calvin believed there were four distinct biblical offices — teachers, pastors, elders, and deacons.[5] Paul seems to list seven types of leaders in the early church — apostles, prophets, evangelists, pastors, and teachers in Ephesians 4:11, and elders and deacons in Philippians 1:1 and 1 Timothy 3. Even if one takes a cessationist view that apostles and prophets no longer exist (as I do, though no case on this topic is a clear-cut one to make), we still have several different kinds of leaders in the church.

Evangelists seem to have been preachers of the gospel, and pastors were shepherds. Teachers seem to have been a separate group of leaders. Despite some efforts to combine them with pastors as a single group of "pastor-teachers," this view isn't exegetically likely. P. T. O'Brien believes that evangelists, pastors, and teachers were all officers in the earliest church, along with elders and deacons.[6] First Corinthians 12:28 seems to confirm this. Since Scripture indicates that some, though not all, elders teach (1 Tim 5:17; Titus 1:9; Heb 13:7), it is possible that some were teachers who were not also elders (2 Tim 2:2). The apostle Peter calls himself an "elder" under Christ (1 Pet 5:1). And the pastoral responsibilities of leaders such as Paul, Timothy, and Titus, were wider than those of congregational elders (2 Cor 11:28; Titus 1:5). They functioned in a more bishop-like capacity.

represent a *non*organic metaphor. But Peter tells us that the stones of this temple are alive, and so the temple does, indeed, "grow" (see Eph 2:21). This suggests we should understand the church to be both an organism (which grows naturally) and an organization (which is structured and ordered).

It is vital to recognize the Holy Spirit as the author of both aspects of the nature of the church. Sometimes the ministries that directly produce converts and visibly changed lives (e.g., evangelism, worship, preaching) are seen as more spiritual than ministries of administration and ongoing programs (e.g., governance structures, church discipline, church management, rules of operation, membership assimilation programs, finance, stewardship, building maintenance, and so on). This is an understandable error.[4] Centuries of experience have taught us that it is very difficult to keep order and ardor together. The proponents of order tend to see only the advantages of stable institutions and only the disadvantages of spontaneous movements. They see pride and arrogance in radical new movements and dismiss them as unstable, shortsighted, and self-important. Often they are right, but just as often they are wrong. On the other hand, the proponents of more dynamic, less hierarchical movements tend to see only the disadvantages of institutions. They see self-interest, rigid bureaucracy, and idolatry, and dismiss the institutions as dead or dying. Sometimes they are right, but just as often they, too, are wrong. The church, at its healthiest, is both organized and organic. Because the author of both aspects is the Holy Spirit, they must be able to exist in harmony with one another.

MOVEMENT DYNAMICS IN THE LOCAL CHURCH

In the previous chapter, we identified four key characteristics of a movement: vision, sacrifice, flexibility with unity, and spontaneity. What does it look like when these characteristics are present in individual churches and ministries? How do we encourage movement dynamics in the local church that are biblically balanced with institutional dynamics?

THE VISION AND BELIEFS CREATE ONENESS

A church with movement dynamics is driven by a clear vision for a particular future reality based on common beliefs. Vision is a set of strong beliefs animating a concrete picture of a future. So, for example, one compelling vision could be to increase the number of evangelical churches in a city tenfold within a generation. (A vision of this magnitude may seem outrageous in the United States, but it is quite possible in Western Europe, for example.) The concrete picture in this case is the tenfold increase, a picture of what the city would look like with an enlarged church in its midst within the span of a generation. This vision is wedded to strong beliefs — the classic evangelical gospel of the revivals and the Reformation.

Contextualization bears heavily on the communication of a church's vision. A compellingly articulated church vision is, in reality, a contextualized way of expressing the biblical teaching about the gospel and the work of the church. For example, a church may say that its vision is to "seek the peace and prosperity of the city" and then spell out clearly what this means. This vision expresses the biblical call to the people of God in Jeremiah 29 and Romans 12. Another church may express its vision as "changing lives with the gospel" and then clearly and attractively describe what this changed life looks like. This vision expresses the biblical call to the church to make disciples with the power of the Word and Spirit. Each of these vision statements, though they emphasize different aspects of the biblical call, will be galvanizing if they are stated in ways that are clear and persuasive to people of a particular culture.

DEVOTION TO GOD'S KINGDOM OVER SELF OR TRIBE ENABLES SACRIFICE

People in a church with movement dynamics put the vision ahead of their own interests and needs. What matters to the members and staff is not their own individual interests, power, and perks, but the fulfillment of the vision. They want to see it realized through them, and this satisfaction is their main compensation. The willingness to sacrifice on the part of workers and members is perhaps the key practical index of whether you have become a movement or have become institutionalized. Members of a church with movement dynamics tend to be more self-motivated and need less direct oversight. They are self-starters.

How does this happen? Selfless devotion is not something that leaders can create — indeed, it would be dangerous emotional manipulation to try to bring this about directly. Only leaders who have the vision and devotion can kindle this sacrificial spirit in others. A dynamic Christian movement convinces its people — truthfully — that they are participating in God's redemptive plan in a profoundly important and practical way. Participants say things like, "I've never felt more useful to the Lord and to others." Church meetings in movement-oriented churches feel deeply spiritual. There is much more "majoring in the majors" — the cross, the Spirit, the grace of Jesus. People spend more time in worship and prayer.

EMPHASIS ON UNITY CREATES COOPERATION ACROSS LINES

Openness to cooperation is another essential movement dynamic. Because members of the movement are deeply concerned with seeing the vision accomplished, they are willing to work with people who are also materially committed to the vision and share primary beliefs but who differ in preferences, temperaments, and secondary beliefs or are members of other organizations. Because institutions are more focused on protocol and rules than on results and outcomes, their members tend to look askance at groups or people who don't do things in the same way. In the Christian world, this means Christian groups with movement dynamics are more willing to work across denominational and organizational lines to achieve common goals.

Movement-oriented churches think more about reaching the city, while institutionalized churches put emphasis on growing their church's particular expression or denomination. In general, leaders of churches with movement dynamics have a high tolerance for ambiguity and organizational messiness.

EXTERNAL FACTORS THAT FOSTER MOVEMENT DYNAMICS

When listing factors that create movement dynamics, some thinkers list environmental and cultural factors. In *The Forgotten Ways*, Alan Hirsch, speaks of "missional DNA" that largely follows the description of movement dynamics in this chapter.[7] However, he also speaks of the experience of "liminality" as a factor. He notes that social ostracism, marginalization, and persecution can create solidarity and energy within the church. Christians are indeed becoming more and more persona non grata in post-Christian cultures, though there is little or no overt persecution. It is within elite society — e.g., major research universities, global center cities — that Christians feel the most despised and ostracized. Hirsch argues that an experience of liminality or marginalization can be an important influence leading the church to form around risky, dangerous mission.[8]

Observe the unusual amount of creativity and influence from two relatively small minorities in our society — gays and Jews. Both groups grew strong through the experience of social rejection. In this chapter I've chosen to focus on factors that are internal and, at least to some extent, under the control of church leaders, but Hirsch is right in suggesting that these types of external factors can also enhance movement dynamics.

What matters is that people hear the gospel and are converted and discipled, which results in cooperation with people from outside their own membership and involves learning from them.

As always, balance is crucial. A sectarian, highly institutionalized church or agency may refuse to cooperate with bodies that don't share all its beliefs, including secondary and tertiary ones. We rightly criticize this posture as being antithetical to movements. But so is the opposite posture. It is important to be doctrinally vigilant and willing, when necessary, to respectfully contend for important theological truths when we believe that ministry partners are losing their grasp on those truths. A cowardly refusal to speak the truth in love is neither cooperative nor loving. The critical truths that ministry partners must hold in common should be clearly stated, and if there is movement away from them, there should be straightforward conversation about it. But how do we talk about doctrinal differences in a way that is not unnecessarily destructive to unity? See the sidebar on "Gospel Polemics" on pp. 372 – 73.

SPONTANEITY WITHOUT TOP-DOWN COMMAND ENABLES GROWTH

A church or organization with movement dynamics has spiritual spontaneity; it constantly generates new ideas, leaders, and initiatives within and across itself — not solely from the top or from a command center outside of itself. As we noted, spontaneous combustion means ignition from within, not from outside. A church or organization that is highly

institutionalized, however, is structured so that individuals cannot offer ideas and propose projects unless asked or given permission. A church with movement dynamics, however, generates ideas, leaders, and initiatives from the grassroots. Ideas come less from formal strategic meetings and more from off-line conversations among friends. Since the motivation for the work is not so much about compensation and self-interest as about a shared willingness to sacrifice for the infectious vision, such churches naturally create friendships among members and staff. These friendships become mini-engines powering the church, along with the more formal, organized meetings and events.

Another aspect of the spontaneity dynamic is the natural growth in leadership. This doesn't mean a church should not have formal training programs. Rather, it means (1) that the vision of the movement (especially as its content is disseminated) attracts people with leadership potential and (2) that the work of the movement naturally reveals emerging leaders through real-life experience and prepares them for the next level of leadership in the movement. An example is Reformed University Fellowship, a campus ministry of the Presbyterian Church in America. RUF recruits recent college graduates to be campus interns, many of whom go on to become full-time campus staff.[9] Working on college campuses trains workers to be evangelistic, to work with the emerging edge of culture, and to do ministry through fluid, nonformal processes. All of this makes campus ministers who leave the RUF staff more comfortable planting new churches than merely taking positions in established ones. As a result, RUF has created a continual flow of dynamic, fruitful church planters and young laypeople (former Christian university students) who are excellent core-group members for new congregations.

RUF is typical of dynamic movements in that it was not originally founded to produce church planters; the powerful "church planter formation" dynamic happened spontaneously, as the natural fruit of an excellent campus ministry. Most denominations, of course, create institutionalized agencies to recruit and train church planters, but organic leadership development pipelines such as RUF are often more productive. When a denomination experiences these gifts from God, it should recognize them and do what it can to support and enhance the experience without strangling it. Many churches are so institutionalized in their thinking that it makes it difficult to do so.[10]

CREATIVE TENSION

Scripture suggests that churches cannot choose between being a movement or an institution; they must be both. And yet in this book we are emphasizing movement dynamics over institutional ones. Why? Because over time, movements inevitably become institutions. Therefore, it is necessary for churches to *intentionally* cultivate the dynamics that characterize a healthy movement.

This process is difficult not only because movement dynamics push against organizational inertia but also because the movement dynamics themselves can be in tension with one another. Consider two movement dynamics we have identified: vision and spontaneity. On one hand, if everyone gets to define the *vision* according to what seems correct in their own eyes (Judg 17:6; 21:25), the movement falls apart. The vision and beliefs are the glue that must be guarded and rearticulated. They can evolve and be sharpened, but usually only gradually and by the top leaders. They must be codified and committed to media, and leaders must subscribe to them in some way. So the need for unity almost always pushes a movement toward structure in this area. The *spontaneity* dynamic, however, means new initiatives and creative ideas — aligned with and in pursuit of the vision — must emerge from everywhere. Making people wait a long time for "orders from headquarters" only suppresses their contributions, and much of the movement energy is lost. This spontaneity dynamic tends to get suppressed as the organization becomes more formal and codified.

The pursuit of unity and spontaneity will inevitably lead to change as the movement grows in size. If a church has four elders, then most decision making will take on a flat, collaborative shape.

Elders have a lot of time to discuss issues and come to consensus. But what happens when the church grows and now has a team of twenty elders? The meetings become interminable, and reaching consensus can take months. It is only natural, then, for the church to designate groups of elders that make decisions to be routinely approved by the entire elder board. This looks suspiciously like a committee structure, which many (especially authors of Christian movement literature) believe is an unhealthy form of institutionalization. But from another perspective it can be seen as a form of trust, motivated by a desire to avoid controlling everything from the center. So delegation can be more of a movement dynamic than a sign of institutionalization.

How difficult it is to maintain this dynamic balance! Churches, laypersons, and ministers regularly have bad experiences in imbalanced churches and in response flee to the opposite extreme — an equally unbalanced form of ministry. When a lay-driven ministry goes off the rails, its victims tend to move toward a much more authoritarian, tightly controlled ministry. Meanwhile, refugees from "top-down" churches often rush to the opposite kind of church. Each kind of imbalance chokes the *movement-ness* of the church.

On the surface, the description of the church as a movement seems far more attractive than the description that focuses on the institutional aspects of a church and its ministry. In movements,

---

A practical key to maintaining an organized organism is experiencing a season of renewal in the church or organization that parallels the way an individual person is spiritually renewed.

---

the structure clearly serves the cause, whereas in institutions, the cause tends to serve the structure. And ultimately, this is how it should be. Some church or ministry structures are directly biblical (and therefore nonnegotiable), but most are

humanly made (and therefore negotiable). The Bible instructs churches to have elders, for example, but it says virtually nothing about how this team is to be organized. A key to navigating the creative tension of Scripture is to avoid allowing humanly made structures to become idols — relative, finite things elevated to the status of unquestioned divine authority.

For a movement to stay a movement, then, it needs to achieve and maintain balance as an "organized organism." On the continuum below, a movement-driven church would need to have its **X** toward the right. Since churches always migrate toward institutionalism, they often must be brought back toward a movement dynamic.

institution   movement
|———————————————————✖———————————|

A practical key to maintaining an organized organism is experiencing a season of renewal in the church or organization that parallels the way an individual person is spiritually renewed. There must be times for what the Bible calls "covenant renewal." Israel was brought into its original covenant relationship with God at Mount Sinai in Exodus 19 – 20, and the nation was formed as God's people and called to live in a particular way in the world. Whenever Israel faced a major new chapter in their journey, however, they were led through a season of covenant renewal — in Joshua 24, before they entered the promised land; in 1 Samuel 12, before they received a king; and in Nehemiah 8 – 9, as they returned from the Babylonian exile. These times of covenant renewal always had three parts: (1) the people returned to biblical texts in order to remember the things God had called them to do and be; (2) they looked forward to the next chapter, to the new challenges facing them; and (3) they rededicated their lives and resources to God for the next stage of the journey. This renewal must happen frequently in any church for it to remain an organized organism. It also prepares the church to be an active and generous participant in the movement dynamics in its city.

1. Describe the difference between the *general* office and the *special* office. What are the three aspects of ministry that belong to every believer as part of the general office? What are some of the functions and roles given to the special office? How does the distinction between these two help you to better strike the balance between the church as a vital organism and a structured organization?

2. Keller writes, "The willingness to sacrifice on the part of workers and members is perhaps the key practical index of whether you have a movement or have become institutionalized." Take a moment to check the temperature of your volunteer culture. Look at the faces in your church directory and ask how aggressively they are sacrificing. Is the answer indicative of a movement or have you become institutionalized? How might this relate to the vision of your church, or the lack of vision?

3. Keller writes, "Churches, laypersons, and ministers regularly have bad experiences in imbalanced churches and in response flee to the opposite extreme." Are there any conflicts or dysfunctions in your church that you now understand better in light of this statement?

CHAPTER 28 — THE CHURCH AS AN ORGANIZED ORGANISM {pages 344–53}

1. See E. P. Clowney, "Perspectives on the Church," in *Living in Christ's Church* (Philadelphia: Great Commission, 1986); idem, "Doctrine of the Church" (unpublished course syllabus); Lon L. Fuller, "Two Principles of Human Association," in *Voluntary Associations*, ed. J. Roland Pennock and John W. Chapman (New York: Atherton, 1969); Lyle Schaller, "Tribes, Movements, and Organizations," in *Getting Things Done* (Nashville: Abingdon, 1986); idem, *Activating the Passive Church* (Nashville: Abingdon, 1981).

2. See Edmund P. Clowney, *The Church* (Downers Grove, Ill.: InterVarsity, 1995), esp. 199 – 214; see also idem, *Living in Christ's Church*, 111 – 12.

3. See the important essay by Alan Kreider, " 'They Alone Know the Right Way to Live': The Early Church and Evangelism," in *Ancient Faith for the Church's Future*, ed. Mark Husbands and Jeffrey Greenman (Downers Grove, Ill.: InterVarsity, 2008), 169 – 86.

4. Books such as *The Trellis and the Vine* by Tony Payne and Colin Marshall (Kingsford, Australia: Matthias Media, 2009) give the strong impression that institutional forms and structures are, at best, a necessary evil and that management and governing gifts are not really involved in our carrying out the work of the Spirit or our building up the church. On the other hand, many of the critics of revival and broad evangelicalism who call for a greater emphasis on the ordained ministry and the institutional church can make the opposite mistake.

5. John Calvin, *Institutes of the Christian Religion*, ed. John T. McNeill (Philadelphia: Westminster, 1960), 2:1053 – 1084.

6. See P. T. O'Brien, *The Letter to the Ephesians* (Pillar New Testament Commentary; Grand Rapids: Eerdmans, 1999), 113.

7. Alan Hirsch, *The Forgotten Ways: Reactivating the Missional Church* (Grand Rapids: Brazos, 2006).

8. Ibid., 277.

9. RUF produces church planters and missionaries for the PCA, along with Campus Outreach, which is a nondenominational campus ministry with strong ties to the denomination.

10. Most effective leadership pipelines grow organically out of movements rather than institutions. I once learned about a denomination outside the United States that had an evangelical wing. For a number of years, this evangelical wing had leadership "nurseries" in the college ministries of prominent, vital congregations in two or three university towns. College students were drawn to these ministries in great number, and many were inspired to reproduce the community and ministry of the Word they experienced. Dozens of young people from these churches went into the preaching ministry because they experienced movement dynamics there. However, when those churches installed new pastors who weren't as interested or successful in college ministry, the pipelines dried up, and the whole evangelical cause in that country suffered.

11. Spend some time with Richard F. Lovelace, *Dynamics of Spiritual Life* (Downers Grove, Ill.: InterVarsity, 1979); C. John Miller, *Outgrowing the Ingrown Church* (Grand Rapids: Zondervan, 1986, 1999).

CHURCH PLANTING AS A MOVEMENT DYNAMIC

A church that is an organized organism will exhibit movement dynamics not only *inside* itself but also *beyond* itself. So it will naturally be involved in church planting. Church planting is mentioned in many places throughout the New Testament. For example, Paul refers to his work of planting and watering churches with Apollos (1 Cor 3:6 – 7). But the primary place in Scripture to learn about church planting is the book of Acts. All orthodox Christians agree that prescriptive statements of the Bible are normative for us, but the descriptive histories of the Old and New Testaments contain both good and bad examples. Are we always certain which is which? The safest approach, I suggest, is to take the church planting practices of Paul in Acts very seriously while recognizing that this Bible book does not give us a fixed rule book for church planting in all times, places, and contexts. It is best to look for general principles rather than rules or detailed practices.[1]

NATURAL CHURCH PLANTING

In Acts, planting churches is not a traumatic or unnatural event. It is woven into the warp and woof of ministry, and so it happens steadily and normally. Paul never evangelizes and disciples without also planting a church. For decades, expositors have looked to Acts to make lists of the basic elements of ministry: Bible teaching, evangelism, fellowship, discipleship, and worship. I have always found it odd that right there in Acts, along with everything else the church is doing, is church planting — yet this element of ministry is consistently ignored! I believe there is a dubious, tacit cessationism at work. Almost unconsciously, readers of the book of Acts have said, "Yes, but that was for then. We don't need to do that now." I believe this conclusion misses a key aspect of a healthy church, namely,

that church planting must be natural and customary, not traumatic and episodic.

The normal ministry of Paul had three phases that are easily seen in Acts 14. First is *evangelism*. Acts 14:21 states that "[Paul and Barnabas] preached the good news," but it does not use the common word for "preaching." Instead, a more comprehensive word is used: they *euangelizō*-ed or "gospeled" the city. This Greek word connotes a great deal more than simply preaching sermons. The book of Acts describes Paul in the act of spreading the gospel through preaching in synagogue services, sharing in small group Bible studies, speaking out in marketplaces, leading discussions in rented halls, and simply talking with people one-on-one.

In the second phase of Paul's ministry, we see a clear incorporation into *community*. Immediately after "gospeling" the city, Paul goes to the converts to strengthen and encourage them (Acts 14:22). These two verbs (*epistērizō* and *parakaleō*) are also used together in Acts 9:31 and 15:32. John Stott refers to these verbs as an "almost technical" term for building up new believers.[2] So how did Paul do this? He taught them "the faith" (Acts 14:22) — a definite body of beliefs and theology. But also he "congregated" them. New believers do not simply go on living their lives as they were, but they are brought into a community that assembles regularly.

Finally, in the third phase, we find *leadership development*. In each place Paul visited he chose elders, a plurality of leaders out of the converts, who now took on the task of teaching and shepherding the people in the faith. In other words, Paul routinely organized his converts into *churches* in their own right — more than just loosely knit fellowships directly under his leadership. These churches

UNNATURAL CHURCH PLANTING

With the exception of the original persecution of believers (Acts 8), there was no "unnatural church planting" in the book of Acts—but there certainly is today. Two forms are prevalent today, and the results are seldom ideal.

Defiant church planting. Some people in the church may get frustrated and split off to form a new church because of alienation over doctrine, vision, or philosophy of ministry. This kind of move usually includes clashes among oversized leader personalities or culture-based splits (where second-generation leaders leave to start a church in opposition to the will of the first generation of leaders in the church).

Reluctant church planting. Circumstances may force a church's leaders to plant a church against their will. For example, a church may outgrow their building, and even though they don't want to leave, they eventually must. Or some members may move to a new area and begin to lobby for a church "out here" that is similar to the one they left. Some members with a different vision (younger, different worship style; more focused on individual discipleship; etc.) may also begin to drop out or push for a new service or church. Though leaders may give begrudging permission or even money and active support, these examples are "unnatural" because church planting is unlikely to happen again—unless circumstances again dictate it.

As Tim Chester points out in his essay "Church Planting: A Theological Perspective," we find two basic avenues for launching churches in Acts.[3] In Paul and his companions, we see an example of the first avenue: *pioneer church planting*. Though the Antioch church sent Paul out, and he was accountable to them for his doctrine and behavior (Acts 13:1–3), his work in every city was by definition a pioneering work. Paul did groundbreaking evangelism in each place he visited, without the cooperation of other churches.

The other form is *churches planting other churches*. This more implicit example is present in the New Testament, but we have to avoid screening it out by thinking anachronistically about the word *church* when we see it in the text. The churches Paul planted (in fact all of the Christian churches for almost two hundred years) were *household* churches. For example, Lydia's conversion immediately becomes a bridge to the conversion of her household, making her home the first church in Philippi. By Acts 16:40, Paul and Silas are going to Lydia's home to meet the brethren. The same thing happens in Acts 18 with the household of Crispus. What did this mean? It meant that the church at Philippi, Corinth, and everywhere else could only grow naturally by multiplying new assemblies or house churches. Though Paul writes to the "church" (singular) at Corinth, it is obvious by the end of the book that he is addressing a number of household churches—Chloe, Stephanus, et al. Because in the early church the household church was the basic building block of the movement, church planting was built into the church's very nature. You could only grow churches by multiplying new household-based assemblies of Christians who met under elders.

Today as well, these two basic approaches are still the main avenues for church planting (see table).

MAKING CHURCH PLANTING NATURAL

A natural church planting mind-set means that church leaders will think of church planting as just one of the things the church does along with everything else. Church planting should not be like building a building—one big traumatic event followed by

had their own leadership and structure. When Paul began meeting with them, they were called "disciples" (Acts 14:22), but when he left them, they were known as "churches" (see Acts 14:23). To put it simply, the multiplication of churches is as natural in the book of Acts as the multiplication of individual converts.

PIONEERING CHURCH PLANTING	CHURCH-LED CHURCH PLANTING
Ministers/leaders are often self-initiators	Church leaders are selected by church body, but a church can also call and send
No core members; pioneer gets all core members through networking and evangelism	Members come from (1) pooling cell groups and (2) hiving off distant families
Money from (1) mission agency, (2) raising of personal support from friends and churches, (3) tent-making/self-employment, or (4) two or all of the above	Money from (1) core group pledge, (2) gift/subsidy from mother church, (3) outside grants from distant churches or individuals, or (4) two or all of the above
Mentor is a distant pastor or leader, seen infrequently; or reading-only mentor (dead or distant)	Regular meetings with nearby mentor; often peer supervision possible
Model is often innovative, forging new models or imitating distant ones	Model is similar to mother church, though never identical

a deep collective sigh of relief that it's done. Paul was continually engaged in evangelism, discipleship, *and* church planting. In fact, I believe church planting is actually a fifth "ministry front" that works alongside the four aspects of integrative ministry outlined in part 7. There we said that every church should connect people to God (worship and evangelism), to one another (discipleship and community), to the needs of the city (justice and mercy), and to the culture (integrating faith and work). But the fifth ministry front is the multiplication of a church into new churches with the other four ministry fronts. So church planting should be as much an ongoing, natural part of your ministry as worship, evangelism, fellowship, education, and service.

A natural church planting mind-set can be described in terms of three key mind-set shifts. The hard truth is that if you and your team can't make these mind-set shifts, it is highly unlikely that your church can plant churches naturally and effectively.

1. You must be willing to give away resources and lose control of your money, members, and leaders. I hesitate to use the cliché, but it's true in this case: Paul "empowered" these new leaders. He gave them ownership, and in doing so, he surrendered a lot of control. Many churches cannot bear the thought of losing key leaders, money-giving families, or even just friends. Ministers are also afraid of giving away some of their glory. If your ministry adds people who are assimilated into your church and incorporated into Bible studies and new ministries in your church, it swells your numbers, and you gain both control and glory. But if you organize new people into new churches, you lose money, members, numbers, leaders, and control. Yet this is exactly what Paul did! An additional issue is that when we let go, we lose direct control but can't avoid responsibility for the problems that arise. It's a bit like being the parent of an adult child. We are not allowed to directly tell them what to do, but if a problem arises, we are expected to help clean it up.

An evangelical church in our area occupied a small, historic building. They had filled one hundred seats to maximum capacity for four years in a row but had resisted church planting, fearing it would result in the loss of money and people. Eventually, they sent fifty people to a new town to form a new church. Just two years later, close to 350 people were coming to the daughter church. Meanwhile, the mother church once again filled its seats — in about three weeks! Soon they were kicking themselves, realizing that over the course of this time, they could have planted another three churches with nearly a thousand people in the church family, all able to do missions, youth ministry, and many other initiatives together. They realized they needed to make the transition to a natural church planting mind-set.

2. You must be willing to give up some control of the shape of the ministry itself. Doing so is especially scary for those of us who care deeply about the preservation of biblical truth. But it's a simple fact that the new church will not look just like the original. It will develop its own voice and emphases.

The natural church planting mind-set is not as much a matter of trusting new leaders as it is a matter of trusting God.

On the one hand, you must take pains to be sure that the difference is not too great, or else fellowship and cooperation will be strained. We must not forget that the book of Acts speaks of "the faith." There is *one body of true doctrine* at the heart of Christianity. On the other hand, if you insist that the new church must be a clone, you reveal that you are not willing to admit the reality of contextualization in the biblical sense of adapting and incarnating. Different generations and cultures *will* produce a different kind of church. This does not undermine the soundness of the mother church; it testifies to it.

As noted above, Paul appointed elders in each church, giving them a certain amount of independence. He was able to do this because the natural church planting mind-set is not as much a matter of trusting new leaders as it is a matter of trusting God. Paul does not call the new churches to fend for themselves or leave them to the care of others. Rather, he "committed them to the Lord" (Acts 14:23). Paul's heart and character were such that he did not need to keep control; he had faith that God would continue

the work he had started in the church. A natural church planting mind-set requires a high level of spiritual maturity and trust in God's providence.

3. You must be willing to care for the kingdom even more than for your tribe. We see this demonstrated in the way Paul speaks of Apollos, who is affirmed even though he is not his disciple (Acts 18:24 – 28). Paul refers to him in the warmest terms (1 Cor 3:6; 4:6; 16:12) even though his disciples evidently considered themselves a particular party, distinct from Paul's (1 Cor 1:12; 3:4). We also see this in the way Paul willingly takes his hands off the new churches he plants (see Acts 16:40: "Then they left."). Paul is concerned not about his or his party's power (even then, different apostles had their followers and emphases) but about the kingdom as a whole.

A new church in the community usually leads existing churches to face this issue of kingdom-mindedness. New churches typically draw most of their new members from the ranks of the unchurched, but they will also attract some people from existing churches. When we lose two to three families to a church that is bringing in a hundred new people who weren't going to any other church before, we have a choice! We must ask ourselves, "Are we going to celebrate the new people the kingdom has gained through this new church, or are we going to bemoan and resent the families we lost to it?" In other words, our attitude to new church development is a test of whether our mind-set is geared to our own institutional turf or to the overall health and prosperity of the kingdom of God in the city. Any church that bemoans its own small losses instead of rejoicing in the larger gains of the kingdom is betraying its narrow interests. Yet the benefits of new church planting to older congregations can be great, even if that benefit is not initially obvious.[4]

We began with a warning that we must be careful not to read the book of Acts as a strict rule book for church planting. Yet our secular, urbanized, global world today is strikingly like the Greco-Roman world in certain ways. For the first time in fifteen hundred years, there are multiple, vital, religious faith communities and options (including true paganism) in every society. Traditional, secular, and pagan worldviews and communities are living side by side. Once again, cities are the influential cultural centers, just as they were in the Greco-Roman world. During the Pax Romana, cities became furiously multiethnic and globally connected. Since we are living in an Acts-like world again rather than the earlier context of Christendom, church planting will *necessarily* be as central a strategy for reaching our world as it was for reaching previous generations.

Ultimately, though, we don't look to Paul to teach us about church planting, but to Jesus himself. Jesus is the ultimate church planter. He builds his church (Matt 16:18), and he does so effectively, because hell itself will not prevail against it. He raises up leaders and gives them the keys to the kingdom (Matt 16:19). He establishes his converts on the word of the confessing apostle, Peter — that is, on the word of God (Matt 16:18). When we plant the church, we participate in God's work, for if we have any success at all, it is because "God made it grow." Thus, "neither he who plants nor he who waters is anything, but only God, who makes things grow" (1 Cor 3:6 – 7).

ANSWERING OBJECTIONS

There is a common objection to reading the book of Acts the way we suggest here: "That was then! Now, at least in North America and Europe, we have churches all over the place. We don't need to start new churches; we should strengthen and fill our existing churches before we do that." Let me give several answers to this common objection.

FULLY EVANGELISTIC CHURCHES

The way to evangelize a city is not through evangelism programs but through fully evangelistic churches.

Evangelism programs aim at getting people to make a decision to follow Christ. Experience, however, shows us that many of these "decisions" disappear and never result in changed lives. Why? Many decisions are not true spiritual conversions; they are only the beginning of a journey of seeking God. (I must add that some decisions definitely

mark the moment of new birth, but this differs from person to person.) Many people come to full faith through a process of mini-decisions. Only a person who is hearing the gospel in the context of an ongoing worshiping and shepherding community can be sure of finally coming home into vital, saving faith. Evangelism programs, grafted onto a church that is unable to embrace and support inquirers and doubters, cannot do the job. What the city needs is not more evangelism programs but far more wholly evangelistic churches.

GROWING THE NUMBER OF CHURCHES IN THE CITY

The way to grow the number of Christians in a city is not mainly through church renewal but through church planting.

When stagnant churches go through a renewal phase and begin to grow, it is typically through transfer growth from other churches. Strong programs attract believers who are suffering under poor preaching, poor discipleship offerings, or other signs of unhealthy discipleship elsewhere. But even older renewed churches cannot integrate unchurched persons like a new congregation can. Studies confirm that the average new church gains one-third to two-thirds of its new members from the ranks of people who are not attending any worshiping body, while churches over ten to fifteen years of age gain 80 to 90 percent of new members by transfer from other congregations.[5] The average new congregation, then, will bring new people into the life of the body of Christ at six to eight times the rate of an older congregation of the same size. Why is this so?

As a congregation ages, powerful internal institutional pressures lead it to allocate most of its resources and energy toward the concerns of its members and constituents rather than toward those outside its walls. This is natural — and to a great degree desirable. Older congregations have a stability and steadiness that many people (especially long-term residents) thrive on and need. They also have the trust of the local community. Older congregations are inevitably more influenced by the people groups that have been in the neighborhood for a long time. They do not contain (or typically open their leadership ranks to) the members of the growing people groups in the area — new ethnic groups, new generations. As a result, many people can only be reached by churches with deeper roots in the community and with the trappings of stability and respectability.

Nevertheless, these same dynamics explain why most congregations thirty to forty years old or older are experiencing numerical decline. Older congregations of necessity must focus on the needs and sensibilities of the churched and the long-term residents, even at the expense of any appeal to the unchurched or newer people groups. New congregations, by contrast, have no organizational traditions they must honor or oppose. In general, they are forced to focus on the needs of their *non*members simply to get off the ground. There are no members with many years or decades of tenure, and so new Christians and newer members are able to get their voices heard in ways that would not happen in an older congregation. This is generally why new churches do a far better job of outreach.

Thus, the only way to significantly increase the number of Christians in a city is by significantly increasing the number of new churches. Here's a thought experiment that illustrates this point. Imagine Cities A, B, and C are the same size, and each has one hundred churches. In City A, all the churches are more than twenty years old, and so the overall number of active Christian churchgoers in this town will be shrinking, even if four or five of the churches catch a wave and grow in attendance. The most likely reason is that they are pulling Christians from the other churches. Most churches in City A will be declining, and the renewed churches will likely simply be retaining Christians, not reaching the unchurched. Overall, the number of Christians in town is shrinking steadily.

In City B, let's say ten of the hundred churches are less than ten years old. Roughly one new church is being planted per year — a mere 1 percent. These churches will likely be bringing in three to five times more unchurched people (proportionally) than the

rest, and some of the renewed older congregations will also be winning new people to Christ. But it is likely that the growth experienced here will merely offset the normal declines of most of the older churches. Thus, the number of active Christian churchgoers in City B will be staying the same or perhaps slowly declining.

Finally, in City C, twenty-five of the hundred churches are less than ten years old. In other words, new congregations are being planted at 2 to 3 percent the rate of the existing total per year. In this city, the overall number of active Christian churchgoers will be on a path to grow 50 percent in a generation.

RENEWING EXISTING CHURCHES

The way to renew the existing churches of a city is by planting new ones.

In any discussion on new church development, this question often arises: "What about all the existing churches in the city? Shouldn't we be working to strengthen and renew *them*?" The answer is that planting a lot of new churches *is* one of the best ways to renew existing churches.

1. New churches bring new ideas to the whole body. They have freedom to be innovative, and so they become the "Research and Development" department for the whole body in the city. Often older congregations are too timid to try a particular approach, convinced it "could never work here." But when the new church in town succeeds with a new approach, other churches take notice and muster the courage to try it themselves.

2. New churches raise up new, creative Christian leaders for the city. Older congregations attract leaders who support tradition, have tenure, appreciate routine, and have kinship ties. New congregations, on the other hand, attract a higher percentage of venturesome people who value creativity, risk, and innovation. Older churches often box out people with strong leadership skills who aren't comfortable working in traditional settings. New churches thus attract and harness many people in the city whose gifts wouldn't otherwise be used in the body's ministry.

3. New churches challenge other churches to self-examination. Sometimes it is only in contrast with a new church that older churches can finally define their own vision, specialties, and identity. Often the growth experienced in a new congregation brings about humility and repentance for defeatist and pessimistic attitudes.

Indeed, it is also often the case that a daughter church does so well that the mother church is renewed though its influence, resources, excitement, and vision. Though some pain may be involved in seeing good friends and gifted leaders go away to form a new church, the mother church often experiences a surge of self-esteem and an eventual influx of new enthusiastic leaders and members. Some of the new leaders, ministries, additional members, and income "wash back" into the mother church in various ways and strengthen and renew it.

4. New churches can be an evangelistic feeder system for a whole community. The new church often produces many converts who end up in older churches for a variety of reasons. Sometimes the new church is exciting and outward looking but is also unstable or immature in its leadership. Some converts cannot stand the tumultuous changes that regularly happen in the new church, and so they move to an existing church. Sometimes the new church reaches a person for Christ, but the new convert quickly discovers that he or she doesn't fit the socioeconomic makeup of the new congregation and gravitates to an established congregation where the customs and culture feel more familiar. In general, the new churches of a city produce new people not only for themselves but also for the older church bodies.

To summarize: Vigorous church planting is one of the best ways to *renew* the existing churches of a city, as well as the best single way to *grow* the whole body of Christ in a city.

ADDRESSING DIVERSITY

The way to reach the sheer diversity of the city is through new churches.

New churches are the single best way to reach

THE 1 PERCENT RULE

Lyle Schaller talks about the 1 percent rule: "Each year any association of churches should plant new congregations at the rate of 1 percent of their existing total; otherwise, that association is in maintenance and decline. If an association wants to grow 50 percent plus [in a generation], it must plant 2 to 3 percent per year."[6]

(1) new generations, (2) new residents, and (3) new people groups. *Young adults* have always been disproportionately located in newer congregations. Long-established congregations develop traditions (such as time of worship, length of service, emotional responsiveness, sermon topics, leadership styles, emotional atmosphere, and dozens of other tiny customs and mores) that reflect the sensibilities of longtime leaders who have the influence and resources to control the church life. These sensibilities often do not reach the younger generations.

In addition, *new residents* are typically better reached by new churches. In older congregations, it may require years of tenure in the city before a person is allowed into a place of influence, but in a new church, new residents tend to have equal power with longtime area residents.

Finally, *new sociocultural groups* in a community are generally better reached by new congregations. For example, if white-collar commuters move into an area where the older residents were farmers, a new church will probably be more receptive to the multiple needs of the new residents, while older churches will continue to be oriented to the original social group. And a new church that is intentionally multiethnic from the start will best reach new racial groups in a community. For example, if an all-Anglo neighborhood becomes 33 percent Hispanic, a new, deliberately biracial church will be far more likely to create "cultural space" for newcomers than will an older church in town.

Brand-new immigrant groups can normally only be reached by churches ministering in their own languages. If we wait until a new group is sufficiently assimilated into American culture to come to our church, we will wait for years without reaching out to them. Remember that a new congregation for a new people group can often be planted *within* the overall structure of an existing church — perhaps through a new Sunday service at another time or a new network of house churches connected to a larger existing congregation. Though it may technically not be a new independent congregation, it serves the same function.

You see, church planting is not only for frontier regions or pagan societies that we are trying to help to *become* Christian. Churched societies will have to maintain vigorous, extensive church planting simply to *stay* Christian. One church, no matter how big, will never be able to serve the needs of such a diverse city. Only a movement of hundreds of churches, small and large, can penetrate literally every neighborhood and people group in the city.

Church planting is not only for frontier regions or pagan societies that we are trying to help to *become* Christian. Churched societies will have to maintain vigorous, extensive church planting simply to *stay* Christian.

SELF-SUSTAINING MINISTRY

The way to establish ministries that become self-supporting and expand the base for all other ministries in a city is through new churches.

A city needs many ministries — youth work, Christian schools, missions to new groups, and so on. All of them are charities that need to be supported from outside of their own resources. They will require funding from Christian givers indefinitely. A new church, however, only requires outside start-up funding at its inception. Within a few years, it becomes the *source* of Christian giving to other ministries, not its

target. Because new churches bring in large numbers of nonchurched people, church planting is by far the fastest way to grow the number of new givers in the kingdom work in a city. New church development helps all the other numerous ministries in a city thrive and grow. These ministries need a constant stream of new volunteers, workers, and givers to keep them going, and new churches are the headwaters of this stream.

HOW MANY CHURCHES DOES THE CITY NEED? FAR MORE THAN YOU THINK.

So how many churches does your city need? The reality is that churches are institutions. Some of them endure because they are continually revitalized, but all of them lose some flexibility; many of them stagnate for long periods between revitalizations, and a certain percentage die every year. We have seen, then, that it requires at least modest church planting in a city just to keep the body of Christ from steadily declining, and aggressive church planting is needed to grow the whole body — meaning ten to twenty relatively new churches in relation to every hundred existing churches.

There is a problem with answering the question in this way, however. The goal should not be to conserve Christianity's "market share" in a given area; it should be to serve, reach, and influence the entire city. How will this be done? Studies and anecdotal evidence indicate that if there is one church per ten thousand residents, approximately 1 percent of the population will be churchgoers. If this ratio goes to one church per one thousand residents, some 15 to 20 percent of the city's population goes to church. If the number goes to one per five hundred residents, the number may approach 40 percent or more. The relationship of the number of churches to churchgoing people is exponential, not linear.[7] We should not, then, simply aim to maintain the church's traditional place in a city or society. We long to see Christianity grow exponentially in conversions, churches, and influence in our city. While it requires many kinds of ministries to achieve this outcome, aggressive church planting is the trigger for them all.

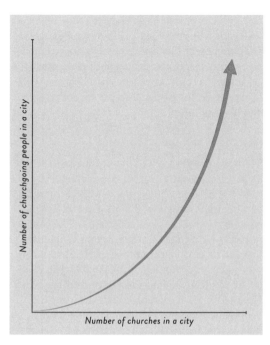

Number of churchgoing people in a city (vertical axis)

Number of churches in a city (horizontal axis)

THE STAGES OF CHURCH PLANTING

In the final section of this chapter, I offer practical advice about how to approach the church planting journey. What are the stages in the process of preparing to launch a new church? You must learn, love, link, and then launch.

LEARN

First, it is necessary to learn as much as you can about the people in the community where you feel called to plant. Seek to know the people you will serve and the culture they live in as effectively as you know the gospel. Create a profile of their interior life. What are their greatest hopes, strengths, aspirations, and pleasures? What are their weaknesses, fears, idols, and prejudices? Begin with personal interviews and make use of relevant periodicals and sociological research.[8] You will also want to develop a "contextual life" profile. Which people groups live in your community? Which groups are declining, and which are growing? Use demographic studies to discern the economic groupings in your

area, the arranging of social structures, and the power relations evident among people, as well as the education and psychological groupings of people.[9]

You will also want to create a profile of the common worldview of the people in your area. What aspects of truth do they have some grasp of (through common grace)? What aspects do they deny or miss? What symbols or myths function deeply? Where are tensions or pressure points in view? What is the people group's narrative and identity? Who do they see themselves to be — where are they from and where are they going? Understanding the common worldview of the people will help you develop the raw material for apologetics.

You will want to ask questions related to the process of contextualization outlined in part 3 (Gospel Contextualization):

1. What are the "defeater beliefs" that make Christianity implausible?
2. What are the tension/pressure points in their defeater beliefs (i.e., where do they fail their own criteria)?
3. What are the "A doctrines" (biblical beliefs similar to what they already accept as true)? What are the "B doctrines" (biblical truths they reject but that are in line with "A" doctrines)?

Finally, you will want to create a profile of the various religious institutions in the area that are involved with the people you seek to reach. How are the religious bodies and churches within this people group doing? How are they organized? What ministry models seem most effective? Successful church planting begins with learning as much as you can about the people you wish to reach with the gospel message.

LOVE

The second stage of the church planting process is continuing to grow in your love for God through learning to maintain a healthy spirituality. It is necessary to be actively engaged in healthy spiritual disciplines, maintaining balance as you implement your strategy for evangelism and mission. Apply the gospel to yourself regularly and grow through the

In 1820, there was one Christian church for every 875 U.S. residents. But from 1860 to 1906, Protestant churches planted one new church for each increase of 350 in the population, bringing the ratio by the start of World War I to one church for every 430 persons. In 1906, over one-third of all the congregations in the country were less than twenty-five years old.[10] As a result, the percentage of the U.S. population involved in the life of the church rose steadily. For example, in 1776, 17 percent of the U.S. population were religious adherents, but that number rose to 53 percent by 1916.[11]

Since World War I, especially among mainline Protestants, church planting plummeted. Older churches strongly resisted new ones invading "our neighborhood." New churches can be highly effective at reaching new people during their first couple of decades. But most U.S. congregations reach their peak in size during the first two or three decades of their existence and then plateau or slowly shrink.[12] During this period, they feel vulnerable to the competition from new churches. Mainline church congregations were the most effective in blocking new church development in their towns. As a result, mainline churches have shrunk remarkably in the last twenty to thirty years.[13]

Church attendance overall in the United States is in decline. The only way to reverse this is by rediscovering the way the church originally and remarkably increased: we must plant churches at such a rate that the number of churches per one thousand residents begins to grow again rather than decline, as it has since World War I.

tearing down of your idols. Begin to share the gospel and spiritually direct people in your neighborhood and community. Model the gospel through community service and in your family life. Pray through the gospel as you bring your requests to God, and begin to experience the gospel in deep community as you develop friendships.

LINK

The third stage in the process is to link as you build your emerging insights into a contextualized strategy for reaching people with the message of the gospel. The goal of this stage is to develop a strategy to serve the particular needs of the people (embodying the gospel) while also challenging the flaws, fears, and hopes of the people (communicating the gospel). Think carefully about how to go about effectively linking the gospel to the heart. How will you incorporate Christ's story into the people's story? Consider the viability of communication modes for the culture: Are they rational, intuitive, or concrete-relational? Consider how you will make your points at each stage of the communication process. Begin with the familiar and point to the culture's strengths, proceed to challenge and destabilize around the points of weakness, and then offer comfort with the gospel.

Embodying the gospel involves discerning how best to link the gospel to the community beyond direct communications. How will you work for the common good of the neighborhood? What will make the people in your neighborhood be glad you are there? Connect with individuals and leaders in the community and begin to meet the perceived needs of the community. Be sure to show the people there what *they* would look like as Christians. Strive to have your leadership structure, infra-community structure, and music incarnate the gospel in that culture.

LAUNCH

Finally, you are ready to launch your church. Begin by developing action steps and goals that can be used as benchmarks to track your progress. In your planning, always be sensitive to God's sovereignty.

What matters is not so much the final detailed plan itself as the actual process of planning. Reality will always alter your plan, but the planning process will equip you to deal with surprises and new realities in a way that is informed by and consistent with your model and vision. Your specific action steps and plans should include these basics:

- goals for funding and how to reach them
- goals for concrete ministries/programs and how to reach them
- goals for leadership development and how to reach them

When it comes time to finally launch your church plant, there are generally two approaches you can take — the top-down or the bottom-up approach. Each has strengths and weaknesses, depending on the context and the gifts of the planter. Consider the approach that is best in your situation, and brainstorm ways to employ the best of both approaches in your launch strategy.

The top-down approach typically begins with a formal worship celebration (congregational singing, teaching). This works well for daughter plants where a substantial group from a mother church is present, as well as with a church planter who has strong onstage speaking gifts. If left unbalanced, this approach carries within it the temptation to skip the *learn* and *link* stages and simply focus on reproducing the mother church.

In the bottom-up approach, the church planter lives in the community and begins with some evangelistic ministry. He sees some conversions and organizes people into either midsize parish groups (fifteen to sixty people) or small groups (four to ten people). After growing into several small groups or two to three midsize groups, the church launches a Sunday worship time. This approach works best with church planters who have good interpersonal, empowering, and evangelistic gifts. If left unbalanced, this approach can make it difficult to attract people who want to "see something happening." Often the church planter feels significant financial pressure because the congregation may not be producing much income to support the work of ministry.

New church planting is the best way to increase the number of believers in a city, and one of the best ways to renew the whole body of Christ. The evidence for this statement is strong — biblically, sociologically, and historically. Nothing else has the *consistent* impact of dynamic, extensive church planting. This is not, however, to demote all the other things we must be doing — church renewal, theological education, justice and mercy, cultural engagement, and many other kinds of ministry and mission. To show how all these things fit together — and how sectors of the whole body of Christ in a city can begin to exhibit movement dynamics — we turn to our final chapter.

1. This chapter asserts that in a healthy church "church planting must be natural and regular, not traumatic and episodic." To make church planting a more natural aspect of ministry, begin by honestly considering three questions:

   - *Resources* — Are you able and willing to give away resources and lose control of your money, members, and leaders?
   - *Control* — Are you ready to give up some control of the shape of the ministry itself?
   - *Fear* — Are you more concerned about the kingdom or the opinions of your own tribe?

   Which of these three areas presents your current ministry team with the greatest barrier to planting a new church? If you are preparing to plant a church, how can you build these attributes into the life of your church from the very beginning?

2. How would you answer the objection that "we don't need to start new churches; we should strengthen and fill our existing churches before we do that." Do you find this chapter's answers to this objection compelling? Why or why not?

3. Keller writes, "The only way to significantly increase the number of Christians in a city is by significantly increasing the number of new churches." What insights do you draw from the comparison of cities A, B, and C in this chapter? When you consider the kingdom math involved, are you convicted? Is your city more like A, B, or C?

4. Review the profiles described in the "Learn" church planting stage (interior life, contextual life, common worldview with defeater beliefs and "A" and "B" doctrines, area religious institutions). What can you learn from this process? Regardless of whether you are currently involved in church planting, how might creating these profiles help you apply what you are learning in new ways?

CHAPTER 29 — CHURCH PLANTING AS A MOVEMENT DYNAMIC {pages 355–66}

1. The general rule when discerning which practices of Scripture to apply today is that "the purpose of God in Scripture should be sought in its *didactic* rather than its *descriptive* parts." (John Stott, *Baptism and Fullness: The Work of the Holy Spirit Today*, 3rd ed. [Downers Grove, Ill.: InterVarsity, 2006], 21). The cardinal rule of biblical interpretation is that the meaning of the text of the Scripture is determined by the author's intent, i.e., what the biblical writer was intending to say. This is why in the didactic parts of the Bible — where prophetic and apostolic writers directly address how God's people should live — it is easier to discern authorial intent than in the historical narratives, where many things are described as having happened but may not be exemplary or serve as a model of behavior for all times.

    Christians have argued for centuries about the "normativity" of the book of Acts — mainly over issues of church government and the operations of the Holy Spirit. But Acts is focused on missions, evangelism, and church planting. I believe we can learn much from the material for our own ministries, but since it is written in narrative form, we must be careful not to apply too rigidly the things we learn. See, e.g., David Peterson's remark that the patterns of the laying on of hands and tongues speaking "are not to be regarded as normative for ongoing Christian experience" (*The Acts of the Apostles* [Grand Rapids: Eerdmans, 2009], 532).

2. John R. W. Stott, *The Message of Acts* (Bible Speaks Today; Downers Grove, Ill.: InterVarsity, 1994), 234.

3. Tim Chester, "Church Planting: A Theological Perspective," in *Multiplying Churches: Reaching Today's Communities through Church Planting*, ed. Stephen Timmis (Fearn, Scotland: Christian Focus, 2000), 23–46.

4. In Redeemer's early days, we were joined by people who came from other congregations in the city. But as we've gotten bigger and older, we have often seen our own members go off to newer and younger congregations where they felt their gifts could be well utilized. They go with our blessing. Older churches are always tempted to resent the loss of members to newer churches, but if we care about reaching the whole city for Christ, we must be glad that we trained people in our congregation who then opt to become involved in new mission opportunities.

5. See Donald McGavran and George G. Hunter III, eds., *Church Growth: Strategies That Work* (Nashville: Abingdon, 1980), 100; see also C. Kirk Hadaway, *New Churches and Church Growth in the Southern Baptist Convention* (Nashville: Broadman, 1987); Ed Stetzer, *Planting Missional Churches: Planting a Church That's Biblically Sound and Reaching People in Culture* (Nashville: Broadman and Holman, 2006). Stetzer writes, "Churches under three years of age win an average of ten people to Christ per year for every hundred members … Churches over fifteen years of age win an average of three people per every hundred members" (p. 8).

6. See Lyle Schaller, *44 Questions for Church Planters* (Nashville: Abingdon, 1991), 12.

7. These numbers are taken from a study — conducted by the Values Research Institute of New York and commissioned by Redeemer City to City — that looked at church attendance and church growth in New York City over the past several decades. These figures, while inexact, should be taken seriously as general patterns. The figures basically align with churchgoing and church-per-capita figures in the parts of the United States that are far more religious and traditional than New York City. We have not done research in other countries.

8. Two useful resources for guiding this process are James P. Spradley, *The Ethnographic Interview* (New York: Harcourt, Brace, Jovanovich, 1979), and Ed Dayton, *Planning Strategies for Evangelism* (Monrovia, Calif.: MARC, 1974).

9. A helpful resource is Craig Ellison, "Addressing Felt Needs of Urban Dwellers," in *Planting and Growing Urban Churches*, ed. Harvie Conn (Grand Rapids: Baker, 1997), 94–110

10. See Schaller, *44 Questions for Church Planters*, 14–26.

11. See Roger Finke and Rodney Stark, *The Churching of America 1776–1990* (New Brunswick, N.J.: Rutgers University Press, 1992), 16.

12. Schaller, *44 Questions for Church Planters*, 23.

13. Schaller (*44 Questions for Church Planters*, 24–26) contends that a lack of church planting is one major cause of the decline of mainline Protestantism. Finke and Stark (*Churching of America*, 248) show how independent churches (such as the Baptists, who have had freedom to plant churches without interference) have multiplied their numbers..

chapter 30

THE CITY AND THE GOSPEL ECOSYSTEM

How can a city's churches become unified enough to be a movement of the gospel, even a movement of movements? They need to be part of a citywide movement of churches and ministries that exist in a supportive, mutually stimulating relationship. The assumption behind this idea is that no one kind of church — no one church model or theological tradition — can reach an entire city. Reaching a city requires a willingness to work with other churches, even churches that hold to different beliefs and practices — a view sometimes called "catholicity."

Many evangelicals have been conditioned to cringe at the "holy catholic church" phrase in the Apostles' Creed. The Greek word *katholikos* is not used to describe the church in the New Testament, but it certainly expresses a biblical teaching that, as Edmund Clowney put it, "the church as a whole is more than the local church."[1] In Acts, the various local gatherings of believers are constantly called *the* church in a city or region: "Then the church throughout Judea, Galilee and Samaria enjoyed a time of peace. It was strengthened; and encouraged by the Holy Spirit, it grew in numbers" (Acts 9:31; see 11:22; 15:3). In Acts 1:8, the task of healing the long-standing breach of the northern and southern kingdoms is given, and the summary statements at 6:7; 12:24; 19:20; and 28:31 demonstrate the "peace" described in 9:31. All of this communicates that it is the restored kingdom alluded to in 1:6 that marches into Rome. It is the unified people of God whom the Spirit uses to reach the far ends of the earth (1:8; cf. Isa 8:9; 48:20; 44:6; 62:11) with the gospel — even Rome! In other words, unity is not simply the work of the Spirit but the very instrument through which the Spirit works. This is why it is vital to maintain the unity of the Spirit (Eph 4:3; Phil 2:1 – 4).

Catholicity-denying *sectarianism* results in un-

necessary division. If two churches differ in their beliefs and practices of baptism and the Lord's Supper, then two different churches they will have to be — but it doesn't mean they cannot cooperate in other ways. To be estranged in ministry from other true believers who are members of the "wrong" denomination is to fail to welcome those whom Christ himself has welcomed. A movement needs the dynamic of cooperation that encourages people of different temperaments and perspectives to come together around their common vision and goals. In fact, part of what we see in the dynamism of a movement is people who "knock heads" and then come up with creative new initiatives because they *share a vision* and yet are very different in terms of denominations, temperaments, and personalities. If this bias for cooperation is absent in a city, the movement dynamic typically stalls or erodes.

Catholicity-denying *racism* reflects a lack of cultural flexibility and gospel humility. Embracing people of different races and cultures requires each cultural group within the church to flex as it serves the others. Cultural differences will range from the small (punctuality, for instance) to the great (music's form and words or the illustrations and applications of the preaching of the Word).

Catholicity and nonsectarianism are important for an additional reason. Unlike the Christendom era that fostered a sense of Christian distinctives among Christian groups, it is much more illuminating and helpful today for churches to define themselves in contrast to the values of the non-Christian culture. As noted earlier, if we bash and criticize other kinds of churches, we play into the common opinion that all Christians are intolerant. If we are not united, the world writes us off, and perhaps, in light of Jesus' high priestly prayer in John 17:23 ("May they be brought to complete unity to let the world know that you sent me"), they have a right to do so! While we must continue to align ourselves in denominations that share our theological distinctives, at the local level our bias should be in the direction of cooperation with other congregations.

Because of this belief, Redeemer Presbyterian Church has for a number of years given money and resources to churches of other denominations that are planting churches. We have helped to start Pentecostal churches, Baptist churches, and Anglican churches, as well as Presbyterian churches. For our efforts we have received sharp criticism and a lot of amazed stares. We believe this is one clear way to practice the kind of catholicity that turns a city of balkanized Christian churches and denominations into a movement.

CHURCH MODELS AND MOVEMENTS

There is no single way of doing church that employs the right biblical or even the right cultural model. What the Bible tells the church to do — witness, serve the needy, preach the Word, disciple people, worship — is so rich and multifaceted that no church will ever do all of them equally well, simply because no single church has all the spiritual gifts

> There is no single way of doing church that employs the right biblical or even the right cultural model. So the city as a whole needs all kinds of churches.

in equal proportions. While no church should stop trying to do everything that God calls it to do, no one church will fulfill these roles perfectly. So the city as a whole needs all kinds of churches. Recognizing the reality of multiple church models humbles us — we see we can't be all things to all people — and also encourages us to reach out and cooperate with other churches.

In our discussion of the need for balanced ministry fronts in chapter 23, we looked at the five models of church proposed by Avery Dulles: "the church as

---

CLOWNEY ON CATHOLICITY

Catholicity means that the church is Christ's. We cannot exclude those whom he welcomes, or welcome those whom he excludes … Sectarianism denies catholicity, for by its refusal to recognize other communions as true churches of Christ, it denies the fellowship that Christ requires.

Edmund Clowney, *The Church*

Racism also denies Catholicity. Not long ago, white American churches stationed "color guards" to bar black worshipers, directing them to a suitable congregation on the other side of the tracks.

Edmund Clowney, *The Church*

The catholicity of the church may also be denied, not out of prejudice but in order to facilitate church growth. It has been convincingly demonstrated that numerical growth takes place most readily when appeal is made directly to one "people group" — one unit sociologically defined … It has the effect of making the church a subset of secular society rather than the manifestation on earth of the kingdom of Christ.

Edmund Clowney, *Living in Christ's Church*

---

institution" (which we might call *doctrine driven*); "the church as mystical communion" (*worship driven*); "the church as sacrament" (*community driven*); "the church as herald" (*evangelism driven*); and "the church as servant" (*justice driven*). In a later edition of his book, Dulles offers a model called "the church as community of disciples" in which he envisions a church that combines all the elements in proper balance.[2] Naturally, I concur that all good churches include these five elements and emphases to some degree. This is why the healthy example of each model emphasizes its main element(s) while also giving some weight to the emphases of other models. An unhealthy version of each model emphasizes one or two of these aspects and virtually ignores the others. Above all, a church's gift mix and context will dictate what it will do best in certain ministries and at certain seasons in its life.

Not only is it important to enlarge your vision to see the necessity of all models in a city movement; it is vital to identify the features of the church model where you presently serve. Many problems arise if we minister as though we are in one particular model when we are really in another. When I was in college and seminary, I participated in fairly healthy churches that were closest to the doctrine-driven model. They stressed excellent public teaching and preaching and intense Bible study. After seminary, the first church I served was in a small, blue-collar factory town in the South. At that time, almost none of its members had attended college, and most of the older members had not finished high school. It had been a church of 100 to 150 people for thirty years and was relatively unhealthy. Although I had a strong notion of the difference between unhealthy/stagnant and healthy/renewed, I had no concept of different church models. I had only seen healthy churches within the framework of one particular church model worked out only in college towns filled with professors and students. My vision for this church's renewal was great Bible exposition, seminars and classes on Christian subjects, and intense small group Bible studies.

Over the years I came to discover that this was a congregation filled with diaconal gifts ("priestly" gifts, not "prophetic" gifts of teaching, knowledge, and evangelism). It was fundamentally a community-driven model. Grasping this was a slow and frustrating process. As I look back, my emphases did help the church because they contributed to balancing its community model with better (but never excellent) teaching, education, and evangelism. Eventually, I stopped trying to force things and began to accept more of what the church actually was. I was very slow and stubborn, but in the end I gave in before anyone lost too much patience with

me. A key to this process was staying at the church for nine years.

Years after I left this church, the congregation hosted a reception for Kathy and me on the twenty-fifth anniversary of my ordination. At one point in the festivities, a number of people shared one thing they remembered hearing me say during my ministry among them. It struck me afterward that not one person quoted my words from a sermon! Every single person shared something I had said during one-on-one pastoral care. This experience vividly illustrates the difference in church models. In New York City, people let me pastor them because they appreciate my preaching. In Hopewell, Virginia, people let me preach to them because they appreciated my pastoring. In a community-driven model, the pastoring sets up the preaching; it earns you the right to preach. In the doctrine-driven model of Redeemer in New York, the preaching sets up the pastoring and even the leading. People will let you into their lives and follow you if you demonstrate your expertise in communication.

In New York City, people let me pastor them because they appreciate my preaching. In Hopewell, Virginia, people let me preach to them because they appreciated my pastoring.

Why is understanding church models essential in enabling a city's churches to work together in unity? Without this understanding, *there will be no catholicity in your city*. Unless you accept the fact that there is not one exclusively biblical church model, you will not see the need for strong fellowship and connections to other denominations and networks, which usually embody different emphases and strengths than the ones that characterize your model. What's more, *there also will be no catholicity in your church, denomination, or movement*. Without an acceptance of multiple biblical church models, your own movement and network may plant cookie-cutter churches in neighborhoods where that model is inappropriate or may employ leaders whose gifts don't fit it. Your own movement would risk becoming too homogeneous, reaching only one kind of neighborhood or one kind of person, and fail to reflect the God-ordained diversity of humanity in your church. As much as we want to believe that most people will want to become *our* particular kind of Christian, it is not true. The city will not be won unless many different denominations become dynamic mini-movements.

GOSPEL CITY MOVEMENTS AND GOSPEL ECOSYSTEMS

We have seen the prerequisites for churches and ministers to contribute to gospel city movements — including an understanding and appreciation of various church models and a spirit of catholicity that is nevertheless doctrinally robust and sensitive. But what exactly is a gospel movement in a city?

When a church or a church network begins to grow rapidly in a city, it is only natural for the people within the ministry to feel that God is making a difference in that place. Often, however, what is really going on is "Christian reconfiguration." When churches grow, they typically do so by drawing believers out of less vital churches. This can be a good thing if the Christians in these growing churches are being better discipled and if their gifts are being effectively deployed. Nevertheless, if this is the key dynamic, then the overall body of Christ in the city is not growing; it is simply reconfiguring. Reaching an entire city, then, takes more than having some effective churches in it, or even having a burst of revival energy and new converts. *Changing a city with the gospel takes a movement.*

When a gospel city movement occurs, the whole body of Christ grows faster than the population so that the percentage of Christians in the city rises. We call this a *movement* because it consists of an energy that extends across multiple denominations and networks. It does not reside in a single church or set of leaders or in any particular command center, and its forward motion does not depend on any one organization. It is organic and self-propagating, the result of a set of forces that interact, support,

sustain, and stimulate one another. We can also call it a *gospel ecosystem*. Just as a biological ecosystem is made of interdependent organisms, systems, and natural forces, a gospel ecosystem is made of interdependent organizations, individuals, ideas, and spiritual and human forces. When all the elements of an ecosystem are in place and in balance, the entire system produces health and growth as a whole and for the elements themselves.[3]

Can we produce a gospel city movement? No. A movement is the result of two broad sets of factors. Once again I'll refer to the metaphor of gardening (see 1 Cor 3:6 – 8). A garden flourishes because of the skill and diligence of the gardener *and* the condition of the soil and the weather. The first set of factors — gardening — is the way we humanly contribute to the movement. This encompasses a self-sustaining, naturally growing set of ministries and networks, which we will look at in more detail below.

Just as a biological ecosystem is made of interdependent organisms, systems, and natural forces, a gospel ecosystem is made of interdependent organizations, individuals, ideas, and spiritual and human forces.

But the second set of factors in a movement — the conditions — belongs completely to God. He can open individual hearts ("soil") to the Word ("seed") in any numbers he sovereignly chooses. And he can also open a culture to the gospel as a whole ("weather"). How does God do this? Sometimes he brings about a crisis of belief within the dominant culture. Two of the great Christian movements — the early church of the second and third centuries and the church in China in the twentieth and twenty-first centuries — were stimulated by crises of confidence within their societies. The belief in the gods of Rome — and belief in orthodox Marxism in China — began falling apart as plausible worldviews. There was broad disaffection toward the older "faiths" among the population at large. This

All Christian movements must be characterized by a willingness to unite around commonly held central truths and to accept differences on secondary matters that—in the view of the partners—do not negate our common belief in the biblical gospel. To maintain a healthy movement over time, we have to engage in direct discussion about any doctrinal errors we perceive. Yet in doing so, we must show respect for the other party and aim to persuade them, not punish them.

How can we do this? I suggest the following principles for "polemics"—contending over doctrine—seasoned in tone and strategy by the gospel itself. As I've read respected Christian authors over the years, I've distilled some "rules of engagement" to avoid polemics or pursue it in spiritually constructive ways.

1. **Never attribute an opinion to your opponents that they themselves do not own.** Nineteenth-century Princeton theologian Archibald Alexander realized that doing so would harden opponents in their views. "Attribute to an antagonist no opinion he does not own, though it be a necessary consequence."[4] In other words, even if you believe that Mr. A's belief X could lead others who hold belief X to hold belief Y, do not accuse Mr. A of holding belief Y if he disowns it. You may consider him inconsistent, but this is not the same as insisting that he actually holds belief Y when he does not. A similar move happens when we imply or argue that if Mr. A quotes a particular author favorably at any point, then Mr. A must hold *all* the views held by the author. If through guilt by association we hint or insist that he must hold other beliefs of that particular author, then we are both

alienating and misrepresenting our opponent. Similarly, take full responsibility for even unwittingly misrepresenting others' views. When we accuse Mr. A of promoting view X, and someone observes that Mr. A didn't mean X because over here he said Y, often we merely apologize—if that. Be sure you know what Mr. A believes and promotes before you publish.

2. **Take your opponents' views in their entirety, not selectively.** A host of Christian doctrines have an "on the one hand/on the other hand" dimension—and without both emphases we can fall into heresy. What if we find Mr. A making what appears to be an unqualified, unbalanced statement? If that is all Mr. A ever said about the subject, it would be right to conclude something about his position. But what if Mr. A was speaking or writing to an audience that already believed certain things, and therefore he was able to assume those balancing points of doctrine without stating them? At minimum, we must realize that Mr. A simply can't say everything he believes about a subject every time he speaks. We should not isolate certain statements by Mr. A while overlooking or even concealing explanations, qualifications, or balancing statements he may have made elsewhere.

3. **Represent your opponents' position in its strongest form, not in a weak "straw man" form.** This may be the most comprehensive rule of all in polemics, because, if you adhere to it, most of the other principles will follow. Do the work necessary to articulate the views of your opponent with such strength and clarity that he or she could say, "I couldn't have said it

better myself." Then, and only then, will your polemics have integrity *and* actually have the possibility of being persuasive—which leads to our next point.

4. **Seek to persuade, not antagonize—but watch your motives!** John Calvin was a Reformer in Geneva, Switzerland. His comrade in this work was William Farel, who was outspoken and hotheaded by temperament. At one point, Calvin wrote Farel a letter in which he urged Farel to do more to "accommodate people"—i.e., to seek to win them over. Calvin then distinguished two different motivations for seeking to be winsome and persuasive: "There are, as you know, two kinds of popularity: the one, when we seek favor from motives of ambition and the desire of pleasing; the other, when, by fairness and moderation, we gain their esteem so as to make them teachable by us."[5] The Farels of the world believe any effort to be judicious and prudent is a cowardly sellout. But Calvin wisely recognized that his friend's constant, intemperate denunciations often stemmed not from a selfless courage, but rather from the opposite—pride. Writing to Pierre Viret about Farel, Calvin said, "He cannot bear with patience those who do not comply with his wishes."[6]

So it is possible to seek to be winsome and persuasive out of self-centeredness—a desire to be popular—rather than God-centeredness. It is just as possible to be bold and strongly polemical out of self-centeredness rather than God-centeredness. And therefore, looking closely at our motives, we must take care that our polemics do not unnecessarily harden and antagonize our opponents.

We should seek to win them, as Paul did Peter, not to be rid of them.

5. **Remember the gospel and stick to criticizing the theology—because only God sees the heart.** Much criticism today is marked by scorn, mockery, and sarcasm rather than careful exegesis and reflection. Such an approach is not persuasive. No one has written more eloquently about this rule than John Newton in his well-known "Letter on Controversy," where he states that before you write a word against your opponent "and during the whole time you are preparing your answer, you may commend him by earnest prayer to the Lord's teaching and blessing." This practice will stir up love for him, and "such a disposition will have a good influence upon every page you write."[7] Later in the letter, Newton writes:

> What will it profit a man if he gain his cause and silence his adversary, if, at the same time, he loses that humble, tender frame of spirit in which the Lord delights, and to which the promise of his presence is made?... Be upon your guard against admitting anything personal into the debate. If you think you have been ill treated, you will have an opportunity of showing that you are a disciple of Jesus, who "when he was reviled, reviled not again; when he suffered, he threatened not."[8]

Newton also reminds us that it is a great danger to "be content with showing your wit and gaining the laugh on your side," to make your opponent look evil and ridiculous instead of engaging their views with "the compassion due to the souls of men."[9]

combination of cultural crisis and popular disillusionment with old ways of belief can supercharge a Christian movement and lift it to greater heights than it can reach in a culture that is indifferent (rather than hostile) to Christians. There can also be catastrophes that lead people of a culture to look to spiritual resources, as when the Japanese domination of Korea after 1905 became a context for the large number of conversions to Christianity that began around that time.

In short, we cannot produce a gospel movement without the providential work of the Holy Spirit. A movement is an ecosystem that is empowered and blessed by God's Spirit.[10]

What is the ecosystem that the Holy Spirit uses to produce a gospel city movement? I picture it as three concentric rings.

FIRST RING — CONTEXTUALIZED THEOLOGICAL VISION

At the very core of the ecosystem is a way of communicating and embodying the gospel that is contextualized to the city's culture and is fruitful in converting and discipling its people, a shared commitment to communicating the gospel to a particular place in a particular time. Churches that catalyze gospel movements in cities do not all share the same worship style, come from the same denomination, or reach the same demographic. They do, however, generally share much of the same basic "DNA": they are gospel centered, attentive to their culture, balanced, missional/evangelistic, growing, and self-replicating. In short, they have a relative consensus on a Center Church theological vision — a set of biblically grounded, contextual strategic stances and emphases that help bring sound doctrine to bear on the people who live in this particular cultural moment.

SECOND RING — CHURCH PLANTING AND CHURCH RENEWAL MOVEMENTS

The second layer is a number of church multiplication movements producing a set of new and growing churches, each using the effective means of ministry within their different denominations and traditions.

Many look at cities and see a number of existing churches, often occupying buildings that are nearly empty. It is natural to think, "The first thing we need to do is to renew the existing churches with the gospel." Indeed, all of part 2 (Gospel Renewal) is dedicated to how this can be done. But as we saw in the previous chapter, the establishment of new churches in a city is a key to renewing the older churches. New churches introduce new ideas and win the unchurched and non-Christians to Christ at a generally higher rate than older churches. They provide spiritual oxygen to the communities and networks of Christians who do the heavy lifting over decades of time to reach and renew cities. They provide the primary venue for discipleship and the multiplication of believers, as well as serve as the indigenous financial engine for the ministry initiatives.

THIRD RING — SPECIALIZED MINISTRIES

Based in the churches, yet also stimulating and sustaining the churches, this third ring consists of a complex set of specialty ministries, institutions, networks, and relationships. There are at least seven types of elements in this third ring.

1. A prayer movement uniting churches across traditions in visionary intercession for the city. As noted in part 2, the history of revivals shows the vital importance of corporate, prevailing, visionary intercessory prayer for the city and the body of Christ. Praying for your city is a biblical directive (Jer 29:4 – 7). Coming together in prayer is something a wide variety of believers can do. It doesn't require a lot of negotiation and theological parsing to pray. Prayer brings people together. And this very activity is catalytic for creating friendships and relationships across denominational and organizational boundaries. Partnerships with Christians who are similar to and yet different from you stimulates growth and innovation.

2. A number of specialized evangelistic ministries, reaching particular groups (businesspeople, mothers, ethnicities, and the like). Of particular importance are effective campus and youth ministries. Many of the city church's future members and leaders are best found in the city's

A GOSPEL ECOSYSTEM FOR A CITY

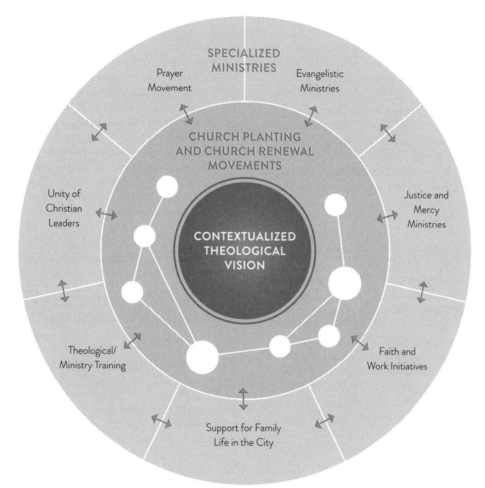

SPECIALIZED MINISTRIES

Prayer Movement

Evangelistic Ministries

CHURCH PLANTING AND CHURCH RENEWAL MOVEMENTS

Unity of Christian Leaders

Justice and Mercy Ministries

CONTEXTUALIZED THEOLOGICAL VISION

Theological/ Ministry Training

Faith and Work Initiatives

Support for Family Life in the City

colleges and schools. While students who graduate from colleges in university towns must leave the area to get jobs, graduates of urban universities do not. Students won to Christ and given a vision for living in the city can remain in the churches they joined during their school years and become emerging leaders in the urban body of Christ. Winning the youth of a city wins city natives who understand the culture well.

3. An array of justice and mercy ministries, addressing every possible social problem and neighborhood. As the evangelicals provided leadership in the 1830s, we need today an urban "benevolent empire" of Christians banding together in various nonprofits and other voluntary organizations to address the needs of the city. Christians of the city must become renowned for their care for their neighbors, for this is one of the key ways that Jesus will become renowned.

4. Faith and work initiatives and fellowships in which Christians from across the city gather with others in the same profession. Networks of

Christians in business, the media, the arts, government, and the academy should come together to help each other work with accountability, excellence, and Christian distinctiveness.

5. Institutions that support family life in the city, especially schools and counseling services. Significant communities that inhabit cities — such as Jewish and Catholic populations — have long known the importance of having their own schools, recreational and cultural centers, and agencies that provide services to help people stay and raise their children in the city.

6. Systems for attracting, developing, and training urban church and ministry leaders. The act of training usually entails good theological education, but a dynamic city leadership system will include additional components such as well-developed internship programs and connections to campus ministries.

7. An unusual unity of Christian city leaders. Church and movement leaders, heads of institutions, business leaders, academics, and others must know one another and provide vision and direction for the whole city. They must be more concerned about reaching the whole city and growing the whole body of Christ than about increasing their own tribe and kingdom.

When all of these ecosystem elements are strong and in place, they stimulate and increase one another and the movement becomes self-sustaining. How this happens, and what can happen as a result, is our final subject.

TIPPING POINTS THAT LEAD TO CHANGE

Isolated events or individual entities crystallize into a growing, self-sustaining movement when they reach a *tipping point*, a moment when the movement dynamics for change become unstoppable. A tipping point is a sociological term — "the moment of critical mass, the threshold, the boiling point."[11] For example, neighborhoods stay largely the same if new types of residents (richer, poorer, or otherwise culturally different from the rest) comprise less than 5 percent of the population. When the number of new residents reaches somewhere between 5 and 25 percent

(depending on the culture), the whole neighborhood shifts and undergoes rapid and significant change.

An *ecosystem tipping point* is reached in a city when the ecosystem elements are largely in place and many churches have the vitality, leaders, and mind-set to plant other churches within five to six years of their own beginnings. If God blesses, at this point the movement has begun to be self-sustaining. Enough new believers, leaders, congregations, and ministries are being naturally produced for the movement to grow without any single center of control. The body of Christ in the city largely funds itself, produces its own leaders, and conducts its own training. A sufficient number of dynamic leaders is emerging. The number of Christians and churches doubles every seven to ten years.

The next threshold of the movement's advance is a *citywide tipping point*. This occurs when the number of gospel-shaped Christians in a city becomes so large that Christian influence on the civic and social life of the city — and on the very culture — is recognizable and acknowledged. In New York City, minority groups — whether of the ethnic, cultural, or lifestyle variety — can have a palpable effect on the way life is lived when their numbers reach at least 5 to 10 percent *and* when the members are active in public life. I have heard it said that when the number of prison inmates following Christ reaches 10 percent, the very culture and corporate life of the prison changes. There is no scientific way to precisely determine a city's tipping point — the point at which the gospel begins to have a visible impact on the city life and culture. In New York City, we pray for and work toward the time when 10 percent of the center city population is involved in a gospel-centered church. In Manhattan, this would amount to about 100,000 people.

Today, in a place like Manhattan, the vast majority of residents do not know an orthodox Christian believer (or at least one who has made their spiritual identity known). As a result, it is very easy for them to believe negative stereotypes. Evangelical Christians (as a stereotype) are as strange and off-putting to urban residents as gay people used to be to most Americans. As a result, Christianity isn't even a plausible option as a way to live for most center city dwellers. But imagine what would happen if a place like Manhattan contained so many believers that most New Yorkers would actually know a Christian they respected. The strong attitudinal barriers that block many urban residents from the message of Christianity would come down. Tens of thousands of souls could be redeemed.

In New York City, we pray for and work toward the time when 10 percent of the center city population is involved in a gospel-centered church.

How likely is it that an urban gospel movement could grow so strong that it reaches a citywide tipping point? We know this can happen through God's grace. The history books give us examples. We see how the exponential growth of Christianity changed the Roman world in the first three centuries AD and how it changed pagan northern Europe from AD 500 to 1500. We have stories of how the evangelical awakenings in the eighteenth century changed British society in the nineteenth. But we don't yet know what it would look like for one of the great culture-forming global cities of our world today to become 10 percent (or more) gospel-believing Christian in its core, with believers playing key roles in the arts, sciences, the academy, and business, while at the same time using their power, wealth, and influence for the good of those on the margins of society.

Every city in the world needs Jesus Christ. But our cities do not merely need a few more churches and ministries here and there; they need gospel city movements that lead to citywide tipping points. So urban ministers enthusiastically and passionately give their lives to these goals, even though they may not see their consummation in their own lifetimes. As we wait with confident expectation and faithful patience, we keep pursuing our vision to see our cities loved and reached for the glory of Christ.

QUESTIONS FOR DISCUSSION AND REFLECTION

1. Keller writes, "Reaching a city requires a willingness to work with other churches, even churches that hold to different beliefs and practices — a view sometimes called 'catholicity.'" How have you partnered with other congregations that have historical traditions or theological distinctives different from your own? What led you to partner together?

2. The sidebar on "Gospel Polemics" gives several guidelines for discussion with those who differ from you. Which of these guidelines is most helpful for you? What do you most struggle with when you engage in discussion with others?

3. Take some time to envision what the gospel ecosystem looks like — and might look like — in your community. Which elements are strongest and weakest? How can you move beyond ministerial alliances you have made in the past? Which key leaders, congregations, and organizations would need to be on board?

CHAPTER 30 — THE CITY AND THE GOSPEL ECOSYSTEM {pages 368–77}

1. Edmund Clowney, *The Church* (Downers Grove, Ill.: InterVarsity, 1995), 79.
2. This chapter ("The Church: Community of Disciples") was not in the original 1978 edition; see Avery Dulles, *Models of the Church*, expanded ed. (New York: Image, 2002), 195 – 218.
3. Likening a gospel city movement to a biological ecosystem is an analogy, of course, and no analogy illumines the concept at every point. Biological ecosystems consist in some part of stronger animals eating weaker ones. No one should think this means stronger churches should eat weaker ones! Actually, a city in which some churches grow only by drawing members out of other churches is the very opposite of the kind of evangelistic gospel city movement we are seeking. The image of the ecosystem conveys how different organisms are interdependent, how the flourishing of one group helps the other groups flourish.
4. Quoted in David B. Calhoun, *Princeton Seminary: Faith and Learning, 1812 – 1868* (Edinburgh: Banner of Truth, 1994), 1:92.
5. Bruce Gordon, *Calvin* (New Haven, Conn.: Yale University Press, 2009), 151.
6. Ibid., 152.
7. John Newton, "Letter XIX: On Controversy," in *Forty-One Letters on Religious Subjects* (Pitttsburgh, Pa.: Loomis, 1931), 107.
8. Ibid., 111.
9. Ibid.
10. Thanks to Dr. Mark Reynolds for his valuable insights that enhance this section.
11. Malcolm Gladwell, *The Tipping Point: How Little Things Can Make A Big Difference* (New York: Little, Brown, 2000), 12.

structured organization
tradition and authority

fluid organism
cooperation and unity

A Center Church is both an organism and an organization. Because the church is both a stable institution with inherited traditions and a dynamic movement of the Holy Spirit, we minister with balance, rooted in our ecclesial tradition yet working cooperatively with the body of Christ to reach our city with the gospel.

- Avoid the twin errors of trying to re-create a Christian society and withdrawing from society into the spiritual realm.
- Acknowledge the core ideas animating the "missional" church without abandoning the classic doctrines of sin and grace that create joy in the heart and an urgency for evangelism.
- Incorporate both the individual/vertical and corporate/horizontal aspects of sin into the motivation for mission, recognizing that the former is what creates space for the latter.
- Allow all the biblical metaphors for the church to inform our practice of church life.
- Acknowledge that our preference for certain worship styles is based on culture and temperament as well as on biblical principle.
- Ensure that worship will be both edifying and evangelistic by centering on the gospel and conducting worship in the vernacular.

- Maintain a balance on both individual and churchly piety through ecclesial revivalism.
- Emphasize both word ministry (gospel messaging) and deed ministry (gospel neighboring), and ensure there are venues to do them both together.
- In rhetoric about acts of mercy and justice, acknowledge the role of both systemic injustice and individual responsibility and show that the gospel of grace can help address both.
- Highly value secular work and still call people to work out of a distinctive Christian worldview.
- Strive to keep the church balanced between the characteristics of a freewheeling organism and a disciplined organization.
- Honor and value the general and special offices of ministry, understanding that the Holy Spirit is at work in both.
- Find common ground to work together with non-Christians, while still offering prophetic critique of cultural idols.
- Reflect both the order and ardor of God's Spirit, balancing the need for spontaneity with the need for unity.
- Support the Spirit-equipped gifting and calling of every believer (the general office), while recognizing the special gifts and callings given to some to exercise leadership (the special office).
- Recognize that it takes all kinds of church models to reach a city, and celebrate the healthy versions of each model.

LATE MODERNITY AND THE CENTER CHURCH

What is a "Center Church"? Throughout this book I have particularly had in mind churches and ministries who labor in urban and cultural centers and the peculiar and formidable difficulties these settings pose for gospel communication. But this is not a volume only for churches in cities. It is intended just as much for churches and ministries that find themselves, regardless of their geographic location, ministering in the late modern culture that now issues from the great global cities of the world.

The root idea of modernity was the overturning of all authority outside the self. In the eighteenth century, European Enlightenment thinkers insisted that the modern person must question all tradition, revelation, and external authority and subject them to the supreme court of his or her own reason and intuition. Still, for years, modern society continued to enjoy relatively stable institutions inherited from the past. People were able to root their identities to a large degree in their family and their nation. Yet today, even these institutions are eroding, worn away by the "acid" of the modern principle that individual happiness and autonomy must come before anything else. People's identities constantly "shape shift" as they move through life episodes. They always stand ready to change direction and abandon commitments and loyalties without qualms and to pursue, on a personal cost-benefit basis, the best opportunity available to them. The underlying thread that ties all of this together is the inconceivability of a moral order based on an authority more fundamental than oneself.

In the great cities of the world, this is the cultural air we breathe. But because of the pervasive influence of cities, more and more churches and ministers in nonurban areas discover that this is also their milieu. This book has been written for them as well.

How can we do gospel ministry in such an environment? We have seen that the key is not merely sound doctrine, though this is a nonnegotiable foundation. But the key is also not some new magic-bullet ministry program that will "reach postmodern people." It is something in the middle — more specific than doctrine but less specific than particular ministry programs. As we have seen, it is a particular *theological vision* that enables Christians to communicate the gospel to our time and place. This Center Church theological vision includes a much greater understanding of contextualization than Christians have needed in the past, a greater familiarity with the character of cities and urbanization, a sophisticated understanding of church models and of different ways of relating Christianity to a hostile culture, an ability to integrate ministries of word and deed, and a commitment to disciple laypeople not only for their private

POSTMODERN OR LATE MODERN?

Countless books today tell church leaders they are now in a *postmodern* culture. The danger of this term is that it lulls us into thinking our present culture is the opposite of modernity. This may be true in some domains (the visual arts, for example). Yet strictly speaking, it is probably more accurate to say we now live in a climate of *late modernity*, since the main principle of modernity was the autonomy of the individual and personal freedom over the claims of tradition, religion, family, and community. This is, indeed, what we have today — intensified.[1]

and church life but for their public life and vocations as well. Undergirding all of this is the key to fruitful ministry in all times and places — a commitment to the biblical gospel and the ability to apply the gospel to minds and hearts so as to bring life, light, and power to the church.

ONE MORE BALANCE

If you have made it this far, you are probably experiencing two contradictory and conflicting emotions. I want to affirm them both!

On the one hand, you may be (I hope) inspired. Many doubt that it is possible to embrace robust, orthodox Protestant doctrine and still engage in holistic, fruitful gospel ministry in places that seem to have rejected Christianity. Many doubt that you can be rooted solidly in a historic theological and ecclesiastical tradition and still learn humbly from other churches, or that you can contextualize to the culture. We have argued in this book that indeed you can do all of these things — not despite classic, orthodox theology but because of it.

On the other hand, you may be (I hope) humbled by the task before you and somewhat overwhelmed by it. As you have read some of what is written here, you may have thought, "This is well beyond my abilities." Of course it is. It is not a cliché to say that a sense of inadequacy is a prerequisite for any success you will ever have in such a ministry.

The way forward is to let the sense of opportunity *and* the sense of inadequacy coexist in creative tension, held together by your belief in the gospel that tells you that you are, at one and the same time, a helpless sinner and a loved, adopted child of God.

You must reject both pride and discouragement.

A vivid illustration of this principle is found in a brief fictional story titled "Palm Monday" which I once read in a Christian magazine. Here is my paraphrase.

The little donkey awoke with a smile on his face. He had been dreaming of the previous day. He stretched and then happily walked out into the street, but the many passersby simply ignored him. Confused, he went over to the crowded market area. With his ears held high with pride he strutted right down the middle of it. "Here I am, people!" he said to himself. But they stared in confusion, and some angrily struck him to drive him away. "What do you think you are doing, you ass, walking into the marketplace like this?"

"Throw your garments down," he said crossly. "Don't you know who I am?" They just looked at him in amazement.

Hurt and confused, the donkey returned home to his mother. "I don't understand," he said to her. "Yesterday they waved palm branches at me. They shouted 'Hosanna' and 'Hallelujah.' Today they treat me like I'm a nobody!"

"Foolish child," she said gently, "don't you realize that without him — you can do nothing?"

You *can* do this ministry with God's help — so give it all you've got. You *can't* do this ministry without God's help — so be at peace. Jesus captured both of these truths in one verse recorded in John's gospel: "I am the vine; you are the branches. If a man remains in me and I in him, he will bear much fruit; [but] apart from me you can do nothing" (John 15:5).

EPILOGUE — LATE MODERNITY AND THE CENTER CHURCH *(pages 381–82)*

1. For the case that today's culture has more continuity with the modern past than discontinuity, and thus that a better description of our culture would be "late modernity" (often called "second modernity" or "reflexive modernity"), see Zygmunt Bauman, *Liquid Modernity* (Cambridge: Polity Press, 2000); Edward Docx, "Postmodernism Is Dead," *Prospect* 185 (April 20, 2011), www.prospectmagazine. co.uk/2011/07/postmodernism-is-dead-va-exhibition-age-of-authenticism/ (accessed March 8, 2012); Luc Ferry, *A Brief History of Thought: A Philosophical Guide to Living* (New York: HarperCollins, 2011), 143 – 254; Anthony Giddens, Ulrich Beck, and Scott Lash, *Reflexive Modernization: Politics, Tradition, and Aesthetics in the Modern Social Order* (Palo Alto, Calif.: Stanford University Press, 1994).

ACKNOWLEDGMENTS

At first glance, this seems to be a book about what I've learned during my ministry in New York City, or perhaps about what we at Redeemer have learned in our church planting efforts. The truth is, the material in this book is just as much the fruit of what many others have learned and accomplished in major global centers around the world over the past fifteen years. To a much greater degree than with any of my other books, this one was written in and with a community — a network of practitioners across the great cities of the world from whom I have learned much.

The kernel of this book derives from a set of lectures I gave in London during 2008 and 2009 to an international gathering. Even those talks had been the product of what others had taught me, but since then, this material has been rigorously critiqued by others in the trenches around the world, and so it has expanded and been revised multiple times during the past three years.

I have had many interlocutors because of the work of the staff of Redeemer City to City. They have done a remarkable thing in helping to advance gospel movements in cities by emphasizing a Center Church theological vision, *not* by simply importing specific programs from the United States and from Redeemer Presbyterian Church. Through their humility and generosity, they have helped to make a lasting impact on the cities of the world for Christ. I particularly want to thank my colleagues Terry Gyger, Al Barth, Jay Kyle, and Mark Reynolds for their leadership.

Some of the colleagues in ministry who carefully read chapters and provided a wealth of feedback included Enoch Wong, Fong Yang Wong, Darrin Patrick, Siebrand Wierda, Richard Coekin, Dan Macdonald, Andrew Jones, and Mike Wittmer. Their extremely helpful insight shaped (and probably delayed!) this book more than they know.

Above all, I want to thank Scott Kauffmann of Redeemer City to City's Content Labs for serving as the project manager who brought this book into existence but also for the enormous amount of editing he did to turn this ungainly mass of material into an orderly, readable volume. Any elegance of presentation should be attributed to him. I also thank Ryan Pazdur, John Raymond, and the team at Zondervan, as well as David McCormick and the team at McCormick and Williams — we are deeply grateful for your committed and skillful partnership. As you saw in the introduction, I am indebted to Rick Lints (and his book *The Fabric of Theology*) for his seminal thinking on theological vision. Finally, thanks to Michael Thate, David Denmark, Cindy Widmer, and John Thomas — each of you made significant contributions that enriched this book and made its publication possible.

Finally, one of the joys of writing books is to have more places to thank my wife, Kathy, for her innumerable contributions, both seen and unseen. This book, as with all the others, is indebted to her ideas and her encouragement in ministry.

SUBJECT INDEX

contextualized theological
vision, 374
gospel city movements and, 371,
374–75
specialized ministries and,
374–75
tipping points that lead to change
in, 376–77
Edwards, Jonathan, 16, *68*, 73, 74, 77,
78, 123, *307*, 315, 327
elders, Christian, 112
elites, *256*
cultural, 161
governing, 112
Ellul, Jacques, *312–13*
emergence of models and culture
shift, 186–89
emotional intelligence, *121*
enemies of the gospel, 31–32
engagement, cultural, 230–32
act, don't react, in, 241–42
following one's convictions in,
238–40
knowing the seasons and,
237–238
remembering the difference
between organized and
organic in, 240–41
seeking the center for, 235–37
Enlightenment philosophies, *183*,
253, 330
entering and adapting to the culture,
120–24
Ephesus, 148–49, 278
epistemological challenge, 113
eschatology, 228
Eternal Word and Changing World,
104
European culture shift, *182*
evangelicals
and the culture shift, 182–83
individualism among, 224
pietism and, 184–86
strength in the United States,
264–65
evangelism, 49–50, 79, 82, *146*, 185,
203. *See also* missional living
bias for complex, 176–77
church planting, 359–60
Counterculturalism and, 208–9

crusade and personal, 317
gospel ecosystem and, 374–75
missional church and, 256–57
through mini-decisions, 281–82
Evangelism in the Early Church,
277–78
evangelistic worship
deeper teaching in, 307–8
seeker sensitive versus, 301–3
three practical tasks for, 303–7
Eve, 226–27
examination of candidates for
membership, 315–16
exile, 41–42, 146–47
city of, 141–43
existential perspective, 301
experience meetings, 74–75,
75–76
extended biological family, 147
extraordinary prayer, 73

F

Fabric of Theology, The, 104, 105
faith, 35–36
integration of work and, 175–76,
375
sanctification and, *69, 69–70*
works and, 30–31, 40
faithfulness, 13
Faith in the Halls of Power, 235
fall, the, 227–28
Falwell, Jerry, 187
family, 49, 375
extended biological, 147
fearfulness, 69
financial resources, *325–26*
Finney, Charles, 56
Fitch, David, 206, 265
flexibility
of movements, 340–41
toward culture, 110–11
following one's convictions, 238–40
Foolishness to the Greeks, 253
forgetting, spiritual, *58*
forgiveness, 50
forms of ministry, 16–17
"forward-back" aspect of the gospel,
47–48, 85
frontline prayer meetings, 72
fruitfulness, 13–14
books on, 14–16

frustration, 242
fulfillment of the covenant, *41*, 42
fully evangelistic churches, 359–60
functionalism, *103*, 104
future of cities, 157–58

G

Gandhi, Mahatma, *140*
Gathercole, Simon, 33, 39–40, 46
generations in cities, 160–61
Gibbs, Eddie, 17, 277
Glaeser, Edward, 138, *140*, 156, *156*
globalization, *256*
and renaissance, 154–57, 159
God, 33–34
connecting people to, 297–309
covenant and fulfillment, *41*, 42
growing to better know, 313–14
holiness and love of, 76–77
integrative ministry connecting
people to, 297–309
kingdom of, *229–30*, 269, 348–49
love and judgment, 125–27
sovereignty of, *338*
three ways of responding to, 63–64
God's Politics, 223
Goheen, Michael, 216, 217, 239
Gordon, T. David, 211, 214
gospel, the, 22, 23–24, 27, 28. *See also*
renewal, gospel
announcing we have been
rescued, 29–30
application, 74–75
attitudes toward class and, 51
balance, 85
behavior change, 67–70
changes everything, 48–51
for the city, 166–79
community and, 319–20
contextualization and, 43–44,
115–16
different presentations in the
Bible, 39–40, 113
discouragement and depression
changed by, 48
ecosystem, 371, 374–75
on faith, 35–36
family changed by, 49
"forward-back" aspect of, 47–48
on God and the Trinity, 33–34
as good news, not good advice, 29

guilt and self-image changed
by, 50
as heraldic proclamation, 37
human authority and, 48–51
innovation, 75–76
"inside-out" aspect of, 47
on Jesus Christ, 34–35
loss of a clear understanding of,
267–71
love and relationships changed
by, 48–49
as news about what Jesus has
done to put right our
relationship with God, 30
as not the results of the gospel,
30–31
polemics, 372–73
rediscovery, 73–74
religion compared to, 65, 76
revival, 54–61, 82–83
richness of, 46–48
right relationship of all ministry
to, 36–37
self-control and, 49
sexuality changed by, 49
shaping our work, 330–32
on sin, 34
tied to the Bible's story line and
themes, 40–43
two equal and opposite enemies
of, 31–32
"upside-down" aspect of, 46–47
witnessing and, 49–50
*Gospel in Life Study Guide: Grace
Changes Everything*, 318
Gospel in a Pluralist Society, The, 253
governing elites, 112
grace, 66, 125–26
the heart and, 57
preached to nonbelievers and
believers, 306
renewal dynamics, 351
richness of, 76–77
Two Kingdoms model and,
212–13
Great Awakening, 55, 74, 75
Green, Michael, 277–78
Grounded in the Gospel, 56, 316
Gruder, Darrell, 203, 255, 256
guilt and self-image, 50

H

Harry Potter, 131
Hauerwas, Stanley, 189, 205, 206,
207
Hays, Richard, 206
heart, the, 57
gospel renewal focused on,
58–60
Heclo, Hugh, 240, 339
Henry, Carl F. H., 186
hermeneutical circle, 105
Hesselgrave, David J., 104, 122
Hippolytus, 316
historical offices of the church, 348
historic worship form, 298, 299
Hodge, Charles, 315
Holy Spirit, the, 33–34, 73, 347
job of, 60
revival and, 58
homecoming and exile, 41–42
hope, cultural, 129
Horton, Michael, 188, 211, 214, 216,
217
household churches, 357
human authority, 50
human flourishing, 202
human rights, 129
humility, 116, 287
humor and joy, 50–51
Hunter, James D., 109, 185, 197, 200,
206, 207–8, 223, 239
Hybels, Bill, 16, 203, 206

I

idolatry, 70–71
freedom and, 44
human authority and, 50
missional church confronting,
271–73
sin as, 127–28
image and likeness, 44
immigrants in cities, 157, 159, 161
incarnation, 34–35, 46–47
missional church and, 257
individualism, 102, 259
Industrial Revolution, the, 55–56
inevitability of contextualizing,
93–96
informal missionaries, 277–79
inner reality, 58–59
innovation, gospel, 75–76

"inside-out" aspect of the gospel,
47, 85
institutions and movements, 337–42
integrative ministry
balance of ministry fronts in,
291–95
connecting people to God,
297–309
connecting people to one
another, 311–20
connecting people to the city,
322–27
connecting people to the culture,
330–35
defining the poor in, 327
level of priority, 326–27
roles, 324–26
integrity, relational, 282–85
intercanonical themes, 40–41
irreligion, 31, 48
Israel, 140, 146

J

Jacobs, Jane, 170–71, 175
Jerusalem, 135–36, 140, 146
Jesus Christ, 30, 31
atonement, 47, 130–32
enemies of the gospel and, 31–32
faith and, 35–36
gospel renewal and, 59–60
incarnation of, 34–35, 46–47
kingdom of, 42–43
preached from every text, 77–79
proclamation of, 113
redemption and restoration
through, 228–29
resurrection of, 47–48
Jews, 112
exiled, 146–47
John, apostle, 39–40
Jonah, 147, 169
Joseph, 172
joy and humor, 50–51
Julian, Emperor, 327
justice, 204, 213, 274, 305, 322–24,
375

K

Käsemann, Ernst, 91
katholikos, 368
Keller, Timothy, 78, 318

missionaries
    in cities, *160*
    informal, 277–79
mixed nature of culture, 108–10
models
    of the church, 292
    Counterculturalist, 194, 199,
        205–9, 223, 226, *231*,
        231–32, 235, 238, 239
    crossover among, 223–24
    emergence of, 186–189
    finding a way forward through,
        224–25
    following one's convictions and,
        238–40
    knowing the season and, 237–38
    movements and church, 369–70
    problems with, 194–95, 199–200,
        203–5, 206–9, 212–15
    Relevance, 194, 200–5, 223, *231*
    remembering the difference
        between organized and
        organic in, 240–41
    seeking the center and, 235–37
    Transformationist, *188*, 194, 195–
        200, 230, *231*, 235, 238
    Two Kingdoms, *188*, 189, 194,
        209–15, 230, *231*, 231–32,
        235–36, 238, 239
Models of Contextual Theology, 104,
    207
modernity, late, 381–82
Moody, Dwight, 185
moralism, 31, 48–51, 63
moralistic behavior change, 66–67
morality, common, *68*
Motyer, J. Alec, 141
Mouw, Richard, 199
movement(s), 22, 23, 24–25, 249–50
    balance, 379–80
    church as an organized organism
        and, 344–53
    church planting, 355–66
    creative tension and, 351–53
    dynamics in the local church,
        347–51
    gospel ecosystem and, 368–77
    and institutions, 337–42
    vision and, 339–40
music. *See* artistry and creativity

N

naïveté, 242
Natural church planting, 355–57
    mind-set, 357–59
naturalism, *93*
Nature of True Virtue, The, *68*, *78*
neighborhoods and justice,
    commitment to, 174–75
neighbors, engaging, 283–84
Neo-Anabaptists, 208
Neo-Calvinists, *187*, 196–98, 199,
    211, *212*, 224–25
Newbigin, Lesslie, 46, *188*, *207*, 223,
    239, 251–52, *256*
    on apologetics, *272*
    -Bosch rescue, 252–55
    missional movement today and,
        256
New Monasticism, The, *318*
new social realities, *183*
Newton, John, 373
Nicholls, Bruce, 96–97, *105*
Nicodemus, 64
Niebuhr, H. Richard, *109*, *194*, 195,
    196–97, 201–2, 209, 237, 241,
    256, *256–57*
Nine Marks of a Healthy Church, 15
nonbelievers, worship for, 302–7
non-Christians, preaching to, 79
normative perspective, 299–300

O

O'Connor, Flannery, 288
Open Secret, The, 252, 253
organization, church, 344, 352–53
    general and special office in,
        344–47
    general office of believers,
        345–46
    special office of minister, 346–47
Origen, *278*
Owen, John, 30

P

Packer, J. I., 30, 31, 32–33, *56*, 316
pagans, sophisticated, 112
Parrett, Gary, *56*, 316
Pascal, Blaise, 130
pastoral counseling, 75
pastoral support for lay ministry,
    285–88

patriarchs and the city, 139–40
Paul, apostle, 29, 172
    contextualization of the gospel
        by, 44
    on grace, 67–68
    ministry in Ephesus, 148–49
    on mixed nature of culture,
        111–12
    on natural church planting,
        356–57
    on pagan sources, 124–25
    presentation of the gospel by,
        39–40
    speeches in Acts, 112–14
    on worship, 302
peasant polytheists, 112
personal challenge, 113
personal gospel renewal, 54
persuasion, 122–23
Peter, apostle, 39, *300*, *300–1*, 320
Peterson, David, *58*, 113
Pietism, 184–86, 205
piety, 314–15
polemics, gospel, 372–73
politics, 187, 197, *256*
    Counterculturalism and, 208
    Transformationism and, 200
Politics of Jesus, The, 206
poor, the, 162
    defining, 327
post-Christendom age, *256–57*, 258,
    281
postmodernity, *93*, 128, 158, 270,
    381–82
pragmatism, 31, 49, 50–51
prayer, extraordinary, 73
preaching, 74
    to both Christians and non-
        Christians at once, 79
    for conversion yet honoring
        communicant status, 315
    for gospel renewal, 76–79
    grace, 306
    inevitability of contextualization
        in, 93–96
    Jesus Christ from every text,
        77–79
    to make the truth real, 77
    that both attracts and challenges
        urban people, 177–78

GOSPEL. CITY. MOVEMENT.

Global cities are the greatest missional challenge of our generation. For the first time in the history of the world, more than 50% of the world's population lives in cities. Five million people a month are joining them.

Cities are the best place to reach the next generation, the culture makers, unreached people groups, and the poor.

To bring the gospel to the nations, we need hundreds of new churches in the great cities of the world.

Learn more about gospel movements in global cities.

REDEEMER
CITY to CITY

redeemercitytocity.com

The Prodigal God Curriculum Kit

Finding Your Place at the Table

Timothy Keller

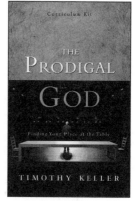

The Prodigal God Curriculum kit contains everything that your church needs to experience a four- or six-week preaching and small group campaign.

In this compelling six-session DVD study, pastor and bestselling author Tim Keller presents a new way of looking at this well-known parable.

Where most teaching focuses just on the younger "wayward" son, Dr. Keller challenges us to consider both the role of the elder brother and the father as well.

Even Jesus began his parable with "a man had two sons," so, you see, the story is not just about the younger son who leaves home and squanders his inheritance before eventually returning home.

The story is as much about the elder brother as the younger, and as much about the father as the sons. To this end, Dr. Keller contends that the story might better be called "Two Lost Sons."

In six sessions your group will explore the prodigal who spent until he had nothing left, the self-righteous and offended elder son, and the father who forgave with reckless abandon.

And in it all, your group will learn the love of the heavenly Father, who lavishes his love on his children and welcomes us back into his loving arms.

Session titles include the following:
1. The Parable
2. The People Around Jesus
3. The Two Lost Sons
4. The Elder Brother
5. The True Elder Brother
6. The Feast of the Father

The kit contains one (1) each of the following: *The Prodigal God* DVD, *The Prodigal God* Discussion Guide, Getting Started Guide, and *The Prodigal God* Curriculum Kit Box.

Available in stores and online!

ZONDERVAN®
.com

The *Reason for God* Discussion Guide with DVD

Conversations on Faith and Life

Timothy Keller

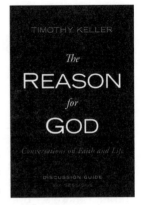

In the *New York Times* bestselling book *The Reason for God*, Timothy Keller established himself as a modern-day C. S. Lewis who brings together faith and intellect, theology and popular culture, modern-day objections and historic Christian beliefs. Now fans of the book will find resources to help them engage with those same objections, drawing on recent scholarship and debates. *The Reason for God* curriculum can be used individually, in groups, or by any believer who is engaging with friends' who don't share his or her beliefs. Christians will be challenged to wrestle with their friends' and neighbors' hardest questions and to engage those questions in ways that will spark an honest, enriching, and humbling dialogue.

    The Reason for God DVD captures a live and unscripted conversation between Timothy Keller and six panelists discussing their objections to Christianity. The discussion guide will help small groups and individuals dig deeper into these objections and learn about both sides of the issues.

Session titles include the following:

1. Isn't the Bible a Myth?
2. How Can You Say There Is Only One Way to God?
3. What Gives You the Right to Tell Me How to Live My Life?
4. Why Does God Allow Suffering?
5. Why Is the Church Responsible for So Much Injustice?
6. How Can God Be Full of Love and Wrath at the Same Time?

Awards:

2011 Christian Retailers Choice Award for Curriculum (Nontraditional)
2011 Outreach Magazine Resources of the Year for Small Group (Curricula)

Available in stores and online!

Gospel in Life Discussion Guide with DVD

Grace Changes Everything

Timothy Keller

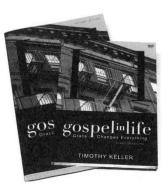

Join author and pastor Tim Keller in an eight-week, video-based study of the gospel and how to live it out in everyday life. In Week One, you and your group will study the city, our home now—the world, that is. Week Eight closes with the theme of the eternal city, our heavenly home—the world that is to come. In between, you'll learn how the gospel changes our hearts, our community, and how we live in this world. *Gospel in Life* is an invitation to all who seek to live the message of Jesus right here and right now ... in our hearts, in our homes, and in the community around us.

Session titles include the following:
1. The City—The World That Is
2. Heart—Three Ways to Live
3. Idolatry—The Sin beneath the Sin
4. Community
5. Witness—An Alternate City
6. Work—Cultivating the Garden
7. Justice—A People for Others
8. Eternity—The World That Is to Come

Available in stores and online!

Share Your Thoughts

With the Author: Your comments will be forwarded to the author when you send them to *zauthor@zondervan.com*.

With Zondervan: Submit your review of this book by writing to *zreview@zondervan.com*.

Free Online Resources at
www.zondervan.com

Zondervan AuthorTracker: Be notified whenever your favorite authors publish new books, go on tour, or post an update about what's happening in their lives at www.zondervan.com/authortracker.

Daily Bible Verses and Devotions: Enrich your life with daily Bible verses or devotions that help you start every morning focused on God. Visit www.zondervan.com/newsletters.

Free Email Publications: Sign up for newsletters on Christian living, academic resources, church ministry, fiction, children's resources, and more. Visit www.zondervan.com/newsletters.

Zondervan Bible Search: Find and compare Bible passages in a variety of translations at www.zondervanbiblesearch.com.

Other Benefits: Register to receive online benefits like coupons and special offers, or to participate in research.

ZONDERVAN.com/
AUTHORTRACKER
follow your favorite authors